THE OFFICIAL CENTENARY HISTORY
OF THE FOOTBALL LEAGUE

1888~1988

LEAGUE FOOTBALL

and the men who made it

SIMON INGLIS

Willow Books
Collins
8 Grafton Street, London W1
1988

ACKNOWLEDGEMENTS

This Centenary History would have been impossible without the tremendous help and co-operation of the Football League staff at Lytham St Annes. They have not only furnished me with every possible reference, but also withstood my continuous stream of obtuse questioning. I am particularly grateful to the Secretary, Graham Kelly, for his time, understanding and help with the manuscript, and to staff members David Dent, Norman Thomas, Glynis Firth, Andy Williamson and Marion Ainge. Liz Ashforth's excellent management of the League's records was also much appreciated.

For advice and extra research on the statistical and historical background, Ray Spiller of the Association of Football Statisticians was a tower of strength. I am additionally beholden to the following AFS members for statistical work which is quoted in the book: Wallace Chadwick, Chris Fincham, John Fowles, Ian Laschke, Robert McCutcheon, Paul Marsh and Jack Rollin.

Many people have shared their personal reminiscences with me and given me invaluable advice. Among them I thank Patrick Barclay, Pam Beaumont, Arthur Charnley, Matt Gillies, Jimmy Hill, Florence Mabel Holt, Alan Howarth, Cliff Lloyd, Roley Orton, Len and Mary Shipman, Enid Sutcliffe, Gordon Taylor, O. T. Wisden and Prof. Sir John Wood.

Appreciated too was the assistance of the Football Trust, the Football Association, Linda Fletcher, Ted Griffith, Jonathan Inglis, Ian Rigby, David Walker and Keith Warsop.

For much of the biographical detail in this book I have leaned heavily upon a countless number of journalists and club historians, plus the resources of local history and reference libraries all over Britain. No praise is too high for the staff at Colindale (newspaper library), Birmingham, Bolton, Blackburn, Burnley, Edmonton, Grimsby, Liverpool, Manchester, Newcastle, Preston, Stoke, West Bromwich, Wolverhampton and Woolwich libraries.

The illustrations in the book have been obtained from the following sources: BBC Hulton Picture Library, *Blackpool Gazette*, David Chadwick, Lynda Emmanuel, Football League, Hammersmith and Fulham Public Libraries, Photo Source, Popperfoto, Press Association, Sport and General, P. Sweeney, Syndication International, Alan Walter and Terry Weir. I am grateful to all of the above for helping to uncover such excellent material.

Finally, most heartfelt thanks to my family and friends for putting up with my one-track conversation and sporadic bouts of gloom; to my dear friend Stephen Lavell for sharing with me his deep knowledge of the game; and, as ever, to Jackie Spreckley, the best supporter I have ever known.

Willow Books
William Collins Sons & Co Ltd
London · Glasgow · Sydney · Auckland
Toronto · Johannesburg

First published 1988
© Simon Inglis 1988

British Library Cataloguing In Publication Data
Inglis, Simon
    League football and the men who made it:
    official centenary history of the Football
    League, 1888–1988.
    1. Soccer – England – History
    I. Title
    796.334'63'0942   GV944.G7

    ISBN 0 00 218242 4

Set in Garamond by Butler & Tanner Ltd, Frome
Printed and bound in Great Britain by Butler & Tanner Ltd, Frome

Contents

Introduction

Such a simple concept, and all it needed was for someone to invent it. The idea of a group of teams playing a pre-arranged schedule of games against each other, home and away, seems so natural to us today that it's rather hard to imagine why it took the Victorians so long to stumble upon it.

In fact, it was cricketers who first hit upon the idea, then baseball players in America.

But such is the power and popularity of Association football that no sooner had William McGregor formed the Football League on 17 April 1888 than leagues started sprouting up all over Britain, and within a few decades in every corner of the globe. There isn't a footballing nation in the world today which doesn't run a league in some form or another.

Nor are leagues confined to football. The idea has spread to hockey, rugby, speedway, basketball, ten-pin bowling, and no doubt shove ha'penny and tiddlywinks too; from the very highest levels of professional international sport down to the humblest group of enthusiasts.

In 1987 the Football Association had ties with some 1500 leagues in England (not including schoolboy football), of which the Football League is only one. The FA has 41,569 affiliated clubs, of which only ninety-two are in the League. There are Sunday leagues, Wednesday afternoon leagues, leagues for the unemployed, leagues for local factories, five-a-side leagues, six-a-side leagues, and leagues for women. Only 0.1 per cent of the people playing football in England in 1987 were full-time professionals.

But the Football League is the daddy of them all. It is also the largest national professional league existing in the world today.

This Official Centenary History of the Football League is not a history of English football, nor is it a survey of the current state of the game. Many other writers have already tackled these subjects quite expertly enough.

Instead, this is the history of rather a small organization which, by dint of its membership and the quality of its weekly programme, happens to dominate football in England and Wales and intrigue massive audiences from Scandinavia to Sydney, from Malta to Madagascar.

It is a history with three main strands:

• the origins and development of the Football League itself, from the small group of volunteers who ran it from a terraced house in Hanley to a multi-million-pound concern with a staff of thirty-one at Lytham St Annes and London;

• the interplay between the League and its constituent members, both at club level and on an individual basis, and the relationship between the League and other bodies such as the FA, the PFA and, lately, the Government;

• The stories of The Men Who Made It; that is, the men who conducted the League's business. Not players, not managers, but officials of the League and the elected members of its governing body, the Management Committee.

Because the League is a democratic organization, and because club chairmen are invariably powerful men who have 'made it' in their own right and who aren't always willing to compromise, change is a slow process in the Football League. One of the measures agreed in 1986, for example, to reduce the majority required for rule changes from three-quarters to two-thirds, was first proposed in 1895! It matters not how brilliant or vital a proposal from the Management Committee may be; if the clubs don't agree, then it will not become part of League regulations. In this sense, the history of the Football League is a chronicle of one hundred years of disputes and dissent, with just the occasional outbreak of *détente*, all played out to a gallery of continual criticism and abuse from onlookers.

From the minute it was born the League has been on the defensive. 'Just a money-making circus' sneered one reporter in 1888, and the stigma has remained ever since. Even amongst the League's many friends there has always been someone who can run it better ... until he tries himself, that is. Many a rebel director has joined the Committee only to realize how different life seems from the other side of the rule-book.

The current Management Committee meets every three weeks, each meeting taking hours of preparation beforehand and the best part of a day to conduct. Motorway dashes and last-minute shuttle flights are all par for the course for the average Committee man today.

But for the first seventy to eighty years of the League, a Management Committee member had to know the rail network backwards and be prepared for many a late night trek home on a cold, foggy night. For years, the Secretary Tom Charnley and Committee member Charles Sutcliffe would travel overnight to save hotel fees, working in a dimly-lit railway compartment with foot-warmers and blankets as their only comforts.

The Men Who Made It had to be dedicated indeed to go through all that for the honour of attending long-winded meetings, following which there would rarely be any thanks and invariably plenty of brickbats, once their decisions were made public.

Because of this, not surprisingly, The Men Who Made It formed closely-knit units in which friendship and bonhomie abounded. How many times have I heard former Committee men sigh dreamily: 'Ah yes, we were a grand bunch in those days!'

The main source for this book has been the minutes of the Football League; that is, the public and private accounts of every single Management Committee meeting, every Annual General Meeting, every Extraordinary General Meeting and every Special General Meeting.

League minutes are not easy to digest, and I have highlighted only a few of the more unusual extracts throughout the book. However, the following, from June 1976, is not untypical of the kind of language in which weighty football business is often phrased:

'The constitution of the various Football Association committees was discussed, in particular the Executive Committee which, it was suggested, might usefully comprise the Chairmen of all standing committees. It was left to the President to speak to the FA Chairman about the constitution of the committee which appointed committees.'

In debate, the language was invariably a little more, shall we say, direct. Nevertheless, one cannot escape the fact that running a ninety-two-club Football League is a devilishly complex bueaucratic business which makes quite exhausting demands upon its voluntary elected representatives. Energy, devotion to the game, and above all, a sense of humour, are vital prerequisites for any prospective Committee man.

Using the League minutes as my basic source, I have then consulted any newspaper I could find which showed an interest in the League's affairs. In the period 1888–1930 that meant predominantly the sporting press (daily papers were not greatly interested until the 1920s), and more specifically the weekly *Athletic News*, which for many years seemed to serve as the League's very own in-house publication. One of its editors was a President of the League, and several members of the Management Committee contributed regularly to its columns.

Nowadays it seems astonishing how minutely these men would discuss quite arcane aspects of the game in such a public forum. Or how deeply they were involved at every level. At one point League President J. J. Bentley was reporting in *Athletic News* on matches he had himself refereed, while elsewhere in the 'paper commenting on the affairs of the game in his capacity as editor.

It is said that today's leaders in the game are too powerful. By the standards of men such as J. J.

Bentley they are but supporting actors.

A major secondary source of material has been the various memoirs and histories already compiled by League officials and journalists. In 1938 the League produced *The Story of the Football League*, written by Charles Sutcliffe (a leading figure on the Management Committee), Fred Howarth (the League Secretary) and J. A. Brierley (a Preston journalist), on the occasion of the League's fiftieth anniversary. This invaluable reference book is referred to in the text as Sutcliffe's history.

I have also leant heavily on the works of Ivan Sharpe, a former League player who became the leading football journalist of his time. No outsider ever enjoyed the confidence of the League more than Sharpe, and it was no surprise when he was asked to write the League's seventy-fifth anniversary history in 1963. Alan Hardaker's autobiography, *Hardaker of the League*, has proved to be another excellent source, since it is the only candid account ever to emerge from the inner sanctum of the League.

My fourth major source has, of course, been The Men Who Made It themselves, their families and friends. Talking to these past and present stalwarts of the League has given me a very real sense of the strengths which hold it together.

I liken the League, as did men such as Sutcliffe, to a family. Families do not always get on well; they bicker, they fight – over money, pride, jealousies – and they don't always like each other. But the best families overcome these differences and stay together. Sometimes they even kiss and make up and have a jolly good laugh about it afterwards. And there is nothing finer than a family that is happy, contented and celebrating together.

Football is more than a family, however. It is an industry, but an industry quite unlike any other, for the following reasons.

Firstly, the Football League has ninety-two clubs, the same number as it had in 1950. How many other industries in Great Britain can claim to have maintained the same number of outlets for thirty-eight years? Over a third of those clubs have, at one stage or another in their history, defied all the normal rules of financial survival by clinging on to existence long after most other businesses would have thrown in the towel (or had it thrown in for them by an exasperated bank manager).

Secondly, unlike most competitive industries, football cannot afford to see its losers go under. There is no point in one club putting others out of business by buying up all the best players and attracting all the spectators. Liverpool need Everton as much as Everton need Liverpool, and both depend on the likes of Tranmere to bridge the gap between a kick around in Stanley Park and a place in the limelight. Everyone wants to win, of course, but winning has no meaning if the contest has no depth.

The third factor which makes League football so unlike any other industry – or sport for that matter – is its capacity to play the most wicked and wonderful tricks on clubs and individuals. It can cast a club such as Wolverhampton Wanderers from the First to the Fourth Division without a moment's regard for the club's honours or traditions, yet thrust a homely little outfit like Wimbledon from the outlying branches of non-League football to the top of the tree, all within a decade. No other sporting framework has maintained this facility for toying with the hopes and dreams of so many millions of people with such startling unpredictability.

Such is the enduring fascination of the Football League. May it live on for another hundred years, and so, too, may the names of The Men Who Made It. We owe them all a great debt. It is a precious heritage.

Simon Inglis
London, April 1988

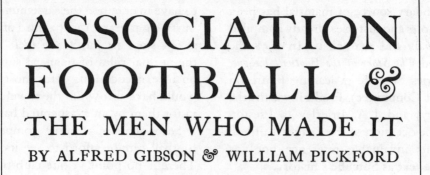

ASSOCIATION FOOTBALL &
THE MEN WHO MADE IT
BY ALFRED GIBSON & WILLIAM PICKFORD

IN FOUR VOLUMES
VOL. III

FULLY ILLUSTRATED

LONDON
THE CAXTON PUBLISHING COMPANY
CLUN HOUSE, SURREY STREET, W.C.

*The title and presentation of this book is unashamedly
based on a four-volume set entitled* Association
Football and The Men Who Made It, *first published
about 1906. 'So long as the Empire lasts,' wrote its
authors Gibson and Pickford, 'football will rejoice its
robust, manly, sport-loving millions.' Dedicating their
work to all who loved the game and manfully strove to
keep it free from reproach, the authors intended the
books to be 'a monument for the men who have made the
game'.*

CHAPTER ONE

William McGregor – Father of the League

*I*n 1905, William McGregor wrote:

'Football has seen many changes. Beginning as quite a desultory pastime, club matches were for long deemed the highest form of football fixture because no other kind of fixture was known. Then, with the increase of interest, came International matches; then district associations took shape, and we had interesting games between picked forces of those associations, and very attractive the games were. Then there came the professional era, and with it came the Football League.

As the founder of the Football League, I suppose I am naturally looked to as its apologist. Well, there is not much to apologise for; there is much to explain.

I suppose no institution ever founded in connection with a national pastime has been girded so freely as the Football League. To some the very term "league" seems to act as a red rag is currently supposed to act to a bull.

I have heard people say they hated, detested, and loathed the word "league". I have usually put these people down – I was going to say as brainless asses, but perhaps that would be too strong a term, so I will say as foolish people.

I do not see that the title of an organisation matters much; its scope and objects matter vitally. I wonder what would happen if you could blot out the league system from sport from this day onward? I wonder who would be better for it? Ninety-nine players out of every hundred, and ninety-nine clubs out of every hundred, would be infinitely worse off, because no principle ever formulated in connection with sport has caused so much really genuine, bona-fide competition as the league system.

No sooner was the League formed than it was copied throughout the country, and now it is the accepted form of football strife. The colleges at Oxford and Cambridge play their matches on the league system, and they gain greatly in interest by reason of that. The man who says he loathes the word "league" is foolish, and there is an end to the argument.'

The father and founder of the Football League was, by all accounts, a quite remarkable man. When commentators noted that he was without enemies and never lost a friend they were not, it would seem, indulging in gratuitous flattery. Throughout his life William McGregor won friends and influenced people.

That he possessed the power, energy and determination to form the League and yet still remain a man of faith, humour and kindness is to his eternal credit. William McGregor was undoubtedly one of the greatest men ever to serve the game of football.

Born in the Scottish village of Braco, Perthshire, in 1847, McGregor first saw football being played by stonemasons when he was aged about seven. While the men were at work one day, young William and his friends borrowed their ball and tried to emulate the masons. The attempt put William in bed for a week afterwards, but he was soon joining his friends in games which lasted from morning till night.

Thereafter, McGregor didn't see another football again until around 1870 when he was drawn south to Birmingham, then in the midst of a trade boom brought on by the Franco-

Prussion war.

With his brother Peter, who, it is thought, had arrived in the city earlier and was working as a nurseryman in Harborne, McGregor opened a linen draper's shop on the corner of Brearley Street and Summer Lane, then a busy thoroughfare a mile or so from the city centre. A warehouse now occupies the site, with a public telephone marking the shop's exact location.

Summer Lane, Newtown, was then a cobbled, gas-lit street, set amid the type of dense housing and small workshops that typified industrialized Victorian cities. In later life McGregor recalled how the area began to deteriorate with the activities of the so-called Harding Street Gang. He said, 'Ruffianism became so rampant that the lower end of Summer Lane became a very dangerous quarter. It was no uncommon thing for the police to be stoned there, and often severely handled.' The same gang had been mentioned in Parliament in connection with the Aston riots, which broke out after a Tory party meeting at Aston Lower Grounds (the site of Villa Park).

Sixty years later, poet John Douglas described Summer Lane as 'a blue-bricked street of slums and shame, of back-to-backs and drunken fame, the toughest street in Brum ...'

McGregor would barely recognize Newtown today, but he would be familiar with the problems facing its people. He was a passionate and at one time active member of the Liberal Party. He was also a dedicated Methodist, at a time when Christianity, combined with a concern for social welfare, often manifested itself in the promotion of sport. As a small-time shopkeeper McGregor didn't have the resources to be a philanthropist on the grand scale of many leading Victorians; he lived and worshipped among the poor and was certainly never affluent himself. But as a self-employed man with a natural gift for leadership and rapport it was inevitable that he would leave

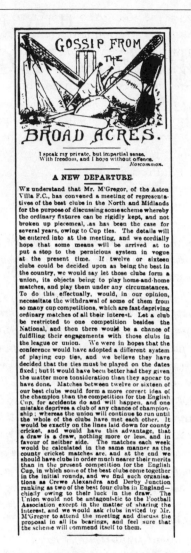

'Gossip from the Broadacres' in Athletic News, 20 March 1888, backs up McGregor's plan for a new competition, and confirms that the idea was based on cricket rather than American baseball.

his mark in one way or another.

That football became the focus of his attention was initially due to the Glasgow club Queen's Park, whose exploits he'd read about in the Scottish press. Anxious to see what all the fuss was about, soon after arriving in Birmingham he started to watch a club nicknamed the Quilters, at the Aston Lower Grounds. Unfortunately, kick-off was often too late for the young shopkeeper, so he wrote to a newspaper to complain. He later reckoned this might have been the first letter of complaint against a football club!

McGregor then organized his half-day closing on Saturday, to allow him to watch the city's strongest team – Calthorpe, founded by another Scot, J. Campbell Orr. But he always had to return to the shop to reopen at 6 p.m.

Had he directed his energies towards Calthorpe or the Quilters, the history of football might have been quite different. Instead, McGregor made contact with Aston Villa after hearing they had three Scotsmen in the team. One of them was club captain George Ramsay, who had come to Birmingham, very much like McGregor, in search of work.

Some accounts contend that McGregor was primarily attracted to Villa by their skilful play and their uniform dress. McGregor was always an admirer of neatness on the pitch. But Villa's Wesleyan Chapel connection may also have impressed him.

McGregor was no footballer himself. He occasionally played in goal during practice matches, but was never picked for Villa's first team. It wasn't long, however, before George Ramsay recognized his other qualities and invited McGregor on to the committee. Villa were so badly off at that time that bailiffs once seized all their possessions. To prevent a recurrence, McGregor thereafter stored them at his shop for safe keeping.

THE
CHEAPEST HOUSE IN THE TRADE
FOR
CARDIGAN JACKETS, WOOL SHIRTS, VESTS &C.
(ENGLISH AND SCOTCH MAKE.)
Strongly recommended by the Medical Faculty.

P. & W. McGREGOR,
306, & 307, Summer Lane,
BIRMINGHAM

A very large stock of
Football Jerseys always in stock.
Special patterns made to order.

'What a place for gossip that used to be!' But while William devoted more and more time to football, Peter was left to mind the shop. Eventually he took on an assistant, Andy Hunter, the brother of Aston Villa's inspirational Scottish captain, Archie.

The linen draper's shop on Summer Lane soon became a favourite gathering place for sports enthusiasts, and not merely because it sold football shirts. 'What a place for gossip that used to be!' recalled one journalist.

'Genial Mac', according to one who knew him well, was 'a grave, thoughtful Scotsman, with a benevolent face of Father Christmas type, built on those ample lines, both bodily – which carry weight in any assembly – and mentally, which prove that the weight carried is not everything. Mr W. McGregor has the goodwill of everyone and the enmity of none.'

Supported by George Ramsay and another exiled Scot, Charles 'Fergus' Johnstone, McGregor went on to hold every office at Villa. He often acted as umpire (in the days before match officials had to be neutral), and once recovered a piano stolen from the Villa's meeting room, by placing advertisements in local papers and tracing the thief to London.

Until the turn of the century, McGregor, his wife Jessie – 'a most estimable and lovable woman' – and their two children lived in a terraced house on Witton Road, within sight of the famous Aston Lower Grounds. The 1870s and 1880s saw the Lower Grounds reach their heyday as pleasure gardens, offering not just football but all kinds of sporting entertainment, from athletics to cricket. There was also an aquarium, a boating lake, a skating rink, a restaurant, a concert hall and a theatre.

Villa played in those days a couple of miles

away at Perry Barr, and as they grew to prominence, so too did McGregor. For example, with English football at a crossroads in the early 1880s, McGregor fought for the exemption of major clubs from the opening rounds of cup competitions. Whilst active in local charity and the Birmingham and District Counties Association, he also inaugurated various local schools' and junior competitions.

But the major issue of the decade was professionalism, which by 1885 threatened to tear the British football world apart. Although not an early supporter, once McGregor realized its spread was inevitable he soon lent his voice to the cause; and a powerful voice it was, too. At a special FA conference he was the only delegate from the Midlands prepared to stand up and openly advocate professionalism, and to admit that his club was paying players. His was not the sole voice – Major Sudell of Preston North End was almost certainly more prominent – but McGregor was amongst the most respected and eloquent.

Having helped to secure the recognition of professionalism in 1885, McGregor was subsequently keen to curb what he feared might be its effects upon both the players and unity within the game. McGregor was never a rebel; he remained loyal to the FA all his life.

But it is as father of the League that McGregor will always be remembered, and to appreciate how and why he evolved the idea it is important to discover something of McGregor's life in the 1880s.

Until football took up more of his time, McGregor was a member of the local Liberal Association. His membership until 1882 coincided with a period when Joseph Chamberlain was the local president, and men like John Bright, the fiery MP from Rochdale, would come to address the party faithful. Oliver Vaughton, whose family was long associated with Villa, was also a member, as were other Birmingham notables such as J. S. Reynolds, the industrialist, and Councillor Cadbury, of the Bournville family.

Birmingham in those years was a thriving and influential centre of liberal and radical ideas. The need for civic improvement, the betterment of the worker's lot, the virtues of temperance, faith and diligence were all planks of late Victorian urban life. Football clubs, which promoted sport, kept men off the streets, enhanced local prestige and inspired loyalty, ostensibly helped towards these goals – even if they were often tainted by the twin evils of drinking and blasphemy.

In common with several eminent figures in early football, William McGregor was a lifelong teetotaller (as were Blackburn's John Lewis, Sheffield's Charles Clegg and Small Heath's Walter Hart). But he was no dour evangelist. Indeed, he was renowned for his sense of mirth. Referee Harry Walker recalled that on one foreign tour to Budapest, the FA party was invited to visit a champagne cellar, where samples were 'temptingly arrayed' for the visitors. McGregor tactfully requested mineral water, but by a misunderstanding was given instead a large glass of 'medicinal water', which he consumed innocently. The next day he was confined to his bed, and he told Walker afterwards: 'I assure you, it was not sham pain!' Mr Pooter would have been proud.

A few doors from the McGregors' shop stood the local Liberal club, and a hundred yards further down the road, at 91 Alma Street, was the coffee shop of McGregor's close friend, fellow Liberal and Villa enthusiast, Joe Tillotson. (The coffee shop was on the site of what is now the Cross Guns pub car park, on Rodway Close.) Tillotson was a popular referee and linesman who stayed on the League list until he was fifty-two, in 1909. He became President of the Birmingham County FA, an active Liberal city councillor, and lived to the age of eighty-eight.

Tillotson's shop and the Liberal club were popular meeting places where it is believed that the first conversations about the League took place. In fact, according to some reminiscences, it was Tillotson who first gave

McGregor the idea for a regular competition, one winter's evening in 1886. Peter Morris's history of Aston Villa (Naldrett Press, 1960) says that Tillotson complained 'that Villa supporters were getting tired of watching one-sided friendly games at Perry Barr'. McGregor then discussed the problem with fellow Villa committee men Charles 'Fergus' Johnstone and J. E. Margoschis.

Although Tillotson may have voiced the supporters' discontent, there can be little doubt that McGregor was already aware of the problem. 'A great many people saw the difficulty which football and footballers were in; I happened, luckily, to be the one man at that particular time who saw the way out.'

But was MacGregor really the first man to think of a football league? In later years, the columns of the *Sunday Chronicle*, *Athletic News* and *Sporting Chronicle*, all from the Hulton Newspapers stable in Manchester, reckoned that credit for 'the ardent advocacy' of the league system should have been due to a Manchester journalist called W. H. Mounsey. John Bentley of Bolton Wanderers, another Hulton journalist in Manchester, refuted this. Bentley was involved with McGregor's plan almost from the very beginning and always maintained that the idea of the League was McGregor's alone.

Certainly, McGregor was the only man to take any action. What he sought above all was to bring about 'a fixity of fixtures' which, he argued, would eliminate the uncertainty plaguing professional football in the 1880s.

This uncertainty was strangling the infant game. For example, advertised games would often be cancelled or postponed at the last minute, not due to bad weather, transport problems or illness – common enough obstacles anyway – but because one of the clubs had been lured into another fixture which promised to attract a higher gate. The guilty club might send a scratch eleven to the original venue for appearances' sake; they might not.

In newspapers of the period, dozens of adverts can be found from club secretaries desperately seeking games to help them raise money to pay their best players. A cancelled fixture or an empty Saturday meant not only a loss of income but also a risk of losing players to whoever else came up with the offer of some cash and a game. Before professionalism was legalized in 1885, therefore, the players held the whip hand. After 1885 the pressure increased, and this resulted in too many games with no competitive spirit (for example, contrived Married *v.* Singles matches).

Not surprisingly, fans grew frustrated, not always knowing which team was going to turn up, or at what time. And they were bored with friendlies and one-sided contests. McGregor wrote of this time:

'The lax and loose system which prevailed became intolerable. It is on record that in one season in the early 'eighties West Bromwich Albion refrained from issuing a fixture-card because they found that the match list was so cut up by Cup ties and replayed Cup games that it was farcical to have a printed list.

Usually a club like the Albion would enter for four or five cups, and make provision for a reasonably long run in each. If they were thrown out in the first round they had blank days; if they kept in longer than they expected to remain, then fixtures already arranged had to go by the board. Spectators, too, became disgusted with the intermittent character of the fare provided for them.'

Contemporary sources go as far as claiming that by 1887–8 professional football was all but dying on its feet. As Everton's chronicler, Thomas Keates, put it, 'How can we vitalise the torpid? That was the question.'

The answer came from cricket.

A regular, competitive system of fixtures involving only the top clubs, along the lines of the County Cricket Championship, was the obvious solution. It would still leave room for local and national cup games, but maintain interest throughout the season if a team was knocked out in the early rounds. (Some sources suggest that the idea for a league came from the then recently formed National Baseball League in the United States. McGregor, however, always cited the County Championship as his model.)

After discussing his idea for a new competition with fellow Villa committee members, McGregor probably started testing the climate of opinion in early 1887, during the second full season of legalized professionalism. The League was not, therefore, conceived in haste.

Nor, indeed, was the concept eagerly embraced by all. McGregor had to tread warily. In Sheffield, for example, he found that Wednesday were not only afraid that any new organization might antagonize the FA, but also that regularized fixtures would be too expensive to stage. McGregor's priority was to interest the most powerful club in the land, Preston North End. If they would agree to join, then the other major northern clubs would soon follow.

After various travels around the country, and with the backing of his committee at Aston Villa, McGregor made the first formal move on 2 March 1888 with a letter sent to five clubs: Blackburn Rovers, Bolton Wanderers, Preston North End, West Bromwich Albion and Aston Villa. According to J. A. H. Catton (Tityrus of *Athletic News*), McGregor wrote this circular in pencil on the back of a draper's fashionplate.

'*Every year it is becoming more and more difficult for football clubs of any standing to meet their friendly engagements and even arrange friendly matches. The consequence is that at the last moment, through Cup-tie interference, clubs are compelled to take on teams who will not attract the public.*

I beg to tender the following suggestion as a means of getting over the difficulty – that ten or twelve of the most prominent clubs in England combine to arrange home and away fixtures each season, the said fixtures to be arranged at a friendly conference about the same time as the International Conference.

This combination might be known as the Association Football Union, and could be managed by a representative of each club. Of course this is in no way to interfere with the National Association. Even the suggested matches might be played under Cup-tie rules. However, this is a detail.

My object in writing at present is merely to draw your attention to the subject, and to suggest a friendly conference to discuss the matter more fully. I would take it as a favour if you would kindly think the matter over, and make whatever suggestion you may deem necessary.'

In this one letter McGregor set the scale and the tone for future developments: the limit of twelve clubs (calculated simply on the basis of available Saturday afternoons), the concept of democratic representation, and the implementation of FA rules.

McGregor was, of course, addressing himself to old friends and fellow campaigners, men he'd met many times at matches, at meetings on the issue of professionalism, and under the auspices of the FA.

At the foot of his letter McGregor asked correspondents to suggest the names of other clubs who might be suitable members. He received only two replies. One was from Bolton's secretary, John Bentley, who was to become such an important character in the League's development. Bentley's list proposed eight clubs: Wolverhampton Wanderers, Accrington, Burnley, Halliwell (from Bolton), Notts County, Mitchell St George's (from Birmingham), Stoke and, surprisingly, an amateur team from the South, Old Carthusians.

McGregor wasn't interested in amateurs, nor clubs like Halliwell or Mitchell St George's. He envisaged inviting only one club from each town or city. But after such a poor response to his letter, he doubted whether the idea would reach fruition at all. That was until three weeks later, when the first exploratory meeting was successfully held, at a time when McGregor knew most club representatives would be in London – the eve of the 1888 Cup Final at The Oval, between prospective members West Bromwich Albion and Preston North End. The first ever minutes of the Football League read as follows:

'*In response to a circular letter issued by Mr McGregor of the Aston Villa FC the following gentlemen met at the Anderton Hotel London on Friday evening March 22nd.*
  Messrs W. McGregor, Aston Villa, chair
  A. T. Ashwell, Notts County
  J. T. Birtwistle, Blackburn Rovers
  W. Allt, Wolverhampton Wanderers
  Geo Armistead, Burnley
  T. Smith, W. Bromwich Albion
  H. Lockett, Stoke. Hon Sec protem'

Of the twelve founder members, Preston were presumably too wrapped up in Cup Final preparations to attend, or maybe they were simply playing hard to get. Bolton were also absent, although John Bentley's personal involvement suggests that this was not significant. Derby's delegate attended, but only to observe. He was thus omitted from the minutes, as was another onlooker, Fred Rinder, McGregor's neighbour in Birmingham and fellow Villa committee man who had accompanied his friend 'Mac' on fact-finding visits around the country. George Ramsay also attended.

McGregor was then aged forty-one, a modestly successful shopkeeper. Of the other men around the table on 22 March, the only 'gentleman' as such was the former Rugby schoolboy Arthur Ashwell, a former Notts footballer, referee and cricketer, now a solicitor of Fletcher Gate, Nottingham. He was aged thirty-five.

John Birtwistle, aged thirty-two, was an inspector of Factories. He later became a prominent freemason and director of the Blackburn Philanthropic Mutual Assurance Company. His son Thomas was also a director of Blackburn Rovers.

George Armistead, then aged thirty-four, was an auctioneer who lived a few doors away from Turf Moor.

Thomas Smith, aged thirty-three, was a former Albion half-back known to the fans as 'Razor'. He had been Albion's club secretary since 1884 and continued in office until a paid official took over in 1890. Like many Albion players, he became involved in the club through his employment at George Salter and Co., manufacturers of springs and scales. Razor Smith was credited with suggesting in 1884 that Albion adopt the thrush (or 'throstle', as known locally) as the club's emblem.

Apart from McGregor, only two of the men minuted at this first gathering would continue to be involved in League affairs.

Bill Allt, the Wolves secretary, was a boot and shoe maker who owned two shops, in Worcester Street and North Street (opposite Molineux). Like McGregor, Allt supplied some of his team's kit. His son, the wonderfully named Dr W. Greenhouse Allt, became a celebrated musician.

Harry Lockett, a printer from Hanley in the Potteries, also had a famous son, but more of that later. Harry became the League's first secretary, and it is from his copperplate handwriting that we learn how the 22 March meeting confirmed McGregor's opinion:

'. . . *a strong feeling was evinced that something should be done to improve the present unsatisfactory state of club fixtures & to render them more certain in their fulfilment & interesting in character.*'

Several suggestions were made, with Lockett underlining the word 'suggestions', no doubt to emphasize McGregor's desire not to appear elitist or dictatorial.

The main points were these:

● *That the following twelve clubs be invited to form a League or Union to play 'home and home' fixtures: (in Lockett's order) Preston North End, Burnley, Accrington, Blackburn Rovers, Bolton Wanderers, Stoke, Aston Villa, West Bromwich Albion, Everton, Wolverhampton Wanderers, Derby County and Notts County.*

(Thus there were to be six from the Midlands and six from Lancashire, each having professional players. Although Preston had missed the meeting, McGregor still hoped they'd join.)

● *That these twelve clubs be invited to a conference at the Royal Hotel, Manchester on Tuesday 17 April at 6.30 p.m. Their representatives should be in a position to arrange fixtures for the coming season (1888/9).*

● *That all matches be played under the Cup Rules of the Football Association but that 'any bona fide member of a club shall be allowed to play providing he shall not have played with any other club in the Union or League during the same season'.*

● *That each club shall be expected to play its full strength team in all matches.*
(This is the only rule among the original suggestions which survives today.)

● *That the gross gates be divided in all matches, apart from the income derived from reserved stand members and season tickets.*

● *That the price of admission shall be at the option of the home club.*

● *That the average shall be taken from wins, draws and losses and not from the number of goals scored.*

● *That the four clubs having the lowest average shall retire but shall be eligible for re-election.*

Once these 'suggestions' were released for public appraisal – and it must be said that the matter aroused almost no publicity at all, not even in the sporting press – the most controversial element proved to be the choice of clubs.

Like so many big-spending clubs since, Preston were not popular, especially for having such a high number of imported players. West Bromwich Albion, who beat them in the Cup Final the day after the meeting, were, on the other hand, a team of pure Englishmen. Preston had also just refused to play Accring-

ton in the Lancashire Cup Final because the venue was Blackburn, where they claimed they had been given a hostile reception recently. (As a result of this refusal, North End were suspended for two weeks, during which time they managed to play eight games!)

The selection of Accrington also met with criticism. *Athletic News* commented on 3 April 1888 that Accrington were 'not particular whether they win or lose matches with clubs admittedly inferior to them'.

Notts County were another controversial choice. 'They are distinctly fortunate in gaining admission to the "ring"', it was said. Their recent performances proved incontrovertibly 'that Notts have just closed their absolutely worst season. I have no hesitation in declaring that their prestige alone saved them from an ignominious collapse . . .'

Athletic News continued, 'Some of the "twelve most prominent" Association clubs, who are to form the new League, have been knocked into smithereens by teams who, so far, have been left out in the cold.' Those clubs included Everton's neighbour, Bootle. Everton at the time were regarded as the weakest of the twelve invited clubs.

A week later, *Athletic News* reported that Mr J. G. Hall of Crewe Alexandra, another of the overlooked clubs, was trying to gather support for a parallel league, to be known as the Combination. In fact, on the very day the League was officially born, 17 April 1888, the newspaper reported that Hall's 'second ring' might yet prove 'very little inferior to the other one'.

This was a faint hope, however. The list of eighteen clubs invited by Hall included only one FA Cup winner, Blackburn Olympic, whose glories had already been entirely eclipsed by their neighbour, Blackburn Rovers.

Of the other clubs Hall invited, Crewe Alexandra and Derby Junction had reached the FA Cup semi-finals that year, Mitchell St George's and Small Heath Alliance were Aston Villa's closest rivals and Bootle, as we have noted, had better credentials than Everton.

Hall's other targets were Walsall Town Swifts, Derby Midland, Notts Rangers, Burslem Port Vale, Leek, Newton Heath, Witton, Darwen, Sheffield Wednesday and Long Eaton Rangers. Nottingham Forest and Halliwell, it was thought, were unlikely to join the Combination. 'Having been overlooked as among the chosen twelve, they will probably refuse to place themselves amongst the second-class clubs.'

Second-class or not, the alacrity with which Hall copied McGregor's example showed one thing: this league business was going to be mighty popular. But, as William McGregor was soon to discover, it was no easy matter being a pioneer.

For a start, Preston still refused to respond. The biggest club in the country, McGregor complained later, and they wouldn't even reply to a letter. Without them he was convinced the League was doomed to failure. But North End were not alone. Other club secretaries also failed to respond.

His message did sink in, however, because a second meeting did take place, on 17 April, this time in Manchester at the Royal Hotel (a famous coaching inn which until 1908 stood where Lewis's department store is now located in Manchester's Piccadilly, on the corner of Mosley Street and Market Street).

Tuesday 17 April 1888 marks the birth of the League in every way. If McGregor thought that clubs who had so often squabbled over fixtures, rules, results and receipts in the past would immediately call a truce under the aegis of his new organization, he was very much mistaken. Having formed an instant family, they were squabbling from the off.

According to the minutes, the historic meeting at the Royal Hotel saw the attendance of eleven of the twelve founder members (unless Harry Lockett simply forgot to record West Bromwich's attendance, by no means impossible for this often wayward first secretary).

The men we know for certain attended the inaugural gathering were as follows: William McGregor (Villa), who took the chair, Major William Sudell (Preston), Harry Lockett (Stoke), Bill Allt (Wolves), John Bentley (Bolton), John Lewis (Blackburn), Alex Nisbet (Everton), Edwin Browne (Notts County), J. H. Richardson (Derby) and George Armistead (Burnley). There is no record of who attended on behalf of Accrington, but it was almost certainly their charismatic secretary, Joe Hartley.

First on the agenda was the choice of a name for this new organization. This brought McGregor's first defeat, albeit a minor one, at the instigation of William Sudell. Sudell proposed the title 'Football League'. McGregor favoured the term 'union', but this was felt to be too similar to that of the Rugby Football Union.

According to Charles Sutcliffe's *Story of the Football League* (see Bibliography), McGregor 'was not impressed by the term "league", owing to its use by political and other bodies'. McGregor's distaste was presumably that of many a citizen of the day. The term was reminiscent of the Land League, which had been responsible for various agrarian outrages in Ireland, and the Home Rule League, led by Charles Stewart Parnell in the 1870s, which had tried to disrupt Parliament in order to advance the cause of Irish home rule. Equally, Sudell might have argued that McGregor's favoured term, 'union', would be associated with the growing numbers of organized radical workers, some of whom, perhaps, were to be found smouldering with discontent in the cotton mill which Sudell managed.

Having lost over the issue of the name, McGregor next found that his plan for clubs to divide up gate money was also rejected. Instead, the delegates agreed that the visiting club should be guaranteed a sum of £15. Thus, McGregor's egalitarian ideal was quickly sacrificed in the interests of profit. As Sutcliffe commented quite rightly fifty years later: 'This rejection of the sharing principle is of historic interest and importance.'

These two matters apart, the meeting agreed upon all the other recommendations laid down on 22 March. John Lewis proposed that the number of clubs be increased if sufficient dates could be found for fixtures. Until such a time, it was decided that the personal applications of three clubs 'could not be entertained'. The clubs were Nottingham Forest, Halliwell and, surprisingly in the light of their earlier misgivings, Sheffield Wednesday. Although each had been approached by J. G. Hall, they were all still obviously hoping to grab a late place in the League.

Nowadays, it would seem astonishing that Accrington should have been considered a better proposition than Sheffield Wednesday, but in truth local and personal contacts in Lancashire were probably too pervasive to admit outsiders from Yorkshire at such an early stage, especially when free Saturdays were so precious.

Athletic News reported afterwards: 'The supporters of the Forest are pardonably sore about their exclusion', particularly because Edwin Browne of Notts County hadn't spoken up on their behalf. But the Nottingham correspondent, 'Ubique' (actually J. A. H. Catton, later known as 'Tityrus'), felt that Forest's exclusion was more sinister than that.

McGregor had apparently admitted that some of the excluded clubs were superior to ones among the chosen twelve, but that the privileged few had been selected for their having the highest gates. 'Here we have it in one word,' complained Ubique. 'The whole thing is a mere money-making scheme, a speculation.' Forest had big gates, too, he argued. The difference was that County played at Trent Bridge, which had a better tram service than Forest's ground at Lenton.

Bootle were also still riled at being left out. 'They have a splendid record, a splendid ground, and get good gates,' wrote one *Athletic News* correspondent.

For their part, *Athletic News*' editorial writers continued to question the details, but applauded the overall concept, which, they noted 'without claiming any credit', was exactly along the lines they had laid down a few months earlier.

Perhaps the most important proposal made on 17 April came from John Bentley and William Sudell: 'That the clubs forming the League shall support each other and bind themselves to carry out in the strictest sense the arrangements for matches between them, and not allow them to be cancelled on account of any cup competition or other matches.' So crucial was this resolution to the success of the League that each representative present had to agree on it individually.

Thus, if Aston Villa had an important Birmingham Cup match replay, it would have to take second place to a pre-arranged League fixture. Similarly, if a club was tempted to arrange a lucrative friendly, perhaps against Glasgow Rangers or Sheffield Wednesday, they couldn't do it at the expense of a less attractive League fixture.

Other proposals agreed at this historic meeting were that players who had played for another team during the season could play in the League only with the committee's permission, and 'That any offending club or player shall be dealt with by the League, in any manner that they may think fit.' With these two proposals, the League made its first tentative steps towards establishing an authority independent of the FA.

Membership fees were set at £2 2s per annum, and three men were elected to office: William McGregor naturally became chairman, William Sudell was the first treasurer, and Harry Lockett was confirmed as honorary secretary.

Three further matters remained for discussion. McGregor proposed the setting up of a competition for second teams, but because of the likely expense, the scheme was left in abeyance. It was resolved to prepare a list of referees for the League, and finally, to arrange a further meeting for the Grand Hotel, Birmingham, on Tuesday 1 May to organize the first list of fixtures.

Thus, although the forthcoming months were to demonstrate just how complex running this new organization might become, in April 1888 the League seemed just about the simplest and most obvious step football had taken since the formation of the FA and the birth of the English Cup.

And all it had needed was someone to invent it.

Slapping a child's backside at birth is no guarantee of lifelong obedience. So it was with the infant Leaguers. No sooner had the inaugural meeting taken place than teething problems began. First, the fixture meeting in Birmingham had to be put back three weeks, and second, when it was held, four Lancashire clubs – Preston, Blackburn, Bolton and Burnley – didn't bother to attend.

'Rumour has it,' noted the Birmingham correspondent of *Athletic News*, 'that there is not perfect unanimity of opinion amongst members of the newly fledged League, as might be desired, and from what I can gather they are not such a happy, contented family as the outside public would suppose.'

In this, little has changed in the course of a hundred years. Nor, indeed, has criticism of the League. Another Birmingham journalist wrote on 21 April: 'The League, as at present constituted, is not formed for the purpose of encouraging football. It is formed so that the allied clubs may make more money than they already do. As matters stand, many of our leading clubs are nothing better than circus shows.'

Money was, indeed, a major issue. At the 17 May meeting, referees were the first to be disappointed; their proposed fees were halved to one guinea before a ball was even kicked. West Bromwich objected to the £15 visitors' guarantee. Notts County argued that no alterations should be made to any rules except at annual meetings.

But there was some accord, and that was in deciding how to respond collectively to various measures threatened by the FA. This was the beginning of a relationship which would never be easy, that of a body within a body: the League beholden to the FA, but forever trying to establish itself as an independent authority.

For example, it was agreed that League members would oppose *en bloc* a proposal at the forthcoming FA annual meeting to replace studs (or knobs, as Lockett wrote) with bars on players' boots. The League clubs also decided to object 'most strongly' to an FA proposal that 'all clubs entering the Challenge Cup must be members of some affiliated Association'. (This was an attempt to make Preston toe the line. After their suspension for refusing to play in the Lancashire Cup Final, Preston had left the Lancashire FA in a storm of protest. In support of Preston, the League decided, therefore, to argue that membership of a county FA should be optional.)

A further point of contention between the infant League and its parent body was a proposal which promised to give the FA a greater share of Cup semi-final gate receipts. 'It does appear to the casual observer that the FA and other associations get all the cream, and water the milk plentifully besides', commented *Athletic News*.

Looking back on that 17 May meeting, Sutcliffe remarked: 'When it is remembered that

> 'The League should never aspire to be a legislating body ... by the very nature of things the League must be a selfish body. Its interests are wholly bound up in the welfare of its affiliated clubs, and what happens outside is, in a sense, of secondary importance only ... The League has its work to do; the Association has its work to do and there need be no clashing.'
> *William McGregor*

the national and affiliated associations did not view the bantling with any real affection, and that there was division between, if not actual dissent amongst those who were to profit from it, the wonder is that the project did not fall through completely.' That it did not was mainly due to the fact that the League was such a brilliant idea, and its founders knew it.

So did its rivals. On 27 April the Combination was officially established at Crewe and was occasionally referred to thereafter as the 'second league'. The Combination's president, H. Mitchell (of Mitchell St George's), stressed, however, that there should be no antagonism between the two organizations, nor any attempts to prevent his members from facing League clubs in friendlies. (In the event, the twenty-strong Combination did not operate as a league. Its clubs were obliged to play only eight fixtures each, and after a poor first season it disbanded in disarray.)

The fourth meeting of the League took place on 7 June 1888, once more at the Royal Hotel, Manchester. Ten clubs attended on this occasion, the missing members being Preston (again) and Everton.

Gate money was the first issue for debate. The clubs had agreed on 17 April that visiting clubs should receive a guaranteed £15. Louis Ford of West Bromwich proposed a rule change (before the League had even started!) to commit each club to an equal share of gate receipts, after expenses had been paid. This attempt to restore something of McGregor's egalitarian spirit was voted down, so John Bentley proposed instead, with Ford seconding, that the £15 guarantee should apply, but that if clubs wanted to share gate money they could, if both agreed.

Ford may have been worried about low gates. Any attendance below 2000 would not have left much change after paying a £15 guarantee. But his opponents' argument was more powerful. Equal share of gates in the past had frequently given rise to disputes. A set guarantee at least avoided the League having

to become involved in arbitration.

A century later, as we look back at the summer of 1888, it seems rather odd that the birth of one of the most influential bodies in world football should have been greeted without banner headlines or detailed analytical articles in the press. *Athletic News* sounded a rare note of enthusiasm on 12 June by reporting that 'The coming season will be of the most brilliant and successful character.'

Otherwise, the most publicized effect of the League's formation was a change in the structure of the FA Cup. From 1888/9 it was agreed that twenty-two clubs (eighteen seeds and the previous season's four semi-finalists) should be exempted from the early stages, which were now to be categorized as Qualifying Rounds. This change would not have come about without the agitation of the League clubs, who needed to be able to guarantee their League fixtures in the earlier part of the season.

'Now, instead of the leading clubs being compelled to go through the ordeal of slaughtering the innocents in the initial stages, the innocents will have all the fun to themselves until Christmas ... then the real fight for supremacy will commence', wrote 'Brum' in *Athletic News*. (The exemption scheme was drawn up by Richard Gregson of Blackburn Rovers, with the help of Mr W. E. L. Gaine, who was then Town Clerk of Blackburn.)

Although it was by no means certain that all twelve League members would be placed among the twenty-two exempted clubs, the very fact that the League was able to influence the organization of the venerable Cup itself was a measure of how far professional clubs had begun to wield the balance of power in English football.

And as would soon become apparent, the Cup and the League proved to be the perfect foils for one another. As Geoffrey Green wrote in his *History of the Football Association* (Naldrett Press, 1953): 'While the League beats with a steady prosaic throb from week to week, the Cup brings sudden bursts of fresh air and a new impulse to the season in the New Year.'

Once the FA had agreed to rearrange the Cup, the League clubs were then able to draw up their fixtures with confidence, at a fifth meeting on 23 July, again at the Royal Hotel. Six weeks later, the arrangements were complete, and on Saturday 8 September 1888 the first five Football League fixtures kicked off.

Played in perfect weather and in front of enthusiastic crowds, these were the first results:

Bolton	3	Derby	6
Everton	2	Accrington	1
Preston	5	Burnley	2
Stoke	0	West Bromwich	2
Wolves	1	Aston Villa	1

Accounts differ as to who scored the first ever League goal. Some give the credit to Preston's 'lean and sinewy' right-winger Jack Gordon, whereas more reliable reports suggest that Gordon's team-mate Fred Dewhurst claimed the honour. If this be the case then it is a wonderful irony. The League was born out of professionalism, yet the first League goal was scored by an amateur! Dewhurst, a large, physical player who also played for Corinthians, was indeed the only amateur in the Preston team. Meanwhile, George Cox of Aston Villa won the unenviable distinction of scoring the first own goal.

Highest crowd of the day was at Anfield, where an estimated 10,000 watched Everton v. Accrington. 'That's something to make a treasurer smile', commented *Athletic News*. How the crowd reacted to Accrington arriving an hour late was not recorded. Preston attracted 6000, and 3000 each turned up at Wolverhampton and Bolton.

A week later, Notts County and Blackburn joined the fray. County were obviously less of an attraction at Everton, where they lost 2–1 in front of only 3000 spectators. Rovers managed a 5–5 draw at home to Accrington. Bolton's gate rose to 4000 for Burnley's visit,

but Villa's encounter with Stoke drew a mere 2000. That League status was no guarantee of large crowds was emphasized by the fact that on the same afternoon there were equal or higher gates at Newton Heath, Bootle and Birmingham St George's.

Three weeks later came confirmation that not all the chosen twelve were considered among the country's top twenty-two clubs. Despite having League fixtures already arranged, three clubs were forced to play in the first round of the FA Cup's new Qualifying Competition on 6 October 1888. All three had falsely assumed that they'd be exempted until the competition proper. Stoke suffered the most from this presumption: the second eleven they were forced to field in the Cup lost 2–1 at home to the barely known side Warwick County, while in the League the first team went down 7–0 at Preston. Notts County's reserves went through the formality of a 4–1 victory over Eckington, while the seniors drew 3–3 at home to Blackburn in the League. The third club, Everton, who had been drawn at home to Ulster FC, decided to scratch from the Cup and concentrate on their League fixture against Aston Villa.

Three weeks later Notts County had to field two sides again when Cup and League fixtures clashed, and on 17 November County became the first club to have to rearrange a League match, exactly the situation McGregor had hoped to avoid. County reached the Qualifying Competition's Third Round and, no doubt because they were drawn against tough opposition – Derby Midland from the Combination – they gave it priority over their scheduled home match against Derby County. If it was any consolation to McGregor, Combination fixtures suffered similarly from clashes with the Qualifying Competition.

One other aspect of the early matches is worth recording. In several League games the referee was quite openly listed as 'J. J. Bentley, *Athletic News*'. Bentley was assistant editor of the newspaper at the time, which might not

The first League matches were conducted in a rather different way from today's. Until 1891 the referee stood on the touchline, acting as time-keeper and arbitrating whenever the two umpires, each nominated by the clubs, could not agree on a decision. At half time the players stayed on the pitch for their permitted five-minute break, although if the light was failing they might simply change ends and carry straight on with the game. There were no team-sheets or programmes, no numbers (until 1939) and no clocks visible in the ground. League matches might take place on Mondays or Thursdays, and some Saturday games might not start until four o'clock. And if any club official ever knew the exact size of the attendance, he was not supposed to make it public.

seem so surprising except for the fact that he also reported on the games under the *nom de plume* 'Free Critic'. When not judging players on the pitch or in print, Bentley was also among the arbiters of the League's business, which in the opening months mainly concerned transfers and disciplinary problems.

Scottish full-back Alec Dick of Everton became the first footballer to be cautioned by the League, after allegations that on 13 October he had struck a Notts County player and used foul language. After discussing his case, Louis Ford – a committee man *par excellence* judging by the volume of proposals he initiated – proposed 'that Dick be requested to apologise for the ungentlemanly language he used on the Notts ground', but that the charge of striking an opponent was not proven. Significantly, County were requested not to report the case to the FA. The League obviously wanted to keep its dirty linen as well hidden as possible.

Surprising as it may seem, one matter remained unresolved until the eleventh week

of the season, and that was perhaps the most crucial issue of all – how to fix the system of points.

By the time the matter was finally resolved, at a meeting in Birmingham on 21 November, each club had played between nine and eleven games, without a League table, as we know it, appearing. Until then, the newspapers had simply given a list of clubs in order of who had won the most games.

The question of how points should be attributed had long occupied officials, journalists and supporters alike – newspaper columns were full of all sorts of convoluted systems – but by far the most popular method was that proposed by John Bentley: that a win should earn two points, with one point for a draw. Louis Ford once again attempted to fight against the tide, by proposing instead that only a win should earn points. Draws should carry no reward, he argued, and in the end he was only narrowly defeated, Bentley's proposal winning by just six votes to four.

That decision, by just two votes, was to set the pattern for just about every league in the world thereafter, with only a few adjustments being made in more recent years. How different might football have been had Ford's thinking prevailed!

For every one major decision, there were countless other smaller problems to solve, and it didn't take long to ascertain just how time-consuming and complicated running the League would be.

Naturally, those who could both cope with the tedium and spare the time for committee work emerged as the most influential, and in particular the referee and 'Free Critic', John Bentley, seemed to be the most active. McGregor, one suspects, was already adopting a more paternal and watchful role. Certainly, his health was suspect.

On 11 January 1889, the first sub-committee was appointed under Bentley to formulate the first official rules of the Football League. Point by point, these are worth considering:

1. This amalgamation of Clubs shall be called 'The Football League'.

(The term 'English League' was avoided, because McGregor hoped one day to include Scottish clubs.)

2. The League shall consist of one representative from each Club, such representatives to appoint a Chairman, Treasurer and Secretary, and also a Management Committee, consisting of two from each class (see point 4 below), in addition to the Officers, who shall have power to appoint Referees and Umpires, who must be neutral.

(Before 1891, the referee stood on the touchline and acted as arbiter between the two umpires, who were both on the pitch and were usually members of the competing clubs.)

3. The Management Committee shall also conduct the business of the League, and also have power to convene a meeting of the General Committee at any time they may deem it necessary. On receiving requisition signed by one half the Members of the League, the Secretary shall also call a meeting of the General Committee.

4. That there be two classes of League clubs – First and Second – each to consist of Twelve Clubs.

(Although the principle was agreed upon in 1889, it was not until 1892 that a 'second class' came into being. The word 'division' was a later usage, while the term 'Second League' was often used casually between 1888 and 1892 to refer to the Combination, or its successor, the Football Alliance.)

5. There shall be first and second class Championships, the last four in each class to retire, but be eligible for re-election. The League shall have power to order any of the retiring Clubs, or the first four of the second class, to compete in order to decide the question of superiority.

(This rule laid the basis for the end-of-season test matches, an idea borrowed from county cricket and introduced in 1893 to decide which teams went up and down between the divisions. It seems extraordinary to modern observers that the apparently fair and obvious principle of promotion and relegation was so delayed in its application, in England until 1898/9 and in Scotland until 1921/2.)

6. All matches shall be played under the Rules of the Football Association. Any bona fide Member of a Club shall be allowed to play, providing he has not taken part in a League Match for another Club the same season. If he has so played, permission for his transfer must first be obtained from the Management Committee. A bona fide Member of a Club is one who has been registered with the Secretary of the League as such, seven days before playing.

(The first player whose transfer was approved by the League was Archie Goodall, who joined Aston Villa from Preston in October 1888. 'Goodall's arrival at Perry Barr', said *Athletic News*, 'led to a good deal of bickering', which might, in addition to his health, have been a contributory factor in McGregor's decision to resign from the Villa committee. Certainly, McGregor was always opposed to the idea of players being imported to solve a team's problems. Later in life, he told J. A. H. Catton, 'Tityrus' of *Athletic News*, that he had only one regret about the League: that from the very beginning he hadn't insisted on players having a 'territorial qualification' before being allowed to play.)

7. All League matches shall be arranged in a manner decided upon by the General Committee, and the fixtures shall not be made until the Annual Conference of Football Association Secretaries. When possible, the matches shall be so arranged as not to clash with the conference fixtures.

(Since the *raison d'être* of the League was 'a fixity of fixtures', it was vital for games not to clash with other competitions, as they had done in late 1888. To ensure this didn't happen again, in March 1890 the League asked the FA to allow McGregor and Lockett to attend the Annual Conference of Secretaries in London.)

8. Each Club shall play its full strength in all Matches, unless some satisfactory explanation be offered.

(It was crucial that the League didn't become just another competition. Clubs had to give it priority.)

9. Each club shall take its own gate receipts, but

shall pay its opponents a sum of £12.

(This rule, with the guarantee reduced from £15 to £12, was again opposed by West Bromwich, who continued to argue that all gates be shared equally. The matter would not be brought up again until 1908, this time by Preston, but it still won no support.)

10. Averages for the Championship shall be taken from wins and draws (not from the number of goals scored) to be counted as follows: two points for a win and one for a draw. In the event of two or more clubs being equal in points, the best goal average to count.

(By introducing goal averages, the League inflicted upon the public a calculation which, before the advent of electronic calculators, caused all kinds of torment. Mercifully, it was replaced in 1976 by the simpler system of goal difference. The first goal average calculations were made at the end of the opening season, when three pairs of clubs finished level on points.)

11. Any infringement of the League rules shall be dealt with in such a manner as the Management Committee may think fit. Aggrieved clubs shall have the power to call a meeting of the General Committee on payment of a deposit of £5, which shall be forfeited in the event of the complaint not being sustained. The League may also order the complaining club to pay the expenses of the members of the General Committee and those of the opposing clubs.

(The early years of competitive football were characterized by an astonishing level of bickering among clubs over all kinds of matters: the height of crossbars, dimensions of pitches, the state of pitches, eligibility of certain players, legality of particular goals, and so on. Clubs would exploit any conceivable loophole to try to salvage a bad result. In formulating the above rule, therefore, the League hoped to reduce the squabbling and perhaps, just perhaps, cement some kind of higher loyalty to the organization.)

12. At each meeting of the General Committee the representatives pay their own expenses, but the expenses of the Management Committee shall be paid out of the funds of the League, such expenses being third-class railway fares and hotel expenses.

13. A match shall be played each season between teams selected by the Management Committee of the League, the proceeds of which shall be devoted to the funds of the League.

(Such matches, after 1891 in the form of Inter-League games, continued until the 1970s in various forms, and until 1939 formed the League's chief source of revenue. See Appendix Three.)

With the printing of these rules – by Harry Lockett's firm, naturally – the League confirmed its position as the premier force in English professional football. The Football League embraced most, if not all, of the nation's leading teams, and most, if not all, of the nation's leading football administrators. Fixity of fixtures was at last a reality. There could be no holding back now.

CHAPTER TWO
The League Proves Champion

What a proud event the Football League's first ever Annual Meeting must have been, both for William McGregor and for everyone associated with its opening season. Held on 3 May 1889 at the Douglas Hotel, Manchester, all twelve clubs were represented, and for the first time it was agreed to admit members of the press.

Had the inaugural season been a success?

On the playing side, Preston had walked away with the Championship, finishing eleven points clear of runners-up Aston Villa without losing a single game; a record which has never been equalled and probably never will be. Sudell's team of Invincibles also won the Cup without conceding a goal, another astonishing feat.

But there was more to the League than just Proud Preston. A total of 586 goals in 132 matches – over four goals per game on average – was prolific by today's standards (in post-war years, 3.44 goals per game was the record, in 1960/1). Indeed, during the entire season only two League matches ended up goalless.

Off the field, as an organization the League was now well set in its ways, drawing up new rules, discussing discipline, money, procedures and so on – the very stuff of committee life. Within two months of the first rules being circularized, alterations and additions were already being proposed.

Most pressing for the Annual Meeting was the problem of what to do with the four retiring clubs: Burnley, Derby, Notts County and Stoke. Mr Barclay of Everton proposed that these four clubs be allowed to vote in the re-election process. Mr Dewhurst of Preston (was

this the scorer of the first League goal?) and John Lewis of Blackburn disagreed. Since opinion was equally divided, McGregor, as chairman, had to give his casting vote. This he did, in favour of the four.

There then followed, for the first time in League history, an election of new clubs. Apart from the retiring clubs, personal applications were made by Bootle, Newton Heath, Sheffield Wednesday, South Shore (from Blackpool), Birmingham St George's, Sunderland Albion (an offshoot of the present club) and Sunderland. Written applications were also received from Grimsby Town and Walsall Town Swifts. Each club was given five minutes to state its claim, after which the twelve members cast their votes.

The result was as follows: all four retiring clubs were readmitted (Stoke received 10 votes, Burnley 9, Derby 8 and Notts County 7). Of the new applicants, St George's fared best with 5, Wednesday gained 4, Sunderland and Bootle 2 each, Newton Heath 1, and the rest received no votes at all. Thus, what later came to be nicknamed 'the Old Pals' Act' was first seen to operate, with no new members admitted at the inaugural annual meeting.

A measure of early solidarity was a proposal that members again vote *en bloc* at a forthcoming FA meeting, once more on the question of how gate receipts at Cup semi-finals and finals be distributed. Why should the parent body get a bigger slice of the cake, asked the clubs, especially as, in the words of *Athletic News*, the FA had enough money to open a bank?

League clubs now dominated the FA Cup. Since 1886, the final had been contested solely by professional teams, and after 1888 only six non-League clubs would ever reach the semi-final stage. In short, League clubs now dominated English soccer almost entirely. They were soon to prevail north of the border also.

Abolition of the FA's residential qualifications for professionals in 1889 effectively gave League clubs the pick of Scottish players, so that within months the League scene was awash with new faces from north of the border. Knowing this would happen, the FA president, Major Marindin, resigned in protest.

Only the English national team remained beyond the total influence of the League. For example, in the international against Scotland on 13 April 1889, shortly after the League's first full season, six of the eleven came from League clubs: Allen and Brodie (Wolves), Forrest (Blackburn), Goodall (Preston), Bassett (WBA) and Weir (Bolton).

Yet even though the skills of these professionals were coveted by the FA selectors, the men were still treated differently from their amateur team-mates. This division between professionals and so-called 'gentlemen amateurs' was as offensive to men such as McGregor and Bentley as it no doubt was to the players themselves.

William Pickford, a bastion of the FA and the southern amateur game, was suitably dismissive about the new League. Looking back at 1888 he wrote; 'We, in the South, did not for a time take much interest in it. Twelve clubs struggling under the handicap of having to pay players' wages, as a consequence of their success in securing the recognition of professionalism, bound themselves by three simple rules, to meet home and away, to keep their fixtures as arranged, and to play their best available teams. That was about all.'

It was no different in Scotland, where professionalism was officially outlawed until 1893. When the Scottish League formed in 1890, the magazine *Scottish Sport* wrote: 'Our first and last objection to them is that they exist. The entire rules stink of finance – money making

and money grabbing.'

In England, similar scorn from London, no doubt strengthened by a chip or two upon certain shoulders in the North, gave rise to what was seen as a quite straightforward division: the League representing working men from the industrial North and Midlands, and the FA representing amateur gentlemen from the South.

But it would be false to categorize the relationship so simply. The North-East and Yorkshire remained strongholds of the amateur game long after the League spread to those districts, just as the South soon caught up with the North and Midlands when it came to professionalism.

The League certainly provoked considerable interest in the South. Clubs like Bolton and Stoke were regarded in awe if they ever ventured south of Birmingham. As Gibson and Pickford recalled in 1905: 'Year after year the League clubs and their doings formed the chief football topic not only in their own towns, but in the South. To have paid a visit North and seen an occasional match was a memorable event to the average Southerner...'

One wonders if they would have felt the same had they sat in on the deliberations of the Management Committee.

Each meeting brought with it new problems; rules were being broken by the very men who had helped draw them up, while each fresh situation showed up the inadequacies of the existing regulations.

Fielding ineligible players was the most common offence, even amongst those clubs whose representatives sat on the Committee. This apparently hypocritical stance, to be repeated countless times in the future, was no better illustrated than at a meeting on 2 December 1889 when the first punishments were handed out. Wolves, Bolton and Stoke were each fined for fielding ineligible players, by a four-man meeting consisting of Messrs Allt (Wolves), Bentley (Bolton), Lockett (Stoke) and, of course, McGregor.

Could it have escaped these gentlemen's minds that fines were the League's main source of income? Surely not. During the second season, fines amounted to just over half the League's total earnings of £141 11s. Of that, £20 went on Harry Lockett's salary. The Stoke man's living thus depended to a large extent on the misdemeanours of League members, his own club included. It was rather like drawing one's wages from a swear box.

Notts County ended up covering the secretary's entire salary when they were fined the then substantial sum of £25 for fielding Tinsley Lindley, a Cambridge and England centre-forward whom they signed apparently for just one game. The Committee had originally decided to fine County only £5, with one point deducted. By calling a special meeting of all twelve clubs, however, County managed to win back their point, but at the cost of an extra £20 on the fine. Such was the price of a League point in 1889.

(Lindley, an amateur who later signed for Preston, was referred to in the minutes as Mr Tinsley Lindley, confirmation that he was a gentleman. Other players were called by their surnames only.)

But there were no rules to control the weather, or what should happen when matches had to be postponed or abandoned. Nor did the rules dictate what other fixtures clubs could arrange when not on League duty. In September 1889, Stoke were rather miffed that a fellow member, West Bromwich, had arranged 'to visit the neighbourhood of Stoke' (presumably to play Burslem Port Vale) on the same day as Stoke's home match against Preston. A few months later, Wolves were warned that if they did not rearrange their friendly at non-League Nottingham Forest so that it didn't coincide with a Notts County home match, the Committee would have to cancel all friendlies against Forest by way of retaliation.

Clashes of interest over fines, postponements and fixture arrangements built up

to such a level that by Christmas 1889 the Management Committee reached a minor crisis of confidence.

Yet when they annulled all the previous meetings' business and in desperation called a full meeting of clubs to sort out the confusion, what, did it transpire, was all the fuss about? A few fines here and there? A few complaints about the state of grounds, the matter of crowds encroaching upon pitches? No, these were relatively routine details. The real bone of contention was the share of receipts from games disrupted by fog earlier in the season. Money, as ever, was the dominant issue.

Modern observers of the game complain that football is too much of a business nowadays. It was ever thus. Indeed, McGregor paraded the fact with apparent satisfaction, not least because it confirmed that professional football was an expanding, thriving industry.

Business being business, the problem of 'poaching' players arose from the very beginning. William Sudell proposed 'that any League club offering inducements to a player of another League club to leave the club of which that player is a member, or engaging a player of a League club without the consent of the club of which that player is a member, shall be deemed guilty of objectionable conduct and dealt with as provided by Rule 11'.

No doubt the assembled gentlemen nodded gravely as this proposal was carried. Yet once the meeting was over, several of them emerged like schoolboys from a lesson on the evils of theft. Unabashed, they went out in search of greater plunder.

It was in this atmosphere of experiment – testing the rules to see how they would bend, testing the Committee to see how the members would react – that the second League season ended, as had the first, with Preston as Champions.

Since the Invincibles had nothing tangible to show for this marvellous achievement, the Committee suggested that 'a flag bearing the winner's name, together with the English coat of arms and the town motto, shall be presented to the champions'.

This was obviously not enough for Preston's mentor and benefactor, William Sudell, who, having seen his club win the Cup the year before, had obviously developed a taste for silverware. He proposed at the annual meeting in May 1890 that instead of a mere flag, a Championship trophy should be purchased, but for no more than fifty guineas (Sudell was treasurer, after all). His proposal was carried and, as fortune would have it, Preston have never won the Championship since.

Having resolved in 1888 to determine League placings on goal average, should teams tie on points, the end of the second season brought a compromise which would have seemed unthinkable in later years. Aston Villa and Bolton were together lying in eighth place, equal on nineteen points each. Villa's goal tally read 43–51, compared with Bolton's 54–64. The goal averages were thus 0.84314 and 0.84375 respectively, meaning that Villa should have finished below Bolton and thus have had to apply for re-election – an embarrassment particularly to William McGregor.

So small was the margin, however, that had the two clubs been separated it would have been the closest decision ever made in a hundred years of the League. The Annual Meeting thus decided unanimously that in view of the extraordinary circumstances, the standing orders and rules would be suspended and the two clubs allowed to stand equal.

(As it happened, later calculations corrected Bolton's goal tally to 54–65, giving a goal average slightly worse than Villa's. Early records were often inaccurate – the League's own results summary shows several corrections – partly due to the fact that on occasions clubs, newspapers and referees reported different scores for the same match. Disputed goals were common in the early days.)

With Villa and Bolton tying in eighth place, it was then left to consider the fate of the remaining three clubs, which were, for the second year running, Stoke, Burnley and Notts County.

New applicants in 1890 included five of the previous year's hopefuls – Bootle, Grimsby Town, Sunderland Albion, Sunderland and Newton Heath – together with Darwen, neighbours of Blackburn. (Apart from Sunderland, all the applicants belonged to the Football Alliance, formed in 1889 by twelve clubs, most of whom played in the earlier Combination.)

Unlike the previous year, the votes were not recorded in the minutes. Harry Lockett merely recorded the fact that 'after consideration Sunderland was elected a member of the League in place of Stoke'. How painful it must have been for him to record these words, for not only had his club finished bottom in both seasons and become the first to drop out of the League, but now his position as secretary must also have been in jeopardy. Was he too stunned by this realization to note down the voting figures?

Lockett had no need to worry. He was immediately re-elected to his post, and the Committee was so pleased with him that its members then voted him a bonus of £30 for his services over the previous two years. There was a catch however. Since Stoke were no longer members of the League, Lockett would no longer be able to vote. Thus, in 1890, the Secretary of the Football League became a servant of the organisation, relieved of any split loyalties. He has remained so ever since.

While Stoke were out (they joined the Alliance), new members Sunderland had to promise to pay any additional travelling expenses that clubs would incur through their membership. These included the cost of teas, hotels and breakfasts, plus the difference in rail fares between Sunderland and that of the longest distance travelled to any of the other League clubs.

Having welcomed the Wearsiders, the ever-growing problem of discipline persuaded the Committee to add to the rules a clause giving them power to deal with any offending party 'as they may think fit', should the offence not be covered by existing rules. In other words, the League awarded itself emergency powers; normally the prerogative of a dictator, but in this case more the desperation of a headmaster losing control of his first formers.

Other rules introduced in 1890 were as follows:

● The common misdemeanour of fielding ineligible players was now made punishable by a fine of £25 and the loss of two points. (Newcomers Sunderland were the first to suffer, three weeks into their first season, when they fielded goalkeeper John Doig, newly signed from Arbroath, in their 4–0 win at West Bromwich.)

● Poaching another club's player was now made punishable by expulsion (a rule that was, of course, never put into practice, or the League would soon have been reduced to a handful of clubs).

● Since one of the main reasons why the League came into being was to regularize fixures, when members started to break engagements during the 1889/90 season the Committee had to exert its authority. At an earlier meeting in February, Notts County, Stoke and Wolves were each fined the relatively small amount of £5 for this offence, but the annual meeting in 1890 set the fine at £50, surely enough to dissuade any club from reneging on its commitments.

● A fine of £50 was also set for the crime of playing a weak team without being able to offer a strong excuse.

● For the first time, a minimum admission fee was imposed, another break with the ideals of McGregor, who always maintained this was a private matter for the clubs themselves to determine. The minimum fee set was 6d (2.5p), the only concession allowed being to boys under fourteen and 'ladies'. (In fact, women constituted such a high percentage of some clubs' gates that from being allowed free entrance originally, then half-price, by 1900 in most cases they had to pay the same as men.)

Finally, the 1890 Annual Meeting considered the FA's impending debate on the import of Scottish players. To stem the flow begun the year before, and to appease the much concerned Scottish FA, the Association wanted to limit the period of each season

THE
Football + League.

SEASON 1890-1.

RULES.

Chairman:
Mr. W. McGREGOR, Summer Lane, Birmingham.

Treasurer:
Mr. W. SUDELL, Holm Slack, Preston.

Secretary:
Mr. H. LOCKETT, Harley Street, Hanley.

Telegrams—"LOCKETT, HANLEY."

The New Press Printing Co., Foundry St., Hanley.

The first published set of rules consisted of 22 regulations and totalled around 1400 words. In 1987–8 there were 86 regulations, which when added to two appendices, the rules of the Littlewoods Challenge Cup, the Articles of Association and various other agreements and rules, amounted to approximately 40,000 words. Only one rule has survived the 100 years; that each club play its full strength in all League matches unless some satisfactory explanation is given.

during which Scottish players could be signed.

League clubs, not surprisingly, objected vehemently to this limitation. Without Scottish imports few could have maintained their standards. But even though restrictions were not subsequently imposed, Scotland took the first step towards self-protection that year, simply by establishing its own league competition.

Why had it taken so long? R. M. Connell, writing in 1905, gave this view: 'Sandy is slow to move. He likes to "bide a wee" to see how the thing works out ere following a lead ... Scotland has always played the part of following the leader.'

(Before modern Scots tear up this book in protest, it should be pointed out that Connell was a Scot himself, and that his country's FA persisted in shunning professionalism for a further three years – that is, eight years after the English FA saw sense. This fact alone helps explain why so many players came south. The money was better, and it was up front.)

League clubs did not have it all their own way, however. Since no transfer agreements existed as yet between the various leagues around Britain, clubs such as Wednesday or Forest from the Alliance could poach League players with impunity. To resist this, in December 1890 the Committee resolved that member clubs should be prohibited from organizing fixtures against any outside club found guilty of poaching.

Ardwick (later Manchester City) were the first to suffer from this resolve. They poached Walker of Burnley, and immediately found themselves on the League's blacklist. It worked; two months later they apologised and offered Walker back to Burnley. As soon as they came off the blacklist, Walsall went on it, having illegally signed one of Wolves's players. Sheffield Wednesday and Stockton joined them in May 1891.

But how could the League maintain this stance when its own clubs were frequently guilty of the same crime? West Bromwich, for example, complained in May that no sooner had J. Reynolds signed registration forms than he was approached and tempted by another League club, 'to the player's discontent and the Albion's annoyance'.

Sure enough, in July 1891 the FA secretary, Charles Alcock, complained about the blacklist, and the League promptly rescinded the measure. Not for long, however. Within three months Glasgow Celtic were boycotted for poaching Doyle and Brady from Everton.

Of course, this situation could not continue indefinitely. Some sort of *modus vivendi* had to be achieved between the League and its rivals, if only for the sake of good public relations. Nor did it help that at the time, solidarity within the League appeared to be strained. In January 1891, statements appeared in the press hinting that Blackburn Rovers and Accrington were considering seceding. This rumour alone was enough to prompt a full emergency meeting on 30 January at the Royal Hotel, Manchester.

Faced by an angry Committee, both clubs denied ever having threatened to leave. Representing Accrington, Joe Hartley expressed his club's 'hearty allegiance' to the League by reading out a loyal message from Alderman

---

The first colour clash in League football occurred when Sunderland became members in 1890, their red and white striped shirts clashing with Wolverhampton Wanderers' strip. It was resolved that thereafter the *home* club should change its colours. To avoid future colour clashes, in September 1891 home clubs were instructed to have a set of white shirts available just in case, and all clubs had to register their colours with the League at the beginning of each season. Today's ruling that away clubs change their strip in the event of a clash was introduced in 1921. The colour of socks had to be registered after 1937.

D. W. Sprake, chairman of the club. On Blackburn's behalf, Mr Mitchell apologised for a colleague's remark which had obviously sparked off the newspaper story.

Clearly irritated by the washing of the League's dirty linen in public, the emergency meeting resolved to condemn any representative who might promulgate rumours of dissension. Grievances should be aired in the privacy of League meetings, said the Committee, not in the press. How often has that plea been made over the course of a hundred years?

A further indication of the League's fragile sensibilities came in March 1891, when Derby and Sunderland objected to a report of their match which appeared in *Athletic News*. John Bentley promised to take the matter up, as only he could, since he was the newspaper's assistant editor.

The season 1890/1 saw the Committee meet at two new venues, Nottingham and Preston, both marked by ceremonial dinners. At the Lion Hotel, Nottingham, Notts County laid on oysters, mock-turtle soup, turbot and lobster sauce, chicken patties, salmis of pigeon, mutton, turkey, tongue, pheasant and grouse, followed by jellies, blancmange, mince pies, plum pudding, and finally ... macaroni cheese. All this was washed down by chablis, sherry, champagne, port and claret.

At Preston a month later, an equally sumptuous repast awaited at the Bull and Royal Hotel. One of the courses included an intriguing dish entitled 'Pouding á la North End'. An 1847 port finished the meal and no doubt aroused a hearty glow of self-satisfaction among the assemblage. Not so among the club secretaries: in the post-prandial haze of cigar smoke, it was resolved to place a levy of £5 on each League club to keep Harry Lockett's accounts in the black.

The dining went on. To celebrate Everton's Championship win in 1891 – they were the first to be awarded the new trophy – the club invited the Committee to a dinner at the Compton Hotel. North End pudding was off the menu this time, but 'diplomatic pudding' no doubt made a satisfactory alternative.

But back to business. There were radical matters to discuss.

First came suggestions from the sub-committee appointed to revise the rules (a never-ending process, as it transpired). Their most ambitious proposal was to expand the League to three divisions of twelve clubs each, with the so-called first-class clubs having two votes each at Annual Meetings, the remainder one each.

But, as was to occur so many times over the next ninety-seven years, the Committee's 'best laid schemes' went 'aft a-gley' at the hands of the clubs. Weighted voting would have to wait until 1986, but the principle of expansion was agreed at the 1891 Annual Meeting, even if the number of clubs was modestly settled at fourteen rather than thirty-six.

This meant that the bottom four clubs – Aston Villa, Accrington, Derby and West Bromwich – were competing for six places with Darwen, Newton Heath, Notts Forest, Stoke, Sunderland Albion (all from the Alliance) and Ardwick.

Hardly surprisingly, Aston Villa received the maximum eight votes, as did Accrington. Derby and West Bromwich were also re-elected, but only just. Both Stoke (who had just won the Alliance) and Darwen received seven votes each, so they made up the extra numbers. Harry Lockett's club was back, and

> 'One pleasing fact to announce is that out of the 132 matches in which the League clubs have taken part and in which about 300 players have taken the field, not a single fatal accident has to be recorded, and in fact, not a serious case [of injury] in any way, a point that shows that the higher the quality of bootlace the less liability is there of accidents.'
>
> *William McGregor,*
> *summing up the 1890/1 season*

> **The subject of crowd violence was first discussed by the Management Committee on 18 December 1891 when Harry Lockett was authorized to print posters for all League grounds, warning spectators not to demonstrate against the referee or players. Throwing mud and stones at referees appears to have been the commonest form of attack.**

with Darwen's arrival the new fourteen-strong League was divided thus: seven from Lancashire, six from the Midlands and one from the North-East.

Also at the 1891 Annual Meeting, both McGregor and Sudell were re-elected unopposed to their posts as chairman and treasurer respectively, while Harry Lockett had to enter a ballot for the post of Secretary, for which the salary was now thirty guineas. He had two rivals, a Mr Roscoe of Bolton and a Mr Heath, who lived near Lockett in Hanley. In the event, the Secretary only just kept his job, on McGregor's casting vote, an indication that not everyone was satisfied with his efforts. (Since then League Secretaries have been appointed rather than elected.)

One of Lockett's first duties after re-election was to open up a bank account in Preston, where treasurer Sudell resided (this only partly explains why the League headquarters were eventually settled in the town).

There were two further developments in 1891. First was the formation of a Board of Appeal, a neutral body of senior FA councillors appointed to arbitrate in certain League disputes. Charles Clegg, a referee and solicitor from Sheffield, was chosen, along with Charles Crump of Wolverhampton and W. J. Forrest of Turton.

Secondly, on 11 December 1891, the League finally met with the Alliance to discuss the widespread poaching of players. The result was an historic agreement, both sides resolving that no player should be paid more than £10 as a bonus or signing-on fee. In 1891 that represented about a month's wages for the average player, hardly a great incentive to uproot one's family and home.

But the most surprising part of the agreement was that, despite enormous inflation, £10 remained the official limit for the next seventy years! Even in 1891/2, the measure was none too popular, and because it was virtually unenforceable, it became one of the greatest bones of contention between the clubs and the Management Committee.

As Charles Sutcliffe wrote in his 1938 history, although any club found guilty of paying above the limit should technically have been expelled, no club ever was. Nor was the threat any deterrent whatsoever, the rule being flagrantly disregarded as soon as it was passed. That this should have been so was less a discredit to the clubs than an indictment of the rule itself.

Nevertheless, in 1891/2 the League administrators felt that they had to act to control the movement of players, and when the £10 limit came into effect for League and Alliance clubs, on 18 January 1892, the Northern League also fell in with the rule.

The next step was to agree on an end to poaching, and again clubs continued to ignore the agreed resolutions. A month after the compact betweeen the League, Alliance and Northern League, Wolves were supplying firm evidence that Ardwick had tried to poach one of their players and had paid him £5 to visit Manchester. A few months later, Preston were officially censured for arranging a fixture against Ardwick. Middlesbrough and Middlesbrough Ironopolis were the next clubs to come under suspicion.

If existing agreements were tenuous, next on the agenda was another problem, more fraught than anyone could possibly have imagined. In December 1891, a new concept, one destined to plague League football for so long, first reared its ugly head when the three major Leagues decided to look into the possibility of imposing a maximum wage for players.

Their initial recommendation, made three months later, was to prohibit all bonuses, limit the weekly wage to £3, and stop all wages during the close season. Even by the standards of the day it was a draconian proposition, totally out of step with the prevailing economic doctrine of *laissez faire*. It allowed for no free market forces, and offered no incentive whatsoever to individuals. Nearly a century later we hear much of so-called 'Victorian values', but these proposals seemed to hark back to feudalism.

Fortunately for the players they were soon forgotten, although Derby County would raise the discussion of a maximum wage once more in September 1893. Meanwhile, on 22 April 1892 it was agreed to form a second 'division' (the first time the term was officially used). The First Division would be enlarged, once again by election, to sixteen clubs, and these sixteen would then vote for twelve members of the Second Division.

Lockett went through the motions of advertising the vacancies in four newspapers, but in truth the matter was wholly predetermined. The final words of the first volume of League minutes state quite plainly: 'It was felt that the Alliance as a body (except St George's) should be admitted to the League.' In that one sentence the League's hegemony within British football was confirmed. The Alliance, born in 1889, was to be completely absorbed.

Not that this was any cause for concern. The Alliance had never been more than a waiting room for the League. Newspapers often referred to it as 'the Second League', and there is little doubt that its senior committee men never intended to rival the League or to expand their own sphere; they wanted only to join forces.

Events on the field gave them reason enough to believe that Alliance clubs could compete on equal terms. Apart from success in friendly fixtures, in 1890 Sheffield Wednesday reached the Cup Final (although they were humiliated 6–1 by Blackburn), and in 1892 Alliance champions Nottingham Forest reached the semifinals where they took the eventual winners West Bromwich to a third replay. Four Alliance players won England caps between 1889 and 1892.

The expansion programme was finally settled at the 1892 Annual Meeting, held at the Queen's Hotel, Sunderland, in honour of the Wearsiders' first Championship. Enlarging Division One was the first step. West Bromwich, who had finished in twelfth place, were excused from having to apply for re-election in recognition of their Cup Final victory (the only time such a concession was ever made). That left five places to be contested by six clubs: Accrington, Stoke and Darwen applying for re-election, in competition with Forest, Wednesday and Newton Heath from the Alliance.

Forest announced that before applying they had reached an agreement with neighbours Notts County. This stated that County would support Forest's application provided that Forest, plus five other clubs to be selected by County, played their fixtures at County before Christmas and before they visited Forest's ground. County also insisted that home fixtures should never clash.

There were three other applications. One was from the newly formed Liverpool FC, who were rejected before the vote on the grounds that 'they did not comply with regulations'. (One assumes that Everton's opposition was decisive in this matter. Everton had recently been forced to leave their Anfield home by a greedy landlord who was now sponsoring the new club.) The other applicants were Newcastle's East End and, making a joint challenge, Middlesbrough and Middlesbrough Ironopolis (who had agreed to amalgamate if accepted). Both applications failed, and rather than enter the Second Division ballot the North-Easterners withdrew 'on account of the great expense incurred in travelling' – an odd

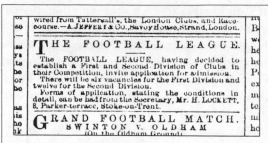

*It was an advert such as this which John McKenna
spotted in* Athletic News, *and led him, although he
had no authority to do so, to apply for League
membership on behalf of his club, Liverpool. The other
Liverpool committee members had wanted to wait
awhile!*

reason, since the First Division would have
entailed four more away trips.

The voting resulted as follows: Sheffield
Wednesday (10 votes), Forest (9) and Newton
Heath (6) were newly admitted to the First
Division. Accrington (7) and Stoke (6) were
both re-elected. This left Darwen as the odd
ones out with only 4 votes, and they therefore
had to enter the ballot for the new Second
Division. No votes were recorded. We simply
read that Darwen were to join Burton Swifts,
Grimsby Town, Bootle, Walsall Town Swifts,
Small Heath Alliance, Crewe Alexandra,
Lincoln City and Ardwick, all from the
Alliance, plus Burslem Port Vale, Sheffield
United and Northwich Victoria.

(Apart from poor, slighted Birmingham St
George's, only two other earlier members of
the Alliance failed to gain League status: Sunderland Albion and Long Eaton Rangers. All
three disappeared from the football map soon
after their rejection.)

Thus, the League expanded to Manchester,
Cheshire, Lincolnshire and South Yorkshire.
It had taken four years for the founder's original
plan for two divisions to come to fruition, and
with this accomplished, McGregor decided the
time was right to step down as chairman.

He missed the Sunderland meeting through
illness, and there may have been several there

who thought, as they sent a telegram wishing
him a speedy recovery, that they may never see
the old Scottish warhorse again. They were
wrong; he remained heavily involved for
several years to come.

But even McGregor at his peak was never
able to devote the time and energy his successor managed to invest in League affairs. John
Bentley of Bolton Wanderers was a League
referee, an FA councillor, and assistant editor
of *Athletic News*. In 1892 he was elected chairman of the Football League. No man ever held
such an influential position in English football.

The founder was not forgotten, however.
In his absence, William McGregor was unanimously elected to the new honorary position
of President, while Harry Lockett had his
salary doubled to £60 per annum. His workload doubled too, since the League's finances
were now made his sole responsibility. The
former treasurer, William Sudell, was thanked
for his voluntary services and as far as the
League was concerned, there ended the Preston
man's involvement. His subsequent fate (see
page 28) helps to explain why this should have
been so.

Thus, on 13 May 1892, the position of Secretary was formalized and firmly established
as a full-time occupation. From now on, Mr
Lockett, with the League office in his terraced
house in Hanley, would have to spend even
more time away from his printing business to
keep an eye on the growing clan. It was a tall
order.

On 1 July 1892, at the Royal Hotel, Manchester, the League's first ever full meeting of
two divisions took place. From the small table
and familiar faces that Messrs Lockett, Bentley,
Lewis and McGregor had been used to since
1888, suddenly there were twenty-eight men
around the room.

Hardly surprisingly, arranging fixtures to
suit everyone proved to be one of the main
difficulties. Even friendlies had to be carefully
scheduled so that none took place within a
month of the same team appearing in the dis-

trict for a League match.

But the most irksome problem lay with that most controversial £10 limit on signing-on fees. As Newton Heath's Mr Albut pointed out, the rule was barely a year old and was already being flouted, usually by clubs giving players a large advance on wages.

Sheffield Wednesday were the first to be investigated for a breach of this rule, when it was reported in May 1893 that they had paid two players £120 to sign on. They made a feeble excuse, and to their relief escaped with no more than a censure. But then, how could the Committee judge otherwise when the members knew full well that their own clubs were often as guilty?

If clubs had the cash to make illegal payments to the tune of £120, they must also have had the money to bolster the League's own depleted funds. The cost of holding successive meetings in Sunderland and London forced the Committee to raise another levy, £5 this time, to keep the organization solvent. Needless to say, several members refused to pay up and were later threatened with a one-guinea surcharge.

The League's main source of income at this time came from Inter-League representative matches. These started in April 1891 with a match against the Football Alliance at Olive Grove, Sheffield. A year later, a League XI met the Scottish League at Bolton. (For a full list, see Appendix Three.) But by mid 1892, it became apparent that one match a season would be insufficient to keep the newly expanded organization in funds.

Desperate for money, Lockett wrote to the Scottish League suggesting another match – and received no reply. Instead, the League settled for a North v. Midlands match at Bramall Lane, but only on condition that Sheffield United made no charge for the ground.

With fourteen new clubs paying membership fees, why was the League so hard up? The main reason appears to have been the cost of calling more Committee meetings to deal with the increase in business. For example, one meeting in August 1892 confirmed a total of twenty-five transfers, more than in any other previous month.

Inevitably, the number of disputes rose, too. During the 1892/3 season, the following protests or complaints were recorded: against the state of a pitch (3 cases); late arrival or short time being played (10); teams playing with men short (6); poaching (3); against referees (3) and players (2); against clubs for non-payment of fees or fines (8), and against clubs for breaches of rules other than those mentioned above (7).

But while clubs continued to squabble amongst themselves, it should be said that the quality of their own organizations improved gradually during this period. By the start of the 1892/3 season, seven of the twenty-eight member clubs had formed limited liability companies. Around the same time, Lord Kinnaird, president of the FA, officially opened Everton's new home at Goodison Park, the country's finest football ground and a model for all to copy.

On the pitch, the 1892/3 season showed a further consolidation of the League's overall strength and drawing power. Champions for the second year running, Sunderland, became the first League team to score a hundred goals in a season, and with the Alliance now absorbed the League had no rival anywhere in England.

Financial matters also seemed brighter, after a bumper gate at the Inter-League match in Scotland on 8 April 1893, which earned the League more in receipts than all its other income put together that year.

Having expanded so much in 1892, the 1893 Annual Meeting was a much less dramatic affair. The bottom four clubs in the Second Division – Lincoln, Crewe, Port Vale and Walsall – were re-elected, and the Second Division expanded by the election of Rotherham Town and Newcastle United. It was also resolved that in future no club be elected to

William Sudell – Honorary Treasurer 1888–92

No individual in our history suffered such an ignominious fall from grace as Major William Sudell of Preston North End. Sudell it was who led the fight for professionalism in England and then built the team which dominated the League's first two seasons, 'The Invincibles'. Yet within a few years of these triumphs he would be languishing in prison before leaving football and this country behind for a new life in South Africa.

None of this could have been remotely foreseen when Billy Sudell, a handsome, well-built eighteen-year-old, joined a sports club called Preston Nelson in August 1867. He was then a rugby enthusiast who seemed to possess every advantage a youth could want; he hailed from one of Preston's better-known families, he was a natural leader, a popular and generous character, and at his work in the Peel Hall cotton mill he was soon recognized as a high flier, said to have been able to make lightning calculations in his head and to add up three columns of figures at the same time.

At the mill he rose to become manager. In the local volunteer rifles he rose to the rank of major. At Preston Nelson, who became North End, he became committee chairman at the age of twenty-five, seven years before the club had even considered swapping the oval ball for the spherical version.

Two years after North End did make the transition, in 1881, however, Sudell threw himself into football management. While other clubs were recruiting raw footballing talent in Glasgow, Sudell plundered the Edinburgh clubs. His greatest scoop was the demon defender Nick Ross, the first exponent of the passback to the goalkeeper and the man who, with Sudell, introduced the blackboard into the dressing room, adding tactical know-how to strength and commitment.

It was not a popular ploy, and in 1884 Preston's amateur Cup opponents Upton Park accused Sudell of paying his Scottish players. The FA upheld the charge – which was quite true – and Preston were expelled from the competition, as Accrington had been earlier. But while others were content to keep professionalism under a shroud of deceit, Sudell exposed the whole sham by leading thirty-six prominent clubs out of the FA to form a rival association. With Machiavellian cunning he also signed an amateur goalkeeper from the South, to increase national interest in Preston's affairs.

'Gentlemen,' he told a gathering of the FA in January 1885, 'Preston are all professionals, but if you refuse to legalize them they will be amateurs. We shall all be amateurs and you cannot prove us otherwise.'

His honest determination, combined with the efforts of William McGregor and Richard Gregson of Blackburn, forced the FA to capitulate finally in July 1885. Yet even after professionalism was legalized and Sudell had joined the FA Council, he continued to defy the Association whenever it suited him, for example by refusing to release players for internationals, and by demanding that the FA pay the wages of players participating in Cup semi-finals and finals. And he would twist the Lancashire FA round his little finger when it came to County Cup matches.

By 1886 Sudell's team were the most feared side in the north of England. Then they beat Queen's Park of Glasgow 6–1, and there were no other giants to topple, north of the Trent. And although West Bromwich defeated North End in the 1887 Cup semi-finals and in the 1888 Cup Final,

Preston were rightly deemed to be the first giants of British professional football, as all-powerful as Arsenal in the 1930s and Leeds in the 1970s. 'Major Sudell's appetite for success was insatiable', wrote Preston's historians Harry Berry and Geoff Allman.

Naturally, this success brought jealousy and bitterness in its train, a situation which Sudell hardly eased by remaining apparently aloof when McGregor invited North End to join the new League in 1888. Sudell wouldn't answer letters or attend meetings until the very last moment. It was as if he were deliberately playing hard to get.

But once Preston did throw their hat into the ring, as an acknowledged financial whizz-kid Billy Sudell was the natural choice as the League's first honorary treasurer.

Preston's record in those first two seasons of League football is well known, and it would be wrong to ascribe it all to one man. Nevertheless, the genius and energy which Sudell invested in tactics, team-building and financial matters had transformed Preston North End from a rugby club of little note to the very pinnacle of British football within the space of just seven years. Even in the 1880s, that was quite a feat.

But it couldn't last. Sudell's health began to deteriorate, the mill's business declined, and by 1893 he was said to have been a broken man. 'He had run North End as a virtual dictator', wrote Berry and Allman. He had also, it transpired, diverted some of the mill's funds into the club, partly through ambition, partly through his penchant for lavish hospitality.

Sudell's fall was almost as swift as his rise. Having stepped down as League treasurer in 1892, in August 1893 he left North End amid acrimony and suspicion.

He moved to Morecambe soon afterwards and in July 1894 received £50 from the League towards a testimonial. A year later he was charged with and found guilty of embezzling his former employer's funds – largely to help finance North End – and he spent the next three years in prison. (There were no suggestions that his alleged embezzlement ever involved League monies.)

John Bentley wrote movingly in *Athletic News* of his former colleague's ruination.

'We are afraid that what Major Sudell spent on old North End Football Club formed the nucleus of the deficit which afterwards terminated so fatally, for he was badly supported by Preston. But the real mistake seems to come after that.

Whilst, however, we think it is wrong to hold this up as a terrible example of the awful effects of football, we think footballers will do well to remember that the unfortunate man was once one of the leaders in English football and if they will remember this, to support and not to kick one down, they may indeed do something worthy of the best spirit of the game. They can help by extending the hand of generous benevolence in aid of those whom Major Sudell's fall had not only crushed almost to hopeless despair, but left wholly unprovided for. Those are the events which are worse than death. This is one of them, for it leaves Mrs Sudell and a large family altogether unprovided for, children absolutely without resource.

We do not want to say more than can be helped, that would only be rending heartache, but the pathetic spectre of a woman left suddenly to face the world alone, without a penny and with many hungry mouths to fill, should appeal to every heart. Let us then as footballers, do what we can for those who find themselves hurled from comfort to penury and let us send in our little to help.'

Sudell left prison around 1898, disgraced, probably impoverished, and suffering with lung problems. But he was no quitter. From Morecambe he took his family off to a new life in Cape Town, where football was still undeveloped and his misfortune was little known. Starting out as a freelance journalist at the age of about fifty-two he returned to his first love, rugby, and eventually became sports editor for the *South African News*.

He died in 1911, literally pen in hand, after a strenuous day's reporting of a rugby tournament, and was mourned by a large section of Cape Town's journalistic fraternity. One of his former colleagues wrote: 'Sudell was a true gentleman, a valued friend and co-worker, and a man of unselfish, kind-hearted, amiable character who will be sorely missed and long remembered with affection.'

Another wrote a quite sycophantic elegy, including the words: 'You never injured in word or deed God's creatures, great or small.'

Was this the same man found guilty of dishonesty? Was this the man who so single-mindedly set out to create an invincible football team? Or was Major Sudell's reputation deliberately scarred in this country by those who wished him harm, who wished to sully his achievements and thus darken the very name of professional football? Someone, somewhere, sometime, hatched the notion that Sudell had in fact committed suicide in Cape Town on 9 May 1911. Where the date or the details came from one can only guess, but the truth is quite different: William Sudell died on the evening of 5 August 1911 of pneumonia; he was a happy, successful and popular man, who appeared to have put all his former woes behind him.

J. A. H. Catton ('Tityrus' of *Athletic News*) never doubted Sudell's innocence of the charges made against him. 'Honest as the day, in my opinion,' he wrote, 'and frank to a degree... I respect him for the man I knew him to be, and I can never believe that he forfeited his honesty and self-respect. In disposition he was noble enough to have borne the burden of another man's misdeed. Indeed, he was a great gentleman and responsible for the finest football team I ever saw.'

the First Division without having first competed in the Second Division.

The question of movement between divisions was not so clear cut. The year 1893 saw the first of the test matches, played as a knockout competition between the bottom three in Division One and the top three in Division Two.

Notts County and Accrington, who finished in fourteenth and fifteenth place respectively in Division One, both lost their test matches; County 3–0 to Darwen at Ardwick, Accrington 1–0 to Sheffield United at Trent Bridge. But when it came to the Annual Meeting several weeks later, neither defeated club would confirm that it deigned to join the Second Division. Given until the following Wednesday to make up their minds, both of, course, opted to stay in.

The third test match indicated the potential inequalities of the system. Newton Heath, who had a miserable debut season and finished five points below Accrington, faced the top club in the Second Division, Small Heath. The first test match between them at Stoke resulted in a 1–1 draw, but in the replay at Bramall Lane Newton Neath scored a decisive 5–2 win. Small Heath thus stayed down, while the two teams below them went up. By way of consolidation, Small Heath at least became the first recipients of the new Second Division shield.

With Rotherham and Newcastle elected to Division Two, there were now sixteen teams in the First Division and fourteen in the Second. It was resolved, therefore, to place an advertisement for two more clubs to even up the numbers, the entries to be selected by the Management Committee on the following Wednesday.

Once again, there was hardly any need to advertise. Within a day or two of the announcement, applications were received from Woolwich Arsenal, Middlesbrough Ironopolis, Liverpool, Doncaster Rovers and Loughborough. After some debate, it was decided to admit Liverpool and Arsenal. With this decision, the League made its first foray into the South, a brave decision in view of the expense that Second Division clubs would incur by travelling to London, but a sensible one for the League's future prospects as a national entity.

Arsenal's election put the onus on London's only other professional club, Millwall Athletic, to campaign for the creation of a league for southern clubs. They succeeded in 1894, when the Southern League was formed, with nine clubs in its First Division and seven in the Second. Among the originals were future League members Millwall, Luton, Southampton, Reading, Swindon and New Brompton.

* * *

Until 1893, those who ran the League's affairs were often referred to as the emergency committee. The first officially titled Management Committee was elected in May, with two representatives from each division.

William McGregor was confirmed as President. John Bentley (the *de facto* chairman) and Edwin Browne (Notts County) became Vice Presidents, and Louis Ford (WBA), Dick Molyneux (Everton), W. Starling (Small Heath) and Josh Parlby (Ardwick) were elected as Committee members (for biographies of these Committeemen see Appendix Two).

The newly elected Committee faced its first crisis on 3 August 1893 when the League recorded its first resignation, that of Accrington. 'Th' Owd Reds', no relation to the later club Accrington Stanley, had for some time

been labouring under heavy financial losses. They were occasionally unable even to raise a team.

Instead of being sympathetic or offering aid, as one might have expected in an era when sentimentalism still governed much of the League's behaviour, the Committee reacted with surprising coolness, treating Accrington more like defectors than helpless defaulters. First, it demanded that the club pay £7 7s worth of expenses incurred at the last two meetings. Then, all members were instructed not to play any matches against Accrington until the debt was paid.

Excommunication took immediate effect, as the stricken founder members begged the League to drop its boycott so that they could play a pre-arranged game against Burnley. But the Committee proved implacable. Only when Accrington paid up on 16 November were they removed from the blacklist, by which time all their good players had been transferred. It was a sad end to a brief and otherwise unremarkable League career.

In Accrington's place, Middlesbrough Ironopolis were elected, but then, as if to foil the League's attempt to balance up numbers, a few days before the start of the season Bootle tendered their resignation. They, too, had been unable to keep pace with their stronger neighbours, Liverpool and Everton.

At the same time, another resignation was accepted, this one with deeper regret. William McGregor had shrugged off his illness, but he was no longer fit enough to shoulder both his League and business responsibilities (it is possible that his brother Peter either died or went his own way at this time). On 16 August, the Management Committee placed on record 'their great appreciation of the services rendered to the League by him both in organising that body and the valuable work done since its formation'.

No fears were raised for the League when this news was announced; John Bentley was already firmly in control. But before we get acquainted with the new President, let us briefly return to the founder.

Although he took a back-seat role in committee business from 1893 until his death in 1911, McGregor's steadying influence could often be seen in League affairs, as a mediator, as a commentator in the press, and simply as a figurehead.

In August 1894, just before his testimonial at Perry Barr (see Appendix Three), he was made the League's first Life Member, and from then until 1899 he attended Management Committee meetings infrequently. Thereafter, however, he rarely missed a meeting until becoming ill in March 1910.

McGregor remained active in his other work. As an FA councillor he took an England team abroad. He became a Vice President of Aston Villa, and President of the Birmingham Works Association, and was also said to have been keen on the Old Villans club, an organization formed to look after former Villa players.

Happily for the Committee, there was a complete absence of any rivalry between McGregor and his successor, John Bentley. They were firm friends who worked well together. McGregor's characteristic, wrote Bentley in later years, was 'the smile on his face and the twinkly in his eye'. Bentley claimed that he and

---

McGregor's newspaper jottings were full of wit and wisdom. He spared no one his criticism if he felt it justified, not even his beloved Aston Villa. In 1908 his comments were enough to inspire 'Frank' of the *Villa News and Record* to pen this poem:

Hail! for the bold McGregor here will pass
To view his beard in 'The Looking Glass';
To notice with a kind of mild surprise
Time takes no sunshine from his merry eyes;
But to discover here and there some creases
Where laughter leaves a wrinkle when it ceases.

Though all the world may worry, still he smiles
To think perchance upon his ample files
That liabilities are nearly nil,
And assets would a pond'rous volume fill;
For he will sell you 'kerchiefs or a 'column';
A flannel shirt or Scottish jokes as solemn.

Our daily papers glisten with his name
In comments or critiques upon the game;
And tremblingly we view the columns o'er
To see our sins discovered by the score;
Till one is half inclined to think McGregor
Is nothing but a bold, bad, bearded beggar!

For sometimes he will dip his pen in gall,
To add another anguish to our fall;
And show us in a manner most abhorred
The nimble nib's still mightier than the sword,
And cut us to the quick with fearful phrases,
Or damn our virile virtue with faint praises.

Time was, before the Chieftain took to print
And found some profit from the inky mint,
That kindly thoughts of us were uppermost,
And Aston Villa was his weekly boast.
They're uppermost to-day, but scarcely gentle;
Is this a sweet revenge – or, accidental?

McGregor never exchanged one cross word.

This may have had something to do with the fact that 'Genial Mac' was apparently silent throughout most Management Committee meetings, contributing only when he felt necessary. 'He was always practical and thoroughly enthusiastic', wrote Bentley, nevertheless.

Freed from the burdens of office in 1894, the founder was able to spread his wings a little. He became, ironically, much more of a public figure in his later life than he had ever been during the League's earlier years.

It helped that McGregor had a great many friends in the press, to whom he gave tips and stories quite freely. Eventually, he decided to try his own hand at writing, with the result that he soon became a popular critic of the game as weekly correspondent for the *Birmingham Gazette*. Thus, McGregor eventually became a household name in Britain and Europe, never knighted or publicly honoured, but known to every schoolboy in the land as 'father of the League'.

Although this measure of celebrity did enable McGregor and his wife to move to a greener suburb of Birmingham, he always remained true to his religious and political roots. The *Birmingham Post* said of him: 'He had a broad and tolerant mind, but was inclined to be scornful of those who gave way to excesses or who rendered themselves unfit for service by over-indulgence.'

One theme dominated his writings, and that was the defence of the League against the steady stream of abuse which flowed, usually from irate amateur sportsmen or disgruntled outsiders. More than any newspaper, the *Birmingham Gazette* knew how much this never-ending abuse annoyed and upset McGregor.

'Some people may say that the Football League turned a pastime into a business, but that is hardly correct. McGregor was a personality in Birmingham, beloved by all who knew him ... an astute judge of character ... a born leader of men ... simple in his tastes, conscientious in his business capacity, a man of the highest integrity and one who never sought publicity or notoriety. We do not believe he ever made an enemy; he certainly never lost a friend.'

One Villa regular remembered McGregor for his vitality and sportmanship, as a

'handsome descendant of the Clan McGregor, as a sportsman of the old school, with a heart as merry and gay as that of a lad ... who could spin yarns in the Doric dialect with a refreshing humour that was good to listen to.

Footballers of the top grade were his heroes, and he could watch a match and extend admiration for the clever doings of the opposing side almost as much as his own; and he could lose with smiling grace and dignity ... he knew a trier and was never hard upon him: he carried his religion into practice and spoke well of his neighbour every time he had the chance.'

It was, indeed, a hard act for John Bentley to follow.

CHAPTER THREE
J. J. Bentley – Free Critic and Autocrat

If William McGregor was father of the League, John James Bentley should rightly be called its governor. 'No man could ever love an organization more than he did the League', Liverpool's John McKenna said of Bentley, and certainly no man, not even McGregor, gave more of himself to the League in its first thirty years. He sat on the Committee from 1888 to 1918, and attended more meetings than any of his contemporaries.

Devotion alone achieves little. What Bentley brought to the League was administrative acumen, toughness and authority. 'JJ', as he was widely known, was, according to William Pickford, 'a man of very strong views who, as they say, called a spade a spade'.

He could be an autocrat, but was rarely unpopular because he drew men towards him like a magnet. Once persuaded, they were ever loyal. At one stage, between about 1895 and 1900, he was probably the most powerful man English football has ever known.

To his friends, however, like football correspondent 'Red Rose' of the *Manchester Evening Chronicle*, JJ was 'just a Lancashire lad' who ruled with both unwavering persistency and kindliness. His roots were those indeed of Lancashire football, for he was raised in the village of Turton, where, in effect, it all began.

Born the third of four sons in June 1860, John Bentley was named after his father, the local church organist and grocer whose shop on Chapeltown High Street was next door to the Chetham Arms in this barely altered hill-top village.

Chapeltown became the focus of Lancashire football when J. C. Kay, son of the local squire at Turton Tower, returned from Harrow school in 1872 and set up the first Association club in the county, on a pitch which lay directly behind the terraced cottages where Bentley lived. (This pitch is still used today, by Old Boltonians, and might well claim to be the oldest pitch in continuous use in Britain.)

JJ's elder brothers Tom and William joined in with the first games, which were played to vague Harrovian rules and used a ball which was flat on two sides. The goalposts were lamps borrowed from the railway station. Perhaps because he was a member of the local school board and saw its educational advantages, Mr Bentley the grocer encouraged this new public-school game, and young John soon grew accustomed to the sight of muddied players tramping through his parents' house to change and wash after matches.

His chance to join in came in November 1874 when, it was said, Turton were a man short for a match against West Houghton. The fourteen-year-old turned out to be quite a half-back, and by the time he was twenty, JJ had been appointed first captain, then secretary and treasurer.

By this time, he had started working in Bolton with his brother William as clerk for the London–North and North-Western Railway. Although Bolton Wanderers were keen on him, it was with the lesser-known Bolton Association that JJ furthered his footballing career. This led to county caps, along with his brother Tom, with whom it was said that he formed 'the cleverest left wing in the county'. In one match, against Staffordshire in 1878, JJ found himself playing alongside a lad called Tom Sutton, of whom more later.

Bentley never forgot Turton, however, and

his proudest moment for them was to lead the side against Sheffield Wednesday in the FA Cup Third Round in 1881.

Eventually, the time came for JJ to leave his Chapeltown home and settle in Bolton. After serving as clerk to the Bolton School Board, he set up on his own as an accountant at 22, Acresfield (the site of which is now submerged under Bolton's Arndale Centre).

Business thrived, and JJ gave up playing before he was twenty-five. He was appointed a collector of income tax, and in 1885 became secretary of Bolton Wanderers, with immediate results. By the end of his first season, Wanderers had £100 in the bank and three cups to their name. He was described then as a genius who lived in the future, inspired by a vision of what football could become. 'He appeared bold, but extravagant,' wrote one Bolton historian.

It was thus a considerable shock when, the following year, Bentley was ousted at what was called 'one of the stormiest gatherings in the history of the club'. (For a full account, see P. M. Young's history of Bolton Wanderers, see Bibliography.) Bentley was back within a year, however, persuaded to return when the club slipped into disarray.

It was at this point in his career that William McGregor contacted him about the possibility of forming the League. In fact, the two men had already met in 1885, at one of the meetings held to debate professionalism. By that time, Bentley was more than just a club committee man. Since 1877, JJ had been sending in match reports to local newspapers, and as with everything else he tried, he soon became proficient. For years he wrote up Turton's matches under the pen-name of 'Free Critic', completely unknown to his team-mates. To make certain they remained unsuspecting, he was always careful to be freely critical of his own performances.

So popular was his writing that in 1884 he started contributing regular critical essays to the much respected Bolton weekly journal, *Cricket and Football Field*, and by 1886 had established enough of a reputation to concentrate most of his efforts on journalism. Leaving his Bolton office, he started working in Manchester as assistant editor of a small and little-known newspaper called *Athletic News*. The editor was Tom Sutton.

Athletic News then had a circulation of some 10,000. It came out on Wednesdays and cost two-pence. With Sutton, Bentley revamped the paper entirely, bringing is publication forward to Monday mornings, cutting the price to a penny and gradually raising circulation to 230,000 by 1897.

He did this by using all the conventional tools of popular journalism; making the paper bright and chatty, offering prizes, and signing up all the celebrity names (which in those days meant reporters, administrators and referees rather than players). In some issues, one can find articles by three or four members of the Management Committee, all arguing the League's case.

Having become editor in 1895, Bentley was able to use *Athletic News* as the virtual mouthpiece of the League, a power that no other president has enjoyed since. Since he was also a League referee of some rank until the mid 1890s, the situation often arose whereby Bentley, a member of the Committee, would be officiating at a League match, reporting on it in *Athletic News* under the name of Free Critic on one page, before adding further editorial comments on another! A few days later he may well have discussed a disciplinary matter arising from the game at a Management Committee meeting.

Not surprisingly, therefore, it is almost impossible to separate Bentley's period of office at the League from the contents of *Athletic News*. Surprisingly, however, it is rare to find him abusing his power. One contemporary observed: 'His writings are noted and admired for mildness and for a desire to give credit where credit is due; and even his adverse critics confess that he has never used his paper as a means of pushing forward the interests of his club . . .'

Of his club, maybe not. In the same year that he became editor, Bentley also became chairman of the newly incorporated Bolton Wanderers. However, a difference of opinion in 1897 led to him leaving the club, a departure he always deeply regretted, even if it gave him, at last, a greater freedom to express himself.

In one respect Bentley was never afraid of treading on toes, and that was when it came to defending the interests of the League. One such occasion came on 1 April 1895, when he used the columns of *Athletic News* to criticize the FA's Appeal Committee for its verdict on a dispute between Everton and Sunderland. 'In our opinion,' he wrote (which usually meant in the League's opinion), 'Sunderland have been treated in a most shameful – we don't know any more appropriate adjective – manner!!'

The Appeal Committee did not appreciate the comment – April Fool's Day or not – and responded by protesting that they had not sought appointment nor were they prepared to keep it if they did not enjoy the confidence of the clubs. But if that confidence did exist, they were entitled to ask the League for protection from attacks such as the one from Bentley. The Appeal Committee added pointedly: 'We cannot undertake to discuss our decisions with newspaper correspondents.'

This was not the only occasion on which JJ clashed with the FA. He was often caught in debates with the equally fiery Yorkshireman Charles Clegg, champion of the amateur game.

Bentley was, apparently, frequently portrayed as a rabid anti-amateur, but this was a false impression. He was, in fact, vehemently opposed to sham amateurism. He wrote in the *Windsor Magazine* in 1902:

'Pure amateurism in every sport I hold to be the higher state, but unfortunately, in football it is impossible. Amateurism can only exist in sports which are followed exclusively by the wealthier classes, such as hunting or shooting, for example, where those who
indulge in them pay all their expenses out of their own pockets. But this is impossible in any popular sport like cricket and football, which are games of rich and poor alike. I have always been an advocate of professionalism in football, because I am convinced that open professionalism is better than bogus amateurism.'

However assertive Bentley was in the FA council chamber, after being elected in 1888, he was no great orator. His speeches were short and to the point. And as Geoffrey Green wrote of him in relation to the FA: 'His power was such that had be been wanting in real loyalty to the parent body he could well have precipitated the most violent complications.'

But, like McGregor, Bentley was no rebel. However much he fought for the League's rights, he always did so within the context of the existing hierarchy. Thus, his pre-eminence at the League was mirrored by his status in the Association. He became the first League official to be appointed a vice president of the FA (in 1905). He was also elected vice president of the Lancashire FA, president of the Manchester & District FA, president of the Lancashire Amateur League, president of the Bolton Charity Cup Committee, a member of the Sheriff of London Charity Shield Committee, and president of the Manchester, Bolton & District Referees' Association.

P. M. Young relates a curious tale concerning Bentley in April 1892, when he was on FA business with the England team in Glasgow, as one of the international selectors.

'After the match, in which Scotland were beaten by 4–1, the winners assembled to be photographed. When a count was taken, however, there were only ten men present. The one amateur (Dunn of Cambridge University) was absent. Possibly this was accidental, possibly not, for the relations between amateurs and professionals were not quite easy. But an England ten could hardly be handed down to posterity. So Bentley was pushed into the group. In a literal sense the resulting record is false; but a bigger truth, no doubt, is thereby stated.'

Sir Frederick Wall, secretary of the FA, recalled Bentley as a staunch defender of professional footballers, 'most of whom he regarded as thoroughly decent fellows'. Apparently, Bentley was out walking with a company of ladies and gentlemen one day. Several young men, well dressed and groomed, passed them by, raising their hats in greeting. One of Bentley's companions enquired as to the young men's identities, to which he replied, 'only those disreputable football professionals you sometimes talk about'. (As Wall added: 'He could be very relentless with his dry wit.')

Before proceeding to look at Bentley's work with the League, it would be appropriate to focus upon his contribution to sporting journalism.

Above all, J. J. Bentley was known for being a precursor of modern reportage, as this account from *Association Football and the Men Who Made It* (1906) suggests:

'He is to the point with the pen as with the tongue, and calls a football "the ball". Such things as "inflated spheres", "tegumentary cylinders" and "the leather globe" he leaves to others. A champion of his day is to him "a good player" or a "sound one". He does not deal in superlatives, nor is he led to place the football player of momentary eminence on a pedestal.'

In a series called 'Popular People', the *Lancashire Review* said of Bentley in October 1897:

'There is no more popular personage in Lancashire ... in football or cricket circles. He is the pioneer of modern go-ahead athletic journalism.

In the years before the League was formed, reports of cricket and football matches were perfunctory, inaccurate and dull in the extreme. Mr Bentley was one of the very first to infuse enthusiasm, animation, technical accuracy and literary skill into his reports, with the result that footballers got into the habit of saying that the next best thing to playing was reading Mr Bentley's account of it.

His opinion is so much respected that he receives letters from all parts of the world, asking his advice on football matters.'

Bentley seems to have left *Athletic News* around the turn of the century, after which he contributed to a wide variety of publications, including *The Umpire, C. B. Fry's, The Royal, Windsor Magazine*, the *Daily Express* and the *Daily Mail*.

He then returned to club administration in 1902 by becoming chairman of Manchester United, when the extremely wealthy businessman J. H. Davies began the transformation of the club from a bankrupt operation in Clayton into a major power at Old Trafford.

Despite many tempting offers from Fleet Street, Bentley succumbed only once, in 1909, when he agreed to become editor of the London-based weekly magazine *Football Chat*, which was primarily the mouthpiece of the Southern League. How seriously he took this appointment is impossible to say. He certainly never strayed far from Bolton, where he had a wife, Betsy, and three daughters (one of whom married the Manchester sports journalist Cyril Luckman). In his later life he was also much restricted in his movements by severe attacks of rheumatism.

Remembering John Bentley at the peak of his powers. 'Red Rose' recalled being amazed at the League President's unruffled calm. JJ made mistakes, of course, but often because he was too generous. Money meant little to him; he was a soft touch, especially when it came to former players, whose requests he rarely refused. To Red Rose he was 'a man of real worth, blind to the faults of his friends, eager to exaggerate their virtues. I can honestly say that I have never met a kinder, or more easy-going man.'

CHAPTER FOUR

Tests of Strength

John Bentley's accession came at a time of great experimentation and change in the League. The test match system was changed, debated, then finally dropped after a scandal. Clubs dropped in and out of the Second Division with every new season, and the spectre of crowd disorder appeared on the horizon once again.

But the most difficult part of the growing process involved the League's relationship with the FA, with the players and with rival competitions such as the new Southern League. No sooner had Bentley become President than he clashed with Charles Clegg at the FA. Two issues divided the camps: wages and transfers.

Bentley's position was that, in order to protect the clubs, their right to retain a player had to be guarded while at the same time wages and incentives were strictly regulated. Only in this way would wealthy clubs be prevented from snapping up all the best players and unbalancing the overall strength of the competition. On the other hand, if a wealthy club wanted a player, it was only fair that the other club should gain compensation for their loss, at the best possible price.

Representing the FA, Clegg took a completely different view. Abhorring professionalism as a concept, the Sheffield solicitor saw the player as an individual whose personal rights should be protected. That meant no limitations on his earnings or his freedom of movement. It also meant that the FA could keep well clear of unsavoury involvement in financial wrangles.

Against the FA, Bentley won this first round of the argument, but when faced by the League clubs he lost another.

The first significant move to restrict players' wages came at the instigation of Derby County in September 1893 (Derby were so strapped for cash that on one occasion they couldn't afford to pay even their League subscription). A month later, Bentley was asked to hear the players' case, and in November a set of proposals was drawn up, 'to secure an equitable and permanent basis of remuneration to players, which shall be advantageous to both clubs and players'.

The proposals were as follows:

1. That no player in the employ of a League club shall receive more than a maximum sum (£140) for one year. It shall be optional to any club to pay a player during the close season so long as such payments do not exceed £1 per week.

2. That no club shall pay more than £10 bonus on engaging a player, and then only to players not previously registered with the League. In the event of the transfer being desired by the player and the club to which he belongs, the amount of such transfer to be decided upon by the Management Committee.

3. That every club shall keep a full and true account of its payments to players, which shall be ordered for production at any time.

4. Any club discovered to be infringing these rules shall be fined the sum of £200, in addition to having six points deducted, and also be liable to expulsion without appeal.

Deterred by the draconian threat of the last clause and the implied restraint of transfer fees in clause 2, the clubs threw out these proposals at a meeting in Manchester. This was the first, but by no means the last, time that a Management Committee package would be rejected because it had not gained the necessary three-quarters majority, as required by League rules.

Nowadays, of course, the League can decide the value of a player's transfer through a formal tribunal, and as Charles Sutcliffe pointed out in 1938, had the independent valuation scheme been adopted in 1893 it may well 'have prevented the bargaining over them, and probably the swollen prices paid'.

Derby were angry that their groundwork had come to nought, and in May 1895 called a Special General Meeting to propose that the majority required for rule changes be reduced from three-quarters to two-thirds. Unfortunately for future generations, Derby's proposal failed – it didn't gain the necessary three-quarters majority – and it took until 1986 for the change to come about, a delay which brought about the scotching of many a progressive move.

Of 1895, Charles Sutcliffe wrote:

'Seven years after the establishment of the League, clubs were yet careless and recalcitrant. They were still negligent in compiling their retain lists, in playing unregistered players, in returning their result forms, in paying fines, even their annual subscriptions, and generally in complying with instructions.'

They also frequently clashed with the Management Committee, and often used every available pretext to complain about a result: pitch, weather, referee, bad light and so on. Disputed goals were, however, fewer than one might imagine.

One long-standing mystery concerns the question of whether Notts County beat Bolton by 3–0 or 4–0 on 26 October 1889. An even more controversial goal was that allegedly scored by Everton against Small Heath. The Heathens complained that Mr Ashmole had allowed Everton a fourth goal (in a reported 5–0 victory) when they considered that the ball had not passed between the posts. The Committee ordered the scoreline to stand (as

it invariably did when there was a dispute), but, unusually, set up an enquiry into the incident, with the result that referees were instructed to inspect goal nets before each game. This practice has continued ever since.

After first discussing the issue in 1891, crowd trouble came to the Committee's attention again in January 1895, when the highly controversial referee John Lewis, Blackburn's representative on the Committee, complained about the ungentlemanly behaviour of Derby's supporters. Any recurrence, warned the League, 'may result in the withdrawal of League matches from the Derby ground'.

The word 'may' was significant, for the League rarely clamped down on members when it came to crowd trouble. This was shown a few weeks later, when a referee was assaulted at Arsenal. As always, the FA dealt with the disciplinary aspect of the incident

Was this Birmingham Sports Argus *cartoon trying to score a point against a rival newspaper? J. J. Bentley, then assistant editor of* Athletic News, *kept the Villa and Albion teams waiting for their match at Perry Barr on 2 September 1893, but, unlike most unpunctual referees, was not fined by the Management Committee.*

(usually by issuing a caution or ordering the ground to be closed for a period), while the League merely suggested – but did not order – that clubs with ropes surrounding their pitches install rails instead, 'and take every precaution to prevent spectators crossing the playing pitch at the conclusion of their matches'.

Olive Grove, the home of Sheffield Wednesday, had what was described as a 'massive iron railing' around its pitch, but this didn't stop spectators pelting the referee (John Lewis again) with mud, or using unseemly language during a match against Stoke, which Lewis had to abandon after seventy-five minutes. Again, a verbal reprimand was handed out, but, as history has shown repeatedly, it amounted to a virtual admission that the League alone was relatively helpless in the fight against hooliganism.

Similarly in October 1895, after yet another assault on a referee, at Wolverhampton, all clubs were ordered to provide a dressing room for the referee and visiting players 'in a convenient position on the ground'. A relatively innocuous provision, one would have thought, but no sooner had the order been made than it was revised to read 'It is desirable', rather than 'required'.

For all his power and authority, it was clear that John Bentley still had to bow to the sensitivities of his members. But he did at least establish one important principle as a result of these unsavoury incidents. For the first time, the League decided to hold all host clubs responsible for any assault on visiting teams or referees, a principle which has remained in effect until today.

What should not be overlooked is the fact that many clubs were simply caught out by the rapidly growing popularity of League football. Few grounds could cope, and it is no coincidence that the 1890s saw the majority of clubs form themselves into limited liability companies and issue shares in order to finance extensive ground-building programmes.

The second series of test matches was scheduled for 28 April 1894, with replays to be played 'to a finish' (whatever that entailed) on the following Monday. In fact, no replays were necessary. The results were:

Newton Heath 0 Liverpool 2 (at Blackburn).

Whereas Newton Heath had finished bottom again, Liverpool had been a stunning success in their debut season, losing not a single game.

Darwen 1 Small Heath 3 (at Stoke).

This time Small Heath reaped the reward of another excellent season, having become the second club to finish a campaign without drawing a match. More creditably, they scored a record 103 goals in 28 games.

Preston North End 4 Notts County 0 (at Olive Grove).

Victory was a tremendous relief for the former Invincibles, who in their five previous seasons had been champions twice and runners-up three times.

This series of test matches, therefore, saw justice being done, with the top two and bottom two clubs changing divisions.

Elections to the Second Division were not quite as straightforward. Firstly, one extra club was needed to balance numbers to sixteen in each division. Secondly, Crewe, who finished fourth from bottom and should have been up for re-election, pleaded that they had in fact finished twelfth out of a list of sixteen, not fifteen, Bootle having dropped out just before the season. It was a brazen ploy, but it worked.

Since Northwich Victoria did not re-apply for membership, having finished with the worst record of any club to date, this left only Ardwick (who had just been renamed Manchester City) and Rotherham Town to stand for re-election. City sailed through with 20 votes, largely thanks to Josh Parlby's eloquence, but Rotherham dropped out with 15 votes, beaten by Midland Leaguers Leicester Fosse with 20 votes.

Bury (from the Lancashire League) and Burton Wanderers (Midland League) took the remaining two vacancies, with 17 votes each. Unsuccessful applications were made by Accrington (7 votes), Blackpool (8), Loughborough (8) and Rossendale (0).

As in 1893, however, the story did not end there. On 11 June the Management Committee read a letter from hard-up Middlesbrough Ironopolis, resigning their membership with regret. Having earned more votes than any of the other unsuccessful applicants, Rotherham were thus invited back into the fold (where their first act was to complain quite justifiably that ten of their first twelve matches were away from home!).

In stark contrast to their reaction when Accrington resigned, the Committee showed a a rare touch of sympathy on hearing of Middlesbrough's plight. Expressing 'regret at the unfortunate position that the "Nops" club were placed in', Ironopolis were assured that 'if at any time they should be in a strong position and apply for a place in the League, such application should be treated as favourably as possible.'

But surely, we modern democrats ask, wasn't it beyond the powers of the Management Committee to favour an application for membership? Technically yes, but in practice, while it was up to the clubs to do the voting, the Committee quite often made its preferences quite plain (especially once the Third Division was formed).

The 1895 test matches resulted as follows:

Stoke 3 Newton Heath 0 (at Port Vale).

Stoke finished third from bottom of Division One. Newton Heath were third in Division Two.

Derby 2 Notts County 1 (at Leicester).

Derby finished second from bottom, Notts County second from top.

Bury 1 Liverpool 0 (at Blackburn).

This was a real reversal of roles. Having run away with the Second Division Championship in their debut season (by eight clear points), Liverpool failed miserably in Division One. It was therefore doubly painful that this defeat should come at the hands of a club who not only emulated them by capturing the Second Division title in their first League season, but did so by an even greater margin of nine points.

Up for re-election in 1895 were Lincoln (22 votes), Port Vale (22), Crewe (18) and Walsall Town Swifts, who were ousted by Loughborough (18). Walsall's total was not recorded. We merely learn that along with Blackpool and Fairfield Athletic they were unsuccessful, which, considering they had finished only third from bottom, level on points with Lincoln, much have come as a considerable shock.

Walsall's record was not entirely unblemished, however. On one occasion, at home to Newcastle, their team took the field thirty minutes late, because they hadn't yet been paid. On another, they arrived at Darwen with only eight men.

The last year in which the test matches operated as straight play-offs was 1895. Soon after, it was decided to experiment with a 'mini-league', in which the top pair from Division Two faced the bottom pair from Division One. Also, in order to participate in test matches a player now had to have played in at least four League matches for the club or have been resident in the town for at least four weeks beforehand. This was, of course, to stop clubs trying to buy their way out of trouble.

The 1896 test matches resulted as follows:

Man City	1	WBA	1
WBA	6	Man City	1
Liverpool	4	Small Heath	0
Small Heath	0	Liverpool	0
Liverpool	2	WBA	0
WBA	2	Liverpool	0
Man City	3	Small Heath	0
Small Heath	8	Man City	0

The final table therefore read:

Liverpool	4	2	1	1	6	2	5
WBA	4	2	1	1	9	4	5
Small Heath	4	1	1	2	8	7	3
Man City	4	1	1	2	5	15	3

Thus, Liverpool bounced back to the First Division at the expense of Small Heath, whose record (set in 1894) for the most goals scored in a season Liverpool had just, coincidentally, bettered. Liverpool found the net 106 times in 30 League games. West Bromwich, meanwhile, kept their First Division status, despite having finished bottom, one point behind Small Heath.

A few weeks after this first experimental series, there was another alteration to League rules at the 1896 Annual Meeting in Birmingham. It was agreed that instead of four clubs, only three from the foot of the Second Division should be required to stand for re-election.

In 1896, because Rotherham Town had already decided to drop out (was it all those successive away games?), only Port Vale and Crewe were left to fight it out with a record number of eight non-League applicants.

It might amuse the current generation to note that a certain Tottenham Hotspur won only two votes on this occasion, the same as Macclesfield and less than both Fairfield Athletic and Glossop North End. At the time, it will have amused neither Crewe (4 votes) nor Port Vale (10) to have been unseated by Blackpool (19), Walsall (16) (back after one season), and Gainsborough Trinity (15). The highest-placed challengers were Luton Town (10).

The 1897 test matches resulted as follows:

Notts Co.	1	Sunderland	0
Sunderland	0	Notts Co.	0
Newton Heath	2	Burnley	0
Burnley	2	Newton Heath	0
Burnley	0	Notts Co.	1

Notts Co.	1	Burnley	1
Sunderland	2	Newton Heath	0
Newton Heath	1	Sunderland	1

The final table therefore read:

Notts County	4	2	2	0	3	1	6
Sunderland	4	1	2	1	3	2	4
Burnley	4	1	1	2	3	4	3
Newton Heath	4	1	1	2	3	5	3

Sunderland thus kept their First Division place, while Second Division champions Notts County replaced Burnley, who had finished bottom.

The prospect of Second Division football seemed to frighten Burnley so much that a few weeks later they proposed an extension of both divisions to eighteen clubs each, a move which would conveniently allow them to maintain their higher status.

Alternatively, did they know something which would have put the whole test match series into question? Why else would they also have proposed an addition to Rule 7, to read: 'Any club or players offering a bonus or any inducement to another club or the players of another club to win, lose or draw a League or Test Match, shall be guilty of misconduct and liable to be dealt with under this rule.'?

Grimsby were also concerned about the test matches. They proposed giving automatic promotion to the top two Second Division sides and letting the third and fourth placed clubs fight out the test matches with the bottom two of the First Division (similar to the play-offs of today).

Quite what happened to these proposals, or indeed any of the elections to the League in

> **'The Management Committee wish clubs to understand that kicking off by outsiders is illegal, and clubs are desired to discountenance such practices.'**
> *League minute, 8 October 1897*

1897, we discover only from newspaper reports, for in a rare lapse of duty Harry Lockett failed to write up the minutes of the Annual Meeting. Since he was at the time a volunteer sergeant awaiting a call to the Boer War, we can, perhaps, excuse him.

According to *Athletic News*, neither Burnley's nor Grimsby's proposals were carried, so Burnley were down to the Second Division for the first time

In the votes for re-election, Lincoln (21 votes) and Burton Swifts (15) were each successful. Burton Wanderers, who finished second from bottom, won only 9 votes and thus lost their place to Luton Town, who polled 13. Other unsuccessful applicants were Port Vale (11), Nelson (7), Glossop North End (5), Fairfield (3), Crewe (2) and two-time winners of the new Southern League, Millwall Athletic (1).

Although the minutes of the 1897 meeting have not been handed down to us, Charles Sutcliffe expressed something of its mood: 'A new sense of [the League's] mission and its future animated the clubs ... There was a keener realization of the common interests of the members, of the broad interests at stake, as opposed to the narrow and selfish.'

A sign of this new era was the setting up of the Inter-League Board, to co-ordinate matters of mutual interest with the Scottish League. The Board's first priority was to make retain and transfer lists binding on both sides of the border. This was to avoid the existing situation whereby, to avoid having to pay possible transfer fees, dozens of players were registered with League clubs in both England and Scotland (usually without even having visited or played for one of the clubs).

The League also tried to persuade the Scottish League to adopt the maximum signing-on bonus of £10, but the Scots were having none of this Sassenach nonsense (nor did they ever adopt the maximum wage rule).

With the setting up of the Inter-League Board at Douglas, Isle of Man (the Committee always chose holiday resorts for summer meetings), the League took an important step towards its modern state. A further step was the abandonment of the test match system, albeit in circumstances which left the League little choice.

The 1898 results were as follows:

Newcastle	2	Stoke	1
Stoke	1	Newcastle	0
Burnley	2	Blackburn	0
Blackburn	1	Burnley	3
Blackburn	4	Newcastle	3
Newcastle	4	Blackburn	0
Burnley	0	Stoke	2
Stoke	0	Burnley	0

The final table thus read:

Stoke	4	2	1	1	4	2	5
Burnley	4	2	1	1	5	3	5
Newcastle	4	2	0	2	9	6	4
Blackburn	4	1	0	3	5	12	2

It was the final game at Stoke which brought about the system's downfall. On Thursday 28 April Blackburn had beaten Newcastle 4–3, leaving both Stoke and Burnley on four points and Newcastle on two points. Stoke and Burnley players knew, therefore, that a draw in their match at the Victoria Ground on the following Saturday would be sufficient to keep Stoke in the First Division and lift Burnley out of the Second.

Despite the fact that everyone knew an 'arrangement' was in the offing, Stoke and Burnley made their intentions so patently obvious that they gave the League no choice but either to revamp or drop the test match idea completely.

'The game proved a complete fiasco', reported the *Staffordshire Advertiser*. *Athletic News* called it a fraud: 'The teams could have done without goalkeepers, so anxious were the forwards not to score.' Played in wet and windy conditions on a shocking pitch, the players kicked the ball into the crowd so often that the disgruntled fans 'gave themselves up to unlimited fun with the ball on their own account'.

To stop this happening for the umpteenth time, one of the linesmen tried so hard to stop the ball reaching the crowd that he ran headlong into a policeman, who went head over heels. To make this afternoon doubly humiliating for the League, the linesman in question was William Bellamy of Grimsby, a member of the Management Committee.

Something had to be done, if only to restore public confidence and placate both Newcastle and Blackburn, victims of the fraud. The chance came three weeks later at the Annual Meeting in Manchester, but because of the need to keep to the pre-set agenda it came about in a very roundabout manner. Follow this if you can:

Three Second Division clubs were up for re-election: Lincoln City (for the fourth time in six seasons), Darwen and Loughborough. Despite their poor record, Lincoln gleaned the most votes (21), followed by Burslem Port Vale (18), who had been in non-League football for two seasons, and Loughborough (16). Thus Darwen lost their place (with 15 votes). Other unsuccessful applicants were New Brighton Tower, Nelson and Bristol City (then referred to as plain Bristol).

After Harry Lockett had announced these results, discussion then turned to the expansion of the two divisions.

Arsenal's Mr Beardsley suggested two Second Divisions of sixteen clubs each, to be divided into North and South. Mr Rinder from Aston Villa proposed a First Division of eighteen clubs and two Second Divisions of twelve clubs each. Rinder also put forward the apparently obvious idea of straight promotion and relegation, two up and two down.

However, 'after considerable discussion' (a favourite term of Lockett's) and a vote, easily the most popular suggestion was that of Charles Sutcliffe to expand both divisions to

eighteen clubs. Sutcliffe's commonsense approach and his ability to dominate proceedings would show increasingly from this meeting onwards. He was also elected on to the Management Committee for the first time.

Most important of all, Sutcliffe – who represented Burnley, one of the guilty parties on 30 April – ensured through his diplomacy that Blackburn and Newcastle were voted into the newly expanded First Division, thereby rendering the recent test match series meaningless.

Blackburn's and Newcastle's promotion meant that there were now four vacancies in the newly expanded Second Division, so, in effect, the previous elections to the Second Division were also nullified. One place was immediately filled by Darwen, who returned from the shortest ever recorded sojourn in non-League circles (probably half an hour).

The remaining three places were filled at a meeting eight days later, when New Brighton Tower, Glossop North End and Barnsley were elected, apparently uncontested. Thus, in exactly one decade, the League had expanded to thirty-six members, three times its original size.

Hard though it is for us to imagine, when Grimsby proposed in 1898 that goalkeepers wear shirts of a different colour from their team-mates, they won little support. Distinguishing colours were not introduced until 1909. Then only scarlet, royal blue or white were allowed. Oddly enough, although clubs were regularly fined for fielding 'keepers in the wrong coloured shirts, the League XI itself played its next three games with 'keepers in the normal team colours. At that stage the goalkeeper was still allowed to handle the ball anywhere in his own HALF! He was not confined to his penalty area until 1912. Also in 1912, he was allowed to wear a green jersey, the colour which soon became the most popular among custodians.

More clubs meant more registered players, who therefore gained greater bargaining power, and the season was only three months old before the Committee had its next confrontation, with a group of players attempting to form a union.

The deputation's main concern was the operation of the retain and transfer system. After discussion, the Committee agreed to consider the question, but pointed out that if a player ever had a grievance he could always raise it through official channels, that is, through the Committee. The League would use this same anti-union argument repeatedly over the ensuing decades.

On the other hand, the players were no firebrands. They assured the Committee that they 'had no desire at all to be antagonistic to the League but wished to assist so far as lay in their powers'.

Four months later, in March 1899, that arch anti-professional, FA chairman Charles Clegg, rekindled the great transfer debate by sending the following proposals to every league in England:

1. That players could in future be signed on for more than just one season.
(This was to ease the uncertainty under which every player laboured, never quite sure of his security from one year to the next and always aware that a club could drop him in May without having to pay summer wages.)

2. That after existing transfer arrangements had been completed, no transfer fee be demanded for a player which exceeded his original price.
(Clegg and the FA regarded the whole business of purchasing players as being 'objectionable', but accepted that those clubs which had already bought players should at least be able to sell them for what they had paid.)

3. That players for whom no fee had ever been paid should not in future be bought or sold for fees.

4. That no payments ever be made to agents or any other people involved in arranging transfers.

The Management Committee's response was predictably wary, especially in view of the sudden appearance of the Players' Union. But they did recognize that the system was open to abuse among players and clubs, and suggested instead:

1. To abolish the system of publishing transfer lists and to make private and confidential all details of transfer deals.
(This was accepted. Fees mentioned in the press have always, therefore, been estimates, unless a club has been prepared to divulge an exact sum.)

2. To allow the cancellation of League forms of any player who has not played or been paid within six months of signing.
(This was designed to stop clubs selfishly holding on to large numbers of players rather than release them to rival clubs. In 1905, League clubs retained on average seventy-one players each. None of them could possibly hope to use that many, even allowing for the fact that many of the individuals concerned had long since given up the game or moved on to non-League clubs.)

3. That players should have the right to appeal directly to the Management Committee in the event of a dispute with the club, with the Committee having fullest powers to adjudicate, subject to appeal.

4. That a one-year agreement was preferable, and the Committee strongly advised the FA to pass a rule fixing the maximum bonus at £10 (as the League had already done). The proposal stated: 'We feel that the offering and paying of large bonuses to players is detrimental to the best interests of clubs and players alike and a source of much mischief and unsportsmanship.'

Clegg would not be appeased, however. He was determined to exert the FA's power, and therefore resolved that, although unable to abolish the fee system, the FA could at least demand that one of its rules be adhered to, namely that once a player's annual registration expired he would be free to move to another club, without a fee. The FA wrote:

'In the opinion of (our) Committee, the practice of buying and selling players is unsportsmanlike and most objectionable in itself, and ought not to be entertained by those who desire to see the game played under proper conditions.

During our enquiries it was stated that some clubs derived considerable pecuniary advantage from training young players and then selling them to the more prominent clubs. We think the practice in such cases, when applied to human beings, altogether discreditable to any system bearing the name of sport.'

The maximum transfer fee the FA could tolerate, to halt the inflation of fees and to cover what it regarded as legitimate expenses, was £10 (this at a time when several players were changing hands for around £200–300).

The Management Committee's response was again uncompromising. Bentley asserted that the League rules worked quite satisfactorily, and that most of the grounds for complaint from players had been ironed out. As in 1894, Bentley won, Clegg lost. At the 1899 FA Annual Meeting, the £10 bonus limit became enshrined in the FA rules, and the farce which McKenna and Sutcliffe had tried to avert in 1897 carried on.

The conflict had one interesting side effect. We noted earlier a comment that John Bentley and William McGregor had never shared a cross word. This was not quite the case. When Bentley supported the £10 limit, old Mac wrote articles against it, mainly because he felt it was unenforceable. And just as he had done during the fight for professionalism in 1885, McGregor admitted, this time in print, that his own club, Aston Villa, had paid one player £50 to sign on.

Bentley did not appreciate the founder's contribution. Writing in *Athletic News* shortly after the 1899 FA Annual Meeting, he commented pointedly:

'If Mr McGregor knows everything why doesn't he buckle on his armour and attend meetings, as he has the right to do? If he has the time to think and to write, he surely has the time to act? He prefers not to do so, but to sit afar off and to criticise . . . now that he has left the ship he would seek to navigate it from the shore.'

If such a stinging rebuke was intended to stir up the 'old warhorse', it had just the right effect. McGregor had indeed been a distant figure since Bentley took over in 1894. But from this moment until his death in 1911, William McGregor hardly missed a meeting. JJ's barb had obviously struck a sensitive nerve.

Thus, the Football League approached the twentieth century: its founder shamed back to the fray, its clubs still squabbling among themselves about transfer fees, rearranged dates, compensation, poaching and all the other matters which had occupied the first twelve years of the League's existence. McGregor will not have found it hard to pick up where he left off.

To some clubs, the idea of being able to afford even a £10 signing-on fee was laughable. Loughborough sent their subscription for the season, but the cheque bounced. Darwen were so hard up during 1898/9 that they asked for extra time to pay their two guineas entrance fee. Eventually, the League had to lend them £20 just to keep them afloat. Hardly surprisingly, Darwen finished bottom of the League that season with just nine points from thirty-four games, the worst record yet. Included among the 141 goals they conceded – also a record – were three 10–0 defeats. Suffice it to say that when it came to the Annual Meeting in May, Darwen did not apply for re-election.

While Darwen were offering their opponents shooting practice, one of the oddest events in League history occurred. At the game between Sheffield Wednesday and Aston Villa on 26 November, the referee, Mr A. Scragg, blew for time 10½ minutes early, because of bad light. On this occasion, however, neither team was to blame. Mr Scragg had delayed the kick-off by being late himself.

Two weeks later the clubs took their case to the Management Committee. Wednesday argued that the final $10\frac{1}{2}$ minutes should be played. Villa thought the entire match should be replayed (but then, they were losing 3–1 at the end). Similar cases in the past had always ended with the League ordering the result to stand, but in this instance, to everyone's surprise, the Committee ordered the remaining minutes to be played.

Villa were subsequently told by the FA's Appeal Committee that the only comparable case was that of Wolves *v.* Stoke on 25 November 1893. On that occasion the referee also arrived late and the two clubs were ordered to play the remaining three minutes. Both refused, so the result stood.

After Villa's appeal in 1899, however, the FA did advise the Committee to settle a general principle for unfinished matches, with the result that from thereon it was resolved that any match not completed would have to be replayed for the full ninety minutes.

Mr Scragg was meanwhile reprimanded, and on 13 March 1899 the famous $10\frac{1}{2}$ minutes were played in front of 3000 fans at Olive Grove. Wednesday actually scored another goal, to make the final score 4–1. (Of course, Villa didn't travel all that way just for ten minutes' football. Once the League business was settled, the two sides played a benefit match. Wednesday won that one too, 2–0.)

The final Annual Meeting of the nineteenth century, at the unfortunately titled Old Boar Hotel, Manchester, was that of a relatively secure organization showing a healthy balance of £367 in the bank. The word 'loyalty' pops up throughout the minutes in this period. Bentley demanded no less.

With Darwen retiring, shell-shocked, to the Lancashire League, the other two bottom clubs, Loughborough and Blackpool, joined Chesterfield, Coventry City, Chorley, Middles-brough, Stockport County, Ashton North End and Wigan County in the election. Loughborough won the most votes (28), followed by Chesterfield and Middlesbrough with 17 votes each. Thus, Blackpool (15) lost their place after three seasons in the League (and cheekily asked to have their expenses for attending the meeting reimbursed).

The year 1899 also saw the League's first promotion and relegation issues being contested. Sheffield Wednesday and founder members Bolton shared the dubious distinction of being the first relegated clubs. Manchester City and Glossop North End were the first to be promoted. Glossop thus became the smallest town in Britain ever to have had a First Division club (even if it was only for one season).

A year later, the first relegation battle of the twentieth century sounded alarm bells that a scandal even worse than that of 30 April 1898 might have occurred, and, to Charles Sutcliffe's acute embarrassment, Burnley were involved once again.

The Management Committee meeting of 30 April 1900 was to have been in Manchester, but John Bentley switched it to Preston so that members could attend the vital relegation match between Preston and Blackburn. Rumours were rife that the match was going to be fixed to enable Preston to stay up.

Suspicion had been aroused by an occurrence on the previous Saturday. Just before Burnley's vital match at Forest, goalkeeper 'Happy' Jack Hillman had reportedly offered the Forest captain a bribe to lose the game so that Burnley could stay up in the First Division.

If anything of this nature had occurred before, this was certainly the first time it had become so widely known. When Hillman faced a joint FA and Football League commission in Manchester on 9 May, he claimed that his offer had been no more than a joke. 'It was all chaff', he insisted. Messrs Clegg, Bentley and Charles Alcock (the former FA secretary and founder of the FA Cup) failed to see the funny side, however, and banned Hillman for one year.

Out for other reasons in 1900 were Luton, who finished second bottom and didn't apply for re-election, and Loughborough, who had performed even worse than Darwen the year before, gaining only eight points from thirty-four games and winning only one match. Unlike Luton, Loughborough would never return to the League fold. Blackpool and Stockport County were elected in their places, and the second re-election candidates, Barnsley, were comfortably returned. Unsuccessful applications came from Doncaster Rovers, Kettering and Stalybridge Rovers.

January 1901 was just another month for the Football League. The minutes record the usual number of disputes and arguments between clubs. For the nation as a whole, however, it represented a watershed in history. Queen Victoria had died after a reign of sixty-four years, years in which the game of football had been transformed almost as greatly as the country itself. Football had moved from fields and public schools to municipal parks and great stadia. Britain had been transformed from a predominantly rural country to an urban industrial monster, choked in soot but decked in imperial honours.

The FA reacted patriotically to Victoria's death by postponing the Cup programme, a measure which much annoyed the League because a fixture pile-up was thus created. But on the day of Victoria's funeral on 2 February, the Management Committee could hardly do other than to postpone the entire fixture programme.

A great era had passed, indeed. While the Empire mourned the Queen, in football the people of Preston were about to mourn the passing of the Invincibles. By the end of the 1900/1 season, Proud Preston were down into the Second Division for the first time, and not even a proposal by their director, Tom Houghton, to increase each division to twenty clubs could save them. His last-ditch attempt

failed by just a few votes to win the necessary majority.

So Preston were doomed to relegation, along with fellow founder members West Bromwich Albion, whom they had faced at The Oval in the 1888 Cup Final; now they were to compete with the likes of Gainsborough and Glossop. Truly, no club could ever survive on reputation alone in the League. New clubs would forever steal the limelight; 1901, for example, saw the first of many a Championship win for Liverpool, while of the original twelve clubs only Notts County finished in the top six.

Three clubs sought re-election in 1901; Walsall, Burton Swifts and Stockport County. Walsall, with a new committee, no proper home and a recently held enquiry into their transfer dealings, received only 7 votes and were banished into non-League football for the second time in six years.

Meanwhile, Burton Swifts, who had finished bottom, won 23 votes and were re-elected, along with Stockport County, who originally tied with applicants Doncaster on 16 votes each, but won a second vote by 21 to 13. The successful new applicant was Bristol City, who became the League's second southern club after Arsenal, with 23 votes.

The other failed applicants were Crewe, Darwen, Stalybridge and Southport Central. (As it transpired, Doncaster did find a place for the following season when New Brighton dropped out within hours of the opening matches. The only other change involved Burton Swifts, who changed their name to Burton United after merging with neighbours Burton Wanderers.)

So the League entered the Edwardian age, only thirteen years old but already showing signs of substance and permanence. Despite a balance sheet which recorded only a token profit of £19 13s 3d on the season, the major source of income had been two Inter-League matches which had yielded a very healthy £743 17s 3d (67 per cent of the total income).

THE FOOTBALL LEAGUE.

Abstract of Cash Account for Season 1900-1901.

Dr.   Cr.

RECEIPTS.	£ s. d.	£ s. d.	PAYMENTS.	£ s. d.
To Subscriptions and Entrance Fees		309 15 0	By Balance from last Account...	196 12 2
„ Fines and Appeals	68 3 0		„ Expenses—General Meetings	170 1 8
„ Less Appeals returned	13 4 10		„ Expenses—Management Meetings...	256 6 6
		54 18 2	„ Printing, Stationery, Advertising, &c. ...	58 1 4
„ Inter-League Matches—			„ Secretary's Salary	100 0 0
Irish	150 17 3		„ Rooms for Meetings	8 11 0
Scotch	593 0 0		„ Stamps, Telegrams, &c.	40 6 5
		743 17 3	„ Bank Charges and Sundry Expenses, including Medals...	67 14 10
„ Luton Football Club—Loan repaid ...		10 0 0	„ Arrangement of Fixtures	23 15 0
			„ Shorthand Notes	10 0 8
			„ Expenses—Inter-League Matches	128 1 7
			„ Expenses—Inter-League Committee	14 6 0
			„ Luton Football Club Transfer Fees	25 0 0
			„ Balance	19 13 3
		£1118 10 5		£1118 10 5

We have examined the Secretary's Cash Book, with the Vouchers and Papers relating thereto, for the period
May 1st, 1900, to April 30th, 1901, and certify the above is a correct abstract of the same.

J. HENRY STRAWSON,
J. H. RICHARDSON, } Auditors.

Chartered Accountant.

The Football League.

REPORT FOR SEASON 1900-1901.

The Management Committee, in presenting their report, congratulate the Members on another successful season, the interest in the competition being sustained quite to the close of the season, especially so far as the position of the top and bottom clubs in the First Division were concerned, it being during the last week that these places were definitely decided. Liverpool by winning their last match secured the championship, Sunderland being the runners-up—two points behind, but with a better goal average.

Preston North End and West Bromwich Albion retire by rule into the Second Division, their places being taken by Grimsby Town and Small Heath, the latter returning to the First Division after an absence of five years.

Both these Clubs have merited their promotion, Small Heath having the better goal average, though Grimsby finished a point in front.

Walsall, Stockport County, and Burton Swifts being the last three clubs in the Second Division, retire, but offer themselves for re-election.

The Inter-League Matches have resulted in a win against Ireland and a loss against Scotland, both being played away, the defeat by Scotland being the heaviest ever sustained by us. The interest taken in these matches increases each year, the attendances being very large.

Your Committee were instructed at the last Annual Meeting, to devise a scheme for the amalgamation of The Football League and Southern League, but, unfortunately, after several informal meetings, the matter has had to be abandoned for the present.

Financially, the year has been a successful one, the Inter-League Matches bringing in a large sum of money, which has enabled us to turn the large deficit of last season into a small balance in hand.

It is still thought advisable that some scheme should be formulated to improve the finances, and thus avoid the calling of levies.

There has been Fifteen Meetings of the Management Committee, the Attendances are as follows :—Mr. J. J. Bentley, President, 15 ; Mr. D. Haigh, Vice-President, 14 ; Mr. T. H. Sidney, Vice-President, 11 ; Mr. J. Lewis, 15 ; Mr. H. S. Radford, 14 ; Mr. W. W. Hart, 15 ; Mr. C. E. Sutcliffe, 15 ; in addition, Mr. W. McGregor (Life Member), has attended on 8 occasions.

Into the 20th Century, into the black, and all looked healthy, mainly due to large receipts from the Inter-League match at Ibrox, which, despite ending in an unprecedented 6–2 defeat, attracted a record attendance of 37,668. The League's finances would depend almost entirely on such fixtures until the Second World War.

The other major source of funds was from subscriptions and entrance fees (28 per cent), with fines, once a major source, now yielding only 5 per cent. The single largest expense was the holding of Management Committee meetings, which cost a quarter of the total outgoings.

The League now issued an annual report with a printed agenda, League tables and a balance sheet. Minutes of all the Committee meetings were also, for the first time, printed and circulated to every club.

Only less seemly items were omitted from these more public minutes; for example, those which revealed why Secretary Harry Lockett had to bid the League a hasty and unexpected farewell. Lockett had not missed a single meeting of the League since 1888, a record no other official could match. So it was that the minutes recorded, apparently with great regret, in January 1902, that, 'having acquired an extensive business, [Lockett] was desirous of devoting as much time as possible to it'.

Unfortunately that was only the official version. In reality Lockett was forced to resign in the wake of a potential scandal, none of which was reported in Charles Sutcliffe's history nor, indeed, in any published source until now.

Apparently, before the Management Committee meeting in London on 8 November 1901, Lockett gave Bentley a letter in which he admitted having used £50 of League funds to help him in the expansion of his business. He wanted Bentley to cover up this moment of weakness by advancing £50 so that he could balance the League's accounts. Lockett's plea was that he had urgently required the money, was full of regret, but hardly considered it a serious matter.

He was wrong.

Harry Lockett was then aged around forty-six. He had come to prominence in the football world as the man who really put Stoke on to a firm footing, arranging attractive fixtures and introducing professionalism two years before

it was legalized. When appointed honorary secretary of the League in 1888, he had just the right credentials. He was also, until November 1892, a League referee.

It is possible that Harry was the father of Arthur Lockett, who was once capped for England in 1903 and played for Stoke until a £400 transfer to Aston Villa. Certainly, Harry remained actively involved with Stoke's affairs during his period as League Secretary.

What time he had left was devoted to a printing and stationery business in Foundry Street, Hanley. Naturally he printed the League's first balance sheet, and when William Sudell gave up the role of honorary treasurer in 1892, Lockett's own Hanley bank took over the League's account.

As League Secretary, Lockett was not always an accurate recorder of minutes. He occasionally got names or dates wrong or left them out completely, his spelling and arithmetic were sometimes erratic, and as time went by his handwriting became increasingly difficult to read. But no complaints were ever recorded, and by 1894 he was receiving £100 a year salary. So why, in the space of a few months, did he put his career and good name into such jeopardy by tinkering with the League's finances?

It would seem that Lockett had simply been unable to run the League and his own business affairs at the same time. In 1901 the printing company of which he had become a director in 1897 had gone into liquidation, and in September 1901 he started business on his own.

It was to fund this new business that he started borrowing funds from the League, without the Committee's knowledge. Whether he owned up due to pressure from outside or from within his own conscience we will never know. What we do know is that once informed, the Committee immediately appointed Charles Sutcliffe and Harry Radford (of Nottingham Forest) to look into the League's books. In the meantime, John Bentley was appointed honorary treasurer.

Lockett's misdeeds were confirmed by the two men's enquiries. Briefly, a detailed breakdown of the League's bank account showed that from May to October 1901 Lockett had repeatedly held on to the League's money for longer than necessary, and instead of banking large amounts as they were received he deposited them in small portions, a bit here, a bit there.

The accounts also showed that after Lockett had confided in Bentley on 8 November he paid in £55 to the League's account on 13 November, apparently to cover the deficit. On one occasion, Lockett had written one amount on the paying-in slip counterfoil, but had actually paid in less. Sutcliffe's and Radford's report to the Committee summed up their findings thus: 'The Account speaks for itself. Comment is unnecessary.'

The report was considered at a meeting in Derby on 6 December 1901, and the unanimous verdict was that Lockett be asked to resign. This he did on 7 January at Bentley's home in Bolton. Thus it was that among the last words Lockett wrote in the League's minutes were these:

'*Mr Harry Lockett the League Secretary tendered his resignation as Secretary to the Committee stating that having acquired a large business he was desirous of devoting as much time as possible to it, he at the same time offering to give all necessary assistance to anyone who might be appointed to the office.*

The resignation was accepted with great regret and his offer of assistance accepted.'

But once the ink had dried and Lockett had packed his bags, the words 'with great regret' were purposefully struck out by John Bentley. The President was clearly furious.

So it was that the man who for fourteen years had battled with the tardiness, forgetfulness and downright meanness of clubs when it came to fines, subscriptions and levies was now disgraced before the Committee over a matter of some £50. All his hard work had

evaporated in a few months of madness. Perhaps desperation had set in. Perhaps he had felt justified in manipulating the funds of an organization to which he'd given so much in terms of time and effort.

Lockett did not become an immediate outcast, however. The League continued to pay him occasional sums of petty cash for helping out the new secretary, Tom Charnley, and at the 1902 Annual Meeting he fought for a seat on the Management Committee. He failed, attracting only five votes.

By 1904 he must have been forgiven, for he was awarded a League season ticket by the Management Committee. Yet when next we hear of him, in early 1907, he is trying unsuccessfully and unreasonably to use that season ticket to gain access to the referee's room 'and all parts of the Stoke ground'.

Rather like his own business, Stoke were then in considerable financial difficulties, and Lockett again proved to be the man to save them. Stoke had been in trouble twice before, in 1892 and 1895, but in 1908, a year after the team had been relegated, apart from the directors only three Stoke shareholders attended the club's Annual General Meeting. The meeting was adjourned to the next day, when even fewer turned up! Port Vale had already resigned from the League, and with Stoke suffering from a £1100 deficit, it was decided to go into liquidation and resign from the League.

So much consternation did this arouse in the Potteries that Lockett called a public meeting in the town hall, where to a packed audience he announced that a new company could be formed if twelve men would come forward to meet the liabilities. In a scene straight out of Arnold Bennett, Lockett himself volunteered, as did a League referee, A. J. Barker. Eventually, the target was reached an hour before deadline.

But, having resigned from the League, Stoke couldn't get their place back, so they played their first team in the Birmingham

League. Lockett became a director of the club. It was typical of the man's devotion (or was it sheer recklessness?) that he put money into Stoke at the very time his own business was floundering.

Also in 1908, he had been persuaded by several priests to take on the printing of the *Staffordshire Catholic Chronicle* newspaper. It proved an impossible burden. With debts of over £500, and having been pressed by creditors for two years, in January 1911 Harry Lockett filed for bankruptcy, an ignominious fate for a man once regarded as one of the most important personalities in League and local football.

Of course, he was also forced to resign from the Stoke board, and the next record of his activities was on 31 March 1911 when the Management Committee considered a letter informing them of his 'financial difficulties'. Charles Sutcliffe agreed to deal with the request, but by 30 April it was clear that nothing had been done. Stoke tried to raise funds for him, and in December 1911 the League received letters setting forth the costs of Lockett's possible discharge as a bankrupt, estimated at £10–12.

We know virtually nothing of Harry Lockett's subsequent life. All we can be sure of was that his printing business was eventually sold to a Mr Sherwin, who became a director of Stoke in 1913. In 1916 a new company appeared in Hanley called The Lockett Printing Co. Ltd. It might have been Harry trying to get back into business, it might not. The rest is a blank.

CHAPTER FIVE
Maximum Wage, Limited Company

With Harry Lockett's departure under a cloud, John Bentley took over the chequebook and the show went on.

Clubs continued to poach, dispute goals and haggle over compensation for rearranged matches. Their claims for the latter were often wildly over-optimistic. West Bromwich, for example, demanded over £192 for the postponement of a match against Lincoln, whereas the Committee calculated an award of only £37, this being the difference between the actual gate and Albion's average gate. Similarly, Blackburn tried to gain £260 for a postponement, but had to settle at £145. The attitude of Rovers and Albion was typical of the period – ask for the maximum and hope to get away with it.

Wages were another matter. In May 1901, the Committee was given another rod for the clubs' backs in the form of the maximum wage. As we have seen, the concept was first mooted seriously in 1893 by Derby County. In 1900 the idea was revived at the FA's Annual Meeting by one W. Heath of the Staffordshire FA. Heath proposed, and it was agreed, that from season 1901/2 no professional footballer should receive more than £4 a week. At the same time, no bonuses for results would be permitted and the £10 signing-on bonus would remain in force.

Once this became enshrined in the FA rules, the clubs had to obey it, but this didn't stop several prominent League chairmen from opposing the maximum wage. Fred Rinder of Aston Villa and John McKenna of Liverpool were the first to oppose the rule. As representatives of wealthy clubs they knew full well that a wage limit was not only unen-

forceable but also damaging to their own interests. How could a player be lured to Villa Park or Anfield if he could earn only the same £4 as at another club, regardless of how well or how badly his team fared? The only answer was to reward that player under the counter.

What annoyed men like Rinder and McKenna even more was that the maximum wage rule gave the Association power to govern the private business of League clubs. It was as if the FA had performed a complete *volte face*; first, it had wanted no involvement in the 'objectionable' financial affairs of League clubs, but now, because they wouldn't toe the line on transfers, it wanted to dictate to them exactly what they could pay to their employees.

Rinder asked, what experience did the amateurs at the FA have in professional matters? The maximum wage was not an aid to professional football but a hindrance. It would hold the bigger clubs back. In fact, for many First Division players it would actually mean a reduction in their wages.

Rinder's argument nearly won the day, but not quite. Although a majority voted to delete the maximum wage rule at the FA's Annual Meeting in 1901, the majority was insufficient. Thus was introduced a regulation such as existed in no other profession, and one which was to be the cause of countless breaches of rules over the next sixty years of its troubled existence.

In one way the FA did back down, however. Fed up with all the haggling and disputes which arose because of the legislation, in 1904 the FA effectively handed over to the League all responsibility for its clubs' financial affairs. After that, as Geoffrey Green wrote, '... it adopted the role of referee, contenting itself with seeing, or trying to see that there was fair play between the clubs and their employees. . . . When all is said and done, the Association, in that year of 1904, took the line of least resistance.'

But if the League regained control of its own financial dealing, why then did it not bring to an end the maximum wage, neither in 1904 nor in 1910, when the FA belatedly amended its rules to confirm that it no longer had control over financial arrangements?

The answer is probably this: by 1904 the maximum wage rule was three years old. Richer clubs who had found a way round it were happy not to rock the boat, as indeed were poorer ones who benefited from the restriction. What developed was a kind of silent conspiracy in which subterfuge became the accepted norm; the public face nodded approval while the private hand slipped cash into the players' pockets. It was at the onset of these developments that Harry Lockett's successor was appointed, in May 1902. He was Tom Charnley, the forty-two-year-old secretary of Preston North End. (Three other men were nominated, the closest contender being J. H. Richardson of Derby County, one of the League's auditors. Charles Sutcliffe also applied, but came third in the vote.)

The League's official address thus moved from Lockett's house in Hanley to Charnley's terraced home a few hundred yards from Deepdale, and it remained in Preston for the next fifty-nine years. But because Charnley was a full-time employee, on the same £100 a year salary as Lockett but with no outside business interests (he severed all his work connections with North End), it was no longer feasible to run the League from a private address. Within a few months of his appointment, therefore, Charnley found a proper office at 13, Winkley Street. To help him with the expanding business he also took on the League's first office worker, a Mr A. H. Downs. (Harry Downs had been Bentley's right-hand man at Bolton.)

The League was now well on its way to becoming a truly respectable bureaucracy.

Tom Charnley proved to be conscientious and exact in his duties. In the minutes he sometimes detailed the precise time, location and duration of each meeting. His handwriting was florid and expansive, with key notes neatly underlined in red. He also made a summary of fines paid by clubs and individuals.

His first Annual Meeting as Secretary was at the Tavistock Hotel, London, soon after his appointment. Embarrassingly, Harry Lockett attended and tried to win a place on the Management Committee. He failed, but there were a few other changes.

'Honest John' McKenna of Liverpool was a newcomer who would serve the League for many years to come (but would never manage to end the maximum wage). Charles Sutcliffe suffered a second blow when, having already been outvoted for the secretaryship, he also lost his place on the Committee (although he remained involved as a legal adviser).

The three bottom Second Division clubs – Chesterfield, Stockport and Gainsborough – all successfully applied for re-election. A fourth, unsuccessful, application was made by Walsall.

But the major surprise came from Charnley's old club, Preston. Still apparently unhappy with Second Division status, North End repeated their attempt to engineer a return to Division One by changing the League structure. First, they proposed expanding the League to forty clubs – having finished third that season they might therefore have sneaked up on a vote. When this proposal failed, Preston's blatant self-interest was not to be deterred, for they then tried to introduce a system of three up, three down (which would definitely have won them promotion). That would have to wait another seventy-one years, however, by which time Preston were on their way down to the Third Division.

Charnley's first year in office went relatively smoothly, the minutes giving every indication

Tom Charnley – League Secretary 1902–33

Tom Charnley was one of Billy Sudell's protégés. He started as an office boy at Sudell's cotton mill, and was soon doubling up as office boy at Preston North End. In 1881 we see Charnley seconding the motion that the club should concentrate on soccer, and in 1893 we find him permanently engaged as North End's secretary.

When chosen to be Harry Lockett's successor, Charnley's priority was to find suitable offices, a quest which took him to four different premises in Preston over the next thirty-one years. During this period, Charnley nursed the League's affairs along calmly and without fuss.

'A perfect Secretary', Charles Sutcliffe said of him, but then the two were close friends, travelling many miles together by train. Both had cars, but neither of them liked driving. Both were Liberals, with strong Christian beliefs.

Charnley was remembered as a quiet, retiring man who never swore, barely touched alcohol and whose main source of relaxation was a game of bowls. But when the occasion demanded he could command attention. Certainly, the Management Committee was delighted with him. They upped his annual salary over the years from £250 in 1908 to £700 twenty years later, awarded him a long-service medal in 1918 after twenty-four years at Preston and then the League, and allowed him a virtually free hand at the League offices.

With that freedom, Charnley took on his son-in-law and next-door neighbour, Fred Howarth, as assistant in 1921. But even though Fred was groomed for the succession, Tom remained at the helm until he was seventy-three, standing down in May 1933 only on medical advice, a few months after the death of his wife.

He was granted a retirement allowance of £350 per year, a £200 cheque and an engraved silver tray. Sutcliffe said of him at the presentation: 'He made countless friends and never an enemy.' But it would have escaped no one's attention that when Sir Frederick Wall retired as Secretary of the FA a year later, he received a golden handshake of £10,000, a massive sum even in the 1930s. Such was the gulf between the League and the FA.

The League's second secretary died on 8 February 1936, aged seventy-six, but as we shall see, the Charnley/Howarth family connection with the League would continue for another thirty-seven years.

that the League was cracking down on minor infringements by imposing regular but token fines. Charnley's own contribution was marked by the award of a £25 honorarium for his year's work, and a rise in salary to £150.

At the 1903 Annual Meeting in London, the three Second Division clubs up for re-election were Doncaster, Stockport, and for the first time ever, Burnley. That a founder member should have floundered so was sad enough, but that Charles Sutcliffe himself should have had to be the one to go cap in hand was quite humiliating. Of course Burnley were re-elected, and Sutcliffe's day was made when he was re-elected on to the Management Committee. But it had been a close-run affair, with Burnley actually coming in third place, one vote behind Stockport, who were themselves ten votes behind the most popular of all the applicants, Bradford City, who gained 30 votes.

Bradford's attraction was obvious; they

were representatives of a rugby stronghold, in a part of Yorkshire yet untouched by the League. And if football caught on in Bradford, places like Hull, Leeds, Halifax and Huddersfield would surely soon follow. In this way the League plotted the colonization of England at the expense of every other rival organization in both football and rugby.

But it was big city clubs the League wanted, as was shown by the list of unsuccessful applicants in 1903. Apart from Doncaster (who had survived only two seasons), these were Crewe, Southport Central, West Hartlepool and Willington (County Durham).

Now that the League had its own office and a permanent staff of two, it decided in 1904 to follow the example of most of its members and the FA (in 1903) by becoming a limited liability company. Charles Sutcliffe was put in charge of the legal arrangements, and in May he drew up a list of forty-four shareholders. These comprised the eight members of the Management Committee, twenty-three clubs who were already limited companies, and personal nominees of the remaining thirteen clubs. Among these nominees were the well-known names of all-powerful Manchester United chairman, J. H. Davies (who despite his wealth and interest in the club never became involved

in League affairs), Fred Everiss, the West Bromwich secretary, and John McKenna of Liverpool.

The first gathering of shareholders was the 1904 Annual General Meeting – now grandly called the Statutory Meeting of the Football League Limited. Charnley and his fellow officials clearly revelled in their new status; the word 'Limited' was used whenever possible, and club representatives were now referred to as 'shareholders' in the minutes. Members of the Management Committee became directors.

The new company was at least solvent, having made a profit of £424 for the year. As in previous years, the only difference between profit and loss was the income derived from the Inter-League matches, although the cost of staging these games now ate away two-thirds of the receipts. It is also interesting to note from the company's first accounts that fines, once the League's main source of income, were now relatively unimportant, representing only £22 17s of the overall income of £2169 3s 6d.

As fines decreased, it also becomes noticeable how the petty squabbling which had so characterized the League's first fourteen years or so reduced during the early part of the twentieth century. This was partly because in 1902 the Committee started to charge clubs £2 2s every time they made a claim, in the hope that they would think twice before sounding off. But it was also clear that club officials were beginning to accept and respect the bureaucratic processes of the organization, a process begun by Bentley but cemented only by the arrival of Tom Charnley.

Only an omniscient superman could have prevented clubs from breaking the new maximum wage rule, however. When, between 1904 and 1911, the FA came to judge upon the financial misdemeanours of at least seven League clubs, it became clear that, as in the early 1880s when professionalism had been outlawed, the guilty clubs' major crime had not been to *do* anything especially base, but to be caught in the act. Glossop, Manchester City,

> One of the oddest proposals concerning team colours came from Liverpool, who proposed in 1904 that in order to avoid colour clashes every home team should play in red shirts and every away team in white shirts; extremely convenient for the Reds, who tried the same proposal again two years later, backed by those other Reds, Manchester United. The polychrome lobby won. Meanwhile, Burnley complained in 1903/4 that Gainsborough Trinity's shirts had been so washed out that in a recent match it had been hard to distinguish them from Burnley's own green shirts.

Middlesbrough and Sunderland were to suffer most from fines and suspensions – mainly for payments above the £4 maximum, payments of match bonuses or simply for not keeping their books in well-enough-disguised order. Manchester City lost practically their entire 1904 Cup-winning team from suspensions after a major investigation in 1906 into the alleged 'fixing' of a match by star winger Billy Meredith. In the course of the investigation it was discovered that most City players were paid above the maximum. Meredith himself had been receiving £6 a week since 1902.

In cases of this nature, the FA as parent body passed sentence, and it was then up to the League how it acted on any breaches of League rules. Coming second in the process, however, the League proved unwilling to make the clubs suffer further.

Glossop were thus fined only an additional £5 by the League, after they had suffered a £250 fine from the FA in 1904. In the same year, Sunderland were fined another £50 to add to their £250 punishment. They appealed, but the League stood firm. Sunderland's illegal payments, it was said, 'gave them a decided advantage over League clubs when re-engaging their players'.

However, the Committee soon softened. In March 1905 it was stated in the private minutes, although not in the printed version, that the fine had been reduced from £50 to £5. No wonder clubs tried it on!

But, warned the League, suddenly toughening, in future the Committee would investigate clubs and take action of its own, independently of the FA. An immediate opportunity to test this resolve came after Alf Common's famous £1000 transfer from Sunderland to Middlesbrough in February 1905.

Middlesbrough were desperate – near to the relegation zone and badly in need of a proven goal-scorer. Even so, the transfer shocked the football world and provided ample ammunition for the game's opponents.

At the time, the highest transfer fees reached around £400, and most clubs subscribed to the view that buying one's way out of trouble was somehow unsporting. Middlesbrough, who had been elected in 1899 and had recently spent £10,000 on a superb new stadium, were thus looked upon as *arrivistes*. But the main objection to Common's transfer was that it threatened to set off an uncontrollable surge in transfer fees.

A major source of opposition to Middlesbrough's action was Charles Clegg, senior Vice President of the FA, who as we have already seen was bitterly opposed to most forms of transfer payments. Clegg had a personal interest because his own club, Sheffield United, had sold Common to Sunderland only a few months earlier, and now felt entitled to a share of the massive fee. Showing their resolve, the League refused United's plea, and to make Clegg angrier, when Common returned to Bramall Lane a few weeks after his controversial transfer, he scored Middlesbrough's winning goal. Middlesbrough were not, therefore, among Charles Clegg's favourite football clubs.

He had several opportunities to wreak his vengeance over the next six years, as Middlesbrough were hauled before both the League and the FA for financial misdemeanours so often that they went through more directors and paid more fines than any other club. In short, Clegg and the Management Committee soon grew heartily sick of the Ayresome Park brigade.

Clegg still believed he could stem the rise in transfer fees, however, so on 31 March 1905 an FA rules committee proposed, and later had accepted, the following provision:

'After the 1st January 1908, no club shall be entitled to pay or receive any transfer fee exceeding £350 upon or in respect of the transfer of any player.'

This gave the League nearly three years to argue the case against the FA, so that by the time the rule came into effect it was quickly

As this cartoon from the Birmingham Gazette
indicates, life in the Football League, let alone at
Molineux, has never been plain sailing.

seen to be ineffective. It was dropped within three months, and has never been revived since; another example of how the wishes of the League have prevailed over those of the Association.

We have noted that expansion of the League's national coverage was, by 1903, generally accepted as desirable. There were no further territorial gains made in 1904, but 1905 proved a bumper year.

In the 1904 re-election process, Stockport County lost their League place and thus their short-lived shareholding, having received only 11 votes. Leicester (33) and Glossop (27) were comfortably re-elected, and Doncaster

returned to the fold with 21 votes after a season's absence. Crewe were unsuccessful with 10 votes.

(Stockport's share, in the name of Thomas Axon, was automatically transferred to S. Balmforth of Doncaster, a process neatly reversed twelve months later when Doncaster dropped out in favour of Stockport.)

The year 1905 promised a marvellous opportunity for the League to widen its net, when it was proposed to expand the divisions to twenty clubs each (this was not another ploy by Preston – they had won promotion legitimately the year before).

Applications from Leeds City, Hull City,

Clapton Orient and Chelsea were bound, therefore, to be viewed favourably, even if Chelsea's claims were somewhat controversial since all they had was a ground and money in the bank. The club had no players and no playing record whatsoever. Whatever their potential, however, both Chelsea and Clapton Orient had to offer member clubs some financial incentives for travelling south.

But before the proposal for expansion could be voted upon, the Committee insisted that according to procedure, the three vacant Second Division places had to be filled first. Port Vale, Burton United and Doncaster were up for re-election, with the result that only Port Vale kept their place, with 21 votes. Leeds City joined the fold with 25 votes, together with Chelsea, who won 20 votes. Hull (18 votes) and Stockport (3) and Clapton (1) failed to gain election.

As expected, this vote was immediately rendered academic, as next on the agenda came Charles Sutcliffe's proposal to increase membership by four clubs. The proposal was carried, and thus further elections were necessary.

Four of the original five unsuccessful applicants won a place: Hull, Burton, Stockport and Clapton Orient; while poor Doncaster, who had finished bottom of the League that season with only eight points, were sent back to the Midland League for the second time in two years.

Elections for the two extra First Division places were a formality. Bury and Notts County, who finished in the two relegation slots, were voted back in.

Bradford City then proposed that because the divisions were now larger, promotion and relegation should be three up and three down. The proposal was lost, as it would be when Derby took up the fight in 1908. (Two years later, Derby upped their sights to four up, four down, and tried several more times before the Second World War. Tottenham carried on the crusade after 1946.)

The new forty-strong membership in 1905 was the most widely representative the League had yet known. London now had three clubs: Arsenal in the South, Chelsea in the West and Clapton Orient in the East, while in the North of England, the Lancashire stronghold now had a rival pack of clubs across the Pennines.

Still to fall under the League's influence were East Anglia, Wales and the entire area south of Birmingham apart from Bristol and London. But there was no doubt where the power lay. For 1905/6, the members of the Management Committee were from Bolton, Blackburn, Liverpool, Everton, Notts Forest, Burnley, West Bromwich and Villa. In short, the founders of 1888 were still firmly in the driving seat.

New members invariably took some time to settle into the routines of the League. Hull, for example, were often late with their results sheets. Clapton Orient proved to be the League's greatest liability. In their first season the East Londoners were repeatedly in trouble for late payment of transfer fees and fines, and on one occasion for their secretary making adverse comments in the press about a referee. By January 1906 the League told Clapton not to transfer any more players until they had paid off their debts. By February, they were bottom of the Second Division.

After setting up a special bank account to administer Clapton's debt, the Committee noted ruefully that the club's apparent inability to manage its own affairs was 'a source of

> 'The Secretary was instructed to write to the Leeds City chairman and point out that the word "transferred" opposite D. Nelson's name in the result sheet, for the match in which Nelson played and was injured, and his death took place before the close of the game, was uncalled for and entirely out of place, as this was a national calamity.'
>
> *League minute, 5 November 1906*

trouble and annoyance to this Committee'. Yet no action was taken to expel Orient, even though they continued to avoid paying transfer fees. It got to the stage where, in April 1907, the Clapton secretary had to attend a Committee meeting and show the members a pile of cheques all filled in and ready to post to various debtors. It was only a temporary respite, however. The following January Clapton were so broke they couldn't even afford to pay a one-guinea fine which had been imposed on them for failing to pay another fine of £25.

These were, however, minor infringements compared with those discovered at, for example, Manchester City and Middlesbrough during the same season. In fact, so many clubs committed technical breaches that in 1905/6, fines were six times greater than the previous year.

By the end of the season the League's new intake had experienced mixed fortunes. Chelsea's gate and playing record showed them to be worthy newcomers. They finished third in their first season. Hull and Leeds were close behind. Clapton Orient not surprisingly finished bottom, and therefore had to join Chesterfield and Burton United in seeking re-election. All three succeeded, with Clapton amazingly squeezing in just one vote ahead of

Oldham Athletic, who polled a very respectable 20 votes. Wigan Town's application attracted only 5 votes.

Expansion was not without its problems. For a start, it promoted even greater rivalry with the Southern League, whose territory the League had now penetrated with great success. One of the biggest problems facing clubs during this period was the complete lack of any agreement between the two organizations. This enabled clubs on each side to snap up the other's players without paying a transfer fee. The League had already formed an agreement with the Scottish League to avoid this, but relations with the Southern League always seemed more fraught.

This can be seen from a meeting which took place between the two leagues on 11 March 1907, at the Tavistock Hotel, London. According to Charles Sutcliffe's brief typewritten report of the meeting, it was the Southern League who called the meeting 'to enter into arrangements for the formation of a new National League on the basis of fusion between the Football League and the Southern League. The (Southern League's) opinion was that such a fusion would end all troubles as to transfers, maximum wages and bonuses.'

The Management Committee was not so sure, and greeted the suggestion coolly. After an informal discussion it was resolved that Tom Charnley would circularize the clubs asking if the Committee had their approval to continue the talks.

Three days later, thirty-eight clubs had replied, of which twenty-six were in favour of negotiations with the Southern League. But although at that stage nothing remotely concrete had been put forward, the Committee decided not to take the matter further, on the rather spurious grounds that a three-quarters majority had not been reached.

Interestingly, of those against talks, three were from the South: Chelsea, Clapton Orient and Bristol City. They obviously did not welcome a widening of the League net.

Charles Sutcliffe's devotion to the League was never more apparent than when it came to hunting down breaches of his beloved regulations. In 1910 Tom Charnley alerted Sutcliffe to a letter making certain allegations about the transfer of a player called O'Hagan. The pair set off to Scotland in search of clues and, having found none, discovered on their return that the letter was a hoax, sent by O'Hagan's brother after a family feud. Another stint of detective work took Sutcliffe to the dressing room of a famous London music-hall artist.

But why did the Management Committee seem so reticent? Were they jealous of their powers? Did they see a sudden influx of southern clubs as a threat to the northern dominance of the League? Probably it was a combination of such sentiments, laced with a hope that the best Southern League clubs would eventually join the League anyway and thus enable their own offices to prevail.

We should not forget that for most members of the Management Committee, the League represented the most exciting and interesting part of their lives. For John Bentley, Charles Sutcliffe and John Lewis in particular, football was practically their life. They congratulated each other warmly before each Annual Meeting, they spent many a tedious hour travelling to onerous meetings, most of which were spent dealing with disputes, and they made no profit on their time. They loved football, of that there can be no doubt, but they also loved the power and prestige of office. They had helped to build up the League and to secure it, and thus they were loath to see a bunch of outsiders muscle in on the act.

If Southern League clubs were to join up, therefore, it had to be on the League's terms. The Committee seemed to be saying: apply to join us if you wish, but we shall not suffer if you don't. For their part, the Southern League officials knew that if their best clubs were lost to the League, their ability to negotiate a share of the power would also diminish.

The 1907 Annual Meeting showed the validity of such fears when Southern League champions for the two previous seasons, Fulham, applied successfully to join the League. Like Chelsea and Clapton in 1905, they too had to offer Midland clubs an extra £15 and northern clubs £20 for travel expenses to London.

Fulham were the only southern applicants that year. Burton United, who had finished bottom of the League, lost their place with only 7 votes, and Burton hasn't had a League club since. Chesterfield (23) and Lincoln (28)

were both re-elected.

Unsuccessful applications were made by Oldham Athletic (17), the newly-formed Bradford Park Avenue (11), who despite their location opted to play in the Southern League for the following season, and Rotherham Town, Salford United and Wigan Town, none of whom attracted any votes.

London now had four League clubs, two of them close neighbours in West London. The irony of Fulham's success was that when Stamford Bridge had been established as a football stadium, Fulham had been invited to take it over. Only when they decided to stay at Craven Cottage did the Bridge's owners set up their own club, Chelsea.

Within a few weeks of the 1907 Annual Meeting, the Management Committee members were called at short notice to the Lane End Hotel, Blackpool, to discuss an unexpected crisis: Port Vale had resigned.

An angry set of members demanded to know why Vale hadn't made their position clear at the Annual Meeting. The club's chairman and secretary explained humbly that they had appealed to the public in early May, hoping it would tide Vale through their difficulties. Unfortunately, the response had been poor, and they could no longer afford League status. Under the circumstances, the Management Committee had no choice but 'very reluctantly' to accept the resignation.

Two clubs applied to fill Vale's place immediately after the news was announced: Oldham Athletic and Burton United. Rotherham Town also sent a representative, who instead of seeking his club's election merely wished to enquire if the League would consider setting up a Third Division and introduce a system whereby clubs could join the League on merit rather than by voting. He was wasting his time – election on merit would have to wait another eighty years.

Port Vale's misfortune proved to be Oldham's lucky break. All six Committee members present voted for them in preference to Burton, and so Lancashire gained its eleventh League club. But in sympathy with Port Vale's plight, it was suggested for future consideration that entrance fees to the League be raised and that £200 be made available to any retiring club, depending on its financial circumstances.

CHAPTER SIX

John Lewis —
Chief Constable of Football

League football has never been short of controversial characters, but none can match the record of John Lewis. In thirty years at the top, Lewis managed to fall out with just about everyone. From Accrington to Antwerp, John Lewis was showered with abuse and pelted with bottles. Even close friends weren't immune from his often savage temper.

But John Lewis was no tyrant. He was, rather, a puritan who swept aside all who confronted him with boundless energy and unflinching honesty. As one newspaper described him, he was 'straight as a die and absolutely fearless. His great ambition was to keep football sweet and clean.'

John Lewis would thus appear to have been a sanctimonious, self-righteous busybody. But because no one loved football more than he did, or was prepared to do more for it, John Lewis rose to the highest echelons of the game. It became almost like a crusade to him.

Football, he said in a speech in 1925, was a means of keeping young men in order and helping to create an A1 nation. It cemented the Empire and promoted citizenship.

Don't drink to that, however, because John Lewis was also a militant abstainer who, according to the *Daily Dispatch*, 'hardly missed an opportunity to speak out against drinking, smoking and gambling. This irritated many, but those who got to know him grew fond of him. A remarkable man, he was a fascinating subject for the student of psychology. He was, in short, a Puritan, living hundreds of years after his time.'

John Lewis was born in 1855, the son of a Methodist preacher and the youngest brother of Elizabeth Ann Lewis, who was known nationally for her work in the Temperance Movement. John did not let the family down. 'I have ever worked hard – and played hard. It is an excellent combination. Add to it that I am a life abstainer and have never felt the slightest inclination for what is picturesquely called the "fragrant weed" and you have the recipe for my health and vigorous constitution.'

At grammar school Lewis was a talented sportsman, and when he met up with Arthur Constantine in 1874 the result was a gentlemen's club called Blackburn Rovers.

Few were able to match his enthusiasm. 'I wanted to be chasing the ball every Saturday', he recalled, so when Rovers had no game or if his team-mates didn't fancy turning out in bad weather, Lewis played for Darwen or anyone else who'd have him. As one who defended the shoulder charge all his life, he must soon have developed a reputation, for in one match he kept getting knocked over, only to discover later that his marker had been offered a shilling for every time he floored Lewis. The match lasted two and a half hours!

A skating accident ended his days as a centre-forward, so while setting up as a coach builder in Blackburn, Lewis took up refereeing, a task well suited to a man of his moral certitude.

Lewis was a fine, upstanding citizen in every way. He acted as a special constable during the cotton riots in 1878, he never missed church, and was often to be seen lecturing the populace on the evils of drink. His charity and social work commitments alone would have exhausted most men, but for Lewis they were mere interludes between matches.

In all, he was reckoned to have officiated at over a thousand games in twenty-five years. He took charge of the first Cup Final at Crystal Palace in 1895 – the first time someone other than a member of the FA Council had officiated at a final. He also refereed the 1897 and 1898 finals. At his peak, Lewis was probably the most famous referee in the world, and he added to that celebrity in later life by becoming a prolific writer on the laws of the game.

But John Lewis never made a penny from being a referee. He gave all his fees to charity (as did Charles Sutcliffe), so no one could accuse him of not practising what he frequently preached.

*John Lewis –
straight as a die and absolutely fearless.*

More than once at a match he jumped the rails and chased spectators who had thrown mud or clinker at him. At Deepdale he once refused to resume a game until someone who had blown a whistle in the crowd was detected and removed. He demanded honesty from everyone, and when it didn't come he could explode with rage.

Lewis was insatiable when it came to refereeing. Once, on football business in England, he covered 2200 miles in fifteen days, spending five nights in trains and steamers, but managing to attend church on both Sunday mornings. 'For years he must have been one of the best known men on the railway ... he was prepared to referee football matches anywhere and at any time', remembered Charles Sutcliffe.

Only a man of strong conviction could have sustained such a busy programme, for it is doubtful whether any other League referee ever became the subject of more physical attacks, hate mail or protests from angry clubs than John Lewis.

Among numerous incidents, at Barley Bank, Darwen, he was surrounded by a mob, kicked and battered, despite being an ex-player of the club and married to the sister of a former mayor of Darwen.

At Gigg Lane, Bury, Lewis had to hide in a ticket box after his clothes had been ripped by an angry crowd, one of whom accused him of being drunk. This insult so infuriated the teetotal Lewis that he emerged from the box, whipped off his jacket and shaped up to thrash the man. Fortunately, Joe Hartley of Accrington interceded before blows could be exchanged.

None of these attacks put him off, however. If anything, he seemed to thrive on adversity. As Charles Sutcliffe wrote: 'There were times when I almost felt that he went out of his way to interfere with matters that did not concern him.'

'Tatler' in the *Blackburn Weekly Telegraph* described Lewis thus in 1900:

'the referee par excellence ... he knows what he knows and though there were 60 million people there you wouldn't get a nervous tremor out of John.

He claps his teeth together like a rat-trap, looks as fierce as a drill sergeant. He would send his own brother to the block if he caught him in any shady practices. Better be wrong and firm than right and weak.

Many people would like to "square" this sturdy

hot-tempered little man, but find that he is vulnerable neither to fear nor favour.

In his spare time, Mr Lewis is a coach builder; but his serious role in life is Chief Constable of football. Is there a knotty problem in the offside rule to be unravelled? John is the man who will unloose it.

[He could talk cheerfully] by the hour or by the week, as you may desire, about penalty-kicks. You cannot please him better than by setting him a problem that would make your head ache. It is meat and drink to him, light and life, air and water ... Mr Lewis's eye is not for the spectacle [of football] but for the nice legal points that arise in its progress. A clear, unwinking eye it is.'

At one point, the League actually struck Lewis off the referees' list after he had attacked the Committee for being corrupt. No sooner had they reinstated him than he resumed his tirade and was hauled up again to apologise.

In fact, he eventually won sufficient support to be elected to the Committee, so that at the turn of the century he was the last serving referee to hold League office. Only in 1905, at the age of fifty, did Lewis finally stand down from the League list.

Not that this prevented him from getting out his whistle for the odd special occasion, for example the Olympic Games in London in 1908, a soldiers' international at Blackpool in 1917, and on Christmas Day of that year a ladies' match at Preston, watched by 10,000.

He was also much in demand abroad, long after his League days were over. The Olympic Games committee begged him to referee the football final in Antwerp in 1920, despite the fact that he was then aged sixty-five. Controversial as ever, in the course of that match he ordered off a Czech player for foul play. When the rest of the team followed and refused to return, Lewis had no choice but to award the game to Belgium.

There seemed no limit to his energy. Ignoring pleas for him to take life easier, on the day on which he had a seizure which led to his death a week later, he was preparing his regular articles for half a dozen newspapers, including *Athletic News*.

John Lewis died on 13 January 1926, aged seventy. Appropriately, he had only just been at the centre of yet another major fuss, after delivering speeches at Bradford and Blackburn claiming that the English cricket team would have done better in Australia had they stayed away from drink.

On his death, the *Manchester Evening Chronicle* commented: 'His personality was too autocratic and his nature too reserved for him ever to be loved as some strong men are loved. His fine qualities commanded deep respect and some affection, but he never courted easy popularity and it is doubtful he ever wanted it. Very few men could claim really intimate friendship with him.'

Perhaps that is why we can discover only one small weakness in the man. It was said that as a referee he did rather enjoy eating a few raisins at half time.

CHAPTER SEVEN

Coming of Age

League football by 1907 was big business littered with anomalies. For example, players could not receive more than £10 for signing on, or any match bonus for a win or a draw. Yet crowds were now approaching a level similar to that of the mid 1980s, while overheads were still relatively small for most clubs. Above all, the players' lot was the most precarious of all.

The League had already, in 1902, studied the obligation of clubs to players under the Workmen's Compensation Acts of 1897 and 1900 and the Employers' Liability Act of 1880. Counsel's opinion then was that League clubs were not liable should a player suffer serious disability.

By 1907 this position was increasingly untenable from a moral standpoint. Large sums were being made from football, and it was only right and proper, in that Edwardian period of liberal social reform, that footballers, like all workmen, should be given proper financial protection in the event of accidents.

In truth, many players had been looked after on an informal basis, but in 1907 there was a move to regularize the situation by holding a joint meeting of the League, Scottish League and Southern League. This resulted in the setting up of the Football Mutual Insurance Federation, designed to protect the players of those clubs who joined. Membership was not compulsory, but in practice most clubs did participate.

While one hand gave, the other remained clenched. When transfer fees and wages again came up for consideration at an FA conference in May 1908, the League showed a hardening of its attitude towards the players. This was mainly because the Players' Union had just been revived.

At the same time, the Management Committee also aimed to be stricter about new clubs joining its ranks. It was agreed, therefore, to hoist the entrance fee from five guineas to a massive £300. Of that amount, up to £200 would be granted to any club losing its membership, thus providing them with some financial compensation.

The new entrance fee certainly seemed to deter aspiring non-League clubs. When the Committee was instructed by the members to form a new Third Division, only ten clubs responded to Tom Charnley's advertisement in *Athletic News*.

After this failure, the League clubs seemed happy to forget expansion for a while. At the 1908 Annual Meeting they rejected a proposal to enlarge the Second Division by one club, then approved a measure to reduce the number of clubs having to seek re-election from three to two. Consolidation was the order of the day, and would be for the next decade.

This last rule change came about largely as a result of Grimsby's situation. They had finished third from bottom of the Second Division, but hoped to avoid seeking re-election on the grounds that they were in that position only on goal average. On the one previous occasion when this had been the case, the club concerned, Aston Villa, in 1890, had been excused. But that was in the early days.

John Lewis, acting chairman in the absence of John Bentley (who had fallen ill in Vienna some weeks before), sympathized with Grimsby, but would not relent. As it happened, they were then comfortably returned with 32 votes. Chesterfield (23 votes) kept their place too, but Lincoln City were out at the sixth time of asking (in sixteen seasons), having polled only 18.

Their only consolation was to become the first retiring club to receive the new £200 grant (just as in 1987 they became the first club to be compensated for losing League status under the new system of automatic promotion and relegation). Lincoln's place was taken by Bradford Park Avenue, with 20 votes. so Lincoln now had no League club, while Bradford had two.

Other applications came from Tottenham Hotspur (14 votes) and Burton United, whose ostracism was confirmed with just one vote in their favour. Rotherham withdrew their application, as did Queen's Park Rangers, at the last minute, after complaints about certain inducements being offered for travelling expenses.

Tottenham's fate was not yet sealed, however, because Stoke promptly emulated their neighbours Port Vale by announcing only days after the Annual Meeting their inability to remain in the League due to lack of support. As in Vale's case exactly twelve months earlier, the Management Committee had no choice but to accept Stoke's resignation. League status, said one member ruefully, was still no guarantee of support, even in a heavily populated place like the Potteries (which was to be deprived of League football until 1919).

Immediately, the Committee called a Special General Meeting in order to elect a replacement, a meeting which became rather confusing when it transpired that Stoke had changed their minds and wanted to struggle on after all (thanks to Harry Lockett's efforts – see page 51).

By that stage it was too late to cancel the meeting, and too serious a matter for the League to readmit Stoke without a vote, so along with Lincoln, Tottenham, Rotherham and Southport, the team from the Potteries found themselves up for election for a place they need never have forfeited.

The members' response was unforgiving. Stoke lost out in the first ballot, leaving Tottenham and Lincoln to finish level twice on 20 votes each before the Management Committee settled the matter amongst its members, resulting in a 5–3 vote in favour of the Londoners.

The 1908/9 season was a busy one for the Management Committee, dominated by simmering disharmony between the FA and the League. The main point of contention was still the payment of bonuses, which the majority of League clubs now approved (and practised, though illegally) and which the FA prohibited.

A conference was organized, then postponed, then the Management Committee convened a Special General Meeting, at which the majority of clubs called for a change in the FA's Rule 31. Fulham wanted to go further and delete all restrictions, but that was too radical. All most clubs desired was to legalize a situation which existed anyway between the doctored lines of balance sheets.

After long debate, several drafts and much circular writing, the Management Committee finally settled upon the following proposal to put forward to the FA: that any league or combination should, if approved by the majority of its members, allow payments to players which went beyond those allowed by Rule 31.

This seemed reasonable enough. Was not payment on merit the right of any worker in a liberal era, especially those already bound by other petty wage limitations?

Clearly the FA was aware of the League's resolve on this issue, because in July 1908, after several years of investigations and hefty fines, it offered a full amnesty to any League club which had made illegal payments, in an attempt to clear the air and start afresh.

While finally accepting the amnesty in February 1909, without admitting any guilt, the League was keen not to lose its momentum. Now that the board had been wiped clean, it was important to change the rules once and for all, and thus League clubs met for a special meeting at the Grand Hotel, Birmingham, to draft a letter to the FA.

In accepting the amnesty, League clubs pledged loyalty to the FA but maintained their right 'to use any and every constitutional means to obtain such alterations in the FA rules as they shall think desirable'.

Only two of the thirty-seven clubs in attendance abstained from signing the letter – Sheffield United and Sheffield Wednesday. This was hardly surprising, since Charles Clegg sat on the boards of both clubs.

At the same time, the Southern League made further overtures to the League at a meeting in March 1909. Their proposals were to amalgamate the two leagues into a competition sixty strong, comprising a first division of twenty clubs and two equal second divisions, North and South. Complicated promotion and relegation systems were also suggested, plus (those who believe the Super Leaguer to be a modern animal might be surprised to learn) a new voting system giving more power to First Division clubs.

If none of that was acceptable, the Southern League at least hoped that the League would agree to the same mutual recognition of players' registrations as existed with the Scottish League.

Charnley again circularized the clubs, but the tone of his letter was hardly enthusiastic. Not surprisingly, all forty members rejected the Southern League's proposals, and only eight would consider any other schemes. Furthermore, not one club was prepared to recognize the Southern League's retain and transfer lists. From this it seems clear that it was League clubs who benefited most from the unfettered traffic of players from one league to another.

A more startling rebuff can hardly be imagined. Yet at the same time the formation of a third division was not ruled out. Thus, another meeting with the Southern League resulted in the Management Committee putting forward the following proposals:

● That a third division be formed of twenty clubs, eighteen of which would be nominated by the Southern League.
● That the entrance fee be five guineas (not £300 as for the Second Division), with an extra £100 payable on promotion.
● Two clubs to be promoted, and two to be eligible for re-election.
● The third division clubs to have one representative on the Management Committee, but only the top ten clubs in the division to have a vote at general meetings.
● If these proposals were accepted, no Southern League clubs would apply to join the Second Division at the next Annual Meeting.

Never had the two League Committees gone into such detail, or had such serious intent. They even discussed the possibility that the FA might object to the scheme. John Bentley and J. B. Skeggs of Millwall were asked to meet the FA in that event.

The climax of this movement towards forming a third division arrived on 30 April 1909 at a Special General Meeting held at the Midland Hotel, Manchester. It proved to be no picnic for the Southerners. John Bentley reminded the clubs that when his Committee had been instructed unanimously to form a third division the year before, only ten applications had been received. Now, after two meetings with the Southern League, he felt the proposals on the table were the best that could be expected.

The northern clubs, led by Tom Houghton of Preston and Lt Col Gibson Poole of Middlesbrough, begged to differ. According to *Athletic News*, Houghton couldn't understand why the Committee had taken the liberty of foisting Southern League clubs upon the Football League, when League members knew the southerners always to have been their greatest enemies – in the football sense, of course. Praising clubs in the South for their sportsmanship, Houghton reminded members that for years Arsenal had remained faithful to the League, while 'all sorts of baits were tried' to tempt them away. The Southern League clubs had now realized that the Football League was 'the football of the country', and so they wanted to enter 'the camp'.

He found the whole business utterly strange, and added with emphasis: 'I don't understand it at all.'

Feelings then heightened when Houghton criticized the Management Committee for the manner in which Tottenham had recently been elected (by a Management Committee vote), at which point Bentley called him to order twice. But the Preston man was not to be silenced. Older members of the League should have taken priority, he protested. 'As to the Southern League, we wish them well, and we wish them to get on. We want antagonism. We don't want the football world to ourselves.'

He called on the clubs to oppose the motion handsomely, and was answered by some hearty applause. There then followed a debate as to how the proposals might be amended to gain more satisfaction. For example, could the twenty new third division clubs be nominated by the League rather than by the Southern League? Captain Wells Holland of Clapton Orient suggested a twelve-month adjournment, especially since some of the eighteen clubs nominated by the Southern League had claims far inferior to several others from the North and Midlands.

Still smarting from Houghton's criticisms, John Bentley defended the Management Committee. A settlement with the Southern League, he argued, would help solve the wage question with the FA by bringing all professional football under the League's banner. Clubs would feel more secure, and players more settled.

Messrs Branston of Chesterfield and Walford of Leeds suggested that if the members were in favour of a third division, then surely it was best simply to invite applications from both North and South, then vote on the merits of each, as was normal practice at Annual Meetings.

Argument then broke out over the procedure governing clauses and amendments, proposals and counter-proposals, until finally Bentley silenced everyone and put the basic issue to the meeting. Should a third division be formed or not?

As *Athletic News* reported melodramatically, all hope was 'ruthlessly shattered' when a show of hands produced twenty-seven in favour, thirteen against, the necessary three-quarters majority not being reached. The Southern League would have to wait, yet again, and watch helplessly as its best clubs defected over the next decade.

The passions raised by the third division issue illustrate clearly how divided the League could be, with the Management Committee often coming into open conflict with a group of outspoken club chairmen. Colonel Poole was a constant thorn in the Committee's side – his club, as we have seen, was frequently found guilty of illegalities – and in the end Poole himself was banned after a bribery scandal. Fred Rinder of Aston Villa and Tom Houghton of Preston were also vocal critics of the Committee. And yet Bentley's position as President was rarely challenged, and the same faces adorned the Committee year in, year out, after each annual election.

That did not mean that Bentley could afford to be complacent, as was shown at the 1909 Annual Meeting when 'a somewhat painful matter' arose.

Apparently, several clubs had convened regional meetings to discuss the composition of the Management Committee, which some felt was too biased towards Lancashire. If this were the case, Bentley told the Annual Meeting, it was hardly the fault of the Committee but of the members who voted. 'I like peace and harmony', he said, but it hardly smacked of peace or harmony to have cliques in such a small body as the League. The League should work together as a unit of forty clubs. Any other way would mean 'grave danger'.

Nevertheless, the clubs did demand more

representation on the Management Committee, and a motion by Everton to increase its composition from four to six club representatives was carried. These Committee men would no longer be elected on the basis of divisions (as introduced in 1893). 'The merits and character of the men themselves should be the only points to consider', advised Everton's W. R. Clayton. He cared not who managed the League so long as they were men of integrity. Recalling a former member of the Management Committee, he said that if they were all like T. H. Sidney he would be quite satisfied to accept them, whether they came from Wolverhampton or Timbuktu.

So the Committee was now to be composed of ten men: the three Johns – Bentley as President (still unopposed), McKenna and Lewis as Vice Presidents; William McGregor, of course,

stayed on as a Life Member; but who would be the other six?

The 'cliqueists' can't have been too dissatisfied, because they immediately re-elected all four sitting members: Charles Sutcliffe (Burnley), Dr James Baxter (Everton), Harry Keys (West Bromwich) and John Cameron (Newcastle), while voting in Arthur Dickinson (Sheffield Wednesday) and Tom Harris (Notts County) to the two newly created positions.

Significantly, the two unsuccessful nominees were Captain Henry Wells Holland of Clapton Orient and Henry Norris of Fulham, whose failure only served to emphasize the northern and Midland domination of the League.

As the previous Annual Meeting had decided, in 1909 re-election concerned only two clubs. Blackpool kept their place with 27

The Football League, **Coming of Age .**
1888-1909. **. Celebration.**

A Banquet will be held in the Royal Venetian Chamber,
Holborn Restaurant, London,
on June 8th, 1909, at 6·30 p.m. for 7 p.m.

The League will be pleased if you will attend as its guest.

Please reply on or before June 1st to T. Charnley, Secretary,
47, Tithebarn Street, Preston.

H. A. Mears, Esq

MORNING DRESS.

This was H. A. 'Gus' Mears invitation to the League's
Coming of Age Banquet in 1909. Hock, Burgundy and
champagne flowed almost as freely as reminiscences, but
the day after it was back to business with a feud at the
F.A. Mears was the man who transformed Stamford
Bridge into a major football stadium.

votes, while Lincoln returned to the fold with 24, in place of Chesterfield. Of two other applicants, Rotherham failed to attend and Stoke mustered only 6 votes. How deeply they must have regretted their withdrawal twelve months earlier.

For the first time since 1904, no southern club applied for membership. The reason was simple: in retaliation for the League's recent snub, the Southern League's committee had threatened large fines on any member applying to join its rivals.

The meeting over, members had a few hours to return to their hotel rooms and dress for dinner. A 'Coming of Age Banquet' awaited them at the Venetian Chambers of the Holborn Restaurant, with an 'exceedingly interesting musical programme' laid on by Henry Norris, chairman of Fulham.

What a splendid occasion it was. Twenty-one years of the League, and almost every leading figure in British football was there to celebrate, including five of the original six committee members from 1888. Long-service gold medals were handed out, vellum addresses presented to Messrs McGregor, Bentley, Lewis, McKenna, Charnley, and even Harry Lockett.

The founder told the story of the early days – one suspects for the umpteenth time – and concluded by warning clubs to beware of 'the clever, sharp men' who were creeping into the game. McGregor said that business acumen could go too far. 'Give me the honest plodder, the straightforward man. That is the kind of man we want for League football and every other kind of football.'

Toast followed toast. Charles Sutcliffe assured the FA of the League's loyalty. 'With the attainment of manhood comes the period of reflection', he commented.

Charles Clegg took up the theme in a much longer and more pointed speech in which he compared the FA to a magisterial body, which was not often popular, and the League to entertainers, who usually were. 'Mr Sutcliffe has

hinted at the childish things somebody has been doing [laughter]. May I express the hope now that, having become a man, you will put away childish things?' ['Hear hear' and applause]

The next morning, on 9 June, these fine words meant little as antlers were locked at the FA's Annual Meeting. Facing the same men who had applauded him the night before, Charles Clegg more or less admitted that he was at the end of his tether and wanted the FA to have no more to do with the financial arrangements of the League or, for that matter, any other league. If the League or whoever wanted to delete Rule 31 (governing the maximum wage and prohibiting bonuses), he and almost all his councillors were quite happy to reverse their stance of a year before and support its removal.

There were men, said Clegg, who would scorn to do anything dishonourable in their own business or private affairs, but who in football voted for laws which they repeatedly broke themselves. Why should the FA be troubled by such dishonesty? Let those people make their own rules and be put in charge of carrying them out.

Wasn't this exactly what the League clubs so earnestly wanted, control over their own financial affairs?

Not entirely, it would seem. T. H. Sidney of Wolves thought that Rule 31 should be kept. If it was not, the Association would be leaving poorer clubs to the mercy of the more powerful ones. Small clubs needed the FA's protection.

'Removing the prohibition of the bonus for winning matches is the most objectionable suggestion of all', Sidney was reported to have said. To dangle a purse of money before a team before they would do their best was degrading football to the level of prize fighting. If a match was lost, he argued, someone was blamed, not for losing the match but for robbing his comrades of their bonus. This would almost certainly lead to corruption, as it had done in the past. It would also start up 'the whole miserable business of poaching', claimed Sidney. His own club would be ruined.

Replying, John Bentley could foresee neither ruin nor damnation. He stated that the maximum wage had been an experiment, and it had not, as intended, reduced clubs' wage bills. The £4 maximum had simply become the minimum, and that wasn't fair on top players. The only way round the maximum was to pay illegal bonuses, and there was hardly a player who hadn't been paid in this way.

This last comment brought Tom Houghton to his feet. Bentley's remarks had been, he claimed, 'damaging, untrue and unsportsmanlike'.

There then followed an exchange involving Charles Sutcliffe, who unlike Bentley supported the maximum wage and the ban on bonuses. He cited the example of two clubs who at that time had been unable to re-sign practically all of their first-team squads. These were not poor clubs, said Sutcliffe, but the League champions and the Cup winners, no less. If they couldn't sign their players with the protection of the maximum wage, what would it cost to sign them without it?

Sutcliffe then stirred up a veritable hornets' nest by accusing the FA Council of failing to prosecute clubs against whom they had definite evidence of illegal payments. Amid angry shouts and demands for proof, Sutcliffe refused to divulge his sources.

But if Sutcliffe was sure that proof existed, why did he not take any action, called out one of the members. According to *Athletic News*, Sutcliffe replied, 'If a member of the Council did not consider it his duty to report the case, it certainly was not mine. I am not a member of the Council, and don't want to be.' (Cries of 'Oh! Oh!')

Tom Houghton of Preston turned again on John Bentley. North End had not once offered a bonus, not even to keep hold of their goalkeeper Peter McBride, whom Houghton called the best in Britain (to more laughter). Bentley, he sneered, had started to support bonuses

only since he became involved with a wealthy club (Manchester United).

From another wealthy club, Fred Rinder of Aston Villa argued in favour of deleting Rule 31. Bristol City and Manchester United had earned about £3000 for appearing in the recent Cup Final, he estimated, yet they could not give the players even a £5 note out of the profits. He resented Mr Sidney's suggestion that bonuses led to corruption. During Villa's greatest period in the 1890s, before all these restrictions had been introduced, bonuses had always been paid, and there had never been any scandals or dirty play, unscrupulous methods or arrangements.

Rinder's comments were particularly noted because it was he who had led a movement of bigger clubs against the FA regulation, which in turn had led to considerable speculation about the possibility of a breakaway movement. The so-called Super League was talked of even in 1909.

So the members of the League were themselves divided over the wages and bonus question, and so, too, were the members of the Management Committee.

No wonder Clegg summed up the position as intolerable. What it boiled down to, he regretted, was that there was no longer any trust. Just one example sufficed. Mr Skeggs of Millwall and the Southern League had stood up earlier in that very meeting to beg the FA chairman to stop being so pessimistic and give the clubs some credit for being honest. The Southern Leaguers professed their loyalty to the FA, Skeggs had declared. Yet, as Clegg now reported, only a few weeks earlier he had found a Southern League club guilty of paying bonuses. And Skeggs knew it. That was why Clegg was so sick of the whole business.

These were Clegg's final words on the subject: 'If this game cannot be carried on under honourable conditions, the sooner it goes to the wall the better for everybody.'

In fact, it was the delegates who went to the wall – literally. So close was the voting on this issue that each representative was ordered to line up on either side of the room, according to his intentions. The result was as follows: 108 votes for deletion of Rule 31, 70 against. Thus, the resolution was lost by 11 votes, having failed to reach the FA's minimum requirement of a two-thirds majority. Clegg's torment was not over yet.

But it was forgotten temporarily when the summer delivered another crisis to the game. This was in the form of a threat by the Players' Union to go on strike. Like squabbling neighbours thrown together by some natural disaster, the FA and League administrators instantly dropped their differences and formed a coalition to fend off this greater challenge to the fabric of the game.

Briefly, the Players' Union had been given official FA sanction in March 1908. The League, though wary, did not oppose the decision, and allowed a match between Manchester United and Newcastle to be staged in aid of the union's funds.

In early 1909, however, the union decided to affiliate with the Federation of Trades Unions. This meant that if the Federation were to call a general strike in support of, for example, the railway workers or the miners, the Players' Union would have to join in.

This prospect so appalled both the Management Committee and the FA Council that recognition of the union was immediately withdrawn, its chairman and secretary were suspended from football for life, and any players already signed up for the union were ordered to resign by 1 July or be sacked by their clubs.

Far from caving in to these measures, the union responded by calling a strike. As the summer wore on and the crisis heightened, League representatives met for a tension-filled conference in Birmingham, on the very eve of the new season. Each club came armed with a list of amateur players it would field in the event of strike action (a ploy again held in readiness in both 1945 and 1961 when strikes

were also threatened).

But 1909 did not see a players' revolution, nor, indeed, did the union make any real capital from its actions. Divided at club level (like its bosses), and unsure of its ground, the union backed down at the eleventh hour. It left the Federation, pledged loyalty once more to the FA, and thereafter assumed the role it would play for the next fifty-two years, that of relatively moderate agitators rooted to the sidelines.

The players' cause was hardly helped by events on the pitch. Complaints about rough play were heard so often, especially against Clapton Orient, that on 13 January 1910 Tom Charnley sent a circular to all referees, an unusual step given that matters of discipline on the field were primarily the FA's concern.

Dear Sir,

Reports are continually being received that the many unfair and unscrupulous tactics indulged in by some of the players engaged in League football are allowed to pass unpunished by referees. In other instances the punishment is inadequate.

The Management Committee are of the opinion that referees are not exercising full powers as required by laws of the game, and desire to further point out that they are remiss in their duties as referees in not taking cognisance of these offences, which they should penalise as to have a salutary effect on the offenders.

Rough and dangerous play, likely to injure players should be at once stopped, discrimination being made between 'robust' and 'rough' play. Firmness should be used at the start of the game and little trouble, generally, will be afterwards experienced.

*The Management Committee not only **ask** but **expect** referees to at once penalise actions which are calculated to injure the general character of the games.*

Yours truly,

T. Charnley, Secretary.

Meanwhile, the year 1910 saw a remarkable degree of accord off the pitch.

Firstly, at a Special General Meeting in Birmingham on 18 February, the League agreed not only to an Inter-League match against the Southern League but also, at last, to entering into a working agreement on transfers.

Immediately afterwards, the Southern League's representatives joined the League delegates for a joint meeting. After sixteen years of mutual distrust, the two sides of English professional football were finally moving closer together.

Secondly, the FA finally managed to end Charles Clegg's nightmare by agreeing to delete that controversial Rule 31. In a letter dated 10 January 1910, Frederick Wall, secretary of the FA, wrote: 'It is incompatible with the position of the FA as the governing body of a national sport that it should be concerned in the financial arrangements between clubs and players other than seeing that the engagements which they enter into are observed.'

Rule 31 was finally amended on 22 April, and from that moment onwards the Association became no more than a mediator. But this was not a complete victory for the likes of Fred Rinder and John Bentley, because FA Rule 30 still contained a reference to the maximum wage. League clubs could still pay only £4 a week maximum. Whatever else they offered was entirely up to them.

This brings us to the third major agreement of 1910.

Still enjoying something of a honeymoon period, the League and Southern League now began to negotiate jointly on that 'whatever else' with the Players' Union, a process which would continue in much the same fashion, on and off, until 1961; the players trying to abolish the maximum wage, the League granting just enough concessions to keep them sweet. The result was harmony, of sorts.

Meticulous as ever in his approach, in March 1910 Sutcliffe drew up the following proposals, all of which were approved:

• *The present right of a club to retain a player on*

offering a wage of £208 a year to be continued in the FA rules.

(This meant that so long as a club offered a player the maximum wage of £4 per week, he could not seek a transfer.)

• *It shall be permissible for any League, by resolution at its annual meeting, to extend the maximum to £5 per week or £260 per annum, but the increase shall not operate more quickly than a rise of 10s per week after two years' service, and a further 10s per week after four years.*

(This was to encourage loyalty and to ease the potential burden on clubs.)

• *If the player is transferred at the request of his club for financial reasons, he may be allowed to start for his new club at the same wage he was receiving from his old club. If a player is transferred at his own request, he must start with his new club at no more than £4 a week.*

• *That no bonus shall be permissible to a player on re-signing for his club. Clubs may pay only a bonus of £10 on his first signing.*

(Of all rules, this remained the least observed.)

• *The top five clubs of the League's First and Second Divisions, and of the Southern League's First Division, may distribute as talent money for meritorious service, sums not exceeding the following:*

No. 1 club £275, No. 2 £220, No. 3 £165, No. 4 £110 and No. 5 £55.

In like manner, clubs may distribute sums not exceeding the following for meritorious service in the FA Cup:

Winners £275, Runners-up £220, Defeated semi-finalists £165, Clubs reaching the Fourth Round £110, Third Round £55 and Second Round £22.

(Thus were established the first bonus payments allowed since 1901. As the *Aston Villa News and Record* commented, talent money would lead 'to increased energy and zeal on the part of players, and as the natural consequence, to better and brighter football all round'.)

● *After three years' service with a club it shall be permissible for a club to enter into an agreement with a player providing for a benefit after five years' service. A player shall be eligible for a second benefit after ten years' continuous service.*

● *Where players are transferred by a club for financial reasons, such club may pay to the player a percentage of any transfer fee in lieu of accrued benefit, not exceeding the following scale:*

After 1 year's service − 10 per cent, 2 years' − 15 per cent, 3 years' − 25 per cent, 4 years' − 35 per cent, and 5 years' − 50 per cent.

● *Clubs shall have the right to insert a clause in all players' agreements allowing the club to terminate the agreement with fourteen days' notice, if the player proves palpably inefficient or is guilty of serious misconduct or breach of disciplinary rules. Players have the right of appeal to the Management Committee, and a further right of appeal to the Appeal Committee on making a deposit of £5.*

(This would lead to many an appeal from players who felt wrongly dismissed, and because the three main leagues in Britain were now in agreement over transfers, it meant the player accused of 'palpable inefficiency' was unlikely to find a new club in senior football, unless he went to Ireland − as a few did.)

At the end of such a relatively peaceful season, the League took on another convert from West Yorkshire when Huddersfield Town (26 votes) won a place at the expense of Grimsby (12). Birmingham, who finished bottom, sailed back in with 30 votes, while former members Chesterfield (6) and Stoke (3) were rejected, along with Hartlepools United (1). No Southern League clubs applied, for fear of incurring the heavy fine which, despite the new relationship, remained in force.

But the main event of the 1910 annual meeting was the retirement of John Bentley from the presidency. He was still aged only fifty, but after a second long illness in the spring decided to stand down on the advice of his doctor. Bentley had missed very few meetings since 1888, and like McGregor, his resignation did not signal the end of his involvement with the Committee. He, too, was elected a Life Member, and would continue to attend whenever possible.

Nor did he retire from his other activities. He continued to write for various newspapers and magazines, and although no longer chairman of Manchester United he played a large part in the club's historic move from Clayton to Old Trafford, also in 1910. Bentley, it was said, was responsible for toning down the architect Archibald Leitch's grandiose plans for the new stadium so much that he halved the cost. Even then, it still cost £60,000 to build, a colossal sum for the period. Once United had settled in, Bentley spent four years as the club secretary, thus returning to a role he had occupied at Bolton twenty-three years earlier.

Back at the League, the 1910 succession was a smooth affair. John McKenna proved to be the clear favourite with 37 votes, the only other nomination being John Lewis, who polled just 4. (Curiously, William McGregor's name was put forward but the founder diplomatically withdrew.)

Lewis was re-elected as a Vice President, however, and was joined by Harry Keys. And since Bentley kept his place on the Committee, as did the other five sitting members, in effect the composition of the Management Committee remained exactly the same. Only the titles changed. (This conservative voting pattern must have been very frustrating for outspoken chairmen like Fred Rinder and Captain Wells Holland, who yet again both narrowly failed to win a seat.)

Before we learn more about the League's new President, it should be noted that the 1910 Annual Meeting approved one rule which has remained in force ever since. This was the imposition of a transfer deadline, then set at 16 March, to prevent clubs buying their way out of trouble, as Chelsea had tried, unsuccessfully, to do in the previous season.

The Men in Black

In the early days of League football, players and clubs were not the only ones to need an occasional dose of League discipline. For example, in 1919 three referees were struck off the list for having lied about their ages. Six years later, the League demanded proof of each referee's date of birth, and discovered that twelve of the seventy-six had been lying. When the same check was made in 1946, twenty were found to be older than they had claimed and six had actually falsified their birth certificates. One man was so keen to remain on the list that he took on his younger brother's identity!

One could forgive a man for not wanting to give up his whistle, but fiddling expenses was another matter altogether. Between the wars a dozen or more referees and linesmen were sacked for this reason, including eight in 1924 alone.

Before 1939, the clubs' usual complaint against referees was either bias (seldom proved) or unpunctuality (usually blamed on the trains). But far from cheating on their expenses, many of the earliest referees refused to accept any fees at all, or insisted on donating the money to charity.

Several prominent pioneers of the League were on the list of referees, including J. J. Bentley, John Lewis, Charles Sutcliffe, Louis Ford, Arthur Ashwell, Harry Lockett, Tommy Hindle and John Strawson. Countless other club officials served as umpires before linesmen took over in 1891.

By 1902 only one club secretary was still on the referees' list – James West of Manchester United. Arthur Sutcliffe, the former Burnley secretary and brother of Charles, was also still officiating. Hull City's secretary, J. F. Haller, was still a League linesman as late as 1907. Such men were never appointed as officials in their own club's division, however.

Complaints about referees were fairly common, even though the League rarely judged against the man in the middle. But when Darwen made a five-point complaint about Mr Jefferies after their game against Wolves in October 1893, the Management Committee was incensed. It rejected two points as unproven, and two others as being within the referee's sole judgement. The fifth charge – 'that in our opinion he was under the influence of drink' – the League regarded as 'outrageous and totally unfounded', and Darwen were ordered to withdraw it unconditionally, make a public apology in specified newspapers and pay all the expenses of the maligned Mr Jefferies and other witnesses.

The linesman came of age in 1896, for the first time receiving a fee (5s or 25p) plus third-class railway fares. For this he was given the responsibility of acting as an emergency referee (a burden he still shoulders), and for the first time he could be consulted at any time by the referee on points of the game. But he was always a local man, having to live within a twenty-mile radius of the ground.

To ensure against possible bias, in October 1901 all linesmen were advised to register with their local association and qualify as referees. This became compulsory in June 1905, together with the instruction that linesmen who wore glasses would be taken off the list. Two men lost their League status as a result.

In the earliest years of League football, referees would often report on their matches for local newspapers. John Bentley did this while he was President, and editor of *Athletic News*. But in time the practice came to be frowned upon by the Management Committee, who after several warnings banned it in November 1904. J. W. Horrocks of Bury persisted with his reporting, however, and was immediately struck off.

It was around this time that dissent started to become a real problem in League football. If it wasn't a case of players constantly questioning decisions, it would be clubs demanding that certain referees were not appointed to their games.

By 1907, referees were sufficiently fed up with all the criticism and extra public scrutiny that they took the unprecedented step of sending a petition to the League, signed by thirty-eight League referees. It read:

'We the undersigned members of your official list of referees for 1906/07 do hereby respectfully ask you to seriously consider whether the time has not arrived when the remuneration given shall be more commensurate with the work done.

We think the duties have become more onerous; the amount of criticism we are subject to, and the great responsibility resting upon us in competitive matches, justify us in making this appeal for a considerable augmentation of the present rate of payment.

The majority of your referees, in order to fulfil engagements, often involving tedious railway journeys, make considerable financial sacrifices so far as their business callings are concerned.

In presenting this petition we have every confidence that you will give the matter your careful consideration, and we hope and feel assured that it will meet with a favourable result.'

It did not. But were referees really hard done by? According to Stoke's official programme in December 1904, certain referees were given appointments 'not through merit but through favouritism, and because they are particular nominees of some member of the Committee'. Since the article had already criticized a Mr Stott of Rawtenstall, the inference was quite clear: Charles Sutcliffe, the little lawyer from Rawtenstall who drew up all referee appointments, was abusing his position.

Though angered by this suggestion, instead of castigating Stoke the Management Committee started watching Mr Stott's performances. Stoke had been right. He was struck off almost immediately, and the Committee drew up a new system for choosing match officials, whereby each club nominated a number of referees and then, from the whole list, thirty were chosen by a ballot conducted

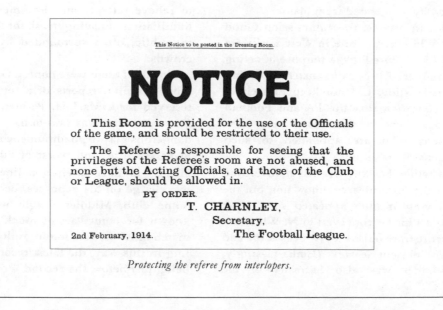

This Notice to be posted in the Dressing Room.

NOTICE.

This Room is provided for the use of the Officials of the game, and should be restricted to their use.

The Referee is responsible for seeing that the privileges of the Referee's room are not abused, and none but the Acting Officials, and those of the Club or League, should be allowed in.

BY ORDER.

T. CHARNLEY,
Secretary,

2nd February, 1914.   The Football League.

Protecting the referee from interlopers.

amongst all the clubs. The Management Committee was allowed to nominate six referees whose place on the list would be guaranteed for a season.

The first voting took place in June 1907. Ninety-eight were nominated, the most popular choices being J. T. Howcroft of Bolton (35 votes), Thomas Kirkham and J. Mason, both of Burslem (32 each), Nat Whittaker of south-east London and T. P. Campbell of Blackburn (31 each).

The system was grossly unfair. None of the Committee's nominees polled more than 17 votes – one got only 9 votes – and yet all were guaranteed places, whereas Arthur Kingscott of Derby, a former Cup Final referee, won 17 votes and could still not get a place. Similarly, the experienced A. G. Hines of Nottingham lost his place, with 14 votes.

Events the following season were to prove that the clubs could indeed make the wrong choice. The popular Mr Whittaker was at the centre of a disturbance on New Year's Day at Barnsley, where the crowds were said to have 'exhibited hostility' towards him. At the subsequent enquiry, Barnsley were fined £10 for the crowd trouble and Whittaker was officially exonerated from blame.

But in private, the commission found that Whittaker, 'while in West Yorkshire and Lancashire for the purpose of acting as referee in certain matches during Christmastide, did not keep himself in the condition that the FA and Football League have a right to expect from persons who are appointed to such responsible positions'.

Whether he was overfed or overtired after the festivities we know not, but the following minute appeared soon after: 'that a hint be conveyed to N. Whittaker to retire from our list of referees at the end of the present season'. (Embarrassingly, Whittaker was also Secretary of the Southern League at that time.)

In the same season, another popular choice, A. Millward of Leyton, was struck off. Another referee, Mr A. Green of West Bromwich, was ordered to have his eyes tested by two members of the Management Committee and a doctor. Their report was, however, favourable, as was another on referee J. H. Perks, also of West Bromwich, whom one malicious correspondent had accused of having only one eye.

On three occasions the League boobed with its appointments: two referees turned up at one Christmas Day game, and three linesmen turned up at both Newton Heath and Bradford.

Referees and linesmen in this period came from all walks of life. There was a sergeant-major, the Reverend W. S. Strange of Small Heath, a teacher, a café proprietor, a gas worker, and Howard Spencer (the ex-player), whose address was given as Aston Villa, Hucknall Torkard, Nottingham.

All of them benefited from one change in the rules. In January 1908 club secretaries were instructed to pay match officials in their dressing rooms. This was to relieve referees and linesmen of the humiliation of having to ask for their fees in public, often surrounded by hostile crowds.

Not all of them were honest. One of the most damning reports of a referee was reserved for a Mr J. H. Palmer, who in December 1913 was said to have allowed dangerous play to go unpunished, players to harass him, and worst of all he was alleged to have advised a linesman to overcharge on his expenses, because the home club, Middlesbrough, were well known for being 'a soft touch'. Several match officials were found guilty of fiddling in this way, the latest recorded case being just before the Second World War.

The Committee was always extremely strict about moral standards. Linesman T. Hogg was ordered to resign when it was discovered that he was a publican. Another was sacked for betting on a football match, another after being found guilty of stealing a vehicle in order to reach a match on time. Linesman S. Young of Newcastle was sacked for being 'helplessly drunk in the street' outside Roker Park after a match in which he had officiated. In 1907, J. Scott of Sunderland was found to have been inebriated on his line at Bradford. But it *was* New Year's Day.

Referee J. Winter of Crewe received a letter from the Committee asking if he was getting 'a good night's sleep before taking up matches'. A month later he resigned. In 1948 a referee was struck off after a divorce court judge had accused him of 'disgraceful conduct'.

Match officials had always to be careful not to accept favours. Both Bradford clubs were fined in 1920 for providing pre-match meals. Referees were also forbidden to fraternize with players, on or off the pitch. The Committee wrote to Mr Bamlett of Gateshead pointing out 'the undesirableness of speaking to a player during a game'. W. Bristow of Stafford was told not to compliment players on their play. Meanwhile, Gainsborough were ticked off for writing to several referees congratulating them on their being elected to the League's list in 1910. 'Sinister and unsportsmanlike', thought the Committee.

CHAPTER EIGHT
John McKenna – Honest John

William McGregor was a Scotsman, John Bentley an Englishman, and now the third President of the Football League was an Irishman. A big, round, smiling Irishman at that. But as J. A. H. Catton wrote: 'John McKenna always appealed to the public as the personal embodiment of John Bull, as straight as a ramrod, as blunt and as frank as a man can be, and yet full of the milk of human kindness and of Irish humour.'

John McKenna has two claims to a prominent place in football history. He was the League's longest serving President, in office for an astonishing twenty-six years. He was also a driving force behind Liverpool FC in its formative years.

In his own younger days, however, he very nearly devoted himself to the game of rugby. Born in County Monaghan in May 1854, McKenna arrived in Liverpool as a seventeen-year-old. After starting as a grocer's boy, he soon embarked upon a career as a vaccination officer in the West Derby district of Liverpool.

Like many white-collar workers in the city at that time, his main sporting interest was rugby union. He also joined the South Lancashire Artillery Volunteers, becoming sergeant-major, and eventually, chairman of the rugby club. He was also a member of the West Lancashire Rugby Union.

As a soldier he was remembered for being a strict disciplinarian, but very considerate to the men. 'A man of action', recalled one former soldier. 'His smartness when on parade, sparkling eyes, light red hair and moustache' all made him stand out. And, of course, there was his ever-present smile, which in photographs might just as easily be a scowl.

In 1885 McKenna started to follow one of the growing numbers of clubs trying out the round-ball game. The club he chose was called Everton, and they won him away from rugby completely.

Seven years later, when Everton's landlord John Houlding precipitated the famous split within the club, McKenna took Houlding's side and thereby sealed his fate. Like Houlding, McKenna was both Irish and an active freemason. But the division was never one of religion. There were Catholics and Protestants on both sides.

At the final, decisive and noisy meeting in March 1892, McKenna 'the traitor' was met with 'terrible howls of execration and yells of "Lie down, McKenna!"'. Every time he tried to explain himself, he was forced to sit down amid loud jeers.

As is now well known, the result of this hot-tempered confrontation was the removal of Everton to Goodison Park, and the foundation at Anfield of a new club – Liverpool.

But the differences were soon patched up, and McKenna became a close friend of Everton's, especially of their secretary Will Cuff (who would, coincidentally, follow McKenna as League President).

McKenna's first major coup at Anfield was the shrewd signing of Sunderland's Tom Watson as Liverpool's secretary/manager. He was also renowned for his many scouting trips to Scotland, which were so successful that Liverpool's first squad of players was known as the team of the 'Seven Macs' (it included MacOwen, MacLean, McCartney, McQueen, McBride, McQue and McVean). John Bentley had good cause to curse McKenna's diligence, because on one occasion he and McKenna arrived at Hibernian at the same time, hoping to sign the same player (who was, needless to say, another 'Mac' – James McGeacham).

Despite his predilection for Scots, McKenna apparently often found it hard to lure his finds to Anfield. He told J. A. H. Catton once that 'it seemed to require the wealth of Croesus and a Liverpool shipyard thrown in to tempt them South'.

In 1893, when his fellow directors were content to spend another year in the Lancashire League, it was McKenna who thrust Liverpool into senior football with a nifty piece of opportunism. As soon as he spotted Harry Lockett's advertisement inviting applications to the newly expanded Second Division, McKenna dispatched a telegram saying 'Liverpool make application to the Second Division of the League.' Since he had no authority to do this, he signed the telegram in the name of W. E. Barclay, who was then secretary of Liverpool (a post he had also held for Everton).

Later that night a bemused Barclay called on McKenna and handed him a wired reply which read 'Liverpool elected. Come to London meeting at 3 o'clock tomorrow to arrange fixtures.'

Presented with this *fait accompli* the other directors had no choice. McKenna persuaded them to allow him to go to London the following day and, as we know, Liverpool prospered greatly thereafter.

So did the presumptuous McKenna. Elected to the Management Committee in 1902, he became a Vice President in 1908, and in 1910 was the natural successor to John Bentley. Of the other senior members, John Lewis was too controversial and Charles Sutcliffe, for all his technical knowledge, did not command a large following.

By the time he took over, McKenna was fondly known as 'Honest John'; a man who always had an opinion and who could be relied upon to stand by it. Unlike John Lewis, he also maintained a steady approach at all times.

'Neither blowing hot nor cold, he preserves the even tenor of his course', was how one contemporary put it.

It is true that he had a somewhat brusque exterior, but it was, apparently, relatively easy to break through this. His work brought him into contact with all classes of people, rich and poor, great and humble, and he was known to chat amicably with all on equal terms. This made him a particular favourite among the players.

As a president he was not in John Bentley's mould, but then he didn't have to be. Rarely did he deliver a long speech, rarely did he get deeply embroiled in football politics. Rather, he took on the role of statesman, a role he was able to play if only because at his right hand stood Charles Sutcliffe, who was always eager to do the talking, brow-beating and political manoeuvring.

But if someone wasn't pulling their weight, he wouldn't hesitate to tick them off. Journalist Ivan Sharpe reported how at one particularly long Committee meeting one of the members suggested that perhaps the time had arrived for refreshments. McKenna replied caustically: 'That's about the only contribution to our deliberations you ever make.'

Both loved and feared, McKenna stayed on the Liverpool board until 1922, by which time he was sixty-eight. He retired the following year and was made a Life Member of the League. The silver gilt casket and illuminated address he was presented with are now displayed in the League's offices.

Honest John was a humble man. He lived modestly, in a terraced house which still stands near Anfield. He left no family, and like so many of the League's prominent men, his wife died some years before him. When the Management Committee wanted to mark his twenty-one years as President, he refused any gift. Then, in March 1931, he tried to stand down to let in a younger man, by which he generously meant Charles Sutcliffe, who was not so young but desperately wanted to become President before he died. But the Committee would have none of it, so John McKenna remained League president until the day of his death, in March 1936. He was eighty-one.

His last years were not easy. He suffered miserably from rheumatism, as did his predecessor John Bentley, and by 1935 was confined to a wheelchair. Charles Sutcliffe often tried to lend him an arm, but he remained fiercely independent, even though it often took him some time to get in and out of trains and taxis. On one occasion, so the story goes, he arrived by cab at an Annual Meeting and when his fellow passenger offered a helping hand it was, as usual, refused. Perhaps his companion could assist by holding back the taxi door? McKenna refused again. More entreaties elicited the same response until McKenna finally snapped, 'Get out of my way!'

'I can't Mr McKenna,' came the reply, 'you're standing on my foot.'

The first League medals and trophies were supplied by the Birmingham firm of Vaughtons, owned in 1888 by the father of Villa and England forward, Howard Vaughton. Vaughton junior later took over the firm and became a director at Villa, but when it came to business he had a rival in the person of J E Fattorini, who represented Bradford City at the 1904 Annual Meeting. In 1911 Fattorini's firm was chosen to supply a new FA Cup (of which, coincidentally, Bradford City became the first holders), and two years later the League decided to give its business to Fattorini's also. In 1914, however, champions Blackburn sent their medals back to the League, claiming they weren't up to scratch, while Second Division winners Notts County complained that the coat of arms on their medals was out of date. By 1918 Vaughtons were back in favour, and apart from the period 1939–45 have supplied the League ever since. In 1987 each of the nine-carat gold championship medals ordered from Vaughtons cost the League £148. That represents a hundredfold increase on the 1889 price and just over twelve times the cost in 1953. Each championship-winning team is now allowed seventeen medals, compared with twelve in 1889 and thirteen in 1953.

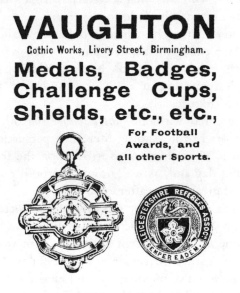

VAUGHTON

Gothic Works, Livery Street, Birmingham.

Medals, Badges, Challenge Cups, Shields, etc., etc.,

For Football Awards, and all other Sports.

CHAPTER NINE
Trouble then Strife

John McKenna's first season saw the Committee busier than ever before. There was a disturbing growth in the number of sendings-off, and those great sinners of the Edwardian period, Middlesbrough, were back in trouble no less than three times, for poaching two Scottish players, for allegedly offering a bribe to a Sunderland player, and for fiddling their books.

Middlesbrough were by common consent extremely lucky not to have been expelled from the League, as John McKenna told the club's Annual Meeting in 1911. But any more sharp practices and they would be out, he warned. The message must have struck home, because thereafter the club members behaved like perfect cherubs.

But the main reason the Management Committee was so busy was that as a result of the agreements reached in 1910, more and more of its time was taken up with processing a flood of demands from players, for transfer requests to be granted, fees to be reduced or benefits to be sanctioned.

By the end of the season the Management Committee had grown so tired of this paperwork that Charles Sutcliffe – not usually one to shirk bureaucracy – drafted a circular to all clubs:

The Management Committee of the League, as the result of their experience in dealing with a considerable number of applications by players for reduction of transfer fees, feel that it is very desirable that all our Clubs should thoroughly revise their retain and transfer lists.

They notice that many players who have long finished football are still included in such lists, and in many instances fees are fixed that clubs can never hope to realise.

They desire that in fixing the transfer fees the Clubs should place them at such a figure as they can reasonably hope to obtain and thereby save the Management Committee much unpleasant work in reducing fees.

The circular did have an effect, but not the one intended. Such was the clubs' respect for their elected leaders that a few weeks later Tom Charnley reported that many clubs had actually increased fees!

Meanwhile, the Players' Union remained active. In March 1911 Colin Veitch, the union's chairman, submitted a set of radical demands to the Management Committee. These included free transfers for all players not offered re-engagement, automatic freedom of contract after five years' service, a compulsory share of transfer fees, a rise in the maximum wage, and, most notably, an introduction of match bonuses – £2 for a win, £1 for a draw. Having heard Veitch's proposals, Charnley noted that 'a long discussion took place in a very friendly spirit'.

This soon evaporated. After consultations with the Southern League, the Management Committee rejected every single one of the proposals and then, in haughty fashion, threw down the promise of one scrap of compensation; that members of the union's committee be given free passes for all League matches. Now there was real generosity – except that when the idea was put to the clubs at the next Annual Meeting it too was rejected.

The players were also refused permission to wear the union badge on their team strips (just as, in 1987, the clubs rejected a request for all shirts to bear the logo of the centenary's sponsors, Mercantile Credit).

At that same meeting, John McKenna struck a defiant note in his first presidential address. His Committee had done all in its power to maintain the dignity and the purity of football, he said. Whenever the good of the game had been at risk, the Committee had not been afraid to strike. Football's prospects, he concluded, were brighter then than they had been for many years.

Not for Lincoln City, however. For the second time in four years Lincoln, with 17 votes, lost their League status, this time to Grimsby, who polled one extra vote (Lincoln joined the newly formed Central League). The other re-election seekers were, surprisingly, Barnsley, who only a year before had been Cup finalists. Not so surprisingly they were returned comfortably, with 28 votes.

With the Southern League ban still operating, there were again no applicants from the South, while Darlington, Chesterfield, Hartlepools and Rochdale managed only 15 votes between them. Within days of their rejection these four clubs met up with Lincoln and decided to ask the League to reconsider the idea of a third division. Their hopes were raised when they received backing from thirty-four of the forty League clubs.

So, once again the Management Committee went through the motions of putting advertisements in *Athletic News*. This time, however, they imposed two specific conditions, both of which were 'heartily accepted' by the five-club deputation. Firstly, the minimum number of clubs required would be sixteen. Secondly, these clubs would not be given a vote at Annual Meetings, except in the election of new clubs.

Applications arrived from twenty clubs. Apart from the five instigators, these were: former members Port Vale, Rotherham Town, Crewe Alexandra and Walsall; from the North and Midlands, Burton Town, Macclesfield, St

Helen's Town, South Liverpool, Southport Central and South Shields Adelaide; from the South, Croydon Common, Portsmouth and Southend United; and for the first time in League history, there were applications from Wales, from Cardiff City and Merthyr Town.

The Southern League was incensed at this development. After all the arguments two years earlier and all their efforts to bring the two leagues closer together, that the League should now independently consider forming a third division was, they told the Management Committee, 'an unfriendly act'.

Whether this stricture caused a rethink, or the Committee simply didn't rate the applicants highly enough is impossible to determine – the twenty hopefuls certainly did form a mixed bag – but the Committee did then drop the idea.

Undeterred, Lincoln's John Strawson persisted so much with the campaign that the Management Committee finally relented and put the matter to the members. Given that thirty-four of them had backed Strawson the previous May, a positive response seemed assured.

Not a bit of it. When the votes were cast, only eleven clubs were in favour, twenty-six were against, and one club opted to stay neutral (an act which the Committee regarded as disrespectful and worthy of censure).

Stunned though Strawson was by this reversal, his disappointment was soon forgotten when sad news united the entire football world in mourning. William McGregor, the founder of the League, was dead.

Although not so actively involved with Aston Villa or League affairs in his later life, McGregor had remained a much-loved and respected father figure. We learned how John Bentley's comments in 1899 stung him into more frequent attendance at Management Committee meetings, but it would seem that after the turn of the century, McGregor became more of a celebrity than a leader. He gave speeches, wrote articles, and even gave

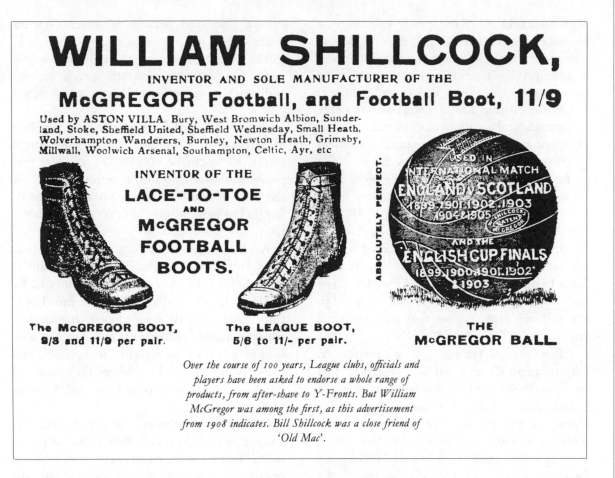

WILLIAM SHILLCOCK,

INVENTOR AND SOLE MANUFACTURER OF THE

McGREGOR Football, and Football Boot, 11/9

Used by ASTON VILLA, Bury, West Bromwich Albion, Sunder-
land, Stoke, Sheffield United, Sheffield Wednesday, Small Heath,
Wolverhampton Wanderers, Burnley, Newton Heath, Grimsby,
Millwall, Woolwich Arsenal, Southampton, Celtic, Ayr, etc

INVENTOR OF THE
LACE-TO-TOE
AND
McGREGOR
FOOTBALL
BOOTS.

ABSOLUTELY PERFECT.

USED IN INTERNATIONAL MATCH ENGLAND v SCOTLAND 1899, 1901, 1902, 1903, 1904 & 1905 AND THE ENGLISH CUP FINALS 1899, 1900, 1901, 1902 & 1903

The McGREGOR BOOT,
9/3 and 11/9 per pair.

The LEAGUE BOOT,
5/6 to 11/- per pair.

THE
McGREGOR BALL.

*Over the course of 100 years, League clubs, officials and
players have been asked to endorse a whole range of
products, from after-shave to Y-Fronts. But William
McGregor was among the first, as this advertisement
from 1908 indicates. Bill Shillcock was a close friend of
'Old Mac'.*

his name to various products, such as Billy Shillcock's 'McGregor football' and the 'McGregor lace-to-toe football boot'.

After his wife Jessie had died in December 1908, McGregor had gone to live with his daughter not far from Villa Park, but his health, which had never been robust, soon deteriorated. On occasions he had rallied, and his appearance at the 1911 Annual Meeting had been warmly received.

McGregor's last appearance in public was on 4 December 1911, when he managed to attend a Management Committee meeting in London. On the same day he was presented with the FA's long-service medal and was reported to have been looking forward to attending the Scottish League's 'Coming of Age' banquet in Glasgow on 28 December. But within days of his trip to London he was

taken ill again, and he died on 20 December 1911, at Miss Storer's nursing home in Newhall Street, Birmingham. He was sixty-five.

The list of mourners at his funeral read like a chapter from the history of football. Among the coffin bearers were two of his closest friends, Bill Shillcock and Joe Tillotson, the man in whose coffee shop McGregor had first talked of forming the League.

William McGregor was buried next to his wife at St Mary's church, Handsworth. Typical of the man, his grave gives no clue as to his achievements. It simply reads: 'William McGregor, beloved husband of Jessie – Thy will be done'. But his daughter summed him up at the funeral when she said, 'He had the spirit of a schoolboy and the heart of a true, full-grown man.'

'His death is an irreparable loss', John

McKenna told the Management Committee a few weeks later. 'Knowing him as we did, as a thoughtful, tactful and wise counsellor and legislator, full of the highest ideals for the game to be played and controlled in clean, honest and manly fashion, a true friend of every grade of football, and a willing adviser and friend of everyone associated with the game, he was held in universal affection and goodwill.'

To 'honour and revere' McGregor, their loving friend whose 'striking personality, his unvarying geniality endeared him to all', the Committee resolved to endow a bed in the Birmingham Hospital, at an estimated cost of £1250. That sum was finally handed over by John Bentley in June 1912, and the McGregor bed with its commemorative plaque stood in the children's ward from that time until the late 1940s.

After its unveiling, at a dinner in Birmingham, Charles Sutcliffe remarked that this was the second time the game had donated a bed. Aston Villa had raised £25,000 for charity in the previous twenty years, a fact which, surely would silence all the 'knockers'. As Sutcliffe spoke, William McGregor's bearded visage looked down upon the assembled Committee men from an oil painting. His eyes seemed to urge them: 'Never give in to the knockers!'

That painting is now displayed in the McGregor Suite at Villa Park. Next to it is a section of the McGregor memorial drinking fountain. This was unveiled in October 1913 by Charles Crump, Vice President of the FA and another close friend of Old Mac. The fountain was set in the wall of a bank in Six Ways, Aston (where the Midland Bank is now), a stone's throw from McGregor's first home on Witton Road, and within sight of Villa Park. The fountain narrowly escaped destruction during the blitz, and after the war was removed to Villa Park.

There are two other memorials to the founder. One is the silver casket which he received on becoming a Life Member. This is now displayed outside Secretary Graham Kelly's office in Lytham St Annes.

The other is, of course, the Football League itself, born in 1888 and still going strong. William McGregor has no better monument.

* * *

However noble the sentiments expressed at McGregor's memorial dinner mentioned above, there can be no escaping the fact that professional football in the period just before the First World War was a particularly hard-fought business, subject to every kind of uncertainty and manipulation.

As McGregor lay dying, his club, Aston Villa, was being investigated for financial irregularities. In 1912 they were followed by Chelsea, Bradford Park Avenue and Leeds City. Leeds actually came close to a complete collapse, as did Huddersfield and Arsenal, who sought salvation by moving lock, stock and barrel to north London, where they incurred the joint wrath of Tottenham and Clapton Orient.

In addition, between 1909 and 1912 the League had to fine seven clubs a total of £1075 for fielding weak teams on twenty-one separate occasions. As one would expect, all the offenders were involved in the later stages of the FA Cup.

The Committee did have one cause for celebration in this period. In April 1912 a cloud which had hung over the League for two years was finally lifted when Aston Villa won a court case brought against them by a former player called Lawrence J. Kingaby (bafflingly also referred to as George Kingaby and H. C. Kingaby in other sources). This was a complex and long-winded affair, but the essential points were these.

Kingaby signed for Villa in March 1906, failed to settle, and by the end of the season wanted away. Villa wanted their £300 investment back, but no other club would pay that much. As long as Villa paid him the maximum £4 a week and held out for the full fee, Kingaby could not leave for another League club, so instead he joined Fulham in the Southern League. This was at a time when the two leagues did not recognize each other's retain and transfer lists. Villa, therefore, received no transfer fee.

The years passed; Kingaby moved to Leyton FC in the Southern League and went down to £2 a week wages. Then, in 1910 as we have read, the League and Southern League reached agreement over transfers and suddenly Kingaby found that he was still on Villa's transfer list at the now larger fee of £350.

No club in either league thought he was worth it, and the only ones who would offer him reasonable terms were Southern Leaguers Croydon Common, but only if he could get a free transfer.

Kingaby therefore had no choice but to drop out of the Southern League, and after some time without a club he joined Peterborough, who could pay him only thirty shillings a week. All this because Villa had put a large fee on a very ordinary player, for no particular reason other than that the rules allowed them to.

It was not a unique case, nor was Kingaby a militant. But it typified the kind of restrictions under which all players laboured because of the retain and transfer system. And so it developed from a private feud between player and club into a test case between the Players' Union and the Football League itself.

The union argued that the system brought slavery to the players, a situation which had worsened since the League and Southern League had reached agreement in 1910. This was because players were being forced to accept wages which had been lowered in the knowledge that less senior clubs might be able to pay similar wages but certainly couldn't afford the transfer fees. Kingaby, argued the union, had effectively been thrown out of work by Villa's 'preposterous' valuation.

Every club director held his breath as the case was heard in London in March 1912. Charles Sutcliffe was the League's main hope, for it was he who briefed the counsel for Aston Villa. On his own admission, Sutcliffe was aching for a chance to give evidence in the High Court, and spent weeks searching for letters, proposals, schemes and minutes to back up his argument.

Like every man on the Committee, he was convinced that the retain and transfer system represented the central pillar of the League's existence. Without it the whole structure of football would come tumbling down, with clubs being put to the mercy of the union. 'The League,' wrote Sutcliffe, 'could not be dictated to by any organisation.'

As it happened, victory came rather quicker than he had anticipated, Justice Lawrence not even calling upon Aston Villa to defend themselves. He simply heard Kingaby's case and decided that there was, after all, no case to answer. Victory for the League, but such sweet sorrow for Sutcliffe, who was not called upon once! All that preparation for nothing.

Nevertheless, the success was described as 'a personal and professional triumph for Mr Sutcliffe', a tribute to which Sutcliffe was happy to lend credence by recalling a little snippet from the case.

He had the onerous task of explaining the intricacies of the retain and transfer system to counsel for the defence, Mr Montague Shearman. A good job he did, too, because Shearman confided later that before the Kingaby hearing he had been asked to take up another case, this time on behalf of the Players' Union. On that occasion he had studied the facts and concluded that the retain and transfer system was, in fact, contrary to law. Thank goodness Mr Sutcliffe had put him right on the matter.

So the London lawyers had their bit of fun in the football world, while the defeated Players' Union picked up the bill. Many felt that it had picked the wrong case, and then made the mistake of fighting it on legal principles rather than introducing a personal element. The union secretary put on a brave face – 'We do not squeal or complain, but take defeat as sportsmen' – but he couldn't avoid the fact that the legal costs of nearly £1000 would cripple his organization (in fact, it took the union over eight years to pay off its debts, which perhaps helps to explain why no other player attempted to challenge the system in court until 1963).

A month after the Kingaby case, Leeds City and Gainsborough Trinity went on trial themselves, but this time for purely footballing reasons. They were up for re-election. Leeds emerged from their cross-examination with 33 votes, but the case for Gainsborough was found badly lacking. They attracted only 9 votes, and thus became the third Lincolnshire club to lose out in three seasons. Lincoln City became the second to step back, with 27 votes. Chesterfield Town (6 votes), Darlington (1), Newcastle City (1), Cardiff City (1) and Doncaster (0) were the other applicants.

On the Management Committee there was one change. As usual, Fred Rinder and Captain Wells Holland narrowly failed to win a seat, both being beaten by Preston North End's outspoken director, Tom Houghton.

Houghton's joy at being elected was short lived. Three months later he died of a heart attack, aged forty-nine, leaving John McKenna almost speechless with sorrow (Houghton, like the President, was an ardent Freemason who shared McKenna's passion for travelling on scouting missions). William Hall of Fulham took Houghton's place, thus becoming only the second representative of a southern club to join the Committee.

Hall's election coincided with the League's best ever financial year, with a profit for the season 1912/13 of £1567. Over half of that came from fines, most of which came from clubs fielding under-strength teams.

Prosperity brought with it the need for prudence, and the Management Committee decided for the first time to put £1000 into some sort of investment (they chose the Sheffield Gas Light Company, which was paying interest of 3.5 per cent). But success also brought new costs. The League now had to pay income tax (then a mere 6d in the pound).

Profits were still sufficient, however, McKenna told the 1913 Annual Meeting, to justify a 20 per cent pay rise for Tom Charnley – taking his earnings to £300 per annum – an announcement which was greeted with hearty cries of 'hear, hear'.

Self-congratulation being the order of the day, there were therefore no surprises in the Management Committee elections. All were re-elected, even Tom Harris of Notts County who had been ill for some time and had missed several meetings. It almost goes without saying that Captain Wells Holland and Fred Rinder were, for the fourth year running, the closest challengers.

There were no changes in the Second Division either. Blackpool (32 votes) and Stockport (22) were comfortably re-elected. Blackpool's case was argued by their secretary, Tom Barcroft, who reported that despite finishing bottom on goal average, profits that season had reached a record £1100. How modern strugglers would envy such failure!

The other applicants were Chesterfield (10), Stalybridge Celtic (6), Darlington (4), Gainsborough Trinity (4), South Shields (0) and Nelson, who withdrew before the vote.

If there were no actual surprises at the 1913 meeting, voices were raised throughout the proceedings, not through anger but because the room was uncomfortably overcrowded, and workmen were hammering and chiselling noisily next to the meeting room. *Athletic News* reported: 'The complaint against this Bedlam cannot be too strongly emphasised.' It was so bad that when the chairman of League champions Sunderland stepped up to receive the First Division trophy, he made only a brief speech, saying that his 'voice was not a good accompaniment to a blacksmith's anvil'.

Voices were raised in fury, however, when the subject of Arsenal's move to Highbury came up. Earlier in the year, when Woolwich Arsenal's new chairman Henry Norris had

William McGregor, father of the League. He was, by all accounts, a quite remarkable man who had no enemies and never lost a friend.

Andertons Hotel, Fleet Street, has a special place in football history. The crucial FA meeting which legalized professionalism took place here, on 20 July 1885, as did the first gathering of parties interested in McGregor's 'union' on 22 March 1888. Andertons was demolished in 1939, and replaced in 1956 by Hulton House, which appropriately enough became the home of Charles Buchan's Football Monthly. *Another coincidence was the fact that Hulton Newspapers published* Athletic News, *the League's mouthpiece for 42 years.*

In response to a circular letter issued by Mr McGregor of the Aston Villa FC the following gentlemen met at the Anderton Hotel London on Friday evening March 22nd 1888

Messrs W. McGregor Aston Villa, chair.
A. S. Ashwell Notts County
J. H. Birtwistle Blackburn Rovers
W. Allt Whampton Wanderers
Geo Armistead Burnley.
T Smith W Bromwich Albion
H Lockett Stoke. Hon Sec pro tem

After considerable discussion the following suggestions were made & a copy of them was to be forwarded to each of the 12 clubs named therein.

"At a meeting of representatives of some of the leading clubs in the

RIGHT

All that remains of the drinking fountain erected in William McGregor's honour in October 1913, at Six Ways, Aston. It is now displayed in the McGregor Suite at Villa Park.

BELOW

The official record of the first League season, as it appears in the minutes. The compiler, one R. H. Richards, inadvertently deprived Notts County of one goal in their 5–3 defeat at Derby County.

Plaque inscription:

ERECTED BY
THE BIRMINGHAM COUNTY FOOTBALL ASSOCIATION
IN MEMORY OF
WILLIAM McGREGOR
OCTOBER 1913

Position.	The Football League 1888 · 1889 (Alphabetically Arranged.)	Accrington	Aston Villa	B'burn Rovers	Bolton Wanderers	Burnley	Derby County	Everton	Notts County	Preston N.E.	Stoke	West Brom: Albion	Wolverhampton Wanderers	WON	LOST	DRAWN	For	Against	Points	Position.
7	Accrington	· ·	34 / 11	55 / 02	45 / 23	51 / 22	11 / 62	23 / 31	30 / 12	04 / 02	42 / 20	22 / 01	44 / 04	6	8	8	48	48	20	7
2	Aston Villa	43 / 11	· ·	61 / 15	32 / 62	42 / 04	42 / 25	21 / 02	91 / 41	11 / 02	51 / 11	20 / 33	11 / 21	12	5	5	61	43	29	2
4	B'burn Rovers	55 / 20	16 / 51	· ·	44 / 23	71 / 42	20 / 30	30 / 13	33 / 52	01 / 22	52 / 12	62 / 12	22 / 22	10	6	6	66	45	26	4
5	B'lton Wanderers	41 / 32	23 / 26	44 / 32	· ·	34 / 14	43 / 32	66 / 22	62 / 73	40 / 25	13 / 22	21 / 12	51 / 21	23	10	10	2	63	59	22	5
9	Burnley	15 / 22	24 / 40	17 / 24	43 / 41	· ·	10 / 01	22 / 23	16 / 10	25 / 22	34 / 21	34 / 20	14 / 04	7	12	3	42	62	17	9
10	Derby County	11 / 26	24 / 52	02 / 03	63 / 23	01 / 10	· ·	24 / 26	32 / 52	23 / 05	21 / 11	12 / 05	14 / 30	7	13	2	41	60	16	10
8	Everton	21 / 13	12 / 20	03 / 31	26 / 21	22 / 32	42 / 62	· ·	21 / 13	03 / 02	00 / 11	14 / 02	05 / 12	9	11	2	35	47	20	8
11	Notts County	33 / 21	19 / 24	33 / 25	04 / 37	61 / 01	23 / 25	12 / 63	· ·	07 / 14	03 / 03	24 / 21	30 / 12	5	15	2	39	73	12	11
1	Preston N.E.	00 / 20	41 / 20	10 / 04	23 / 22	45 / 51	23 / 22	30 / 50	70 / 20	· ·	70 / 30	20 / 50	40 / 52	18	·	4	74	15	40	1
12	Stoke	24 / 02	15 / 11	25 / 21	12 / 22	43 / 11	42 / 12	20 / 13	03 / 00	07 / 03	· ·	02 / 02	01 / 14	4	14	4	26	51	12	12
6	West Brom. Alb.	22 / 12	02 / 33	26 / 21	15 / 21	43 / 02	21 / 50	41 / 10	41 / 12	03 / 05	20 / 20	· ·	12 / 13	10	10	2	40	46	22	6
3	Wolverhampton Wanderers	44 / 40	11 / 12	22 / 22	12 / 12	32 / 40	41 / 03	41 / 21	50 / 25	03 / 41	04 / 31	01 / 21	· ·	12	6	4	57	37	28	3
	For / Against	48 / 48	61 / 43	66 / 45	63 / 59	42 / 62	41 / 60	35 / 47	34 / 73	74 / 15	26 / 57	40 / 46	57 / 37	110 / 110	110 / 110	44	586	586	264	

Results of 132 Matches. No. of either 22 Each. GOALS.

April 1889. R. H. Richards.

① North End. ② Aston Villa ③ Wolverhampton Wand. ④ B'burn Rovers ⑤ Bolton Wand. ⑥ West Brom ⑦ Accrington ⑧ Everton ⑨ Burnley ⑩ Derby City ⑪ Notts City ⑫ Stoke.

The League Championship trophy on display in Lewisham in the late 1950s. After Preston won the first two championships, their benefactor William Sudell proposed that the League buy such a trophy 'for no more than fifty guineas'. Preston have never won the title since. Vaughtons, whose works were just around the corner from McGregor's shop in Birmingham, designed and manufactured the trophy in 1890, and with the exception of a few years have been supplying the League with championship medals ever since.

A meeting of club secretaries and Committeemen in 1891–2. Back row, left to right: John Bentley (Bolton), G. Winfield (Derby), R. Molyneux (Everton), Edwin Browne (Notts Co), Josh Parlby (Stoke), J. Addenbrooke (Wolves), T. B. Mitchell (Blackburn), Tom Watson (Sunderland). Front row, left to right: Louis Ford (WBA), J. Coe (Accrington), Fred Dewhurst (Preston), James Marr (Sunderland). Seated on floor: George Ramsay (Villa), C. S. Grime (Darwen). (Burnley were absent)

RIGHT

J. J. Bentley. With a referee's whistle, a seat on the FA Council, the editorship of the leading sporting newspaper of the day and the League Management Committee under his command, no man has ever enjoyed such an influence in football affairs.

BELOW

The League's first venture north of the border resulted in a 4–3 win against the Scottish League at Celtic Park in 1893. With the players in the back row are (l to r) Messrs McGregor, Bentley, Molyneux and, looking very dashing, Harry Lockett. Members of the Management Committee often ran the line for Inter-League matches, while Bentley refereed two of the first four games in the series. William 'Billy' Bassett (front row, far left) scored the winning goal at Celtic Park and was the only League representative player who would eventually serve on the Management Committee.

Harry Lockett at work. For the first decade or so the League's address was that of Lockett's home, whereas this picture appears to have been taken at his printing works in Foundry Street, Hanley. Although there is a telephone on the desk no number was ever listed for the League until the offices moved to Preston.

Tom Charnley in the League's office at 47, Tithebarn Street, Preston. A meticulous man by nature, he deliberately displayed the League's Appearance Book for season 1910–11 to give an idea of when the photograph was taken.

The Management Committee circa 1903. Standing, l to r: W.W. Hart (Small Heath), John McKenna (Liverpool), Harry Radford (Nottm Forest). Seated, left to right: William McGregor (Life Member), T.H. Sidney (Wolves), John Bentley (President), John Lewis (Blackburn), Tom Charnley (Secretary). George Leavey (W. Arsenal) was absent from the photograph, which was presented to the League by William McGregor Junior in 1955.

Honest John McKenna was not above using his power to aid Liverpool's cause. At an F.A. disciplinary meeting, Sir William Clegg wanted to suspend a Liverpool player for six months, after he'd been sent off for striking an opponent. McKenna protested that the player had been called 'an opprobrious name, which to Liverpool people is the greatest insult a man can suffer. He would not have been a Britisher if he had not retaliated. I would have taken the same action in the same circumstances,' declared McKenna. The result? Case dismissed with a caution.

John Lewis: the Chief Constable of Football, 'a sturdy, hot-tempered little man'.

Resplendent with their moustaches and watch chains, this unique photograph of the Management Committee in 1910 shows the first four presidents together, probably at John McKenna's first meeting in the chair. From left to right: John Cameron (Newcastle), Harry Keys (WBA), Dr James Baxter (Everton), Charles Sutcliffe (Burnley), Tom Charnley (Secretary), John McKenna (President and Liverpool), John Lewis (Blackburn), William McGregor (Life Member), Arthur Dickinson (Sheff Wed), Tom Harris (Notts Co), John Bentley (Man Utd). Bentley served as an ordinary Committeeman for two years before being elected a Life Member.

Charlie Sutcliffe (on right) photographed in Preston with John McKenna (centre) and his close friend and fellow traveller, Tom Charnley. Although his hair had turned white by the 1920s, Sutcliffe's moustache turned brown, stained with the nicotine of 60 cigarettes a day.

> 'The power of the League strengthens the Association and the authority of the Association safeguards the League.'
>
> In theory, these words, spoken by just about every League president since William McGregor, hold good. Once in a while, however, the two organizations have a tiff. Nowadays it's more likely to be over the release of players or the postponement of League fixtures to help the national team. Before 1914, the issues were often more basic.
>
> For example, in 1911 the Cheshire FA fined Stockport for not fielding their first team in a Cheshire cup tie. The League retorted that County Associations had no right to arrange cup matches which clashed with League games.
>
> In April 1913 Fulham were incensed when the FA chose to stage an England *v.* Scotland match at Stamford Bridge on the same afternoon as Fulham had a home League match.
>
> When the FA held their Jubilee Banquet that year, Management Committee members were sent personal invitations, rather than ones which acknowledged their official standing. This was regarded as a snub for the League, and for a while the Committee threatened to boycott the dinner. Of course, everyone attended in the end, and on behalf of the League pledged their 'unabated and unswerving loyalty'.

this matter was somewhat ironic, considering that in 1905 Spurs had opposed Orient joining the Southern League, with the words, 'We are not going to have them on our doorsteps.')

Captain Wells Holland of Orient said he couldn't conceive of anything more ridiculous than Arsenal's move. It was one of the first principles of the League for a club to represent a certain district. According to the existing rules, there was nothing to prevent Newcastle United moving to the Isle of Wight, or Stockport County to Manchester. 'Any millionaire can buy up a poverty-stricken club, form a company and then where does the sport come in?'

Arsenal's move had clearly upset many of the delegates, because Orient's motion, which sought to prevent a recurrence, was then passed by a large majority. But Henry Norris was still not off the hook, because he and Committee member William Hall (who was in reality no more than Norris's henchman) were then attacked by Morton Cadman of Spurs for being on the boards of two clubs at the same time – Arsenal and Fulham. This had resulted, among other things, in the transfer of one player, T. Winship, back and forward between the two clubs without third parties being allowed to bid. Surely, said Cadman, the League was not going 'to allow wealthy men to monopolise clubs and do as they jolly well pleased'?

Henry Norris took immediate offence at this remark. He pointed out that Charles Clegg sat on the boards of both Sheffield clubs, and no one had suggested a scandal in that. Besides, both he and Mr Hall were going to retire from the management of one of the clubs (Fulham, as it turned out, a month later), and there the matter would rest.

(There are strong parallels here with the events at Fulham in February 1987. In 1910 Norris, a property developer, tried to merge Arsenal and Fulham. In 1987 another property developer, David Bulstrode, tried to merge Fulham with Queen's Park Rangers. In both

announced the club's intention of transferring from Plumstead in south London to Gillespie Road in north London, Clapton Orient and Tottenham (with Chelsea's backing) had complained to the Management Committee, which replied that it had never prevented clubs changing grounds in the past and could not therefore object in Arsenal's case. In the Committee's opinion, there was 'ample population and opportunity for three League clubs within the area'. (Orient's collusion with Spurs over

instances the League refused to grant permission.)

Whenever modern-day commentators talk about the good old days they rarely take into account the periods during which football went through a difficult patch. The season 1913/14 was one such patch. Sendings-off were up, while complaints about referees reached startling levels. In one three-month period alone, no fewer than thirty complaints were lodged against twenty-one of the League's thirty-five referees. A handful were subsequently warned after having been watched by members of the Committee, but the majority were exonerated, suggesting that the clubs were more at fault than the referees. (There was one notable exception. One particularly weak referee was alleged to have told a linesman that Middlesbrough were 'a soft touch' when it came to making false expenses claims.)

Referees in turn had their own complaints. At several grounds club officials 'grossly abused' the sanctity of the referee's room, while some secretaries had still not adopted the long-recommended practice of paying match officials in their dressing room rather than in a public place.

William McGregor would certainly have raised a weary sigh over that, as he would over one item in the minutes of February 1914, calling clubs' attention to the fact that it was a serious offence to kick off *before* the advertised time, thus breaking faith with their spectators. This was exactly the kind of laxity which McGregor had intended the League to eradicate.

Similarly, Clapton Orient were fined £25 for fixing their kick-off against Leeds City in March 1914 so late, at 4.30 p.m., that the last part of the game was played in near darkness and the City goalkeeper claimed that he was, literally, unsighted when two late goals were scored against him.

Yet another attempt to form a third division was made in that fateful close season of 1914.

This time, a delegation was formed by representatives of Stoke, Chesterfield, South Shields and Walsall, who had gathered applications from a further thirteen clubs from the North and Midlands. Remembering the previous failure, the Management Committee refused even to consider the idea.

And so the squabbles, the bureaucracy, the problems on the pitch, the difficult day-to-day business of the Secretary carried on as war clouds gathered over Europe.

The last Annual Meeting before the outbreak of hostilities was held at the Connaught Rooms, Great Queen Street, London, where there was no building work to disturb the delegates and plenty of room for onlookers.

Worries about declining standards of behaviour on the pitch were immediately brushed aside by John McKenna, who commented that attendances were on the rise so the product on offer 'was good enough for the public'.

Nottingham Forest and Lincoln were up for re-election and succeeded in keeping their places, polling 34 and 24 votes respectively. Lincoln were by now old hands at the election process, having been in the hat no less than ten times in twenty-two seasons. Stoke (16) were their nearest challengers. For the seventh year running, Chesterfield (1) failed, as did Darlington (2), for the fifth year in succession. The other applicants were South Shields, Gainsborough and South Liverpool.

Those perennial also-rans, Captain Wells Holland and Fred Rinder, failed yet again in the elections for the Management Committee, which was returned to office *en bloc*, and the Orient man was never to apply again. Rinder would not be deterred, however, as we shall see.

In view of the impending crisis in Europe, one other feature of the 1914 Annual Meeting is worth noting. In the previous two or three years, foreign tours had become quite the fashion in League circles. But the Management Committee insisted that clubs should not use the trips as a means of providing players with hidden benefits. So, after fining Newcastle £100 for overpaying their touring team in 1912, the Committee took it upon themselves to vet the advance plans and final accounts of every single tour.

In 1913/14 Newcastle, Middlesbrough, Leicester, Burnley, Tottenham, Bristol City, Liverpool, Bradford City and Notts County were all given permission to travel overseas, but only on condition that their players received no more than five shillings pocket money per day. Manchester City were ordered to stay at home, however, because their intended trip had turned out to be no more than a holiday, with no matches scheduled at all. Quite scandalous!

It is quite possible that some of the clubs mentioned above were still abroad when news came through that in a remote town which few people had ever heard of, called Sarajevo, a Bosnian schoolboy called Gavrilo Princip had assassinated the rather brutal, unpleasant heir to the Austro-Hungarian Empire, Archduke Ferdinand, and his wife Sophie. That was on Sunday 28 June 1914.

The following day, Austria declared war on Serbia and began bombarding Belgrade. On 31 July, the Russians mobilized in support of Serbia, so Germany declared war first on Russia, then on France, and on 4 August invaded Belgium. By nightfall, Britain responded by declaring war on Germany, and Sir Edward Grey, Britain's Foreign Secretary, made his famous, though inaccurate, statement: 'The lamps are going out all over Europe. We shall not see them lit again in our lifetime.'

On Thursday 6 August, the Management Committee gathered at the home of Blackburn's chairman Mr L. Cotton, at Clayton Green, near Preston, and from the opening exchanges one wonders if anyone had told them about the war. It seemed just like business as usual; transfer fees were fixed, benefits sanctioned, dates arranged and the venue for an Inter-League match decided.

Only near the end of the meeting did the outside world infringe upon League business: 'It was reported that a number of football grounds were being used for mobilisation purposes, and it was doubtful as to how it might affect the opening games.'

Opening games? With the British Expeditionary Force preparing to enter the fray? Apparently so. The League had every intention of carrying on, Huns or no Huns. John McKenna was empowered to summon a special meeting by wire, as he thought fit, and a hearty vote of thanks was tendered to Mr Cotton for his hospitality. One can almost hear the members as they gathered up their papers muttering confidently amongst themselves, 'Be over by Christmas...'

Two weeks later, on the day the first British Expeditionary Forces landed in France, Frederick Wall of the FA wrote to Tom Charnley granting permission for League clubs to play matches in aid of war relief funds. Clubs were also urged to make collections and do all they could to help the war effort. Charnley himself advised clubs that, although not legally liable for players' wages once they had joined the armed forces, it was hoped that they would be as generous as possible to the players' wives and families.

Meanwhile, contingency arrangements were made with the railway companies to ensure that bookings would still be honoured, although clubs were warned to make alternative arrangements in case troop movements prevented them from travelling by rail.

But the League did not have its head entirely in the sand, as the following eve-of-season pronouncement from 31 August indicated:

'At this grave crisis in the history of the British nation the Management Committee of the Football League desires to make the following public pronouncement:—

Thousands on thousands of the flower of British youth and manhood who on the playing fields of this country have acquired and developed the splendid characteristics of the fearless and undaunted warrior are now, at the peril of their lives, fighting the battle of honour, honesty and uprightness against military despotism in the greatest struggle the world has ever known.

Not merely from the responsible officials of this country, but from the decimated towns and villages of the grievously wronged yet heroic and sacrificing people of Belgium, comes the call for help. It is the call of patriotism, justice, and redress, and we trust that in this hour of England's need every young man who can possibly do so will respond to his country's call. There lies the path of duty. While scores of thousands have gone and scores of thousands must follow, there will be millions of people who must remain behind and in other ways lend all possible aid.

In considering the course to be adopted with reference to our great National winter game, we are not unmindful of the days of deep sorrow now with us, and yet to come — days when the dark clouds that surround us will oppress and appal us. To sit and mourn is to aggravate the nation's sorrow. Any sport which can minimise the grief, help the nation to bear its sorrow, relieve the oppression of continuous strain, and save the people at home from panic and undue depression, is a great national asset which can render lasting service for the people.

Just as we look, hour after hour, for the latest news from the theatres of war, our vast armies in the field will, week by week, look for papers from home, and in so far as their minds may be temporarily directed from the horrors of war, and the intense strain of days and weeks of almost unrestricted fighting, much will be done to give them fresh heart, fresh hopes, and a renewed vitality for the work before them.

At home our clubs are in a helpless position. The contracts entered into with all the formality and security of legal contracts must be performed as far as possible. We feel that the advice offered by politicians, press and commercial authorities that business should be carried on as usual is sound, well considered advice.

We, therefore, without the slightest reservation, appeal to the clubs, the press and the public that our great winter game should pursue its usual course. Especially do we appeal to the press that the same

prominence and publicity should be given to reports of the games as of old.

Sacrifices will be necessary. Let them be cheerfully and willingly made, and let every club remember that football must discharge to the full its duties and obligations to the war, those engaged therein, and those who suffer therefrom.

Every club should do all in its power to assist the war funds. Every player should especially train to be of national service — at least, in national defence — and while we unreservedly authorise the due fulfilment of the League programme, we must accept to the full every obligation that we can individually and collectively discharge for our beloved country and our comrades in arms who in this fight for righteousness and justice at the risk of their lives have answered to duty's call.

Signed on behalf of the Committee,
J. McKenna, President and T. Charnley, Secretary.'

These were noble words which did great credit to the Committee, and at the time found few detractors. But as both the season and the war progressed, the League's position would grow increasingly untenable.

The League was not alone in carrying on its affairs. In the first few months of the war, the official government advice to every organization and company was to carry on normally as much as possible. So the Committee was not being heartless or mercenary. Rather, it saw itself as providing a welcome diversion, in the same manner as did music halls or those newfangled cinemas. By staging games, the clubs were also able to raise large sums for the war effort.

THE WAR AND FOOTBALL.

In view of requests from certain people to stop football, the Management Committee have taken counsel with their Clubs. The Committee are even more decidedly of the opinion that in the interests of the people of this country football ought to be continued.

The League stands firm, with this announcement in September 1914.

This was still not good enough for some. Was it not distasteful to play games while fellow countrymen died at places like Mons and Ypres? And was it not disgraceful that so many able-bodied footballers should be seen in their team colours rather than those of the country?

To read the League's response in late September, one would imagine League football to have been some kind of magic potion, blessed with all manner of properties. As if from an advertisement in a penny dreadful, the public were informed that football was 'a healthy antidote to the war'. It helped the nation 'to preserve an equable mind' and 'counteracted any tendency to panic and monomania'.

'Notwithstanding the early opposition to football being played,' the Committee announced, it was now 'confident that the failure to continue League football would be a national calamity.'

One man who disagreed, and disagreed loudly, was an east London temperance worker called F. N. Charrington. He was given permission to address the crowd during half-time at Craven Cottage on 5 September, provided that 'he confined himself to advocating enlistment'. He did not. He started to rail against the playing of football and was thus 'ejected pretty speedily and unceremoniously', while Frederick Wall looked on uncomfortably.

Among numerous letters and articles protesting against the continuation of all forms of organized sport, one from 'an old rugger man' in *The Sportsman* had particular spice:

'It has been abundantly and painfully evident since Germany won the toss (with a double faced coin) and took first innings on a carefully prepared wicket, that the genus Pro-Boer is still very much alive in our midst. Every bachelor under 45 who has not been declared unfit for service by Government medical authority belongs to that hateful family, whether he knows it or not.

This being so (deny it who may), may I ask who cares one straw whether the Coventry XV for the coming season (ye gods! a football season in progress with the Motherland in real danger!) will be the same as that which represented the club last season?

Signed,

"Britain Uber Alles"'

Whether the public cared one straw or not for Coventry's rugby prospects, they certainly seemed to desert League football. A detailed breakdown of gates compared with the previous three seasons' confirmed that takings were down by more than 50 per cent. In the Second Division, season ticket sales were down from an average of £516 to only £177. (Only one of the forty clubs showed an improvement on gates, that being Arsenal, whose receipts had in any case been rising steadily since their move to Highbury.) If the falling trend continued, the League estimated, total receipts would drop from £326,017 in 1913/14 to £210,620.

The Sportsman *added its voice to the recruitment drive with this cartoon, 2 September 1914.*

THE IDLE, THE IDOL, AND THE IDEAL.

Something had to give, and inevitably it was the players' wages. The League called 'for sacrifice on the part of the best paid professional players ... in the interests of players whose position is precarious ... The players must show that spirit of brotherhood which immediately compels the rich to help the poor. The strong clubs must come to the help of the weak ... devotion to the League is of paramount importance ... The situation brooks no delay. There is no time for argument or cavilling ...' Otherwise, they warned, the Second Division would soon collapse and 500 players find themselves unemployed.

Hardly in a position to refuse – though some did, at Bradford City and Tottenham, only to be met with 'some straight talk' – players on the then maximum of £5 per week took a 15 per cent wage cut, with a sliding scale down to 5 per cent for those players earning under £3 per week. The amounts deducted (around £300 a week) were then sent to the League and put into a fund to assist those clubs struggling to pay wages. As a gesture of solidarity, club secretaries also agreed to pay a percentage of their wages to the fund.

On 9 October 1914, just as the troops in Europe were digging themselves in for a new phase in the conflict – trench warfare – a special general meeting of the clubs at the Grand Hotel, Manchester, approved another batch of contingency arrangements. Each club would contribute 2.5 per cent of gross gates to the League's relief fund, while the League and Southern League would press the FA to forego its usual 5 per cent share of Cup-tie gates.

So the League steeled itself for the inevitable crisis. Telephones were installed in the homes of McKenna and Sutcliffe. A special emergency bank account was opened in Preston, just in time to meet the first requests for aid. Blackpool, Leicester and Lincoln received £50 each from the relief fund, then Lincoln were given a further £40, followed by Bristol City (£108) and Stockport (£61). Within a fortnight, a further eight clubs' applications were made,

including one by Fulham, who asked for a £500 grant, only to be told that there wasn't £500 left in the kitty.

Clapton Orient were more public spirited. Under the influence of their chairman, Captain Wells Holland, they returned one of their grants as a donation to the fund. In fact, no League club gave more to the war effort than Orient. Apart from raising money, forty-one of its players and officials joined up with the Footballers' Battalion (formed in December 1914), of whom three did not return.

Keeping the League competition going proved to be a real struggle. Clubs were late in their contributions, disruptions in train timetables meant officials and players arriving late, and on one occasion a match at Newcastle was delayed ten minutes because the military had taken over the dressing rooms. At the same time, the transfer system all but collapsed because clubs were unable to pay the fees.

Leicester Fosse were in a particularly bad way. They were found to have debts of £3550 and owed nearly £600 in wages. Apathy was the root of the trouble, concluded a Committee report. The mood at the club was 'shrouded in an atmosphere of pessimism ... The club lacks vitality and confidence. New friends should be introduced and efforts made to create greater local interest. There must be energy and enthusiasm, and it must commence with the club's officials.'

Unusually, the League ordered this report to be made public and sent copies to all Second Division clubs, no doubt to serve as a rallying call to the troops from HQ.

Meanwhile, the League itself faced a crisis: by December 1914 it had less than £65 to its name and desperately needed a top-up from the relief fund.

Not everyone suffered, however. In the Southern League, Watford's and Luton's gates were both up, in Luton's case because of the proximity of a large number of recruitment camps. And while some League clubs were reporting a fall in attendances of up to 60 per cent, others reported near normal gates. Only eighteen of the forty clubs ever actually drew money from the relief fund.

Even so, by March 1915 it was clear that however closely they tried to budget, several clubs were on the verge of total collapse. Radical action was called for. So, as the Commonwealth forces prepared for their fateful landings at Gallipoli, the Management Committee laid its battle plans on the table at a Special General Meeting on 29 March.

The proposals were that a club could terminate a player's contract with twenty-eight days' notice; that once a player joined His Majesty's Service the contract was terminated but the club retained his registration; and that no summer wages would be paid. Furthermore, the maximum wage was to be reduced from £208 per annum to £156.

Once again Charles Sutcliffe reiterated the League's position, which was coming under increasing pressure from several quarters. 'The spirit of patriotism,' he told the Special Meeting (and a bevy of journalists), 'must be placed first and the game take second place.'

Nevertheless, it was still the League's intention to carry on playing the following season.

Criticism mounted. Colonel C. F. Grantham, Commander of the 17th (Service) Battalion, the Duke of Cambridge's Own Middlesex Regiment (Football) – otherwise known as the Footballers' Battalion – wrote to the League on 26 March from his headquarters at the White City Stadium, London.

'You are aware that some little time ago there was much controversy in the papers with regard to the manner in which the professional football player had failed in his duty by not coming forward to serve his country in its time of stress. The laxity of the football professionals and their following amounted to almost a public scandal. Mr Johnson Hicks MP therefore raised the Footballers' Battalion, and public opinion died down under the belief that most if not all of the available professionals had joined the Battalion.

This is not the case, as only 122 professionals had

joined. I understand that there are 40 League clubs and 20 in the Southern League with an average of some 30 players fit to join the Colours, namely 1800. These figures speak for themselves.

I am also aware and have proof that in many cases directors and managers of clubs have not only given no assistance in getting these men to join but have done their best by their actions to prevent it ...

It is no use mincing words. If men who are fit and capable of doing so will not join, they and also those who try by their words and actions to prevent them will have to face the opinion of their fellow men publicly. I will no longer be a party to shielding the want of patriotism of these men by allowing the public to think they have joined the Football Battalion.'

Relations with those players who remained with their clubs now steadily worsened as the reduction in wages began to bite. In an open letter, the Management Committee accused the Players' Union of indulging in 'flattering platitudes to the players' and refusing to be of any practical assistance to the clubs and governing bodies. 'Through the distressing trials in the early days of the season, when it was apparent that the difficulties would grow rather than diminish, the Players' Union adopted a policy and attitude calculated to hinder us in our purpose to keep the game going and complete our competition.'

But what had the union done? It had suggested that the players might go on strike if contracts weren't honoured. That it could even consider such a suggestion during the emergency led the Committee to conclude that it could 'never imagine the union being of any practical service to the game'.

Relationships were further exacerbated when, with the season drawing to an uncomfortable close, two events brought disgrace and discredit to both the players and the game. With the public attitude already increasingly hostile towards football, the incidents seemed to indicate a mood of almost reckless self-destruction.

One of these occurred during Middlesbrough's game against Oldham on 3 April. It had been a tetchy match, played in the rain in front of 7000 spectators. At one point, angry because they felt two of Middlesbrough's goals should have been disallowed, the Oldham players childishly kicked the ball away from the centre spot when the referee tried to restart the game. Then, in the fifty-sixth minute, with the score 4–1 to Middlesbrough, Oldham's right-back William Cook was sent off for a foul. For some reason – perhaps he thought he might be able to get the match replayed – Cook stubbornly refused to leave the pitch, leaving the referee, Mr H. Smith of Nottingham, no choice but to abandon the game.

There had never been anything like it in League football. Although the Committee wanted to ban Cook permanently, the FA suspended him for one year. Oldham were also censured for continuing to play him after the incident, and, finally, the 4–1 scoreline was ordered to stand.

A curious aspect of this incident was that Oldham were then top of the First Division and stood an excellent chance of winning the Championship for the first – and only – time in their history. In the end, Everton eclipsed them by one point. Furthermore, Cook was generally considered to be an intelligent man who, though near to the end of his footballing career, was still a popular cricketer for Lancashire.

But the more serious event of that Easter weekend in 1915 came at Old Trafford, on Good Friday, where relegation-threatened Manchester United were playing middle-of-the-table Liverpool. United won 2–0, but the whole match was a complete fraud. The result had been prearranged by a handful of the players, and like the 1898 test match at Stoke, this was patently obvious to most of the 15,000 rain-soaked spectators.

'Too poor to describe', was one reporter's verdict. It wasn't the war that was killing football, he wrote. Football was killing itself, with matches like this. It was so bad that United's

secretary/manager John Robson left in disgust before the final whistle.

The story of how this match was rigged is a long and rather pathetic tale (told fully in *Soccer in the Dock* by the same author, see Bibliography). Suffice it to say here that when the Football League's commission of enquiry finally managed to reach a verdict in December 1915, four Liverpool players, three Manchester United players and one from Chester were all suspended *sine die* from football.

But why should a Chester player have become involved? The reason was this. By Good Friday it had become apparent that whatever the future held for League football, there would be no summer wages for the players, most of whom had already taken large cuts in their pay-packets. For some, there was no avoiding the armed forces any longer. For others, there was only the prospect of long hard shifts in munitions factories.

Faced with this miserable scenario, a group of players clubbed together to make a quick killing with a betting coup. At that time it was possible to make a bet on the result of one League match at a time, so the conspirators put their money on United to win 2–0.

Not all of them were due to play in the game, but by drawing in others who were, they made quite sure that the result would be 2–0. The conspirators kicked the ball into the stands, one of them appeared to miss a penalty deliberately, and when one Liverpool player who was not in on the act nearly scored a late consolation goal, he was torn off a strip by his angry team-mates.

Had the bookmakers not provided pretty conclusive evidence against the players, the League might never have settled the case. But they did, and were thus able to clear both clubs completely of any involvement in the conspiracy. Remember that John McKenna was on Liverpool's board at that time.

As a result of United's pre-arranged win, they finished one point ahead of Chelsea, who would have been relegated had the League not decided soon after to suspend the competition. But for the next four years a great dilemma simmered in League circles. Would Chelsea be relegated as a result of this, undoubtedly the worst scandal to afflict the League in its twenty-seven seasons?

That will become apparent in due course. For the time being, however, we must return to the sad, tainted days of 1915.

The official suspension of League football was announced on 3 July 1915 at an historic conference at the Winter Gardens, Blackpool. Attending together for the first time were representatives of the League, the Scottish League, the Southern League and the Irish League.

Apart from the pressure of public opinion, several factors led to the suspension. More players had by then joined up or were engaged in munitions work, long railway journeys were becoming an impossibility, and the financial strain on clubs was proving intolerable. In such circumstances, declared the Management Committee, 'a competition providing for promotion and relegation would be grossly unjust, would produce the greatest hardship to those who have made the greatest sacrifice, and would favour the club whose players have failed to realise their higher duty to the nation'.

The delayed 1915 Annual Meeting, elections and all, would take place, however, and plans were discussed for an alternative method of keeping the game alive. 'We feel we owe a duty to the game and to those who perforce must stay at home,' said John McKenna. 'There is a limit to physical and mental strain; and football has proved a great mental relief.'

The result of the Committee's deliberations was the setting up of regional competitions to last for six months over the winter, followed by a two-month League competition. All registered professionals would play as amateurs, for expenses only.

The final official Management Committee meeting of the war took place on 19 July at the Regent Palace Hotel, London, in emotional circumstances. Who could say when Europe would be restored to calm and the League allowed to continue its business? The Committee members were not young men. Would they be fit enough to retain office when hostilities ended?

As the minutes recorded, John McKenna could only hope and pray that 'ere long the cloud which hung over the game would be removed, and that conditions very beneficial in the game would return.'

There were just a few matters left to resolve. The relief fund was wound up, with these words of praise from the Committee: 'It is impossible to express in words our heartfelt thanks for the willing and whole-hearted assistance of clubs who have lost very seriously during the season yet made no request for assistance.'

How their attitude contrasted with that of Derby County. Derby had actually requested and been granted £350 from the fund, only for it to be discovered that the club had made a profit of £501 during the previous season and had not at any time called upon its capital of over £2600. Profiting from the relief fund was grossly unfair on those clubs in need, especially in the light of the fact that Derby had won the Second Division that season.

An air of unreality hung over the 1915 Annual Meeting when it did eventually take place, but for one club the re-election results were to prove only too real.

Leicester Fosse were comfortably re-elected with 33 votes, but for Glossop the war proved to be the final blow in a long, drawn-out struggle. Indeed, so appalling had gates been that if it hadn't been for the relief fund, the club would not have lasted the season. They finished bottom of the League with the worst record of any Second Division team since its expansion to twenty clubs in 1905.

Even so, after seventeen seasons' membership, poor Glossop might have been expected to win more than just a single vote. No other club seeking re-election has ever been so emphatically rejected. Glossop's place was taken by Stoke, who won 21 votes but were then fined £250 by the Southern League for leaving without its permission. South Shields (11), Chesterfield (8) and Darlington (4) were the other applicants.

And so the League competition went into hibernation until 1919. But for one man, Charles Sutcliffe, there was still plenty of work to be done. Indeed, it was at this point that Sutcliffe's tireless efforts were at their most crucial.

His chief concern was that the power of the League should not be allowed to diminish during the war years. As long as clubs organized themselves into regional competitions there was always a danger that they might grow accustomed to independence. This applied especially to the London clubs, over whom the League could have least control, not only for geographical reasons but because both the London FA and the Southern League were in a much stronger position to win them over.

In 1915/16, thirty League clubs participated in the regional competitions under the League's jurisdiction, all from the North and Midlands, including four clubs from outside the League – Southport Central, Rotherham County, Rochdale and Chesterfield (in at last!), who were each asked to pay small subscription fees.

(Southport were the subjct of unique concession during this period, when they asked permission to change their name to Southport Vulcan, in recognition of a local factory's support. In view of the club's financial circumstances, and 'as a war expedient', this was allowed. Thus, Southport became the only club under League auspices ever to have a commercial name.)

League clubs not participating in the League's regional competitions in 1915/16 were Sunderland, Middlesbrough and Newcastle (for geographical reasons), Blackburn, West Bromwich, Aston Villa, Wolves and Birmingham (mainly for ideological reasons), all

five London clubs (who joined with Southern League clubs to form the London Combination), and Bristol City, who complained to the Management Committee about feeling rather left out. In 1916/17 Birmingham joined the Midland section, and Newcastle and Blackburn joined the Lancashire section.

Ever anxious to stay involved as much as possible, a skeleton Committee vetted the rules for the Lancashire and Midlands regional groups, appointed referees, approved insurance schemes, and reminded clubs 'that the same honest spirit of effort will be looked for as in the usual League games'.

But old habits died hard, and the Committee men simply couldn't resist continuing their role as guardians of the game. In fact, apart from the almost total lack of transfers, the Management Committee (albeit never actually calling itself that) seemed to carry on its routine work as if nothing had changed.

For example, despite the wartime conditions, it scolded Bradford for having put their assistant trainer in goal for the start of a game at Sheffield Wednesday and then substituting him when their regular 'keeper, Scattergood, finally arrived.

Additionally, it was so determined the public should never be given the impression that any individual was living off the game that when Derby wanted to field one of their players whom they also happened to be paying for other services, permission was refused.

From October 1915 the Management Committee split into two groups to supervise each regional section, reporting directly back to Tom Charnley in Preston. Often these reports were just jotted down on hotel notepaper, and in one such report came the sad news that Vice President Harry Keys' son had been killed while serving with the navy.

Human suffering apart, the war was forever creating new problems. Clubs couldn't raise eleven players, or find dates when all the workers would be off duty. In January 1918 the Government banned the use of petrol-driven vehicles in connection with sport, except where life or limb was endangered. In the winter months games were restricted to eighty minutes, often without a half-time break if the referee considered the light was poor.

Long or short, the games were at least fulfilling the function for which they were intended – entertaining the public. Indeed, some commentators who had criticized the general standard of play before the war suggested that because players were now playing only for fun, without hope of remuneration or reward, the games were much more enjoyable.

Often, players were so keen to play that they were known to go straight from an arduous night shift to a game. One player paid for such enthusiasm with his life. Bob Benson of Arsenal had just finished a seventeen-hour shift in the Woolwich munitions factory when he took his family to watch a game at Highbury. When an Arsenal player failed to turn up, Benson took his place, despite being tired, unfit and ill prepared. Just before half time he was seen retiring to the dressing room, where his heart gave out. His last wish was for the game to go on.

A total of £400 was raised for Benson's family, and, indeed, throughout the war football clubs and supporters contributed large amounts to charity. The main beneficiary was the Red Cross, who were given a fully equipped ambulance called 'The Football League', costing £600. The YMCA received £250 for a special tent, which was also named after the League.

While giving freely itself, the League's own funds were maintained by a 1 per cent levy on gate receipts, introduced in 1916. Thus was established a principle which has survived until today (although the amounts have varied throughout the years). An extra 5 per cent was added to the levy for charities, dropping to 4 per cent in 1917/18.

In addition, each club was required to pay 20 per cent of its gate money to the visitors in the Principal Competition (which took the first half of the season), and to donate 20 per cent of takings in the later Subsidiary Competition to a pool which was then divided equally among the members.

Although forced upon the clubs because of the war, the principle of pooling a percentage of gates for the greater good, which would have been rejected out of hand before 1914, proved in post-war years to be one the most unifying and beneficial measures the League had ever taken.

Again, the credit for its introduction must go to Charles Sutcliffe.

Meanwhile, admissions rose from 6d to 9d because of the introduction of the so-called Amusement or Entertainment Tax, introduced as a wartime measure on 1 October 1917 (and not lifted until half a century later).

The Annual Meeting of 1917 brought the first changes on the Management Committee since 1912, with the deaths of two members, John Cameron of Newcastle and Tom Harris of Notts County. The President, Vice Presidents and the four remaining members were all re-elected unopposed, the two vacant places being filled by John Oliver of Newcastle, and, after fifteen years of trying, Fred Rinder of Aston Villa.

It was his rightful place. Rinder was one of the surviving pioneers of the League, along with John Bentley and John Lewis. He had accompanied William McGregor during the attempts to form the League back in 1887, and had attended the very first meetings. So there was no prouder man than Rinder on that July afternoon at the Grand Hotel, Manchester – with the possible exception only of the Arsenal chairman, who had just been knighted. Sir Henry Norris was warmly congratulated. After all, the League had never before been honoured by the presence of a knight.

There was a change in the voting system in 1917. Rather than every Committee member having to stand for election each year, in future the three junior members and the junior Vice President would come up for election one year, then the other three members and the senior Vice President the year after. The President would stand for election every two years. Although hardly a radical measure, since precedent amply demonstrated how few personnel changes were demanded by the clubs anyway, the new system did at least guarantee some measure of continuity.

The First World War ended on 11 November 1918, eight weeks after the start of the season. The war everyone hoped would be 'the war to end all wars' was over, and Britain entered into two days of riotous celebration.

It is difficult to confirm exactly how many players and officials of League clubs died in the war. The League itself kept no record, although casualties were occasionally mentioned. The most comprehensive list appeared in *Athletic News*, which gave the names of forty-four players who had given their lives. These included Donald Bell of Bradford, who was awarded a posthumous Victoria Cross for his bravery on the Somme. Clapton Orient's loss of three players was the greatest for any one club.

But no club was able simply to switch from a war footing to normal operations overnight, so that however great the spontaneous desire of some to return immediately to the *status quo ante bellum*, the Committee urged caution.

It was agreed that there was little point in rearranging the fixtures to provide for a normal League season, but several clubs wanted at least to end all the wartime regulations so that they could pay their players the full rate once again.

Speaking at length against any such hasty plans, at a Special General Meeting in Manchester on 29 November, Charles Sutcliffe warned: 'Before clubs can pay normal wages they must get back to normal gates and normal players.' Clubs had to remember not only those players who 'had been loyal to their country and played the Greater Game' – not all of whom would be fit enough or still young enough to carry on where they had left off –

but also those men who had kept the clubs going during the war. The needs of both sets of players had to be carefully considered.

Instead, suggested Sutcliffe, since few clubs could afford wages for the time being, it was better to continue paying 2s 6d for each training session plus £1 expenses for each match. Gates were already on the increase after the armistice, he said, and a return to normality could not be far off. 'Be patient!' was his message.

Support for the FA was also discussed. Since the FA depended largely on Cup and international receipts – non-existent since 1915 – and had given most of its money to the war effort, in 1918 the League had leapt to its rescue with a grant of £1000. How ironic that the League, from being disowned by so many gentlemen at the FA in 1888, should now prove to be its saviour.

One of the men who had worked hard to put the League into such a strong position was John Bentley, and one of the great sorrows of that first post-war gathering in Manchester was that Bentley had not lived to see the dawn of peace.

Bentley had been an active man since his retirement from the presidency in 1910. He had continued to attend Management Committee meetings, and after being made a Life Member of the League he spent four years at Old Trafford as secretary, finally retiring in 1916 when he was fifty-six.

A year later, he found his wife of thirty-five years dead at home, and was said never to have recovered from his grief. As McGregor had done, he sought refuge with his daughter, in Lytham, but his health deteriorated rapidly. He rallied the following autumn, and told a friend; 'See you at Turton Fair', an annual event he had rarely missed since his childhood. Three days before the fair he was paid a visit by a footballer friend, George Livingstone, who was home on leave from active duty, and it was Livingstone who saw him die the following morning, on 2 September 1918.

So it was that while the guns in Europe fired their last salvoes of the long, drawn-out war, in perfect peace at Turton's hilltop graveyard, J. J. Bentley was laid to rest next to his beloved wife Betsy and their son Harry, who had died, aged two, in December 1892. Looking on were all the great names of football, including all the Management Committee (apart from Sutcliffe, who was ill), Billy Meredith and J. A. H. Catton, Bentley's successor at *Athletic News*. The grave was a stone's throw from both the house where JJ had been born and brought up and from the football pitch where Turton FC had set him off on a lifetime's work in football.

Standing in that graveyard today, the scene seems so little changed that it's hard to believe that seventy years have passed. And as the wind swirls about the blackened headstones, one almost imagines that the sound of a farmer's voice from a nearby field is instead the squire's son, J. C. Kay, calling to the Bentley brothers in their terraced cottage for another practice of this new game he'd learnt at Harrow.

* * *

Three other issues faced the League at this crucial point in its history.

First, as the *Manchester Evening Chronicle* put it, 'How are all these uncontrolled clubs which have sprung into life to be brought into the official fold?' The clubs referred to were Rochdale, Southport Vulcan, Chesterfield, Rotherham County, and in the final wartime season, Coventry City.

Secondly, the Players' Union reformed itself after the war and decided that, in common with other trade unions, it now wanted to retain the right to strike. As in 1909/10, to the authorities this radical approach smacked of dangerous extremism, and even worse, since 1917, possibly of Bolshevism.

Finally, on 6 January 1919, a deputation from the Southern League put to the Management Committee a proposal that the Football League take over all its members, either as a third division or as a regionalized second division. In effect, they were offering their total submission.

But why the self-sacrifice? The plain truth was that during the First World War the Southern League committee had been apathetic. It let its members fend for themselves, gave out no official advice, and took no part in organizing the London Combination.

Athletic News also noted pointedly that while the League gave £1000 to the FA, the southern clubs contributed only £105. 'The one is a handsome sum and the other is – well, not quite so handsome. We say no more.'

So, while the League emerged in 1918 as a strong, confident organization with almost complete mastery of its members (if not its players), the Southern League was apparently ready to throw in the towel.

The difference between the two leagues was quite simple. The Southern League committee had depended entirely upon J. B. Skeggs of Millwall, and he had been wrapped up in war work since 1914 (for which he was awarded an OBE). The League's Management Committee also had members heavily committed to the war effort. But it had the one man who kept the League alive and strong – Charles Sutcliffe.

So, before we see how the League emerged from the clouds of war to a new era in 1919, let us discover more of this remarkable little lawyer from Lancashire.

John Bentley had certainly never doubted Sutcliffe's voracious capacity for hard work. Once, when the Management Committee had been gathered at Lytham to work out an insurance scheme with fellow officials of the Scottish and Southern Leagues, Bentley had announced: 'It's a beautiful day gentlemen, much too fine to be cooped up here. I move that Mr Sutcliffe and Mr MacAndrew (of the Scottish League) be asked to draft a scheme and submit same on our return . . .' And with that, Bentley led the party off for a drive on the seafront.

Most men would have fumed at such treatment. Possibly MacAndrew did. But not Charlie Sutcliffe. It would be fairly certain that when the others did return, not only had he drawn up a scheme but, furthermore, he had probably enjoyed himself a lot more than Bentley's party.

CHAPTER TEN

Charles Sutcliffe – the Little Lawyer from Lancashire

*B*y 1918 Charles Edward Sutcliffe, 'CE' or 'Charlie' to his friends, was an exhausted man. The strain of the war and of all his unpaid efforts to keep the League intact had led him to a breakdown. It was hardly surprising. He looked a frail man; so small, so thin, that it's hard to believe that he ever commanded such power or achieved so much. If it hadn't been for the outbreak of war, Sutcliffe admitted in 1918, he would almost certainly have given up his football work (although he never explained why).

Speaking in a tribute to Sutcliffe's twenty-one years' work on the Committee, in July 1919, the Manchester City secretary/manager Ernest Mangnall called him 'one of the greatest Leaguers, one of the greatest workers, and one of the most gifted men our game has ever known'.

With the benefit of greater hindsight we can go further, and say that with the possible exception only of Alan Hardaker, the League's secretary from 1957–79, no man ever had a deeper or longer lasting impact on the League than Charles Sutcliffe.

By the time it came for Mangnall to pay his tribute to Sutcliffe in 1919, the little lawyer from Lancashire had recovered his health sufficiently to attend a reception at the Grand Hotel, Manchester, where he was presented with a massive silver rose bowl and a cheque for £426, which had been raised among the clubs in gratitude for his wartime efforts. (It could have been more, since several players, referees, linesmen and other organizations had wanted to contribute.)

If not for Sutcliffe, Mangnall said, there would have been no football during the war. But his devotion went much further back than 1914. From the time of his first election in 1898, Sutcliffe had been 'in at everything'. Always at the beck and call of everyone, 'any knotty points that required elucidation, any rule that required interpretation has almost invariably been referred to Mr Sutcliffe....' Mangnall went on to say:

'I don't think I am going too far when I say that, in a sense, he has been regarded as The League, and the great wonder to me and to all of us is how he has managed to cope with the work. Money could not have paid him for what he has done, for I am sure no paid official would have put in the time, care and thought that the demands of the League have made upon Mr Sutcliffe.

A record of his daily day would be worth reading. Physically as well as intellectually he must be something of a marvel.... The name of Mr Charles E. Sutcliffe will live on in football history, and will always be honoured. His work will live after him.'

Mangnall was quite right. To Charles Sutcliffe the League is still indebted, because in many ways the League of today is the League for which Sutcliffe laid the foundations.

It was Sutcliffe who worked out the details of four expansion programmes, in 1898, 1905, 1919 and 1920–3, taking the League from thirty-two clubs to eighty-eight. When the League was called upon to investigate its legal responsibilities towards the insurance and welfare of injured or retired players, Sutcliffe undertook the task and brought about the formation of the Football League's Mutual Insurance Federation. This was the first legal bond between the League and its players, a bond which has survived until the present day.

It was Sutcliffe's idea, too, to set up the Jubilee Fund, which led after his death to the foundation of the Provident Fund. Both these measures, flawed though they became in later years, represented real improvements in the players' lot.

But Sutcliffe's major concern was the preservation of clubs so that the League could remain 'a family', supporting both rich and poor. This was the prime motivation in the 1890s when Sutcliffe, with T. H. Sidney of Wolverhampton Wanderers, successfully defended the transfer system against the opposition of men such as Charles Clegg at the FA. Then, in 1912, Sutcliffe almost single-handedly organized the League's defence of the retain and transfer system in the Kingaby case.

When the First World War broke out, despite the fact that he was already contemplating giving up football, it was Sutcliffe who drew up the emergency regulations which effectively kept most clubs in business and allowed wartime regional football to proceed. Had the League slipped into the background, as did the Southern League during this crucial period, it would almost certainly have become a fragmented and weakened organization by 1918.

Instead, guided by Sutcliffe, the League emerged strong enough to become a truly national body, absorbing all those leading professional clubs which had until then remained beyond the League's jurisdiction.

In addition, in the immediate post-war period, Sutcliffe more or less rescued the Lancashire FA, reorganized it, and by introducing a new cup made it profitable enough to buy its own premises (he had already set up the Lancashire Combination and donated its first trophy, worth £40).

The First World War also found Sutcliffe in court on several occasions in connection with the Enoch West case. West was one of the Manchester United players banned *sine die* for their part in rigging the game against Liverpool on Good Friday 1915. West took the League to court over the matter, lost his case, then made an appeal and lost a second time. On each occasion, as a leading member of the original commission of enquiry, Sutcliffe gave evidence.

Sutcliffe also undertook another interesting legal case during the war. We may recall how a Mr F. N. Charrington was forcibly evicted from Craven Cottage in September 1914 after trying to speak out against wartime football. Charrington eventually sued the two men who had shown him the door, Fulham's secretary/manager Phil Kelso and their chairman, W. G. Allen. Sutcliffe won the case and Charrington had to pay two guineas costs.

Finally, and just as importantly, Sutcliffe took on, quite voluntarily, the two enormously complicated tasks of organizing referee appointments and drawing up League fixtures. In fact, it was Sutcliffe's own scheme for compiling the fixtures upon which the League and Central League depended entirely between about 1915 and 1968 (when computers took over – see p. 366 ff.), based on a system of charts which he guarded jealously. Few other people ever saw the charts, and few would have understood them either. Once a year, Charles shut himself away in his office for a couple of days to draw up the fixtures, calling only upon his son and daughter for help.

Journalist Ivan Sharpe reported that Sutcliffe would often work out the fixtures while sitting on a bench in Lord Street, Southport, near the bandstand, 'poring over pieces of card that looked like a pocket chessboard'. It is a charming image, but although Sharpe knew Sutcliffe well, the family have no recollection of Charles ever tackling the fixtures 'away from home'. Wherever he did work, though, when he died in 1939 he bequeathed those precious pieces of card to his son Harold.

If we add to these achievements a further list of Charles Sutcliffe's football commitments, it becomes apparent just how great his capacities were. Apart from his long-standing devotion to the League and to Burnley, Sutcliffe was active in the Lancashire FA, becoming its president in 1926 (in succession to John Lewis), and for the FA (for whose Council he held little regard), where he worked on the Referees' Committee, International Selection Committee and Rules Revision Committee.

He was also on the International League Board and the Anglo-Irish League Board. He was president of the Northern Counties Amateur Championship, served on the Appeals Committees of about twenty different leagues, and just in case anyone thought he was shirking his parochial duties, he was chairman, then vice president of Rossendale United.

But the League was always his first love, and those who knew him said that he never really cared for the FA. Ivan Sharpe tells this story to illustrate the point (in *Forty Years in Football*, Hutchinsons, 1952):

'One evening I was sitting beside Sutcliffe in the official motor-coach after an International match at West Bromwich. Into the coach came B. A. Glanvill, a gentleman of the old school – buttonhole, genial bearing, white hair, revered figure on the Stock Exchange.

"Who does he represent?", someone whispered.

"The Public Schools."

"Who do we represent?"

"The public houses," C. E. Sutcliffe quietly intervened.'

As Sharpe added, Sutcliffe was of the harder, northern school. He was a man of the people, and proud of it.

Apart from football and the law, Sutcliffe was also keen on cricket. As a youth he played for Burnley CC (whose ground adjoins Turf Moor), and on one occasion guested for the touring Australians when they were a man short. In later life he became a vice president of Rawtenstall CC.

As F. Hargreaves wrote in the *History of the Lancashire FA 1878–1928*: 'How he, in addition to being engaged in a large legal practice, can find time to devote to all the football matches, meetings, functions, etc., is a mystery to his closest friends.'

But fit them in he did, for Sutcliffe never seems to have taken on a position without giving it his best. In 1926/7 he attended all fifty-eight meetings of the Lancashire FA. At the League's Annual Meeting in 1920, Sutcliffe admitted that in his twenty-one years on the Management Committee he had missed two meetings; one because he was in London for the Kingaby case, the other, he had to confess, because of his own work commitments. It was still on his conscience, he said and he probably wasn't joking.

Will Cuff wrote of Sutcliffe in 1938:

'He does not know the meaning of idleness. I doubt even if he can relax. Some subject, some new plan for the betterment of the League or the game keeps him in a constant state of activity.... Often I have watched him when a perplexing matter has been under review and he has sat silently listening to others. Was he pitying their lack of understanding and waiting puckishly to reveal it, or simply taking his own time to reach a decision? I could never be sure, but on occasions it has seemed as if he has taken a delight to wait his opportunity to show how much better was his own way to deal with the matter.'

This indefatigable man, Charles Sutcliffe, was born in Burnley in 1864, one of four sons of a prominent local solicitor, John Sutcliffe. The whole family were achievers, heavily influenced by a strict Methodist upbringing. On Sundays there were no games and Charles was never allowed to read a newspaper at home. He appears to have developed only one vice, and that was tobacco. He smoked up to sixty Senior Service cigarettes a day.

For the first thirty years of his life, Charles seems to have followed in the footsteps of his elder brother Arthur. Both played for a rugby club called Burnley Rovers, which in 1882 decided to switch to the Association code, and thus became Burnley FC. Both were early committee members, and Charles was one of Burnley's first directors in 1897. Arthur was at one time club secretary, and later the club's solicitor. Both brothers qualified as solicitors and went into their father's office, and both later became Football League referees.

Charles' playing career ended in the 1880s, probably around 1886 when he qualified as a solicitor. His last game, he recalled, was against Blackburn at their old Leamington Road ground. As a left-half, Sutcliffe was detailed to mark Joe Lofthouse, Rovers' international forward. 'It was months before I got rid of the bruises I collected. I shall never forget it. I am not suggesting that Lofthouse was unfair. I had nothing to complain of, but the top and bottom of it was, I could not stop him.'

If fame never came his way as a player, Sutcliffe soon made up for it as a referee. Yet his career with the whistle came about purely by accident.

According to his own reminiscence – Sutcliffe was an inveterate story-teller who seemed to change his facts according to the listener – one afternoon, Burnley and Preston North End were kicking the ball about at Turf Moor waiting impatiently for the referee to arrive.

'*Major Sudell and Mr Tom Heaton, who was then the treasurer of the Burnley club, came to me in the stand, explained the difficulty and invited me to referee the game. I dissented, because I had never refereed a game in my life. Major Sudell soon made me feel quite at home by saying, "You know the laws of the game. I am sure you are competent and honest and that is all we want".*

I consented. Burnley lost, and as I left the field a section of the crowd desired to express their view of my conduct of the game and declared that I had backed Preston. Major Sudell came to me and in the spirit so significant of a true sportsman assured me that I had convinced him that I should make good as a referee and advised me to take it up seriously.'

Sutcliffe took Sudell's advice, and no doubt that of his brother Arthur, who was already a referee, and joined the League's list in 1891.

Despite his small stature, Sutcliffe proved to be a fearless referee. Once, at Ewood Park on 5 September 1896, he had sufficient conviction to disallow *six* goals in succession, during Blackburn's 1-0 win against Liverpool. As 'Quiz' in *Athletic News* commented: 'The fact that the ball was put into the net seven times for one goal is, I fancy, something like a record. I think it is only fair to add that there could be no doubts about the justice of Mr Sutcliffe's decision.'

There were plenty of doubts about his decisions in a game between Sunderland and Small Heath, however, after which, legend has it, he was forced to escape from the ground disguised as a policeman, no small feat for such a small-footed man! According to Sutcliffe, several hundred Sunderland youths made their way to his dressing room, 'evidently with no friendly intentions'.

As there were several piles of stones lying nearby for the repair of the roads, it was deemed inadvisable for Sutcliffe to face the mob so, on the suggestion of Inspector Watson, he donned an officer's overcoat and helmet, and was thus able to nip out from another gate into a waiting taxi cab.

Sutcliffe apparently presented a 'grotesque appearance' in the oversized coat and helmet. His stiff, upright shirt collar was quite visible underneath the coat, and no sooner had he leapt into the cab than someone in the crowd spotted the ruse. But before they could catch up with him, the driver whipped up his steed and transported the unfortunate fugitive to safety.

It made for a wonderful after-dinner story, but since Charlie was known to love a good yarn and be prone to embellishment, he was

Sutcliffe's getaway from the Sunderland mob, recalled in the Liverpool Echo.

phone in Lord Street, Rawtenstall, was forever ringing with enquiries from referees as to their appointments. Mabel Sutcliffe, who helped in the office, recalls one man who was on the supplementary list anxiously telephoning every Saturday on the offchance of a game.

Sutcliffe once said: 'All referees are good, and all are bad. A referee only needs to make one mistake, or an assumed mistake, against a club and if he lives till he is a hundred he never gets over it.'

After giving up refereeing in 1898, Sutcliffe was immediately elected on to the Management Committee. One of his first contributions was to propose the abolition of the test matches. No doubt the involvement of his own club, Burnley, in that fraudulent match at Stoke hurt him deeply. Indeed, all his life Sutcliffe fought against corruption with the ardour of an evangelist and the nous of a detective. Once, he and John Lewis tracked down the perpetrators of a football scandal by following an anonymous tip-off which led to the dressing room of a famous performer at a London music-hall.

In 1900 Charles left Burnley, but not because of football. His brother Arthur dispatched him to a new branch of the family law firm in Crawshawbooth, between Burnley and Rawtenstall, apparently jealous that Charles had proved such a success that most clients were now asking for his services. A year later, Charles moved again a mile or so down the hill to the centre of Rawtenstall, where he soon became one of the busiest solicitors in this small, but then thriving mill town (there is still a C. E. Sutcliffe solicitor's office in Bank Street, Rawtenstall).

Charles was said to have loved court work, being so adept with words that he would often gain an acquittal completely against the odds. In time everyone in Rawtenstall came to know him, and it was generally recognized that had he not neglected his practice so much because of football, he could have become an extremely wealthy man. Even so, he was a regular at Burnley police courts, and when he

often asked if the Sunderland incident really happened. Being a mischievous sort of man at times, he was known to reply with a twinkle in his eye, 'Why spoil a good story?' But the events related did happen (although sometimes the location was given as Birmingham), and as his daughter Mabel recalls, the family all enjoyed a huge laugh when he returned home safely to tell the tale.

Unlike John Lewis, as a referee Sutcliffe never achieved the ultimate accolade, the chance to officiate at a Cup Final, but for four years he did referee every home international match in which England were not playing.

Sutcliffe retired to the touchline in 1898 and continued as a linesman in League matches until 1907. Thereafter, he was seen running the line at Inter-League matches until 1914 (when he was fifty), and once in an emergency at a League match at Blackburn in 1912.

As with everything else he became involved in, Sutcliffe could not resist tackling the problems facing match officials. Thus, he was a founder member of the Referees' Union, and was its first president. In 1909 he drew up a system of appointments by which no referee had to visit the same ground twice in a season.

Because of this involvement, his office tele-

retired from the law in 1936 he received a warm letter of appreciation from the Ministry of Labour for his work with industrial cases in Rossendale.

But football always seemed to come first, even to the point where he once moved the family home to be nearer to the tram-line. Although he had his own motor car, Sutcliffe hated driving. On one occasion shortly after the First World War, he decided that he would drive his daughter Mabel and her new husband to the Cup Final in London. They had travelled only a few miles down the road when some sheep jumped in front of the car, appropriately enough at Ramsbottom, at which point his much relieved son-in-law took over the wheel. Charles never drove his car again, thus explaining why he always liked to be near to the tram-line.

The tram took him to Rawtenstall railway station (this was in the heyday of the local network) and from there, Britain was his oyster. He covered thousands of miles by railway, often returning from yet another meeting in London in the early hours of the morning and having to walk home from the station. Almost everyone else on the Committee lived on main lines, in towns large enough to have taxis awaiting them at the station, so Sutcliffe's devotion was continually tested by this early morning homeward trudge.

'On one occasion,' Sutcliffe once told Ivan Sharpe, 'I attended a Football League meeting in London on Friday and refereed an international match in Aberdeen the following day. I returned to Burnley on Sunday and on Monday refereed a League match at Newcastle.'

Wherever he travelled his pockets were always bulging with documents, and he was said to have been able to work happily in any railway compartment, which was just as well since he spent so much time in them. 'I know all the telegraph posts by Christian name', he once joked.

In May 1902 all this might so easily have come to an end when he lost his seat on the Management Committee (less through unpopularity, one suspects, than owing to limitations in the system of divisional representation). Forever needing to be involved, he hovered in the background, continuing to offer advice and legal back-up. But perhaps this wasn't enough, because the following March Sutcliffe stood for a seat on the Rawtenstall town council, losing by a single vote. Two months later he was back on the Management Committee, but by then he had obviously become too involved in local affairs to back out completely. So in November 1903 he stood again for the council, and this time was elected unopposed.

In both his politics and religion, Charles, and indeed Arthur Sutcliffe, showed striking similarities to William McGregor. Firstly, the brothers were both active Liberals, as was the founder of the League. Charles, in particular, rose to become president of the local Liberal party and as a town councillor gave much support to Rossendale's Liberal MP, Sir Louis Harcourt, before the First World War. In 1905 he was appointed an alderman, a role he fulfilled until 1911, and for one year, 1906–7, he was deputy mayor. So when he said in 1918 that he had been on the point of giving up football in 1914, it may well have been to pursue a political career.

Like McGregor, the Sutcliffe brothers were also devout Methodists, and like both McGregor and John Lewis, both campaigned ardently for the Temperance Movement. Indeed, as a youth Charles was a leading member of the Curzon Street Mission's minstrel troupe in Burnley. He taught in Sunday School, once gave evidence to a Royal Commission on the problem of alcoholism, and having served his apprenticeship in the Langholme Methodist Church in Rawtenstall, Charles became a much sought after speaker on religion, the Temperance Movement and, of course, football.

Clearly, therefore, Sutcliffe had much in

common with his fellow members when he joined the Management Committee. T. H. Sidney was also active in local politics, Harry Radford was a corporation official, Walter Hart was another teetotaller, and G. H. Leavey of Arsenal, it is thought, was a Liberal. John Lewis and Sutcliffe shared the experience of having been somewhat controversial referees, and Walter Bellamy, whose family firm produced health-enhancing mineral water, was a League linesman. Amongst all these clean-living, upstanding citizens, Josh Parlby, a larger-than-life publican from Manchester, must have been either a breath of fresh air or a pariah. (Whatever his standing, he stood down in 1899.)

We have seen how Sutcliffe helped keep the League alive during the First World War. Afterwards, once he had recovered from illness, Sutcliffe returned to the offensive, as we shall see in the following chapters. Although John McKenna remained President until his death in 1936, Sutcliffe was undoubtedly the power behind the throne. He continued to make all the difficult speeches, force through several unpopular measures and fight the hardest for the League's rights.

But all this hyperactivity leads one to ask certain questions about the restless, chain-smoking figure of Charles Sutcliffe. What was it that drove him so hard, and was he, like other unusually energetic individuals, a rather unlikeable or unsympathetic character? No man was ever presented with so much silverware by the League or FA – caskets, cutlery (two sets), plates, bowls and so on – but were these gifts given in gratitude and respect rather than affection?

Sutcliffe's personal life may help to shed some light on his apparent dynamism. However much he was driven by his religious and political ideals, it is doubtful whether he'd have thrown himself so wholeheartedly into work had he not been married to a woman who can at best be described as an invalid, but was more probably a hypochondriac.

Annie Sutcliffe took no interest in football, which is entirely excusable, but she also paid very little attention to either her husband or her children. She had her breakfast in bed every morning, spent the afternoon asleep, and only got up after tea to do a little baking.

As a result, she and Charles led separate lives. But was she led to this type of existence by the fact that her Charlie was never at home? Or that he was a chain-smoking workaholic? Like the wives of so many of the leading football figures at this time, she would have been almost totally excluded from his male-dominated world. When they married he was simply a young solicitor who liked football. Only when he was about thirty-five did the real marathon begin. Perhaps her indifference drove him to it. Perhaps she simply gave up, unable to fight any longer against his obsessive devotion to the game.

But Sutcliffe was not a cold man. He was loyal and generous to his close friends and doted upon his daughter Mabel, who in many ways fulfilled her mother's role as his companion. Fortunately for Charles, Mabel loved football (her brothers did not) and gladly accompanied him every Saturday afternoon, to Burnley, Bury, or often to Preston, where he met up with his lifelong friend Tom Charnley.

As a child Mabel often went with her father to meetings, and when she was older, she accompanied him on social occasions. She would spend hours with him in his office, often until two o'clock in the morning, typing up referees' lists or fixtures, and in 1913, when she was sixteen, the Management Committee presented her with a watch bracelet 'as a token of their esteem' for all her work.

Mabel remembers how, after each game, her father would sit on the train feverishly writing a match report which would have to be delivered to a Manchester newspaper by 6.00 p.m. Sutcliffe was a regular correspondent on football matters, in common with all the early leading figures of the League, and as to be expected it was *Athletic News* which published most of his articles, ones which invariably attempted to explain some obtuse point of League regulations. He didn't have Bentley's style nor McGregor's flow, but he wrote clearly and in depth, and it would certainly be unfair to judge his writing by the 1938 *Story of the Football League*, a badly arranged book full of dull, convoluted passages. Sutcliffe was old and infirm by the time he compiled that book, and in the end was too ill to complete it.

Probably Charles' greatest skill was in his oratory, the power of which lay not so much in its volume or its humour (which was described as 'homely') as in its appeal to reason. It was a style which apparently came over well in occasional broadcasts, and many was the time he would use his gift to rally the clubs or cajole them into accepting some unpleasant home truths. And many was the time John McKenna would step aside to let Sutcliffe do the explaining.

Perhaps this explains why Sutcliffe was known variously as 'the brains of football' or the 'football dictator'. William Pickford, a leading figure at the FA, described Sutcliffe as 'quiet, and yet with an incisive way of piling up convincing arguments in debate. Charlie's "A moment, please" has often heralded a statement always commanding attention.'

Another man who knew him well said: 'He knew how to speak quiet words of praise, encouragement or appreciation, or he could demolish opponents by logic, cold facts and sometimes sarcasm.'

But he could arouse passions also. When Burnley were once at a very low ebb in the 1930s, he was said to have rekindled the town's enthusiasm with a stirring speech at a public meeting.

Annie Sutcliffe died in November 1924, when Charles was aged sixty. Many of his fellow Committee men also outlived their wives – for example McGregor, Bentley, McKenna, Rinder and Charnley – but Sutcliffe decided a couple of years later to remarry. His second wife was an old friend and former housekeeper, Miss Pickup, whom the family suspected was after Charles' money. If this was true her plans came to nought, for she died in January 1932. Thereafter, Sutcliffe depended on his family. His eldest son Frank had died in Canada, Mabel was now married with children – upon whom he lavished affection – and Harold, who followed his father into the legal profession, was also tragically bereaved in 1933 when his young wife died (although he later remarried, and carried on his father's fixture work until his death in 1967).

The last few years of Sutcliffe's life were a mixture of great disappointment and deep satisfaction. First, his ardent advocacy of Will Cuff's proposal for a two-referee system floundered in 1935 when the clubs voted against it. He was upset by this, and by the fact that McKenna was the only one on the Committee to oppose it. 'The referee now needs a Bluebird car to keep up with play', Sutcliffe had argued in a broadcast. One club official's response was: 'It's bad enough with one referee, never mind two!'

Then, in 1936 Sutcliffe initiated, fought and lost the so-called Pools War (of which more later), and thus bore the brunt of much hostility from several clubs. But in the same year he did at least achieve the ambition for which he'd waited so long when he was unanimously elected President of the League, a role to which he lent great dignity during the Jubilee celebrations in 1938.

Despite his age, he supervised almost every element of these celebrations, particularly the foundation of a £100,000 Jubilee Fund to help players once their careers were over. Afterwards, he admitted to the Burnley Annual Meeting that he was 'dead tired'. The hardest work, he remarked, had been to shake hands with 1600 people.

Eight months after this, his proudest moment, Charles Sutcliffe died, on 11 January 1939. If he had been 'football's iron leader', as some had written, he certainly didn't want for any respect or affection. A crowd of 11,000 sang 'Abide with Me' and stood in silence at Turf Moor the following Saturday. At his funeral, the cameras of Gaumont British Newsreel filmed enormous crowds lining the road from Langholme Methodist Church to Rawtenstall Cemetery, where his coffin was borne by four Burnley players.

Five cars were needed just to carry the wreaths, and hardly a League club was unrepresented. Dignitaries had travelled hundreds of miles, some from Ireland and Scotland. The procession brought Rawtenstall to a complete halt.

On his grave are engraved the words 'President of the Football League'. Sutcliffe had been so proud of this title that on his deathbed he asked, had a successor been appointed yet? Assured that no such step had been taken, he replied that in that case he could die as he'd wished, still President of the Football League.

At his funeral the Methodist minister said, 'It is almost true to say that he lived and died for football.' It is fitting, therefore, to conclude this chapter with a story about Charles Sutcliffe which expresses rather poignantly something of his devotion, his times and the people with whom he dealt.

(I have chosen Sutcliffe's version as told to 'Jax' of the *Rossendale Free Press* in preference to the one he related to Ivan Sharpe, if only because the former, no doubt embellished by Sutcliffe, is by far the richer.)

As we learned before, Sutcliffe was in charge of referees' appointments, not just for the League but for many competitions in Lancashire. One Christmas Eve shortly after he'd given up the whistle himself, he received a call from a referee who had fallen ill. Knowing he couldn't find a replacement at such short notice during the holiday period, Sutcliffe replied wearily, 'Well, I'll have to go myself.'

So he cancelled his plans to spend Christmas Day with the family, and set off in the freezing cold at nine o'clock in the morning to catch a long, slow, stopping train which deposited him in some small Lancashire town at noon. After whiling away the next couple of hours in the deserted streets – no pubs for him, remember – he refereed the match and afterwards, as always, told the club they could keep his fee and expenses. (Like John Lewis, he never once pocketed his refereeing dues.) The club secretary thanked him heartily, put the money in the players' Christmas box, and then asked, 'Will tha have some 'ot-pot with us in t'dressing room?'

Sutcliffe accepted the offer gratefully, and then at five o'clock started to wend his lonely way down the long, dark lane which led to the railway station. The only illumination came from Christmas lights peeping through the curtains of nearby houses, from where he could hear the sound of Christmas parties in full swing.

At the station he had to wait an hour for the train. There was no fire in the waiting room, and as he paced up and down the dimly-lit platform to keep warm, he said to himself, 'I have left my family and can't get home until nine o'clock. I must be fond of football to make such a sacrifice as this. Still, it was nice of the club to provide that hot-pot. . . .'

At that point came the sound of a man scurrying down the lane towards the railway station. It was the club secretary.

'Oh Mr Sutcliffe,' he gasped breathlessly in the cold evening air, 'Ahm reet glad ah caught thee. Tha's forgotten to pay us for th'ot-pot!'

CHAPTER ELEVEN
Southern Comforts

Like so many important phases in the history of the League, the post-war era began at the Grand Hotel, Manchester, on 13 January 1919. All forty clubs attended the meeting, plus the five clubs co-opted during the war, and, for the first time in an official capacity, representatives of the reconstituted Players' Union (including Charlie Roberts of Oldham and Jesse Pennington of West Bromwich).

The union attended to join the debate on players' wages. John McKenna stated that clubs still couldn't afford normal wages, not even £2–3 a week, and that anyway he was not prepared to deal with the union if it insisted on retaining a 'right to strike' clause. The League, he said, could not contemplate the possibility of a sudden strike with a crowd of 30,000 spectators waiting for a game.

Had the players chosen to be militant at that moment, the inter-war period might have been very different. In the event they were divided. After considering McKenna's statement, they returned to the meeting to announce that they had passed a resolution asking for players' expenses to be doubled to £2 per week and for clubs to be permitted to pay above that amount if able.

Considering that they were talking not about wages or bonuses, but merely a token sum for expenses, and considering that gates were rising sharply in the euphoria of the immediate post-war period, these demands hardly betokened Bolshevism.

But when placed in context with the union's adoption of the strike clause, even these mild demands were seen as potentially dangerous. Some of the players were anxious, too. One of them, H. T. W. Hardinge, announced to the

League meeting that he and the players representing London clubs had decided not to associate with the strike clause 'and by doing so had dropped forthwith the old trade union influence in their London movement'. (If Charlie Roberts did not mutter 'scab' under his breath, no doubt many politicized supporters did when they read reports of the meeting.)

With that, the players and the press were asked to leave, and Charles Sutcliffe stood up to evaluate the financial welfare of the clubs. His suggestion was as follows: if every club paid each player £2, as Roberts had proposed, ten of the well supported clubs would have to subsidize seventeen of the others. The remaining thirteen would neither pay out nor receive help. It was the typical Sutcliffe formula: the rich helping the poor, to keep the family strong.

Had such a proposal been mooted ten years earlier, it would have been rejected, no doubt. But the war had had a salutary effect on the clubs. They had grown accustomed to paying regular contributions and supporting the weaker clubs when called upon. And they had also grown to trust Sutcliffe's judgement.

The proposal was accepted, therefore, but the union's demand for a minimum wage and freedom of contract were ridiculed as pure fantasy. Sutcliffe described them as being 'as impossible as they are unreasonable'. Major Frank Buckley, who had been second-in-command of the Footballers' Battalion and was wounded in action, said: 'Fancy players talking about £6 per week minimum and not six clubs in England solvent!'

A week later, Charlie Roberts (a leading

union activist since the threatened strike of 1909) wrote in *Athletic News* that his fellow players, 'if not exactly thirsting for a fight were not altogether averse to one'. After all, during the war, club secretaries had been earning about £10 a week while the players received only meagre expenses. Calling upon the breakaway 'New Union' in London to return to the fold, he wrote: 'We are not unreasonable and we are not bloodsuckers.' He also added that both McKenna and Sutcliffe had been courteous and sympathetic towards his members.

Another player said of McKenna: 'He talked like an American. He quoted figures, income, expenditure, gates and liabilities that simply floored those who imagined the clubs were rolling in wealth and could afford to pay us the old wage right off.'

But there can be little doubt that with gates rising, some clubs did slip their players more than the stipulated £2 (rumours circulated that Everton and Manchester City players were on £4 a week).

Meanwhile, many players were still engaged in work they had taken up during the war, and this was to be actively encouraged by clubs. It reduced the players' dependence on football and at the same time, claimed some observers, helped to make them into better footballers.

After wages, next on the agenda at the 13 January meeting came the Southern League's proposals for the League to absorb all its leading clubs. But so discredited had the Southern League become during the war that *Athletic News* (still effectively the League's mouthpiece) called its proposals a 'miserable

Football club directors were maligned in 1921 as in 1988. This image of the rotund capitalist, argued the Sports Post *in Leeds, was grossly unfair. 'In the dark days of defeat, the directors' lot is not a happy one. They get an abundance of blame and very little syumpathy.*

document ... so thin that sensible men doubt very much the sincerity of its sponsors'.

The Southerners, it said, should 'set their house in order and save themselves, a much finer ambition than to hang on to the coat tails of their brethren in the Midlands and the North'.

In view of this, and the fact that League clubs were loath to rock the boat just as it was about to be relaunched, the result of the debate was the same as in April 1909: the President moved that the Southern League's proposals 'should not be entertained', and the League clubs agreed with him unanimously.

A crucial element in this response was the position of Chelsea. We may recall that the 1914/15 season left Chelsea second from bottom in the First Division, a point behind Manchester United, who had gained two points from the rigged game against Liverpool on Good Friday. There was never any question of punishing United. As a club they had been innocent and had done all within their powers to track down the villains. But, had Chelsea been relegated after this scandal, they might just have been persuaded to join a new London League. This was no idle speculation. Consider the following facts.

From 1915-19, all five League clubs from the capital had played in the London Combination and had grown used to their separation from League headquarters in Preston. In addition, the London players were also out of sorts with their more militant northern counterparts.

Bottom of the first Division in 1915 had been Tottenham, so if they and Chelsea had been relegated there would have been no London club in Division One for the first time since 1904.

Finally, Second Division Arsenal were by now heavily in debt. Even worse, their support was still insufficient to promise any immediate relief. Unless, of course, by some miracle they could be spirited into the First Division, somehow....

Of course, if that was not possible, *and* Chelsea were also rebuffed *and* Tottenham went down with them, Arsenal's powerful chairman Sir Henry Norris might just have considered risking his own club's future on a London League, formed among the wartime London Combination clubs. Only Norris could have done this. The Southern League was certainly not strong enough to organize such a major coup.

Faced with these potential threats, the Management Committee, and Sutcliffe in particular, made it absolutely clear that Chelsea were the key to unity. 'Come what may the innocent must not suffer,' said Sutcliffe. 'It is the duty of every man who loves justice to demand Chelsea's return. Wrong must not triumph over right.' And he added wearily, 'I am growing old in service, I glory in my record'; but his crowning glory would be the restoration of Chelsea. Chelsea returned his faith by vowing their own loyalty to the League, come what may.

On 22 February the Management Committee answered Sutcliffe's entreaty and agreed to propose an extension of the First Division by two clubs, thereby allowing Chelsea to keep their rightful place. All well and good, so far.

With Derby and Preston being promoted by right, that left the question of who would be the twenty-second club. Tottenham were the obvious choice, and precedent was certainly in their favour; expansion programmes in both 1898 and 1905 had seen the two bottom clubs stay up. Simple, wasn't it?

Not with Sir Henry Norris and talk of a London breakaway still in the air. Fore-

warnings of a sensation appeared as early as 13 January 1919, when *Athletic News* commented that Spurs should not stay up. Instead, promotion should be given to Arsenal as 'the oldest League club' who had been most loyal, who now faced financial difficulties and who had, after all, only just missed promotion in 1914 on goal average. All these factors seemed to weigh more heavily than the fact that Arsenal had managed only fifth place in 1915.

Athletic News continued to support Arsenal's cause right up until 10 March, when a Special General Meeting was held, again at the Grand Hotel, Manchester, to discuss the matter.

There was no objection to the expansion programme, the Committee's proposal for two divisions of twenty-two clubs each being carried unanimously. It was at the next stage that controversy arose – controversy which was to have repercussions for years to come and for which no definitive explanation has yet been found. In short, the League appeared to break with all tradition on that March afternoon in 1919 by electing Arsenal, rather than Tottenham, to the First Division. As far as we know, this was what happened.

Once the clubs had rubber stamped Chelsea's restoration, the Management Committee proposed that one club be elected from the Second Division to even up the numbers. Crucially, the Committee didn't offer the clubs a chance to discuss or even vote upon the best method of choosing this twenty-second club, as might have been expected with legalistic minds like Charles Sutcliffe's around. The Committee simply made it an open vote, which suggests that they were well prepared for a club other than Tottenham to win majority support.

Nevertheless, Tottenham were still in by far the strongest position. Although they had hardly set Division One alight since being promoted after their debut League season in 1908/9, they had at least avoided relegation until 1915. Within living memory, Tottenham's greatest achievement had been to win the FA Cup in 1901, while members of the Southern League. It was true that their ground at White Hart Lane had been in considerable disarray during the war, with industry taking up one stand and most of the pitch, but by March 1919 the damage was healing and would certainly be repaired in time for the 1919/20 season.

For their part, Arsenal's record was reasonable, if not spectacular. Relegated in 1913 – the year they arrived as unpopular intruders upon Tottenham's doorstep – they had just missed promotion on goal average in 1914 (as *Athletic News* kept reminding readers), and in 1915 finished in fifth place, above Birmingham and Hull on goal average but seven points behind second-place Preston.

Of their twenty-two seasons in the League, Arsenal had spent twelve in the lower division and unlike Spurs had no major honour to their name. But they had a weapon far mightier than trophies or tradition. They had Sir Henry Norris, one of the sharp money-men that William McGregor had warned against in 1909.

Norris, a tall, thin, domineering man with large, bull-terrier features and a white, walrus moustache, first came into contact with the League as chairman of Fulham. It was Norris who took Fulham to two successive Southern League Championships and then into the League in 1907. In 1910, he and William Hall also became directors of Arsenal, and until 1913 they effectively controlled both clubs.

We have already seen how proud the League was in 1917 to have, for the first time, a knight in its midst. By 1918 Sir Henry had become a Coalition Unionist MP for Fulham East (where he was already mayor), and thus he outshone all fellow club chairmen and members of the Management Committee, who, for all their powers, had not a fraction of Norris's wealth or influence.

By 1918 Sir Henry was in a major fix. Having ploughed £125,000 into Arsenal since 1910, he

had spirited the club to Highbury, built a new stadium and then seen the First World War rob him of any chance to recover even a small part of his investment.

As a result, Arsenal were £60,000 in debt, a huge amount for that period when one considers that the highest transfer fee up to that point had been less than £3,000. Norris needed success for his club and he needed it quickly. He still had money, but more importantly, he had influence. At a time when his was the only voice for football in Parliament, the game was subject to the new Entertainment (formerly Amusement) Tax, it was struggling for money after the war, and it needed all the allies it could muster to fight the menace of betting and re-establish its credentials after the bad press of the early war years.

In the *Official Centenary History of Arsenal* (Hamlyn, 1986), Phil Soar described Norris's strategy as 'the single most outrageous enterprise ever to be conceived in the history of English football'. His aim, wrote Soar, 'was to talk The Arsenal back into the First Division', by canvassing club chairmen and influential men in the game, by 'showing remarkable stealth and political judgement' and, one might add in cynical conjecture, by offering handsome inducements to other clubs or individuals.

Another Arsenal chronicler, Leslie Knighton, wrote of Norris: 'His influence was enormous ... [he would] speak to an important person there, suggesting a favour, remind a certain financier who was interested that he had once done him a good turn and been promised something in return.'

Above all, Norris had a great ally in the person of his friend, the League president, 'Honest John' McKenna.

Is this to suggest that McKenna was somehow not so honest after all? Almost certainly not. There is no evidence, for example, that Norris was a fellow Freemason seeking a brotherly favour and with men like Lewis and Sutcliffe on the Committee, it is inconceivable that any attempt to bribe or offer an inducement would have met with anything other than a haughty and swift rejection. Unless history has been totally and utterly deceived over the characters of these men, which seems highly unlikely, money was never a factor.

However, Sir Henry had done the League a very good turn during the war. In 1916, clubs were asked to contribute 1 per cent of their gate receipts to keep the League afloat. Because the London clubs were then outside the League's jurisdiction, there was no compulsion on their part to pay that levy. But Sir Henry Norris insisted that Arsenal would contribute, and was said to have persuaded the four other League clubs in London to do likewise. This gesture of solidarity came at a vital time for the League, and we can be fairly sure that once the war was over Norris didn't fail to remind the Committee of what had happened. In effect, they owed him a favour.

With all this in mind, we now return to the March 1919 meeting in Manchester, and the vote to see which club won First Division status.

Of those clubs nominated, the least hopeful was Nottingham Forest, who finished the 1914/15 season third from bottom of the Second Divison. Surprisingly, Forest received 3 votes. Hull City (seventh in 1915) won 1 vote (their own), Birmingham (sixth in 1915) polled 2, Wolves (fourth in 1915) received 4, and Barnsley (third in 1915) managed 5. The remaining votes were split between the two north London rivals, Tottenham and Arsenal.

At that point, the President, John McKenna, threw his weight behind Arsenal's claim. In an astonishing speech, he asserted that Arsenal should be given the remaining First Division place because of their service to the League and their longevity. On both counts he was patently twisting the facts to support his friend Norris.

In terms of 'service', it is true that during the war Arsenal had been loyal in contributing to the League and its related charities. But so

had a dozen other clubs. On an individual level, only one Arsenal official had been active in League affairs – G. H. Leavey, who sat on the Management Committee from 1901–4. So if 'service' was a criterion for winning promotion, Second Division clubs like Orient and Forest were just as, if not more, deserving.

McKenna's second assertion, that Arsenal had been members longer than Spurs, was true. But then Wolves, who finished above Arsenal in 1915, had been founder members, so why not elect them to the First Division instead?

The simple answer was that none of these clubs had a chairman like Sir Henry Norris.

When the votes were counted Tottenham had polled 8 votes, Arsenal 18. Had Spurs been better prepared they might, by canvassing the other 15 votes, have beaten Arsenal. Instead, Norris was the winner.

The real losers were not Spurs, but the League. However one massages the facts of the case, the result is always the same: the President, the Committee and the clubs had succumbed to a rich and powerful politician and property dealer. Current critics of the League may decry the present-day influence of such men in football, but never has the League been so manipulated as it was in 1919. One can only ask, what were puritanical men like Sutcliffe and Lewis doing throughout this unseemly business?

Phil Soar suggests that McKenna's backing was the deciding factor. Once clubs saw that the President 'was prepared to support so unlikely a cause', they might have assumed that there were sound reasons for Arsenal's promotion: favours to be gleaned in Parliament, gifts to the League ... no one ever put a name to the potential benefits, they simply accepted McKenna's judgement.

If financial inducements were offered to individual clubs nothing has ever been proved, and there are no surviving documents to provide clues. And although Norris was later banned from football in 1927, for financial irregularities, in 1919 it could well have been that his personality was sufficient to sway opinion.

'Everyone was afraid of Sir Henry,' remembered Leslie Knighton. 'And no wonder! I have never met his equal for logic, invective and ruthlessness against all who opposed him.'

Thus, Arsenal became the first and last club to win promotion in the Football League other than by merit, and to their credit, having reached the First Division, they have never left it – an unbroken spell unmatched by any other club.

And in case we feel too sorry for Tottenham, fired by the injustice of it all they proceeded to win the Second Division Championship in record-breaking fashion in 1920, the FA Cup in 1921, and in both 1921 and 1922 they finished above Arsenal.

Returning to the slightly stunned Manchester gathering in 1919, there was one other set of elections, for the four extra places in the Second Division. This time, however, there was no controversy.

Eight clubs applied: the five co-opted members from the war, plus West Ham (from the Southern League), South Shields (North-Eastern League) and Port Vale (Central League).

Chesterfield failed to attract a single vote (they'd been involved in an unfortunate financial entanglement with a restaurateur during the war and had had to be taken over by the local council – the first time such a move has ever been recorded). Southport and Rochdale polled 7 votes each and Port Vale were unlucky not to succeed with their 27 votes. The successful newcomers were therefore South Shields and Rotherham (28 votes each), West Ham (32) and Coventry City (35).

Thus, the League expanded evenly throughout the country: in the South, Midlands, Yorkshire and the North East. After the Arsenal travesty, this election was at least seen to be even handed.

The Special General Meeting made one other significant change. Instead of clubs paying an annual subscription fee, it was agreed that they would pay 0.5 per cent of net gate and stand receipts to the League for its general expenses. This principle, introduced in 1916, has remained in force ever since (at varying levels). Another wartime innovation was continued in limited form, with the agreement that clubs pay the visitors 20 per cent of net receipts.

The Arsenal sensation seems to have blown over rapidly, so that the Annual General Meeting of June 1919 found the League in buoyant, optimistic mood. The first post-war season of reconstruction had proved beyond doubt the game's popularity, and it was likely, claimed John McKenna expansively, that the rise in gates of recent months would increase tenfold!

Despite the war's draining effect upon the League's finances, the bank balance showed a quite startling recovery. Even after donating £1000 to rescue the FA the League's account for 1918/19 showed a balance of £2136, of which just over half had come from the levy on gates.

But there was one note of dissent, from Blackpool. They had issued a circular suggesting that the system of electing the Management Committee provided insufficient guarantees of representation for Second Division clubs. Blackpool clearly had their supporters, for in the subsequent elections Blackpool's Tom Barcroft just ousted Everton's Dr Baxter, who had sat on the Committee for the previous fifteen years.

As clubs prepared to resume League action in the summer of 1919, it became clear that the transition from war to peace would, after all, be no easy process. Burnley, for example, were still awaiting the release of players from the army. Several other clubs were given special dispensation to pay players extra travelling expenses because of housing shortages in their areas.

Then, when the season opened in September, a rail strike and petrol shortages threatened to disrupt the entire fixture list.

This gave Sir Henry Norris his first chance of repaying the League by leading a deputation to try to extract concessions from the railway companies. He failed, and as a result the Inter-League match against the Irish League fixed for 6 October had to be postponed.

Norris and his right-hand man on the Management Committee, William Hall, also visited the Transport Minister, Sir Eric Geddes, to impress upon him the need for football teams to be given special permits to travel by road, but industrial action ended soon afterwards and the League returned to normal.

As if this were not enough, the League then found itself embroiled in a bitter argument with the Southern League, which was angry at not being invited to a special conference with the Scottish League. It also claimed that a threat had been made that if the Southern League didn't agree to certain changes made at this conference, 'there would be a fight'. Above all, however, it was mightily upset that West Ham, one of its top clubs, had applied to join the League in 1919 while still a member, contrary to its own rules.

In retaliation, therefore, the Southern League refused to allow the players of its three former members, Stoke (who left in 1915), Coventry City (in 1917) and West Ham to be registered with the League. This was, of course, contrary to the 1910 joint agreement on mutual recognition of retain and transfer lists, but the Southern League was in no mood to be humbled.

In response, the League simply ordered the three clubs to ignore the matter, which prompted an angry letter from the Southern League secretary, H. Bradshaw, in July 1919. After detailing the League's discourteous behaviour, Bradshaw gave notice that the Southern league intended withdrawing from the original 1910 accord as from 26 July.

The Management Committee's reply was icy. They stated that the conference with the Scottish League previously alluded to in the Southern League's complaint had never taken place (there are certainly no records of it). Furthermore, stated the Committee, West Ham had resigned their membership of the Southern League some time before joining the Football League. The letter ended tersely: 'We approve the termination of the agreements.'

Only in one sense, therefore, had the Southern League been right: there was going to be a fight – but this time it was going to be for their very survival.

A written offer from the FA's honorary treasurer, former League refereee Arthur Kingscott, suggesting arbitration, was politely declined. Then, the Southern League wrote back to say that West Ham had not resigned before applying to the League. Tom Charnley admitted to having been misinformed on that particular point, but emphasized that in all other matters there was no possible room for doubt and misconception'. The letter ended with the words 'Further correspondence is needless.'

Never had the two Leagues been at such loggerheads.

With this potentially serious rift simmering in the background, a further headache faced the Committee. This was the case of Leeds City, which first arose in July 1919 when the FA received a letter from a Mr Copeland alleging that City had paid certain players above the regulated amounts during the war. Three Committeemen, John McKenna, Harry Keys and Arthur Dickinson were immediately appointed to join three FA councillors to investigate the matter.

The issue became not so much the illegal payments – it was generally recognized that several clubs had been similarly guilty – but the fact that Leeds refused to hand over their books for inspection. In many previous cases of misconduct the League had been fairly consistent; where a club or individual admitted to errors, they were invariably treated with sympathy. But whenever an obvious misdeed was denied, the League's wrath knew no bounds.

The axe fell on Leeds on 13 October 1919: 'After the repeated warnings of the President and Committee they regard this violation of the financial regulations and the failure to produce documents vital to full and complete enquiry so serious that expulsion from the League can be the only fitting punishment.'

So Leeds City were out, the first club ever to be expelled by the FA and by the Football League, and Port Vale (who ironically became the second club to be expelled) took over their fixtures with eight games played.

City died almost instantly. Within weeks, most of the team had gone and by 8 December the entire Elland Road playing staff had been sold off for £8650 to pay off the club's liabilities.

But before the dust of this quite stunning judgement could settle, another issue came to the fore when struggling Huddersfield applied for permission to play its games at Elland Road. Immediately the Committee was confronted by an angry deputation of Huddersfield supporters opposing the move, to which the Committee's response was quite unyielding: if the Huddersfield public couldn't raise sufficient money to pay off Town's owner, Mr Hilton Crowther, by 31 December, then the League could have no objection to Crowther taking his team to Elland Road.

It was a tall order. An attempt to raise £25,000 was still in progress, and the Supporters' Committee begged for more time. But time was running out, because Hilton Crowther had in the meantime bought Elland Road and effected repairs of over £2,400.

The deadline passed, by which time, backed by a now growing set of frantic supporters, the team miraculously started to climb towards the top of the Second Division. By the end of the season, gates had risen from 3000 to 47,000, Town had gained promotion (behind Tottenham) and, incredibly, reached the FA Cup Final after several record-breaking crowds at Leeds Road.

So Huddersfield stayed at Leeds Road, while down the road a new club called Leeds United was formed at Elland Road. The moral was plain – never write off a football club when it's down and almost out.

And in March 1920, a month before Huddersfield's Cup Final appearance, came proof that nor could one write off the Management Committee as being hidebound. After cordial negotiations with the Players' Union it was decided to reform completely the players' wage structure. No one had expected the Committee to go so far.

One of the proposals it put forward at a Special General Meeting (once again at Manchester's Grand Hotel) was amongst the most radical conceived since the turn of the century – that all restrictions on wages (not including bonuses or signing-on fees) be lifted. That is, the Committee was prepared to consider abolishing the maximum wage in 1920, a full forty years before it eventually happened.

Whether it put this forward as a sop to the union, knowing only too well that the clubs would reject the proposal, is not entirely clear, but reject it they did, almost without discussion.

There was no denying, however, that wages had to rise, not only because of massively increased gate receipts but also because the cost of living was rising. Even so, the players must have been exceptionally pleased, if not absolutely amazed at the terms which were finally agreed.

They were as follows:

1.   The maximum wage previously set at £234 (£4. 10s per week) was doubled.

2.   A sliding scale of wages was set, the maximum rising from £5 in a player's first year to £9 after four years. Thus the new first-teamer in 1920 was able to earn more than the veteran of pre-war days. Also, if a player was being paid below the maximum but was then transferred, his new club could raise his wages to the limit in mid-season. These new allow-

ances alone give an idea of how football's finances were entering a new era. (It should be stressed, however, that maximum payments were not obligatory, nor were minimum wages specified.)

3.   Years of service with associated leagues – Scottish, Southern and so on – would now count towards the rising wage scale. Army service would also count as service.

4.   Talent money, previously payable only to clubs finishing at the top of the table, was now payable on a weekly basis to all first-team players plus one reserve at the rate of £2 for a win and £1 for a draw. (The payment of one reserve was to encourage players not to lie about their fitness in order to keep their place.)

5.   The new wage scale was to be made payable over the full fifty-two weeks of the year (not thirty-nine plus three training weeks as before).

6.   From then on, the Management Committee would not approve any club paying a player a larger share from a transfer fee than he was entitled to as part of his accrued share of benefit. Nor would it sanction any payments to players who had been put on the transfer list because of misconduct or making demands on the club. Thus, the Committee hoped that loyal players wouldn't be penalized by staying put, and that others would cease to gain by constantly seeking moves. It also put the onus on clubs not to make offers they couldn't legally fulfil. In the past, clubs had promised large sums, only to add a later rider stating 'with the consent of the Football League', knowing only too well that such consent would not be forthcoming.

All in all, it was a remarkable package, and proof that the Committee was entering a new period of trust in its relations with both the clubs and the players.

There were two further innovations in this eventful year. First, instead of club chairmen being presented with championship trophies at Annual Meetings, on 1 May 1920 John McKenna started a new tradition by presenting the League Challenge Trophy to First Division winners West Bromwich Albion after their match against Chelsea at The Hawthorns. The practice has continued ever since, whenever possible.

Second, after over a decade of proposals, deputations and debates, the campaign for the formation of a third division finally reached a successful conclusion at the 1920 Annual Meeting. It was not, however, quite in the form many observers had anticipated.

The time for expansion was certainly ripe. Football had recovered its pre-war status and even improved upon its popularity. Gates had never been higher, and public interest was at a peak. The League's own finances had grown enormously, with a record surplus that year of over £3600 (mostly from the levy on gates). As John McKenna announced at the Annual Meeting, congratulations were due all round. Never had the players been so contented, and this was to their credit as well as the clubs'.

But the Management Committee still felt that, although a third division would be viable, a northern section would not as yet be strong enough, both financially and in terms of its playing strength. Sutcliffe said that the Committee didn't wish to seem unkind or unfriendly in this judgement, and nor did it wish to deprive the northern clubs of all incentive. It nevertheless proposed that for 1920/1, a third division be formed only of the twenty-two clubs then belonging to the Southern League's First Division.

The League would then consider afresh the merits of forming a northern section, and if a sufficient number of suitable clubs was forthcoming, a final decision would be made in February 1921. To prepare themselves for this eventuality, Sutcliffe said, the seventeen northern clubs who had already applied should use the interim 'to put their houses in order, mould their purpose, centralise their aims and ambitions and work to make themselves worthy of acceptance'.

He also suggested that just because twenty-two Southern League clubs were joining didn't mean there would have to be twenty-two northern clubs. Perhaps eighteen or twenty would be enough.

In the meantime, the new third division's entrance fees were fixed at £100 each, plus £10.10s annual subscription. The top club would be promoted to take the place of the bottom club in the Second Division.

But the new clubs would not become Full Members with voting rights. Instead, they would be considered Associate Members, with their interests looked after by the Management Committee. Full membership would be granted only on promotion to the Second Division, when a further entrance fee of £200 became payable. If a club dropped back to the third division and was later promoted, the re-entry fee would be only £20. The bottom two clubs in such a third division, in each section, would have to apply for re-election.

That was the package before the clubs. But would they accept it this time?

Everton and Preston were the first dissenters. Everton argued that in a spirit of democracy the third division clubs would eventually demand and receive a vote in the League's affairs. This would mean the existing members being outvoted. Furthermore, if a northern section was not formed immediately and a club like Bury, for example, was relegated to a third division, it would find itself playing against southern clubs only. That, said Everton's Mr Clayton, rightly, 'would be a great hardship'.

He proposed that the whole question be discussed in greater detail at a later date. John McKenna refused to accept any further delay, but he was then faced with further objections.

Earlier in the meeting, voting had taken place for the two vacant places in the Second Division. Grimsby and Lincoln, both regarded as northern clubs, were up for re-election and

both, with 20 and 7 votes respectively, were ousted. (For Lincoln it was their ninth application since 1893 and the third time they'd been unsuccessful. For Grimsby it was their second failure in four attempts.) Walsall's application also failed, attracting only 3 votes.

Instead, the two places went to newly constituted Leeds United, clear winners with 31 votes (most of them in sympathy after the expulsion of Leeds City), and Cardiff City, with 23 votes, who thus became the League's first representatives from Wales. (There is a suggestion in the League minutes that both clubs took certain steps before the meeting to win votes, perhaps à la Norris. Sheffield United brought this to the Committee's attention, but we have no record of what actually occurred.)

Once the debate about a third division was under way, Tottenham's delegate, Morton Cadman, pointed out that it seemed unfair that twenty-two Southern League clubs should be admitted while long-standing members like Grimsby and Lincoln were left out in the cold.

But then Charles Sutcliffe realized that there was still a glimmer of hope for the two outgoing clubs. Cardiff City, he remembered, had been members of the Southern League. Now that they were elected to the Second Division there would be only twenty-one Southern League clubs eligible to join a third division. This meant one free place, and there could be another if not all the Southern League clubs decided to join (an unlikely prospect, however).

If neither Lincoln nor Grimsby could join a third division, Sutcliffe, now speaking on his own account, suggested that the Management Committee might support them in non-League football for one season, until a northern section could be formed. 'All League clubs would give them every encouragement', he predicted, to much applause.

'The League should comprise all the great clubs in the country', Sutcliffe went on, and once in, clubs could be guaranteed 'even more than mutual aid, friendship and helpfulness'.

He assured the gathering that if formed, the interests of third division members would be given full consideration.

'As a League we have always been making progress,' declared Sutcliffe, now clearly in his stride. 'We have never gone backwards and will continue to go higher and higher until we have reached that perfect organization which should be the ambition of every national body.'

Such stirring words drew loud applause, and clearly illustrated how Sutcliffe, rather than the President, acted as both the brains and voice of the Committee. Few individuals could match him for commitment or resolution, and few tried.

Sutcliffe's speech carried the day. The Committee's proposals were approved. Division Three at last.

On behalf of the disappointed northern clubs, the aptly-named Councillor Cropper, representing the now municipally-owned Chesterfield club, expressed his regret that they would have to wait another season, but accepted the decision in the proper spirit. Cropper told the meeting that the northern clubs would prove their worth and ability, and would try to earn the confidence of the League.

For the Southern League clubs, Mr F. J. Walton of Queen's Park Rangers cordially accepted the conditions laid down by the League and expressed hearty thanks for their support.

But if he was delighted, how must the members of the Southern League Management Committee have felt? The League now had sixty-six of the top clubs in England and Wales, while they were left to do the best they could with a mixed bag of thirteen reserve teams and a few assorted Welsh clubs. From then on, the Southern League would never be anything more than a subsidiary competition.

The League had also gained the services of the Southern League's top administrators, two of whom were now co-opted on to the League's Management Committee, to be called as and when necessary to discuss the affairs of

Associate Members. The two elected men were A. J. Dernell and J. B. Skeggs. Skeggs, from Millwall, had been the Southern League's leading official before the war.

To add to the Southern League's (albeit self-inflicted) malaise, there were still plenty more clubs anxious to join the League. As soon as news of the Third Division's formation was released, the Welsh League approached the Management Committee with a view to securing automatic promotion for their top two clubs to the Third Division. Predictably, the request received short shrift.

In fact, Wales was now well represented in the League. Apart from Cardiff, the new Third Division included Swansea Town, Merthyr Town and Newport County. Of the new influx there were also six from the London area (Crystal Palace, QPR, Millwall, Brentford, Watford and Luton), four from the South West (Swindon, Bristol Rovers, Exeter and Plymouth), six from the South and South East (Southampton, Portsmouth, Brighton, Southend, Reading and Gillingham), Northampton from the Midlands and Norwich from East Anglia.

We should also mention that twenty-second place in the Third Division was taken by Grimsby, because they had polled more votes than Lincoln in the earlier re-election ballot. (Poor, rejected Lincoln then slunk back to the Midland League.)

Thus, the League took one step further

Complaints were received after the First World War that linesmen were not using their flags properly. To make their actions clearer, therefore, each club was issued with two brand-new white flags. The symbolism must have been too inhibiting, however, because only a few months later, in December 1920, the Committee had to remind linesmen that they should unfurl the flags and not leave them rolled up.

towards becoming a truly national competition, stretching its influence from Plymouth to Newcastle, from Gillingham to Blackpool. Only one problem remained: an impending coal strike threatened to disrupt all rail services, with the real possibility that fixtures would have to be postponed unless the Ministry of Transport relented on petrol shortages and allowed clubs to use charabancs. Sir Henry Norris once again tried to wield his influence at Westminster, and once again failed to win any realistic concessions.

A national League was all very well, but if teams couldn't actually travel across the nation it wasn't worth twopence.

The sudden rise from forty-four to sixty-six clubs placed great strains on the League. A sub-committee was formed of the Secretary, John Lewis and Charles Sutcliffe to filter Management Committee business in order to shorten meetings. Help was also needed for Tom Charnley in the office. Rather than advertise the post, he simply appointed his son-in-law, Fred Howarth, who began duties on 1 February 1921 and stayed around for the next thirty-five years.

The League's office, at Castle Chambers, Preston was also in need of a bit of modernization. An office sub-committee was therefore authorized to purchase a typewriter, an index cabinet and more modern general office equipment.

The twentieth century had arrived.

Whether it had arrived at those northern clubs anxious to join the Third Division was another question. To vet each application, the Management Committee decided to print questionnaires and undertake ground inspections, the first time the League had ever done this.

Having rooted out a few of the weaker clubs, the Committee was left with fourteen candidates whom, it was suggested, should be proposed for membership *en bloc*. These fourteen included six with strong League connections:

- Lincoln City (Midland League) – who had been promised a place in the northern section after their disappointment in 1920
- Accrington Stanley (Lancashire Combination) – although no relation to founder members Accrington, Stanley's local inheritance was generally recognized
- Rochdale (Central League) – co-opted members during the war
- Walsall (Birmingham League) – former members 1892–5 and 1896–1901
- Chesterfield (Midland League) – former members 1899–1909
- Crewe Alexandra (Central League) – former members 1892–6

The eight others were: Nelson and Tranmere Rovers (Central League); Ashington, Hartlepools United, Darlington and Durham City (North-Eastern League); Barrow (Lancashire Combination) and Wrexham (Birmingham League). Note that the last two were in areas hitherto unrepresented in the League, Cumbria and North Wales.

The fate of these fourteen was to be decided at a Special General Meeting in the Connaught Rooms, London, on 7 March 1921, where one representative from each club was called upon to state their case.

The meeting began, however, on an unexpectedly sombre note. John Oliver, Newcastle's chairman and a member of the Management Committee, had suffered a stroke just before breakfast and was now lying seriously ill at the Euston Hotel.

After earnest wishes for his swift recovery, John McKenna told the gathering of thirty-four Full Members that for once the Management Committee had not brought forward its own recommendations on the formation of a northern section. Its members were, unusually, publicly divided on the matter, some believing that several of the applicants were not strong enough to do credit to themselves or the League.

Chesterfield's Councillor Cropper immediately reassured the doubters that each club was prepared to pay a deposit to guarantee that they would fulfil their obligations. This seemed to put everyone's mind at rest, and the formation of a northern section of twenty clubs was therefore given unanimous approval. All fourteen clubs in the selected group were then elected *en bloc*.

That left six more places to fill. Grimsby Town, the only northern club in the Third Division during 1920/1, took one of the places, as promised by the League a year earlier. Another place would be filled by one of the bottom two clubs from the Second Division at the end of the season.

Four extra clubs had therefore to be elected, and voting results were: Wigan Borough (Lancashire Combination) – 34 votes, Halifax Town (Midland League) – 25, Southport Central (Central League) – 25, and Stalybridge Celtic (Central League) – 25 were elected. In addition to the entrance fee and annual subscription, each had to pay £50 as a guarantee to the League, a small price to pay for the potential rewards.

It is interesting to note who the unsuccessful applicants were for those four last places: Castleford Town (18 votes), Rotherham Town (13), Blyth Spartans (9), Gainsborough Trinity (8), Doncaster Rovers (6), West Stanley, from Liverpool (6), Wakefield City (4), Lancaster Town (3), Scunthorpe and Lindsey United (3) and South Liverpool (1).

Thus, the League grew from forty-four clubs in 1919 to eighty-six clubs in 1921 (seven times its original size in 1888). More rugby strongholds had been 'colonized', and the League had therefore to negotiate for the first time with rugby clubs to ensure that local fixtures didn't clash. A further settlement was made with the Northern Rugby Union by which Football League grounds were made available for rugby internationals.

So the northern campaigners returned home, happy at last, John Oliver following them a few days later to convalesce in New-

castle. And when it next met, the Management Committee was joined for the first time by the two elected representatives of the new Northern Section: E. Clayton of Southport and Councillor Cropper of Chesterfield. (Cropper was later awarded a gold watch in recognition of his efforts to form the Third Division North.)

There was one further set of elections in 1921.

In theory, the two bottom clubs of the Third Division in 1920/1, Brentford and Gillingham, should have been up for re-election, but Arsenal's representative Lt-Col. C. D. Crisp, proposed that they should keep their places, and since the League seemed to bow to most of Arsenal's requests, this was carried with only one dissenter.

But there still had to be an election for new members to the Southern section, which was now two clubs short. These vacancies were created by Crystal Palace's promotion (as

The new regional Third Division, as explained to Yorkshire sports fans, still involved long distances for its members. But only one Yorkshire club, Halifax, gained entry, and Walsall found themselves crossing the border on several occasions to balance up the numbers.

inaugural Third Division champions), Grimsby's switch to the Northern section, and Stockport County's relegation, also to the Northern group.

Applicants for the two places were predominantly Welsh, but only one of them succeeded. Aberdare sailed in with 38 votes, followed by Southern League Charlton Athletic with 30. Charlton's election was quite remarkable considering the club had turned professional only the year before. The failed applicants were Bath City, Abertillery, Barry and Bridgend, and Pontypridd. Another Welsh club, Aberaman, a village team from just outside Aberdare, sensibly withdrew beforehand.

Since Wales now boasted six League clubs, Charles Sutcliffe reminded clubs to advertise their matches not as being in the 'English League' but the 'Football League', the true title, and one of which they should be proud.

The culmination of all this post-war prosperity and expansion was a Football League dinner, held at the Hotel Cecil, London, after the 1921 Annual Meeting. A total of 278 guests was present, with special prominence being accorded to the FA's representatives, Charles Clegg and William Pickford, and, of course, to Sir Henry Norris MP.

Clegg spoke of how the game's growing popularity made everyone's responsibilities greater than ever before, but the general mood was ebullient. League finances had never been healthier, and there was much back-slapping all round, joyfully rounded off with 'an excellent musical programme contributed by Miss Winifred Lawson, Miss Kathleen Bramwall, Mr George Baker and Mr Rex Harold'. Little did the happy gathering realize how suddenly the good times would end, not just for them but for the whole country.

Meanwhile, for the representatives of Rochdale, Aberdare, Brentford, Norwich and Southampton, the affair must have been a touch too celebratory, for when the clubs reconvened the following morning to arrange the fixtures, they were unaccountably late, and were fined on the spot!

The implication was that they were not in non-League football now. This was the big time, where standards had to be maintained, as the new Associate Members soon discovered as they tried to come to grips with the rigours of League bureaucracy (and Sutcliffe's extremely high standards).

Apart from the Management Committee being faced with an inevitable litany of late result sheets, refereeing complaints, wage irregularities and unregistered players, Wigan, Walsall, Halifax and Accrington each had to undertake hurried developments to bring their grounds up to standard, with members of the Committee making regular visits to report progress.

Two days after the 1921/2 season began Halifax were reported as having no stand at all, and conditions at Wigan and Wrexham were evidently quite primitive. Accrington Stanley had managed to sell more season tickets than they could accommodate (how times were to change), while both Brentford and Newport had to be reminded three times each to pay their annual subscriptions before they were eventually fined and ordered to pay up (even then Brentford appealed, which makes one wonder what sort of laxity they had been accustomed to in the Southern League).

Crystal Palace's pitch was reported as being unsatisfactory (but then, so was Chelsea's, and

---

Although it became common in the late 1970s and early 1980s for the PFA to lend clubs money to aid their survival, when the Players' Union first offered financial help to a club – Stockport County in August 1921 – the Committee was most angry. 'The League is the place to come to for such a purpose', it informed the Stockport secretary testily, even though it knew that it was against League policy to give hand-outs to struggling clubs.

that was used for Cup finals). At Cardiff a crush of late-arriving fans demolished a turnstile. Astonishingly, the receipts showed afterwards that most of the gate-crashers had paid as they clambered into the ground.

But a more serious sign of the times was seen at Barrow, where riots nearly broke out on several occasions after unemployed people had been allowed in free (contrary to League regulations). 'This resulted in a rush of hooligans, who broke down the fence and entered the ground', reported the Committee. Barrow claimed in their defence that the unemployed were allowed free entrance to the local rugby ground, that the club had sought police protection, and that they were prosecuting the ring-leaders – shades of the 1980s.

Several of the new northern clubs begged the League to allow them to admit the unemployed at reduced rates (as is permitted nowadays), but the League held its ground, McKenna stating that the numbers were so great that clubs would almost certainly be inundated. He had a point. Lloyd George's so-called 'fit country for heroes', promised in November 1918, was rapidly evolving, in the North especially, into an ailing country with two million out of work.

While the jobless were priced out of League football, the Committee then quite unexpectedly ordered a reduction in the players' wages. Having fought so hard to improve conditions immediately after the war, the Players' Union was understandably enraged, but there was little it could do in the rapidly worsening economic circumstances.

In April 1922 the maximum wage was reduced from £9 to £8, and even worse, a new maximum of £6 was set for summer wages. (This differentiation between seasonal and summer wages survived until 1961.) Bonuses for League matches remained at £2 for a win, £1 for a draw (half that in the Third Division), but Cup-tie incentives were to be slashed. For example, Cup winners would now receive only £8 bonus each, compared with £35 agreed only a year earlier.

The clubs endorsed this cost-cutting package unanimously, and thus at a stroke brought the post-war boom to a hollow end. Football was, of course, not alone. Politicians' great hopes for national reconstruction also lay in ruins and if the rest of the nation was starting to yearn for the good old days before 1914, club directors showed themselves to be no different. Some things would never be the same, however. McGregor's and Sutcliffe's beloved Liberal Party, for example, never recovered from its post-war failures.

Was every club affected by the 1922 slump?

A comparison of match receipts for the season 1921/2 helps to provide an interesting counter to those modern critics who feel that the League is becoming too weighted towards the South. The truth is that amongst the smaller clubs, this has always been the case.

In 1921/2, southern clubs, especially those in the Third Division, earned on average almost twice as much as their northern counterparts. Even the Welsh clubs, who suffered so much later in the decade, were relatively comfortable in the early 1920s.

The following figures represent total earnings from League matches, that is, including 20 per cent of receipts from away matches but minus the same percentage given to visiting clubs. Full Members also paid a half-per-cent levy to the League. The figures do not, therefore, show net home receipts but reflect a team's earning capacity (and therefore partly its popularity), both at home and away.

Champions Liverpool earned £32,852, roughly the same as Tottenham and Newcastle. But the top earners were, surprisingly, Chelsea, who finished only ninth but netted receipts worth £34,043. The lowest total in the First Division belonged to Oldham, with £13,647, just below Huddersfield.

In the Second Division London clubs also reaped rich rewards. West Ham, who finished fourth, earned £18,710 (higher than six First Division clubs), while Fulham, who managed only seventh place, received £16,955.

There appeared to be prosperity in the Midlands also, with Forest (who were champions), Stoke, Leicester, Derby, Wolves and Coventry each showing healthy returns. Worst off were Rotherham, with receipts amounting to only £6885, just under Bradford Park Avenue and Bury.

But the real contrast lay between the two sections of the Third Division. Southern clubs averaged £7625, almost twice as much as northern clubs, who received on average only £3900. Plymouth (runners-up) were the top southern club with £13,553 (almost the same as First Division Oldham). The top northern club, by comparison, were champions Stockport with £7422.

Portsmouth, Millwall, Southampton (champions) and QPR each gleaned receipts in excess of £10,000, while the lowest earnings of any southern club were those of Newport County, with £4235 (still above the northern average).

In the Northern section, only five clubs managed to earn more than Newport: Stockport, Grimsby, Hartlepools, Darlington and Wigan. The lowest in the League was Durham City, with net receipts of a mere £1472. (Yet Durham still somehow managed to undertake a foreign tour in the summer of 1922, as did Hartlepools and their wealthier neighbours Newcastle.) Also under £3000 were Halifax, Rochdale, Nelson and Stalybridge.

These figures show clearly that in earning power alone (if not in playing strength), the northern clubs were at a disadvantage from the very earliest days of the Third Division.

> 'The Committee considered a letter from Mr Belcher requesting members to meet him at dinner and talk over the new ground at Wembley. The Committee decided that no useful purpose would be served by accepting the invitation.'
>
> *League minute, 5 December 1921*

The 1922 Annual Meeting was the first in which two sets of elections had to be held, for each section of the Third Division. Southend (36 votes) and Exeter (32) were comfortably returned to the Southern section. Pontypridd (21), Bath (1) and Llanelly (0) were the challengers. In the Northern section both Halifax (42) and Rochdale (31) were re-elected, the unsuccessful applicants being Doncaster (9), New Brighton (7) and York City (1).

So no changes in the Associate Membership, nor on the Management Committee, but there was an alteration in the regulations governing transfers. Charles Sutcliffe explained that the Committee wished to ensure that the amount of money paid for a player remained a confidential matter between the buying and selling clubs. Too often, fees had been disclosed to the public for no real purpose, said Sutcliffe, and there was no reason for the Management Committee to know the scale of fee either.

This proposal was carried unanimously (and remains in force still), but another motion put forward by Sir Henry Norris was more problematic. This was a proposal to place a ceiling of £1650 on transfer fees and to prohibit a player transferred in mid-season from playing against a club against whom he had already played that season. (How Norris arrived at the figure of £1650 is not clear.)

Having got his way in the past, this time Sir Henry was rebuffed, and when he put forward a similar motion in 1923 the response was the same. Was his influence waning? Perhaps so, for just before the crucial general election of November 1922, Norris resigned his parliamentary seat after a disagreement on tariff reform.

The transfer question was again in the news in June, when a commission of enquiry found Preston guilty of paying A. Doolan more than he was entitled to after his transfer from Bradford City in 1920. Preston were fined the enormous sum of £500, the largest fine ever meted out by the League, and four of their former directors, including the well known W. E.

Ord, were suspended from football for twelve months. Doolan was ordered to return the £100 signing-on fee he had received, and for their part, Bradford City were fined £250.

Clearly the League meant to clamp down on illegal inducements – Rotherham was the next club to suffer suspensions at board level in April 1923 for a similar offence – but at the same time more clubs were finding their way around the regulations by subsidizing players' removal expenses and advancing them loans for furniture and similar items.

Clubs were also repeatedly asking permission to buy players presents, such as gold watches. The League allowed this if the value did not exceed £20, but there can be little doubt that many of the gifts were immediately redeemed in exchange for money. The Committee was ever vigilant in this matter. For example, when Plymouth asked if their players could be presented with miniature silver cups, donated by a supporter, permission was refused. Similarly, Everton's Dixie Dean was ordered not to accept a supporter's gift offered in recognition of his goal-scoring feat in 1927/8 (when he scored a record sixty goals in one season).

Yet wedding presents were a common incentive allowed by the League, both Liverpool and Everton were allowed to lend money to players in financial difficulties, and Cardiff City were known in 1922 to be buying a house for one of their team. One of the most unusual requests granted by the Committee was for Preston to lend T. Roberts £25 'for the purchase of hen pens'. But overall, if there was any method behind the Committee's reasoning on this question of gifts and loans, it certainly isn't discernible from the records.

What we can say for sure is that all these payments, which had to be individually sanctioned, plus the inevitable increase in the number of transfers, insurance claims, forms, reports, complaints and letters, created an appreciable growth in the League's workload.

No one could ever accuse the Committee-

Before the Second World War, the League was constantly organizing collections and special matches to raise money for disaster appeals, particularly those involving coal-miners. Pit accidents at Hulton, Bolton, Pretoria, Whitehaven and Maltby were each met with generous donations from the League and supporters. For the Gresford (Wrexham) Colliery appeal in 1934, the League and its members raised an astonishing £5900, the equivalent of the League's entire annual income at that time. Also well subscribed were appeals following the *Titanic* sinking and floods in London and Fleetwood.

men of slackness in this period, however. They wanted to investigate and solve everything, be it concerning poor sanitary arrangements at Sunderland, Bury and Forest, indiscreet comments in a Swansea programme, a betting advertisement at Crystal Palace's ground, the lack of hot water for visitors at Durham City, or bad language on the terraces at Halifax and Brentford.

They were frequently generous. Benefit games (see Appendix Three) were arranged for the families of E. Hodgson (Burnley), John Robson (Manchester United), T. Meehan (Chelsea) and J. Howarth (Burnley). Donations were often given to former players, club officials, referees and to charities, such as the British Olympic Association, which received £100 towards its preparations for the 1924 games.

Charity or otherwise, some northern Third Division clubs needed any help they could get as the economic slump continued to bite deeply into their resources. Lincoln and Durham were each on the verge of ruin by 1923. Wage cuts were the order of the day, as at Halifax, where there was nearly a walk-out when players refused to accept a reduction of 20 per cent. Tranmere players were even worse off. Their club was so poor that no wages at all were paid during the 1923 close season.

It was in the midst of this hovering uncertainty that the last expansion of the League until 1950 took place in 1923, with the addition of two extra clubs to the Third Division North.

Beforehand, however, came the re-election campaign, and it is of particular note that prior to the 1923 Annual Meeting each Third Division section met to decide (also by ballot) which of the applicants to recommend to the Full Members. This practice continued right up until recent years, and as in 1923, often resulted in the four retiring clubs being given the green light (which in turn gave rise to the accusation that the League was a closed shop).

However, we must remember that in 1923 both third Divisions were still very much at an experimental stage, and quite naturally everyone wanted to give the newcomers the best possible chance of establishing themselves. So it was that Aberdare and Newport (Southern section), Ashington and Durham (Northern section) were re-elected, with not a single vote against them.

Elections for the two new clubs were more complicated. Firstly, there were in fact three vacancies, since Stalybridge Celtic had become the first of the new intake to fall by the wayside. Despite finishing seventh in 1922 and eleventh in the year after, their gates had been poor, so they decided to switch to the Cheshire County League. But because both of the Second Division's relegated clubs – Wolves and Rother-

ham – were allocated to the Northern section, this meant that Stalybridge's place was allocated to the Southern section.

Boscombe (28 votes) filled the vacancy, ahead of Llanelly (9), Pontypridd (8) and Torquay United (0). (No sooner had Boscombe won membership than they applied to change their name to Bournemouth United. A few weeks later they changed their minds and adopted the lengthier but homelier title, Bournemouth and Boscombe Athletic.)

Finally, there were the two extra Northern section places to fill. Again, recommendations were made, and these resulted in Doncaster and New Brighton polling the maximum 45 votes each. Nuneaton Town and Wallasey United were the unfortunate, voteless challengers.

So we leave this hectic post-war period with the League comprising four neatly-balanced divisions of twenty-two clubs each. Liverpool had just won their second Championship in succession, while former no-hopers, Huddersfield, were about to embark on the most successful period any League club had ever known. Manchester United were in Division Two, while Wolves became the first founder members to fall into the Third Division (where they stayed just one year). Thus, a pattern for unpredictable mobility between the divisions was set, and the League assumed the shape and form it was to retain for the next thirty-five years.

CHAPTER TWELVE
Associate Aspirations

The 1920s were years of great changes on the pitch – a change in the offside law in particular – and for the Committee. The period saw a continuing battle to keep the clubs in order during the depression.

Some clubs may have become more efficient, but others grew much cleverer at side-stepping the rules (sending post-dated cheques for transfer fees was a favourite). Fines would continue to be an important source of revenue, except that now they were used to build up the League's Benevolent Fund rather than the organization's own coffers. Newcastle made the biggest contribution to date, with a record fine of £750 for fielding weak teams on seven different occasions in 1923/4 (on their way to winning the FA Cup that season).

The mood of the so-called 'roaring twenties' seems to have affected some players, for there was a constant stream of suspensions for misbehaviour. Their crimes were listed variously as drunkenness, betting, bad language, 'physical inefficiency', breaches of training rules, failing to turn up, and in two cases, those of J. Lyons of Derby and H. McCracken of Charlton, insubordination so great that both were permanently suspended.

Equally, footballers were victims of unfair treatment, and both the Management and Appeal Committees were often known to judge in a player's favour. One cannot help but feel, however, that they might have prevented Southend from slapping a permanent suspension on A. Jackson, whose sole offence was to attempt suicide. There were other cases, like that of Barney Travers of Fulham who was banned for life for his part in a bribery attempt in 1922.

In 1927 Sir Henry Norris bowed out of the game in disgrace after being suspended for his unorthodox management of Arsenal's finances. It was an ignominious end to a remarkable career, but in truth his influence had been waning for some time. After his repeated inability to persuade the clubs to impose a limit on transfer fees, at the 1924 Annual Meeting his further demands were publicly brushed aside by Sutcliffe. Two years later his attempt to bring forward the transfer deadline from March to December was also rejected. The last record of Sir Henry in the League minutes is from October 1931, when he was refused entry to a club boardroom. How the mighty had fallen.

As Norris left the scene, several of the pioneers were also lost to the game. Daunting John Lewis died in January 1926. Charles Crump and Lord Kinnaird of the FA also passed away. But there were always men of ability and presence coming forward. Will Cuff, for example, an Everton supporter in their St Domingo days, joined the Management Committee in 1925.

Charlton were the first of the Southern section's Associate Members to flounder, after their disastrous and short-lived move to Catford. It was still tough in the North, but as the decade wore on, previously sound Welsh clubs also started to feel the pinch. In 1924, therefore, the Committee decided again to vet all applications and recommend which clubs should or should not be favoured. Despite claiming that it didn't wish the League to become 'a closed corporation', the Committee also made it harder by dispensing with the custom of allowing each club the chance to address the Annual Meeting in support of their application.

These new conditions, plus the increasing economic hardships of smaller clubs, meant that in 1924 the four retiring Third Division clubs, Bournemouth, QPR, Barrow and Hartlepools, had no challengers, the first and only time this has ever happened in League history.

In 1925 Mid Rhondda tried for the Southern section, but gained not a single vote. Brentford and Merthyr were re-elected with 44 votes each. For the Northern section there was less unanimity. Rotherham (42 votes) and Tranmere (32) were re-elected. Mansfield Town (13) and Blyth Spartans (3) were the challengers.

In 1926 a similar pattern emerged. Both Charlton and QPR were unopposed in the South, but in the Northern group Walsall (33) and Barrow (25) had to fight it out with Carlisle (12), Blyth Spartans (10) and Mansfield (10).

Thereafter, the Committee made it even harder by asking each outside applicant to supply balance sheets for the two previous seasons, a list of members and shareholders, average attendances for both first and second team matches, and details of the ground, its capacity, location and dressing-room facilities.

In 1926 the thorny issue of exemption from earlier rounds of the FA Cup came to a head. The FA proposed that all eighty-eight League clubs should go into the hat in the first round (which consisted of 128 clubs overall). This the First and Second Division clubs opposed vehemently; it put them on the same footing as Third Division clubs, and increased their chances of meeting non-League opposition.

Sutcliffe called the FA's proposal absurd, and when it became clear that the idea had emanated from the Third Division clubs he launched a long and scathing attack upon the ring-leaders. They may have been unhappy with their limited voting rights and representation on the Committee, said Sutcliffe, but they still enjoyed all the benefits and advantages of the League, especially in the form of generous insurance awards.

So Associate Members they would have to stay, he warned. They simply could not be allowed to 'clog the wheels of progress and thwart changes desired by the First and Second Division clubs'. (In this, Sutcliffe was using a similar argument to the one used by First Division clubs to procure greater voting rights in 1986).

Sutcliffe was always a great champion of the smaller clubs and of the 'family of the League', but he also recognized where the power base had to lie. Yet the Third Division clubs were still not content, claimed Sutcliffe in 1926. They wanted full membership and direct representation.

Both sections of the Third Division had formed executive committees, which Sutcliffe presumed had been intended to be helpful. Instead, he said, they had only pressed forward schemes which 'palpably prejudiced' their own interests. The proposal concerning the FA Cup was one of them. So was a proposal to promote two clubs from each Third Division.

Sutcliffe showed nothing but contempt for such presumption on the part of the Associate Members. If the Third Division clubs were unhappy with the League's rules and government, then they should leave, he told them plainly. If not, they should express their loyalty. Unless there was a change of attitude he would recommend that the two sectional committees be disbanded forthwith.

Harsh words, but the Full Members approved his sentiments unanimously. Sutcliffe, the headmaster, had put his youngest pupils in order. But he patently realized that

> F. W. Laycock of Barrow was severely censured for leaving the pitch in the middle of a Third Division North game against Rotherham on 16 March 1925, ostensibly to have an injury treated but in reality to sign transfer forms for Nelson. Nelson were fined five guineas for their novel attempt to beat the transfer deadline.

none of the clubs would break away. He was merely, he said in response to some humbled and battered Third Division chairman, laying down the ground rules. And as if to confirm Sutcliffe's suggestion that they should concentrate on consolidation, not gain, the first of the Southern section's early intake dropped out in 1927.

Despite the group's recommendation that the Full Members re-elect them, Aberdare lost out in a controversial second ballot to Torquay United. In the first vote, Watford (44 votes) had been unanimously returned, but Aberdare and Torquay tied, with 21 votes each. Then Sutcliffe found one spoilt ballot paper, so it was decided to take a second vote, which gave Torquay an advantage of 26 votes to 19.

Aberdare's secretary was furious, pointing out that one of the scrutineers was an interested party, but McKenna dismissed the protest, and thus Wales lost its first, but by no means last, League representative. The other applicants, Kettering, Yeovil and Petters United and Ebbw Vale, mustered only 2 votes between them.

The vote for the Northern section was more straightforward. Both retiring clubs, Barrow (30) and Accrington Stanley (36), were re-elected. Mansfield (8) and Blyth Spartans (3) failed for the third year in succession, along with York City (6) and Carlisle (5).

But it was only a matter of time before the depression would overtake some of the struggling northern outfits.

Durham were so badly supported that on one occasion they asked Accrington to forward £25 as an advance to allow the City players to travel to Accrington for their match. Struggling on through the general strike of 1926, then the gloomy, storm and flood-ridden winter of 1927/8, when Durham eventually came up for re-election in 1928 they finished a poor third behind Nelson, re-elected with 37 votes, and Carlisle United, voted in by 33 votes. Durham managed only 11, and with York (7) and Chester (2) also failing, it proved

to be a poor year for cathedral cities. Meanwhile, Carlisle became the League's furthest outpost in the North West.

The novel suggestion of a purely amateur club joining the League was put forward during the 1927/8 season by a London amateur player, Dick Sloley, who was told that, subject to the club having a proper ground, the League would welcome them. After all, had not Queen's Park in Glasgow achieved greatness (albeit some years before), while the Corinthians had won enormous respect for their Cup exploits in 1924 and 1927.

But when the proposed amateur club – wonderfully titled Argonauts FC – did form soon after, it was announced that they hoped to play at the White City Stadium, right next door to Loftus Road. Naturally, Queen's Park Rangers were totally opposed to this, as were Brentford. Even so, the Argonauts gained a surprising 16 votes at the 1928 Annual Meeting.

It was still insufficient to outseat the two retiring clubs, Torquay (42) and Merthyr (47), but it was higher than any of the other applicants, Kettering Town (3) and Peterborough and Fletton United (2).

The Southern section clubs, much more than their Northern section counterparts, continued to hector the Management Committee throughout the late 1920s and early 1930s, especially in their demands for votes at Annual Meetings and an increase in the number of clubs promoted from each Third Division. Apart from repeating Sutcliffe's earlier warnings, McKenna was able to scotch at least the first demand by stating that it would violate FA rules, 'which the League was the last body in football to break'. The rules in fact stated that no League should have more than forty-four full members.

Nevertheless, continued pressure on the Committee did eventually reap a reward when it was agreed in 1929 to give each section of the Third Division two votes at Annual Meetings. As a result, FA regulations had to be amended.

The 1929 Annual Meeting saw a whole crop of new clubs trying their luck. Argonauts applied again for the Southern section, but this time managed only 6 votes. Recently-formed Aldershot (5) made their first application, as did a new east London club called Thames, who polled just one vote. Kettering (1) and Llanelly (0) were the other applicants. Exeter (42) and Gillingham (35) were both re-elected.

For the Northern section, a club called Connah's Quay and Shotton FC, from Queensferry, withdrew its application at the last minute, while Manchester Central (who played at Belle Vue), Prescot Cables, Workington, Chester and Rhyl gleaned a meagre 3 votes between them. Mansfield managed 16, but the highest number went to Hartlepools (33), who were re-elected, and Midland Leaguers York City (24), who thus won a League place at their fourth attempt. York's gain was Ashington's loss. The North-Eastern club dropped out with only 14 votes after an undistinguished run of eight seasons, despite a brave attempt to help the club with a one penny per week levy contributed by local miners.

By 1930 the Third Division clubs were well accustomed to meeting independently to discuss their own problems. The first time this happened amongst Full Members came in April 1930. All but six of the First and Second Division clubs gathered independently of the Management Committee's aegis to debate a whole range of issues they wished to take up either at the Annual Meeting or with the FA (a practice which is now quite common and accepted, but was then regarded as tantamount

to anarchy).

The most important proposal to emerge from these discussions was that clubs should no longer be obliged to release players for Irish, Scottish or Welsh international matches (or English matches, too, in the case of the Welsh clubs), if they clashed with League fixtures. Fed up with releasing players on Saturdays, the clubs also wanted internationals other than those between England and Scotland to be played mid-week and preferably nearer the start of the season.

Since the national associations' income depended largely on international match receipts, this challenge by the League clubs bordered on insurrection. They were in effect saying, you cannot always have our best players, and nor may you play on Saturdays, even though they are, of course, far more lucrative than mid-week afternoon fixtures.

Not all the clubs were prepared to go so far. At the 1930 Annual Meeting, Mr Bendle Moore of Derby County called the demands the most retrograde he could ever recall the League considering. Mid-week internationals, he argued, would attract more men away from their places of work, reduce the importance of the games, and show the League up as a self-interested body. 'We are all selfish,' he said. 'Every one of us. We always play for our own hands. But I do ask you to think a little bit better of the game.'

His speech almost swung the vote, but not quite, and thus Amos Brook Hirst of Huddersfield was given the green light to put the League's proposals forward to the FA.

It was at this point that Charles Sutcliffe spoke up. He had supported the original motion, but now apparently changed his mind (or was he plotting behind the scenes?). He spoke instead of loyalty to the FA and the need for football to present a united face to the world.

So, after the preliminary meeting and all the debate and press interest, another vote was taken, and this time the proposal to propose

> **'An application that the League should take part in a World's Football Championship organised by the Uruguayan F.A. was turned down as it would not be in the interests of the League's competition.'**
>
> *Response to World Cup invitation,*
> *16 December 1929*

the proposals to the FA was defeated, and Saturday internationals survived.

The League's behaviour was similar to that of a teenager, conjuring up all kinds of radical demands in his bedroom, only to be cowed into silence when standing on the threshold of his father's study.

Naturally, the FA was delighted not to have to discuss the matter at its meeting. A loud 'Hear, Hear' was heard when it was announced by William Pickford that the League had stepped back from the brink.

But in fact the matter was far from resolved. Once more at the instigation of Amos Brook Hirst, another meeting of Full Members was arranged, again independently of the Committee, whose members were not even invited. Such discourtesy, wrote the Committee to Brook Hirst, 'may be thought suggestive of disloyalty'.

But before open anarchy could break out, further ill-feeling was pre-empted by a settlement of the international match dispute, on 7 January 1931. At a conference in Liverpool of the four national associations and the Football League, the following, quite remarkable set of concessions was agreed:

● All international matches, apart from those between England and Scotland, in which the services of a League player would be required, would have to be played before 14 December each year.

● Any national association wishing to select a Football League player who was registered with a different association would have to apply for clearance from the Management Committee twenty-one days in advance. This applied, for example, if Scotland wished to pick a man based in England, or Ireland wished to pick a Welsh club's player. The Football League retained the right to refuse permission if the player was needed for an important League match.

● All League players taking part in international matches had to be properly insured

by the national association.

● If a national association selected a League player for a Saturday international, it would have to pay the player's wages for that week.

Accepted unanimously by the clubs in March 1931, these proposals confirmed, if ever there had been any doubt, that the Football League had achieved *de facto* dominance of not just English, but all British football. It had the football associations of four countries eating out of its hands, for the simple reason that its clubs possessed most of the best players.

And as if to prove how inextricably linked were the fates of the League and the FA, at the Liverpool conference which approved these proposals, John McKenna represented not the League, of which he was President, but the FA, of which he was Vice President.

Indeed, the two bodies had never been closer. In 1929 the FA had agreed to the League automatically having four seats on the FA Council, in addition to McKenna and any other Management Committee members (such as Phil Bach) who happened to be on the Council at various times (representing interests other than those of the League). This was a major concession, especially as the League itself was allowed to choose who those four representatives would be.

Then, in 1930, the FA went one further by doubling the number of League representatives on the Council, so that every member of the Management Committee would now automatically become a councillor by right and not by election.

Athletic News pointed out that this rule change made the League the single most powerful group within the FA. 'The FA sowed the seed. The plants grew. This was all the work of enthusiasts. Then the professional gardener stepped in and the amateurs were content to hand over the estate and nursery ... the FA are growing feeble.'

But as Geoffrey Green wrote in his *History of the FA* (Naldrett Press, 1953): 'This fusion, as it were, of the two most powerful bodies in the game, though unpopular in certain quarters at the time, was in fact to bring great benefit in due course, for henceforth each was able more intimately to keep its finger on the pulse of the other.'

So it was that the League achieved its highest level of power in 1930, and thus was able to exert its influence on the national associations when it came to international matches.

But if the League had such new-found power on the FA Council, why did Sutcliffe stymie Brook Hirst's proposal at the 1930 Annual Meeting? Was it really because be believed in loyalty to the FA, as he stated at the time?

More likely was the fact that Sutcliffe could never tolerate any group of clubs or individuals challenging the authority of the Management Committee. Furthermore, the intention of Brook Hirst's original proposals had been to give each club the right of refusal to release players for internationals. The agreement finally reached, however, after Sutcliffe's intervention, gave the right of refusal only to the Management Committee, through which all applications now had to come.

Sutcliffe had enforced his principal doctrine once again: the League before everything, the Committee ruling supreme.

Before leaving this intriguing episode in the League's history, we should point out that the 1931 settlement did not include Inter-League games involving Scotland or Ireland. These would still go ahead on Saturdays. Furthermore, the agreement didn't actually work terribly well, and in January 1934 was subject to another set of negotiations. But whether good or bad, the 1931 settlement proved one thing: if League clubs wanted to score a few goals on their own account, independently of the Committee, Charles Sutcliffe would be there to rule them offside in an instant.

But some things were beyond even his control – the election of clubs at the 1930 Annual Meeting, for example. Much criticism was voiced over the re-election to the Northern section of both Halifax (40 votes) and Barrow (22), mainly because Halifax were in dire financial straits at the time and Barrow's application was their fourth in seven seasons. 'The Northern Section are making their competition a farce', commented *Athletic News*. Mansfield (15), Manchester Central (13) and Prescot Cables (0) were the challengers.

But the real controversy occurred in the elections for Division Three South. For the first time, the Southern section's Associate Members collectively recommended that a non-League club be elected in place of one of the retiring clubs, Merthyr Town. Times were hard in South Wales, reflected in Merthyr's terrible gates and poor record. So while Gillingham (33 votes) were comfortably re-elected, Merthyr dropped out after ten seasons, with just 14. Perennial also-rans Llanelly polled 4 votes, despite having just won the Welsh League and Cup double, while the gallant amateur Argonauts received no votes at all, mainly because their representative refused to state who their players were, on the grounds that he didn't want to breach confidences.

Merthyr's departure, though sad, was no great shock. What really caused the controversy was the identity of the club which gained the Southern section's coveted recommendation. Thames FC played at the West Ham Greyhound Stadium, very close to both West Ham's and Orient's grounds. Apart from the fact that there seemed to be no demand for a third east London club, Thames's credentials were so weak as to be almost insulting to the League.

Firstly, they were almost certainly a subsidiary company of the greyhound stadium's owners. Secondly, they were £2800 in debt at the time of their application. Thirdly, their playing record was quite ordinary. Since forming two years earlier, they had played in the Southern League's Eastern section, coming third in 1930 out of seventeen clubs. Finally, their average gate was 900, at a time when other non-League clubs like Mansfield, for example, were averaging about 5000.

Yet even with all these facts operating against them, Thames won a place in the League, eclipsing Aldershot by just one vote (20 to 19).

Contemporary sources give no clues as to why this happened, so we can only speculate. Perhaps Thames's stadium owners were able to offer certain incentives to other Southern section members. Perhaps clubs were interested to see how a football club could co-exist with this new craze of greyhound racing. Or maybe Aldershot's directors were unpopular. All we know for sure is that the election of Thames was the oddest ever in the League's history, and was proven to have been a mistake from the very beginning.

The club kept only six of their former players, signed on another twenty, and although their pitch was neat and surrounded by beds of geraniums, the atmosphere on the wide-open terracing was deathly. After three months of playing they managed to attract the lowest ever gate in this century for a normally scheduled League match. Only 469 turned up to see them play Luton (although Thames did actually win 1–0).

Lack of interest was Thames's problem. Elsewhere, gates were dropping simply because of the hardships brought on by mass unemployment. But as soon as League clubs started admitting the jobless at reduced prices, the Management Committee stepped in. For example, New Brighton were fined eight guineas in 1930 for doing this on four occasions. Times were so hard at New Brighton that when they were fined the usual nominal fee of ten shillings for sending in a late result sheet, the club secretary called the punishment 'a grave imposition'.

Meanwhile, only a few miles from struggling Thames, Clapton Orient found themselves in 1931 in the hands of a receiver called Major Swears, after a season in which they had to play two home games at Wembley and one

at Highbury because their own pitch at the Lea Bridge Speedway Stadium was found to be a yard or so too narrow. In a move unprecedented in League history, Arsenal stepped in to save Orient with a cheque for £3450, at the same time giving the Management Committee an assurance that they had no intention of interfering with Orient's affairs.

Nevertheless, the League investigated the connection and found Arsenal to be somewhat embarrassed by the invidious position in which they had placed themselves.

Arsenal's John Edwards, a solicitor, thought that one way out would have been to sell Orient lock, stock and barrel to a non-League club such as Aldershot (who refused the offer). Otherwise, Arsenal were stuck with a heavy investment in a bankrupt club which no one wanted to buy and which had a manager, Jimmy Seed, appointed by the receiver but beholden to Arsenal for his future.

Of course, since the activities of Messrs Norris and Hall it had been against League regulations for any individual to have a controlling interest in more than one club, so in the end Arsenal had to convert their £3500 into shares which carried no voting rights in a new Orient company.

Modern readers will be interested to note that the men Arsenal wanted to take over Orient were Stanley and Albert Gliksten, timber magnates in east London. When the Management Committee and FA rejected Arsenal's rescue package and formulated their own, this paved the way for the Glidkstens and Orient manager Jimmy Seed to transfer their attentions to Charlton, which in the next two decades they transformed from a run-of-the-mill Second Division outfit to runners-up in the First Division (in 1937) and Cup winners (in 1947). And to think it could so easily have been Orient...

Orient survived however, largely through the vigilance of the League, the bounty of the receiver, the efforts of the supporters (who paid the players' wages for a few months), and a gift of £400 from a tobacco firm.

Mass unemployment, big business involvement, the threat of extinction or mergers, worries about the future of grounds; if any member of the Management Committee from the early 1980s had been transported back half a century he would have found little changed in the outlook for some of the League's struggling clubs.

Further north the story would have been quite familiar too, even if the names have changed. In 1931 Wigan Borough were so behind in paying wages that the FA threatened to expel them. Accrington Stanley were often on the verge of collapse – a bazaar saved them in 1932 – while Port Vale couldn't pay transfer fees and several clubs, including Halifax and Rochdale, were repeatedly unable to pay their players.

At the same time, there were plenty of clubs still anxious to join the struggle. Merthyr wrote saying they would be prepared to join the League at a moment's notice should any club fall by the wayside. Others went much further, so that John McKenna, celebrating his twenty-first year as President, had to warn non-League clubs at the 1931 Annual Meeting to stop 'touting for votes' and 'keeping open house'. Was this a trend started by Thames, one wonders?

Whichever of the six applicants McKenna's reproach was directed at, two of them, at least, succeeded. In the Southern section, Norwich City (38 votes) were re-elected, but Newport County (19) became the third Welsh club to lose their League place after finishing behind Mansfield Town (25). This was Mansfield's sixth attempt but the first time they had applied to join the Southern section. They were hardly obvious candidates, especially in a division whose northernmost member was Walsall, but at least they had some pedigree, unlike Thames. In 1929, Midland Leaguers Mansfield had beaten Second Division Wolves to earn a Fourth Round tie against Arsenal, which they lost 2–0. The team had trained on a special

THE FOOTBALL LEAGUE,

30, WINCKLEY SQUARE,
PRESTON,

Nov. 4th, 1932.

PRIVATE AND CONFIDENTIAL,

Dear Sir,

FOOTBALL CLUBS and DOG RACING.

The Management Committee have discussed on several occasions the effect on The League Clubs of the spread of Greyhound Racing. The Committee are definitely of the opinion that Dog Racing is a menace to our game and that it is a mistake to permit it on any League Club's ground, but would welcome the opinion of the Clubs on this point.

Will you please be good enough therefore to ask your Board to submit their views on this matter to me at an early date, so that the Management Committee may be guided as to any future action they may contemplate.

Yours faithfully,

T. CHARNLEY,

Secretary.

Since the people were going to the dogs, the League decided to stop the dogs coming to League grounds. Only those clubs who already had agreements, such as Bristol Rovers and Chelsea, were allowed to continue staging racing after 1932.

diet, which prompted the message on the cover of their election pamphlet: 'Plump for Mansfield Town, the Egg and Milk Team.'

Perhaps Aldershot (14 votes) should have tried a similar regime, or maybe they should have just applied to the Northern section instead. Merthyr tried both, but it didn't help. They received 2 votes for the Southern section, none for the North.

For the Northern section, Rochdale (40) were comfortably re-elected, Manchester Central (4) failed again, and there was a tie between Nelson, who had finished bottom, and Cheshire County League members Chester, at 27 votes each.

Technically, the President could have decided the matter with his casting vote but, wisely perhaps, McKenna declined to play the role of arbiter. A second ballot ensued, this time giving Chester a majority of 28 votes to 20. Nelson thus became the first Lancashire club to lose membership since Darwen in 1899.

They were joined, sooner than anyone might have anticipated, by Wigan Borough. In September 1931 the Wigan board laid out their balance sheet before the Management Committee at Blackpool and revealed debts of nearly £20,000, an astonishing amount for that period. Their only hope of salvation, Wigan Corporation, had decided against buying the ground at Springfield Park, and now the directors were at their wits' end. So they turned to the Management Committee in the worst possible way: with no ideas of their own and with an appeal for money.

That just about finished them off. The hapless Wigan directors were given four days to come up with something, failing which the club would have to resign by the end of the month. Never before had the Committee shown such apparent firmness with an ailing club – Orient had at least shown some fighting spirit – and on 26 October, after all other attempts to stave off collapse had failed, the Management Committee were shown Wigan's letter of resignation.

No club had ever resigned before in mid-season. In October 1919 Port Vale had taken over the fixtures of Leeds City, but City had been expelled. In October 1931, Manchester Central offered to take over Wigan's fixtures, and the Committee went so far as to seek the views of both Manchester clubs, since Central played their Lancashire Combination home games at Belle Vue, a few miles from both City and United (and close to City's old ground at Hyde Road). But as a result of the 'emphatic objections' received, Central's offer was turned down and their name was never again seen in League records. Prescot Cables and Merthyr Town also applied to fill the vacancy, but the

Management Committee decided instead to declare Wigan's games null and void.

(Wigan had actually played twelve games, including two defeats at the hands of Lincoln City. The deletion of their results therefore made the outcome of the Championship extremely close, Lincoln eventually beating Gateshead on goal average instead of by what should have been a four-point margin.)

After Wigan, Rochdale were reported in December 1931 for being on the brink. Response to an appeal fund was dismal, the manager and some of the directors were unpopular, and since players' wages were constantly in arrears it was hardly surprising that they recorded the worst points per match ratio since Doncaster's disastrous season in 1904/5. Rochdale also managed to concede 135 goals in forty games, marginally worse than even Nelson in 1927/8 (136 in forty-two) or Merthyr two years later (135 in forty-two), though just behind Darwen's all-time blundering record of conceding 141 goals in thirty-four games in 1898/9.

Wigan, possibly Rochdale, New Brighton ... where would it end? Some press reports went so far as to suggest that the Northern section was about to disband. But somehow, as has happened so often in the League's hundred years, clubs like Rochdale managed to survive.

Thames did not. While greyhounds and speedway prospered at the West Ham stadium, no one seemed too bothered about the football team. An appeal for support was ignored by the public, and after finishing bottom of the division Thames decided in May 1932 to

---

In April 1932 it was resolved that any continental club outside England, Scotland, Ireland and Wales trying to sign a League player 'will be regarded as having committed an unfriendly act towards the League and all friendly relations will cease'.

disband. (Their neighbours had a poor season too, Orient finishing only six places above them and West Ham being relegated from Division One.)

After the Thames debacle and the experience of Wigan, no one on the Committee wanted to take any risks. All clubs applying in 1932 had to have their accounts vetted, with the result that the Committee recommended that only three of the six southern applicants be considered at the Annual Meeting. These were: Gillingham, re-elected with 41 votes; Newport County, returned to the fold after a year's absence, with 36 votes, and – to fill the vacancy left by Wigan – Aldershot, newly elected at the third attempt with 35 votes. Llanelly did well at their fifth attempt by attracting their highest ever total of 25 votes, but this was still not enough. Guildford City (8) and Merthyr Town (2) were the other challengers.

In the Third Division North there was only one vacancy, Mansfield having been switched to that section (where they should have been in the first place). A newly reformed Wigan club gained no sympathy whatsoever with their application, which received not a single vote. Rhyl managed 2, which left the way clear for Rochdale's re-election, with a surprisingly high total of 47 votes.

Why were Rochdale so popular after such an abysmal season? Simply because the Spotland club had made great efforts towards rehabilitation, and such commendable self-help invariably won the League's warm support.

A year later, and attention had switched back to London. Herbert Chapman's Arsenal won the first of their trio of championships, Tottenham won promotion to the Second Division, Brentford went up from the Third Division, and West Ham only narrowly missed taking their place.

Meanwhile, at Orient . . . well, little seemed to have changed. On 8 May 1933 they were suspended by the FA for non-payment of wages and fees. Once more the directors made desperate attempts at fund raising, negotiating

with creditors and formulating new schemes to revive the club. But promises alone would not impress the FA, warned the Management Committee, and if Orient's situation was not improved by 27 May the League would have no option but to report them under Regulation 72, which governed the expulsion of defaulters.

Someone must have had a soft spot for the East-enders, however, because to help them survive the League decided to conduct any transfer negotiations that might arise on the club's behalf – the club itself could do nothing while under suspension – and hope that the fees thus raised would save them yet again.

The 1933 Annual Meeting was faced, therefore, with the recommendation that although Orient had been guilty of misconduct, they should be allowed until 22 June to pay all wage arrears. If they could then show at least £1000 in hand and could satisfy the Committee of their capabilities, the League would call upon the FA to remove the suspension. 'Orient are a very lucky club in having a generous lot of gentlemen allowing them to continue,' John McKenna told the meeting. 'But I will say clearly now that there will be no further sympathy with them, unless they put their affairs in order by June 22nd.'

In the end, of course, Orient did fulfil the Committee's criteria, helped by a donation from no less a figure than the Prince of Wales (probably because in the First World War, Orient's contribution had been so outstanding). Charlton Athletic also sent £50.

So Orient returned to the fold, while at the same time Tom Charnley, who was now seventy-three, decided to step down after thirty-one years as League Secretary. He had been ill in 1932, and, after losing his wife in January 1933, was advised by his doctor to take life easier. On 31 May, therefore, he moved aside to a consultative role while his son-in-law and assistant, Fred Howarth, was promoted to Secretary. Howarth was then forty-five, exactly the same age as the League.

Apart from the Orient ultimatum, Tom Charnley's last Annual Meeting as Secretary was notable for three proposals, all of which aroused considerable passions.

Firstly, Derby County made the seventh attempt since 1904 to increase the number of clubs promoted and relegated. Bendle Moore contended that four up, four down would lead to a greater interest in the competition. Representing the Northern section, Mr R. Ledsom of Tranmere pleaded with the members to be generous. Change would have to come eventually, so why not make it now? Notts County's distinguished representative, Lord Belper – the first peer to be associated with the League – said that attendance figures had proved that once a club's chance of promotion had gone, interest waned.

This time, the proposal came closer to success than ever before, a 24–24 vote being recorded. (Bendle Moore tried again in both succeeding years, and in 1935 actually won a majority of 28–21, which didn't quite reach the necessary three-quarters.)

The second move in 1933, a proposal to introduce the numbering of players, was less popular.

This was a continental idea, much favoured by Arsenal's manager Herbert Chapman, and first seen in England on 25 August 1928 when both Arsenal at Hillsborough and Chelsea, at home to Swansea, wore numbers. It was another five years until the experiment was repeated officially, at the 1933 Cup Final, where players were numbered from 1–22. Cup winners Everton wore the same numbered shirts when they played a League match at Wolverhampton a week later.

Proposing its official adoption for League matches, Charles Roberts of Tottenham stated that football was an entertainment and that 'every facility should be given to the spectator to identify the players easily'. Claude Kirby of Chelsea told the meeting that after their game against Swansea in 1928, 700 fans had been asked for their comments on numbering

players, and every one had been in favour.

Bendle Moore was not. 'It might be an advantage to the press, but in my view it has definite disadvantages as it tends to stress individuality rather than team spirit.' Here, surely, was the nub of the matter: the deeply-rooted reticence of the English to parade an identity. Better to be a face in the crowd, a cog in a wheel, than a star individual.

Or was it simply a question of money? Leeds United's E. J. Clarke said that numbering the front and back of each shirt would be costly, and club colours would be spoiled. Charles Sutcliffe calculated that each club needed eight sets of shirts. This consideration alone probably clinched the matter. Only four votes were in favour, and numbering had to wait another six years.

A similar lack of support was shown for the third proposal, put forward by E. S. Atkin of Sheffield United. This was the amendment of Regulation 32 to allow clubs to admit unemployed people, on the production of their dole cards, at a charge of 6d, half the stipulated minimum.

Unemployment in 1933 stood at its highest level since records had been kept. An international financial crisis in 1931 had split the Labour Government, itself elected two years earlier largely because of the Tories' inability to reduce unemployment. After the election of a National Coalition in 1931, the dole queues lengthened during the winter of 1932/3 to a peak of around three million, with the total dropping gradually thereafter to just below two million in mid 1935.

Requests from clubs to charge a lower admission for the unemployed were made throughout the early 1930s. Supporters' clubs added their voice in 1932. But, as before, the principal objection in 1933 was that the system was difficult to operate and open to abuse. Mr Clarke of Leeds said that when his club had experimented with reduced admissions for Central League games, it had been widely abused. Leeds Rugby Club had reported a similar experience.

Mr Atkin thought otherwise. Sheffield United had tried it at a benefit match, without problems. The League, he said, had to think of the unemployed man who, in better times, had been a regular attender. Southampton's Mr Muir backed him up, as did two other clubs. The rest were against the proposal, and so the unemployed man had to continue with his usual habit of either begging at the turnstile, offering to work on the ground to prepare the pitch, or entering at half time for 6d.

Were gates affected?

The yield from the League's percentage of net takings – a fair though not entirely accurate measure – actually went up slightly in 1932/3, but it was still below that recorded for 1928/9, when the post-war attendance boom was at its end.

Exact gates are hard to determine, since clubs were forbidden from giving details to the press. Barrow were ticked off for doing this in 1933. The figures given in newspapers were thus, until 1946, no more than approximations.

One innovation of 1933 did succeed, however, albeit only until the outbreak of the Second World War. This was a cup competition contested amongst clubs in each section of the Third Division. The southern clubs gave their competition the uninspiring title of 'Football League Southern Section, Third Division, Challenge Cup Competition'. Modern commentators have therefore much to be thankful for when it comes to the present-day equivalent, the Sherpa Van Trophy: much less of a mouthful. (For details of the pre-war Third Division competition, see Appendix Six.)

There were no other changes that year or in the following two years. In 1933 all four retiring clubs were re-elected: Swindon (45 votes) and Newport County (26) in the South, Darlington (47) and New Brighton (47) in the North. Unsuccessful applications were made by Llanelly (20), Folkestone (5), Merthyr (1), Nuneaton (1) and, making their first bid, Scarborough (4).

In 1934, Bournemouth and Cardiff were re-elected to the Southern section with the maximum 48 votes each. Folkestone thus went home empty-handed. In the Northern section, Rochdale and Rotherham were unopposed.

The 1935 Annual Meeting also saw all four retiring clubs being re-elected: Southend (48) and Newport (43) in the South easily beat off challenges from Bath City (6) and Folkestone (1). Carlisle (46) and Southport (46) were returned to the Northern section, well ahead of Shrewsbury (6), who were making their first application.

CHAPTER THIRTEEN

Fred Rinder – Architectural Agitator

No man tried longer or more persistently to get on to the Management Committee than Fred Rinder, one of the leading figures of the 1930s. It took him nine attempts before he finally succeeded in 1917, but once on board he needed no time to learn the ropes. He had, after all, been involved with the League from its very conception, travelling with his friend William McGregor around the country before 1888, canvassing opinion and being in attendance at the very first meetings.

Even so, it isn't hard to see why Rinder took so long to gain acceptance. By the turn of the century he was known as the 'stormy petrel' of football, an iconoclast who repeatedly denounced John Bentley and others for their support of wage and bonus restrictions. (Rinder was supported in this by William McGregor, incidentally.) Perhaps it was inevitable, therefore, that he had to wait until Bentley's star had dimmed before he could finally win his seat on the Committee.

Rinder's worst clash with the Management Committee arose over remarks he made at the FA's Annual Meeting in 1899. He was alleged to have said that it was a matter of 'common knowledge that the £10 bonus rule of the League was repeatedly broken'. Hauled in front of the Management Committee, he refused to answer any questions unless a shorthand clerk was present to note down everything he said. The Committee refused, and Rinder was found guilty of misconduct.

On 11 November 1899 Harry Lockett issued the following declaration: 'Being the chairman of a leading League club [Rinder's] action is the more regrettable and deserving the most severe censure. In order to mark their sense of his conduct this Committee will in future decline to recognise Mr Rinder as a representative of any League club.'

No senior figure in the game had ever been so publicly excoriated, but in effect it was the Committee men who were making a rod for their own backs. They couldn't possibly hope to silence Rinder, nor apply any real sanctions against him. He hadn't been found guilty of dishonesty or corruption, and most people knew, or at least suspected, that Rinder was right about clubs ignoring the £10 bonus limit.

Inevitably, the November declaration had no effect, and after Rinder had duly appeared at the next Annual Meeting in May 1900, the Committee backed down by agreeing to supply a shorthand clerk should he agree to give evidence in the future.

This he did in October 1900, but contrary to all expectations, instead of courting more controversy he declined to name a single case known to him of a player receiving more than the £10 maximum signing-on bonus, merely saying that he had based his allegations on newspaper reports. Had Rinder been totally honest he would no doubt have mentioned such cases at his own club, but for some reason he seemed unwilling to stir up more trouble and the matter was allowed to slip. The Management Committee made a token gesture by resolving that Rinder had been 'wanting in loyalty to the League', but took no further action.

One possible explanation for his reticence was that he and his brother freemason, John McKenna, were planning a full assault on the much greater issue of the maximum wage, which was due to be approved at the next

Annual Meeting of the FA in May 1901. As we have already learned, their bold attempt to stop the move just failed to win the necessary two-thirds majority, and Rinder was once again placed in direct opposition to John Bentley.

Rinder had an unusual upbringing. 'It is natural that I should be fond of sport,' he liked to say, 'for I was born in Lancashire [Liverpool, to be exact], reared in Yorkshire [Leeds], polished in London [Battersea] and finished off in Birmingham.'

Rinder actually arrived in Birmingham in 1877 at the age of twenty. Following in his father's footsteps he became a surveyor, being taken on by Birmingham City Corporation in 1882. For years he was responsible for helping to clean up many a small and dirty unlicensed premises as part of Arthur Chamberlain's 'fewer and better' scheme for public houses. He later became involved with the new film industry and became an adviser on cinema design. He recalled in later life how the early picture houses, set up in the backs of shops, would show films twice, forwards then backwards, to save rewinding the film.

Between 1909 and his retirement in 1922, Rinder supervised the licensing of sixty-seven cinemas and 2000 pubs, billiard halls, music halls and clubs. It was this experience in public works and planning which made Rinder the perfect man to plot the building and development of Villa Park.

Rinder joined Villa in 1881, and was co-opted on to their committee in 1887 to help build a new stand at Perry Barr. It was such a success that 30,000 people turned up to see it being opened (when gates of 8000 were normal), and chaos reigned. Money had to be collected in water buckets, the crowd spread on to the pitch, and the game had to be declared a friendly. Those who had bought tickets for the new stand but hadn't got near it were given their money back.

When times were hard at Perry Barr in 1892, it was Rinder who organized an historic meeting in Barwick Street at which he made a scathing attack on the 'well-meaning but hopelessly incapable' committee. Villa were 'in a deplorable state owing to utter mismanagement', he declared, before successfully engineering the committee's resignation.

Profits soared immediately once Rinder took over, if only because he built turnstiles at the ground and therefore smashed a widespread ticket racket. With McGregor at his side he became chairman in 1894 and oversaw the most glorious period in Villa's history. Rinder was also largely responsible for forming the club into a limited company and organizing the move to Villa Park. He later claimed to have laid down every 'level and line' when construction began on the site in 1896.

Thus, Fred Rinder transformed Aston Villa from a famous but small-time organization founded upon romance and sentiment into a businesslike and powerful sporting institution. But Rinder still had dreams.

After drawing up grandiose plans for a 130,000 capacity stadium, in association with architect Archibald Leitch, Rinder began the modernization of Villa Park in 1911. It was his drive which led to the building of the splendid Trinity Road stand at a cost of £90,000, a project which a large body of shareholders opposed. This led to Rinder resigning after a stormy meeting in July 1925.

Not content with remodelling Villa Park – the massive Holte End was his idea also – when Rinder was over seventy years of age he turned his thoughts to Wembley, which he felt was too small. So he visited the stadium alone one day to measure up the place, but, sadly for future generations of squashed Cup Final supporters, his plans didn't get further than his notebook.

During his absence from the directors' box at Villa Park, Rinder was reported to have flirted with Bristol Rovers for a couple of years (his brother Sam was chairman at the time), then in 1936, in a remarkable turnaround, he was re-elected to the Villa board when the man who had ousted him originally was himself turfed out. Rinder was then aged seventy-eight.

As one might expect of a club chairman with his record of achievement, Rinder could be a hard man. He might listen to another man's view, but he invariably went his own way. The *Birmingham Mail* wrote of him: 'If he made enemies it was because his quiet forcefulness was often interpreted as autocracy.'

One contemporary teased him with being 'a trifle didactic', as he showed during the League's crusade against the pools in 1936, and once on a train returning from a Villa away match. The team's compartment had filled up with hangers-on, forcing the players to stand up. As soon as he saw this, Rinder cleared the carriage by the simple expedient of throwing three bottles of whisky, which had just appeared, out of a window. 'There were plenty of black looks,' he remembered. ' A reformer is rarely popular.'

But as we have seen, he was not averse to bending the rules if it suited his own purposes. For example, he was once suspended for a month for fielding a brilliant young goalkeeper he knew to be ineligible. He also went to extraordinary lengths to sign players (as did so many of the League's pioneers).

On one occasion, Rinder travelled to a Hednesford coal mine to sign Steve Smith, with whom he eventually made contact hundreds of feet below the surface while working a night shift. Having signed the player in the engine-house, Rinder then lost his way in the dark and after hours of wandering around coal tips and canal sides he ended up creeping into the cabin of a longboat for an uncomfortable night.

On another occasion, being chased by an angry mob in Rossendale (Sutcliffe country) after signing a particularly popular local player, he reached the station and leapt on to a moving train, only to find it was going a long way in the wrong direction without stopping.

After his younger days as the 'stormy petrel' of football (a curious epithet, which seems to have been attached to many a rebel in the game), Rinder rapidly became one of the League's most stalwart and respected Committee men. He succeeded Arthur Dickinson as a Vice President in 1930, and was made a Life Member in 1938. He was also forgiven his earlier outbursts by the FA, who elected him on to their International Selection Committee. In that capacity he led an England tour to Sweden and Finland in 1937, at the age of seventy-nine.

Ivan Sharpe recalled how Rinder joined him on that tour in a radio broadcast from Bergen. Seeing him sporting an Olympic Games blazer, someone asked his age. 'Young enough to tell these footballers how to play!' was his answer.

Fred Rinder so nearly achieved one of his great ambitions. When Charles Sutcliffe fell ill after the jubilee celebrations in 1938, Rinder, as senior Vice President, stood in as chairman of the Management Committee. He would almost certainly have succeeded Sutcliffe as President had he lived, if only in an honorary capacity. Instead, while Sutcliffe hung on to life until 11 January 1939, Rinder died a fortnight earlier.

Despite the cold, he had insisted on watching Villa's junior team play against Leicester City. He had a stroke and died a few days later at his daughter's home in Harborne, on Christmas Day 1938.

But although he never made the presidency, Fred Rinder did at least earn two distinctions in League circles. He was the longest surviving participant of the original League gathering of 22 March 1888. Having then witnessed the birth of the League in April 1888, he missed only one of the next fifty Annual Meetings. No other man could claim such a record. Not bad for someone one accused of 'wanting in loyalty'.

CHAPTER FOURTEEN

The Pools War

The year 1936 was a watershed in the history of the League. Firstly, John McKenna died on 22 March, aged eighty-two. Secondly, he died at a time when the League had just undergone its single biggest crisis – the 'Pools War'.

Had it emerged from this crisis with credit, then McKenna might have died contented. Sadly, however, the Management Committee was humiliated by the whole affair, and was fortunate to escape without being voted out of office.

Nowadays we are accustomed to reading of attempts to extract the maximum benefit for football from commercial interests, pools or otherwise. But in 1936 a moral majority on the Management Committee not only refused to accept a penny from the pools, but they also tried to use their powers to halt the industry completely. They failed, they failed badly, and arguably their stance did great harm to the game.

The problem of betting in football had long occupied the game's senior administrators. In 1892 the League prohibited players and officials from betting on games. A decade later, the FA extended the ban to football grounds, then in 1910 toughened up the rules further so that any player or official proved to have taken part in coupon betting would be permanently suspended.

That year, football betting was found to be rife in the army. Pub landlords were running football lotteries, and coupons were widely circularized, often by workers who were picked out by coupon printers for their popularity and paid a 10 per cent commission.

But once popular newspapers got into the act, it seemed as if nothing and no one could prevent betting on football becoming almost as widespread as it was on horse racing. Newspaper competitions became so popular that agencies bought up massive stocks simply to cut out and distribute the printed coupons. This did wonders for the newspapers' circulation figures until the competitions were finally outlawed in 1928. By then, the coupon betting industry was estimated to have been worth £36,000 a week in postal revenue alone.

The League itself had consistently opposed betting. In 1921, for example, when the Irish club Glentoran invited League clubs to join a sweepstake, the Committee expressly forbade any club from entering. Similarly, when Clapton Orient tried to organize one for a player's benefit, the Committee refused permission. Palace were ordered to remove an advertisement for a coupon company from their ground in 1922. Newport had to remove a comparable advertisement from their programme in 1927, and soon afterwards, one of Hartlepools' directors was questioned about his links with a betting company.

So, when the 1933 Royal Commission on Lotteries and Betting contrived to ignore completely football's part in the industry, the League and the FA were not mightily pleased.

Primarily, betting was regarded as a moral evil, especially by the Management Committee's four most prominent members. John McKenna was a strict disciplinarian who once accused his barber of betting on football, after seeing coupons hanging up in the shop. Persuaded eventually that the coupons were old, unused ones that the barber cleaned his blades with, McKenna forgave him (and loved to tell the story against himself subsequently).

McKenna's close friend, Will Cuff of Everton, and Fred Rinder were also outspoken in their basic objections, although they didn't necessarily share the Scottish FA's view that betting was a factor in corruption. Although there had been several reported incidents of anonymous 'fixers' trying to bribe players for betting purposes, in reality most of the proven cases of squaring had implicated players and officials, acting in their own interests in vital promotion and relegation games.

Even so, few football officials approved of the pools, and Charles Sutcliffe approved least of all. Sutcliffe, the teetotaller, democrat and devout Methodist, had long been the League's leading crusader against corruption.

Once, on a train returning from Newcastle, three men got into Sutcliffe's compartment and persistently pressed him to 'find the lady' (a card trick played for money). The men fleeced everyone else in the carriage, but when they tried Sutcliffe again he took out a slip of paper and wrote on it, 'Deaf and Dumb'.

The Pools War began to simmer, innocuously enough, in June 1934, when a Liverpool accountant, Mr Watson Hartley, approached the Management Committee with a scheme to divert some of the pools companies' profits to League funds. The Committee's reaction was predictable. 'There can be no connection, however vague, between the League and betting.'

The intensity of this moral stance should not be undervalued. The League's coffers were hardly overflowing at the time; indeed, claims on the insurance fund were stretching resources so much that there was even talk of raising the levy on match receipts – a move that no Committee member wanting to hold his seat would ever take lightly.

Hartley was persistent, however, and with cause. According to published figures, pools revenue soared from £9 million in 1934 to £20 million in 1935, still only a fraction of the total spent on betting – estimated at around £500 million – but to Watson Hartley, enough to prove that the League would be foolhardy not to claim some of the profits for itself.

Accordingly, he renewed contact with the Management Committee in October 1935, and two months later presented his scheme a second time. Its basis was the contention that the League held the copyright of its fixtures. Although Charles Sutcliffe devised the fixtures, he did so at the League's request and had to alter them at the discretion of the clubs. No one disputed this.

Hartley explained that advertisers, pools companies and newspapers all used the fixtures in one way or another, without any acknowledgement to the League. Instead, the League should prohibit the printing of the fixtures without its consent, at the same time establishing certain terms and conditions.

Hartley's main target were the pools companies, who paid nothing for the fixtures yet made enormous profits from them. He was not suggesting any connection between the League and the pools; merely that anyone – betting companies, calendar printers, sports publications or whoever – should be charged for using the League's property.

It was at this point that an idea struck Committee member Phil Bach. If the League could control the use of its fixtures, could it not thereby stop coupon betting? Hartley couldn't deny this, but he argued that since pools betting was legal and brought the Exchequer considerable benefit, the League would hardly be advised to stop it altogether. For all his antipathy towards betting, Charles Sutcliffe had to agree. The number of legal actions the League would have to face in such a battle would be far too costly. But he did think Hartley's scheme would be an effective way of at least controlling the pools.

At this stage the Committee seemed well disposed to Hartley's idea, more so when legal opinion was read out suggesting that the League had a strong claim to copyright of the fixtures.

The members disagreed only on how to

proceed. Should a football copyright control board be set up by the Committee, or independently? Wouldn't the Scottish League have to be involved also? They did agree, however, that the first step was to ascertain counsel's opinion on the question of copyright. Until then, the press were to be told only that the matter was under consideration.

That was 3 December 1935. On 16 December, the Committee met again to hear that in counsel's opinion, the League did have copyright of the fixtures as a whole, but not over the listing of individual matches. Charles Sutcliffe would see counsel again on the twentieth of the month.

Meanwhile, John McKenna had been approached in Liverpool by a Mr E. Holland Hughes, legal adviser to the Pool Promoters' Association (which was based in the city). Apparently, the PPA wanted a meeting to discuss the matter. Will Cuff urged caution, Fred Rinder warned against accepting money, but McKenna saw no harm in just talking. So it was that the President went with Messrs Sutcliffe, Cuff and Amos Brook Hirst to meet the PPA on 3 January 1936.

What happened at this meeting was to prove one of the mysteries of the Pools War. We know that the PPA, having sought legal advice, decided to contest the fixture copyright issue. We also know that despite this, the pools companies were prepared to offer 'a reasonable ex-gratia contribution', subject, of course, to the FA's approval, and provided the money was used in the best interests of the sport.

But the real question mark hanging over this meeting concerned the League's demands. Did the Committee delegates ask the PPA for 'a substantial sum' in return for the right to print the fixtures? John Moores, co-founder of the Littlewoods Company, who was present at that meeting, later swore on a bible that the League had indeed asked for a sum of money. The figure of £100,000 was mentioned.

So, was the League prepared to sacrifice its opposition to betting, after all, at a price?

Unfortunately, the League's own records of the meeting have not survived intact. They may even have been tampered with afterwards. All we learn from the surviving part of the record is that the PPA representatives said that they had no power to discuss terms, but would call a meeting of members and report back.

Ten days passed, during which the League received more assurances about its legal right to copyright. Committee member Tom Barcroft reckoned, therefore, that the League should pressurize the PPA to come up with 'a satisfactory proposal', failing which they should be issued with an injunction to prevent them using the fixtures. Thus, a letter was drafted to the effect that unless a concrete proposal was received within seven days, proceedings would be commenced for breach of copyright.

The question is, what was at stake here – the principle of receiving money from the pools companies, or the amount of money itself?

The sum most often touted in the newspapers was £50,000, which was £10,000 below the sum Watson Hartley had originally suggested, and still only a tiny proportion of the PPA's total profits. But as Will Cuff soon discovered when he met Holland Hughes again, the PPA was considering a payment much smaller even than £50,000 and that would be only out of the goodness of their hearts. Their own legal advice directly contradicted that of the League's and they were prepared to defend any legal action strenuously.

As one solicitor to another, Amos Brook Hirst considered that Holland Hughes was bluffing and that the PPA was just trying to evade having to pay out a reasonable sum. They would not dare risk legal action, he reckoned. The League should simply agree a figure and put it directly to the pools companies. If they didn't accept it, proceedings should begin. 'Any damages granted would be enormous', he said.

Will Cuff, also a solicitor, was more cautious. The League's public stance should be that they wanted to eradicate pools betting. Only if this proved impossible should they seek a financial settlement.

By now, several ideas were flying around the table: conferences with the FA, meeting the PPA again, issuing writs, consulting the clubs. Cuff and Rinder seemed to be most hostile to the pools, Sutcliffe and McKenna were prepared to carry on talks, while Brook Hirst was all for legal action.

It was at this point that Charles Sutcliffe revealed a plan which would earn the League nothing financially, but a great deal ethically; a plan to cleanse both football and the nation of this unsavoury pools betting business, once and for all. Instead of negotiating with the pools companies, argued Sutcliffe, the League had the ability to kill them off altogether. And it could achieve this before the season was over, no less, simply by scrapping the existing fixtures and releasing details of the new ones only at the latest possible moment, thereby throwing the week's coupons into complete disarray.

It was an intriguing idea, in principle. Unfortunately, the Management Committee not only took it seriously but was also encouraged by the FA, who pledged financial assistance should the League vote to take action.

Even with the two organizations acting in concert, it was still an awesome task: a handful of men, mainly volunteers, with a joint annual income of less than £50,000, taking on a multi-million-pound business.

Every week, it was reckoned, £800,000 was spent on the pools, compared with only £48,125 on watching football. Over sixteen times more people gambled on the game than watched it. And it was not just a question of numbers. Football betting seemed to have become an integral part of the national psyche, affecting all ages, and both rich and poor.

There were reports of families being broken up as wages were frittered away on pools, of schoolchildren found filling in coupons, of junior club secretaries being bribed by pools promoters to distribute coupons to players in return for equipment.

Yet how could one form of betting be banned while horse racing – the sport of kings – escaped censure? Was there to be one law for the working man and another for the lords and ladies at Ascot? And what about the government income from taxation on pools and from the postal services they used? And all the people employed by the pools companies? The issue was brimming with social, economic and political implications, far too deep for the League to handle, with or without the FA's assistance. After all, the League was an organization formed to stage professional football, not to enforce its moral code upon Britain.

Sutcliffe, Rinder and Cuff were determined, however. Nothing would stop them now.

The Pools War was declared on Thursday, 20 February 1936. That was the date of a private meeting of clubs, summoned by the League with unusual haste to the Midland Hotel, Manchester. Eighty-five clubs attended to hear Charles Sutcliffe, as always, explain the situation.

The League had a choice, he said. The Committee was certain that the League held copyright of the fixtures, but to establish that in law would be a long, difficult and costly business. No doubt in time the League could make large sums of money from the pools, but Sutcliffe asked the meeting to consider the overall cost. It could cripple the League in the short term. The clubs had to decide, he concluded: stop the pools or negotiate.

Will Cuff and Fred Rinder made their views exceedingly clear, the latter stating that in view of the game's popularity and honesty, 'it would be fatal to accept money from a tainted source'.

Bendle Moore of Derby expressed doubts about this. Pool betting was a menace, he agreed, but not to the game itself. Even if the League did withhold the fixtures, the public could still bet on blank coupons.

Alderman Alf Masser, the recently

appointed chairman of Leeds United and himself a prominent lawyer, complained that the meeting had been called too hurriedly, and that the League would only be made to look foolish if it issued threats it couldn't carry out. Besides which, whatever they decided, betting would still continue in one form or another.

The League should not touch a penny of the pools money, Masser agreed, but that was different from trying to wipe out football betting altogether. Instead, he proposed a motion which stated: 'That the representatives of League clubs here assembled view with alarm the growth of betting on Football Pools and they call upon the Parliament of the Country immediately to introduce legislation to deal with the menace.'

Mr Barlow of Stockport was dubious about the will of Parliament. Why would an MP risk alienating his constituents by supporting such a Bill?

Masser's motion was defeated heavily. Will Cuff's motion condemning the pools was passed. The next question was, what could they do about it?

Cuff proposed that the Management Committee 'be hereby empowered to take such steps as it deems expedient to bring about the suppression of betting'. Sutcliffe then explained what those steps might be. After the following Saturday, 22 February, all the fixtures would be scrapped and clubs informed of their schedules late enough to fox the coupon printers, but not too late for away teams to make plans.

Colonel Crisp of Chelsea thought this an ingenious plan. Several others thought it far too drastic, and potentially disastrous for gates. But when a vote was taken only eight of the eighty-five clubs voted against, eleven abstained, and so Sutcliffe's scheme carried the day. The Pools War was on.

But it would depend entirely on secrecy, warned Will Cuff. No one at the meeting should breathe a word to anyone about Sutcliffe's plan.

Some hope. Immediately after the meeting the newspapers caught wind of the secret plan and one club director told them: 'The whole idea is too revolutionary to contemplate. It is cutting off your nose to spite your face.' He begged the Committee to reconsider.

As they prepared to do battle, therefore, the ranks of the League were already divided: solicitors Cuff and Sutcliffe on one side, Alf Masser, with Brook Hirst's tacit support, on the other.

The newspapers were highly sceptical about Sutcliffe's battle plan. If home and away sequences were to be maintained, as he had promised, then surely all the pools promoters had to do was issue lists of home teams, leaving the punter to fill in the away column. And even if the pools were disrupted, the League would still have to establish in law that the fixtures were copyright.

Furthermore, Scottish fixtures were not going to be affected. A Scottish League official said that they had considered taking similar action but felt in the end it wouldn't be worthwhile.

For its part, the PPA was still anxious to avoid coming to blows. After a secret four-hour meeting at the Adelphi Hotel, Liverpool on 22 February, Holland Hughes issued a statement reiterating the previous offer of 'a reasonable contribution', provided it was directed to the best interests of the sport and subject to FA approval. The FA hadn't had the decency to reply to the PPA's offer, Holland Hughes noted, while the League's action was 'a stunning blow … coming as it did without warning. But we are not dismayed.'

Nor were they cowed. The pools companies also informed the public that certain members of the Management Committee had indeed asked the PPA on 3 January for a substantial sum of money for use of the fixtures. This sum was described as 'exorbitant and unreasonable'.

Nonsense, cried the Management Committee in reply. Fred Rinder insisted that no payment of 'any sort, size or description' had been demanded. Strictly speaking, this was probably true. No sum had been *demanded*, but a sum had certainly been *mentioned*. Tom Barcroft admitted as much.

So now the seeds of doubt were planted in the public mind. Was this impending Pools War a moral crusade, or merely an attempt to extort more money from the PPA?

Alderman Masser, meanwhile, issued a protest at the Management Committee's conduct of the affair. Cancelling the fixtures was futile, he complained; the PPA's discomfort would be trivial compared with that of the clubs and the supporters. The pools, Masser repeated, were a matter for Parliament.

In fact, they soon would be. The Liberal National MP for Eddisbury, Mr Richard Russell, had already introduced a Private Member's Bill to make illegal all *pari-mutuel* or pools betting. But that wasn't due for debate in the House of Commons until 3 April, and as press comment indicated, the Bill hardly stood a chance.

'It is only another move to spoil the small man's recreations, while people who can afford big bets on horse racing will still be allowed their amusement', wrote one Yorkshireman.

MPs were divided right across party lines. The Conservative member for Macclesfield, Mr J. R. Remer, said patronizingly: '... to suppress football pools is such a silly thing. The football pool is a poor man's little flutter....' He admitted to indulging a little himself, and was at that very moment awaiting winnings of 12s 6d.

But his fellow Tory, Mr C. G. Gibson, MP for Pudsey and Otley, supported the League's stance. 'It is not just a little sporting matter now, it is a gambling craze.' He personally knew of five divorce cases precipitated by arguments over the pools. The dispute even raised hackles in Sweden, where some 200,000 people were said to enter British pools competitions every week.

Among football commentators, one question was paramount: did the Football League really ask the PPA for 'an exorbitant fee' or not? The public had a right to know, because it was one thing for the League to punish the PPA, but why hurt the supporters more?

Charles Sutcliffe didn't help matters by some of his own remarks to the press. The pools punter wasn't much good as a football supporter anyway, he muttered to one journalist. 'A spade is always a spade to him', said Cuff in his defence.

Sutcliffe had originally intended to start the campaign on Thursday 27 February. On the preceding Monday, as the extent of the opposition became apparent, McKenna, Rinder and Cuff met the FA in a lengthy conference at Lancaster Gate, London.

On the same day, up in Derby, Bendle Moore added his protest to that of Alderman Masser, while in the evening Richard Russell MP spoke at a meeting in Birkenhead to promote his Private Member's Bill. In the audience, Will Cuff, amid much interruption, denied flatly that the League had ever approached the PPA for an 'exorbitant' sum.

But the following day his fellow Committee member, Amos Brook Hirst, told the press that a large enough offer from the PPA would, in fact, be seriously entertained. What did he mean by large enough? Over £50,000 apparently. This sum had already been offered by a group outside the PPA, and was thought to be insufficient.

Did this answer the public's doubt? Was it just a question of haggling over an amount, rather than establishing a principle? Probably not. By this stage men like Cuff, Rinder and Sutcliffe probably had the bit between their teeth and were determined to embark upon a crusade for the national good. Brook Hirst's statement revealed only one truth: the Management Committee was publicly split, an unprecedented occurrence in the League's history at that time.

The clubs were split, too. On the evening of Tuesday 25 February, the northern malcontents – Leeds, Manchester City, Sunderland, Stoke, Blackburn and Newcastle – gathered under the chairmanship of Alf Masser, who contended that the Manchester meeting on 20 February had gone against the rules of the Football League.

This was no casual allegation. To accuse someone like Charles Sutcliffe of breaking rules which he had more or less drawn up himself (the last major revision having been in 1926) was rather like a film extra criticizing Alfred Hitchcock for one of his camera angles. But in matters of law, Masser was at least Sutcliffe's equal.

The Leeds chairman claimed firstly that League Rule 23 would be broken if any of the fixtures were rearranged.

Secondly, Rule 80 had already been broken. This stated that if a change in the rules was planned at a meeting other than an Annual Meeting, the Secretary had to give at least seven days' notice and send out a full agenda in advance. The Manchester meeting had been convened at short notice, by telegram and without an agenda.

Thirdly, stated Masser, Rule 3 allowed the Third Division clubs four collective votes between them, yet in Manchester, Associate Members had voted individually.

How Sutcliffe, normally so punctilious about the rules, had allowed all this to happen without first suspending standing orders is a mystery. Had he become so swept up in the affair that for once he had let his heart overrule his head?

Because of these irregularities, Alderman Masser called for a meeting of all clubs – to exclude members of the Management Committee – to be held on the following Monday, 2 March, at Leeds Town Hall, the same day as the Management Committee was due to meet in London. Although his avowed aim was not to cause a split but to persuade the Committee to drop its fixture plan, an internal dispute of this magnitude had never happened before.

'For all I care, Leeds United and Manchester City can hold their protest meetings', was Sut-

cliffe's chilly response, but he can't have been reassured when the next day further protests came from Brentford, Bristol Rovers, Barrow and Charlton Athletic, whose manager Jimmy Seed said that advanced bookings for Saturday were well down because no one knew who the opposition would be. Some supporters had threatened to boycott the game whoever the visitors were, for as long as the Pools War lasted.

Around the country, preparations were made for what the newspapers billed 'The Big Hush' and 'the Football Fixture Farce'. Posters went up saying 'United *v.* ???', and one pools company issued a coupon with Scottish fixtures only. Another went ahead as normal in the belief that the League wouldn't hold to its plan.

The PPA was taking no chances. It announced from Liverpool that instructions to investors would appear in Friday's papers and that the final hour of postage allowed for coupons would be moved back to 3 p.m. on Saturday, for that week only, thus allowing for the late printing and distribution of coupons.

Meanwhile, at League headquarters in Winkley Square, Preston, Fred Howarth announced that to prevent the Friday newspapers from printing the fixtures, clubs would be telephoned late on Friday as to who their opponents would be the next day. Those clubs which needed to travel long distances would be telegrammed earlier, probably late on Thursday.

The Secretary also insisted that there were no internal divisions in the League, despite the fact that Masser had just announced that twenty clubs had agreed to attend his dissident meeting, including three clubs – Tottenham, Huddersfield and Everton – who had directors sitting on the Management Committee.

The vice-chairman of one Lancashire First Division club told the newspapers: 'The League clubs realize that they have made a gigantic mistake. Everybody knows that Saturday's interference with fixtures will be the last. We shall be back to normal next week. You cannot keep back the tide of public opinion. The League know it must climb down, and will do so. Who are we to dictate the morals of the country? It is the Government's business, not ours.'

It was now Thursday night, and at Winkley Square, Sutcliffe and Howarth prepared to contact those clubs with furthest to travel. But would secrecy prevail? Were there spies about? Could the clubs be trusted to keep their affairs from the press?

Apparently not. By Friday morning it was clear that overnight leaks had occurred. How could it have been otherwise with so many outside parties involved? Telegrams had to be sent, trains booked, meals arranged. Anyone could have leaked the information, especially with so many vested interests eager to pay for information. And even it if wasn't outsiders, within each club were disgruntled directors or secretaries, managers or tea-boys. They had been the ones forced to work overnight in order to make hasty arrangements.

By noon on Friday it was common knowledge that Saturday's fixtures were to be the games originally scheduled for 14 March in the First Division and 11 April in the Second Division. The remaining fixtures were thus simple to work out. Sutcliffe had merely brought forward whole sections of the original list.

But there were complications. Also due to be played that Saturday were the Sixth Round FA Cup games, over which the League had no jurisdiction. As a result, five clubs had no game at all. For example, Bradford Park Avenue's original League fixture against Manchester United had been replaced by another against Barnsley, but Barnsley were already booked to play in the Cup. Understandably, Bradford's chairman, Mr Ernest Waddilove, was furious. 'I consider the treatment meted out to us to be preposterous.' He wondered, did it have anything to do with the fact that his club had voted against Sutcliffe's battle plan? He

assumed that the League would not be compensating Park Avenue for their loss of revenue.

There were other disappointments. Some 3000 Tranmere fans had arranged a whole day out for their visit to Stockport: entertainment, accommodation, meals, the lot. It was to have been the biggest supporters' trip in the club's history. But when Rovers were rescheduled to play Accrington instead, the trip had to be cancelled.

Despite the fact that all the fixtures were known by Friday lunchtime, the League stuck doggedly to its position by refusing to announce the official list until Friday evening. In the meantime, the clubs had been making frantic efforts to complete arrangements. The Pools War was turning out to be very unpopular among the troops at the front.

Sensing this, Fred Howarth issued a circular to all League clubs reminding them of the resolution passed at Manchester on 20 February. It was the clubs who had agreed that pools betting was a menace and must be suppressed. It was they who had empowered the Management Committee to 'take such steps as it may deem expedient'. And the clubs were fully aware that such steps included Sutcliffe's scheme to scrap the fixtures.

As a result of breaches of confidence, wrote Howarth, the secret plan had been leaked to the press, as had the fixtures. Thus, another meeting of all the clubs would be necessary, at the Grand Hotel, Manchester, on Monday 9 March.

But the Committee was already losing ground. As Howarth issued his statement, twenty-seven out of the forty-four Full Members had agreed to attend Masser's meeting, while on the same day, branch meetings of the PPA took place in five major cities.

In Leeds, the newly formed Northern Pool Promoters' Association (consisting of those companies not centred on Liverpool) urged fans not to boycott the following day's games. 'In our opinion football pools, far from being a menace as suggested, give an added interest to the game.' The Public Morality Council thought otherwise, and offered its full support to Richard Russell's forthcoming Bill. So did the Bishop of London, who urged all church members to support a ban on the pools.

And so that fateful Saturday arrived, 29 February 1936, a day when the first real battle of the Pools War would be fought. But who would win?

The Times leader comment on Saturday morning had no doubt. The League had to win, and if it didn't, it was the fault of the clubs. Taking great pains to explain what pools betting was all about, *The Times* pontificated on the PPA, which was, it asserted, not a group of 'trustees' acting on behalf of 'investors', as the PPA liked to portray itself. It was, in reality, sneered *The Times*, 'a combination of bookmakers'. The Football League and the FA were, on the other hand, 'actuated by the loftiest ideals'. They had the purity of sport in mind. The League called the pools betting, the PPA called it investment.

Continuing its lofty tirade, *The Times* estimated that between 'six and seven million of the King's lieges exercise their minds weekly' in pools betting – the assumption being that surely no *Times* readers would stoop so low. It revealed the existence of a vast industry, with offices rivalling Somerset House.

A proliferation of activities was dependent on the pools: newspaper columns which devoted more space to coupon betting than to football itself, plus myriad books and periodicals giving out advice to 'investors'. Thus, the PPA defended itself as the provider of much employment.

'But what of the purity of sport?' asked *The Times*. Lamenting the fact that the 1934 Betting and Lotteries Act had left football virtually untouched, the editorial called for Parliament 'to grasp the nettle . . .' now that football, 'the most popular of all open-air entertainments', had been reduced to 'chaos and public ridicule'.

But had football been reduced to chaos and

The Daily Mail *took delight in leaking the League's secret fixtures, the PPA warned its clients to hold fire, while the* Express *announced a no-score draw after the first day of disruption on 29 February 1936.*

FOOTBALL POOL PROMOTERS ASSOCIATION

Next Saturday's POOL COUPONS

COUPONS for next Saturday's matches have been issued by the leading pool promoters in the usual way, but in view of the possibility of altered fixtures, clients are advised not to fill in their coupons until a further statement is made in the Press.

ISSUED BY THE FOOTBALL POOL PROMOTERS ASSOCIATION

BOTH SIDES LOSE IN THE POOLS WAR

BOTH SIDES IN THE FOOTBALL POOL WAR LOST HEAVILY ON SATURDAY. THERE WERE BIG DROPS IN ATTENDANCES AND GATE RECEIPTS AT MATCHES.

Receipts for most of the pools are stated to be down, although an accurate estimate is impossible until today's mail opening is over.

A number of League clubs will consider their position in Leeds today. It is expected they will urge immediate return to the normal fixture list for next Saturday.

MUDDLE HALVES ATTENDANCES

By TREVOR WIGNALL

BAD weather may have had something to do with the smallness of the attendances at Association football matches on Saturday.

But yesterday the feeling generally expressed that the

SEE HOW THEY FELL

Following figures show how the "gates" fell:—

	Average.	Saturday. day.
Bradford C.	9,500	3,000
...te U.	22,000	8,000
...	18,000	6,000
		15,000

"Secret" Fixtures

First and Second League football fixtures for tomorrow are given on Page Seventeen. The League's "secret," officially due for disclosure this afternoon, is out!

public ridicule? The real test would come on Saturday afternoon. Would the public show its anger with the League by staying away?

Frustratingly, it was impossible to judge. Snow, sleet and rain swept across the North and Midlands, reducing attendances to only 193,000, compared with 318,000 for the corresponding week the year before. Cup attendances were also down, whereas in the South, where the weather was less severe, attendances were hardly down at all.

At Hillsborough, where the crowd was the smallest of the season, a poll was conducted to find out how many people supported the League's action. Only one in ten answered in the affirmative. On Sunday, opinion was divided. Alf Masser declared that the low attendances were partly due to people objecting 'to interference with their liberties'. But most commentators blamed the weather.

Had the pools companies suffered in this first battle? Certainly they reported no casualties, and in truth the only reported disruptions seem to have occurred at post offices, where the usual Friday rush for postal orders – so great that extra staff were often needed to cater for the demand – was delayed until Saturday.

On Sunday evening the Management Committee gathered to assess the damage – what little of it there was. The meeting was reported to have taken all night, but although it left its mainly elderly members exhausted by morning, they emerged with even greater resolve to continue the fight.

The minutes of this marathon meeting confirm that the League and FA were by that stage not even prepared to communicate with the PPA. The issue of whether Third Division clubs should have been allowed to vote at the original meeting in Manchester was sidestepped, but the Committee did discuss an offer of £50,000 for the use of the fixtures, made by a Mr Vince on behalf of 'a City firm of standing'. It was noted approvingly that the firm in question had no connections with betting,

had a senior member who was a director of the Bank of England, and wanted to use the fixtures to help hospitals in some way. Further enquiries were needed.

As the weary Committee members emerged to face the press, they had only one comment to make. Next Saturday's fixtures were still scrapped. 'If you are told anything else during the week,' stated Charles Sutcliffe, 'you can take it you are having your leg pulled.'

That night, representatives from thirty-six of the forty-four First and Second Division clubs gathered at Leeds Town Hall for Alf Masser's meeting. Some of the biggest names in football management were there, including, from the First Division's four leading clubs, George Allison of Arsenal, Johnny Cochrane of Sunderland, George Jobey of Derby County and Clem Stephenson of Huddersfield Town. Only eight clubs declined the invitation: Blackpool (Tom Barcroft's club) and Burnley (Sutcliffe's club), plus Bury, Manchester United, Nottingham Forest, Sheffield United, Swansea and Wolves.

But, despite the build-up, there was no revolution. Instead, after two hours' discussion, during which Masser and his supporters were at pains to emphasize their loyalty to the League and the Management Committee, the following resolution was passed: that while they accepted that the Management Committee had been given a mandate to scrap the fixtures, the clubs now urged the restoration of the fixtures and a return to the *status quo ante bellum*.

On hearing this the next morning, John McKenna announced that if the Leeds resolution was confirmed at the official League meeting on 9 March, then the fixtures would revert to normal the following Saturday.

Yet still the generals would not roll up their battle plans and sound the retreat. On the following Thursday evening, 5 March, the same charade as the week before was enacted at Winkley Square, with the League still vainly confident that secrecy would be maintained.

Once again they were hopelessly wrong.

Fred Howarth cabled seven clubs who had long distances to travel, and all seven leaked details to the press, who were thus able to deduce the remaining games and print the entire fixture list in their Friday morning editions. The Management Committee's plans were in tatters, and once again it was the clubs rather than the pools companies which suffered.

Saturday's attendances were down again. In the pools strongholds of Leeds and Liverpool, Anfield and Elland Road had their lowest gates of the season. At Leeds, Alf Masser addressed the crowd of 10,500 over the loudspeaker system and bellowed: 'Are you in favour of restoring the fixture list?'

'Yes!' came back a huge roar.

When the fans returned home they heard unexpected news over the wireless, but this time the headlines were not about the Football League but the League of Nations. German troops had just re-entered the demilitarized Rhineland. Another war, of far greater proportions, was on the horizon now.

On Monday morning L. V. Manning of the *Daily Sketch* predicted the demise of the Committee's plan at that day's official meeting of the clubs. He wrote; 'The puir wee bairn will die unloved, unmourned. A short life and a stormy one. I hope to be at the funeral.'

Sure enough, the Pools War ended on Monday afternoon 9 March 1936, at the Grand Hotel, Manchester. But it was a stormy, eventful ending, from the moment delegates discovered that the Management Committee would permit entrance to only one representative per club, not two as expected. Dozens of irate men jostled in an adjoining room and passed a resolution demanding entry. Next door, in the crowded hall, the meeting began at 2.30 p.m. under a cloak of secrecy, with the press excluded. Just as the debate developed, there was a sudden commotion.

Charles Sutcliffe, describing it afterwards, wrote: 'During the proceedings ... behind what purported to be closed doors ... a shadow was seen to pass across the glass lights on a floor above, where a window was discovered to be open, and investigation resulted in the discovery of a photographer and reporter from a prominent newspaper, who had succeeded in getting shots and making notes of what had been transpiring. These gentlemen afterwards appeared in the meeting, apologised for their action and surrendered their notes and plates.'

'Newspaper sleuths caught red-handed', reported the *Daily Sketch* the following day. 'Two irresponsible youths', said the *Daily Mail*. No paper owned up, however.

(In his official jubilee history of 1938, Sutcliffe confused the sequence of events and described the journalists' intrusion as occurring at the original Pools War meeting on 20 February. Ivan Sharpe repeated the mistake. Sutcliffe's report of the Pools War is in any case brief and necessarily coloured by his own responsibility for the debacle.)

But what stories these two intruders might have told – and possibly did among their friends – of the real mood at that Grand Hotel meeting. All the public would ever know is that Alf Masser's resolution, seconded by Messrs Waddilove of Bradford and Woolfe of Sunderland, was passed unanimously. The fixtures were to be restored.

The League's own minutes of the meeting tell us much more. Five clubs were absent, and before anything was decided the Full Members voted to exclude the Third Division clubs from speaking or voting.

Derby's chairman Bendle Moore proposed that the resolution passed in Manchester on 20 February be rescinded and expunged from the minutes. It was unwise for the League to take part in politics. He reckoned that fixed odds betting – that is, betting on one particular match – was far worse than the pools. An example was the forthcoming Cup semi-final between Fulham and Sheffield United. A press report had stated that one Sheffield bookmaker stood to lose £75,000 if United won. Should the unfortunate goalkeeper make an error, said Moore, 'every hand would be against him and it would be alleged that he had been "squared".' But the pools companies cared not a jot who lost or won. They drew their commission in any event. Therefore, he concluded, the pools were not such a menace to the game.

Alf Masser accused the Management Committee of inconsistency – negotiating a fee with the PPA one minute, then decrying the pools the next. Sutcliffe insisted once again that they had never mentioned money with the PPA. (John Moores always repudiated this, and the League's own records, it should be borne in mind, were strangely incomplete.)

It was a maxim of business, Masser went on, that the customer was always right, and it was not up to the clubs to ask a spectator at the turnstile whether he filled in coupons or not. Great harm had been done by the Committee's action. Above all, the paying customers had been antagonized.

John McKenna, now almost eighty-two and crippled by rheumatism, vainly tried to defend the Committee, but his only reward was a unanimous vote in favour of Alf Masser's resolution, that the fixtures be restored and not tampered with again. The Pools War was over.

But the debate was not. For once, Charles Sutcliffe was on the defensive. He had lost the war, now he had to explain the matter of who held the copyright. Was it he as compiler of the fixtures, or the League?

Sutcliffe spoke deferentially: 'I cannot help myself in this. I have no desire and I have never had the slightest desire for exploiting your fixtures for my personal profit ... whatever is thought necessary or is advised, whatever the clubs wish me to do, will be done.'

Seldom had the great legislator of the League been so humble. But he maintained his dignity throughout.

'I wish to make clear that the fixtures are not made haphazardly but from a chart,' he continued. 'I am not going to give away the chart which took me years to work out for you

to make fixtures à la carte.... I am going to use plain language. I am not out to exploit the Football League. I have received what the Management Committee have thought fit to pay. If you think it is too much, reduce it. If you want them free, ask me, but don't be surprised at my answer.'

When Sutcliffe spoke so plainly he was, invariably, respected. Bendle Moore accepted his speech without hesitation. A man was worthy of his hire, and Sutcliffe could not be expected to give the chart away. Instead, he proposed that the Committee negotiate with Sutcliffe for the purchase of the chart, and this, too, was agreed.

Finally, and with chilling timeliness, Bendle Moore reiterated the esteem with which the President, John McKenna, was held by the clubs. 'They love him, they love him for the work he has done for the League.'

Moore's words turned out to be the final tribute. As the battle-scarred and aged President awaited a train back to Liverpool after the meeting, he slipped on the station platform. From then on, McKenna's health deteriorated rapidly.

A week later he went to Inverness in his capacity as an international selector for the FA to watch an amateur match between Scotland and England. He was taken ill on the return journey and died soon after, at Walton Hospital, on the morning of 22 March. He was a few weeks away from his eighty-second birthday, had been President for twenty-six years, and had served on the Management Committee since 1902.

But at least McKenna was spared the final flurries of the great pools debate. These began on 28 March, two days after his funeral, when Richard Russell finally introduced his Bill to make the pools illegal. He was supported initially by four Tories, two Liberals, one Liberal National, one National Labour and three Labour members. Russell also had the backing of the Church and the FA, who went so far as to send to every MP a letter signed by the President, Sir Charles Clegg. 'Football,' he wrote, 'should be protected from the parasitical outside organisations that fasten upon it for the sake of profit.'

But where the League had failed, Russell failed too. Only twenty-seven MPs supported him, and 287 voted against the Bill. The pools had survived.

The matter did not quite end there. Out of defeat in the Pools War came the realization that the League needed a firmer control over its own fixture-making process. With that in mind, the Committee agreed on 25 March that Sutcliffe should hand over to the League the rights to his mysterious charts, in return for which a contract was agreed that he and his son Harold (who always helped Charles anyway) would prepare the fixtures for the next ten years, at the usual fee of £2 per club per annum.

That settled, there remained three further questions to resolve in the aftermath of the Pools War.

The first was this. Having established that the League now held the rights to Sutcliffe's fixtures, what was it going to do with them?

Mr Vince's syndicate was still offering £50,000 a year for sole use of the fixtures, for advertising rather than betting, but they now had three rival bidders, including one represented by the editor of *Sporting Life*.

Before Watson Hartley had put ideas into the Committee's head, the fixtures had been no more than a list, freely distributed. Now, however, they offered a possible injection of funds to the League's creaking bank balance; quite a temptation, except that, as it was pointed out at a special meeting in London to discuss the issue, if the League sold the fixtures to one company, would that mean the pools couldn't use them? If so, the League might have to face costly court action.

Opinion veered towards caution. The Pools War had been an own goal of disastrous proportions, so why risk another? It was agreed – no sale.

This brings us to the second major question.

Had the League missed a golden opportunity to stabilize its finances?

Certainly, one cannot dismiss or minimize the moral standpoint taken by Sutcliffe, Rinder and Cuff in particular. Ignoring the financial benefits, they chose to avoid a link between agencies of betting and the game. Yet it seems odd that with three accomplished lawyers on the Committee, and several others such as Alf Masser sitting on the reserves' bench, no one had the confidence to take on a test case. Or could they simply not conceive how lucrative it would be in the long term to establish legal copyright?

This was the course adopted over twenty years later, and it worked. Indeed, it has worked ever since, to the enormous benefit of the League and individual clubs.

It can only be assumed that in 1936 men like Sutcliffe believed that any such test case would cripple the League with legal costs, which the pools companies could no doubt easily bear themselves. And since the clubs also rejected the notion of selling the fixtures, it was very much an idea whose time had yet to come.

The third important issue for the Committee to resolve after the Pools War was the selection of John McKenna's successor, at least until the Annual Meeting.

Of course, there could be only one candidate. Apart from his misjudgement with the pools, Charles Sutcliffe's record as the power behind McKenna's throne was quite outstanding, and so on 3 April 1936 the little lawyer from Lancashire took one further step towards achieving his cherished ambition by being elected acting President of the Football League. He was then aged seventy-two.

But would the clubs confirm him as President? A new order was emerging, and not just in Germany. When the Annual Meeting was held on 6 June, younger, more strident voices were heard. Old traditions were questioned, radical ideas proposed. Clearly, the Pools War had engendered a new spirit of resistance in the ranks.

Bob Smith of Manchester City and Alf Masser of Leeds even challenged the traditional procedure for electing the President and Vice Presidents. In most other limited companies, said Smith, the board of directors was elected first, and the President and Vice Presidents chosen thereafter from among the board members.

The League had always done it the other way round, Smith protested. But Charlie Sutcliffe held his ground, and then won the ballot for the presidency with 25 votes. His challengers were: Amos Brook Hirst (14 votes), who had opposed Sutcliffe throughout the Pools War; Fred Rinder (6), who had always challenged Sutcliffe's monopoly of the fixtures, but was essentially on the same side; and Will Cuff (3), McKenna's companion, whose time was yet to come.

So Sutcliffe was confirmed as President, but for the first time in such an election he was by no means the overwhelming choice. This was almost certainly a legacy of his failed campaign against the pools. He was doubtless the natural choice, however. Conservatism still prevailed within the League, and as he said himself in his acceptance speech, Sutcliffe was now the only living subscriber of the company's original Articles of Association in 1904.

Of the earliest pioneers, only Sutcliffe and Rinder remained, since 1936 also saw the deaths of Tom Charnley, former Secretary and Preston official, and George Ramsay, long-serving secretary of Aston Villa, both of whom had been involved with the founding fathers in 1888.

After Sutcliffe had been forced to fight for his coveted presidency, the League's innate fear of radical change quickly re-emerged with the elections for the Management Committee. Messrs Cadman, Bassett and Brook Hirst were each returned comfortably, and the fourth, vacant seat was closely fought between Arsenal's J. J. Edwards, the vociferous Alf Masser, and eight other nominees. Never before had there been such a fiercely contested election, and four ballots were needed before Edwards just squeezed out Masser by three votes. Significantly however, four of the unsuccessful challengers would eventually claim seats on the Committee.

The same would be true for the applicants to the Third Division North. Shrewsbury (7 votes) would have to wait until 1950 to join the League, and Wigan Athletic (6) had to wait until 1978. Both retiring clubs, Southport (47) and New Brighton (38), were returned.

In the Southern section, Exeter (48) and Newport (40) were also re-elected. Bath City received 9 votes, Dartford 1 and Folkestone none at all.

Some things were still predictable. Bendle Moore tried once again to increase the number of clubs promoted from two to four, and failed – albeit by only a handful of votes. And thus the hectic season of 1935/6 drew to a close, with the Pools War rapidly forgotten; treated as an aberration and nothing more, while a real war was only just beginning, in Spain. As in Winkley Square, so in Europe the tide was turning.

CHAPTER FIFTEEN
Jubilee and the Real War

Despite the ominous signs emanating from Berlin, the years 1936–9 were relatively halcyon for the League. The depression seemed to be over (partly due to rearmament), clubs could afford to raise the level of talent money payable to the top clubs in each division, and relations with the FA could not have been better.

They were further cemented in 1937 when the FA agreed to pay off not only the League's crippling £5446 insurance deficit, but an extra £660 per annum for the next four years. It was a generous offer, lapped up by the Management Committee and heralded by the clubs at the 1937 Annual Meeting. (The size of this debt was a further reason why the Committee was unwilling to embark upon legal action against the pools companies.)

There was one new club among the applicants at that Annual Meeting – Ipswich Town, who had recently turned professional and were now champions of the Southern League. Their 24 votes boded well for the future, but were insufficient to oust either Exeter (40) or Aldershot (34). In the Northern section, Darlington (47) and Gateshead (34) were re-elected, in preference to Shrewsbury (12), South Liverpool (4) and Wigan (1).

Another new name for the future was that of Arthur Oakley of Wolverhampton Wanderers, who fought off another spirited challenge by Alf Masser for a place on the Management Committee. Bill Bassett had recently died, as had Phil Bach, but continuity came in the form of Derby's Bendle Moore, as ever proposing four up, four down. As always, Colonel Crisp of Chelsea opposed the motion, and in the vote, eighteen clubs were opposed, thirty were

in favour, again an insufficient majority. Moore would have to wait yet another year.

One matter couldn't wait, however – the celebrations to mark fifty years of the Football League.

Planning began in June 1937, the main event being a jubilee banquet at the Dorchester Hotel, London, on 30 May 1938, on the evening of the Annual Meeting. But the most wide-reaching part of the celebration was to be the setting up of a £100,000 Jubilee Fund, to assist players and clubs in times of need. The idea seems to have been credited to Charles Sutcliffe, and was the first attempt of its kind to safeguard former players (apart from the insurance scheme for injured footballers).

Of the £100,000 total, it was hoped that about half would be raised by the staging of 'Jubilee Day' matches, consisting of pre-season derbies all over the country.

Once the Jubilee Fund was launched, the football world reacted immediately. Wolves gave £1000 without question, the Lancashire FA gave £200, the Hampshire FA £100, William Pickford of the FA gave £10 and a referee, appropriately named Mr Argent, also made a donation.

Meanwhile, the jubilee history was in production by February 1938, and Aston Villa agreed to lend their oil painting of William McGregor to hang at the jubilee dinner.

But as the League prepared to celebrate, the Players' Union under James Fay had other ideas. A month before the banquet, the players made it clear that they thought it high time the maximum wage was increased. It had been stuck at £8 for exactly sixteen years. The cost of living had risen, transfer fees had spiralled, but the players' lot had not changed at all, despite record gates and receipts in 1937/8. In many cases, long-serving players had not even been given benefits and were paid no wages at all during the close season. Some Third Division players were receiving as little as thirty shillings per week. So the union made its demands, one of which was that the maximum wage should be raised to £9 per week.

The Management Committee listened amicably, but was not greatly moved. As ever, Sutcliffe restated the financial problems of the clubs and reiterated the Management Committee's willingness to protect any player in the event of a dispute. But that was all.

Towards the clubs, the Management Committee approached the jubilee in a more generous mood. Allegations of four clubs playing weak teams were dismissed. It relented on a previous decision forbidding radio commentaries of Hartlepools' matches being relayed to a local hospital. At Winkley Square it raised the junior clerk's wages by five shillings a week, and lashed out a further £15 on a Gestetner duplicator.

So it was that after the disaster of the Pools War, President Charles Sutcliffe looked forward to the jubilee celebrations with justifiable satisfaction; the FA was on good terms with the League, the players were subservient, the clubs seemed mostly happy and under control, and the public continued to flock to games.

On the field of play there had been a significant reduction in the number of players sent off or cautioned; the Jubilee Fund was building up nicely and, best of all, most of the final championship, promotion and relegation issues were not settled until the very last Saturday, producing a nail-biting climax to the 1937/8 season.

Before the banquet could begin, however, there was just the small matter of the 1938 Annual Meeting, itself an historic event. Not only was it the fiftieth Annual Meeting, but it was the first at which representatives of all the other major leagues and associations in the United Kingdom were represented.

Also for the first time, two men on the Management Committee had the honour of Life Membership conferred upon them in the same year: Charles Sutcliffe and Fred Rinder. Sutcliffe's contribution was well known, but for Rinder it must have been an especially emotional moment. He was the sole survivor of the League's very first gathering in 1888, and since then had missed only one annual meeting, and that had been through illness. No other man could claim such a record.

The actual business of the meeting was routine, with one exception. Rarely did the Management Committee voice an opinion on the election of new clubs, but this year Sutcliffe felt it necessary to inform members that Gillingham were applying for re-election for the sixth time. Perhaps the assembled men were overcome by the occasion – or Sutcliffe's aura – since no one corrected him; it was, in fact, Gillingham's fifth time of asking. But even without the President's comment, it is doubtful whether the result would have been different.

Ipswich (36) joined the League at only their second attempt, while Walsall (34) were re-elected. Gillingham (24) thus lost their place, and for Kent at least, the jubilee seemed suddenly rather flat.

In the Northern section, Sutcliffe again made a none too subtle reference to the fact that one of the applicants, Wigan Athletic, had been associated with a draw for Cup Final tickets. That was simply not done. Accrington Stanley had also organized a draw, but it turned out that the Supporters' Club had been responsible and the club had 'entirely disassociated themselves from it'. That seemed good enough for the clubs. Stanley (41) were thus returned with Barrow (35), and for the fourth year running Shrewsbury (15) came third. The other applicants were South Liverpool (5), Scunthorpe (1) and the errant Wigan (1).

As the delegates returned to their hotels to prepare for the evening's banquet, Fred

Howarth sorted out the congratulatory tele-grams. They had come from all over the world: from the Football Associations of Germany, Canada, Australia, New Zealand and Nova Scotia. Jessie Hinchley, William McGregor's daughter, sent her best wishes, as did one of the earliest members of the committee, Louis Ford of West Bromwich. From Sandringham, the King's private secretary thanked the League for its loyalty.

Among several other goodwill messages was one from the president of the Chief Constables' Association, T. Rawson of Bradford, which makes for interesting reading in view of modern crowd problems.

'The value of outdoor games as a safety valve for the release of superfluous energy and as a relaxation from workaday life has always been recognized in this country', wrote Mr Rawson. The League played a valuable part in keeping order, because 'one of the acknow-ledged methods of dealing with delinquency among juveniles and adolescents in particular in recent years has been the provision of organ-ised pastimes by which to divert criminal tend-encies along healthy channels'.

With an eye to the international situation, Rawson added: 'These organised competitions have a further value in assisting to foster local patriotism and mutual esteem on which true national patriotism and the larger ideal of uni-versal brotherhood have their foundation.'

Other messages came from the Archbishop of Canterbury, the Prime Minister Neville Chamberlain, the Lord Chief Justice, the Chan-cellor of the Exchequer, Cardinal Hinsley, The Earl of Derby, the Minister of Transport and a former president of the Federation of British Industries, Sir Francis Joseph, himself a keen follower of the game as president of Stoke City. He wrote:

'Being linked to industries employing hundreds of thousands of men and mixing with them day in and day out has given me exceptional opportunities of knowing what is in their minds in working or leisure

moments. Going around our collieries after a cheery "Good-day" to the men, the first thing they say to me is: "Guvnor, what about our chances next Satur-day? Are we going to win?" No matter how often their team may lose they are still optimistic and turn up hoping for the best from their own team, and as good sportsmen, will applaud the best in their opponents' play.

There is nothing to take the place of football for the people of Britain. It carries them through the days of Winter; it keeps them happy; they will look forward to the match; their only worry is whether they will be late for the kick-off. When the match is over, whether their team has won or lost they talk over the game, "chew the rag" with their pals, as they put it, and then, day in and day out, discuss the prospects of next Saturday. It is the finest safety valve we have ever had. Public interest is great today; it will be greater still in the future.

All honour to the men who founded the League and to those who are now carrying on, maintaining a standard of clean and robust play which is charac-teristic of the British race.'

William Pickford, the recently appointed Presi-dent of the FA (Sir Charles Clegg had died in 1937), had been one of many southern ama-teurs to view the fledgling League as an irrel-evance in 1888. But in 1938, Pickford wrote:

'When our old friend William McGregor took the important step of calling a dozen clubs together for the purpose of starting a novel form of competition, and for some years afterwards, I knew very little about the League. Then I began to share the feeling with others that it was growing rather too fast for the FA to feel very easy with such a big and sometimes, we thought, unruly boy in the house. But we long ago realised that any fears we might have were groundless.

The League and the principles on which it was founded made ours the most popular open-air field game in the world. There were only about 1000 clubs altogether in England then; there are now some 35,000 all playing merrily in leagues, and the system has captured the globe. Casual and desultory football, such as you and I played long ago, could never have *accomplished that.*

If one thinks of the vast assets of the League clubs in property alone, with their serious obligations, of the huge sums they raise and distribute among players and staffs, the Exchequer, the Postmaster-General, the railway and transport companies, and a hundred and one others, and endeavour to visualise the interest, excitement and pleasure that its competitions bring into the lives of millions of people, one can begin to form some idea of its great importance in the life of the nation.'

And so to the packed Dorchester banqueting room, where 657 gentlemen congregated in what was the largest single gathering ever witnessed in British football. The guest list was a veritable *Who's Who* of football.

Among the dignitaries were the Lord Mayors of London and Westminster, the Earl of Granard, Lord Aberdare, the Duke of Gloucester and the Earl of Derby, plus representatives from the home international associations and FIFA. Both rugby codes were represented, as were the BBC, the House of Commons and the military.

Away from the top table sat a host of footballing personalities; among them Stanley Rous, Cliff Britton, George Camsell, Raich Carter, Stan Cullis, Bill Dodgin, Jimmy Guthrie, Eddie Hapgood, Harry Hibbs and Leslie Knighton.

Also present were Archibald Leitch (the Scottish architect responsible for designing most of the major grounds in Britain), William McGregor Junior (the founder's son, who lived in Sheffield) and Harold Sutcliffe (heir to the famous charts).

Among the journalists assembled were Ivan Sharpe of the *Sunday Chronicle* (who would later pen the seventy-fifth anniversary book) and J. A. Brierley ('Perseus' of the *Lancashire Daily Post*), who helped Charles Sutcliffe and Fred Howarth write the 1938 jubilee history.

The Duke of Gloucester proposed the toast to the Football League in a speech filled with good intent and historical references, but sug-

gesting in its tone that he had never been to a League match in his life. No matter, this was an evening for much mutual back-slapping and self-congratulation, and with every reason. Football in 1938 seemed to be on the crest of a wave; embraced by the world, free of violence or corruption, and administered by men of lofty ideals.

After the toasts, Lark's London Band played a selection of light music, while the diners settled into a sumptuous eight-course banquet accompanied by vintage wines, champagne, Taylor's 1920 port and 1865 brandy, all for a mere £2 a head (compared with £75 a head for the centenary banquet in 1987). From the Anderton Hotel to the Dorchester in fifty years; it had been quite an achievement.

After joy came sorrow. After elation, exhaustion. Having climbed the jubilee mountain and reached the peak of their careers in 1938, within less than a year no fewer than ten of the old guard had died.

Among the names of the departed read out at the Annual Meeting of 1939 were those of Sir Walter Raine of Sunderland, who had helped to organize the jubilee; H. L. Fellows of Walsall, after whom their ground was named; E. Clayton of Southport, one of the pioneering spirits behind the creation of the Third Division North; Archibald Leitch, the League's favourite architect; and Thomas Rushton, the League's long-serving auditor.

But most mourned of all were three men of the highest note.

Only a few weeks after the jubilee banquet, the seventy-six-year-old President, Charles Sutcliffe, was taken ill. In his absence, the chair at Management Committee meetings was taken by Fred Rinder, the senior Vice President, who might yet have thought that at the age of eighty-two he could still become President, should his old friend Sutcliffe not return.

In the event, Rinder's health gave out first. After a short illness, he died on Christmas Day 1938. Thus passed away the last remaining link with those first meetings of 1888.

The FA had already lost its own President, William Pickford. Having written the introduction to the League's jubilee history, Pickford died before the book's publication, in November 1938. That the book had been published at all (in early 1939, at 10s 6d a copy) was largely due to journalist J. A. Brierley. With Sutcliffe now too ill to finish the job, Brierley stepped in at the President's invitation.

As if these personal griefs were not enough, as Charlie Sutcliffe lay dying in Rawtenstall, the League became embroiled in another scandal regarding illegal payments. Eleven Carlisle players were fined and suspended for accepting 'incentives' from a Stockport County director in April 1937. County had wanted to secure promotion by encouraging Carlisle to win both their matches against their nearest challengers, Lincoln City.

It was a depressing start to the year 1939, and to the League's second half-century, made worse by the death on 11 January of the President, only a fortnight after that of Fred Rinder. Sutcliffe had managed only three Committee meetings that season, after thirty-nine seasons of almost unbroken attendance. Indeed, it was hard to conceive of any League meeting without his eagle-eyed presence, his plume of cigarette smoke and his usual pile of papers and documents.

Charlie Sutcliffe's contribution to the development of the League was probably greater than any man either before or since his forty-year spell on the Management Committee. To him we owe much of the League's present infrastructure, and to him can be ascribed most of the values upon which the League became established in the twentieth century.

His exhaustive mind took in fixtures, insurance schemes, wages, transfers, refereeing, the Benevolent Fund, the jubilee celebrations and the jubilee history. Only once did he fail to impose his will, and that was during the Pools War.

And when he had gone, there was a very real sense in which the League had to readjust; Will Cuff, a link with the days of the 1890s, took over as President, but under him there was, Tom Barcroft, Morton Cadman and Amos Brook Hirst apart, a set of comparatively inexperienced men.

The two newest Committee members, elected in 1939, were Walter Tempest of Blackburn and Bill Cearns of West Ham. Both had been on the sub-committee appointed to arrange the jubilee celebrations.

Sutcliffe's immediate legacy was an instant success, his book selling out its first edition of 1000 copies within weeks of publication. Even the King received a copy. But there was little time to dwell on the past. The work of the League, as Sutclife had always maintained, had to go on, whatever the looming crises overseas or the personal sadnesses at home.

At the 1939 Annual Meeting, all four retiring clubs kept their places. In the Southern section Bristol Rovers (45 votes) and Walsall (36) were re-elected, ahead of Gillingham (15), Chelmsford (1) and Colchester (1). In the Northern section Hartlepools (38) and Accrington (29) kept their places, with Shrewsbury (22) making a strong challenge. Other applicants were South Liverpool (5), Scunthorpe (4), Burton Town (0) and Wigan Athletic (0).

Cuff made an immediate impact upon the clubs at his first Annual Meeting as President, determined to start as he meant to continue, on the attack. After Bendle Moore of Derby had tried once again to introduce a four-up, four-down system of promotion and relegation, the new President tore into the proposals, detailing their potential effects on standards within the League and concluding that the main benefactors would be the Third Division clubs, who would thus drag the general standard of play down to their level. 'But, gentlemen,' warned Cuff, 'there is another and, in our view, a more sinister

To launch the Jubilee Fund, all eighty-eight League clubs played pre-season friendly derby matches on 20 August 1938. The largest gate was at Highbury, where 41,997 saw Spurs beat Arsenal 2–0. Several reserve games were also played, and all match officials gave their services free of charge. Overall, just under 450,000 watched the forty-four first-team matches, earning the Jubilee Fund £27,443. Sutcliffe had hoped for £44,000. Other donations brought the total to £32,000 by December 1938, but an offer of £5000 per annum from the PPA was rejected by a majority of clubs.

In August 1939 another series of pre-season derbies was played, and both during the Second World War and afterwards, ordinary pre-season practice match receipts were added to the fund.

Throughout the years, the Jubilee Fund has helped dozens of former players to become anything from a bricklayer to a barrister, from a publican to a PE instructor.

One man who was particularly grateful was Harold Shepherdson, who at the age of twenty-nine found his career ended by injury in 1947. His £200 grant from the Jubilee Fund allowed him to move his family back to his native Middlesbrough, take up the post of assistant trainer at Ayresome Park and attend various courses run by the FA. Ten years later, Shepherdson became England's trainer and held the post for their next 169 matches, including four World Cup campaigns. Sutcliffe would have been delighted to know that his little scheme had helped to further such a career.

In 1979 the Jubilee Fund was incorporated into the Footballers Further Education Vocational Training Society, run jointly with the PFA. Nowadays, instead of practice match receipts, the League contributes all its fines to the society, which also receives a share of Charity Shield receipts.

In 1987 it had assets of £164,000 (Sutcliffe's target was eventually reached, therefore) and was run by former Blackpool, Newcastle, Cardiff and Middlesbrough forward Mick Burns, a member of the PFA staff in Manchester.

aspect . . .'

There had, he explained, been lurking 'a subtle attempt on the part of the Third Division, and particularly the Southern Section, to dominate the policy of the League. In other words, the tail is trying to wag the dog.'

Cuff went on to vilify the Third Division clubs for circulating a questionnaire behind the Committee's back on the questions of four up, four down, and Cup-tie exemption. The League had absorbed these clubs in 1920 after they had implored the Committee to create a new division to 'save them from extinction', said Cuff. And how did they repay this gesture? – 'by repeated attempts to alter the constitution of the League, clog the wheels of progress and thwart changes'.

This was straight out of the Sutcliffe textbook, but Cuff appeared to have his own, extra measure of authority. There was almost an echo of John Bentley in his no-nonsense, bullish approach.

The most significant change instituted at the 1939 meeting was the compulsory numbering of players. Tottenham were the leading campaigners for this, while some clubs voiced a preference for optional numbering. But Cuff was not having this. It should be all or nothing, he reckoned, and when twenty-four voted for numbering and twenty against, he declared it carried, not as a rule change (which would have needed a three-quarters majority), but as an instruction. It was a fine distinction, but as events that summer were to prove, a fairly irrelevant one.

The players would get their numbers next season, not only on their shirts but also on their call-up cards. By July 1939 many were already being called for military training and by late August, although the League kicked off as normal, it was becoming obvious that the League would have to take drastic action.

Sure enough, when war was finally declared on 3 September 1939, the Committee knew it had no option. The experiences of the First World War were not to be repeated. The following day, Cuff sent a telegram to all clubs stating 'League Competition suspended'. This was confirmed on 6 September when the Committee met in haste in Crewe and further informed clubs not to keep players standing by. On 8 September another meeting at the FA offices resulted in the setting up of a wartime committee, consisting of Cuff, Brook Hirst, Barcroft and Tempest.

The storm had broken, and the League went on to an immediate war footing. At Winkley Square, Fred Howarth put into operation plans which had been formulated with the FA up to twelve months earlier. He held the fort while first the senior, then the junior clerk left for military service. The Secretary, who at the age of fifty-one was too old to join up himself, dusted down the regional competition arrangements made during the First World War, and by 2 October eight local groupings were agreed. Reports on referees were suspended, players' bonuses forbidden, and players were allowed to play for any club in Britain (but not in the Irish League). Their contracts were also suspended, which meant that dozens were without any form of income.

There was to be no repeat of the 1914/15 season, nor any reliance on one man as there had been on Charles Sutcliffe during the years 1915–18. Not even Adolf Hitler was going to jeopardize fifty years of the League.

War Office measures governed where and when matches could be played, with initial restrictions of 8000 on gates, admittance by ticket only, and no journeys of more than fifty miles. Only six clubs decided to shut up shop totally: Aston Villa (who were also among the first to do so during the First World War), Derby, Sunderland, Exeter, Ipswich and Gateshead. Only one club, Birmingham, was prevented from staging matches at its own ground (by the Public Entertainments Restrictions Order), while Luton, Watford, Portsmouth, Bournemouth, Norwich and Southend all complained that the regional groupings left them out in the cold for much of the season.

But there were considerable difficulties for clubs all round during that first season of the war. Gates remained low while the public were preoccupied by the war and fear of air raids, and bad weather caused the postponement of practically the entire fixture list on several Saturdays during the winter of 1939/40.

Depite all the obstacles, the Committee continued to meet as normal throughout the season 1939/40 to conduct the newly formed Football League (War) Cup Competition. As ever, clubs were fined for minor misdemeanours – late result sheets and so on – while Liverpool and Everton were each fined for admitting juveniles at 4d instead of 6d. The League and FA even found time to conduct a full investigation into the affairs of Millwall, Derby and Leicester City.

In the cases of Derby and Leicester, illegal bonuses were discovered going back over several seasons, with all the attendant doctoring of accounts that that entailed. There is little doubt that most leading clubs were up to the same caper, and Derby and Leicester were

> **Although square goalposts have survived in Scotland, in England and Wales the elliptical goalpost was made standard for all League grounds in 1939.**

caught only because former employees had informed the authorities. In Derby's case the payments went back at least to 1925, and were hidden by the use of wages to fictitious ground-staff and expenses for journeys never undertaken. The Supporters' Club had also played a part in the collection of bonus money for players. Several other clubs would have used similar devices.

No matter, Derby and Leicester were the ones found out, and like Leeds City in 1919 they were to be made an example. Five Derby directors were suspended *sine die* for their involvement, and the biggest shock of all was the first name on the list: W. Bendle Moore, the chairman, a regular, vocal attender of Annual Meetings since the First World War and, of course, dogged champion of the four-up, four-down system. The former manager, George Jobey, was also banned permanently, and Derby were fined £500.

Leicester were similarly punished in 1941. Five directors were suspended *sine die*, four directors received limited bans, the former manager F. Womack was banned for a year, and Leicester were fined £500. Among the three directors exonerated from blame was a certain Len Shipman, who would one day become President of the League.

Indeed, the war saw several future League activists come to the fore. Future President Arthur Drewry of Grimsby was elected to the Committee in 1940, and a year after was joined by Birmingham's David Wiseman and Liverpool's Will Harrop (so, with Will Cuff, the Committee now had double Will power from the city of Liverpool).

The arrival of these novice Committee men made Cuff's paternal approach even more necessary to keep the League afloat during those difficult years, and he lost another experienced henchman in October 1941 when Amos Brook Hirst resigned to take over as chairman of the FA Council.

No one could accuse the League of being an inward-looking organization during the war, however. 'We must subordinate League interests to that of the country.' Will Cuff urged the clubs. 'To act otherwise would be to cast a slur on the name of football.'

Thus, the Committee relaxed its ban on broadcast commentaries, since these brought 'some relaxation to the worker, and to the forces in training'. In fact, the troops in France also benefited, because the Blackpool *v.* Manchester United commentary was relayed to the front on 14 October 1939.

Charity matches were played whenever possible – rules were repeatedly relaxed to help clubs and the public – while the Committee members did their bit to help. Will Cuff, for example, sat on the organizing committee of the Central Council of Recreative Physical Training, which launched a 'Fitness for Service' campaign in 1940.

Also in 1940, a sum of £5000, previously invested on behalf of the Jubilee Fund, was loaned to the Government free of interest. During 1940–1, £4000 of the League's money was invested in Defence Bonds. 'Football can rightly claim a share in the upkeep of the nation's morale during the first nine months of war', Will Cuff told the belatedly convened Annual Meeting on 29 July 1940.

But as the war intensified, by August 1940 twenty League clubs had expressed their inability to compete in the regional competitions, while those who carried on couldn't always guarantee to finish their games. Brighton's match against Southampton, on 21 September 1940, was halted after five minutes because of an air-raid warning. A Cup tie between Grimsby and Barnsley had to stop when the referee was called away to military duties. A month later, Leicester, West Ham, Northampton and Notts County had to play with reduced teams. Clapton Orient solved that problem by asking for volunteers from the crowd – thus earning themselves a rebuke from the Committee. But soon it became the only way for some clubs to put out a team, even with extra players borrowed from army camps and neighbouring clubs.

By mid 1941 the League had no choice but to relax its attitude. In fact, several players were permitted to play in the Cup for a second club, simply to keep the competition going. Venues were also swapped with regularity as bombs rained down on the cities, damaging grounds and their vicinities.

Austerity marked everything the League organized, right down to the choosing of a trophy for the War Cup – they took an off-the-shelf model from Messrs Vaughtons – and the award of saving certificates rather than medals to the winning players. The Cup Finals themselves required everyone to pitch in. In 1941 Luton Town offered to transport the Committee to and from the match. West Ham were asked to provide balls and goalposts, and London clubs provided staff for the match day.

The London clubs were less happy to co-operate when it came to the fixtures organized by the League. The 1940/1 season found them arguing with the Committee over the division of London clubs into groups, and they continued to argue when plans were announced for a two-way North–South competition for the 1941/2 season, which they complained involved too much travelling and inconvenience. Despite several concerted efforts by Cuff to persuade them to show loyalty, they voted unanimously to break away and form their own London War League.

In retaliation, the Committee took the unprecedented step of cancelling the League membership of eight clubs: Arsenal, Brentford, Charlton, Chelsea, Fulham, Millwall, Tottenham and West Ham. The Associate Membership of seven other southern clubs was also cancelled.

London's breakaway had wider repercussions. Portsmouth had to join the breakaway group to save their fixtures (their membership was duly cancelled). Southend had to drop out completely.

This was exactly the scenario Sutcliffe had fought to avoid throughout the First World War, but even he would have found it hard to argue the League's case in the more trying domestic circumstances of this new war. The simple truth was that within London there were enough clubs to sustain a reasonable competition without outside help. They had been independent during the First World War, they would be so again. Not out of disloyalty, but through practicality.

Recognizing this, in November 1941 the Committee made conciliatory gestures towards the sixteen rebel clubs by offering to restore their membership in return for an agreed statement of regret and nominal fines.

There were other pressures the League couldn't resist. In December 1941 the Office of Works requisitioned the League's offices at Winkley Square, forcing a hasty removal round the corner to 102 Fishergate. Also in December, petrol restrictions forced clubs to rely on the railway network. They were already finding kit difficult to obtain, with clothing coupons being in short supply.

Players themselves were hardly plentiful. West Ham alone had twenty-four players in the services in 1941, and during the 1941/2 season, Northampton were found to have fielded so many guest players in their nine Cup qualifying matches that their own registered players had made only four appearances.

In 1942/3 the regional arrangements were changed due to the increasing transport difficulties, and in order to make the Western section viable, non-League clubs Bath City, Lovell's Athletic and Aberaman were allowed to participate. Lovell's were particularly successful, winning the section two years running and finishing second in the North (Second Championship) in 1942/3. Bath City won the latter competition in 1943/4.

After holding the 1942 Annual Meeting in Nottingham – the first time it had been held away from London or Manchester – the 1943 gathering returned to London, to the Holborn Restaurant on 28 June. Until that year, not many footballers had been lost in the war, but the toll had risen quickly during 1942/3. Four former players had died in battle, two had been killed during exercises, three had died of wounds and one had been lost at sea. Of those who died, two were from Fulham, two from Tranmere. And the list would grow.

In August 1944 the sons of the Management Committee's two newest members, Harry French (Middlesbrough) and Phil Wood (Huddersfield) were reported missing whilst on active service, as was a Fulham player, Major J. J. Tompkin. Ipswich's chairman, Lt-Col. J. M. Cobbold, and his son, Major R. N. Cobbold, were killed during the period 1943–4, along with a further twenty-six players, seven of whom were on Arsenal's books.

On the playing side, as German bombing eased in 1943, so attendances rose. But wartime gates were rarely higher than 10,000, and often under 1000 in certain areas. Only representative games and regional cup finals attracted larger gates, and the receipts were invariably handed over to charities.

For example, a match at Chelsea in May 1943 raised the astonishing sum of £8000 for the Navy Welfare Fund. A Footballers' Day collection among the clubs in 1943 raised £1035 for the Prisoners of War Fund, and in 1944, £2124 was collected for the Red Cross and St John Fund.

Increased attendances meant that clubs could now raise the fees payable to players from thirty shillings per match to £2 (although bonuses were still prohibited), and instead of saving certificates the winners of the various championships and cups received £5 each.

Will Cuff's greatest problem continued to be the lack of experience on the Management Committee. Tom Barcroft's resignation in 1943 meant that all but two of the members had been elected since 1939, putting an even greater onus upon both the President and Fred Howarth to maintain the procedures and traditions of the League. Nevertheless, while academics and politicians began to plan for postwar Britain (in the Beveridge Report), the

League, too, embarked upon some forward thinking of its own in 1943.

Under pressure from the clubs to create a wider base for discussion, the Management Committee invited six men to join it on a Post-War Planning Committee. The men were Fred Normansell (Aston Villa), Harry Hardman (Manchester United), A. J. Platt (Sheffield United), J. I. Taylor (Preston), H. H. Merrett (Cardiff) and Joe Mears (Chelsea).

Their first two pronouncements suggested that the Committee's approach would be somewhat less progressive than Beveridge. For a start, there would be no dealings with the pools companies (which would have been unlikely anyway, given Cuff's vehement opposition during the Pools War), and no allowance for competitive football on Sundays.

But when the Post-War Planning Committee reported to the Annual Meeting 'after nine protracted meetings' in 1944, they were able to put forward some fairly detailed proposals, all of which depended on the success of the Allied offensive in Europe. One thing was certain, Will Cuff told the club representatives. Despite grumblings from certain club directors that the pre-war League system 'was obsolete and moribund', the vast majority were quite happy with the status quo.

'The cessation of hostilities might occur at any moment', warned Cuff, rather optimistically – he had described the recent setback at Arnhem as only temporary – and his Committee wanted to be 'in a position of complete preparedness for such an occurrence'.

Thus, he divided the Planning Committee's report into two sections, the first governing the transition period from war to peace, the second covering what were termed 'normal times'.

For the transitional period there would be a Victory League, and a cup competition, unless the FA managed to restart the FA Cup instead; all groupings of clubs would be as per September 1939, with no promotion or relegation at the end of the transitional competition. The practice of fielding guest players would be limited to six only per team, this figure to be reduced gradually as the circumstances allowed; no agreements with players would be made during this period, and the maximum match fee would be £4 – that is, twice the wartime sum.

The reception of these proposals suggested yet again a certain antagonism between the London clubs and the Management Committee, so that when an Extraordinary General Meeting was held in Manchester on 7 May 1945, the day before VE Day and a week after the collapse of the Third Reich, Arsenal were the first to object. George Allison, a thorn in the Committee's side for most of the war, proposed that instead of returning to the 1939 groupings for 1945/6, the First and Second Division clubs should be split, North and South, with only the Third Division remaining as before. Just because peace had come didn't mean that petrol supplies or war work could stop overnight, he argued. Apart from anything, if players weren't going to be paid a full wage, it would be unfair to ask them to take more time off than absolutely necessary.

Allison's argument was carried, but only just. He also won the meeting's approval for the formation of a sub-committee to look into the League's arrangements for insuring players. He claimed to have found many 'apparent shortcomings' in the League's existing scheme (which had been Sutcliffe's brainchild). Clearly, the Arsenal manager was not going to let the Committee off the hook just because the war had ended.

But by far the most extraordinary aspect of this 1945 Extraordinary Meeting was the sheer number and nature of proposals and amendments which, although rejected then, would eventually become part of League regulations, in one form or another.

The reason for this sudden blossoming of ideas was obvious: Victory in Europe, the prevailing air of reform, the perceived desire to sweep away the old world and rebuild anew,

had infected the entire nation. It led to the election of a new and radical Labour Government; perhaps it would also lead to widespread changes in the football world.

As it transpired, this was not the case. Will Cuff kept his office, while Winston Churchill did not. But the Manchester meeting did at least lay down an agenda for the development of post-war football and, as such, was one of the most important in the League's hundred-year history.

First among the reforms to be discussed was the old chestnut of four up, four down, but now that Derby's Bendle Moore was banned from football it was left for Luton to continue his crusade. They were backed by the Third Division's representative, Mr Goodman, who appealed to the meeting 'as sportsmen to give the Third Division their due reward'. This remark incensed Liverpool's R. Williams, who replied: 'What was wrong with football [before the war] . . . were the public dissatisfied?' Luton were even less successful than Bendle Moore had been, only 18 votes being cast on the issue.

But there were other ideas which suggested that the League did encompass at least some innovative thinking.

One scheme raised at Manchester was the formation of a British League. Another came from Tottenham's G. Wagstaffe Simmons, who emerged as champion of the Third Division clubs by proposing that their voting strength at Annual Meetings be increased from four collective votes to twelve. 'Twelve votes out of a total of fifty-seven could hardly endanger the superiority of the First and Second Divisions', he believed. Leicester City backed him up, but the amendment was lost.

So, too, was Birmingham's far-sighted plan to lower the required majority for rule changes from three-quarters to two-thirds.

'The Football League is a progressive body', said W. A. Camkin, and by reducing the required majority he 'merely sought to make it a little easier to progress. At present the majority ruling meant in practice that 13 votes could nullify 36 votes.'

But for Mr Camkin the League was obviously not progressive enough, because only fifteen clubs supported him. Not until 1986 would a two-thirds majority gain acceptance.

Southampton's Mr J. R. Sargantson raised a new issue, one which has been up for discussion ever since. Why were the League's headquarters in far-away Preston (now Lytham St Annes)? Sargantson told the meeting that he wished to make no reflection on Preston nor on the League officials, but wouldn't an office in London keep them in closer touch with important government departments? Plymouth, the most distant club from Preston, seconded the motion, but once more, support was minimal. Only nine clubs voted in favour, and the matter was shelved, no doubt to the relief of Fred Howarth and his staff.

Luton came up with another far-sighted suggestion; the staging of a League cup competition, on the home and away principle. But they weren't prepared to press the matter. Everton preferred instead that the FA Cup should be played on a home and away basis, from the Third to the Sixth Rounds inclusive, an idea the FA had already considered and which had extensive backing among League clubs, who desperately needed the income and could not have forecast the imminent boom in attendances.

Players' wages also came up for discussion, with a suggested increase from £8 to £9 maximum per week during the season and £7 per week during the close season. Several other wage scales were put forward, until Cuff finally put matters in order by bringing up Bolton's cautious amendment which suggested that no decisions on wages, bonuses or similar topics could possibly take place until the general state of the economy was known. No one could argue with that.

And so the debate went on, concerning

> Since 1888 the League had repeatedly argued that the FA took too great a share of the profits from Cup and international matches in which League teams and players predominated. Between 1933 and 1939, said Will Cuff, the FA earned £15,000 a year from these sources. The League's portion was tiny by comparison. But former Management Committee member Amos Brook Hirst, then chairman of the FA, refused to budge, pointing out that the FA had a responsibility for some 35,000 clubs. 'It is not the FA's intention to amass wealth', he told Cuff. But the League would carry on arguing, until finally the matter was settled in 1972.

match officials, the advisability of players finding work, even the sort of kit referees should wear. An all-black uniform, it was agreed, should now be compulsory. Everton proposed, and found favour in, a recommendation that the FA hand over half the receipts from Cup Finals and internationals to the League, a move the FA would clearly never make.

At the same time it was apparent that the League was still adamant over the question of receiving money from the pools companies.

In April 1945 the PPA offered the League £100,000 per annum as a payment for the fixtures, and although this represented only a tiny fraction of its profits and would have solved all the League's financial problems at a stroke (without any risk of legal costs), with Will Cuff at the helm it was inconceivable for the Committee to accept now what they had refused in 1936. In this one act of self-denial, the League arguably made its greatest error of the early post-war period.

But before we move on to those boom years, let us find out more about this man Will Cuff, the fifth President of the Football League.

CHAPTER SIXTEEN
Will Cuff – The Master

*I*n the best tradition of League presidents, Will Cuff of Everton never once shirked a challenge. Whether it involved the pools, the FA, the Third Division clubs, the Players' Union or, the biggest obstacle of all, war, he met each problem head on. Cuff was probably the last League president to rule with an iron fist, before the age of consensus and profit took a grip on football in the 1950s. He was also the last president to have had a personal link with the League of the nineteenth century.

William Cuff was born in Liverpool in August 1868. His family attended the Protestant St Domingo chapel, where his father was a trustee and where the seeds of Everton FC were planted. As a boy, young Will cheered on St Domingo in their Stanley Park days, and later he became the chapel's choirmaster.

After giving up the game because of an injury, he attended Liverpool College and entered a solicitor's office in 1888, qualifying five years later. Thus far, his background paralleled that of Charles Sutcliffe: religion and the law. One description of him, as having 'a restless energy and progressive mind', could so easily have been applied to Sutcliffe. Cuff was also a strict disciplinarian with high moral standards.

But the two men were very different on other levels. Sutcliffe was small and frail, Cuff was stocky and tough. He was no great public speaker either, often using three expressions where one would suffice, and making sweeping statements he couldn't really justify.

He seemed to prefer short, sharp campaigns rather than great, universal plans. His victories were achieved up front, not by background manoeuvring. In fact, he had more in common on a personal level with John McKenna, his friend from across Stanley Park. Both men were freemasons, and both men shared the same Liverpudlian geniality.

Cuff first teamed up with Everton's committee in 1890, took a seat on the board in 1895, and when R. Molyneux resigned as secretary in 1901, Cuff took over (he thus had to leave the board, since no directors could be paid club officials).

It was as club secretary that Cuff really established himself both in Liverpool and in the wider football world. He was, for example, largely responsible for the formation in 1911 of the Central League, becoming its first secretary.

The Liverpool magazine *Porcupine* wrote glowingly of him during this period.

'*Although a solicitor of the Supreme Court of Judicature, there is nothing in his personality that smacks of the hard and crude fossildom of the typical man of the law ... his breezy temperament carries with it an infectious atmosphere of geniality ... he is one of the men who gets things done, done thoroughly, and yet in such a fashion that the disciplinary machinery seems to run on oiled wheels ... he has to dive deeply, and with absolute accuracy, into a mass of statistics affecting fixtures, engagements of teams and heaven knows what besides, which would puzzle the brain of a mathematical professor.*

And yet Will ever "bobs up" with an unruffled exterior, and in his own electric individuality inspires everyone from Chairman of Directors to message boy with that esprit-de-corps which has, in so large a measure, contributed to the success of the world famed Association football club of which he may justly claim to be the bright particular star.'

Cuff resigned as secretary at the end of the First World War, mainly owing to the pressure of his growing legal practice. But he rejoined Everton's board in 1921 and stayed until 1948. He was chairman from 1921 to 1938, during which time he was elected to the Management Committee in 1925. There was no doubting his popularity; he won a remarkable 42 out of 45 possible votes.

Cuff's first main achievement for the League was in 1929 when he campaigned successfully for the automatic election of Management Committee members on to the FA Council. Had he achieved nothing further, this success alone would have won him a deserved place in the annals of professional football.

Meanwhile, as chairman of Everton he saw his beloved team go from the sublime to the Second Division. They won the Championship in 1928, then two years later were relegated for the first time in their history (albeit for only one season).

Dixie Dean said of Cuff: 'He was the master.' He recalled how Cuff sold the Everton training ground for £60,000 to a brewery, then bought a much larger site, the present Bellefield training ground, from the Co-op for only £30,000.

Cuff was both an opponent of the change in the offside law in 1925 and a great believer in Everton's tradition as a pure, attacking side. When the Everton players experimented with the third-back game made popular in the 1930s, Will Cuff walked into the dressing room at half time and told them: 'I don't know what you're playing at, but you'd best stop it. We have always played attacking football. We have a tradition. I don't care if you are beaten 6–5.

As Joe Mercer, who recalled this incident to Everton historian John Roberts, added: 'And we did get beaten, 6–5!'

Cuff was always destined for the presidency. Given a long-service medal by the League in 1932, he was then made Vice President in 1936, and on the death of Sutcliffe in January 1939 was the only real contender for the presidency. He was made a Life Member in 1945.

It was Cuff who kept the League intact during the Second World War, ruling over an inexperienced Management Committee and a gaggle of demanding and, at times, provocative clubs. While a lesser man may have backed away from open conflict with the London clubs, Cuff faced them square on, and although he didn't get it all his own way, he did extract an apology from them.

Len Shipman remembered how once, in his early days as a Leicester director, he had stood up to speak at a meeting. After a couple of minutes Cuff ordered him to stop. 'Sit down and stay down!' ordered the President. And no one argued when he was in that sort of mood.

'Tart and tough', Ivan Sharpe said of Cuff. Jimmy Guthrie of the Players' Union called Cuff 'a doughty opponent in negotiations and a great man for the League. We admired him for his fighting qualities. He stood up for what he believed right.'

But although he kept the League together during the war, once the post-war boom reached its peak life started to turn sour on Cuff.

Just before the war, he had opposed a change in Everton's constitution to allow one vote for each share owned. Cuff felt this gave too much power to wealthy individuals. But when he was re-elected to the board in 1946, some of the other directors accused him of wrongful use of proxies. Over the next three years his relationship with the club deteriorated, and after February 1948 when his wife of nearly fifty-four years died, he seemed to lose the will to fight any longer. A few months later he resigned from the board, bitterly opposed to the way the club was being run.

He spent the last year of his life living in a hotel room in Neston, overlooking the Dee Estuary, still active in both the League and FA and still taking an interest in his law firm in Castle Street, Liverpool. Finally, after returning from London to help make the FA Cup draw, he fell ill.

Scheming right to the last, he spoke to Ivan

Sharpe about a plan he was hatching to halt the rise in transfer fees. 'The transfer system,' he told Sharpe, 'is absolutely necessary. It is the abuse of it we have to consider.'

He then explained his plan of action, which Sharpe thought so drastic that he rang him back an hour later to check the details. Cuff confirmed them and added, in a husky voice, 'I wish I could get rid of this cold. Can't shake things off now like I could when I was under eighty!' Twelve hours later he died in his hotel room, on 6 February 1949.

And though an Evertonian through and through, it was a former Liverpool player who conducted his funeral service – the Reverend James Jackson. The funeral procession was over a mile long.

'So Will Cuff is dead', wrote Henry Rose in the *Daily Express*. '... Will Cuff, the benevolent solicitor who could suddenly whip himself to his feet and quell a League backbenchers' rebellion with a frozen look and a few faltering exhortations. Away from the council chamber he was gentleness itself; inside, when the status quo was threatened by progressives, he was a bear defending its young.'

The Management Committee took such exception to this description of their late President that they banned Rose from the press box shortly afterwards. He was eventually forgiven, but died himself a decade later on a snow-covered runway at Munich.

In that later era of aeroplanes and floodlights, Will Cuff would have been an anachronism. His death in 1949 coincided with both the peak of an era, and the start of a downward slide which would not be arrested fully until the 1960s. Cuff led the League into the post-war world, but he could not have taken it any further, not in his stiff collar.

THE FOOTBALL LEAGUE

Numbering of Players

CIRCULAR ISSUED BY THE MANAGEMENT COMMITTEE TO ACCOMPANY THE MINUTES OF MEETING HELD 23RD JUNE, 1939.

1.—The method of numbering in the League Competition shall be uniform, from 2—11, commencing with the Right Back and omitting the Goalkeeper, thus :—

2   Right Back.
3   Left Back.
4   Right Half-back.
5   Centre Half-back.
6   Left Half-back.
7   Outside Right.
8   Inside Right.
9   Centre Forward.
10   Inside Left.
11   Outside Left.

2.—Numbers shall be *not less* than 8 inch long and *not less* than 1½ inch in width, and should be cut out and stitched on the back of the shirts, thus :

3.—Colours of Numbers should contrast with Colours of Shirts. The following suggestions are for the guidance of Clubs.

Colour of Shirt.	Colour of Number.
White	Black or Navy.
Blue	White or Red or Yellow.
Red or Claret	White.
Old Gold	Black.
Green	White.
Red and White Stripes	Black.
Blue and White Stripes	Red.
Black and White Stripes	Red.
Black and Gold Stripes	White.
Halves, Blue and Gold	White or Black.
Halves, Claret and Amber	White or Green.
Halves, Green and Yellow	Black or Red.
Quarters, Blue and White	Black or Yellow.

F. HOWARTH,
Secretary.

Playing the numbers game, summer 1939. Some clubs wanted numbering to be optional. Will Cuff demanded all or nothing, and, as was usually the case, his will prevailed.

CHAPTER SEVENTEEN

Boom Years

Will Cuff began the 1945 Annual Meeting as he had each of the wartime gatherings, with a silent tribute to those who had died. A further eleven League players had been killed in the war, bringing the total number to seventy-five. Cuff himself was awarded Life Membership, and both he and the Committee were roundly applauded for the work they had done during the trying years of the war. The fact that no new names were put forward for the Committee in 1945 confirmed this general satisfaction.

Discussion of the coming 1945/6 transitional season took up most of the meeting. It was decided to split each section of the Third Division into two regional groups; North West and North East in the North, and Groups 1 and 2 in the South. There was no place for Bath City, Aberaman nor Lovell's Athletic, and neither Hull nor New Brighton were able to compete. Hull had actually gone into liquidation and were in the process of building their new ground, Boothferry Park. New Brighton, as late as June 1946, had no players and only an undeveloped sports field.

And so the much-awaited transitional period began, and for the League's staff also there was a fresh start, with new offices at 6 Starkie Street, Preston being bought for £1500 in August 1945. The new premises, the first ever owned by the League, were opened in April 1946, complete with their own resident caretaker. Secretary Fred Howarth also welcomed back Major Tom Charnley (the former Secretary's grandson), who was appointed Assistant Secretary in February 1946.

'Young Tom', as he was called, had started with the League as a junior in 1937. During the war, his brother George Charnley had worked as a temporary clerk, then in August 1946 Fred Howarth's nephew Eric joined the staff. There was also a distant relative, George Howarth, who began as an office boy at the League and later became secretary of Preston North End.

Major Tom Charnley and Signalman Eric Howarth were among the lucky soldiers returning home to find work. But many of the players had come back from the war only to find themselves unwanted by their former clubs.

Behind closed doors at another Extraordinary General Meeting at the Midland Hotel, Manchester, Cuff told the delegates that since they had last met, the Reinstatement of Civil Employment Act had taken effect. This made it compulsory for a company to re-employ those who had worked for it in September 1939. In addition, the 'sudden and victorious termination of the Japanese War' had allowed the release of more players from the forces. In one of his most powerful addresses, Cuff reminded the clubs of their debt.

'*Owing to the claims created by the war, many of your players have been engaged in the maintenance, at enormous cost, of the priceless inheritance of freedom. Many have given their lives, limbs and health in order that we at home might enjoy the blessings of safety. They have spent in this supreme effort six of the best years of their very short football life. Those who are spared to return to civil life may be desirous of resuming their pre-war occupation. They are conscious that in doing so they are handicapped by six years' abstention from the game and that they are six years older.*

When they do apply for reinstatement, I hope that, remembering the sacrifices that they have made and remembering what might have been our lot had they failed in that effort, we shall – and I hope every club without exception will – hold out the right hand of sportsmanship and fellowship to each of their players ... a unanimous gesture to this end would resound throughout the world of sport as typical of the high standard of Association football in general, and the League competition in particular ...'

There were no dissenters at the time, but once they were back at their clubs the directors refused to take back hundreds of players, despite the Reinstatement Act.

Neither would the clubs relent when it came to the demands of the Players' Union. Despite the sudden huge rise in attendances, and a raising of admission fees from 1s to 1s 6d, the players' call for a maximum weekly wage of £12 throughout the year, with a minimum wage of £5 per week, was barely discussed. Instead the Committee argued for a return to the pre-war level of £8, with match fees for players not signed on to remain at £4, and no bonuses permitted. What a welcome home!

After five years of playing for expenses only, and the prospect of another season, 1945/6, of being tied to their clubs without the security of a contract, it was hardly surprising, therefore, when the fireworks began on 5 November. Refusing to accept this high-handed brush-off from men who for the most part hadn't fired a shot throughout the war, the Players' Union threatened a strike, to begin on 19 November, unless negotiations were reopened.

In a panic, the Committee gathered on 11 November for an emergency meeting, in which the members agreed to offer the players a slightly improved deal: £9 maximum weekly wage (the players had demanded £12), but with no minimum (the players had asked for £5). Match fees for those not in full-time football would go from £4 to £5, while pre-war match bonuses – £2 for a win, £1 for a draw – would be reluctantly restored from 1 December.

The following day at the Midland Hotel, Manchester, League officials presented their hastily-concocted package to the Union delegation, which included chairman Sammy Crooks (Derby), Joe Mercer (Everton) and the future union chairman, Jimmy Guthrie, who had just been sacked by Portsmouth.

Cuff explained that increases in Entertainment Tax had accounted for all but one halfpenny of the rise in admission prices. Only if the tax were reduced – and there was considerable lobbying going on to that effect – would clubs be in a better position to meet the players' demands.

With this, the players' delegation retired to consider the offer, Crooks returning to say that they wanted £10. No deal, said the Committee, and the players retired once again. More discussion followed, and when Crooks returned he announced that £9 would be accepted. A strike had been averted and, according to Will Cuff, with the players showing dignity and tact. From being adversaries the two parties proclaimed themselves to be full of good wishes towards each other.

But it was undoubtedly a victory for Cuff. If press reports from the period are to be believed, some clubs were healthily endowed with funds at that time, and some had even survived the war with no financial loss at all.

Shortly after the Burnden Park disaster of 9 March 1946, in which thirty-three spectators died (the League raised £6500 for the victims' families), partial relief for League clubs from Entertainment Tax arrived with the 1946 Budget. During the war, admission had risen to 1s 6d, of which 8d had been tax. With a reduction of the levy, the Committee proposed at another Extraordinary General Meeting in April 1946 that admission should now be reduced to 1s 3d. This would give a reduction to the public of 3d – one of the Chancellor's conditions for reducing the tax was that the benefit would have to be passed on to the public – and a tax saving for clubs of 2½d.

But if the clubs could ignore the Reinstatement Act, then they were certainly not going to be governed by this new Labour Chancellor, Hugh Dalton. Southampton, backed by Arsenal, argued that admission costs should remain at 1s 6d, especially since higher wages and the need to make their grounds safe after the Bolton tragedy now placed extra demands on their funds. Plymouth supported the argument, since their own ground needed to be completely rebuilt because of bomb damage. Once again, therefore, the Committee was outvoted, by 32 votes to 17, and admission prices were set at 1s 6d. Not for long, however.

As soon as Hugh Dalton heard that the League had defied him, Will Cuff was summoned to the Exchequer and given a dressing down. Why had the master allowed his pupils to run riot? Poor Cuff. In June 1946 he had to urge the clubs yet again to reduce the minimum admission to 1s 3d, but this time, to his relief, they did (though several only grudgingly). So, had the President prevailed again? As we shall soon learn, the clubs still had a trump card up their sleeves for the following season, and Cuff's ordeal was not over yet.

In the meantime, another result of the 1946 Budget was to pave the way for a further rise in players' wages, from the maximum of £9 to £10 per week and from £5 to £6 for newly-signed professionals. Taking summer wages into account, this meant an overall annual rise for top players of just over eight shillings per week (while Fred Howarth was awarded a rise of £3 16s per week). Maximum benefits payable were to rise from £650 to £750.

But still the union declared its dissatisfaction. After all, the majority of players were still being paid below the maximum, there was still no minimum wage, and raised benefits were not much use if they remained optional. A player could still serve for five years and be refused a full benefit if the club felt so disposed.

Were the clubs being unfair? One set of figures from Southampton suggested that even with 14,000 average gates paying the 1s 3d

admission, the club would be unable to make a profit if they paid the new wage rates to their normal complement of twenty-five professionals.

There was also an enormous disparity between the incomes of certain clubs in this immediate post-war period, the most startling example of which was the pooled income from the Third Division Cup competitions in 1945/6. While the Southern section games yielded a total pool of £22,977, or £1044 per club, the Northern section brought in only £3712, or £185 per club. It would be inaccurate simply to conclude from these figures that southern clubs were therefore six times better off than their northern counterparts, but they do illustrate that there was a considerable gulf among the smaller clubs.

Nor should it be forgotten that those clubs

" I understand the hold up is because they refuse to give Simpkins a new jersey until he surrenders coupons."

Rationing left some clubs short of essentials, as the Daily Graphic *noted in January 1948. A League minute in August 1946 read: 'An application to the Ministry of Food, through the F A, for professional footballers to be allowed an increased bread ration, was refused.'*

which did enjoy healthy bank balances invariably found roundabout ways of rewarding their top players, be it above or below the counter. But that wasn't the point. The union believed that players should not have to depend on illegal handouts for their living, and so it informed the Ministry of Labour that it was now in dispute with the League.

This dispute had still not been settled by the time the restored League competition kicked off in August 1946. There were a few changes: Hull City had a new ground and a new set of directors, Clapton Orient were now Leyton Orient, and Birmingham were now Birmingham City. New Brighton had salvaged their operation during the summer by signing up a completely new set of players and restoring their former home, the Tower Athletic Ground, which had been occupied during the war by the US Army.

On the terraces, a large number of supporters discovered to their dismay that despite Hugh Dalton's order to reduce the minimum admission to 1s 3d, large areas of grounds were still being charged at 1s 6d. The commonest ploy was to charge 1s 6d for standing in the paddock or covered areas, where previously only the minimum had been charged.

Once again, the Government was infuriated at this cunning behaviour, and poor Will Cuff was summoned back to HM Customs and Excise, who reckoned that 43 per cent of clubs were not providing their usual amount of accommodation at the minimum price. A further 16 per cent had reduced such accommodation by as much as a fifth. If Government figures were correct, that meant that only thirty-six clubs had obeyed the Management Committee.

Another matter of concern to the Government was the number of mid-week matches being played in front of large audiences, many of whom were leaving their work places under false pretences. It was astonishing, said one factory owner, how many grandmothers were being buried on Wednesday afternoons! To alleviate this, the League suggested an extension of the season by two weeks, so that it would now run from 23 August to 10 May, with certain Saturdays being cleared of League fixtures to allow Cup ties to be played.

What with a new package of austerity measures, rationing still in force, shortages all round, and now a possible ban on mid-week games, it was hardly surprising that there was a flood of protests from clubs and supporters.

The players were not to find much relief either, because when another Extraordinary General Meeting met in the cold and gloom of the Midland Hotel, Manchester – the power supply had been cut off – not one club representative supported the union's demand for a £12 maximum wage. Instead, they proposed £11 per week for 1947/8 and £9 per week during the close season.

But the clubs were prepared to make one major concession. Perhaps placed in a more sympathetic mood by the miserable conditions at the hotel, but more likely under pressure from Government legislation, the clubs did finally agree to the principle of a minimum wage, some forty-five years after the players had first raised the subject. They agreed a scale of minimum earnings rising from £3 to £6, depending on the player's age. Even so, £6 a week in 1947, with attendances reaching record levels, was no king's ransom, and there were still plenty of First Division players earning well below the maximum.

Otherwise, the clubs showed no interest at all in union demands to make benefit payments compulsory or for players to receive a share of transfer fees. Nor were they prepared to allow the players to be represented on certain committees which affected their welfare.

Those were the views of the clubs. Now it was up to a National Arbitration Tribunal, under the chairmanship of Lord Terrington, to settle the dispute. Here was a sign of the times; no outside body (apart from the FA of course) had ever before intervened in the League's financial arrangements. John Bentley would have been horrified enough, Will Cuff wasn't too pleased either. Nor were the staff at Starkie Street, who had to put in hours of overtime to prepare the League's case.

The union chairman, Jimmy Guthrie – labelled a communist by some clubs – took legal advice from Sir Walter Monckton (a man well versed in diplomacy as advisor to Edward VIII during the abdication crisis). Monckton read through a typical League player's contract and said: 'Guthrie, this contract has no validity in law.' If the union could find a suitable test case, then he would help them prove it, once and for all. That test case did not come until 1963. In 1947, however, Monckton and Guthrie were able to negotiate some substantial gains for the union.

The Tribunal's report, issued on 11 April, came as a great blow to the League, which had spent over £800 in legal advice. But there was no doubt as to the result: the players had won a significant victory, and the clubs would have no choice but to comply.

These were the Tribunal's findings:

• The maximum wage was finally settled at £12 per week (£10 in summer).

• Instead of £6, as the union had asked, the minimum wage was set at £7 (£5 in summer) for players over twenty.

• Full payment of benefit money was to become a right, not a concession.

• Clubs would now have to pay players full wages (that is, not summer wages) from the start of pre-season training, instead of from the week of the first League game. (However, players' contracts still ran from May to April, which meant that in May a club could easily offer a player much reduced terms for the following season, knowing that if he refused to re-sign, the club would not have to pay his summer wages. If the player then failed to find a new club he would have to return in August, cap in hand. Either way, the club benefited; no summer wages, or lower wages for the whole

next year. Many players at smaller clubs thus received no income at all during the summer.)

• A negotiating council should be formed between the clubs and their players, to discuss wages and to review the transfer system. (This was the only part of the Tribunal's recommendations that the League was able to delay.)

All in all, it was a satisfying conclusion to a frustrating period for the players, after a winter so bad that many of them hadn't earned a bonus for weeks. Over 140 games were postponed or abandoned, and the season had to be extended by some five weeks to complete the fixtures. Some clubs had to draft in former prisoners of war to help clear snow from the pitches.

From all accounts, the effort was worth it; the standard of play was high, the First Division Championship being decided 'at the post' (Liverpool pipping Manchester United by one point), and gates were higher than they had ever been before, reaching an aggregate of 35·6 million. (Exact pre-war figures are unavailable, except for season 1937/8 when the total was reckoned to be 28·1 million.) The fact that clubs had been forced to accede to some of the players' demands must be seen, therefore, in the context of this sudden boom in prosperity.

Good will and bounty continued to flow at the June 1947 Annual Meeting. Talent money was raised for both League placings and FA Cup performances. In addition, single-match bonuses were raised by 50 per cent to £3 a win and £1 10s a draw. The players had never had it so good, even if their contracts were still feudal by nature and their signing-on fees were still pegged to the £10 limit set in December 1891!

There was no shortage of clubs wanting to enter the League during these boom years. In 1947, applications were received from a record number of clubs: Ashington, Gillingham, Merthyr Tydfil, Nelson and Northwich Victoria were former League competitors; Bath City had joined the wartime league; Guildford,

Llanelly, Peterborough, Scunthorpe, Shrewsbury, South Liverpool and Wigan Athletic were experienced pre-war campaigners; newer claimants were Anfield Plain (from Wearside), Ashton United, Bangor City, Barry Town, Chelmsford City, Colchester United, Consett, Dudley Town, Gravesend and Northfleet, North Shields, Stockton, Worcester City, Workington and Yeovil Town.

Never before had the League been so popular; twenty-seven clubs seeking to win four places. Unfortunately for them, there wasn't even an election. Fred Howarth announced that, because the two relegated clubs from the Second Division (Swansea and Newport) had both gone into the Southern section, that meant only one vacancy in the South and three in the North. If geographically unsuitable new clubs were elected, this would create a further imbalance and require some of the existing clubs to switch from North to South.

Therefore, since the executives of both sections had recommended the re-election of the four retiring clubs – Mansfield, Norwich, Haifax and Southport – and bearing in mind that the previous season had been the first since the war and had been extremely testing (because of the weather), was it not better to re-elect all four *en bloc*? Without a single dissenter, the clubs answered in the affirmative, and all twenty-seven applicants went home in a huff.

As a result of their disappointment, a delegation from the so-called National Association of Non-League Clubs met the Committee in January 1948 to re-argue the case for expanding the League. They made little headway, and at the 1948 Annual Meeting did little better when the eighteen non-League applicants mustered only 15 votes between them. Of those, 8 were cast in Shrewsbury's favour. The League doors seemed as tightly shut as ever.

For the record, Brighton (47) and Norwich (47) were re-elected to Division Three South,

Halifax (47) and New Brighton (38) were re-elected to Division Three North. Apart from Shrewsbury, only Colchester and Scunthorpe (2 each), and Gillingham, Worcester and South Liverpool (1 each) managed to find any favour. Bath, Bridgend, Chelmsford, Lovell's Athletic, Merthyr Tydfil, Peterborough, Yeovil, Nelson, North Shields, Northwich, Wigan and Workington all failed to attract a single vote.

The Annual Meeting did see the introduction of one new face to the League, however. Joe Richards of Barnsley was elected to the Management Committee in place of the late Phil Wood of Middlesbrough, for the start of what would be a long and distinguished career in League affairs.

Richards entered the scene at a time of unparalleled prosperity in the League. Indeed, the entire entertainment and spectator-sport industries had never known anything quite like this post-war boom of the late 1940s. Cinema audiences, for example, reached an all-time high in 1946. During 1947/8, total League attendances rose by some 4·65 million to top the 40 million mark for the first time, an average of 21,785 per League match (compared with 8572 in 1986/7). The Second Division, which accounted for nearly 31 per cent of the total, would never again attract such high numbers, but the overall rise would continue the following season.

'The most phenomenally successful [season]

In 1948 experiments were conducted by linesmen using a novel form of fluorescent flag, made up of material imported especially from the United States by Stanley Rous. At the same time as these swish new flags were made general issue, linesmen also cast off their sixty-year-long anonymity. In 1950/1 they were at last allowed to have their names and the colour of their flags – red or yellow – officially listed in the programme, alongside that of the referee.

since the inauguration of the League,' Will Cuff announced, with obvious glee. 'The level of attendances has, at times, reached such heights that any further increase is barred by existing ground capacities.'

The public's thirst for good entertainment following years of strain and hardship was obviously the main reason for this boom. But a second factor was the Government ban on mid-week afternoon matches. This had forced both the League and FA to switch more games to Saturdays and all mid-week games to evening kick-offs at the beginning and end of the season (when light conditions were better). As Cuff noted, the supporters seemed to like this new arrangement, despite their earlier protests, and it was felt that the League might well be advised to continue it even after normal conditions resumed.

So everything in the League's garden was rosy. Relations with the FA were excellent, especially since both the FA secretary, Stanley Rous (soon to become Sir Stanley), and the chairman, Amos Brook Hirst (a former member of the Management Committee), were patently sympathetic towards the League. Accordingly, in 1948, for the first time a Joint Committee was formed between the two organizations to discuss issues of common interest, such as television, players' welfare, transfers and Entertainment Tax.

Relations with the Players' Union were as stable as might be expected, while at League headquarters the expanded staff of five (including for the first time two female clerks) now had their own pension scheme and were enjoying the benefits of central heating. In January 1949 they all also received handsome wage rises. Indeed, League funds were so healthy that one delegate at the 1949 Annual Meeting thought that the Jubilee Fund could now be much more generous with its payments to former players in need.

It would seem that some clubs were already being too generous, fuelled no doubt by their sudden surge in income, especially once Enter-

tainment Tax was further reduced in 1948. We may recall that the last club to have been caught *in flagrante delicto* was Derby County in 1941. Seven years later Derby were again under scrutiny after various newspaper allegations concerning Billy Steel's £15,000 transfer from Morton. Investigations suggested that Steel had received more than the permitted £10 allowable signing-on fee (surprise, surprise!).

But there was much worse. Derby's books were found to be full of 'gross irregularities', ranging from tax evasion to illegal wage payments and fiddled accounts. The result was much the same as in 1941. The chairman, B. Robshaw, was suspended *sine die*, the former secretary banned permanently, a £500 fine was imposed, and just for good measure, poor Derby were fined five guineas for letting in old-aged pensioners at reduced rates.

Only one threat loomed on the horizon – televised football – and that was met with supreme confidence by the League, despite attempts by the BBC to court the Management Committee's favour by showing it around the Alexandra Palace studios.

Radio commentaries, first heard in January 1927, had, since the outbreak of the war, become part and parcel of Saturday afternoons in Britain, and this was now irreversible. But the Committee refused to allow the televising of matches other than internationals and Cup Finals and the clubs agreed unanimously.

They usually did when Will Cuff put his foot down, which was often, because they recognized that in him lay nearly sixty years of active involvement in professional football. Cuff died on 6 February 1949. 'A great leader, a wise counsellor and a staunch friend', the Committee called him. He was the link between the old and the new worlds.

Yet despite the boom years, Cuff's decade in office had probably been the most troublesome experienced by any president, encompassing as it did six years of war and the difficult period of transition afterwards. Cuff himself euphemistically described the post-war traumas as 'growing pains'.

He was undoubtedly the last of his kind; a leader who was somewhat larger than life, a man whose roots lay with the world of William McGregor but who still managed to impose his stamp upon the vastly more complicated and demanding world of the late 1940s. This was the age of the atom bomb, the welfare state, the nationalized railways, the new health service; austerity at home, prosperity in football.

Not one of the Management Committee members could claim Cuff's remarkable heritage, and it is therefore no slight upon those men nor their successors to suggest that when Will Cuff died, the innate authority invested in the leadership of the League since its inception in 1888 died too. The last of the patriarchs had passed away. Now, League presidents would have to prove themselves in a meritocracy.

* * *

As was customary on the death of a president, the League's senior Vice President moved into the chair until the next Annual Meeting. In February 1949 that role fell to seventy-two-year-old Arthur Oakley of Wolverhampton Wanderers. Oakley's four months as Acting President were dominated by two issues, both affecting relations with the players.

First, the Management Committee met the Ministry of Labour, with the result that Lord Terrington's 1947 recommendation for a Joint Committee to deal with players' affairs was at last implemented, in theory if not in spirit.

Second, after prolonged deliberations with a London firm of insurance brokers, the Management Committee finally arrived at a blueprint for a provident scheme, designed to give players more security after their playing days were over.

The idea for such a fund had originally come from Jimmy Guthrie and Stanley Rous, but it was partly Arthur Oakley's efforts which brought it closer to fruition. The idea was to impose a levy of 4 per cent on gates, the proceeds to be distributed to each player at the age of thirty-five as a lump sum. This sum was calculated on the basis of 10 per cent of his earnings in each year of his League career.

Annual running costs of the provident scheme were estimated at nearly £121,000 per annum, and Fred Howarth calculated that under the prevailing conditions in 1949, a levy of 4 per cent would bring in £148,000. That would give each player about £120 on his retirement from the game, or the equivalent for a top player of just under a year's basic wage.

(In practice, once gates started to decline the fund would be hard pressed to maintain that level of payments, and the Provident Fund became increasingly meaningless over the years. But in 1949 it certainly represented a giant leap forward, for both the players and the League, which had to administer it. And as the Players' Union soon found out, whenever it asked for higher wages during the 1950s, the clubs were able to plead that the Provident Fund absorbed so much of their income that they couldn't possibly afford more wages. Security was a double-edged sword.)

Arthur Oakley worked hard on setting up the Provident Fund, but he soon realized that his health would not allow him to be nominated for the presidency after all. Since three other members of the Committee had already been nominated – Bill Cearns (West Ham), Arthur Drewry (Grimsby) and Will Harrop (Liverpool) – Oakley's decision was accepted.

Thus, for only the third time in the League's sixty-one years, there was to be a contest for the election of a new president (the previous two occasions having been in 1910 and 1938).

But before he stood down, Oakley was able to acquaint the delegates at the 1949 Annual Meeting with a quite astonishing set of statistics. The remarkable rise in attendances had continued throughout the 1948/9 season, with the final aggregate of 41.2 million giving an average gate of 22,333 per league match. This was a rise of approximately 2.5 per cent, even though crowds had been marginally lower in the Second Division. Indeed, the aggregate attendance figure, plus those for the First Division and the Third Division North, reached peaks which were never subsequently equalled. Only crowds in the Third Division South continued to rise after 1949, reaching a record level in 1950/1 (see Appendix Eight).

Oakley went on to detail how this boom was benefiting the players. Apart from a rise in the number receiving benefits, the number of those receiving the maximum wage had risen to almost 600. That represented 30 per cent of a total number of 2000 full-time professionals (an average of twenty-three per club). No wonder Oakley was able to add: 'Relations with the Players' Union continue to be amicable.'

Having been the bearer of glad tidings, it was now time for Oakley to stand down – reluctantly, as he told the meeting. This was not the end of his involvement, however, since he was re-elected without opposition to remain on the Committee (and would return, surprisingly, as president six years later at the age of seventy-eight).

For the presidency, the first ballot resulted as follows: Bill Cearns – 10 votes, Arthur Drewry – 21, Will Harrop – 18. Since none had received the required 50 per cent of the vote, a second ballot was held, in which Drewry succeeded with 28 votes to Harrop's 21. Thus, Arthur Drewry, a fish merchant from Grimsby, became the League's sixth president. More of him anon.

One place on the Committee had to be filled, and this went to David Wiseman of Birmingham City. Otherwise there were no new faces for the 1949/50 season. Aldershot (41 votes) and Crystal Palace (40) were re-elected to the Third Division South. The challengers were Worcester and Gillingham (5 each), Merthyr (3), Yeovil (2) and Peterborough (0). In the Northern section, Bradford City (45) and Southport (42) were also comfortably

returned, the failed applicants being Shrewsbury (5), Scunthorpe (4) and Wigan Athletic, South Liverpool, North Shields and Nelson (all without votes).

It was partly the issue of extending the League, and partly a certain dissatisfaction with the Committee itself, which gave Arthur Drewry his first challenge as League President. On 4 July 1949 directors from forty-one clubs met independently of the Committee to discuss the formation of an association of directors of League clubs. Major Wilson Keys of West Bromwich (son of the former Vice President Harry Keys) was at the forefront, together with W. J. Heryet of Spurs and J. R. Sarjantson of Southampton. Naturally, the Committee saw such a grouping as a direct challenge to its own authority. There had, after all, been no formal independent gathering of League directors since the disastrous Pools War of 1936.

Some club directors felt that a separate organization would help raise matters for the Committee's attention, without being either disloyal or critical of it. For its part, the Committee considered that a meeting of clubs every March, held under the League's auspices, would give the directors sufficient time to debate issues before Annual Meetings. Thus, Drewry called for a conference and hoped that nothing more would come of the independence movement.

But by the time the conference was held, on 27 March 1950 at the Café Royal, two members of the Committee had died: Newcastle's George Rutherford, in December 1949, followed ten weeks later by Bill Cearns. Will Harrop of Liverpool was elected to Rutherford's position as Vice President, but even he was too ill to attend the conference.

No doubt the two deaths, plus the Committee's undoubted commitment to solidarity, put Major Keys in a conciliatory mood. He told the assembled directors that the Committee's plans to hold such meetings annually should be given a trial. But the proof of any harmony was in the talking.

First on the agenda was the extension of the League. That no new clubs had been admitted the previous year had not been to every member's satisfaction. Indeed, Everton carried on their former chairman Will Cuff's predisposal towards an opening of the doors, backed by Sheffield Wednesday. Fred Howarth had himself expressed a similar view in a speech he had made in 1949, so the Committee had to come up with a plan if it were to be seen to mean business.

According to Drewry, the setting up of a Fourth Division was impracticable. There simply weren't enough clubs of the right calibre. Instead, the Committee proposed an extension of each Third Division by two clubs.

That alone was insufficient, however, added Drewry. There had to be a change in the re-election system, so he proposed that the bottom club in each section should be barred from seeking re-election for twelve months. That way, at least two new clubs would have a change to prove themselves every season.

(The Committee did consider various other proposals, some of which make interesting reading. One far-sighted idea was for a premier division of sixteen clubs, First and Second Divisions of twenty-two clubs each, and two regional Third Divisions of twenty-two clubs. This would have entailed the introduction of sixteen new clubs. An alternative was to introduce twenty new clubs, and form a regional Fourth Division.)

Once this discussion began, it became clear that the Third Division clubs were strongly opposed to any automatic relegation from the League. Plymouth felt it far better to debar clubs from seeking re-election twice within three years, while West Bromwich proposed a Third Division split into three sections, Northern, Midland and Southern.

And there, regrettably, the discussion ended, with little support for the Committee's proposals and little agreement on any of the alternatives. But the meeting did illustrate one theme which has surfaced consistently throughout the League's hundred-year history: that it was often the Management Committee which put forward the most radical proposals, and the clubs which rejected them. How different might the League's subsequent history have been had that 1950 plan for automatic relegation from the League been endorsed.

Arthur Drewry's first year as President was not all frustration. On 29 December 1949 the deeds of the new Provident Fund were signed and sealed in Sheffield, and a couple of days later the League showed how proud it was by launching the scheme at a reception at the Great Western Hotel, London. That the League even contemplated such a publicity-seeking event was in itself an indication of how attitudes were changing.

But the effort had been worthwhile. By the end of the season a total of 3618 current and former players had joined the scheme, including virtually the entire playing staffs of all eighty-eight clubs.

As a result, the professional of 1950 was better off and more secure than any of his predecessors. And as if to prove this point, in 1950 the Jubilee Fund (which was a separate scheme altogether) paid out £125 to former national hero Billy Meredith, who was at the time struggling to make ends meet in Manchester. The new Provident Fund couldn't guarantee that that would never be necessary again, but it did at least aim to give retired players a helping hand with their post-footballing careers.

At Starkie Street, the Provident Fund's establishment meant the culmination of months of hard work behind the scenes, especially on the legal side. It also necessitated an extra member of staff being taken on – Norman Thomas, who in 1988 was the League's longest-serving employee. Fred Howarth's office was now busier and boasted more modern equipment than ever.

Indeed, football's prospects remained as rosy as the season before. Season ticket sales

1,272,185!

Packed in at Pompey, heaving at Hull and brimming at Bradford! Tuesday, 27 December 1949 saw the largest aggregate League attendance ever recorded on one day. The record had already been broken the previous day, but Tuesday's crowds were higher by over 46,000.

Of the 1,272,185 spectators who watched the forty-four matches (an average of 28,913), the highest crowd was 70,000 at Villa Park for a local derby with Wolves. Thousands who were locked out stood in the surrounding streets listening to running commentaries from sympathetic fans inside the bulging ground. The lowest crowd was at Hartlepools, where 5000 saw the visit of Barrow. (The figures detailed in the *Daily Express* cutting – see plate section – add up to an aggregate slightly below the official League figure, mainly because several of the attendances were estimated.)

The huge crowds were even more remarkable when one considers that there was a rail strike in London, and that only one club boasted a record attendance – Middlesbrough.

A sign of the times was that one hundred Brentford fans flew in four aeroplanes to Hull. And just to show how action-hungry the English were that day, not far from Hull a crowd of 900 watched a cricket match in freezing conditions.

There can be no doubt as to who was the most surprised man amongst the million and more spectators on that December afternoon.

Arthur Carron, a tenor opera singer, was in the crowd at Swindon when a loudspeaker announcement called him to the club offices. There he was told that the lead singer at Covent Garden Opera House had fallen ill and could Carron rush to London to perform the role in Wagner's *Lohengrin* that evening? One hopes that he hadn't been shouting too much at the County Ground, and that he didn't miss too many of the goals.

---

reached record levels and on 27 December 1949 the aggregate attendance shattered even the previous season's record for one day (see above), although aggregate gates fell by 753,549.

Bad weather was one factor for the slight loss of crowds, but undoubtedly the most critical eyes fell on the gates recorded for 29 April, the afternoon of the Cup Final between Arsenal and Liverpool. Since 1938, all Cup finals had been broadcast live on television, but whereas before the war, viewing figures were no higher than 10–12,000, by 1950 the number of licensed sets had risen to 386,750, meaning a viewing audience of a million or more. This had a drastic effect upon the afternoon's League programme, which attracted the lowest total of the season, only 425,000 (only!)

Sunderland proposed, therefore, at the 1950 Annual Meeting, that the BBC should not be allowed to broadcast matches at the same time as League games were being staged. Instead recorded games should be broadcast in the evenings, as occurred in other countries. Sunderland also pointed out that while the League received only a token five guineas for each match televised, the rights for a recent boxing fight had been sold for £750.

The first episode of football's long-running saga with television had just begun.

New problems, and new faces. The 1950 Annual Meeting saw the election of Joe Mears of Chelsea and Norman Banks of Bolton onto

RIGHT

Sutcliffe photographed in 1938: President at last, but exhausted by nearly four decades of total commitment. Less than a year later he was dead.

BELOW RIGHT

Sir Henry Norris, whose manipulation of the League secured Arsenal's promotion in 1919. Tottenham felt cheated, but it was Norris who ultimately lost favour.

BELOW

Instead of cups, shields were awarded for the winners of each Third Division section. The Second Division also had a shield, replaced by a cup after the Second World War.

ABOVE

*The Management Committee 1926–7,
with Charles Sutcliffe apparently none too
pleased with the intrusion of a
photographer. From left to right, around
the table, are (left foreground) Will Cuff
(Everton), John Oliver (Newcastle), Fred
Rinder (Villa), Arthur Dickinson (Sheff
Wed), Harry Keys (WBA), John
McKenna (President), Tom Charnley
(Secretary), Charles Sutcliffe (Burnley),
William Hall (Arsenal) and Tom
Barcroft (Blackpool).*

ABOVE

Summer 1932, and the Management Committee are guests of Everton at Llandudno. The long established members are getting older, while new faces are increasingly in evidence. Back Row (left to right): Thomas Rushton (auditor), Fred Howarth (Assistant Secretary), Phil Bach (Middlesbrough), Amos Brook Hirst (Huddersfield), William Bassett (WBA), Tom Charnley (Secretary). Front row: Will Cuff (Everton), Charles Sutcliffe (Burnley), John McKenna (President), Fred Rinder (Villa), Tom Barcroft (Blackpool) and Morton Cadman (Tottenham).

RIGHT

An unsuccessful plea to the Management Committee, typed out, oddly enough, on League notepaper.

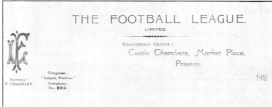

THE FOOTBALL LEAGUE.

LIMITED.

REGISTERED OFFICE :
Castle Chambers, Market Place,
Preston.

Secretary :
T. CHARNLEY.

Telegrams :
"League, Preston."
Telephone :
No. 304.

192

We, the undersigned former Directors of the BRISTOL CITY FOOTBALL CLUB under suspension by the FOOTBALL LEAGUE beg to apply for the removal of such suspension and undertake that if our application is acceded to, to honourably observe the Rules and Regulations of the FOOTBALL ASSOCIATION and the FOOTBALL LEAGUE in future.

Dated this *19th* day of January 1926.

LEFT

Fred Rinder: 'A reformer is rarely popular,' he admitted, having thrown three bottles of whisky out of a railway carriage window.

BELOW

Fred Rinder's silver casket to honour his election as a Life Member in 1938. Such presentations were popular throughout football before the Second World War.

ABOVE

Aboard the Liverpool steamer Ulster Prince, the League party sails to Belfast for an Inter-League match in September 1930. Such trips were always well attended by Committeemen. Notice that some are sporting their Management Committee badges, while Charles Sutcliffe (centre foreground) is again caught in mid-cigarette. Fourteen players travelled in the group (for team line-up see Appendix Three).

ABOVE

The 50th Annual Meeting of the League, at the Holborn Restaurant, 30 May 1938. The Championship Trophy and Divisional Shields await presentation as Amos Brook Hirst honours the 82-year-old Fred Rinder with his Life Membership silver casket. Rinder had collaborated with McGregor in setting up the League in 1888 and up to 1938 had missed only one Annual Meeting. No other man had such a record, or enjoyed Life Membership for such a brief spell. Seven months later he died. Note that the First and Second Division clubs have a table each.

RIGHT

Littlewoods in 1936, where despite the League's best endeavours 4000 employees were at full stretch to cope with the weekly avalanche of one million coupons. Will Cuff would have been aghast to know that his Everton chair would one day be occupied by the owner of Littlewoods.

Charles Sutcliffe with H.R.H. the Duke of Gloucester at the Jubilee Banquet, May 1938. Sutcliffe told his family later that the Duke had been one of the most interesting and well educated men he'd ever met and that he could have talked to him for months. Alas the 76-year-old President only had months to live.

Numbering up in the summer of 1939. A Wilmslow factory worker sews red numbers on to Manchester City's sky-blue shirts.

ABOVE

*TV times are here, as an invited audience
attends the London offices of Rediffusion to
watch the 1948 Cup Final and goes wild
in front of an apparently blank screen. Since
League games were still played on the same
afternoon as the Final, the effect of
television on attendances was disastrous.
Approximately one million people watched
the Final on television that year.*

LEFT

*Will Cuff – 'Tart and tough' in the council
chamber, 'gentleness itself' outside.*

YESTE DAY'J EJULTJ, JCO E J, TA LEJ TO DATE

DIVISION I.

ARSENAL (0) ......0 **MAN UTD** (0) 0
63,000

ASTON VILLA (0) ..1 **WOLVES** (1) 4
Dixon   Swinbourne 2, Smyth
Pye—70,000

BLACKPOOL (0) ...2 **BURNLEY** (0) 0
Mortensen, McIntosh   30,000

DERBY (3) ....4 **BIRMINGHAM** (0) ..1
Mosley, Stamps 3   Brennan—37,459

FULHAM (0) ....0 **EVERTON** (0) 0
34,999

LIVERPOOL (0) ...2 **CHELSEA** (1) 2
Fazad 2   Bentley, Billington
58,757

MAN CITY (0) ....1 **HUDDERSFIELD** (2) ..3
Clarke   Glazzard, Hassall
45,000

MIDDLESBRO' (0) ..1 **NEWCASTLE** (0) 0
McKennan   53,506

PORTSMOUTH (0) ..1 **CHARLTON** (0) 0
Harris   43,650

W.B.A (0) ....1 **SUNDERLAND** (1) ..2
Bowyer, F Mountford   Watson—40,000
(pen)

W.B.A (0) ....1 **BOLTON** (1) 2
Walsh, Barlow   Bradley—45,000

	P	W	D	L	F	A	W	D	L	F	A	Pts
Liverpool	24	6	4	0	27	14	4	5	0	12	33
Man Utd	24	7	3	2	26	11	4	6	4	9	31
Blackpool	23	7	5	1	22	10	4	2	1	7	31
Port'm'th	24	5	6	1	21	10	6	2	3	15	29
Wolves	.24	6	4	2	27	16	5	3	4	20	29
Arsenal	.25	6	2	4	27	16	5	5	3	20	17	29
Burnley	.25	6	4	2	12	6	3	5	10	13	29
Derby	.23	6	1	4	28	17	5	4	3	14	13	27
Sunderl'd	24	8	0	3	24	11	2	3	9	19	30	26
Chelsea	.24	6	3	19	18	4	6	2	22	18	25
Fulham	.24	6	3	3	17	8	5	5	12	18	24
W.B.A	.24	7	2	3	24	9	1	6	12	25	24
Middlesbr	.24	7	4	19	13	3	2	6	11	16	24
A Villa	.24	6	2	14	15	3	6	8	21	23
Newcastle	23	7	2	3	30	18	1	4	6	13	20	22
H'dersf'd	.25	5	4	17	16	2	7	12	26	21
Stoke	.25	5	3	4	15	17	5	7	12	20	20
Bolton	.24	4	1	20	13	0	6	7	18	18
Everton	.24	4	4	3	11	4	7	9	13	18
Charlton	.25	3	3	19	23	4	9	14	20	17
Man City	.24	5	5	5	9	5	19	17
Birm'ham	24	3	5	1	15	10	1	7	28	13

Central League. — Barnsley 4 Derby 0 —
Bolton 3 W.B.A. 0—Burnley 5 Stoke 0—

DIVISION II.

BLACKBURN (0) ...0 **SHEFF WED** (0) 0
30,400

BURY ....0 **BRADFORD** (0) 0
Bodle   22,700

CARDIFF (0) .....0 **PLYMOUTH** (0) 0
Evans   35,000

CHESTERFIELD (0) .1 **TOTTENHAM** (0) ..0
rialton (pen)   Scarth—21,000

COVENTRY (1) ...1 **LEICESTER** (1) 1
G Maxon   Adam, Paterson
36,981

HULL (1) ....2 **BRENTFORD** (0) ..0
Shepherd, Jensen   48,587

LEEDS (0) ......0 **BARNSLEY** (0) 0
Williams   47,500

Q.P.R. (1) .....1 **GRIMSBY** (0) 0
Ardinall   Shearer, Briggs
22,884

SHEFF UTD (1) ..1 **PRESTON** (1) 1
Smith   55,000

SOUTHAMPTON (1) 2 **LUTON** (0) 1
Day, Bates   Kiernan—26,878

SWANSEA (0) ....0 **WEST HAM** (1) 1
McGrorv   20,000

	P	W	D	L	F	A	W	D	L	F	A	Pts
Tottenh'm	24	11	1	1	37	8	3	3	0	21	9	42
Sheff Wed	23	8	4	0	28	12	4	3	14	14	32
Hull City	.24	9	2	1	30	17	1	5	18	25	31
Sheff Utd	.25	8	1	16	13	6	2	5	20	24	26
Bury	.24	8	4	22	12	3	1	7	15	26	25
Sh'mpt'n	23	6	3	2	22	12	3	4	15	19	25
Preston	.25	6	4	2	19	12	3	7	16	19	25
West Ham	.24	6	4	18	17	4	4	15	13	25
Leeds Utd	25	4	6	2	16	12	4	4	6	11	16	24
Ch'st'rf'd	25	7	2	3	15	8	2	4	9	21	24
Cardiff C	.25	7	1	3	15	9	1	4	19	23	23
Swansea	.24	7	2	21	8	3	8	11	26	23
Brentford	25	5	3	26	19	2	7	14	24	22
Grimsby	.24	6	3	3	26	19	2	7	14	24	22
Barnsley	.24	7	3	27	20	0	5	8	19	22
Blackburn	.25	6	3	17	11	3	1	8	16	27	21
Leicester	.25	5	4	20	18	3	7	18	21	19
Luton Tn	24	6	2	16	14	1	5	7	16	19
Q.P.R.	.24	3	6	11	15	2	5	7	18	18
Bradford	.24	4	3	15	21	2	5	7	12	25	18
Coventry	23	4	2	15	13	2	6	18	22	18
Plymouth	24	4	3	14	16	1	4	7	15	27	17

Inter-League Match.—Kent Amateur 4
Middlesex Senior 1.

DIVISION III. (S.)

ALDERSHOT (4) ...4 **NEWPORT** (1) 1
Hobbs 2, McNichol 2   Griffiths—7,318

BRISTOL R (1) ...3 **L ORIENT** (0) 0
Roost 2, Hodges   19,566

IPSWICH (0) .....0 **NOTTS CO** (0) 0
Sewell, Lawton 2.
Johnston—22,983

MILLWALL (1) ...1 **WALSALL** (1) 1
Constantine   Chapman—27,012

N'THAMPTON (1) .1 **PORT VALE** (1) 1
nglish   Martin—19,163

NOTTM FOR (0) ..0 **NORWICH** (1) 1
Ryder—31,844

READING (0) .....0 **BOURNEM'TH** (1) ..1
Amor 2   Cross—22,000

SOUTHEND (1) ...1 **EXETER** (0) 0
Morris   20,000

SWINDON (2) ....2 **BRIGHTON** (0) 0
Simner 2, Dawson   McNicol, Reed
Lunn   18,872

TORQUAY (0) ....0 **BRISTOL C** (1) 1
Shaw, Conley, Lewis   Boxshall, Eisentrager,
Rodgers—13,000

WATFORD (0) .....0 **C PALACE** (0) 0
15,000

	P	W	D	L	F	A	W	D	L	F	A	Pts
Notts Co	22	9	2	0	32	6	7	3	2	22	12	36
Norwich C	23	8	2	2	22	4	4	13	18	30
N'th'mpt'n	23	8	3	1	23	12	5	4	20	19	29
T'rquay	23	8	4	0	23	12	4	1	6	14	22	29
Bo'mouth	24	7	3	2	22	13	4	5	13	22	28
Southend	24	7	4	23	13	3	16	27	28
Nottm F	23	7	0	5	26	15	4	1	5	13	26
Reading	.24	9	2	22	18	1	7	18	26	26
Port Vale	22	6	4	0	19	5	2	3	7	11	25
Watford	.23	5	3	17	10	3	4	14	12	24
Bristol C	22	8	3	17	13	1	3	12	28	21
Walsall	.22	6	3	23	12	1	6	12	15	20
Crystal P	.22	6	2	18	13	1	7	14	21	20
Swindon	.22	6	4	29	13	1	8	7	20	19
Brighton	23	5	4	16	18	4	1	16	28	19
Millwall	.23	7	3	17	11	3	1	8	16	19	18
Bristol R	22	6	2	16	12	0	9	5	19	18
Nwport Co	22	7	2	28	16	2	0	12	40	18
Leyton O	23	6	3	18	12	0	9	13	37	18
A'dershot	22	6	1	15	10	1	2	9	11	26	17
Exeter C	22	3	4	18	19	1	3	8	10	25	13
Ipswich T	22	4	1	8	3	8	25	13

RUGBY UNION

Aberavon 8 Bridgend 6—Bridgwater and A

DIVISION III. (N.)

BRADFORD C (1) ..1 **CHESTER** (0) 0
Kendall   21,000

CARLISLE (2) ....2 **YORK** (3) 4
Billingham, Dick 3   M Patrick, Walker 2
13,000

DONCASTER (0) ..0 **N BRIGHTON** (0) ..0
25,000

GATESHEAD (1) ..3 **DARLINGTON** (2) ..3
Wilbert, Ingham.   Quinn 2, Parsley
T Callender (pen)   8,000

HALIFAX (1) .....1 **STOCKPORT** (0) ..1
Cocker—8,000

H'TLEPOOLS (1) ..1 **BARROW** (1) 1
Sloan, Willetts (pen)   Leach, Woods A
Colline—5,000

LINCOLN (2) .....2 **CREWE** (1) 1
Dodds 2   15,241

OLDHAM (0) .....0 **MANSFIELD** (0) ..0
Gemmell   22,252

SOUTHPORT (1) ..1 **ROCHDALE** (2) 2
Meadows 2, Powell   Brown, Dryburgh
12,000

TRANMERE (0) ...0 **ROTHERHAM** 2
Guest, Noble—14,000

WREXHAM (1) ....1 **ACCRINGTON** 1
Dolan—9,292

	P	W	D	L	F	A	W	D	L	F	A	Pts
Doncaster	22	8	4	0	11	4	7	2	20	13	36
Rochdale	22	9	0	3	20	7	1	7	18	18	30
Stockport	.24	10	1	2	26	7	7	18	18	29
Mansfield	23	7	1	2	26	16	4	18	17	27
Crewe	.22	7	1	28	16	3	4	12	17	27
Southport	23	7	4	22	15	3	12	15	27
Rotherh'm	24	8	3	29	18	4	18	14	26
Tranmere	21	8	7	1	16	9	3	5	10	14	26
Lincoln C	22	8	1	16	8	3	2	7	13	20	25
Carlisle	.22	7	1	2	19	11	5	5	17	18	24
Darlington	23	3	2	28	19	1	7	9	18	22
Oldham	23	5	3	23	18	5	6	21	22	21
Gateshead	23	5	3	18	5	0	6	21	22	21
N Bright'n	23	5	3	15	16	3	0	10	18	21
Halifax	.22	6	4	16	11	2	8	13	34	18
Wrexham	.23	4	2	9	2	9	11	21	17
Accr'ngt'n	23	5	3	19	14	1	2	10	6	26	16
York City	23	4	1	8	15	25	15

BOWLS

ABOVE

1,272,185 spectators! As the Daily Express *reported, this was the record aggregate attendance for one day's League programme, on 27 December 1949. One poor chap at Swindon didn't make it to the final whistle (see page 180).*

RIGHT

Highbury on a packed afternoon in mid-August 1951. Schoolboys at the front, hardly a female in view, no security fencing and only the older supporers and servicemen still wear hats. But as the spectacled man (right foreground) tries to curb a youngster's enthusiasm, the Burnden Park disaster in 1946 was a reminder that crowds were not always well-behaved and nor were all grounds able to cope with the crowds.

the Management Committee, and having approved the plan to extend the Third Division, voting also took place to choose four new Associate Members (all four retiring clubs, Halifax, York, Newport and Millwall were re-elected without having to enter the ballot).

Twenty non-League clubs went into the hat originally, but before a vote could be taken, Bangor City withdrew, and Arthur Drewry pointed out that three of the applicants, Merthyr Tydfil, Llanelly and Cradley Heath, had greyhound racing at their grounds. This was contrary to a 1947 League ruling that no grounds should stage racing other than those which already had agreements, such as Bristol Rovers, Chelsea, Newport and Watford.

Not that this had much effect on the sub-sequent voting. For the Southern section, former League members Gillingham (44 votes) were clear favourites, and Colchester United (28) joined them. The unsuccessful applicants were Worcester City (11), Chelmsford City (8), Peterborough United (5), Merthyr (1) and Yeovil (1). Llanelly, Cradley Heath and Nune-aton Borough received no votes.

For the Northern section, Shrewsbury (30) were at last successful, after having applied on every possible occasion since 1935. For the second vacancy, however, two further ballots were required.

In the first, Wigan and Workington tied on 19 votes each, followed by Scunthorpe (17) and former members Nelson (11). In a second ballot, Scunthorpe and Wigan tied at 15 votes each, with Workington (14) and Nelson (5) dropping out. Finally, in a third ballot, Scun-thorpe, placed third in the first ballot, came from behind and squeezed out unlucky Wigan with 30 votes to 18. So near for Wigan and yet so far. It would be another twenty-eight years before they would finally succeed.

The remaining unsuccessful applicants to the Northern section were former members Northwich Victoria (1) and Ashington (0), plus South Liverpool (1), and North Shields (0).

So Kent was to enjoy League football again, Shropshire was to experience it for the first time, and the Football League now numbered ninety-two clubs, the figure it has retained ever since. How many other industries in 1988 have still as many outlets as they once possessed in 1950? Not many, one can be sure.

As the League settled down into the 1950s, the footballing agenda for the decade soon became clear: wage negotiations, television dis-putes, and a harsh realization that English foot-ball was not quite the world beater everyone had assumed it to be. That was made clear enough when a certain Larry Gaetjens scored the only goal in England's World Cup match against the United States at Belo Horizonte on 29 June 1950. This was England's first World Cup, but it would not be the only humiliation they would suffer at the hands of foreigners before the decade was out. (Gaetjens was actu-ally born in Haiti, and on returning to the island, allegedly as a CIA agent, he was put in jail and never seen again. Perhaps Papa Doc was a closet England fan.)

Back home, illegal payments and sen-sationalism in the press proved to be regular bugbears for the Management Committee. Indeed, the two issues came together when Welsh striker Trevor Ford was fined £100 for allegedly demanding a signing-on bonus, only for Express Newspapers to pay him £100 to 'reveal all'.

At Starkie Street there was an unexpected shake-up when the Assistant Secretary, 'Young Tom' Charnley, left to take up a business post. Since there were no other Howarth or Charnley heirs-apparent on the horizon, for the first time ever the League was forced to advertise the post.

Over 400 applications flooded in, one of them from a thirty-nine-year-old local govern-ment official in Portsmouth who was at the time contemplating his own career prospects.

Alan Hardaker nearly didn't apply at all, especially since he suspected that the League was looking for only a junior clerk. He had

Fred Howarth – League Secretary 1933–56

Fred Howarth, born in Preston just seven weeks after the birth of the League in 1888, in many ways personified the organization he would serve faithfully for thirty-five years. He was a steady, conservative man, making up in honesty what he lacked in flair. The League was seen as a family, and in the League's offices the Howarth family was always to be seen.

As a youth, it had been Fred's intention to follow in his uncle's footsteps as headmaster of St Mary's Methodist School, Preston. But after a short period of teaching the First World War intervened and he enlisted with the Royal Engineers, with whom he spent some time operating searchlights. When his efforts helped to down a Zeppelin one night, he managed to retrieve an ashtray from its wreckage as a souvenir.

After the war, his father-in-law, Tom Charnley, persuaded Fred to join him as assistant at the Football League, where he started work in February 1921. When Charnley handed over the reins in 1933, there was barely a hiccough. Howarth had learnt how to do the job, and saw no reason for changing a thing.

However, he was not as reticent as Charnley in public, and often surprised people with his pungent remarks, especially on the subject of the maximum wage. If the maximum was abolished, said Howarth repeatedly, it would be the end of League football as he knew it.

A small man in stature, Howarth was strong-willed in certain respects, moderate and easy-going in others. For example, like Sutcliffe, a fellow Methodist, he abhorred all forms of betting. He needed no persuading that the Pools War was a moral crusade, or that in the post-war years the League should shun all overtures from the PPA.

But he was no crusader himself. Indeed, he was at times perhaps too self-effacing, for he had ideas about football which sometimes clashed with those of the Committee or the clubs. He favoured involvement with Europe, and foresaw the establishment of a Super League. He also believed strongly in the formation of a Fourth Division.

Howarth's value to the League was as a steward, not an innovator. He formed a link between the League of Charles Sutcliffe and the changing world of the 1950s. After Will Cuff's death, Howarth and Arthur Oakley were the only survivors from the League hierarchy of the 1930s. Howarth was also one of the last of the League's coterie of Freemasons, which may or may not have had an influence during the inter-war period.

Having inherited his father-in-law's mantle in 1933, Howarth was happily grooming young Tom Charnley as his successor when, to everyone's surprise, young Tom decided to seek pastures new in February 1951. Fred's nephew Eric was also at Starkie Street at the time, but was not regarded as secretary material. Hence the advertisement in the *Daily Telegraph* which brought Alan Hardaker into the lap of the League.

In his autobiography, Hardaker describes Howarth as a kindly man who was used to having his own way. The Secretary had created an unflustered world in which everyone seemed underworked and undermotivated. Howarth would start work every day at 10.00 a.m. on the dot, and do only what was necessary. He wouldn't deal with the press if it didn't suit him. He wouldn't file away material, and he would cut out from the minutes of Management Committee meetings any business which he didn't relish, even resolutions which had been agreed by the members.

Since the Management Committee during this period was essentially a passive body of men, none of them ever objected to Howarth's idiosyncratic ways, nor even to the way he would collect up every scrap of paper from meetings so that none of the members could take personal notes away with them.

They also tolerated his accounting system, whereby each member of the Committee signed a series of blank cheques so that Howarth could pay the bills. Only Joe Richards objected to this rather odd way of organizing the League's finances.

Yet for all his rigid methods, the League did function perfectly smoothly during his years as Secretary. And Howarth showed what a fine administrator he was by running the National Savings network in Preston during the Second World War, for which he was awarded the OBE in 1951. It was while fire-watching during the war that he developed the arthritis which forced him to give up his main recreation, golf, when peace-time returned.

Two innovations dominated Howarth's career as Secretary; the establishment of the Jubilee Fund in 1938, and the Provident Fund in 1949. The latter he considered to be somewhat new-fangled, but it hardly mattered since young Norman Thomas was hired to look after it anyway. Thomas, still with the League in its centenary year, remembers Howarth as a rather distant man to whom no one at the office really grew close. There are a few scraps of hearsay about him, but in truth we know little about Fred Howarth as a person because that's how he wanted it to be. He never sought prominence, and never had it thrust upon him.

Much to Alan Hardaker's chagrin, however, he was reluctant to lose power at Starkie Street, holding on to office as long as he could before being forced to retire in December 1956 at the age of sixty-eight. His wife died five years later, leaving Fred to a quiet, rather solitary retirement. Eventually he settled into a masonic home in Lytham, where he died in January 1972 after a long bout of cancer. A year later his nephew Eric left the League, and the family connection was broken after seventy-one years.

cut out the advertisement, put it in his wallet and forgotten all about it until he happened to speak to a friend at Fratton Park, where he was a regular. Hardaker then got in touch with Vernon Stokes, a former Portsmouth director who had just been suspended by the League for making under-the-counter payments. Despite being nominally *persona non grata*, Stokes not only gave Hardaker a reference which helped him get the job, but he also returned to the fold soon after and eventually rose to become chairman of the FA Disciplinary Committee.

As we learn from Hardaker's subsequent autobiography, *Hardaker of the League* (written in conjunction with Bryon Butler, Pelham Books, London, 1977), his initial contacts with the League did not bode well. Arthur Drewry made it clear that they wanted an administrator, not someone who knew about football. That was no problem, but Fred Howarth was. Now aged sixty-five, Howarth was clearly loath to retire, and although given the impression that he would take over after six months, Hardaker eventually had to wait over five years before being appointed Secretary.

Hardaker arrived in Preston just before the 1951 Annual Meeting, and within five minutes had his first argument. Howarth wouldn't give him a proper desk. From being the Lord Mayor's secretary in both Hull and Portsmouth, and Senior Naval Officer during the war, he was suddenly reduced to the role of an office boy, with a salary of £760 a year (lower than he'd earned at Portsmouth) and the promise of a review after six months (a promise which wasn't kept). It was a crushing blow to an ambitious man. He was not even officially confirmed as Assistant Secretary until July 1955.

'I was a salaried outcast,' he wrote. 'I was given no responsibility. I was not allowed to talk to anyone. I was told nothing. I was never asked for an opinion. I was not even allowed to go to Inter-League matches and the only football I saw was at Preston – but even here I knew nobody and nobody, apparently, wanted to know me.'

Hardaker believed that whoever had taken Young Tom's job would have been given the same, unfriendly reception, simply because Howarth was intent on keeping his hands on the reins for as long as possible (which was ironic, since Hardaker himself showed a similar reluctance to let go when he reached retirement age). Also, Hardaker was an outsider in what had essentially been a family firm since 1902, when Tom Charnley Senior had succeeded the disgraced Harry Lockett.

But there was more to Hardaker's frustration than purely personal antagonism. At thirty-nine he'd given up a responsible and busy role in local government to come to the obscurity of a small northern office which seemed more like a rest home.

'Pressure was almost non-existent and a day at League headquarters was slow, uncluttered, peaceful. It often reminded me of an endless patrol at sea – boredom sometimes strangled you. Nobody really had enough to do, but Fred Howarth loved it this way. He was against change of any sort, particularly if it meant more work for him or threatened the familiar, traditional flow of life at headquarters.'

In fairness to Howarth, it must also be said that the Committee members were hardly fiery workaholics themselves when it came to League business. Arthur Drewry had inherited from Will Cuff a smooth-running but essentially antiquated organization, at a time when English football in general was passing through one of its most prosperous and complacent periods (the Hungarians' 6–3 victory at Wembley in November 1953 notwithstanding).

While Hardaker sat contemplating resignation in his isolated office, barely disturbed by the other staff for a couple of years, he whiled away the hours going through the League's minute books from 1888. He began to regard the League as 'a machine covered with rust and cobwebs'.

He also discovered that the minutes were invariably drafted in such a way as to conceal much of the real discussion that took place in Management Committee meetings. As he wrote: 'If Fred Howarth did not like an idea it was never implemented – or even recorded.'

Not that there was much controversy during this period. The League nearly took the Universal Sporting Press to court for publishing fixtures without permission. A handful of players trooped back from South America after a disastrous flirtation with a group of professedly wealthy Colombian clubs. Two of the players, George Mountford of Stoke and Charlie Mitten of Manchester United, were fined the astronomical sum of £250 (the equivalent of about five months' wages) for their part in the venture.

Meanwhile, members of the Committee enjoyed themselves on FA tours to Canada and Australia, several clubs took advantage of improved travel opportunities, and German-born Albert Eisentranger of Bristol City had a wage advance sanctioned to allow him to return home during the summer. Europe was on the mend, and little seemed to disturb the easy calm of Committee gatherings, not even a wrangle between Manchester City, Ashton

United and Chester over an Indian-born winger called Nelson Stiffle.

Amid all these routine matters, the arrival of the League's first company car for Fred Howarth must have caused a rare moment of excitement at Starkie Street. It was an Austin 70 and it cost £974.

Thus was the position of the Football League as it met for its sixty-third Annual Meeting, at the Café Royal on 2 June 1951, with the new recruit Hardaker an anxious onlooker on this, only his second day with the organization.

Gates overall had gone down by about 932,000, a drop of 2.3 per cent, which Arthur Drewry attributed to inclement weather, a lack of transport on Christmas Day and, as in the previous year, a massive drop on Cup Final afternoon. Television was once again clearly to blame, but the wider reality of the situation – unknown to the clubs at that time – was that the boom in attendances was now well and truly over. Nevertheless, opposition to the live broadcast of matches was growing. Sunderland, in proposing a total ban, stated that their gate on Cup Final day had gone down from 40,000 to 17,000.

Alan Hardaker will have been interested to note from Drewry's comments that roughly one in three footballers earned about as much as he would in his new job. But while he was in no position to complain, the Players' Union was again campaigning for the abolition of the maximum wage and, according to its president, there was a distinct possibility of another official dispute. No doubt to reduce the chances of trouble, the maximum was promptly raised from £12 to £14 a week, and to help finance this the clubs also voted to raise minimum

admission charges from 1s 3d to 1s 6d. (There was no longer any need to worry about antagonizing Hugh Dalton. He left office in 1947, and after October 1951 so had every other Labour minister.)

One club which would not reap the benefit of these higher charges was New Brighton. Having finished bottom of the Third Division North, they entered the re-election process with their section's backing, but mustered only 18 votes, compared with Workington's 28. Thus, the League welcomed its fifth new club in two seasons.

In the same poll, Accrington Stanley (46) were comfortably re-elected, while Wigan (4), Nelson (1), North Shields (1), Northwich Victoria and South Liverpool (no votes) were unsuccessful.

In the Southern section, Chelmsford, Hereford United (making their first application), Llanelly, Peterborough and Yeovil also failed to attract any support, and Worcester (1), Merthyr (1) and Bath City (1) made little challenge to Watford (48) and Crystal Palace (45), who were both re-elected.

The following day, the Management Committee and Fred Howarth travelled to Eastbourne for a summer jaunt, leaving the new boy Hardaker to return to his solitary hotel room in Preston. He must have known how New Brighton were feeling.

Soon afterwards, Fred Howarth was awarded the OBE, the first League official to be so honoured.

'Stick it out. You'll be OK', Joe Richards kept reassuring the disconsolate Hardaker, who little realized then that almost exactly twenty years later he, too, would receive an OBE.

CHAPTER EIGHTEEN
Drewry and Oakley – The Two Arthurs

'Stick it out', Joe Richards had said to Alan Hardaker, and he knew what he was talking about, because the years 1949–57 were years of waiting for Richards, too. They form almost an interregnum in the League's history; a period of inertia in Committee circles and complacency amongst the clubs.

Cuff's successor, Arthur Drewry, was a tall, handsome man who was not always in the best of health and often had his mind on other matters. He was followed by Arthur Oakley, a man who was both too old and too weak to meet the challenges of the decade. It is no coincidence, therefore, that the 'fifties saw the League failing to capitalize on the gains made during the immediate post-war years, whilst blithely storing up trouble for the early 1960s.

Arthur Drewry was a different kind of president altogether. For a start, he wasn't based in Lancashire, unlike his four predecessors. He was a Lincolnshire man, a Grimsby man, and in the fisheries trade to boot. Secondly, he did not take the usual route to the top by first becoming a Vice President. He went straight from the Committee to the presidency.

But more significantly, Drewry had already made his mark at the FA before becoming the League's sixth President in 1949, most notably as chairman of the International Selection Committee since 1944.

In November 1945 he accompanied his great friend Stanley Rous to Zurich to negotiate Britain's re-entry to FIFA (which the home countries had left in 1929 over the question of payments to amateurs), and he was subsequently elected a Vice President of FIFA under the leadership of the legendary Jules Rimet.

Drewry was therefore a man of the world game, not merely a baron on his own patch. This was quite contrary to precedent. Previous presidents had always served their apprenticeship on the Management Committee before, if ever, taking a more active role with the Association. League presidents were League men, first and foremost. Drewry was not. His horizons were much wider, and that partly explains why he appears to have left very little mark upon the League in his fifteen years on the Management Committee.

Born in Grimsby in 1891, Drewry's first taste of the wider world was distinctly salty. Posted to Palestine with The Lincolnshire Yeomanry in 1914, his ship was torpedoed en route and he was among the survivors rescued from the waves. After four years in the Middle East, in 1919 he married the daughter of Grimsby Town's chairman and entered his father-in-law's fish-processing business. It was then a natural family progression on to the Grimsby board in 1925 and, a few years later, elevation to the role of chairman.

It was then that his international career began, quite by chance. He was still a relatively young director, aged forty-five, when one of Grimsby's players, Jackie Bestall, was selected to play for the Football League against the Irish League in Belfast in 1936. Drewry decided to accompany Bestall on the trip, and found that he enjoyed the experience so much that a year later he travelled with the England team to Scandinavia 'as a camp follower'. Senior League men were impressed by him, and he was eventually asked to try for the Committee, in 1940. He was successful at his first attempt.

Like most prominent men in football circles,

Drewry wore many hats. Also in 1940 he was elected as a Conservative member of Grimsby Town Council. At the same time, he was head warden and chief fire guard for north Lincolnshire, kept up his duties at the FA, and was active for the Lincolnshire FA and several local amateur leagues.

Had Arthur Oakley been fit enough to seek nomination after Will Cuff's death in 1949, Drewry would undoubtedly have continued to direct most of his efforts towards the FA. In fact, he refused to let his name go forward until Oakley assured him that he didn't want to stand.

Once elected, however, Drewry's presidency of the League began well, with the inauguration of the Provident Fund in 1949 and record gates over the Christmas period. But thereafter he was either hampered by illness or distracted by his other duties abroad. He collapsed after a game in 1950 and had a relapse in mid 1954, which made him absent from the Committee for several months. By the time he had recovered full fitness, the post of chairman of the FA had fallen vacant (on the death of Sir Amos Brook Hirst), and Drewry left the League for Lancaster Gate.

The demands on Drewry as League President were considerable, if only because Grimsby's location made his journeying that much longer. It was just as well that he was an avid reader. Apart from monthly Management Committee and weekly Grimsby Town board meetings, he also had to travel extensively as chairman of the international selectors and as a Vice President of FIFA. In 1952 he was awarded the Olympic Cross of Merit for his contribution to the Helsinki games, and a year later was made a CBE, the highest honour yet paid to a Football League president. Unfortunately, the honour had very little to do with the fact that he was President of the League.

Despite being one of Britain's finest ambassadors for sport and mixing in the highest circles, Drewry never lost his common touch. He once admitted rather shamefacedly that his ideal form of relaxation was to watch a parks game in Grimsby.

'With his easy smile, distinguished good looks and well cut Lovat tweed suit, Drewry conveys an air of casual elegance', noted the *FA Yearbook* in 1956. 'He could meet the Queen and Duke of Edinburgh one day, and be back presenting a cup at a local football final the next,' said the *Grimsby Evening Telegraph*. 'But this gentle, courteous bearing cloaked a firmness and seemingly self-imposed isolation which he knew his duties, often involving discipline, demanded of him.'

Drewry showed this tough streak as President of FIFA, a position to which he was elected in succession to Rodolphe William Seedrayers of Belgium in 1956. (He was thus the second Englishman to hold the post, D. B. Woolfall of Blackburn having been the first from 1906–18.) At a large meeting in 1958, the delegates from China tried to take the floor after they had lost a motion. Drewry ruled them out of order, at which point they announced that they would have to leave. Drewry retorted: 'It is not a question of your wanting to withdraw – you are ordered to do so.'

Will Cuff, a brother freemason, would have approved heartily. That was exactly how he had handled club directors, too.

Arthury Drewry died on 25 March 1961 at the age of seventy after a year-long illness, and was succeeded at FIFA by his friend Sir Stanley Rous. But whereas every other League president has been chiefly remembered for once having held that title, for Arthur Drewry it was just one of many roles he played, and by no means the most important. That was fine for the world game, and a credit to Drewry, but unfortunately it wasn't good enough for the League.

This makes it even more odd that Drewry's successor should have been Arthur Oakley, the man who came back from the shadows. When Will Cuff died in 1949, Oakley had been the natural choice for the role of Acting President.

He had been on the Committee since 1938 and was the senior Vice President. But as we have read, ill health prevented him from seeking nomination four months later and, at the age of seventy-two, it seemed as if he would soon slip into honourable retirement.

He hung on, however, and when Arthur Drewry moved to the FA in 1955 Oakley allowed his name to be put up for the presidency, even though he was then aged seventy-eight, older than any other man who had been nominated before. (Sutcliffe was seventy-two when he became President in 1938.)

It needed four ballots at the 1955 Annual Meeting for Oakley to gain a clear lead over his challenger, Joe Richards of Barnsley. A possible factor was the relative standing of their two clubs at the time. Either that, or the clubs thought that with an old and weak man in the chair they could behave more or less as they pleased . . .

Whatever the reason (Drewry said it was a matter of sentiment), Oakley became the League's seventh and oldest President. But he served only two years, and he did not die in office.

Alan Hardaker describd him as 'a curious chap, a man who had given many years to the game as referee and director but who did not always seem part of it'. Another contemporary called him 'an old stick in the mud' who though thoroughly decent was also obstinate, old fashioned, and worst of all for any member of the Management Committee, lacking in a sense of humour.

Arthur Oakley was born in Wolverhampton in 1877, and was thus, coincidentally, as old as the Wolves. He made his mark first as a useful amateur player for a team curiously entitled the Wolverhampton Early Closers, then as a League referee. During the First World War he served on Wolverhampton Borough council and, being a coal merchant, was appointed the town's emergency coal officer. He was also said to have been a crack shot in the Volunteer Rifles.

Oakley's first involvement with Wolves came in 1923 when the club was at its lowest ebb, just relegated to the Third Division North – the first founder members to fall so low. As one of the new board, Oakley helped to lead the rejuvenated club back to the First Division nine seasons later, and in 1933 was elected chairman. The manager at that time was the famous Major Frank Buckley, the man who deliberately drenched the Molineux pitch to suit his tactics, and was said to have fed monkey glands to his players.

In 1938, Wolves were runners-up in the First Division. Oakley was elected to the Management Committee and then, suddenly, his wife died. A year later, he became a magistrate. Wolves were runners-up again, and against all the odds were beaten by Portsmouth in the last Cup Final before the war.

Oakley certainly lacked the authority and charisma which had so characterized his predecessors, and it is no surprise to learn from Hardaker's memoirs that Oakley was very close to Fred Howarth – both men were seemingly kind, old fashioned and, shall we say, a touch dull. But Oakley must have had his supporters originally, or he would never have been elected in the first place.

By 1957 that support seems to have dried up almost completely. Most sources have it that Oakley finally stood down in 1957 because his health was failing, but according to Hardaker, Fred Howarth actually persuaded him to fight on. After all, no President had, until then, been defeated in an election. But the other Committee members and the clubs made clear their preference for Joe Richards, and thus Oakley stepped down on 3 May. He was not even made a Life Member or elected to stay on the Committee; a sad conclusion to a long and respected career.

One of Oakley's great beliefs was the need to foster young players. Hardaker recalled how complaints were often made against Wolves for the methods they employed in snapping up talented youths. On one occasion, Fred

Howarth read out such a complaint at a Committee meeting, but he loyally refrained from mentioning the identity of the guilty club. Without provocation, Oakley immediately interrupted: 'I don't know anything about it.'

As Hardaker recounted the story: 'Someone else said: "Come on, we must know the name of the club."

Arthur Oakley stubbornly repeated himself: "I don't know anything about it."

"Well as a matter of fact," said Fred Howarth, "it is Wolverhampton Wanderers."

Harold Shentall, another Committee man with a nice dry sense of humour, then chipped in: "Oh yes, I know the player we're talking about ... big lad, with very light hair. Good looking boy. Plays right half."

"No no," said Arthur Oakley, quick as a flash. "He's a little chap. Plays on the wing."'

Oakley's period in office at the League may have been undistinguished, and the manner in which he departed may have been ignominious, but his legacy lived on at Molineux. The young players he so actively encouraged gave Wolves victory in the FA Youth Cup in 1958, the year he left the board after nearly thirty-five years, and they formed part of the sides which won the Championship in 1959 and the Cup a year later. And it was another young Wolves eleven which stepped out at the start of the 1962/3 season to trounce Manchester City 8–1 at Molineux. Oakley missed that one by just a few hours. He was eighty-five.

CHAPTER NINETEEN

Calm Before the Storm

Fred Howarth's final years at the Football League proved to be the calm before the storm. Two issues which had been simmering on the back burner for so long – the maximum wage and copyright of the fixtures – would not be resolved until Alan Hardaker took over as secretary and Joe Richards became President, while the growing international potential of the game could hardly be denied any longer, especially since the advent of floodlighting and easier air travel.

But the dispute with the BBC over the broadcasting of matches at least was settled quickly, at an Extraordinary General Meeting on 27 August 1951, at the Café Royal.

New conditions were imposed. Firstly, from 1952 onwards Cup Finals were to be played on the last Saturday of the season, when few League clubs had fixtures (after 1954 the Final day was kept clear of all League games). Secondly, all advance publicity was to be prohibited. Until then, *Radio Times* had always listed the matches to be covered, but when the League quite sensibly stopped this, *The Times* commented: 'The idea of keeping secret the match to be broadcast is nothing but niggling.'

In fact, the attempt at secrecy failed on the eve of the new season when radio engineers were spotted at St James's Park preparing for the game against Tottenham. Once the story leaked to the press, the BBC made hurried arrangements to switch their coverage to QPR *v.* Swansea.

The BBC would also have to start paying a realistic fee for their coverage, above the nominal five guineas they had previously paid the host club. The sum of £2000 for season 1951/2 was agreed upon, this sum to be divided between the benevolent funds of the FA, the League and the Players' Union.

At the same time, a company based in Luxembourg offered the League £3000 to broadcast to Europe recorded highlights from three matches every Saturday evening. For reasons unknown, this offer was not accepted.

The modern world kept on intruding upon the League in the early 1950s, despite the Committee's best efforts to keep it at bay. Floodlights were mentioned (and dismissed) for the first time in November 1951. Another cold shoulder was given to Brylcreem, who submitted a scheme for sponsoring player awards.

But there were some concessions to modernity. In late 1951, the Committee recommended that each club hold in reserve one of the new white footballs, in case the referee called for it. In 1954, bright orange balls were also recommended for the winter months.

Commercial television appeared on the scene in 1955 and, unlike the BBC, was able to offer substantial sums for each match broadcast. Nor were they alone in seeing the commercial potential of football. Two other independent companies wanted to film League matches, for fees ranging from £100 to £1000 per game. Tempting though these offers were, as Arthur Drewry warned: 'There is a danger of us becoming a nation of fireside football watchers.'

Yet the writing would soon be on the wall, or perhaps, on the pages of the balance books. By 1955, the League's own period of prosperity had come to an end. In March 1952, profits of over £7000 were recorded for the financial year. By 1955 this had turned into a loss of £10,000, mainly due to a decrease in the percentage levy received from gates – which were falling – and the continued high premiums being paid to the Provident Fund.

Attendances began to show the start of a steady, though gradual, decline in the 1951/2 season. They were down then by 1.5 per cent, most of which was due to lower gates in the First Division. In the Second Division and Third Division North, crowds actually grew marginally.

Once again, the live broadcasting of a match, albeit on a wet afternoon, had the greatest effect on the total. This time, however, the match in question was not a Cup Final but the Scotland v. England match on 5 April 1952.

The following season, gates fell by a further 4.5 per cent, representing a total loss of four million spectators in four seasons. Most of the drop occurred in the Second Division, where attendances fell below the ten million mark for the first time since the war. The following season saw a further decline of 2.5 per cent, mostly in the Third Divisions, and in 1954/5 another 6 per cent decrease was recorded, over half of which was from the First Division. Yet floodlit mid-week friendlies were attracting large gates, which suggested that the potential audience was still high.

As gates fell, players' wages rose, a pattern which has continued until the present day. For example, in 1951/2 the number of players on the maximum wage rose substantially from 255 to 730. Admission prices also went up, in 1952, to a minimum of 1s 9d, owing to a rise in Entertainment Tax. (When the League tried to persuade the Chancellor to ease the tax, he responded candidly: 'I need the money!') As a result, the amount clubs paid in Entertainment Tax more than doubled from 9.5 per cent of total gate receipts in 1951/2 to nearly 21 per cent the following season. It would have been more had not QPR successfully contested the payment of tax on season ticket sales.

Higher taxation may explain why the rapid rise of transfer fees after the war seemed to come to a temporary halt in this period. In 1938 the record had stood at £14,000 (paid by Arsenal for Bryn Jones). By 1950 this had more than doubled to £30,000, paid by Sunderland for Trevor Ford. But for the next few years the rise was much less dramatic. It is also worth adding that the vast majority of players were still valued at sums less than £2000.

Under the more radical leadership of Jimmy Guthrie, the so-called 'soccer rebel', the players continued to campaign for an end to wage controls and for players to have proper representation at disciplinary hearings. Once more, in 1953, they took their case to an industrial tribunal, making what Arthur Drewry considered 'irresponsible claims' which followed 'the usual impossible lines'. If this 'continual agitation' were to continue, Drewry told the 1953 Annual Meeting, the League might be forced to reconsider the provisions they had made for players in the Provident Fund.

But the union's pressure did pay off to a small extent, when the appointed tribunal recommended the maximum wage to be raised from £14 to £15 during the season and from £10 to £12 during the close season. International match fees also rose from £30 to £50. But in every other matter – the transfer system, bonuses and so on – the tribunal took the League's side.

Nevertheless, the union's action suggested a growing militancy which would not be easily assuaged, especially as it was now quite widely recognized that most clubs were already paying above the legal limits anyway. Manchester City's chairman, Bob Smith, compiled a dossier of clubs which had admitted to this, but when he proposed twice that an amnesty should be declared, the clubs voted him down.

In December 1953 Mansfield became the second club since the war to incur the wrath of the League and FA for irregular payments. Once again, the cause of their undoing was a disgruntled former employee, whose evidence resulted in the club being fined £500 and most of their directors being suspended either permanently or *sine die*. The former player-manager Fred Steele was fined £250. But the players barely suffered at all.

The Annual Meeting of 1952 proved to be the most disappointing for non-League clubs for years. Darlington (49 votes), Workington (40), Exeter (47) and Walsall (45) were each re-elected, and only Wigan (9) made any serious challenge. Other applicants were Worcester (3), Bath (1), Merthyr (1) and Peterborough (1), with no votes for Nelson, North Shields, Headington United (making their first application) or Yeovil. New Brighton's attempt to return to the fold also found no favour, hardly surprisingly since their next act was to ask the League to help pay off their debts of £2800.

The following year, Wigan increased their share of the vote to 17, while Workington, up for re-election for the second time in only their second League season, attracted only 36. But it was still enough to remain in the Northern section, along with Accrington, who polled 45 votes.

In the Southern section both Shrewsbury (46) and Walsall (41) were re-elected. Peterborough (6), Yeovil (2), Bath (2) and Hereford (1) were the also-rans, along with Nelson, New Brighton, North Shields, Headington and Worcester, who each returned home without a single vote.

The following year, 1954, Chester (48) and Colchester (45) had no trouble being re-elected, but it was much closer for Halifax (28), who were in the hat for the fourth time since 1945, and Walsall (32), who were making their third application in three seasons. Their closest challengers were Wigan (19) and Peterborough (18), suggesting that change might not have been far off. Otherwise, Nelson (3) Worcester (2) and Merthyr (1) failed miserably, and North Shields (for the third year running), Bath and Yeovil attracted no votes.

One had to admire such clubs for their persistence, with only a closed door to greet them year in, year out. Or perhaps their officials just liked having an excuse to visit London every year.

In 1955 Walsall had to go cap in hand for the fourth year in succession, and yet they were re-elected again with 33 votes. Colchester (44), Chester (47) and Grimsby (49) were also re-elected.

Peterborough's votes held up at 16, Wigan's dropped to only 2, Worcester polled 3, Headington 2, and there were no votes for Burton Albion, Nelson, Bedford Town, Yeovil or – it almost goes without saying – North Shields.

Grimsby's need to apply for re-election was ironic in that the 1955 Annual Meeting was their former chairman Arthur Drewry's last as President. Although he had been convalescing for most of the season after a serious illness, that year the FA Council elected him unanimously as their chairman.

His last official duty for the League was to preside over the meeting to elect his successor, on 24 June. There were four candidates from the Committee and it required four ballots to find a clear winner, Arthur Oakley finally emerging with 27 votes to Joe Richards' 21.

Thus, the coal merchant from Wolverhampton became the Football League's seventh President at the end of its sixty-seventh season. To outsiders his election may well have seemed strange. Six years earlier he had turned down the post for health reasons, and yet here he was, at the age of seventy-eight, accepting it.

Arthur Drewry, publicly at least, had no qualms. 'I commend you on your good sense

> Rarely would the Management Committee allow a club to pay bonuses other than those allowed in the regulations, but they made an exception in 1955. Not only did Chelsea's first team win the League Championship, but their reserves, A team and junior team also won their respective leagues – the Football Combination, the Metropolitan League and the South-East Counties League. No other League club has achieved such a feat.

in your choice of President,' he told the clubs. 'None of us can pretend that Mr Oakley is a young man, but he has given long service to the League. During my illness he was most loyal to me, and nothing was asked of him that he did not do. His election today once again proves that there is still a little sentiment left in football.'

Thus, the FA was taken over by a man only just recovered from serious illness, while the League elected an elderly man whose own medical record was suspect. But did it really matter who the President was? If the mood of post-war Britain was in general more egalitarian than in the 1930s, couldn't the Committee have ruled more collectively and by consensus, without needing to be dominated by one man?

The answer has to be in the negative. In fact, the League now needed a strong man as much as it ever had done in the past. Sutcliffe and McKenna had presided over a much narrower organization with few intrusions from without, whereas the League of Drewry and Oakley had constantly to take into account the demands of others; more strident club chairmen, more militant players, more government legislation, the lure of Europe, television and commercial interests, all against a background of high taxation, falling gates and the constant drain of the Provident Fund.

Perhaps it was all too much for anyone on the Committee to grasp fully. The world was changing so fast.

Sunderland – the big spenders of the League at the time – put forward two radical proposals in 1955, both of which were carried but only one of which ever took effect. Firstly, the League was to press the FA to allow Cup replays and postponed League matches to be played under floodlights, if both clubs were in agreement.

The FA agreed, and thus began a new era of competitive floodlit football. In January 1956 the Third Round ties at Highbury, Fratton Park, Hillsborough, White Hart Lane

and Upton Park were played partially under lights, and on 22 February the first ever floodlit Football League game took place at Portsmouth, where Newcastle were the visitors on a bitterly cold night.

There were complaints from cinema owners and publicans. In Wolverhampton some people objected to the arrival of unsightly pylons on the skyline. Otherwise, the football public took to the lights with great enthusiasm.

So why had the League taken so long to sanction their use? The answer is simple; firstly, they had had to await the FA's permission, which was slow in coming, but more importantly, the Management Committee had long argued that until a majority of clubs had lights it was unfair to use them for competitive matches.

Sunderland's second radical proposal was 'That the Management explore the possibilities of erecting a National Stadium'.

As we now know, nothing ever came of this concept, but it was a serious one at the time, nevertheless. Ever since the first all-ticket Wembley Final in 1924, the Management Committee had been trying, not always wholeheartedly, to extract from the FA a greater allocation of tickets for the supporters of each team in the Final. A 'Wembley of the North' was widely held to be a way round the FA's intransigence.

Ticketing was, of course, a perennial sore point, and as far as the clubs were concerned, Jimmy Guthrie, chairman of the Players' Union, was becoming one too. Many of them even banned him from their premises.

Throughout the mid 1950s Guthrie kept up a tirade of criticism against the League in the national press, with the result that the Management Committee decided after a meeting with the Trades Union Congress to withdraw from the Joint Standing Committee in February 1956. Partly in retaliation, the union then instructed its members not to play in floodlit matches until negotiations were resumed.

Then, in July 1955, the Committee was

informed through one of its members, Joe Mears, that First Division champions Chelsea, of which he was chairman, had accepted an invitation to play in the first European Cup competition. Mears was asked to reconsider, 'in the best interests of the League competition', and he did. Chelsea withdrew (Gwardia Warsaw took their place), leaving Hibernian as the sole British representative.

At the same meeting it was also reported that Bristol City had been invited by the BBC to take part in a televised five-a-side knockout competition. The Committee was incensed. Why hadn't the BBC asked its permission beforehand?

It also thoroughly disapproved of another proposed competition, the Anglo-Scottish Floodlit League, due to take place between four Scottish and four English League clubs.

Problems and more problems. Oakley's Wolves were off to Russia that very month. A second televised floodlit Third Division representative match was scheduled for October at Accrington. A new Southern Floodlit Challenge Cup was being planned, while Tottenham left immediately after their League match on 24 September for a friendly in Denmark the following day. Three weeks later, Spurs faced Vasas of Hungary, while in November Wolves entertained Moscow Dynamo in another spectacular floodlit friendly.

This pursuit of the novel, the prestigious, the exotic, prompted one natural question. Was anyone still interested in the old-fashioned, no-frills League competition?

The Committee was taking no chances, and sent every club two reminders of their priorities. In one, the Committee asked clubs to reaffirm the pre-eminence of the League competition. Any club unable to make this pledge would be asked to withdraw.

Clubs were also to be encouraged to install lights as soon as possible, while those who had lights were told to reduce the number of friendlies, in return for which the Committee would allow any mid-week League fixture to be played under lights.

But the decline in League gates was still the most serious issue of all. In a second circular, the Committee wrote:

'It is not necessary to remind clubs that the continued fall in attendances has become a serious matter. Many theories have been put forward to account for the drift of spectators from League matches, but it must be realised that football now has to face keener competition from other forms of entertainment.

Air travel first winged its way on to the League's agenda on 7 September 1932 when Bristol Rovers arranged to fly one of their players, a London schoolteacher called Vivian Gibbons, from Romford to Bristol so that he could play in a mid-week game against Southend. But when Plymouth asked the Management Committee a few weeks later about flying their whole team to a match, permission was withheld because the League's insurance fund did not cover 'travel by air liner'.

The restriction was eventually relaxed in 1957. On Good Friday, 9 April, Chelsea flew to and from Newcastle, while Blackpool flew back from their match at Arsenal. Both had home games the following day. Flying became all the rage in the First Division over the next few years, despite the Munich tragedy – Bob Lord would fly his Burnley team at every available opportunity – but once the motorway network improved in the mid 1960s, road travel soon overtook the railways as the main form of team transportation.

To be successful, every club must provide satisfying entertainment in reasonably comfortable conditions in order to make the customer – for that is what the spectator really is – come again.'

Customers? Entertainment? These were words barely heard before in League circles.

Underlying this concern with gates was the constant need to maintain the Provident Fund. When established in 1949, the percentage paid out to players represented 10 per cent of their income. With gates dropping, this had had to be reduced to 9 per cent, and in 1956 it was dropped further to 7.5 per cent.

To make matters worse, on 7 December 1955 the League recorded its first financial loss on an Inter-League match when the League of Ireland visited Goodison Park. The game was played on a Wednesday afternoon, which hardly helped, but even so, an attendance of 25,000 still resulted in a loss of £181, after costs had been deducted.

It was no wonder, therefore, that to keep the Provident Fund alive the Committee was in 1955 demanding (and receiving) sums of £5000 from the BBC for exclusive rights to televise extracts of League matches, and £4000 for live radio commentaries.

A further £750 was received for live second-half coverage of the Inter-League match against Scotland at Hillsborough on 26 October. This was the first Inter-League match to be played under floodlights.

Not to be outdone by the BBC, ATV promptly offered the League the enormous sum of £40,000 for the privilege of broadcasting live the second half of thirty-five League matches a season, each to kick off especially on a Saturday evening, but for transmission in the London area only. £40,000 represented a third of the required income of the Provident Fund, which made it a tempting offer indeed, and one which confirmed beyond all doubt that a new era – although not necessarily a better one – had truly begun.

An indication of how times were changing can be seen in the 1956 balance sheet. The League was back in the black again, but the dividing line between profit and loss was becoming ever narrower.

Out of a total income for 1955/6 of £156,895, all but £9077 came from the 4 per cent levy on gate receipts, and of the remainder, more than half came from broadcasting and television rights. Once the Provident Fund's outgoings of £127,012 had been accounted for, that left in the bank the price of a moderate centre-forward. Were attendances to decline much further, the balance might easily tip back into the red.

It was for this reason that television began to exercise in the late 1950s the power it has held over the League right up to the present day.

As Arthur Oakley told the 1956 Annual Meeting, television was now a permanent feature of national life and 'its tremendous publicity value cannot be ignored'. But nor could its effect on attendances, especially since, if ATV's scheme was accepted, everyone would know which match was going to be televised because of the later kick-off.

Fulham regarded the offer of £40,000 very small by the standard of modern television. The League had something to sell, and there were people willing to buy it. Fulham were right about that. Shortly after the Annual Meeting, the BBC offered £47,000 for the sole rights to League matches.

Not that anyone was simply prepared to take the money and run, especially while television remained such an unknown, almost awesome entity. There were so many implications. Compensation, for example, was a particular difficulty, until the Committee discovered that it could actually take out insurance against low gates at televised games.

Then, in July 1956, the Variety Artists Federation, the Theatres' National Committee and the National Greyhound Society all urged the League not to authorize live televised broadcasts. Saturday afternoon was the time for football, but leave Saturday night for other forms of entertainment, they argued.

Television, in short, was coming to dominate not just people's lives but the Management Committee's time as well. Finally, on 20 July 1956, an Extraordinary General Meeting gathered in Manchester to thrash out the whole issue.

Joe Richards told the meeting that clubs had a choice – to ban live television coverage, or to authorize it for one trial season. The Committee favoured ATV's offer, not for reasons of greed – it was virtually the same as the BBC's – but because they felt that it covered most of the points clubs were worried about; compensation, payments to players, and extra expenses incurred from 6.15 kick-offs. The fees received would also permit the League to reduce its levy on gates from 4 to 3 per cent.

But the clubs were not tempted. Everton and Liverpool led the opposition with such well prepared statistics that a comfortable majority decided that there would be no live televised matches after all. It was probably one of the most significant victories the Merseyside clubs had ever achieved.

Unfortunately, not all the issues facing football in that period were so confidently decided.

The potential of Europe could no longer be denied. Despite the Committee's best efforts to dissuade them, Manchester United, at Sir Stanley Rous's invitation, became the first League club to enter the European Cup. Another chapter in League football had begun.

Much of the plot remained the same, however. Crowd figures continued to worry everyone in the League, and Arthur Oakley's annual task was no different from his predecessor's. In 1956 he had to announce yet another fall in attendances, this time by 3 per cent. Unable to blame the weather this time, Oakley did suggest that the increased number of matches had possibly made the public more selective. But he sounded one note of cautious optimism: mid-week floodlit games were attracting as many as would have been expected on Saturday afternoons.

Speaking of relations with the Players' Union, Oakley warned: 'There still remains much to be done to remove the clouds of suspicion and mistrust of the past five years.'

Having threatened in March to refuse to play under floodlights, the players had now accepted a £2–3 bonus payment. They also gained agreement on the principle of extra payments for televised matches.

But the Chancellor of the Exchequer proved a much more stubborn adversary than Jimmy Guthrie could ever have been. For years the League had been lobbying to have the Entertainment Tax reduced, especially since other sports escaped the burden. And the tax on football had grown, not lessened, despite the ending of post-war austerity measures. In November 1956, for example, the Chancellor received almost 30 per cent of the gross takings from England's friendly against Brazil. Cricket, meanwhile, paid no Entertainment Tax.

As Oakley told the 1956 meeting, a recent cricket match at Headingley between Yorkshire and Lancashire had yielded receipts of £4483. For Leeds United to have earned the same, they would have needed to take an extra 36 per cent at the gate. Similarly, footballers' benefit money was taxed, cricketers' was not. It was a quite iniquitous situation, which is mirrored today by the huge discrepancy between taxation on football pools and taxation on horse-race betting. The pools pay a rate of tax about five times greater.

The 1956 Annual Meeting saw the beginning of a campaign to reorganize the League into four national divisions. Yet again, the Northern and Southern section clubs were split, the northern Associate Members opposing any change at a time when most of their members were already struggling to keep up their commitments. The southern clubs replied by arguing that reports of extra travelling costs had been greatly exaggerated.

They very nearly won the day. When the

votes were taken, first openly, then by ballot, the result was 33 votes in favour of restructuring, 16 against, thus narrowly failing to win the necessary three-quarters majority.

Having preserved the status quo in the Third Division, the clubs then proceeded to reject all the applicants who wanted to join. Bradford Park Avenue (47 votes) and Crewe (45) kept their place in the Northern section. Wigan Athletic (2), Burton Albion (1) and Nelson (1) were the challengers.

In the Southern section, Crystal Palace (44) and Swindon (42) were re-elected, while Peterborough managed just 8 votes. Boston United and Gloucester City polled a single vote each, and no votes were cast for Bedford Town, Chelmsford, Hastings United, Headington, King's Lynn, Worcester or Yeovil.

Unknown to him at the time, the 1956 Annual Meeting was to be the last for Fred Howarth in his official capacity as Secretary. His assistant, Alan Hardaker, had played an increasing role in League affairs since Arthur Oakley had become President, and it was thus inevitable, with Howarth now of a pensionable age, that the younger man should take over.

On 13 November the decision was taken at a Management Committee meeting: Fred Howarth was to retire. According to Hardaker's memoirs, the man was furious, especially when he read the news in the *Daily Mirror* before anyone had told him. He announced that he was perfectly able to carry on.

As Alan Hardaker recalled: 'A first-class committee row developed, with Fred still insisting his days were far from numbered.' He told the Committee that he would retire, not in December 1956 but in December 1957. It was at that point that the Committee had to ask him to stand down gracefully.

On 27 November Howarth's resignation was officially 'accepted with regret', and from that moment until the official handing-over date, 31 December, Hardaker said that Howarth never once acknowledged that his assistant would be taking his place.

'On New Year's Eve he came into my room, put his keys on my desk and said: "You'd better look after these until the Management Committee decide who my successor is going to be. I'm going home."'

And that was how Fred Howarth's thirty-six years at the Football League ended. He had been Secretary since 1933 and a director of the League since 1948, and although Eric Howarth stayed on at Starkie Street, the family's stewardship of the League in effect came to an end, while at last, Alan Hardaker was given the job for which he'd been waiting for nearly five years. 'I felt as if I had been let out of prison,' he wrote later. 'I went home and slept like a baby.'

From his very first days in the job, Hardaker set about transforming the set-up at Starkie Street. His first action was to revamp the League's antiquated system of banking and accounting, set up by Howarth, it would seem, to save himself extra work. His second act was to increase each staff member's responsibility (and salary), and formally involve one of them in the annual task of drawing up the fixtures – the mysteries of which were still closely guarded by Charles Sutcliffe's son, Harold, in Rawtenstall. Sutcliffe's contract was extended for a further five years only on condition that he instruct someone at Starkie Street as to the system's working.

These, however, were minor matters compared with the greater unease which hung over the League during Hardaker's first six months as Secretary. The reasons were complex, the issues many, and it was probably no coincidence that they all came to the boil at the time Arthur Oakley stepped down from the presidency on 3 May. Too many important issues had been left in abeyance, and at one stage there was almost a call for the mass resignation of the Management Committee.

Matters weren't helped by a continuous stream of articles in the popular press, in which players 'revealed all' in 'no-punches pulled' interviews, chairmen abused each other and the League, and professional football's reputation seemed to sink in direct proportion to the rise in newspaper circulation. Had an outsider based his assessment of the League in the mid 'fifties upon the popular Sunday papers, he might well have concluded that all footballers were rowdy, dishonest, greedy and corrupt, while most club chairmen and League officials were either lazy, ignorant fools or insanely ambitious profiteers.

To illustrate just how scurrilous most of the stories were, in May 1957 one club chairman accused another of making illegal payments to a particular player, based on the evidence of a third party. When the case was investigated by the League it transpired that the player didn't exist and that the third party had been paid by the club chairman to make his accusations.

Sensationalism at one extreme could not, however, mask the myriad problems facing football during this crucial period. Briefly stated, the following were the subjects for contention, as debated by an informal gathering of the clubs on 21 May 1957.

Firstly, under-the-counter payments once again dominated the back-page headlines, with the imposition of a £5000 fine upon Sunderland. No club had ever been so harshly dealt with before; two directors were suspended permanently, two more *sine die*, four were severely censured, five players were suspended for a short time, and ten had their benefits cut. The illegal payments went back several years, but not until Alan Hardaker became Secretary were they fully investigated. (For a full account, see *Soccer in the Dock* by the same author, Collins, 1985.)

Further controversy arose from sensational articles by two famous players, Wilf Mannion and Trevor Ford. When asked to substantiate their allegations, both refused and were subsequently suspended. But Mannion and Ford were no guiltier than most club chairmen of withholding the facts – remember how Manchester City chairman Bob Smith's attempts to

bring the whole sham into the open had been suppressed seven years earlier. The hypocrisy of the maximum wage system had to give, sooner or later.

Secondly, the clubs were now actively seeking reorganization of the League into four divisions. Having rejected the idea a year before, the Third Division North members were finally persuaded, but a minority view still called for the League to absorb a further dozen clubs to create three regional divisions.

Thirdly, there was pressure from Scotland and certain leading English clubs to introduce a fully-fledged floodlit competition. West Bromwich argued for the inclusion of continental teams.

But there was also a fear of 'football indigestion'. With so many clubs now organizing their own lucrative friendlies against top European clubs, and with outside organizations repeatedly inviting League clubs to participate in new mid-week competitions, there was an enormous pressure on the League to exert its authority; to reaffirm the supremacy of its own competition, and if desired, to organize its own floodlit competition to pre-empt all other attempts.

Alan Hardaker's arrival in January 1957 thus came not a moment too soon for the League, just as the Players' Union was rejuvenated itself by the election of Jimmy Hill as new chairman a few months later. Then, in July 1957, Joe Richards of Barnsley became the third of the year's new men when he succeeded Arthur Oakley as President of the League.

The emergence together of these three strong, opinionated men signalled an end to the complacency and drift of the early and mid 1950s. They would clash, of course, but in doing so they would at last put football back on the right road. In this respect, 1957 represented a further watershed in the history of the League. As Joe Richards warned the 1957 Annual Meeting in his inaugural address: 'It has been abundantly clear for a long time now that we are at the crossroads.'

Appealing for a raising of standards overall, he begged club directors, officials and players to sink their differences and focus attention on the good of the game. 'We must all work together so that at the end of twelve months we shall be in a position to start out on a new phase in the history of the League, taking with us many of the good things and shutting the door on all the bad ones.'

It was a speech straight out of Charles Sutcliffe's book, and it came at just the right time.

CHAPTER TWENTY
Sir Joe Richards – Mr Football

Like Alan Hardaker, the League's new President had been forced to wait his turn. But when it came, in 1957, Joe Richards immediately stamped his personality on the League with all the authority of a headmaster wading into a mêlée of squabbling schoolchildren. He stopped the fighting, ticked off the offenders and kept a watchful eye thereafter.

He was hard, he was single-minded, he was energetic, but above all he was a League man to the hilt, and thus he showed himself to be well worthy of a place alongside the likes of those two other great unifying influences, John Bentley and Will Cuff.

He was also the first Yorkshireman to fill the position, and the first one to be a representative of one of the Associate Members. A year after Richards' election, Barnsley were relegated to Division Three, and by the time he stood down in 1966 they were a struggling Fourth Division outfit. Failure at club level exposed Richards to criticism and opposition from First and Second Division chairmen who were only too ready to exploit this weak spot whenever they wanted to challenge his authority. (As happened to a later League President, Jack Dunnett, when his club Notts County were relegated to Division Three in 1985.)

Richards had several characteristics in common with his more illustrious predecessors. He was a freemason and a practising Christian, a town councillor and a magistrate, and when elected to the presidency he was, like Sutcliffe and Oakley before him, a widower. Also in common with several leading football administrators (among them John Lewis and Sir Stanley Rous), as a youth his playing career had been cut short by injury, an injury which

in more ways than one affected his whole life.

Richards was born in the same year as the Football League, the son of Barnsley Main Colliery's pit manager. Following his father into the mine office, one day as a teenager he went underground to feed the pit ponies. One of them reared, sending a heavy coal tub hurtling towards the boy and crushing his leg so badly that at first doctors thought it might have to be amputated.

The accident ended what had been a promising career in local football and put Richards in hospital for seven months. It was during this confinement that he started studying book-keeping and lapped up just about every book on football his family could bring to his bedside.

After leaving hospital, Richards went to Barnsley Technical College to study commerce and mining. He tried to play football again – in one game even playing in goal while on crutches – but sadly his leg never recovered fully and he had to dress it every day for the rest of his life. Not that this stopped him from climbing a tree at Crystal Palace to watch his beloved Barnsley in one of their two Cup Final appearances (in 1910 and 1912), or from cycling to Bramall Lane to see them beat West Bromwich in the 1912 replay.

By that time, Richards had returned to the colliery where in 1920 he was appointed secretary and sales manager, a short while after having been elected to the Barnsley board whilst still only thirty-one. Richards was the true-grit, self-made man *par excellence*. In 1929 he joined Barnsley town council as an Independent – though with Conservative leanings (serving until 1946) – and in 1934 he began a quite remarkable thirty-two years as chairman of Barnsley, possibly the longest unbroken spell ever recorded in League history.

The list of his other commitments says much for both his energies and his commitment, for while Richards was primarily a shrewd businessman, he was also known as an extremely kind man with a particular concern for young people. He rose to become managing director of Barnsley main colliery in 1933 and subsequently had interests in sixteen other businesses, and he also found time to be a governor of Barnsley Grammar School, chairman of the juvenile court, and to serve on the local probation committee for twenty years.

To young offenders, Richards must have presented a daunting figure. Though small in stature he had standards which bordered on the fastidious. He was a stickler for reliability and honesty, and a strict, though loving, father. Personal appearance mattered greatly to him. For example, he was rarely seen anywhere, even at the breakfast table at home, except in a neatly groomed collar and tie. At meetings, his notes were carefully laid out and in perfect order, and he always had his favourite cigar case and a small hip flask of whisky to hand.

Richards was first elected on to the Management Committee in 1948, when Barnsley were a rather average Second Division club whose only major honour under his chairmanship had been to win the Third Division North in 1939. As a great believer in encouraging young players, his first major contribution was to suggest early in 1952 that the League establish its own youth cup. Richards

> **The Youth Cup, first presented by the FA in 1953, was in fact a trophy which the League had purchased during the Second World War but never found a use for. Secretary Fred Howarth came across the trophy in a cupboard at Starkie Street and handed it over to the FA.**

had already helped set up the Northern Intermediate League for 15–18-year-olds, but the League clubs didn't seem interested in a cup competition.

Instead, Richards took the idea to the FA, which immediately recognized its potential, and a few months later the first FA Youth Cup began, with ninety-three entrants. Some 37,000 spectators saw the first two-legged final in 1953, between Manchester United's Busby Babes and Stan Cullis's young Wolves, and the Youth Cup has been staged ever since. All thanks to Joe Richards.

Another cup competition closely associated with Richards was the League Cup (later the Milk Cup and Littlewoods Challenge Cup). After becoming a Vice President of the League in 1955, then President in 1957, it was Richards' support for Alan Hardaker, who first put up the idea, which helped bring about the competition's launch in 1960. He even bought the trophy with his own money, and had his name engraved on it. 'One day,' Richards told Hardaker in his house at Barnsley where the two men planned the new competition, 'the League Cup Final will be played on Wembley turf. But it won't be in my lifetime.' Fortunately, he was wrong about that. Wembley staged the final a year before his death.

Joe Richards' term as President was full of controversy; arguments with the pools companies over copyright of the fixtures, European competitions, television coverage, the abolition of the maximum wage, the first signs of modern-day hooliganism, the loss of top stars to Italy, and two important legal battles. The first of these involved those Sunderland players suspended and fined in 1957; the second concerned George Eastham's challenge to the legality of the retain and transfer system. Both issues were lost, and both completely transformed the relationship between the footballer and his club.

In many ways these events came as an enormous disappointment to Richards. They ran counter to everything he had worked so hard to achieve. In this he was no different from any other member of the Management Committee, but it was Richards who bore the brunt of the negotiations and the penetrating glare of the public spotlight. While Jimmy Hill and Alan Hardaker were adept, in their own very different ways, at handling the media, for Richards this proved to be an alien world in which he could not readily perform or conform to expectations. He came over as a brusque, stubborn little Yorkshireman, and was, in reality, out of his depth.

Having lost the argument over the maximum wage, then the Eastham case – two issues no League president could ever have won at that time, not even Charlie Sutcliffe – Joe Richards remained in power until 1966, even though his health had been failing and there was considerable agitation among the clubs for a change after 1964.

But it is no exaggeration to state that Richards, with Hardaker at his side, guided the Football League into the modern world as no other leading figure of the period could have done. Nor would it be inaccurate to state that after years of stagnation, without Richards' personal strength and leadership the League could so easily have fragmented and been buried under a tidal wave of criticism. He may have made mistakes, but the important thing from the League's point of view was that at least he fought for what he believed in. He looked ahead while others tried to look behind, or not at all.

When he did finally decide to stand down, the League clubs repaid his efforts with one touching gesture of appreciation. Instead of ending his period of office at the Annual Meeting in 1966, they agreed that he should stay on until 30 August 1966.

Thus, Joe Richards was able to take his seat at Wembley Stadium to watch England beat West Germany in the final of the World Cup, still as President of the Football League.

Moreover, he did so as Sir Joe Richards, having been knighted in June of that year, the first League president ever honoured so highly. 'Mr Football' thus became, to the tabloid press at least, 'the Soccer Knight with the common touch'.

The last two years of Sir Joe's life were hampered by deteriorating health. He retired from the chairmanship of Barnsley in December 1966, then saw them promoted from the Fourth Division in 1968. A few days later, his doctor expressly forbade him from making his usual trip down to London for the Cup Final, but Sir Joe went anyway. He always did like to get his own way.

But the doctor was right. Richards was taken ill at the pre-match lunch and had to be driven back to Barnsley before the kick-off. He died six days later at the age of eighty, the last League president to have been born in the nineteenth century but the first to have had the gumption to confront the modern age. So what if he had lost a few battles? At least he had tried.

The League owes Joe Richards a great deal.

CHAPTER TWENTY-ONE
Lights, Lytham, Pools, Posh and Pay Deals

Joe Richards' first act as President was to propose the long-awaited formation of the Fourth Division. It was agreed that it would not come into operation until 1958, to give Third Division clubs a year's notice as to how they would be divided up at the end of the 1957/8 season: the top half of both sections to form the new national Third Division, the two lower halves to form the Fourth.

No new clubs would be competing in that testing season. Norwich (48 votes), Tranmere (48), Crewe (47) and Swindon (42) were re-elected. Peterborough (7) were again the leading challengers, followed by Bedford, Burton Albion, Wigan (1 each), and Heddington, Kettering, King's Lynn, Worcester, Yeovil, Morecambe, Nelson and, yet again, North Shields, with no votes.

After the elections, the main business of the 1957 Annual Meeting concerned players' wages, bonuses, benefits and talent money. In view of the fact that, at long last, Entertainment Tax had been lifted in April 1957, minimum and maximum wages and bonuses were raised slightly, benefits rose to a limit of £1000 (still way behind what most top cricketers were receiving), and talent money was doubled right across the board.

First and Second Division champions would now each share out £1100, while for the first time European Cup games were included in the bonus calculations, a sure sign that the competition was officially recognized.

The Inter-City Fairs Cup was also establishing itself. For the first tournament, held between 1955 and 1958, London sent a representative eleven, while Birmingham City were the first individual League club to participate. Aston Villa, who had just won the FA Cup, were all set to participate in another competition which appeared to be a forerunner of the European Cup Winners' Cup – begun eventually in 1960 – but were prevented when the Management Committee expressed its disapproval.

Even without competitive games, however, it seemed as if every League club was inviting over one continental team or another, or accepting invitations from abroad which meant flying out straight after League matches. Five- and six-a-side competitions (one in Dublin being particularly lucrative) were also gaining in popularity. The *Evening Standard* competition soon established itself, with the *Daily Mirror* trying unsuccessfully to launch a similar event.

Footballers were now becoming marketable commodities, and the Committee often had to consider requests from various companies wanting to hire players for celebrity show-pieces. At the same time, America and South Africa wanted to attract experienced League players to help them establish their own leagues.

In 1957/8, Hardaker calculated, the average attendance at League matches was 16,549, while 135 friendlies and European games had drawn an average gate of 13,475. There was money in them there foreign hills! And if a club couldn't attract a continental team, there was always some other all-star eleven willing to play. The list of floodlit friendlies ranged from an Italian XI *v*. Charlton (in Milan) to Walsall *v*. Rochdale; from Burnley *v*. Lodz to Workington *v*. Blackpool. Did it even matter who were the opposition, as long as the lights were on?

The television companies liked mid-week floodlit games too, so much so that ITV offered the League a staggering £2750 for the right to televise the second half of the Inter-League match against the Scottish League on 28 March 1958 at Newcastle. This was more than half the amount the BBC was already paying for recorded extracts for a whole season (forcing it to increase its offer to £6000 a season plus £7500 facilities fee for the next three seasons).

More significantly, the League actually altered the time of kick-off at Newcastle to suit ITV's programme schedules – the first time this had ever happened.

Wolves hoped that the second half of their League match against Manchester United on 4 October 1958 would also be televised, and in readiness put the kick-off back to 7.00 p.m. In the end the Committee refused permission, but the match went ahead anyway and was thus the first League match in modern times to be staged on a Saturday night.

Also in this period, the League withheld its sanction for an Anglo-Scottish floodlit tournament. Indeed, there were advanced plans for a mid-week competition involving English, Welsh, Scottish and Irish clubs, scuppered only when the Scottish clubs decided to pull out. Had they not, and the subsequent competition had proved a success, it is likely that the League Cup would never have started.

This new era in football had many a drawback as far as the Committee was concerned. For example, clubs repeatedly complained about their opponents' floodlighting systems, while a crop of smaller clubs such as Accrington and Walsall started seeking permission to play their League games on Friday nights, to avoid clashing with their bigger neighbours.

The bubble had to burst sooner or later as, inevitably, floodlit friendlies lost their novelty value once League matches started to be played routinely under lights. Within a year of this happening, the average gate at friendlies dropped to around 11,000. Then, in July 1959, the League and FA imposed a maximum of four friendlies per season on each club.

Another increasingly common item on the Committee's agenda was the matter of air travel. Chelsea appear to have been the first team to fly to a League match, in April 1957, when they flew to Newcastle. More clubs followed suit, even after one of football's darkest moments, on 6 February 1958, when Manchester United's airliner crashed on take-off at Munich airport. Blackpool flew to Portsmouth a short time after the crash, and by this time it was fairly common for teams to criss-cross Europe during the week. But the Munich tragedy brought the entire football world up with a horrifying jolt. Not everything in this modern world was so marvellous, after all.

At its first meeting after Munich, the Committee stood in silent tribute to the dead, after which Alan Hardaker wrote to the doctor at the Munich hospital where more victims were fighting for their lives. 'So long as there is a Football League in England, the name of your hospital will always be remembered with gratitude,' he wrote.

Joe Richards represented the League on the disaster appeal fund and immediately suggested that clubs make collections to help the victims and their families. Over £51,000 was raised.

On 16 March, a forlorn note was recorded in the League minutes on the death of yet another United player as a result of the Munich crash. Duncan Edwards had died of his injuries on 21 February. His Provident Fund number was 5664, and his next of kin were sent the £312 credited to his record.

Death enjoined both the great and the small. Next to the note concerning Edwards was another about Aston Villa's young goalkeeper

Arthur Sabin. He had recently died, aged nineteen, having made just two appearances for the club. A year later, across the city, Birmingham's Jeff Hall also died. Hall had partnered Roger Byrne at full-back in a record run of seventeen games in succession for England, until polio overcame him in 1957. Since Byrne then died at Munich in 1958, it proved to have been a tragic partnership.

The Munich disaster put the Committee into a difficult situation. Because of the crash, United were invited to participate in the following season's European Cup. But the Committee opposed this on principle; Wolves had won the Championship in 1958, not United. However, United then won an appeal against the decision, and were drawn to play Young Boys of Berne in the Preliminary Round.

Still the Committee refused to sanction United's entry, and it threatened to make the issue the subject of a vote of confidence at an Extraordinary General Meeting. But then the FA also turned United down, and champions Wolves were thus the League's sole entry in 1958/9. It was a terrible decision to have to make, and it didn't win the Committee any friends in Manchester or elsewhere in Europe, especially as there had been room for both Wolves and United in the competition. (Joe Richards did, however, establish closer ties with Europe when he and Alan Hardaker attended a conference of European Leagues in October 1958.)

Next to these depressing events, the commission of enquiry into Leyton Orient's affairs seemed petty in the extreme. Nevertheless, the League had to go on, and Orient were fined £2000 for offences similar to those of Sunderland's. As with Derby in the 1940s, Orient's misdemeanours had been revealed by a disgruntled former employee.

The year 1958 did have its optimistic side, though. A new set of League rules was drawn up, the maximum wage rose to £20 a week during the season, and best of all, attendances rose slightly – by just under 3 per cent – the first increase since 1949. This was a great tonic, even if it did prove to be only a temporary respite.

The Annual Meeting of 1958 saw one change in procedure. Now that the Fourth Division was about to operate, with four up and four down being introduced as an experiment, the election of new clubs was conducted in one ballot, instead of separately for each section, North and South.

Not that this change had any effect on the so-called Old Pals' Act. All four retiring clubs were re-elected: Millwall (46 votes), Exeter (43), Southport (41) and Crewe (35). Peterborough (15) were again the leading challengers, followed by Wigan (4), Hereford (3), Bedford (2), Headington (2), King's Lynn (2), Kettering (1), South Shields (1), and Burton, Gloucester, Morecambe and Yeovil (no votes). North Shields seemed to have taken the hint at last, and didn't apply.

It is worth noting the identity of some of the Fourth Division's first members. Five of the clubs would eventually reach the First Division, however fleetingly (Watford, Coventry, Crystal Palace, Carlisle and Northampton). Five would eventually drop out of the League altogether, including Gateshead, the only one of the founder members who would never reach the Third Division.

But how many of that season's First Division elite ever imagined, as they nodded wise approval of the new Fourth Division, that one day they would find themselves in it? Within the next thirty years, seven would know that sinking feeling only too well, including, coincidentally, both the 1958 League champions Wolverhampton Wanderers and the Cup winners Bolton Wanderers.

Such is the glorious unpredictability of the Football League, which turns Wanderers into stumblers, kings into commoners, and transforms the humble into the mighty.

*   *   *

Joe Richards and Alan Hardaker really took a grip upon the League's destiny in the summer of 1958. In his early frustrating years at Starkie Street, Hardaker had studied the League's history in his lonely office, always aware that one day, when Fred Howarth had retired, he might get the chance to make history himself. Now that he was in office, it was almost as if he'd already drawn up a carefully prepared agenda for the future.

First on his list were the pools. The moral stance of previous Management Committees had, he realized, lost the League a fortune. In 1957/8, for example, just £1266 was earned from various commercial interests who reproduced the fixtures. The PPA paid nothing.

No one should criticize the pools companies for this. They had protected their own interests during the Pools War in 1936; they had offered £5000 a year towards the Jubilee Fund in 1938 but been turned away; they had offered a three-year deal worth £300,000 in the late 1940s and been rebuffed again; and as recently as 1955, when the southern Third Division clubs had suggested that the PPA contribute £400,000 a season for use of the fixtures – this money to be used for ground improvements – the Management Committee had again rejected the idea, on principle.

This meant that the Football League was

Whenever the League appeared to slip up or drag its feet, cartoonist Roy Ullyett of the Daily Express *was always ready to pounce. These cartoons appeared in April 1957 after Alan Hardaker had caught Sunderland making under-the-counter payments.*

almost alone in Europe in refusing to accept (or demand) financial help from pools companies. In Eastern Europe the profits from state-run pools went almost entirely into football. No wonder Hungary beat England so convincingly, wrote Ralph Hewins in the *Daily Express*. Since 1946, Hungary's Ministry of Sport had financed through the pools the building of over 6000 sports stadia. Thousands of sportsmen and women had been given free training, equipment and medical care.

Similar stories could have been told all over Europe, but in Britain the pools companies gave nothing back to the game on which they depended, despite the fact that their turnover and profits made them the seventh largest industry in Britain, employing about 100,000 people. In 1948, for example, when they were proposing to pay the League £100,000 a year for three years, the pools companies paid £12.5 million in tax alone.

Since the latest refusal to deal with the PPA, in 1955, two changes had occurred. Firstly, a new Copyright Act had been introduced in 1956, and secondly, a change in the law now allowed individual clubs to run their own lotteries. Several League clubs were already doing this, with such success that a spate of ground improvements soon began.

If clubs could gain from pool betting, why could not the League?

Hardaker began his campaign in July 1958, and this time the League was well prepared. The second Pools War would be a civilized affair fought in the court-room, not in secret meetings.

Legal opinion suggested that the League's best approach was to provoke a test case against one of the pools companies. As a result, Littlewoods were chosen, not only because they were the largest but because their co-founder, John Moores, was now active at Everton and was more likely to be sympathetic. (Moores, later Sir John, was soon to become the Everton chairman, an ironic twist of events when it is remembered who once

held that seat: the arch anti-pools campaigner Will Cuff.)

When the case eventually came before Mr Justice Upjohn, Harold Sutcliffe took over where his father had left off twenty-three years earlier, by arguing that the fixtures were indeed copyright. Littlewoods tried to side-step the issue by rearranging the order in which the fixtures were printed on their coupons, which led Upjohn to comment that it could thus be said that the PPA was only using the information, rather than reproducing it. But he conceded that the League should receive some contribution.

Essentially, the case rested on the question of whether the League fixture list represented a literary work. Facts alone were not subject to copyright; it was the skill which went into presenting facts which counted. The PPA argued that the skill was irrelevant, because otherwise every skilled selection – the choice of an MCC eleven for example – would become subject to copyright.

For the League, Sir Milner Holland replied by suggesting that if the fixtures were not copyright, why did Littlewoods not publish the daily Cause List, which gave details of cases to be heard in the High Court? Perhaps they could take forecasts on whether each case would be won, lost or drawn. 'Surely nobody would be entitled to use such a document by just copying it', he argued.

Harold Sutcliffe said that anyone could draw up the list, but that his job was to do this to the satisfaction of ninety-two clubs, all with specific interests. He had to avoid neighbouring clubs having home games on the same day, he had to prevent whenever possible teams having to travel long distances over Christmas and Easter. Each town had its own holidays which begged for a local derby, or special events like the Grand National which affected attendances, transport and policing arrangements. Mid-week matches at grounds with no floodlights had also to fit in with early-closing days. To satisfy all these separate criteria required 'skill, hard work and ingenuity', commented the judge.

Every attempt at drawing up the season's full list of 2028 matches took Sutcliffe nine hours to complete, but he then needed nine or ten further attempts to finalize it according to various requests from clubs. He did not do this for the sake of it, said Sutcliffe. He did it to enable the League to function.

After weeks of waiting and sifting the evidence, the final judgement came on 13 May 1959. The League had won its case, and, considering all the fuss and niggling memories from 1936, agreement for the use of the 1959/60 fixtures followed remarkably quickly.

'This is the greatest happening in football since the League was formed in 1888', said an elated Joe Richards, as the clubs rubbed their hands with glee at this long-awaited bonus, which above all meant an immediate reprieve from the 4 per cent gate levy. No doubt the ghosts of Messrs Sutcliffe, Rinder and Cuff winced at the very thought of the League accepting such 'tainted' money, but then they, too, might well have reached a similar kind of agreement in 1936 had they only possessed the resources and the conviction to take up the matter in court.

On 1 July 1959 four members of the PPA (Littlewoods, Vernons, Cope's and W. S. Murphy) signed a ten-year agreement to pay the Football League and the Scottish League a royalty of one half per cent of their gross stakes, with a minimum of £245,000 per annum. In fact, the first season's total came to £275,840.

Thus, for the first time in the League's history, its financial well-being was totally assured, especially as subsequent agreements with other firms not in the PPA brought the promised amount up to around £350,000 a year. (These other companies included Empire, Shermans, GIC, Trent and Zetters. Fixed-odds coupons were also made part of the agreement.)

It wasn't long before the League realized

> **The first official proposal for automatic promotion and relegation from the Fourth Division came from the Southern League in 1959.**

just how widely its fixtures were being used. Negotiations held between 1959 and 1961 took in pools companies from Holland, Austria, Yugoslavia, Scandinavia, Kenya, Barbados, Nigeria and Ghana. Pools were also big business in Mauritius, where one rogue company tried to evade the League's copyright by using the Central League and Football Combination fixtures instead. Another company in Norway refused to pay at all, while at home Mr Watson Hartley, the Liverpool accountant who had first put up the idea of claiming money from the pools in 1934, claimed his share of this windfall in a letter to the League. He received a steely response.

The Committee was on a high. The clubs were celebrating and it seemed as if between them Alan Hardaker and Joe Richards had performed a miracle.

This sense of joy was further reinforced when, before even a penny of the pools money had been paid, at the 1959 Annual Meeting Joe Richards was able to present the rosiest balance sheet the League had ever seen.

Over £50,000 of League funds had been invested (mainly with British Gas, Wolverhampton Corporation and Lancashire County Council). Television and broadcasting had earned £8563 during the season, and almost as much came from three Inter-League matches. With £143,315 coming in from the 4 per cent levy, this gave the League, after all its outgoings, a healthy balance of over £33,000.

The accumulation of funds, however, is not, was not, and never has been the League's aim, so it was doubly satisfying for Richards to be able to report another fractional increase in attendances for 1958/9. Richards was also able to soothe any worries about the new Fourth

Division. Although attendances had been slightly down on, for example, the Third Division North's last season, the new national Third Division had proved more or less as popular as the old Third Division South.

One thing was for sure. Midland Leaguers Peterborough United could hardly be denied much longer. In 1959 they attracted 26 votes, only five less than Aldershot, who were re-elected. Barrow did one better with 32 votes. Southport managed 34 and Oldham polled 46. This set of comparatively low votes for the retiring clubs suggested that change could not be far off, especially as the other applicants also received a much wider share of the vote. These were: Headington (7), Worcester (7), Wigan (3), Cambridge City (2) and Gloucester, Kettering, South Shields and Scarborough (1 each). Yeovil yet again received no votes, a fate shared by Bedford, Hereford, King's Lynn and Morecambe.

This constant rejection was too much for some non-League clubs to bear, especially with the pools money now offering an even greater incentive to join the big time. In July 1959 the senior non-Leaguers combined under Wigan's leadership to form a deputation. Their demand echoed that of the non-League clubs after the First World War: they wanted another division to be formed.

But Alan Hardaker and Joe Richards had other priorities. Now armed with ready cash from the pools companies, they started the long overdue search for new premises.

Predicting that this might happen, a *Times* editorial urged the League to spend its windfall wisely, not on the undermining of the FA – which at that stage was not part of the agreement – or on projects like a northern rival to Wembley stadium, or a League knock-out competition.

Instead, said *The Times,* the pools money should be spent on ground improvements, supplementing FA coaching schemes, easing small clubs' overdrafts and, perhaps most important of all, building new League head-

quarters away from 'distant Preston'. The new location should be Dover, commented *The Times* sarcastically, 'nearest to the Continent, where most progressive ideas are to be found'.

As if in response to this barbed comment, the League did the very opposite, by choosing a location more distant than even distant Preston – Lytham St Annes. It was to be one of the most controversial decisions the Management Committee would ever make.

No one could deny that Starkie Street was now totally inadequate for an organization of the League's standing. Apart from its outward appearance in a small Preston street, inside it was bursting at the seams, especially since the League had taken on the trainers' and coaches' pension scheme to add to that of the players. Hardaker's own office was so small, he wrote, that there was barely room to open the door if he had a visitor. There was no real filing system, no amenities for meetings, and nowhere to park.

Hardaker and Richards hadn't quite realized just how antiquated Starkie Street was until they visited their Italian counterparts in Milan in 1958. The English pair could scarcely believe their eyes; the Italian League offices were large, luxurious and well-equipped, a complete contrast with their own cramped and old-fashioned headquarters.

As Hardaker recalled, that night over a drink Joe Richards said to him: 'Alan, we've got to get out of that dump at Preston.'

The logical move would have been to Manchester, home of the Players' Union – now renamed the Professional Footballers' Association – and a convenient centre for rail travel. Manchester also had a long tradition of hosting League meetings, stretching back to 1888.

Birmingham had equally sound historical ties with the League and was more centrally located, although motorways had yet to reach it, and, of course, there was always London. But the capital was never seriously considered, even though the FA and all the government departments were there.

Apart from the fact that moving to London would have cost the League more than it could afford, pools money notwithstanding, the League had always been a provincial body, born in Lancashire and the Midlands and dominated by northern men. It was enough for Annual Meetings and Cup Finals to be held in the capital, but the League had to remain faithful to its roots.

Those roots were not in Lytham St Annes any more than they were in Scarborough, Llandudno, Folkestone or any of the other retreats at which the Management Committee chose to gather during close seasons. But Alan Hardaker had just purchased a house in St Annes, and there, despite his protestations to the contrary, surely lay the crux of the matter.

In his autobiography, however, Hardaker denied outright that the choice had been his. Joe Richards was also extremely fond of the coast around Lytham and spent a lot of time in the region. Hardaker wrote that it was Richards who told Hardaker to look in the Blackpool and St Annes area.

A medium-sized hotel was the chosen ideal; plenty of smaller rooms with one or two large meeting rooms, a formal reception area and good access. Hardaker wrote:

'The curious thing is that when the nine members of the Management Committee met to discuss a new location for the League there were nine different suggestions; and, by the strangest of coincidences, each member nominated a place a short distance from where he lived. Leeds, Manchester, Leicester, Harrogate and Liverpool were among those mentioned, while nobody, to begin with, put London forward. Later on there was a tentative suggestion from Joe Mears of Chelsea that England's capital city was, perhaps, the best place, but this was quickly and positively sat on by the other members.'

Hardaker himself suggested Leamington Spa on the grounds that it was central and that sizeable premises could be bought at a reasonable price. In this he had the support of Michael Gliksten of Charlton (a future member of the Committee). Enquiries were also made in Leeds and Leicester, while Harrogate's town clerk offered the League every assistance in relocating to his town.

Yet each time, the answer was the same. Rented accommodation could be found, but nothing that was suitable for purchase. In September 1959, therefore, after a majority vote of the Committee, Hardaker was instructed to go ahead with a building he and Richards had tracked down in Lytham St Annes.

Known as the Sandown Hotel, on Clifton Drive South, the new offices were close to the sea and the town centre, and about a half-hour drive from Preston. Apart from being large, affordable and close to Hardaker's house, about the only other convenience it enjoyed was that Lytham was then on the main railway line from London to Blackpool (before Dr Beeching had his way). It would cost £11,000 to buy, plus a further £43,000 to adapt to the League's requirements. Flush with money from the pools companies, this was but a small outlay.

Location apart, the greatest need was to revamp completely the League's administrative procedures, and from that point of view the new offices were large enough to accommodate extra staff and modern facilities. For that reason alone, Hardaker was keen that the motives for moving be interpreted correctly.

He reported, 'I should not like the Committee to gain the impression that these suggestions [relating to the move] are in any way intended to be "empire building".' He was concerned for the League's prestige, of course, but he also needed to protect the interests of the five other full-time staff members.

Nevertheless, having made the commitment to Lytham, Hardaker did comment later: 'I still thought Leamington Spa would have been a better choice.'

It was not only new offices which lent the League added prestige. In October 1959 Joe

Richards became Vice President of the newly formed International Liaison Committee of Professional Leagues, a body representing Europe's major leagues. Having banned Chelsea from appearing in the first European Cup, then demanded that Manchester United drop out of the 1958/9 competition, it might have seemed odd that the League was now entering Europe itself on a formal basis. But then, this was the decade of much wider European co-operation, and with air travel now fairly routine for the larger clubs, the League really had no choice but to join in. Besides, it also gave Alan Hardaker and members of the Committee a wonderful excuse to travel themselves.

At the time, there were three League clubs competing in European competitions: Wolves in the European Cup, Chelsea and Birmingham in the Fairs Cup. Then in the summer of 1960, champions Burnley represented the League at a tournament in New York, while the following season they competed in the European Cup and Wolves entered the new European Cup Winners' Cup.

The year 1960 was also of vital importance to the League in that, after long consultation, the Football League Cup was finally approved. It cannot be emphasized enough that when this competition was first envisaged it was a part of a wider package. In the end, the clubs grabbed the Cup but threw the rest of the wrapping in the bin.

In his annual address, Joe Richards described the new competition as 'an interim step' only. The greater issue was, in his opinion, the complete reorganization of the League, 'perhaps by cutting down the number of clubs in each division, as has already been suggested, and even giving more consideration to the system of four up and four down'.

In view of the loss of a further one million spectators that season, Richards went on:

'It must be obvious to all of you that the time has come to do something, and it is up to the Football League to give the lead.

I hope the Press will not immediately assume that the League is going to fall out with the FA, or anybody else. It is a fact, however, that professional football not only in England, but in other countries in Europe, has been used to amateur administrators, who have no experience or interest in the professional game which bears the brunt of criticism. We feel therefore that the time has come for our voice to be heard in every problem which affects the professional game.'

Richards assured the clubs that relations with the FA were harmonious, despite press reports, and that a compromise agreement had been reached on one of the issues which divided them – the playing of internationals on Saturdays. It was agreed unanimously that if any club had two or more players selected for an international, they could postpone their League matches if the dates clashed.

But dealings with the Professional Footballers' Association had been less than satisfactory. The PFA regarded itself as in dispute with the League, and had taken its case to the Ministry of Labour, but Richards made it clear 'that we cannot tolerate any longer the continual barrage of abuse from this quarter'.

Reaffirming the Committee's commitment to the principle of the maximum wage and the retain and transfer system, Richards then delivered a stinging retort to the players, the like of which no President had ever uttered before.

Referring to the European Cup Final in which Real Madrid beat Eintracht Frankfurt 7–3 in a classic encounter watched by 127,621 spectators, Richards said of the players: 'If any of them saw the match at Hampden Park recently, I hope that they took the lesson which is what we have said time and time again – make yourselves masters of your craft, entertain the crowd, and the money will come through the turnstiles, and find its way, as it has done in recent years, to the players.'

Richards' rebuke was by no means an isolated attack upon the players. Contemporary match reports and assessments in the press suggest that not for the first time League football had reached a very low point in terms of entertainment and quality, a factor exacerbated by the number of European clubs coming to our shores and exhibiting a whole range of skills which seemed beyond the average British League professional.

Yet the players could hardly be blamed for making their demands. Since the abolition of Entertainment Tax and the agreement with the pools companies, more money was circulating within the game than ever before, and because of a rise in minimum admission prices – to 2s 6d in 1960 – gate receipts were still rising, despite the drop in attendances. Furthermore, with the rewards of success growing every year – be it from European competitions, lucrative friendlies, television coverage and so on – it was increasingly difficult to blame players for not entertaining when their managers and directors were demanding victory at all costs.

In this sense, football in 1960 was entering a dilemma from which it has never quite escaped, having sought solutions which, it could be argued, have never entirely succeeded in alleviating the game's problems. Messrs Sutcliffe, Rinder and Cuff had argued that the League should have nothing to do with betting interests, whatever the rewards. Now, the League had acted against that legacy, and were, in Richards' words, suffering from 'lost prestige'. They had money, but did they still have their integrity?

The League Cup, it was hoped, would help re-establish some of the League's lost prestige. As 'a shot in the arm', said Richards, it was worth a try. The competition was not going to be compulsory, but it might at least take the place of the numerous meaningless mid-week matches that clubs were now so apparently keen on.

The President hoped that the clubs would not vote hysterically on the matter, having caught a slight dose of what he called 'con-tinental fever'. It was necessary to have strong clubs if the League was to re-establish itself, and to achieve this, more income was vital. 'We must be prepared to put the interests of the League and the game before individual clubs.'

Not everyone agreed that the League Cup was the way to achieve these ends. West Bromwich Albion called it a retrograde step, while several commentators questioned the Cup's attraction for spectators. Was it going to be just a poorer version of the FA Cup, or even worse, an attempt to displace it?

Sixteen clubs opposed the new competition, but thirty-one approved it. The League Cup was therefore born; unloved by many, defied by a few, but here to stay, nevertheless. (For full details of the League Cup, see Appendix Four.)

Another permanent aspect of League affairs from 1960 onwards was the issue of larger clubs being forced to subsidize the smaller ones. This was a principle which the larger clubs had themselves introduced during the Second World War, but now that money appeared to be flowing directly into the League's coffers, some of them resented the way it was distributed.

The Management Committee had suggested that, pools money or no, the 4 per cent levy on gates be continued. But instead of being used almost entirely to finance the Provident Fund, it should now be divided equally between the ninety-two clubs.

Everton opposed the Committee, arguing that since the pools money was sufficient to fund the League, and most smaller clubs were now running their own fund-raising activities, there was no need to continue the levy on gates. Richards countered this by saying that the large clubs had always subsidized the poorer ones, and when it came to the copyright of fixtures, Fourth Division matches brought in as much income as those in the First Division.

On this occasion the Committee won the

day, but Everton's argument would not be so easily assuaged. This issue would run and run.

The year 1960 was in many ways an historic one for the League: the move to Lytham St Anne's in July, the players' struggle to end the maximum wage, the beginning of the footballers' apprenticeship scheme, the first live broadcast of a League match, and the start of the League Cup. But one event particularly stands out in the collective football memory – the election of Peterborough United in place of Gateshead, at the Annual Meeting on 28 May.

The least shocking element of this affair was Peterborough's election. Their record in the Midland League had, for the previous few seasons, been quite remarkable. Champions for the past five seasons, between 1955 and 1960 Peterborough lost just one game at home, scoring 428 goals in 103 matches. During that golden period they had steadily attracted more and more votes at Annual Meetings, so that by 1960 their credentials were irresistible.

To add to their case, a deputation of non-League clubs had met the League in 1959 to state their case for the formation of a fifth division. Their main grouse was this: not one new club had been elected to the League since Workington in 1951. (Alan Hardaker tacitly supported their desire for a fifth division.)

But should Gateshead have been the club to make way for Peterborough? The facts were these.

Since their election to the Second Division in 1919 as South Shields, the club had coasted along in mid-table until being relegated in 1928. As Gateshead, from 1930 onwards, they were twice runners-up in the Third Division North, in 1932 and 1950, and their record thereafter was hardly damning. In their last ten seasons they had finished in the top eight of the Third Division North five times, and in their last season, 1959/60, they had come third from bottom, with 33 points.

Five points below them were Oldham, conducting their second re-election campaign in a

row. At the bottom were Hartlepools, cap in hand for the fourth time. The other club applying for re-election was Southport, for the third year running and for the seventh time overall.

Given these clubs' records, therefore, Gateshead would seem to have been a very good bet to keep their place. In addition, they had applied for re-election only once before, in 1937, and they had never finished bottom.

Imagine their shock, therefore, when the votes were announced. This was the order:

Bedford Town	2
Cambridge City	2
Chelmsford City	3
Ellesmere Port Town	1
Gateshead	18
Guildford City	2
Hartlepools United	34
Headington United	10
Hereford United	0
Kettering Town	1
King's Lynn	0
Morecambe	1
New Brighton	2
Oldham Athletic	39
Peterborough United	35
Romford	2
Scarborough	2
South Shields	1
Southport	29
Wigan Athletic	6
Worcester City	2
Yeovil Town	0

Gateshead were out for the count, after forty-one years in the Football League.

What made the voting even more remarkable was the unprecedented spread of votes. Altogether, 36 votes were recorded for the unsuccessful non-League challengers. It was this, as much as Peterborough's popularity, which sunk the north-eastern club.

Why were poor Gateshead so unloved? There could be only one answer – they were

Gateshead people 'just don't care', or did they simply believe that the other League clubs could never be so ruthless?

so far away. Certainly their name had barely entered the League's bad books, and although gates at Redheugh Park were poor – an average of 3249 in the last season – they were not the lowest in the Fourth Division.

'All true North Eastern sportsmen will be filled with anger and disgust at the League clubs' decision', was the shocked retort from the *Newcastle Evening Chronicle*. They blamed 'a cosy clique' of southern clubs who, like industrialists, saw the North East as 'up in the wilds'. Gateshead's demise came at a time when the town was desperately trying to attract more industry to Tyneside.

Gateshead's bitter chairman, David Absalom, immediately sought a meeting with the Scottish League to see if the club could seek membership of the Scottish Division Two, but nothing came of this and in the end Gateshead joined the Northern Counties league. (They lost their Redheugh Park ground eventually, and now play at Gateshead's new athletics stadium.)

Before Peterborough had even kicked a ball in the Football League (in which they were an instant success), the year 1960 delivered another major shock – the heightening of the campaign to abolish the maximum wage. After years of unrest and increased militancy, the PFA under Jimmy Hill's leadership finally forced matters to a head in the autumn of 1960.

It was a shock to the League, not because it was unexpected, but because of the pro-fessional manner in which the PFA took their case to the public, the press and the Houses of Parliament. But it was inevitable.

Throughout the boom years of the late 1940s, the clubs had made only grudging adjustments to players' weekly wages, so that during the 1950s, resentment grew steadily. As early as October 1950, the Tottenham chairman Fred Bearman had warned: 'We should put wages up before we are compelled to. Most clubs feel their players are underpaid and most can afford a maximum of £20 or even higher.' This was at a time when the maximum was still £12, so the Management Committee was none too pleased with Mr Bearman.

The pressure continued, however, and in August 1951 Joe Richards said of the players: 'they are merely bleating about so-called injustices and doing nothing themselves to ensure a higher standard of play.' An abolition of the maximum wage would ruin the entire League, he claimed.

To this, Danny Blanchflower, who had just left Richards' club, Barnsley, for Aston Villa, replied in the *Daily Mail*: 'Bunkum! Everyone is coached the same way. Everybody is paid the same. Nobody may talk out of turn. Rewards are for long service rather than better ability. The whole system breeds uniformity, and a uniform system leads to a uniform product and mediocrity.'

Before the war, a footballer's wage had been above that of the average worker. By 1960, that gap had closed. In the new age of television, European competitions and commercial exploitation of football, it was no longer enough to expect a footballer to go cap in hand to his club and be thankful for £20 a week while being asked to play in front of large audiences, and then accept £17 a week during the summer with no extra bonuses.

In 1958 the Management Committee had suggested raising the maximum to £25, and asked the clubs to give them full powers to negotiate. The clubs refused. Alan Hardaker wrote: 'It was not a unanimous decision, however, because three chairmen came up to

me afterwards and said: "Alan, we think this is the biggest mistake we've ever made." I replied, "Well, you've been making them all along but I think this is one that's going to cost you more money than any of them."'

In the past, such matters would barely have been the subject of comment from a Secretary of the League, but Alan Hardaker was different. He was becoming a spokesman with independent views of his own.

By December 1959, eighteen months had elapsed since the Management Committee had decided to withdraw from the Joint Standing Committee. But even when the PFA did finally persuade the Committee to hear its case, no progress was made.

'It couldn't really be called a discussion', Jimmy Hill wrote later in *Striking for Soccer* (Peter Davies, 1961). 'It was almost a soliloquy by Jimmy Hill.'

Exasperated by the Committee's attitude, Hill followed Jimmy Guthrie's example by taking the players' case to the Ministry of Labour. Battle thus commenced in February 1960, when an official dispute was declared.

At the heart of the PFA demands was a desire to establish 'two freedoms' – by abolishing both the retain and transfer system and the maximum wage. The union also wanted to improve existing terms of contract.

But, as an Extraordinary General Meeting in London showed quite categorically, the Committee and most of the clubs were totally opposed to such demands; at best, their only concessions could be to raise the minimum and maximum wage limits, reconsider television and special match fees, with no increase in bonuses. Regarding the transfer system, the Committee accepted that some anomalies existed, but considered the basic principles sound.

In past years, such determination on the part of the Committee had usually been sufficient to quell the players for a while. Under Hill, they were determined not to capitulate. There were three further reasons for this.

Firstly, the PFA had challenged the procedure by which the FA and the League had fined and suspended five Sunderland players in 1958. Although the case wasn't settled until two years later, it was already apparent by 1960 that the PFA had a good case and would win. This was a tremendous confidence booster; the law was on the players' side for once.

Secondly, the lure of the Italian lira had already taken John Charles of Leeds United to Juventus in June 1957 for a fee of £65,000. Charles was able to earn far more than his team-mates back in England. His signing-on fee alone was reputed to have been £10,000, as much as many players would make in their entire careers in England. Then, in 1960, Italian agents started to scout for more striking talent, with Brian Clough and Jimmy Greaves the two main targets. If Italian clubs could pay high fees, argued the PFA, wouldn't it be in their best interests for League clubs to raise wages in order to stop a potentially disastrous drain of talent abroad?

Finally, the PFA felt at last that it had the public on its side, after years of newspaper articles and revelations. Jimmy Guthrie had started that process, but it needed the onset of television and European football to bring it home to the British audience.

Thus began months of tough negotiations, culminating in the abolition of the maximum wage in January 1961. This is how Alan Hardaker described the dispute:

'The meetings ticked by, the League putting up one set of proposals and the PFA another, like an endless game of ping-pong, but it should have been obvious to just about everybody which way it was all going. The clubs were wrong in their attitude, they were wrong in the way they handled their case, and public opinion was against them.

Their one hope of salvaging anything was compromise, but they would not or could not see this.

The PFA slowly advanced, the clubs slowly retreated, and in the middle, its teeth drawn, was the Management Committee. Its members had been elected by the clubs to do a job of work but were then prevented by those same clubs from doing it.'

To an extent, Jimmy Hill's own recollection of the negotiations echoed Hardaker's views. In *Striking for Soccer*, the former PFA chairman wrote:

'I realised in the middle of the dispute that there were [directors] who had not the least idea of the implications of the various suggestions for settlement that were made from time to time. Yet these men have an influential voice in the administration of football. The League often arrives at its decisions after a 48-way tug of war. If the clubs cannot agree, however urgent the problem, no action is possible.'

Hardaker cited the main reason for the players' success as their ability to handle public relations astutely, while the clubs and Joe Richards made no appeal to the public.

Jimmy Hill and Cliff Lloyd, the PFA secretary, were on the other hand a perfect combination of persuasive youth and down-to-earth, dignified conviction. They appeared on television and in the press, continually arguing their points, trying to persuade the public that the players wanted to establish basic principles rather than simply to gain an extra pound here or there. Why should footballers have to demean themselves by accepting under-the-counter payments all the time in order to earn a fair wage? Why should they be treated differently from other sportsmen or wage earners? Footballers needed incentives, or the game would drown in a sea of apathy.

The story has been told in detail before, but what is interesting from the League's point of view was how the issue led eventually to a complete split between the Committee and the clubs. Again, this was not the first time this had happened, but in view of the enormity of the final outcome it was significant that when the crunch came, the clubs failed to put their faith in the essential structure of League management.

The President asked the clubs to give the Management Committee full powers to negotiate, but the clubs refused. At another Extraordinary General Meeting on 8 November 1960, a majority of clubs was in favour of raising the maximum wage but could not agree on how it should be done. So nothing was done. The meeting merely agreed to raise minimum wage levels and improve certain other match fees. The players were incensed. Jimmy Hill wrote:

'8 November was the day when the Football League lit the fuse that was to blow up in the headlines of newspapers throughout Britain and even throughout the world; that was to involve battles in Parliament, in courts of law, on television screens, in newspaper headlines – a battle in which, through the statement of their Chairman, Mr Ted Hill, almost every member of the trades unions in this country found himself directly involved.'

A basic anomaly once again came to the fore, one which to an extent remains to this day. Sometimes the League requires a firm hand, a dictator almost, to lead the disparate elements among the members. Yet when real leadership is most needed, the clubs do not always entrust the elected Committee with their fate.

There are, of course, strong parallels in this with any democratic system. And as Hardaker accepted, when the system failed it was the executive rather than the voters who took the blame or faced the flak. Ironically, both Hill and Hardaker spoke of the need for a 'soccer boss', and while many thought that Hardaker was already acting as football's dictator, he was in fact relatively powerless when it came to the final outcome. Joe Richards was the League's dominant figure in the affair, and his was the voice of a man who didn't quite know what had hit him.

Faced with rejection from the clubs in November 1960, the PFA began a series of meetings of players in London, Birmingham and Manchester. Each was well attended by a determined and vocal membership, thereby refuting suggestions that it was only the union leadership who cared. The players clearly meant business, among them men such as Tommy Docherty, Bobby Robson and Don Howe arguing the case on television.

Perhaps the most important source of support, in the public's mind at least, came at the Manchester meeting, when Stanley Matthews finally came out in support of the threatened strike action. If the veteran clean-living superstar of post-war football was on the PFA's side, then surely nothing could stop them now.

Jimmy Hill described the situation.

'All of England was wondering what Stan was going to do. We soon found out. He changed his mind. His hand went up with 189 other players to support the general resolution, and he said at the time: "I was torn between my principles and loyalty to fellow players. I have done well out of the game, but could I ignore the injustice to my colleagues? Rightly or wrongly I made my decision. Loyalty to the players won, my hand went up."'

According to Hill, it was the finest thing Stanley Matthews ever did for football.

'Before, I am sure the public thought the basis of our struggle was Jimmy Hill and his soapbox – that I was always shooting my mouth off about something or other. After these three meetings, in a week that ended with Stan Matthews voicing his support, I think the situation had changed ... however well I presented my arguments, it didn't mean quite the same thing as when Stan Matthews, Bobby Charlton, Johnny Haynes, Jimmy McIlroy, Jimmy Greaves, Phil Woosnam and all the other star players, and the lesser players, made the same argument.'

The players' cause was further helped when a Conservative MP, the appropriately-named Philip Goodhart, made a speech in the House of Commons on 19 November. He described the contracts of professional footballers as documents a fifteenth-century apprentice might view with suspicion. Labour Party and trade union support had been strong all along, but Goodhart's support was almost as heartening to the PFA as Stan Matthews'.

All this helped win the public relations battle, but it barely persuaded the clubs. As 1961 approached, instead of securing a more gradual negotiated settlement which would have brought them more time to adapt to changing circumstances, the clubs almost goaded the players into fighting to the death.

For example, Alan Hardaker, with Cliff Lloyd's initial backing, put forward a plan which was announced to the public on 2 December. Four days later, the Committee discussed and amended it, with the FA's approval, so that when it was finally revealed to the players at the Ministry of Labour on 6 December, it was clearly a different package. The basics were as follows:

● To raise the maximum wage from £20 to £30 a week in annual increments of £2 per week – the biggest wage rise ever suggested in the League's history – this limit to operate for two years, during which time further negotiations could take place. (Fair though this might seem, another clause stated that any player on the maximum £30 a week would, if transferred, have to return to £20 a week and start building up his income all over again.)

● To allow freely negotiated lengths of contracts up to a maximum of three years, but with incentives for players on longer contracts. (Until then, no contract had been longer than a year.)

● To raise the signing-on fee to £150, while recommending that this be paid yearly by negotiation instead of benefit. Players would also be entitled to a testimonial after eight years with one club. No percentage of transfer fees would be payable to the player.

● A retention of the retain and transfer system, but with players to be retained on full wages while new terms were agreed, instead of the existing system whereby if a player refused to re-sign, he was effectively out in the cold.

● The reconstitution of the Joint Standing Committee between the League, FA and PFA.

On one hand, the package could have been seen as an attempt to buy off the players – or at least divide the rank and file from their leadership – while failing to address the basic injustices of the maximum wage and the retain and transfer system. In short, give them as much as we can afford, and hope the fuss will die down. It should be noted that at the time these negotiations were in hand, the average League attendance had gone down from 17,000 to 15,000 in just twelve months. Directors were genuinely concerned for the future.

On the other hand, the Committee's proposals could have been seen as a comparatively generous gesture which would have allowed the clubs to make a smoother transition from a maximum wage to the inevitable moment when wage restrictions were lifted.

In the event, neither supposition could be tested.

Although some players spoke favourably of the proposals, and the League was confident of the PFA's acceptance – after all, they'd never been militant for very long in the past – at a packed meeting of 250 players in London's York Hall (they had to move from the original venue to find more room), there was a unanimous vote to give the League one month's notice of strike action.

At two subsequent PFA meetings in Manchester and Birmingham, the players were equally determined not to back down, now that public opinion was veering their way. In all, 712 players attended the meetings – just over a third of the total number of professionals in the League – and only 18 voted against the PFA's stand.

Faced with such solidarity the clubs then floundered somewhat. Some suggested beating the strike by using amateurs. Joe Richards echoed his predecessor Charles Sutcliffe by pleading for the players to consider the good of the game. 'Strikers will render a grave dis-service to the game and will probably put out of employment a large number of professional footballers', he told the newspapers. Leyton Orient's chairman, Harry Zussman, said: 'I congratulate Jimmy Hill. This could break the greatest game in the country.'

Several leading figures doubted that the strike threat would ever be carried out. 'Strike? They must be barmy', said Arthur Rowe dismissively. Other former players urged the players to accept a £30 maximum, while one First Division chairman questioned the players' vote, suggesting that a secret ballot had not been held. Charlton's manager Jimmy Trotter even claimed that a strike would be beneficial, since postponed games would have to be played later in the season when the weather would be better and thus gates would improve.

Matters took a further turn on 21 December, after a meeting at the Ministry of Labour revived the notion of a two-year transitional period during which a new maximum of £30 a week would operate, after which all limits would be abolished. Three-year contracts would be permitted, signing-on fees would replace benefits, testimonials would be allowed after eight years with one club, and a joint committee suggested by the Ministry of Labour would act as an arbiter in disputes between clubs and players. The 21 December proposals were also significant in that they recognized the invidious position of a player who refused to re-sign for his club. In such a circumstance, the League was to help him find another club.

Overall, the terms represented the best possible compromise for both parties, particularly because they gave clubs breathing space to prepare for unlimited wages. Indeed, several prominent chairmen openly supported the proposals on these grounds alone.

But who could predict how the clubs would really vote when they gathered in London to consider the new terms on 9 January 1961? Many club chairmen appeared to resent the idea of being pressurized into a compromise under threat of a strike, many rejected any change on principle, while only a few seemed at all sympathetic to the players. Nor could the players know that at a Management Committee meeting the day before it had been agreed not to recommend the 21 December proposals. In other words, having hammered out the details at the Ministry of Labour only three weeks earlier, the Committee, under pressure from the clubs, was now having second thoughts.

Thus the proposals were suitably doctored once more, and in this altered state were accepted by the clubs on 9 January. At first glance, one might have thought a solution was in sight. Instead of having a two-year transitional period, the clubs agreed to end the maximum wage immediately. Surely the players would have greeted this with rejoicing? But they didn't, for one simple reason.

Tied to this concession was a complete rejection of any further arbitration on the question of the retain and transfer system. Thus, the League had satisfied only one of the 'two freedoms' demanded by the PFA, while categorically refusing any further talks on the other.

The ball was now firmly in the players' court. Were they united sufficiently to halt the League programme, given that the option of accepting abolition of the maximum wage after sixty years was so tempting? Or should they carry on fighting for a change in the transfer system, and risk splitting the membership? The trades unions advised them to take the money and renew the campaign from there. 'This was the biggest carrot that had ever been offered – a king-size carrot to tempt all footballer donkeys', wrote Jimmy Hill. Could they really afford to turn it down?

The answer came in the following days, when three more PFA meetings were held to frame a response to the League.

According to Hill, the key to the PFA's response was public opinion. If the public thought the League offer was enough, then they could hardly carry on.

'I was scared stiff before the St Pancras meeting,' he wrote. 'I was afraid the maximum wage offer would confuse the players. I knew there was nothing in it for the Third and Fourth Division men.'

As it happened, however, in London the First Division players opted to stick with their fellow professionals and reject the League's offer, by a vote of three to one. Fewer players attended the Birmingham meeting, where Aston Villa's men spoke out for acceptance, but the result was the same. The strike was still on. Then, at Belle Vue in Manchester, the largest meeting of all produced the most overwhelming backing for the PFA stand yet seen, with a horde of journalists invited in to confirm just how strongly the 344 players felt.

Manchester represented another public relations victory for the PFA, while the League scored something of an own goal when Alan Hardaker suggested in the press that a certain Mr X – later revealed to be an agent called Bagenal Harvey – was behind the whole strike threat. It was an unwise and inaccurate statement, but it helped the players by uniting them even further behind the PFA banner.

Joe Richards hit back immediately the PFA's decision was announced. The League would not back down. If the clubs had to field amateurs, they would. 'It is up to the players. It seems we have wasted our time. I think the players are being very foolish', he told the press.

By now, television cameras and journalists were following each of the protagonists, recording their every statement and studying every possible angle of the story, such was the importance of League football to the nation. William McGregor would have been amazed to see his organization so exposed in the headlines.

But with a strike hanging over the game,

there was to be no respite.

The date set for the strike was Saturday, 21 January 1961, and by the beginning of the preceding week the PFA was actively preparing to carry out its threat; players started looking for outside jobs, matches in a Dublin rugby stadium were proposed for star players, sympathetic celebrities offered assistance, and there was even a suggestion that fully-fledged League teams would play in parks or at smaller venues.

Sir Stanley Rous offered to act as peacemaker, while the trade union movement gave the PFA its full backing. Any player breaking the strike would be labelled a black-leg (with all the implications that held for his future employment), and all union members were urged to boycott any League games that might be arranged. Of course, the pools companies were very worried as to what effect all this would have on their coupons, especially when the League revealed that matches for the following Saturday might be moved forward to Friday in order to squeeze in one extra game before the strike.

All these contingency plans came to nothing. On Wednesday afternoon, 18 January, 1961, after a tough meeting in London, the strike was called off. 'Hill's hour of triumph' declared one headline, above a photograph of Joe Richards, forcing a smile, and Hill shaking hands. Next to them, Alan Hardaker glared implacably.

Presided over by John Hare, the Minister of Labour, it was agreed that the maximum wage would be abolished straight away. But if the two parties had thought of settling between them the other details relating to the retain and transfer system, they were completely wrong. The League clubs weren't in the mood to be dictated to by anyone – Hill, Hare or Richards.

These were the main points of the 18 November meeting, which averted the strike but by no means ended the dispute:

● No transfers would take place during the

terms of a player's contract, except by the mutual consent of club and player.

- A player was to be informed by 19 May preceding the end of his contract of the club's offer of a new contract, and he had until 31 May to decide whether to accept. If he did not accept, the club would place him on the transfer list, and if he was not transferred by 30 June, the club would continue to retain him on payment of the minimum wage up to 31 July.

- If not transferred by 31 July, the player would sign a playing contract month by month on the terms offered previously on 19 May, subject to the club's maintaining efforts to transfer him.

- If by 31 August he were still not transferred, the Management Committee, on the application of the player, would deal with the matter.

Thus, the 'soccer slave' was offered the chance to loosen some of the chains which bound him to his master. He could earn as much as the club was prepared to offer, and he was no longer subject to the risk of being unpaid and ignored if he refused to re-sign at the end of his contract. But at the same time, the agreement made it harder for a player to hold out for a transfer to the club of his choice, since the best offer had to be accepted.

The reaction of clubs to these details we will soon discover. Concerning the abolition of the maximum wage, opinion was mixed. The former Wolves and England captain, Billy Wright, said: 'It was the players' fault it didn't come earlier. We weren't 100 per cent behind the union in those days.' There had never been a maximum wage on the continent or in Scotland, so it should work in England.

Matt Busby, Manchester United's manager, felt that the new wage agreement would encourage players to improve themselves, knowing that they would be paid to the best of their abilities. He also thought that the game would now be opened up to all classes of young player, since professional football could now offer a proper career with adequate rewards.

But Stan Cullis, manager of Wolves, disagreed. 'Better money doesn't mean better players', he warned.

At least there was an end to the dispute. Or so it seemed, as the Management Committee met in London on 29 January and approved Alan Hardaker's report of the settlement. All that needed to be done now was to amend the League regulations according to the new circumstances.

Sadly, it was not as simple as that. When the clubs had digested the details of the agreement, it soon became clear that they intended to renege on it, despite the agreement of all sides at the Ministry of Labour on 18 January. To the fury of Joe Richards, the club chairmen met together at London's Café Royal, without the Management Committee, and attempted to establish a maximum wage of their own by gentleman's agreement. The figure mentioned was apparently £50 a week.

Typically, however, they could not agree. Soon afterwards, Jimmy Hill's club Fulham agreed to pay their star international Johnny Haynes £100 a week, five times the previous maximum. Whether it was a wise move or not, the club really had no choice. They had been claiming for a while that Haynes was worth £100 a week, but that they couldn't pay it because of League regulations. Once the maximum was abolished, they could hardly go back on their word.

Not that abolition of the maximum stopped star performers leaving these shores. Haynes' England colleague, Jimmy Greaves, signed for AC Milan at the end of the season for £80,000. Even at £100 a week few British players could afford to turn down Milan's reported offer of a £15,000 signing-on fee (over twice what Haynes could earn from football in a year).

With the question of the maximum wage apparently settled, it now became a question of whether the clubs would abide by the agreement of 18 January on changes to the retain and transfer system.

Alan Hardaker, whose views often clashed with those of the clubs and the players, recognized the validity of the players' case. The clubs, he wrote, 'were fighting to keep a system of retaining players that was not only ludicrous but which, very clearly, would not stand up in law. The system, in short, enabled a club to retain a player against his will at the end of his contract and, not only that, to pay him less money while doing so.'

The clubs' chance to show their true colours came on 14 April 1961, at an Extraordinary General Meeting at the Café Royal.

'What happened on 14 April is now history', an astonished Jimmy Hill wrote soon after. 'The League clubs would not pass the January agreement.'

Even more surprisingly, especially in the light of the enormous publicity surrounding the affair, Joe Richards said publicly: 'Come what may, the Football League clubs will not alter the present retain and transfer system.'

It was as if all the previous negotiations had meant nothing to the clubs, that the Ministry of Labour had no power, and that the PFA's strike threat had been over another matter altogether. 'The Football League, born in 1888, died of shame at high noon yesterday', announced one newspaper.

One of football's greatest allies in the House of Commons, J. W. P. Mallelieu, Labour MP for Huddersfield East, raised the matter in Parliament, and after another meeting with the Ministry of Labour's long-suffering conciliation officer, Tom Claro, another agreement was reached on 16 May, its terms barely different from those agreed on 18 January.

But still the Management Committee had to wait to find out whether the clubs would throw out the package yet again. That was left for the League's Annual General Meeting on 3 June.

A controversial meeting it was, too. Before discussion of the players' agreement, Chelsea proposed that the press be asked to leave, only the second time this had ever happened at an Annual Meeting. So the journalists trooped out of the room, to a chorus of slow hand-clapping from some of the club representatives: a futile and ill-considered gesture, but one which illustrated the mood of the day. Without the press, some chairmen considered, the players would never have won their battle.

Luton Town's representative spoke out against the May agreement as a whole. The League had been forced to give in on the question of the maximum wage: now they were being forced by people outside the game to sacrifice the transfer system.

Chelsea argued that the agreement would allow any player to hold his club to ransom. If he didn't like the terms being offered, then the club would have to transfer him. The agreement labelled that 'a dispute'. Chelsea thought it would just lead to malpractice. Middlesbrough agreed. The proposed agreement put an absolute premium on disloyalty. Burnley suggested that the Ministry of Labour agreement opened the door to agents coming between club and player.

As more clubs spoke against acceptance of the agreement, West Bromwich sounded a note of caution. They, too, disliked the agreement, but hadn't enough damage been done in the previous few months by clubs refusing to act? Every time the Committee suggested something, the clubs rejected it. Rather than go through the whole process again, with all the potential damage to the League's public image that would entail, was it not better to consider each element of the agreement?

Fulham reckoned that the major problem was public relations. The clubs were not afraid of the PFA, they were afraid of the House of Commons and the Ministry of Labour, who listened to people who knew nothing about the transfer system.

And so it came to a vote. Burnley proposed that they ignore the whole agreement; West Bromwich, with the Committee's backing, urged acceptance (with slight amendments). The votes were counted. The agreement was accepted. Only four clubs voted against. Reason had prevailed.

Back came the press and, it could be said, back came sanity to the troubled League. Everything the Ministry of Labour had asked for had been passed, with one exception.

Clause Four, which stated that clubs had to let it be known that a player had refused terms and was available for transfer, was deleted. In theory, therefore, clubs could still hang on to their unsettled player for as long as they liked, keeping him on monthly contracts at minimum wages.

Jimmy Hill was incensed. 'How much longer will we allow such men to go on damaging the game with their pomposity, their inflated egocentricity and their blundering inefficiency? Football deserves better.' In fact, Hill's anger was to be relatively short-lived, since the entire retain and transfer system was to be shattered anyway two years later.

If we can conclude anything from the events of 1960/1, it is this: the clubs had elected a Management Committee and then refused to trust its judgement. Joe Richards had endangered his health passing from one side to another with no thanks from anyone and very little credit at the end. Was it right to expect an aged president to shoulder such a burden? Alan Hardaker clearly felt otherwise; so did Jimmy Hill.

Would a more dictatorial system have avoided any of these troubled events? Probably not. What was the point of imposing an unpopular settlement in public knowing that clubs would flout the rules in private just as they had done since the turn of the century?

As always, it was the Management Committee which was caught in the middle ground. And yet, if the clubs kept on disagreeing with its members, why didn't they elect some new men? In 1961 they re-elected both retiring members, and not once did they raise a motion of no confidence. To be sure, football was, as it had always been, an odd business indeed.

CHAPTER TWENTY-TWO
Hardaker and Stanley's Lament

*A*fter all the furore caused by the threatened players' strike, it would be remiss of this history to overlook the fact that on the field, strike fever had no perceptible effect on the players' performances, at least not at White Hart Lane. Tottenham Hotspur became the first club since 1897 to win the double, while Aston Villa and Rotherham were the finalists of the first League Cup competition.

'It has not made a sensational impact on the public; we never thought it would', Joe Richards admitted in his annual address in 1961. The average gate at League Cup matches (both final legs excluded – they were played the following season) had been 10,556, just higher than the average gate in the Third Division. Hardly a stunning success, but a beginning nevertheless.

In the League, however, attendances had dropped by nearly four million, the single largest decline in one season ever recorded in the League's history.

Was it for this reason that so much controversy was attached to a draft agreement made with ITV, who were reported to have offered £150,000 to broadcast live 26 League games especially arranged for seven Friday and nineteen Saturday nights?

Despite the clubs' anger at the Committee's behind-the-scenes dealing with ITV, the first subsequent experimental live transmission of such a match was scheduled for Saturday evening, 9 September 1960. Had that match been a success, the agreement might have gone further. Instead, all the leading First Division clubs opposed the idea, leaving ITV no choice but to print nervously in *TV Times* the words '7.30 p.m., show to be arranged'.

The public expects to know more, complained a journalist, to which Alan Hardaker replied frostily: 'They may expect, but they will be disappointed.'

He was right about that, although not in the way he had intended. After most First Division clubs had refused to let in the cameras, the lack of lights had ruled out Fulham, and transport difficulties had barred Manchester, that left just Blackpool *v.* Bolton, two clubs destined to struggle all season. Even then, the star attraction was missing – Stanley Matthews was injured.

In the end, viewers saw just the second half, Blackpool winning by a single goal in a dull game, followed by what turned out to be a whole evening of soccer action on the other channel. The BBC showed the Olympic Games' soccer final from Rome, then immediately afterwards on *Sportsview* replayed the highlights of that afternoon's London derby game between Arsenal and Tottenham.

The result? BBC won; ITV lost.

Not surprisingly, ITV's live package was shelved – for the next quarter of a century as it happened – and the League was paid £2100 for the forty-five-minute broadcast, while Bolton and Blackpool received £577 compensation for their loss of gate money.

The newspapers slated both ITV and the League. The *Daily Mail* wrote: 'What the cameras didn't show were the empty spaces for a match that should've brought a capacity gate.' Criticizing the 'treacle commentary', J. L. Manning said: 'Attempts to present the Blackpool match in glowing words fell short of credulity.'

There were plenty of other games for armchair fans in 1960/1, however. But because televised football was never allowed to clash with League fixtures, it remained an added attraction rather than a substitute. To illustrate this, the BBC had a three-year agreement worth £15,000 to film the FA Cup Final, although ITV began broadcasting the match simultaneously from 1961 onwards.

Televised by both television companies in rotation, in part or in whole, were the Charity Shield, the Amateur Cup Final, every England full international, the Inter-League game against Scotland, the Varsity match at Wembley, a schoolboys' international against Wales, and two England under-23 matches. Olympic Games matches in Rome were also shown after 10.00 p.m., as was the case on 9 September, and there was one curiosity, a televised match between Clapton F.C. and a Maori eleven.

However, when Manchester United wanted their attractive friendly against Real Madrid to be televised, permission was initially refused because League games were also being played that night.

After the controversy of the players' dispute and the television negotiations, the voting at the 1961 Annual Meeting was a more predictable affair, with all four retiring clubs being re-elected: Chester (45), Exeter (44), Barrow (35) and Hartlepools (32). Headington United, now called Oxford, showed the strength of their potential by polling 19 votes, and little knew then how soon their ship would come in. The other votes were for Bedford and Wigan (4 each), Chelmsford (3), Cambridge City (2), Hereford, Kettering, Romford, Scarborough and South Shields (1 each), and Bexleyheath and Welling, Gravesend and Northfleet, King's Lynn and Morecambe (no votes). But the most poignant set of figures was for poor, forgotten Gateshead. They attracted just 3 votes, a sure sign that their hopes were lost for a long time to come.

Unless, that is, the League was ever expanded, which in 1961 was not such an improbable thought. The history of the League is littered with attempts to come up with plans for reconstruction along more attractive lines, but none was more carefully considered or more exciting than the one which came immediately after the difficult 1960/1 season.

Called the 'Pattern for Football', the plan had originally been drawn up by Alan Hardaker and Joe Richards two years earlier as part of an overall package which included the establishment of the League Cup. Instead of embracing the plan in its entirety, however, the clubs, smelling extra money, had voted for the new cup and then had thrown out the rest. It was like a teacher offering his pupils sweets if they tidied up their desks, only to find that they grabbed the goodies and left the desks untouched.

The 'Pattern for Football' makes fascinating reading. Even now, some of the findings have relevance.

Hardaker's analysis of gates showed that in the First and Fourth Division, attendances were down, whereas in the Second and Third they were up. Promotion and relegation matches invariably attracted better attendances, so he recommended that a system of four up and four down would add to the public's interest (a point made by Bradford City as early as 1904, and campaigned for consistently over the years by Derby and Tottenham).

'The public likes excitement, tension and "sudden death" in their football matches', Hardaker reported. More clubs had to be involved in meaningful matches at the end of the season. To achieve this, he suggested that each division contain twenty clubs, with an expanded Fourth Division divided into two regional sections.

Not only would this have let the likes of Gateshead back into the competition, but the Management Committee took the idea further by reviving the suggestion that any club seeking re-election two years in a row should automatically lose their place. Such a rule would have saved Gateshead, but cost several other clubs dearly.

Surprising as it may seem, in view of the fact that the League Cup had just begun, Hardaker went on to state that there was too much football. In fact, his original reconstruction plan included the League Cup only because, with five divisions of twenty clubs each, there would be fewer fixtures and therefore more free dates for a knock-out competition.

Hardaker reasoned that in one season, a hundred League clubs would play 1900 League matches, as opposed to the existing structure in which ninety-two played 2028 games. The League Cup would make up the shortfall.

It was a perfect formula for increasing the number of meaningful games; more knock-out cup matches, more promotion and relegation issues to be settled. The League Cup has to be seen in this context. It was never intended to add to the fixture list, it was meant to comp-lement a shorter one.

Furthermore, according to Hardaker's 'Pattern for Football' the League Cup should have been played at the beginning of the season in regional groups, as occurred in Scotland. Hardaker showed that for the past three seasons, gates had shown a 25 per cent deficit during the months of August and September. The League competition should therefore start later – he suggested in October – and reach its climax in late May or early June when better weather could be expected.

It should also be noted that Hardaker's pro-posals included an amendment of the voting system at League meetings, so that a three-quarters majority would no longer be required for changes in the regulations.

Underlying all Hardaker's thoughts was a concern that under the existing system, the public was beginning to regard League fixtures as secondary to European competitions (remember, this was 1961). He might have been able to do something about that, but he was powerless when faced with the fact that leisure habits were changing in an era when the British were supposed to have 'never had it so good'.

Concluding his report, Hardaker therefore posed one question which he clearly felt important: 'Are gates down because the public resent the attitude of the modern player?'

Only a professionally conducted research campaign could answer that, and thus for the first time the League appointed a public relations firm, Garland-Crompton, to look into the whole problem. This was to cost £6800, and the company's findings were, arguably, a waste of time.

But in all its other recommendations, Alan Hardaker's 'Pattern for Football' was the most remarkable document any League official had ever formulated. It represented the start of a new era of self-awareness, and it prodded the Management Committee into reviving the reconstruction plan which had been left in the rubbish bin after the clubs had made a grab for the League Cup.

Had the 'Pattern of Football' been implemented when it finally came to the vote in 1963, the course of League football in the following decades would have been quite different. But, as this history has shown time and time again, it mattered not how pro-gressive the Committee was if the clubs con-tinued to bury their heads in the sand. Hardaker recalled ruefully:

'We were wasting our time. It was defeated by selfishness and shallow thinking. It was rejected because, myopically, too many clubs could see no farther than their own little worlds. They were not interested in the future of the game as a whole. Their one concern was self-preservation. They closed their eyes and minds to anything which even remotely thre-atened their status and life-style.'

Some club chairmen, Hardaker wrote scathingly, would not even accept the arith-metical fact that five divisions with a hundred clubs would play fewer games than four div-isions of ninety-two!

That the package was not accepted was, it must be said, partly due to a slight loss of confidence by the Management Committee. The final paragraph of the 'Pattern for Football' stated that the proposals had to be considered as a whole, not voted upon piecemeal. This was to avoid the clubs running off with the jam but leaving the bread and butter behind, as had happened with the League Cup.

Not wishing to be seen as authoritarian, or for non-acceptance of the package to be seen as a vote of no confidence, the Committee dropped this final paragraph at the last minute. Hardaker called this a major tactical error. He also criticized the Committee for not lobbying hard enough to win support among the clubs.

This was all the more unfortunate in the light of the fact that newspaper and television opinion wholeheartedly endorsed the 'Pattern for Football'.

By the time the proposals reached their final form, the matter had been up for discussion for twenty months. A meeting in March 1963 showed healthy support, but not enough, and so it proved at the vital Annual Meeting the following June. The 'Pattern for Football' needed to attract 37 votes to gain the necessary three-quarters majority. It fell 8 votes short of the target.

Once again, the man they called 'the dictator' had failed to get his way.

This history has already stated that the greatest opportunity ever missed by the League occurred when pools money was resisted in 1936. The rejection of the 'Pattern for Football' in 1963 might well have been the League's second most crucial mistake. Many of the problems the plan aimed to eradicate still exist, most especially the likelihood that every few years one or two clubs will be on the verge of financial collapse.

Few eyebrows were raised when reports of Accrington Stanley's difficulties started to become public in late 1961. Then, in December, the club was prohibited from any further transfer deals, since they already owed £3000 to other clubs. The gravity of their situation was further highlighted when a local alderman launched a £20,000 'Save Stanley' campaign and managed to raise only £450.

By February 1962 Stanley were bottom of the Fourth Division. Gates were down to 1500, when the break-even point was 3000. It really looked like the end for Accrington's second League club, until Burnley's chairman Bob Lord – no friend of the Committee at that time – offered to rescue Stanley. By 23 February the crisis seemed over, as Lord's friend and former Stanley chairman Sam Pilkington stepped into the breach.

But the right hand man of the Lord did'st not valiantly. On 5 March a creditors' meeting revealed that the club was £62,000 in debt, with the telephone, gas, water and electricity on the point of being disconnected. Bob Lord immediately withdrew, admitting that he hadn't realized the enormity of the club's plight, and within twenty-four hours a directors' letter was sent to Lytham, offering Accrington's resignation.

Reaction the next day was predictably horrified, and not only in Accrington. Already newspapers were asking who would be next. (In fact, they haven't stopped asking.) The supporters were especially miffed because Stanley had been one of the first League clubs to run its own pools competition, which raised nearly £28,000 before the police ordered it to close for technical breaches.

Many locals blamed Stanley's demise on the directors' decision to buy a second-hand 4000-seater stand from the Aldershot Tattoo ground in 1958. Although it had cost only £2000 to buy, by the time it had been dismantled, transported and re-erected the cost was nearer £20,000. To pay off this debt Stanley sold their leading scorer, George Stewart (147 goals in four seasons) to Coventry City. Since then, Stanley's fortunes on the pitch had rapidly diminished.

Even so, it was still hard to believe that this wasn't just another sticky patch in the chequered history of yet another struggling northern club.

There was only one chance of a reprieve. Not all the club's directors had been told of the letter of resignation, and on 8 March the club president, Sir William Cocker, sent another letter asking the League to disregard the first one. Cocker maintained that a handful of prominent local businessmen had put up the money to save Stanley after all, and that their action had been approved by the creditors, most of whom were local traders who didn't wish to be cast in the role of executioners.

But which letter would the League accept? Three days of high tension followed, as all Accrington awaited the decision of the Management Committee, which was due to meet in London on 11 March. Accrington's mayor sent a telegram pleading for clemency. One of the directors and the club solicitor put the case for survival in person.

To no avail. As history has recorded, the first letter was accepted. Accrington Stanley thus became the second club in the League's history, after Wigan Borough, to drop out in mid season (Leeds City didn't drop out, they were pushed).

If the football world was astounded, Sir William Cocker was furious. 'The League has treated us shabbily and I regard this decision as a personal affront', he told the press. Above all, he blamed the reconstruction of the regional Third Division in 1958. 'I was always against the plan because I knew the clubs would be faced with crippling expense bills and that many of them would eventually be forced out. Perhaps that is what the League wanted, because football has become big business and the scheme for higher wages for players has not helped small clubs out.'

If the League had intended to make an example of Accrington in an attempt to weed out the weaker clubs, in the light of subsequent events it must be said that it failed miserably. Ever since 1962, each time a club looked like going to the wall the media have raised the spectre of Accrington Stanley. Yet Accrington's experience has never been repeated.

Rather than setting off a chain reaction, their fate has, if anything, acted as a spur to troubled clubs. No one wants to do 'an Accrington Stanley'.

Nevertheless Cocker was wrong in three ways. Firstly, the Management Committee was told by legal advisers that according to established legal precedent, the League had to accept the first letter of resignation. This the Committee regretted deeply.

Secondly, football had not become big business only recently. It had been big business ever since 1888. Had he forgotten that Stanley's precursors, Accrington FC, had dropped out of the League sixty-nine years earlier because of their ailing finances and poor support?

Thirdly, the reconstruction plan mooted by the Committee in 1961 depended on more clubs being in the League, not fewer, and it offered the prospect of a regionalized Fourth Division.

The inescapable truth of the matter was that Accrington Stanley were the victims of circumstance, being situated only four miles from Blackburn and six from Burnley, both of whom were in the First Divison at the time. It was, as a result, impossible for Stanley's fixtures to avoid clashing with at least one of their neighbours'.

Events could, of course, have been quite different. Success and failure in football will always hinge upon the bounce of a ball, a point won or lost, the fitness of a player, or any borderline decision. But bad management can seldom be masked.

During the 1950s the prospects seemed quite rosy for Stanley. As recently as 1958 they had finished second in the Third Division North (with Stewart as top scorer), and at the time they resigned they had been in the Fourth Division for only one full season. The directors had initiated one of the first club pools to operate in the League. But, as Gateshead had discovered, life was seldom fair, and with low gates and mounting debts it would have taken an enormous cash injection to stave off the inevitable.

Sir William bravely announced that he would continue the fight to save Accrington, if necessary in the courts, but events soon overtook him. The best players were quickly signed up by other clubs, including one Mike Ferguson, who moved to Ewood Park. Four years later Aston Villa paid £60,000 for Ferguson, almost exactly the amount Stanley had owed when the axe fell.

(In fact, Accrington Stanley did struggle on in the Lancashire Combination until finally folding in January 1966, while their once well-appointed ground, Peel Park, went into terminal decline until being reduced to a school's playing pitch in the mid 1970s. But Stanley live again. They were re-formed in 1970, and now play at a different ground. Gates are down to a few hundred, but compared with their non-League peers they do quite well, proving that it takes more than just economics to kill off a football club.)

Perhaps the greatest irony of 1962 was that in the same year as Accrington succumbed to their debts, the League itself showed a loss of nearly £23,000, the biggest deficit ever recorded.

Part of the reason for this was the Government's decision to raise the level of the pools betting tax to a swingeing 33 per cent. Soon afterwards, the Government took the opposite course with horse racing, passing the Betting Levy Act by which bookmakers would have to contribute towards the upkeep of horse racing and race courses.

Since 1962 the tax burden on football pools has increased still further to 42.5 per cent, whilst that affecting horse racing has remained fairly constant around 7–8 per cent. As Joe Richards said at the time, echoing the words of Accrington Stanley loyalists: 'It isn't fair!'

Football was being made to carry a burden expected of no other sport in Britain. Representations were made to Parliament, the League even arranging a dinner at Westminster

to brief the Government. But the response after several meetings was the same as it has been until the present day: no deal.

As a result of the League's unprecedented loss in 1961/2, something had to give. As a result, the amount payable from the Provident Fund dropped sharply from 9 per cent to 5 per cent, much to the horror of the PFA.

Clubs also had to make sacrifices. They were asked to resume their responsibility for paying their employees' 10 per cent pension contributions, and for paying talent money, which the League had taken on only a few years previously when the coffers had been full.

Thus, all too abruptly ended the golden age of prosperity, begun when pools money had started to flow in, three years earlier. It was an almost exact repeat of the situation which had existed between 1918 and 1922 – pride coming before the fall.

Yet this time, the cause for concern was not a general depression in the economy. The early 1960s were quite buoyant in Britain generally. What caused the League's dilemma was that more money was being earned from non-footballing sources than ever before – pools and television mainly – but it just wasn't enough. For years the League had refused to accept outside money, and had survived. Now it had more money than Fred Howarth or Will Cuff could ever have dreamed of, but it was still unhappy. Perhaps Charlie Sutcliffe had been right after all.

But still the outsiders clamoured to get in. No sooner had Accrington stumbled than seven non-League clubs swooped in on

---

Between 1888 and 1988 both the Football League and the FA have had five Secretaries. All five League Secretaries were born in the North of England, but with the exception of Derbyshire-born Denis Follows (appointed in 1961), the FA men have all been Southerners.

Lytham with applications to take their place. By June 1962 there were no less than twenty-six non-League clubs vying for election, along with Chester, Doncaster and Hartlepools.

Not surprisingly, in view of Accrington's sudden demise, the members closed ranks at the Annual Meeting and re-elected all three, with 46, 45 and 40 votes respectively. And equally predictably, Oxford United, champions of the Southern League for the second year in succession, were fourth in the list, with 39 votes.

One northern club had gone, and a southern club taken its place. It was a pattern to be repeated several times over the next two decades.

The only other clubs to receive any votes were Wigan (5), Chelmsford (4), Gateshead (4), Cambridge City (2), Worcester (2), and one each for Bath, Hereford, King's Lynn, Morecambe and New Brighton. No support came for Bedford, Bexleyheath and Welling, Corby Town, Folkestone, Gravesend and Northfleet, Guildford, Kettering, North Shields, Poole Town, Romford, Scarborough, Sittingbourne, South Shields, Wellington Town or Yeovil.

Oxford entered the fold at an important stage in the League's development. As it approached its seventy-fifth anniversary (at the same time as the FA prepared to celebrate its own centenary), the appalling winter of 1962 brought the postponement of a record number of matches: over four hundred in the League, and twenty-nine of the thirty-two Third Round FA Cup ties. On two Saturdays, 12 January and 2 February, only four matches in the total League programme were completed.

For four shivering weeks in succession, the pools had to be cancelled. This meant a severe loss of income from both the pools and the 4 per cent gate levy. At one stage the situation seemed so desperate that the Canadian FA offered the use of their grounds to stage League matches during the big freeze.

Another matter facing the League at this time was the selection of clubs to play in the Inter-Cities Fairs Cup. The organizers, under the chairmanship of the new FIFA president Sir Stanley Rous, wanted to invite Birmingham City and Sheffield Wednesday, based on their status as cities holding industrial fairs. The League felt, however, that qualification should be based on a club's League placings.

But while Burnley, who were eligible according to the League, were originally turned down because they represented a mere town, there was consternation south of the border when Dunfermline – from a town smaller than Burnley – were invited by UEFA to join the competition. (It is interesting to note that during the debate on this question, Liverpool, soon to become the conquerors of Europe, stated that they had no interest in the competition.)

If the status of Burnley was hardly an issue in European terms in 1962, no one could ignore the fact that the First Division Championship had just been won by Ipswich Town, who twenty-four years earlier had been in the Southern League. Leyton Orient were enjoying (if that is the right word) their one and only season in Division One, Peterborough were doing well in Division Three, together with Northampton, who were First Division bound, while just-a-town Burnley had nearly won the double.

The League has always given every team a chance, big and small, but the period from 1960 up to the present day has shown the greatest movement of all between the divisions. It began with Peterborough, but Oxford would be the first of the truly upwardly mobile newcomers.

CHAPTER TWENTY-THREE
The Unlikely Revolutionary

The year 1963 provided another watershed in League history. This was the year the Beatles shot to fame, and John F. Kennedy was shot in Dallas. The League celebrated its seventy-fifth anniversary, the FA recorded its hundredth anniversary, and Tottenham Hotspur became the first League club to win a European competiton, the Cup Winners' Cup, at Rotterdam on 15 May.

After the abolition of the maximum wage and the dreadful winter of 1962, optimism reigned supreme; gates were up slightly, England was going to host the 1966 World Cup Finals, and the seventeen-year-old George Best made his debut for Manchester United. Best heralded a new breed of footballer, one which belonged to the Swinging 'Sixties both in hairstyle and lifestyle. The days of the Brylcreem boys were numbered.

At the same time, bingo mania swept Britain, and, surprisingly in view of the League's traditional hostility towards gambling, the Committee allowed clubs to play host to this new craze during the close season. It also relaxed its normally strict attitude towards the staging of other events at League grounds. Birmingham were allowed to host a boxing match, while there was wrestling at Doncaster, Bradford, Scunthorpe and Peterborough.

But for the Management Committee two major events dominated the year. The first was a series of scandals alleging the involvement of between twenty and a hundred players in a well-co-ordinated betting ring. The trail of events seemed to lead back to the late 1950s and a spate of newspaper allegations claiming that at several clubs, one or two players had deliberately thrown matches in order to win fixed-odds bets.

As a result of various tip-offs, Alan Hardaker had himself interviewed one of the ringleaders, the much-travelled striker Jimmy Gauld, in 1961, and handed his findings to the Lancashire County Police. Hardaker later wrote: '. . . even if only half of the information fed to me was true, it still meant football was sick'.

The story has been told in detail elsewhere (for example, in *Soccer in Dock* by the same author – see Bibliography), so suffice it to say here that after three years of difficult but unsuccessful investigations by the League, private investigators and the police, the betting ring was finally broken by a series of sensational articles in *The People* newspaper. The main reason why they succeeded where others had failed was money. They paid Gauld to shop his former accomplices.

The final curtain fell on this unsavoury business in 1965, when ten players were banned from football for life and sentenced to various terms of imprisonment. The most famous of those convicted were three Sheffield Wednesday players, Tony Kay, Peter Swan and David Layne. But, according to Hardaker, 'For every player caught, there were another twenty who escaped for want of evidence against them.'

Thankfully, the bribery scandals of the early 1960s turned out to have been an aberration, precipitated by changes in the betting laws and the selfish greed of a coterie of Third and Fourth Division players who fancied making a quick buck at the end of their careers. Further changes in the betting laws and the draconian nature of the punishments – especially compared with several similar cases abroad – have hopefully ruled out a similar occurrence in the Football League.

But the bribery scandals cannot, and should not, be dismissed. They threatened the entire integrity of the competition, and gave a warning to everyone in the game of the need to be vigilant.

While *The People* was regaling the nation with its shocking revelations about Gauld and his fraudsters, another courtroom drama was about to unfold which was to have deeper consequences for every player.

After the abolition of the maximum wage, two issues on the PFA's agenda remained unsettled: the setting up of a national Negotiating Committee (as agreed in 1961), and the reform of the retain and transfer system.

The first issue was eventually settled in June 1963, when the Negotiating Committee was set up under the independent chairmanship of Ellis Smith, Labour MP for Stoke and a long-standing friend to football (although the position was originally offered to the Chancellor of the Exchequer, Selwyn Lloyd).

The second issue was not so easily resolved.

'There had never been any doubt in my mind that the moment one player stepped forward to challenge the legality of the old retain and transfer system its days were numbered', recalled Alan Hardaker. The Players' Union had tried unsuccessfully with the Kingaby Case in 1912, and since the early 1950s had been on the look-out for another dispute suitable enough to put up as a test case. The problem, however, was not so much finding an aggrieved player; there were many. It was finding the right player, one who was well known, respectable and, above all, determined.

George Eastham was the perfect candidate.

The son of a former player and one of the foremost international midfielders of his day, Eastham had gone into dispute with his club, Newcastle, in 1960. He had asked for a transfer on three occasions, but each time, United had refused. The chairman announced that he'd

sooner see Eastham shovel coal before he left Newcastle.

And when the player appealed to the Management Committee, it refused to interfere, since Newcastle were not actually breaking any rules. Under the retain and transfer system, if the club offered the same terms as before, they could hold on to the man as long as they wanted.

In private, however, the Committee, through one of its members, Wilf Taylor, begged Newcastle to release the player, although not because it approved any change in the retain and transfer system. Far from it. As Alan Hardaker predicted in 1963, without the system there would be 'complete anarchy' in football (even though he accepted its basic unfairness). But bad publicity arising from cases like Eastham's did neither the League nor the system any good at all.

Eastham's dilemma wasn't new, but on this occasion the player was so determined to leave that rather than play against his will, he left football and went to London, where a Surrey businessman, Ernie Clay (a friend of Eastham's father and later chairman of Fulham), found him a job as a salesman.

This was an extraordinary step for a footballer in his prime to take, and showed just how determined he was to leave Newcastle.

Marshall Cavendish's *Book of Football* (1972) described Eastham as 'an unlikely revolutionary. A frail figure on the field ... he was unobtrusive off it. Soberly dressed, he would not have been out of place behind the counter of a bank. But he was also stubborn...'

After five months out of the game, a period in which Eastham was branded a troublemaker by managers, directors and even some of his fellow players, Newcastle finally relented and Eastham signed for Arsenal, in November 1960. The fee was £47,500, of which Eastham was entitled to £20.

Rather than let the matter drop, however, the PFA persuaded him that his case offered the perfect opportunity to challenge the system, if only he would take legal action against New-castle United, its directors and manager, plus the FA and the Football League. Reluctant at first, Eastham eventually agreed. That was just a month or so before the strike threat in January 1961.

Once the maximum wage was abolished, there were many commentators who felt that Eastham had made his point, and now that he was at least able to earn a decent wage wasn't it time for him, in Tom Finney's words, to 'lay down his pistol'? But money wasn't the target. It was the bonds which tied a player to his club which Eastham wanted to shoot away.

Legal proceedings being so slow and complex, the hearing did not actually come to court until 11 June 1963.

For all his deep conviction, Cliff Lloyd of the PFA was extremely nervous as it began. He spent two hours in the witness box, knowing that if the union lost it would face legal bills of £25,000, at a time when its entire assets amounted to less than half that amount.

Wilf Taylor gave evidence for Newcastle, while Hardaker was the League's chief witness. He later recalled that, after having given evidence, he returned to his seat to find that his briefcase had been stolen, in the High Court of all places!

Mr Justice Wilberforce finally delivered his judgement on 4 July. However much the League could argue to the contrary, Eastham had won. Wilberforce found that although the transfer system itself was not illegal, the rule which allowed a player to be retained was, under common law, 'an undue restraint of trade'.

What was legally defensible in 1912 was *ultra vires* in 1963, and the second of the two freedoms for which Jimmy Hill had fought two years earlier finally came into effect. There were now no restrictions on wages, and no holding players at the end of their contracts, against their wishes.

The Eastham judgement did not mean total freedom of contract (which would not come

until 1978). Clubs could still ask for a fee at the end of a player's contract, and wait until they were offered that fee. But it did herald a real revolution in the relationship between the player and his club. Suddenly, the directors had to start dealing with players on a more equal basis.

Naturally, the clubs were greatly perturbed by this interference in their traditional approach to industrial relations. They were like captains of industry suddenly asked to consult with the men on the shop floor. Several direc-tors predicted the end of the game, while small clubs feared that the richer ones would grab all the best players.

But, in truth, there was not too much call for panic. After all, Wilberforce had, in his 16,000-word judgement, defended the prin-ciples of the transfer system. The payment of fees for players would still continue. Some clubs actually welcomed his decision because it resulted, first, in the introduction of option clauses, which allowed them to negotiate longer contracts (previously limited to two years) and second, better bonuses (previously limited to £4 for a win, £2 for a draw).

The PFA secretary, Cliff Lloyd, went so far as to say that the Eastham case and the abol-ition of the maximum wage were among the main reasons for England going on to win the World Cup in 1966. That is arguable. What is irrefutable is that after July 1963 a great many clubs and players had to re-examine their relationships.

Like everything in football, change didn't come overnight. Once Wilberforce had made his judgement, the League and FA had to face the task of redrawing their regulations, a long process which began at a gathering of club chairmen at League headquarters on 5 November 1963. 'Gentlemen, this is probably one of the most – if not the most – important meeting held in connection with League affairs since the foundation', Joe Richards informed the chairmen dramatically.

He reminded them that in the past, the Man-

agement Committee had made recommendations which the clubs had turned
down. This had largely resulted in the PFA's
victory in 1961. But the Eastham case had to
be handled differently, warned Richards, since
if the clubs made the wrong decision it was
only a small step away from the players
winning their ultimate aim, and that was complete freedom of movement at the end of contracts.

Burnley's outspoken chairman, Bob Lord, a
constant thorn in the Committee's side during
this period, proposed stubbornly that the
League ignore Wilberforce's judgement
entirely. Fortunately wiser counsel prevailed
and the Management Committee was voted
full powers to redraw the regulations in consultation with the PFA. It took the best part
of a year to do this, the basis of the agreement
being as follows:

• Players in dispute were to be given the right
of appeal to the Management Committee,
failing which they could then take their case to
an independent tribunal. The biggest breakthrough as far as the players were concerned
was that for the first time the PFA was to be
allowed to represent them. This was a real
advance for the union. No longer would an
inarticulate or shy player be forced to argue
his case in intimidating circumstances.

• Benefit levels were now to be left to the
discretion of clubs, in negotiation with the
player. If the player was then transferred he
would receive a percentage of the fee, unless
he had asked for a transfer in the first place.

• The PFA accepted that transfer fees were
part and parcel of the game, and agreed that a
player could not demand to be transferred to
a particular club, thus giving that club the
chance to offer a lower fee.

• In order not to extend contracts too long,
option clauses were to be for a period of no
longer than the original contract. At the end

of the second contractual period, the club had
to offer the same or better terms.

These new conditions, approved in June 1964,
gave rise to a flood of appeals from players,
which meant, of course, more work for the
Management Committee. For example, in September the Committee had to make judgements on twenty-four individuals.

But Eastham's victory did not herald an
entirely fresh phase in the relationship between
the League and the PFA. In 1965 the League
gave notice that it intended to reduce the scale
of the Provident Fund and replace it with
an all-embracing insurance scheme to cover
players. This decision, combined with an argument over television fees, brought the two
parties into conflict once again, but at least
there was now a Joint Committee to keep the
parties talking and avoid another strike threat.

Having lost one battle in the courts, the
League initiated a minor campaign of its own
in 1963. The Annual Meeting gave notice of
a new, tougher attitude towards non-League
applications. In all, twenty-two clubs applied
that year, but of these, ten were found to
have signed players from League clubs without
going through the correct procedures. To dis-
courage the spread of this practice, the guilty
ten were struck off the list of nominees.

For the twelve left in the hat, the story was
the same as ever, with a handful of votes being
spread across the board. However obvious it
seems in retrospect, had the non-Leaguers
combined to choose just one or two clubs for
nomination they would have vastly improved
their chances of breaking the barrier, as Peterborough and Oxford had done in the preceding
three years.

But non-League solidarity was still a long
way off in 1963, and the list of failed applicants
continued to make weary reading.

For the record, in 1963 the four retiring
clubs were re-elected: Bradford City (47 votes),
Lincoln City (47), Chester (43) and Hartlepools
(34). Followers of Lincoln might note wistfully

that Scarborough's application received only 5 votes. Other unsuccessful applicants were Gateshead (4), Guildford (3), Morecambe (2), Romford (2), and one each for New Brighton, South Shields, Wellington, Weymouth and Yeovil. No votes were recorded for Bexley-heath and Welling, or Corby Town.

The pattern was repeated over the next two years. In 1964, York (48 votes), Southport (45), Barrow (42) and Hartlepools (36) were each re-elected. For Hartlepools it was their fifth application in a row, a dismal record which might have jeopardized their place had a strong enough non-League club been waiting in the wings. As it was, their nearest challengers were Wigan (5), followed by Gateshead and Romford (4 each), Yeovil (3), South Shields, New Brighton and Guildford (2 each), and one vote each for Gloucester, Morecambe and Weymouth. Bexley, Poole Town and Scarborough received no votes. A further eight non-League clubs were deleted from the ballot paper for signing League players without consent.

In 1965 another three clubs were barred for the same reason, not that they had had much of a chance in any event. Lincoln (48), Stockport (45), Barrow (41) and Halifax (41) were comfortably re-elected. Bedford and Gateshead attracted 4 votes each, Guildford 3, Hereford and Wigan 2 each, and single votes were recorded for Cambridge United, Morecambe, Romford, South Shields, Wellington and Wimbledon. Bexley, Corby and New Brighton won no votes.

While the Old Pals' Act kept the non-League clubs at bay for the rest of the decade, the mid 1960s did see great changes to the membership of the Management Committee. After the appearance of only a few new faces throughout the previous decade, and none between 1957 and 1963, in just three years half the personnel changed.

Harry French of Middlesbrough died in 1963, a few weeks before he was due to receive a long-service medal. At the same time, his old friend from Chesterfield, Harold Shentall, stood down. A few months later, Joe Mears of Chelsea resigned when he was elected chairman of the FA. The fourth departure was that of Norman Banks of Bolton, in 1964. Their places were taken by Sydney Collings of Sunderland, Arthur Would of Grimsby, Sam Bolton of Leeds and Michael Gliksten of Charlton. (For short biographies of these men, see Appendix Two.)

The new men were to suffer a baptism of fire, for in October 1964 they faced what amounted to a vote of no confidence from Everton and four other clubs, who objected to the recent signing of an agreement with the BBC.

The rebellion did not succeed, for which a nation can be grateful, because … stand by, cue cameras, run titles and … action! *Match of the Day* had arrived, and Saturday nights would never be the same again in millions of households all over Britain.

Saturday-night televised football was not entirely new. For several years, the BBC had shown up to half an hour of televised excerpts on *Sports Report*, for which they paid the League £8000 per season. But the one-year agreement signed in August 1964 for *Match of the Day* provided for a completely new format, with up to fifty-five minutes of one match being shown on the new channel, BBC 2, which then reached only a very limited audience. For this, the BBC paid £20,000, and agreed to give no advance publicity before 4.00 p.m. on Saturday afternoons.

When it first went out on 22 August 1964, few could have imagined how deeply engrained the programme was to become in the national psyche. That night, a tiny audience of only 75,000 tuned in to see highlights from Liverpool's First Division match against Arsenal, not much more than watched the actual game live at Anfield. But from this humble beginning, *Match of the Day* was to set a pattern which prevailed until the mid 1980s.

Everton's well-orchestrated campaign of

opposition against the television agreement was met with a tough and uncompromising response by the Committee, reminiscent of the days of Sutcliffe and Cuff. At an Extraordinary General Meeting, Everton were told that the Committee resented their high-handed attitude.

If the Committee could not get the clubs' support on this matter, warned Joe Richards, the result 'must be obvious to all – absolute chaos – because the Management Committee would no longer be able to govern the League within the constitutional framework...'

It was the old, old cry. The clubs gave the Committee powers to act, but when it acted, took exception.

Arsenal banned the cameras after an unfavourable remark from one of the programme's commentators about their team. Burnley and Everton refused on principle to have their matches televised. This was fine with the Committee, provided that these clubs didn't expect a share of the television fee, which in 1966 was worth £463 per club – about one-tenth of the sum each club received from the 4 per cent pool.

Meanwhile, anxious not to be left behind by the BBC, commercial television, through its news service ITN, submitted plans to provide a Saturday lunchtime programme with match clips, interviews and news. Then, in 1965, two commercial companies paid the League £3000 to show thirty recorded minutes of a League match on Sunday afternoons.

Thus, football's apparently relentless colonization of the British weekend continued, making it possible for a real devotee to see League matches on Friday evening and Saturday afternoon, then spend a further hour or two in front of the television watching the Saturday preview, plus match highlights on both Saturday and Sunday. There was even a move in 1966 to televise a live game on Thursday evenings.

All this soccer on the box prompted wide discussion as to its effect on gates, which in

Match of the Day's first season slumped by about 3 per cent. Certainly, the fees from television were now becoming increasingly important to the League. For example, the Inter-League game at Villa Park in March 1962, yielded receipts of just under £4000, compared with a television fee of £2500. And the gap would narrow.

One new factor in the decline of attendances was almost certainly the growing number of reports of crowd trouble, first acknowledged in the League's minutes in late 1963. It is not the intention of this book to chronicle the growth of football hooliganism – there are already studies which cover the subject far better than is possible here – but the timing of the League's first reference to the problem is noteworthy.

The year 1963/4 saw unprecedented scenes of gang violence in Britain, recorded with paternalistic horror by newsreels and sensational headlines in newspapers. The violence reached its height with the Whitsun riots in Margate and other seaside resorts between so-called 'mods' and 'rockers'. Swinging London was accompanied by swinging bicycle chains.

Football had nothing to do with this outbreak of modern hooliganism, but it does seem more than coincidental that the fighting spread to the terraces at roughly the same time as the police were clamping down on it in places like Margate. The violence remained, it just switched to a more promising battleground.

The mid 1960s was a period of great intensity in League football. Crowds were becoming more overtly partisan, more vocal. Players were becoming pin-ups, men whose words and deeds were scrutinized by a much wider audience than ever before. Yet, although League football had never enjoyed so much national publicity, its live audience was dropping.

Television and violence were two possible causes. Another, curiously, was the advent of European football. In 1965/6, gates were down by 434,000, of which 415,000 were missing from games at West Ham, Leeds, Chelsea, Everton and Manchester United.

Since these were the clubs competing in Europe that season, the statistics strongly suggest that fans were not deserting the game so much as becoming more selective about which games they went to see. As in the mid 1950s, if there was something novel on offer, the first competition to suffer would be the League programme.

Then came World Cup fever, stimulated by the fact that English football was already feeling rather bullish. In May 1965 West Ham became the second League team to win a European competition, the Cup Winners' Cup, in a thrilling game at Wembley. A year later, the Hammers reached the semi-final of the same competition, and Liverpool were beaten finalists.

Manchester United reached the European Cup semi-finals, while in the Fairs Cup both Chelsea and Leeds reached the semi-finals and were beaten only after play-offs. Thus, English League football had much to feel proud about in the weeks before the World Cup.

It also helped, in the opinion of some, that Britain had in Harold Wilson a prime minister who was a devout follower of football, and Huddersfield Town in particular. Also in his government was a former League referee, Denis Howell, and MPs such as Michael Foot,

almost as ardent a supporter of Plymouth Argyle as he was of nuclear disarmament. Football never had so many friends in government as it had during that glorious summer of '66.

As the World Cup approached, the League did all it could to help with the preparations. Simpson's, a smart store in London's Piccadilly, made a display of League trophies and memorabilia. England manager Alf Ramsey was given full power to use Inter-League matches for his build-up.

In Ramsey's 'Football League' squad for the match against the Scottish League on 16 March 1966 at Newcastle, eight of the members of the final World Cup team were selected (the missing three being West Ham's trio, Hurst, Peters and Moore, who were otherwise engaged in the two-legged finals of the League Cup).

Can one claim, therefore, that contrary to popular belief, Ramsey had in fact hit on his winning team long before the actual final? As the man would have said himself: 'Most certainly not!' The Scottish League won, 3–1.

With six weeks to go before the World Cup kicked off, Joe Richards formally announced his decision to stand down as President of the League, after nine years at the helm. His decision was no surprise; he was now aged seventy-eight and not in the best of health. Indeed, Alan Hardaker later hinted that there had been pressure on him to stand down a couple of years earlier.

But rather than have him retire there and then, and thus miss the honour of representing the League during the World Cup, in a rare display of sentiment the clubs unanimously voted for Richards to remain President until 1 August – that is, two days after the World Cup Final.

It was no more than he deserved. Joe Richards' presidency was arguably more eventful and more difficult than that of any of his predecessors. Under Richards the League at last secured the copyright of the fixtures, he

> **The use of substitutes in League matches was first proposed in 1960, but not accepted until five years later, and then for injuries only. The first number twelve to see League action was Charlton's Keith Peacock at Bolton on 21 August 1965. In 1975, clubs were instructed to hold up boards showing the number of the player to be substituted. In 1971, Everton tried to introduce a rule allowing for two substitutes per team in each match, but this was not sanctioned until 1986 for FA Cup and Littlewoods Cup matches, and not until 1987 for League games.**

oversaw the complete redrafting of the League's regulations, and he was instrumental in the formation of the International Liaison Committee, which did so much to bring the European leagues closer together.

He presided over the League's reorganization in 1958, the move to Lytham, the setting up of the League Cup, the abolition of the maximum wage, the Eastham case, the bribery scandals, the entry of Britain into European competitions, the advent of regular televised football, the introduction of substitutes (for injured players only) in 1965, and, perhaps as troublesome as all of these matters combined, he had had to work with, and often against, a group of demanding, strident club chairmen who rarely allowed the Management Committee a moment's peace.

Despite, or perhaps because of, these enormous problems, Joe Richards emerged as one of the League's strongest ever presidents; not a figurehead like McKenna, not an organizer like Sutcliffe, but a captain, steering his often mutinous ship through stormy waters.

By unanimous decision, Richards' successor was Len Shipman of Leicester City, a man whom the President and other older members of the Committee had been grooming as his successor for several years. But the Barnsley man did not leave the scene altogether. He was unanimously voted a Life Member of the League, and kept his place on the Management Committee as a Vice President.

Richards' last Annual Meeting as President was on 4 June 1966. And an optimistic meeting it was, too. Apart from the success of League clubs in Europe, Richards was able to report a healthy recovery in the League's finances, and, after a few months of negotiation, the decision to hold future League Cup Finals at Wembley Stadium – the dream which he had once said would never come true in his own lifetime.

The use of Wembley, plus the decision a year earlier to grant League Cup winners an automatic place in Europe, was the making of the competition. As a result, several of the clubs who had until then shunned the competition now relented. The League Cup was also proving more popular with the public. Average attendances rose by 16 per cent from the season before (even though League gates dropped slightly, by 1.6 per cent).

This news was met with great satisfaction all round. Those who had scoffed at 'Hardaker's folly' five years earlier, now thought it a jolly good idea after all.

In the 1966 re-election battle, three non-League clubs had their applications rejected on the grounds that they had signed League players without consent. That left fourteen clubs to challenge the four retiring clubs. The results were, as expected, that Lincoln (43 votes), Bradford City (42), Wrexham (40) and Rochdale (40) were each re-elected, ahead of Wigan (5), Cambridge United (5), Hereford (4), Bedford (3), Romford (2), Morecambe (2), Corby (1) and Wellington (1). Future FA Cup winners Wimbledon gained no votes; neither did Scarborough, Yeovil or Folkestone.

The meeting closed with a hearty vote of thanks and best wishes to the retiring Joe Richards, and the sending of a good-luck telegram to Alf Ramsey for the forthcoming weeks.

But if Barnsley's 'Mr Football' felt any twinges of sadness as he left the Annual Meeting, there was surely no prouder man cheering on Bobby Moore's victorious team at Wembley on 30 July. For not only was he President of the League, but he was now, since the birthday honours list, also Sir Joseph Richards.

Of couse, they were accustomed to knights, lords and earls at the FA, where even the Secretaries were given knighthoods. But not one single League administrator had been honoured in this way before. Sir Joe could not have wished for a finer climax to his period of office.

CHAPTER TWENTY-FOUR

Heroes and Villains

Victory against West Germany on 30 July put everyone in good heart for the beginning of Len Shipman's presidency. A crowd of over 35,000 packed into Plymouth's Home Park to see six of the World Cup winning team play for the Football League against the Irish League in a crushing 12–0 victory. Two of the goals were scored by George Eastham, a villain turned hero. Hat-trick man Geoff Hurst also managed a brace.

Meanwhile, many of those who attended League fixtures noticed something new in their progammes – an insert entitled *The Football League Review*. The League had been approached on several occasions during the previous years to bring out a rival publication to the rather dull *FA News* (which frequently printed articles regarded as hostile to the League). A magazine called *Soccer Review* offered itself to the League, and with £4000 guaranteed by the Management Committee, the experiment began under the editorship of Harry Brown, a Leicester-based journalist.

Its first edition, in late August 1966, carried a photograph of Len Shipman and Joe Richards on the cover. In an impassioned message to readers, Richards boldly asserted that the Football League was indeed the best in the world. The entry of English clubs to Europe was, said Richards, the biggest factor in the World Cup victory.

One article marked 'Official' (which came to mean that it was written by Alan Hardaker), decried the growing practice of crowds jeering the opposition. 'This is a juvenile form of mickey-taking and can only result in increased tension', said the *Review*.

Editor Harry Brown introduced himself by sniping at the new language of football, unveiled by 'experts' during the World Cup. Terms like 'sweeper-up', 'overlap', 'laying the ball off' were now common currency amongst those who were trying to baffle us with science, Brown complained. In his opinion, much of the football seen in the World Cup had been 'far less thrilling than the Football League variety'.

In another column, journalist Walter Pilkington reported that several club managers thought that the World Cup hadn't revealed anything they didn't know before. Pilkington called Ramsey's 4–3–3 formation a 'wingless abomination', adopted only as a means of playing the foreigners at their own game.

Such was the mood of August and September 1966. It seemed to proclaim: 'What was all the fuss about? We were the best after all!'

But League managers *had* learned some lessons, and the revolution in tactics which Ramsey had developed in 1966 would permeate the entire Football League within a couple of years, for better or for worse. And the *Football League Review*, from its rather unsteady editorial and financial beginnings, would quickly rise to command a circulation of 250,000 among sixty-two clubs, becoming something of an institution for the next eight and a half years. Editor Harry Brown also became the League's first public relations officer, appointed in February 1967. It was no sinecure.

No sooner had the Jules Rimet Trophy been tucked up at Lancaster Gate than League clubs were making it quite clear to the FA that they would no longer tolerate the existing number of calls made upon their international players.

Football League Review

Not since *Athletic News* ceased publication in 1930 had the League enjoyed the luxury of a national forum for its views. The FA had its own staid, predictable *FA News*, but the League always had to rely on commentators and journalists to put over the League's message.

The Football League Review kicked off in August 1966, and was badly designed, shakily written, but full of good intentions. Within a few years the format and style improved, and those journalists who had scoffed at it in the early days started to offer their own contributions.

Sadly, the *Review* could never quite pay for itself. Despite moving its headquarters from Leicester to Lytham and, at its peak, finding its way into the programmes of seventy-three League clubs, it lost £92,000 in its first year and didn't show a profit until 1970. In 1972 the publishing company was absorbed entirely into the League and the magazine was renamed *League Football*, but it still lost heavily, mainly because clubs were never charged the full rate for each copy. The final issue was on 31 December 1974.

The *Review* will be fondly remembered for many of is features: for Alan Hardaker's bullish articles on League affairs, for Walter Pilkington's statistical analyses, for those pictures of Fourth Division teams with which no other publication bothered, and perhaps above all for the top ten of the best-looking players. Did 36,908 female fans really send in votes for George Best in 1967/8?

Every little detail of the League was covered: from explanations of how the Provident Fund functioned to what a referee carried in his pockets, from details of the backroom staff at Bradford Park Avenue to thoughts from the President, Len Shipman. It was never sensational, it was often a touch earnest, but for thousands of supporters in the late 1960s and early 1970s *The Football League Review* was compulsive reading before kick-off, and a welcome contrast to the shallow trivia churned out in many of the football magazines of the period.

With its passing, there can be no doubt that the League lost a valued bridge between Lytham and the fans.

And as the new season opened, the number of spectators, perhaps overfed on their summer diet of televised football, did not increase as hoped (although later in the season, gates would rise), while the number of incidents of hooliganism did.

Nor was everything in the garden rosy during Len Shipman's first few months of office. Investigations into the affairs of both Peterborough and Port Vale began, Bradford City became the first club to receive a League grant to keep the club afloat (£6000 was handed over on a three-month loan), and Everton renewed their campaign against televised football by sending a circular to every League club, behind the backs of the Management Committee. Everton and Burnley maintained their refusal to be televised, and were joined by Liverpool and Bolton – who both abandoned their objections soon after, however (Burnley finally backed down in 1967).

But 1966/7 was no time to be despondent. If nothing else, the publication of the *Review* and Brown's appointment as public relations officer showed that at long last the League had seen the value of good communications. And the successful staging of the League Cup Final at Wembley on 4 March 1967 confirmed beyond doubt that the competition had come of age. A capacity crowd saw a tantalizing encounter which ended with Third Division Queen's Park Rangers defeating First Division West Bromwich Albion 3–2.

Len Shipman's first Annual Meeting as President was on 3 June 1967, and perhaps the greatest surprise was the election of Burnley's chairman Bob Lord to the Management Committee, in place of Dr Andrew Stephen, who had taken his leave to become chairman of the FA. Two more different men one can hardly imagine, not so much like chalk and cheese as cotton wool and Brillo pad.

Lord's relationship with the Committee had been, since 1956, troubled, to say the least. He was forever complaining about decisions and procedures, or making comments in the press to which the Committee objected. On one occasion he had to apologise for using abusive language to a linesman, on another the League minutes noted: 'It was decided unanimously that the Committee could not tolerate the irresponsible comments of Mr Lord.' The Committee alleged that Burnley seemed to have adopted a deliberate policy of causing annoyance.

In return, Lord accused Hardaker of being biased against his club, argued about expenses, referees, fines and medals, and, as we have seen, suggested that the League even ignore Mr Justice Wilberforce's judgement on the Eastham case.

Yet it could hardly be denied that under Lord's chairmanship, Burnley had enjoyed their best ever spell; champions in 1960, and almost double winners in 1962.

His election in 1967 no doubt caused Alan Hardaker and some of the Committee to wince at the time – it was rather like a stroppy customer being put on to the sales staff – but in fact, once Lord had experienced life from the other side of the counter, he quickly grasped the realities of League management. He may not have mellowed, but he certainly worked hard, and eventually he and Hardaker grew to form a mutual understanding.

There were no other surprises at the Annual Meeting. As usual, the four retiring clubs were comfortably re-elected: Lincoln City, making their third application in a row, received 46 votes, Bradford Park Avenue and York City 45 each, and Rochdale 38. The failed applicants were Wigan and Romford (5 each), Hereford (4), Bedford and Cambridge United (2 each), Chelmsford, Wellington, Wimbledon and Yeovil (1 each) and Cambridge City, Corby, Guildford, Kettering and Scarborough (no votes).

While the rising tide of hooliganism began to occupy much greater space on the back pages during the following season – especially after a referee was attacked at Millwall in October – one of the League's hardest decisions was how to deal with Third Division Peterborough United. After several investigations, it was found that the Posh had breached League regulations on two counts.

First, players had been offered an illegal bonus for a Cup tie against Sunderland, two seasons before. Regulations limited the bonus for Fourth Round matches to £6 per man; Peterborough's players had been offered £100 each. The money wasn't actually paid – Sunderland won the match 7–1.

Second, certain signing-on bonuses had been paid directly to players by the Supporters' Club. Peterborough had also broken two FA regulations concerning payment vouchers.

But, as usual, their biggest crime, their cardinal error, as Geoffrey Green pointed out in *The Times*, was to have been found out.

On the eve of the Management Committee's meeting to decide on the punishment, Peterborough's MP, Sir Harmar Nicholls, begged the League not to expel the club. Didn't the fact that all these illegal payments had been faithfully recorded in the board's minutes suggest naivety rather than calculation on the directors' part? Peterborough were the babes of the League, they knew not what they did.

The Management Committee would not accept that. As Len Shipman later recalled, none of the members flinched when it came to doing their duty that Tuesday in November. 'The Football League had to be master of the situation', he said. Clubs had to be taught a lesson. Clearly, his years of grooming under Joe Richards had not been forgotten.

In the past, such technical irregularities had been punished by heavy fines and the suspension of guilty officials. But this time the sentence was harsher. Not expulsion, but the next worse thing. There was already a £500 fine from Lancaster Gate for breaking the FA's rules, but for breaking League regulations Peterborough were to be demoted to the Fourth Division at the end of the season.

Since this quite devastating judgement was issued when the club was fourth in Division Three, after playing a quarter of its fixtures, the rest of Peterborough's season ceased to have any competitive meaning whatsoever. However well the team did, they would still go down, even if they won the Third Division Championship (which would have been extremely awkward for the Committee).

As a result, the judgement was slated in the press. J. L. Manning was as forthright as ever in the *Daily Mail*. The Management Committee, he said, had turned the Third Division into a farce. They had been 'willing to wound but afraid to strike'. And instead of punishing the guilty directors (most of whom were no longer with the club anyway), the League had punished the players and the fans.

Even worse, wrote Manning, the League would not allow any appeal. Had they been expelled, at least Peterborough could have appealed to a full meeting of the clubs, who would almost certainly have relented. Nevertheless, the club did try to appeal – in vain – and the supporters gathered a 24,128-signature petition to persuade the Management Committee to relent. It would not.

To Peterborough's credit, however, the League's second youngest Associate Members did play their hearts out for the rest of that fateful season, scoring the second highest total of goals in the division. In normal circumstances, their record would have put them in ninth place, with 50 points. Instead, 19 points were deducted and they finished bottom. Once demoted, however, their morale faded, and it took six seasons to claw their way back to the Third Division.

(Before 1967, the only League clubs to have had points deducted had been Sunderland – 2 points in 1890 – and Stockport – 2 points in 1926/7, each for fielding an ineligible player.)

Peterborough were not alone in suffering from the authorities' stern resolve that season. Next on the list came Port Vale. Their misdemeanours were even more serious.

Vale, it was discovered, had paid weekly wages to a number of youngsters whom the club secretary had omitted to register, and who were therefore technically amateurs or associate schoolboys. Illegal bonuses had been offered for a League Cup tie against Chester in August 1967, and three players had been paid bonuses for signing on, contrary to League rules. In addition, a director of the club had made gifts to young players, which was contrary to FA regulations.

Port Vale could have no defence against these breaches, since some were actually recorded in the club's minutes, which suggested that, as in Peterborough's case, Vale's greatest sin was ignorance (or stupidity).

To the public at large, however, the offences were really only very minor. What concerned them was the possible involvement of Sir Stanley Matthews, who happened to be Vale's manager at the time.

Suspicions were heightened when the club directors, instead of facing the press and admitting their errors, as Matthews urged them to do, decided to say nothing, thus compounding their guilt and leading the press and public to think the unthinkable – that Sir Stan himself had been cheating. For a player who hadn't been cautioned once in his entire playing career of thirty-three years, this was a hurtful assumption. What made it worse for Matthews was the fact that he'd given his services to Port Vale free of charge, and yet was being ordered not to speak to the press, as if he were some low-ranking paid retainer.

Eventually, at a commission of enquiry on 20 February 1968, Vale admitted their guilt and were thus severely censured and fined £2000 for breaching FA regulations.

But how would the League punish them? Vale had to wait until 3 March to discover their fate, which turned out to be the worst possible. On top of a further £2000 fine, like Leeds City (the club whose place they had taken in the League in 1919), Port Vale were to be expelled.

Unlike Leeds City, however, Port Vale were not to be expelled until the end of the season, at which time they could simply apply for re-election at the Annual Meeting on 8 June. As a *Times* leader on 7 March commented: 'Port Vale have been treated quite leniently.' They would obviously be voted straight back in.

(*The Times* also thought some of Vale's misdeeds would have been regarded in other walks of life as the mark of an enlightened and imaginative employer. It pointedly suggested that the football authorities direct their 'reforming zeal' to misconduct on the pitch. 'Foul play does more to besmirch the game than Port Vale's misconduct.')

As expected, at the Annual Meeting Vale won their place back in the Fourth Division by a vote of 40–9. But Sir Stanley didn't stay around to celebrate. Disgusted by the club directors' refusal to clear his name, he resigned and effectively turned his back on English football thereafter. What made him additionally angry, he later wrote, was that soon after Vale's punishment, Manchester United were investigated for similar breaches of regulations and were quietly fined £7000 with no further repercussions (as we shall see below).

By that time, United, who had just become the first English side to win the European Cup (beating Benfica 4–1 on 29 May at Wembley), had gained their first representative on the Management Committee. 'Champagne Louis' Edwards took the place made vacant by the death on 24 May of former President, Sir Joe Richards.

Len Shipman paid tribute to his late mentor at the 1968 Annual Meeting. Richards had put the game and the League before everything. 'A more loyal colleague than Joe Richards could not be found anywhere.'

There were other famous names in the 1968 obituary list: E. Holland Hughes, once the League's arch opponent during the Pools War, but later chairman of Everton; Ivan Sharpe, the journalist who for so long had been the foremost confidant of the League (and author of the seventy-fifth anniversary history): and Harold Sutcliffe, the son and heir to Charles Sutcliffe's cherished fixture charts. On the day of his funeral, Alan Hardaker called in at the family law firm in Rawtenstall to collect the famous charts. One could understand his motives, but he might have been more tactful.

Truly, the world was changing. On Harold Sutcliffe's death, the task of compiling the fixtures went to a computer (see page 366 ff.). Colour television was on its way, promising an even better spectacle for the armchair supporter, while in 1969 the BBC would pay £100,000 for the rights to continue *Match of the Day*, five times the sum they had paid five years earlier.

Around the same time, the League offices played host for the first time to a meeting of International League secretaries, and President Len Shipman was allowed to have an official car and chauffeur for the growing number of official functions he had to attend. How Charles Sutcliffe would have envied him this luxury!

On the pitch the focus was well and truly on Manchester, where City had won the League, United had finished runners-up, Matt Busby had just been awarded a CBE, and, not to be forgotten, neighbours Bury had just won promotion, with newcomers Oxford, to the Second Division.

Further proof of how established the League Cup had become came that year when, for the first time, a member of the royal family, HRH Princess Alexandra, presented the trophy, to Leeds United. Apart from attracting a full house to Wembley, the Cup also now guaranteed the winners a place in Europe (provided that they were in the First Division, which of course the 1967 and 1969 winners Q.P.R and Swindon Town were not). Not surprisingly, therefore, 1968/9 saw the highest entry of clubs. Only one, Manchester United, declined to enter.

Len Shipman did have some cause for concern, however. Crowd disturbances continued to receive extensive media coverage, as did an increasing number of disturbing incidents on the pitch. Four League clubs, Leeds, Manchester United, Burnley and Tranmere, had already been hauled before the FA as a result of their disciplinary records.

Debate at the time often focused on the now familiar question of whether bad behaviour on the pitch led to trouble on the terraces. But there was a related issue which had yet to be confronted at all. Did the upsurge in wages and transfer fees have the effect of alienating supporters from the professional footballer?

To the Management Committee this was not merely an academic question. The adoring public expected highly-paid stars like Mick Jagger and Peter Sellers to fool around in their fairy-tale world of glamour, but until the 1960s the footballer had been different. He was 'one of the boys'; a hero, but an approachable one all the same, as much exploited by his own directors as the ordinary worker was by his bosses.

Increasingly, however, the modern footballer was moving away from his roots. He earned much more, he lived in greater style, and was more cosseted from his working-class origins.

This was a theme which seemed to occupy much of Alan Hardaker's thoughts during the 1960s and, it would seem, Len Shipman's, too.

From their discussions in Committee it is clear that they were concerned that this 'cult of the star' was being reflected in attendance figures, since proportionately a greater percentage of the total number of spectators now concentrated on the First Division. It didn't help that the rapidly developing motorway system and wider car ownership allowed more former small-town loyalists to follow the big city teams. Why watch Rochdale when you could be at Old Trafford in twenty minutes?

These were essentially social issues which went beyond the remit of the Management Committee, but that didn't stop it trying to act.

In August 1968 the Committee put forward an astonishing set of proposals on contracts, one of which sought to put back the clock eight years by suggesting the reintroduction of the maximum wage and the imposition of controls on bonuses and incentives. Even when opinion among club chairmen proved to be hostile towards this, the Committee resolved to pursue the matter and drew up sample contracts allowing for wage levels to be set according to division.

Among their other plans was one to reverse one of the consequences of the Eastham case, by allowing a club to withhold wages to any player until a new contract was signed.

In short, the Committee seriously considered trying to undo all that the PFA had fought for in the previous decade.

There were, however, some constructive elements within their proposals. For example, the Committee wished to reward loyalty. Ever since players had been brave enough to emulate Oliver Twist and ask for more, the individual who was transferred the most earned the most, by regularly picking up a share of the fees, whether legally or not. The loyal club man had no such opportunities, and if he relied on a testimonial he was often disappointed (then taxed, unlike the cricketer).

To dissuade the footballing mercenary, and to ease club expenses, it was finally decided after several Extraordinary General Meetings in 1968/9 that if nothing else could be agreed – and it wasn't – the League would at the very least seek to reduce the signing-on levy.

Behind all the Committee's machinations lay one simple truth; football's finances were stretched more than at any other time since the depression of the 1920s. While a handful of clubs at the top of the First Division were making profits, the remainder were feeling the effects of the late-1960s economic squeeze. This manifested itself particularly in the frequency with which clubs paid transfer fees late, or on deferred terms. Combined with the irregularities highlighted at Peterborough and Port Vale, this persuaded the Management Committee to initiate random spot checks on clubs' books.

Notts County were the first to be visited, their books being found in good order by the League's Norman Thomas and a new, young member of staff, Graham Kelly. A few months later, when the League popped in on Manchester United, they found a different story. In all, four League regulations had been broken, each in a manner as serious as in the cases of both Peterborough and Port Vale.

One player at Old Trafford had been given an unauthorized loan, seventeen had been given £200 in lieu of a club tour, and eleven had received £250 appearance money for two World Club Championship matches against Estudiantes of Argentina (which, as the matches proved, might well have been justified as danger money). Finally, United had paid their apprentices' landladies above the League' allowable maximum rate.

This placed before the League a frightful dilemma. Could they really enforce the demotion, or even expulsion, of the European Cup winners? As Louis Edwards sat outside the Management Committee's meeting room when the matter was discussed – members never took part in decisions involving their own clubs – above him hung the sword of Damocles, with the hand of Sir Stanley Matthews

tantalizingly poised around the hilt. The sword had fallen on Peterborough and Port Vale. Why should the mighty Reds be different?

Moreover, United knew that since he had taken over as President, Len Shipman had initiated a real crackdown on clubs. The Committee minutes in 1968 and 1969 are full of the kind of disciplinary action which in the League's first half-century had been common, but which had been noticeably absent in postwar years. The misdeeds, like the subsequent fines, were usually relatively innocuous; teams playing in unregistered colours, turning up late, or failing to hand in correct team lists. Referees and linesmen were repeatedly warned about punctuality.

Individually, these peccadillos meant little, but added together they suggested that laxity had set in. Standards may have been dropping elsewhere in society, but in the League, discipline meant strength and unity. It was one of Shipman's favourite maxims: the Committee had to be master of the situation.

A stern hand of rebuke also fell upon the Associate Members. They were reportedly unhappy that, because several had chosen to stage matches on Friday nights, their share of the pools money was proportionately reduced (by £13,000 in 1968/9). The Committee had no sympathy. Saturday afternoon was the right time for football, it affirmed, besides which Friday-night matches could not appear on coupons (which explains why in 1970 each club was limited to four Friday-night fixtures per season). And if the Third and Fourth Division clubs wanted to make a fuss, warned Shipman, they 'might cause a reaction from the Full Members which would not be to the advantage of the Associate Members'.

Shipman's message was quite clear, as he reminded the clubs at the 1969 Annual Meeting.

'The regulations of the Football League are made and amended at [Annual] Meetings. If a three-quarters majority passes a regulation then it becomes

part of football law. It applies to everyone, and the Management Committee's duty is very clear. This is to see that the regulations are observed by every club, whatever their status may be. They intend to carry out this duty as firmly and fairly as it is possible to do. There is no such thing as a technical breach of regulations. You either observe them or you do not.'

Derby County did not, and were fined £1000 for paying for their team's foreign holiday. Aston Villa received a reprimand for making an unauthorized loan. But when a joint commission finally came round to Manchester United's case in June 1969, the punishment, passed the following September, was the heaviest ever inflicted on a League club in financial terms – a fine of £7000, of which only £500 was for breaches of FA rules. United were also banned from playing friendlies against foreign clubs for two seasons.

But this, surely, was a small price for United to pay in comparison with those fines inflicted on Peterborough and Port Vale. And United had not suffered the humiliation of being demoted or expelled (which is what annoyed Sir Stanley Matthews). So, the Management Committee members were tough, but they weren't that tough.

The purge continued into 1970, with Derby County next on the inspection list. As in the case of Port Vale, the League's roving inspectors, Messrs Thomas and Kelly, found much evidence of poor administration, but there were also some flagrant breaches of regulations, including the payment of a player for writing programme articles after the Management Committee had expressly forbidden it. Bonuses and wages above those listed in contracts had also been paid, and several other smaller payments were given to triallists and scouts.

As the League's report concluded, most of these faults had occurred under a former secretary. The new incumbent was 'well aware of the present situation' and would 'no doubt be able to get matters on a proper basis in time.

He has, however, a difficult job before him'.

He had indeed, for in April 1970 one of the debits he had to enter in his books was a swingeing fine of £10,000, the highest yet imposed by the League. To punish Derby even further, they were banned from playing any friendlies against foreign clubs or competitive matches in Europe for one year. Having qualified that year for the Fairs Cup, this ban represented an enormous loss to the club.

Cynics suggested at the time that Derby and Manchester United were simply unlucky to have been caught out, that like Leeds City in 1919 they were no guiltier than anyone else. This was not the case, however. Several other clubs had their books similarly examined during this period, and they all emerged with a clean bill of health.

A month after Derby's fine, the Committee was sitting in judgement again, but this time the accused, Leeds United, were found guilty not of financial misdeeds, but of breaking the oldest (literally) rule in the book. Weighed down by the demands of challenging for three competitions at the same time, Leeds had fielded weakened sides in three League matches.

The previous highest fine for such a crime had been £2000 (paid by Everton in 1966). In 1970 Leeds were made to pay £5000, and to rub salt in their wounds they finished the season without a single honour. Everton beat them to the Championship, Chelsea beat them in the FA Cup – after Leeds had taken three attempts to beat Manchester United in the semi-final – and Celtic completed Leeds' misery by winning the two-legged European Cup semi-final. A few exhausted Leeds players then flew to South America to join England's preparations for the Mexico World Cup. Not surprisingly, therefore, the £5000 fine was not received kindly in many quarters.

In response to this criticism, Alan Hardaker argued that far from being more sympathetic to clubs like Leeds, the rule should be tightened even further, so that clubs playing under-strength teams would be expelled. There was clearly no love lost between Hardaker and Leeds' manager Don Revie, whom he once described as 'a pain in the neck'.

On one occasion, the former League Secretary wrote, Revie asked the League to postpone a Leeds match

'because he had three players, so he inferred, on the point of death. I refused the request categorically; and four days later (on the day of the match) noted with satisfaction that medical science in Leeds was clearly way ahead of the rest of the world's. The three players concerned made such remarkable recoveries that, not only did all three play, but one of them scored twice and another was widely described in the papers as the man of the match.'

Hardaker also asserted that Leeds would not have suffered from the fixture pile-up which led to their £5000 fine had Revie not insisted on postponing matches earlier in the season. But it was Hardaker who quite unfairly received the blame for depriving Leeds of their three trophies.

Another suggestion from the Committee, arising from Leeds' punishment, was to raise the fine to £20,000 and, if the playing of a weak team was the result of European commitments, to ban the offenders from future participation. In fact, none of these proposals was put into practice; when Liverpool were found guilty of fielding a weakened side in April 1971, just before their Cup Final appearance, they were simply fined £7500.

Even so, Messrs McGregor, Bentley and Sutcliffe would have applauded Shipman and his Committee's resolution – the League competition had to come first in everything. Clubs cannot live on cups alone, as William McGregor knew only too well when he formed the League to save professional football in 1888.

And as if to prove that there was little new in football, also in 1971 a dispute arose over poaching, between Brighton and Birmingham.

Poaching had been a common complaint in the League's early years, but in the post-war period cases were rare, or simply not punished. Not under Len Shipman, though. Found guilty of employing Willie Bell as their coach while he was still registered as a player with Brighton, Birmingham were fined £5000.

Then in July 1972, Derby, who had paid more fines than any other club in League history, had to shell out a further £5000 after their improper attempts to sign Nottingham Forest's winger Ian Storey Moore.

That brought the total amount of fines imposed by the League up to nearly £44,000 in four years. Harry Lockett, whose salary as the first League Secretary largely depended on fines, would have swooned at such a colossal windfall.

Whether clubs stuck to the rules or not, one thing was certain: the financial realities of football had changed irredeemably, not just since Lockett's era, but in the decade since 1961. Largely due to rapidly increasing running costs and wages, plus the effect of government economic measures, clubs which had always survived on the breadline were now finding that they could no longer live on the game alone.

Thus, the late 1960s saw another spate of requests from clubs wishing to use their grounds for other events: concerts, wrestling, military tattoos, bingo sessions, firework displays, hockey matches, even religious meetings. Only the staging of Rugby League remained strictly taboo (although the League did place charges of bringing the game into disrepute against Orient, after they had allegedly staged a cabaret involving male strippers!).

Halifax Town, who opened a golf range at their ground, were among the first to state openly that they now regarded gate money as a mere sideline in their overall operation. But then, soon after saying this, they were found to be £37,000 overdrawn at the bank and losing £250 a week. On 28 February 1971,

Town were warned that if their debts to other clubs and to the League were not settled by 30 April, the Committee would recommend their expulsion. A couple of months later, Halifax beat Manchester United 2–1 in the Watney Invitation Cup; attendance 19,765, receipts £7782. Football clubs do have this curious habit of bouncing back when one least expects it.

This brings us back to Port Vale in 1968. As we have seen, unlike Halifax they were actually expelled, but then voted straight back in. At that same Annual Meeting, the four retiring clubs also emerged with predictable success; York City (46 votes), Chester (44), Bradford Park Avenue (44) and Workington (38) were each re-elected.

The other votes were for Cheltenham (3), Bedford, Cambridge City, Cambridge United, Chelmsford, Runcorn and Wigan (2 each), Guildford, Hereford, New Brighton, Wellington, Wimbledon and Worcester (1 each),

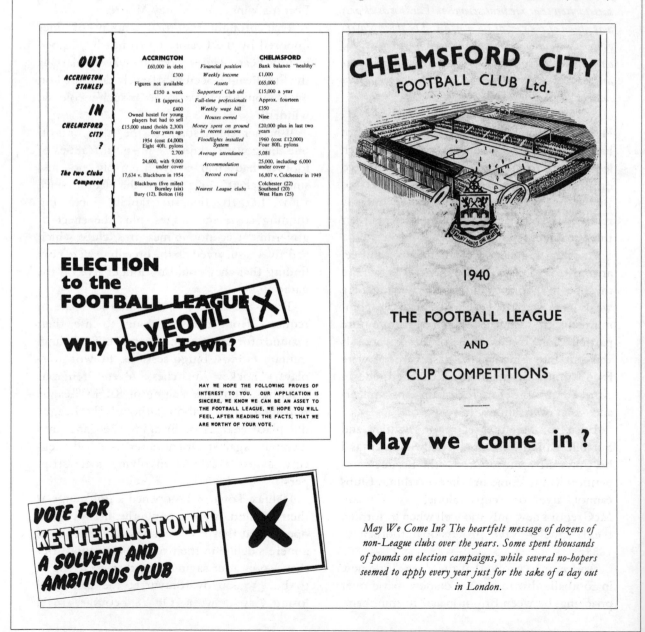

OUT ACCRINGTON STANLEY IN CHELMSFORD CITY ? The two Clubs Compared	ACCRINGTON		CHELMSFORD
	£60,000 in debt	Financial position	Bank balance "healthy"
	£300	Weekly income	£1,000
	Figures not available	Assets	£65,000
	£150 a week	Supporters' Club aid	£15,000 a year
	18 (approx.)	Full-time professionals	Approx. fourteen
	£400	Weekly wage bill	£350
	Owned hostel for young players but had to sell	Houses owned	Nine
	£15,000 stand (holds 2,300) four years ago	Money spent on ground in recent seasons	£20,000 plus in last two years
	1954 (cost £4,000) Eight 40ft. pylons	Floodlights installed System	1960 (cost £12,000) Four 80ft. pylons
	2,700	Average attendance	5,081
	24,600, with 9,000 under cover	Accommodation	25,000, including 6,000 under cover
	17,634 v. Blackburn in 1954	Record crowd	16,807 v. Colchester in 1949
	Blackburn (five miles) Burnley (six) Bury (12), Bolton (16)	Nearest League clubs	Colchester (22) Southend (20) West Ham (25)

ELECTION to the FOOTBALL LEAGUE ☒ **YEOVIL**

Why Yeovil Town?

MAY WE HOPE THE FOLLOWING PROVES OF INTEREST TO YOU. OUR APPLICATION IS SINCERE. WE KNOW WE CAN BE AN ASSET TO THE FOOTBALL LEAGUE. WE HOPE YOU WILL FEEL, AFTER READING THE FACTS, THAT WE ARE WORTHY OF YOUR VOTE.

CHELMSFORD CITY FOOTBALL CLUB Ltd.

1940

THE FOOTBALL LEAGUE

AND

CUP COMPETITIONS

——

May we come in?

VOTE FOR KETTERING TOWN ☒ **A SOLVENT AND AMBITIOUS CLUB**

May We Come In? The heartfelt message of dozens of non-League clubs over the years. Some spent thousands of pounds on election campaigns, while several no-hopers seemed to apply every year just for the sake of a day out in London.

Yeovil and Nuneaton (no votes).

Notice that both Cambridge clubs applied, and failed. No wonder clubs like Halifax survived; their challengers were weak, selfish and divided. The following season saw a hint of change, however, for two reasons.

The formation of the Northern Premier League, to equal the status of the Southern League, was the first step of many which led towards the formation of a non-League 'pyramid'.

Then the Committee decided that from 1969 onwards its members would inspect the ground of any club seeking election, to ensure that it met the standards required (even though at the time there were no official guidelines and none of the members was a qualified inspector).

Possibly as a result of these new conditions, at the following Annual Meeting in 1969 a non-League club made the best challenge since 1962. Grimsby (47), York (45) and Bradford Park Avenue (38) were comfortably re-elected, even though this was Park Avenue's third appeal in a row, but Newport County, seeking re-election for the first time since 1950, polled only 27 votes. For sure, their nearest challengers, Cambridge United, were some way behind with 16 votes, but the voting pattern did suggest that another breakthrough would not be far off.

Cambridge United's neighbours, City, applied again and received only two votes, as did Hereford and Romford. The other applicants were Kettering (3), Bedford, Chelmsford and Worcester (1 each), Nuneaton and Wimbledon (no votes).

How soon the fortunes of many of these 1969 candidates would change! Wimbledon would reach the First Division within an astonishing 17 year period, Bradford Park Avenue and Romford would cease to exist, Cambridge United would eclipse their local rivals and, like Hereford, York and Grimsby, reach the Second Division. For their part, Newport would find themselves playing in Europe. Small wonder that football maintains such a grip upon our imaginations.

Another significant stage in the fight for non-League recognition took place in September 1969, when the Southern League's Management Committee attempted to nominate only one of its clubs for League membership. Although not every member heeded the instruction, the applicants in 1970 were fewer in number and stronger in potential. So much so that for the first time in many years, the Committee announced that Cambridge United, Yeovil and Wigan 'were in every way suitable' should the members decide to vote for change.

They did. Although Darlington (47 votes), Hartlepool (42) and Newport (31) were re-elected, bottom-of-the-League Bradford Park Avenue, with only 17 votes, were soundly beaten by Cambridge United, who received 31. Cambridge had just won the Southern League for the second season in succession while Bradford were seeking re-election for the fourth year running. Their fate came as little surprise, therefore, and even Wigan Athletic, with 18 votes, won greater support.

Of the other challengers, oddly enough Cambridge City did best, with 2 votes. Once United were elected, however, any dream City had of League football evaporated forever. If the city of Bradford was unable to support two League clubs, then sure as eggs is eggs, neither could Cambridge, a third of the size.

(Bradford Park Avenue declined rapidly thereafter, and by 1974 were defunct. Sad though this was, it has to be said that with the exception of New Brighton, all the other clubs to have dropped out of the League since the war have struggled on, even Accrington. Where there's a will, there's a way . . .)

Apart from Park Avenue, Yeovil polled one vote, as did Bedford, Hereford, Morecambe and Romford. No votes were recorded for Boston United, Chelmsford City, Hillingdon Borough, Telford United or Wimbledon.

In February 1971 Alan Hardaker had another try at putting forward a reorganization

The Chester Report 1968

In June 1966, a few weeks before England won the World Cup, the Government set up an eleven-man enquiry into the state of Association Football in Great Britain. Among the members were former Wolves and England defender Bill Slater, referee Mervyn Griffiths of Wales, Labour MP Brian Walden (Birmingham) and Conservative MP Arthur Tiley (Bradford). The chairman was Norman Chester, warden of Nuffield College, Oxford and an expert on government and public administration. As a youth he had started to watch Manchester United in 1922. In 1966 he was a regular at Oxford United.

After two years of gathering information and interviewing dozens of people, including the Management Committee and Alan Hardaker, the so-called Chester Report was issued in 1968. Among its many observations and recommendations were the following concerning the League:

● While Fourth Division clubs were in debt to the tune of £518,000, Third Division clubs £260,000 and Second Division clubs £140,000, the First Division clubs had accumulated surpluses of nearly £1.7 million.

● Pools money and other League revenues were worth roughly £11,000 per club in 1966, a tenth of the current amount twenty years later. Pools money, said the report, had transformed the game, but should not be allowed to rise to a point where clubs lost their incentive to be efficient.

● The League should be increased by six to ten clubs and divided into five divisions; the top three to be national, the fourth to be divided into North and South. The First Division should have only eighteen clubs.

● A system of four up and four down should be introduced, with any club seeking re-election two years in a row automatically standing down.

● Clubs should be allowed to appoint salaried directors, or put their managers or secretaries on to the board of directors (as was finally agreed in 1981).

● A levy on all transfer fees over £25,000 should be imposed, in order to raise money for ground improvements.

● The League should appoint a director of referees, responsible for the training and selection of match officials.

● League clubs should be provided with grants to build sports facilities for 'substantial' community use.

● A Football Levy Board should be established along the lines of the Horserace Levy Board. A 1 per cent levy on the pools, after tax, would be collected and used to improve facilities at all levels of the game.

It took the eleven-man team two years to compile the report, and just a few hours for the majority of League clubs to dismiss it. Chester was asked by the League Management Committee to try again in 1983, and although the response was again lukewarm, several of his recommendations did finally find favour, for example the reduction in the size of the First Division and a reduction in the voting majority required to change League regulations.

The response of club chairmen to the Chester Report went deeper than simply a rejection of his ideas; it was tinged with a strong resentment that an academic could somehow put right a system which, though imperfect, had borne the test of time and adversity. The chairmen might also have noted that Chester himself represented one of the most archaic and tradition-bound institutions in Britain. Were the cloistered dons of Oxford University any more willing to accept radical change than the ninety-two chairmen of the Football League?

plan. This was the mark of a brave man. His first 'Pattern for Football' had been sunk by the clubs, then in 1968 the similarly progressive Chester Report had been given an even frostier reception. Norman Chester, Warden of Nuffield College, Oxford, led a committee appointed by the Department of Education and Science to enquire into the state of British football. Excellent though many of its recommendations were, they were pointedly ignored by League clubs, both in 1968 and when Chester (later Sir Norman) tried again, in 1983.

But Alan Hardaker was nothing if not persistent. Having held talks with the Southern League and the Northern Premier League about the possible formation of an Alliance – essentially a fifth division – Hardaker's new plan was as follows:

● The Third Division to be reduced to twenty clubs.

● Two regional Fourth Divisions of twenty clubs each.

● Two promoted from each Fourth Division, four down from the Third.

● To compensate for the loss of League fixtures (which would number thirty-eight per season), the League Cup to be rearranged to provide for six games for each Associate member in Round One. There might also be room for an additional knock-out competition among the sixty Third and Fourth Division clubs.

Hardaker listed the advantages of this scheme as being: lower travelling expenses, more local derbies, more weekly fixtures for the pools (although the number of League matches would be reduced from 2028 to 1980), and

wider control for the League over professional football in areas then uncovered. A further merit was that the scheme could be introduced as soon as it was agreed, and it would not affect the Full Members, except by giving the Associate Members perhaps one extra vote.

The Management Committee gave the reorganization its full backing, but four weeks later it was killed stone dead by a unanimous rejection by the Associate Members. Yet again, the Committee had tried to take a lead, only for the clubs to dig in their heels. The non-League clubs were understandably downcast, as was the Secretary; here was yet more proof that Hardaker of the League was not the all-powerful dictator his critics liked to think he was.

At least someone recognized his good intentions, however. In June 1971 he was awarded an OBE for his services to football, just like his predecessor, Fred Howarth.

The Associate Members' attitude to reorganization did not bode well for the non-League applicants at the 1971 Annual Meeting, where all four retiring clubs beat off strong challenges by Hereford United (22 votes) and Wigan Athletic (14). Lincoln (47), Barrow (38), Hartlepool (33) and Newport (33) were re-elected, but with a noticeably smaller share of the vote.

The other votes were, surprisingly, for Cambridge City (2), plus Telford and Yeovil (also 2 each), Boston and Romford (1 each), with no votes for Bedford, Chelmsford, Hillingdon Borough and Kettering.

Two other clubs were on the list, and how they must have cried on each other's shoulder. Gateshead, who polled no votes, knew full well how Bradford Park Avenue were feeling: sixty-two years in the League, one year out, and the first time they try to return they receive ... just one vote.

CHAPTER TWENTY-FIVE
Len Shipman – in the Driving Seat

So much happened during Joe Richards' nine years in office that inevitably some matters slipped into the background. Club discipline was one of them.

Whoever succeeded Joe Richards would have faced the same problems, but no one, surely, would have tackled them with more gusto than Len Shipman. While Hardaker played Torquemada to Shipman's Ferdinand, the League clubs had to be on their best behaviour. As the judgements were handed down some of them seemed downright unfair, but that didn't bother either man.

In fact, they shared certain characteristics. Like Hardaker, Shipman was a wily and shrewd operator. He was also a straight talker who wouldn't baulk at any decision if he thought it was for the good of the game. But Shipman also had the reputation for being a bit of a rough diamond. Over six foot tall and with a bluff manner, he could at times present a daunting figure. This was no mere bravado. Shipman's whole life had been a series of difficult and often unexpected challenges.

Born in 1902, Shipman grew up in the back streets of Leicester. As a tall and powerful youth, he played in goal or as full-back for local sides, once in the same line-up as Tommy Clay (later of 'Spurs and England), but soon had his energies diverted to the family business. At fourteen, he started working for his father in a wholesale fruit market, then two years later they entered the road haulage business with just two horses and a dray.

Len quickly showed his ambition and acumen. In 1920 he defied his father by purchasing a one-ton Ford lorry, and when his father died suddenly four years later, the recen-tly-married twenty-two-year-old was left to cope alone. It was an enormous responsibility for one so young, especially as both his brother and sister had died young.

From that one lorry in 1920, Shipman's fleet soon grew to forty-nine vehicles. As a businessman he was tough, uncompromising, but also extremely hard working. He was not one for handing out instructions from an office; he liked to be in the thick of things, in the driving seat. For over twenty years he worked from 3.30 a.m. to 9 p.m. to fulfil his firm's contract for the wholesale delivery of news-papers.

But Shipman rarely had time to sit back and reflect on his success. Having joined the Leicester City board soon after the outbreak of the Second World War, he suddenly found himself and two other young directors saddled with the club when the rest of the board were suspended for life in 1941, after the League had uncovered a series of illegal payments. This experience may well have sown the seeds of his later resolve to clamp down on club finances.

Then, in 1949, the same year he became chairman of Leicester (and they made the first of their four unsuccessful trips to Wembley in the FA Cup), Shipman was dealt a further blow when the Labour government nationalized the road haulage business. Shipman found himself in charge of several different operations, but he was too independent to relish taking orders from above, so he resigned and started all over again with just one lorry. Within three months he had ten, and within a few years his business was thriving again. It still is, under his son Terry, who followed him as chairman of

Leicester City.

Len Shipman joined the Management Committee in 1955, and was soon taken under the wing of Joe Richards, with whom he became very close. Len, his wife Eleanor, Joe Richards and his daughter, Mary, would often go on holiday together, and when Richards retired in 1966, Shipman was his only obvious successor. None of the other Committee men had served longer than he, and only Wilf Taylor had a similar grounding in League affairs. Taylor was then seventy-eight, however, Shipman a mere youth of sixty-four.

From our earlier narrative one might get the impression that once he became President, Len Shipman was little short of being the Judge Jeffreys of football. But there were other strings to his bow, and Shipman was certainly not, as some have suggested, merely a front man for Alan Hardaker, even if Hardaker was more influential during this period than ever before.

During Shipman's presidency, the League managed to negotiate a better agreement with the pools companies. The first sponsorship deals were struck up – with Watney Mann, Texaco and Ford in 1970. The *Football League Review* began in August 1966 from Leicester, and ties with Europe were strengthened further by Shipman's involvement with UEFA's own Executive Committee.

As a result of his services to football, he was awarded an MBE in 1967, then, after twenty-

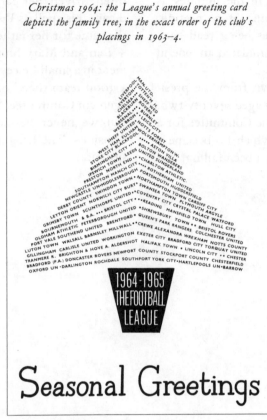

Christmas 1964: the League's annual greeting card depicts the family tree, in the exact order of the club's placings in 1963–4.

one years on the Management Committee, an OBE in 1976.

To many people in the game he was a far more amenable man than his predecessor. Joe Richards was often a reticent man in public; Shipman was anything but. He loved nothing better than to chat about football, whether it was with a workman on the street or a Right Honourable in the boardroom.

'Anyone who visited Filbert Street when LTS was around would be lucky to leave without having had a drink and a natter', said one former manager.

Len Shipman wanted to be liked. He didn't care if he dropped his aitches, nor did he bother about his lack of formal education. At times, however, he could provoke controversy with his outbursts, one of the most famous being when he called for the birching of hooligans.

Cliff Lloyd, former secretary of the PFA, remembered Shipman as creating a new atmosphere between the League and its players. It wasn't always harmonious, but at least Shipman was approachable. He called players and journalists 'm'boy', and on his chauffeur-driven travels around clubs would think nothing of marching into another club's boardroom with his own guest. He was a man used to ruling the roost.

His critics called him 'uncouth'. But there were plenty of other people who would say that despite his being a rough diamond, one couldn't help but like him. As his son Terry remembers, he was the sort of man to give you a good hiding then soften the blow with a sweet. One of his more endearing characteristics was a tendency towards malapropisms and confusing the meanings of words. On one occasion he was recorded in the minutes as having 'intimated' something at a meeting. When he heard the minutes being read back he retorted: 'I've never intimidated anyone in my life.'

Len Shipman stood down from the presidency in 1974, when he was aged seventy-two, although he remained on the Committee for a further three years, after which he became a Life Member. His health had been failing, and

with it his capacity to lead. He had also suffered the loss in 1971 of his wife of almost fifty years, Eleanor.

A year later, however, he married again, at the age of seventy. His bride? None other than Mary Richards, daughter of Sir Joe. Mary had often driven her father around the country during his spell as President, and now she did the same for her father's successor.

Len and Mary Shipman now live in retirement in a small Leicestershire village. 'We were a good team then,' Shipman says of his Management Committee, 'never had a wrong word. But we never hesitated to make unpleasant decisions. The League had to be master of the situation.'

CHAPTER TWENTY-SIX
Points of Order

'The FA is an obsolete battleship and the League is an up-to-date Dreadnought.' Those were the words of Billy Meredith in 1911, but they might easily have been spoken in 1971.

Friction between the two bodies was, of course, nothing new, but from the mid 1960s onwards there were some particularly serious rifts.

The first occurred in September 1965 when ninety-one of the ninety-two League clubs resigned *en masse* from the FA in protest against a directive from Lancaster Gate ordering each club to make a statutory declaration concerning the payment of amateurs. This was a quite unprecedented attempt to interfere in League affairs, and was all the more surprising in view of the fact that the chairman of the FA at the time was Joe Mears of Chelsea (the only club not to resign), a former member of the Management Committee.

The crisis lasted only a couple of days and was over once the FA had realized its error. But the tiffs didn't end there, and nor were they all sparked off by the FA.

In 1968 there was another argument when the League proposed streamlining the procedure for registering players (which involved registration at both Lytham and Lancaster Gate). A year later, the League passed a motion deprecating the FA's action in supporting UEFA's takeover of the Inter-Cities Fairs Cup, without first consulting the League.

Sporadic feuding continued into 1970, when Stoke City led a movement aimed at reducing the FA's power as a disciplinary body. The clubs were also anxious to change FA rules over the allocation of FA Cup Final tickets. By February 1972, the simmering discontent reached boiling point at a meeting of club chairmen in London.

'It was our view,' said Lord Westwood of Newcastle United, 'that the FA was taking too big a slice of the financial cake and we were not prepared to accept this.' He singled out two main issues in the 1972 dispute. From the Watney Cup, begun in 1970 (see Appendix Seven), the FA received a share worth £25,000. From the pools, the FA gained another £75,000 for the use of Cup fixtures. Thus, the FA received £100,000 'without lifting a finger and without having to do anything to get it'.

Moreover, once the FA received their share of the pools money, instead of being distributed immediately to those clubs which had participated in the Cup games, the money was allowed to accumulate interest worth around £7,000 a season. Lord Westwood proposed, therefore, that pools income from the FA Cup and all other monies earned by the League but paid direct to the FA, should go instead straight to the League. The League would then distribute it to the clubs and only then give the FA its share.

Considering this request was an FA committee including some familiar faces: Dr Andrew Stephen, a former Management Committee member, now chairman of the FA, plus three other League club directors. But their loyalty to the FA was obviously paramount, as Lord Westwood reported. No man can serve two masters equally well.

From the profit yielded by international matches, the FA was prepared to pay the League only £1200 for the disturbance of fixtures (that is, when League games were rearranged to help the England team) and for the use of players for pre-match training. For under-23 matches, compensation of £500 would apply. This would still leave the FA with a substantial profit. 'I make no further comment', said Lord Westwood.

Adding up all the concessions the FA was prepared to offer amounted to an extra £45,000 per year for the League. To this, Lord Westwood commented: 'There are sixty-six league clubs losing money, so the FA's offer, gentlemen, works out at just under £700 per club.'

What made the offer more derisory in League eyes was that the FA, with its large profits, had in recent years paid around £300,000 in tax, money that was lost to the game for good. In contrast, noted Westwood, instead of paying tax a few years earlier the Welsh FA had used its surplus to benefit the four League clubs under its jurisdiction.

Antagonism between the League and the FA reached an even lower point as a result of negotiations for the live transmission of England's match against West Germany in April 1972.

The normal forum for deciding on how to approach such negotiations was the Joint FA and League Television Committee. Alan Hardaker, the most experienced negotiator in all such matters, had gained this committee's approval to ask for £100,000 (on the grounds that after bargaining they might have to settle for £80,000). But then, when it came to the actual negotiations, the FA ordered him not to speak, and Andrew Stephen asked for £60,000 instead.

Hardaker was infuriated, not about the

In 1970, match officials were instructed to inspect the studs of each player before a game. To make the task easier, in 1972 the League issued each official with a stud gauge, only then to discover that very few modern standard-issue studs actually complied with the laws of the game!

money but about the breach of faith. After years of being snubbed by Sir Stanley Rous, and seeing all kinds of plots being hatched – one of them to create a super-league in Europe without the League's co-operation – he announced on 29 March 1972: 'Regrettably, there now seems to be a state of war between the League and the Football Association.'

But this was no personal vendetta on Hardaker's part. Bob Lord decried the FA for its attitude. If there was a war, he said, the FA started it, particularly Dr Stephen, who had ignored Hardaker's advice and had interfered in the FA's own democratic decisions.

Southampton declared that this proved it was time to let professionals stand up for their rights. The League should control its own players, not leave it to inexperienced amateurs at the FA.

But what if the FA did not satisfy these demands? Could the League break away? There were certainly plenty of club chairmen urging punitive sanctions. For example, all League clubs to boycott the FA Cup, or, the FA to pay for the privilege of having League clubs in the FA Cup. Len Shipman urged caution, if only because a boycott would cost League clubs their place in European competitions.

The war did not last long. In the end, the quarrel was settled when the Minister for Sport, Eldon Griffiths, arranged for the two sides to meet around a table and hammer out their differences during the summer of 1972. The result was, as always, a compromise.

On the financial front, agreement was finally reached in December 1972 with the so-called Lang Agreement, named after Sir John Lang, who acted as arbitrator. Under this agreement the League was to receive a greater share of the FA's income from international matches and be paid the pools income as soon as it was received.

The other great issue was the control of players' disciplinary proceedings. It was agreed in the summer of 1972 that the FA would retain control of such matters, but in return, the

League would be allowed to introduce their own points system.

As far as the League was concerned, this came not a moment too soon. It now had referees giving pre-match talks in the dressing rooms. It placed warning posters at grounds. Two venues – Elland Road and Old Trafford – had been closed temporarily following recent crowd disturbances. Yet these measures still brought little relief from continual criticism.

The critics were given extra fuel by the introduction of slow-motion action replays. These allowed television commentators to make their own expert judgements on any split-second unsavoury incident caught by the camera. It all added up to an intolerable level of pressure for referees, and a depressing image for the League.

In response, almost every week the *Football League Review* carried a similar message: the referee's verdict *is* final, the referee *is* properly assessed by the League, he *is not* a mere beginner who happens to find himself thrust on to the pitch at a First Division ground, and his foreign counterpart *is* in general a lot less able.

In truth, there was little more the League could do. Several club chairmen argued for professional referees, but then a professional was just as liable to make a mistake as a dedicated amateur, and when the referees were asked to vote on the matter, the vast majority opposed professionalism.

The answer as far as the League was concerned was to tighten up discipline among the players, and that was why it campaigned so hard for the FA to introduce the points system, thereby giving a yardstick to judge players who had been cautioned or sent off.

The basis of the 1972 agreement with the FA was as follows:

● Any player reaching twelve disciplinary points would be suspended automatically for two matches. (Previous suspensions had covered a time period, which meant that some players missed more matches than others.)

● A player sent off would miss three matches. (After a successful first year, the suspension periods were changed to one match for twelve points and two matches for a sending off.)

● The cautionable offences varied from one point for a goalkeeper making illegal markings on the pitch – at one time a common occurrence – to four points for continual dissent, fouling from behind, or deliberate tripping.

One of the main changes brought about by this new system was the ending of all appeals against cautions, many of which were lodged for tactical reasons by clubs, hoping that their players would be freed to play in important matches. Automatic suspension was thus a much fairer method.

The PFA wasn't entirely happy with the scheme, but it did at least manage to secure greater representation for its members at personal hearings and independent tribunals, and the system, with a few variations, has lasted successfully until today.

But that it was necessary at all, did this not suggest that perhaps something about the game had changed? The will to win at all costs, higher incentives for success, the dread of failure....

Some observers regard the early 1970s as a barren period in British football. England were no longer champions of the world (after defeat at the hands of West Germany in Mexico), gates were steadily declining, and the referee's clampdown between 1971 and 1973 suggested (erroneously) to outside observers that carnage on the pitch was a regular event. (The clampdown resulted at its height in the booking of 120 players in eight days, and led to much friction betwen the clubs and Lytham.)

There were even players prepared to commit the heinous sin of refusing to play for their country. Alan Hudson of Chelsea and Colin Todd of Derby actually turned Sir Alf Ramsey down. They were exhausted, they wanted to stay at home. This had never been known before.

Alan Hardaker may not have been an Alan Hudson fan, but he certainly made his own views clear on the congestion of fixtures. In the two months following 1 April 1972, he pointed out, certain League clubs and players could well have had the following schedule: the Easter holiday League programme, two European Cup rounds, the FA Cup semi-finals, the UEFA Cup Final (both legs), the FA Cup Final, the European Cup Final, the European Cup Winners' Cup Final, five England internationals and three Scottish, Welsh and Northern Irish internationals, plus the remainder of the League programme.

In fact, only two League clubs reached the European finals in the end – Tottenham and Wolves, who faced each other in the first UEFA Cup two-legged final in May. But all the other games were squeezed into this busy eight weeks, during which Sir Alf Ramsey wanted all members of the England squad to be released from their clubs two weeks before the game against West Germany on 29 April.

Small wonder it was becoming harder to justify the claim, heralded consistently in the *League Review*, that the Football League was indeed the strongest in the world. Toughest in the world, certainly, but as the tired legs at Wembley showed when West Germany won 3–1, the likes of Alan Hudson and Colin Todd weren't just being bloody-minded in their wanting a rest.

English football was by no means alone in its ills. Reports from Italy showed that violence on the pitch was much worse than in England, and so were gates. A Belgian journalist wrote of how much he envied the English public their weekly dose of League football. Meanwhile, foreign sales of televised League matches continued to rise, as did requests for League teams to tour abroad.

When the Italian FA wanted to re-educate their top managers, they were sent to England. When emerging nations wanted advice on running professional leagues, they turned to Lytham St Annes. The United States tried to lure Alan Hardaker away. Several African Nations sought him as a consultant. It was even claimed once that Bobby Charlton was the most famous individual on the planet, more widely known than the Queen herself (an intriguing proposition, which this author once tested out in the rain-forests of Ecuador and found to be absolutely correct).

So League football wasn't dying. If no one had cared, then it would have died long ago, particularly just before the First World War, when, as in the early 1970s, negative football on the pitch, a negative image in the press, and the usual dissension amongst the clubs, all conspired to create an atmosphere of doom.

'Whether we like it or not,' Len Shipman told the 1972 Annual Meeting, 'We are now in the midst of an industrial revolution ... we have got to find a new approach.' Part of that approach, he suggested, might include reviving Alan Hardaker's 'Pattern for Football'. Had that been adopted ten years ago, hinted the President, many of football's existing problems would have been avoided.

True or not, plenty of new and unexpected obstacles were being thrown in football's path during the early 1970s. Value added tax was on its way, thirteen years after football had escaped from the much-despised Entertainment Tax. The Government's new Industrial Relations Act was also a potential threat to the retention and release of players, and therefore to the whole structure of the League, said Shipman. Alan Hardaker warned that freedom of contract was now inevitable within two or three years.

Just as in 1945/6 the agenda for post-war football was set, so in 1971/2 were raised many of the issues which would occupy the League up to the present era.

For example, sponsorship now became a major theme, beginning in 1970 with the Watney Invitation Cup, the Texaco Cup and the short-lived Ford Sporting League (see Appendix Seven). A new relationship was evolving between commercial interests and football. Football needed the money, it is true. But it should be stressed that many companies also believed that they needed football to enhance their own image.

Every time the Committee met, it seemed to be faced with yet another request from an advertising agency to use League matches or players in its commercials, or from companies wanting to exploit club badges or players' portraits. Tea, soup, razors, bread and wristwatches; football helped to sell them all. But the Committee didn't always approve.

One company's attempt to promote their product by presenting a bottle of after-shave to every player who scored a hat-trick was dismissed as being 'so trivial as to be an insult to the game'.

Another offer from an oil company to pay £35,000 for the use of FA Cup winners' badges ended up with the FA arguing that the League should not receive a share of the money from badges issued for two non-League clubs who had once won the Cup. Whom did the FA mean? Old Carthusians perhaps; Clapham Rovers maybe?

From the antiquated to the ultra modern – 1971 also saw the first discussions taking place about a revolutionary new development called Astroturf. The first synthetic pitch of this type had been laid in Islington, near Arsenal's ground, and a few visionaries – branded as cranks – were even suggesting that one day Football League matches might be played on such a surface.

The term 'community' suddenly became common currency in football circles around this time, mainly inspired by the revamped Sports Council, which had grants available for clubs wishing to lay on facilities for 'the community'. Very few took up the offer, and those who did were rarely able to make the best of the deal. In time, they would embrace the concept, however, because they belatedly realized that 'the community' also meant 'the supporters'.

But no one could ignore the findings of Lord Wheatley's major study on safety at sports grounds, undertaken as a result of the Ibrox disaster in 1971. Its final recommendations would change the crumbling facade of football ground design and ultimately lead to whole new areas of responsibility for football clubs.

Another item on the agenda was the discontinuation of Inter-League matches. Originally designed to provide the League's main source of income, these games were now an irrelevance, no more than a toning-up exercise for the national team, which itself had more commitments than ever, particularly since after 1970 England were having to qualify for the World Cup for the first time since 1962.

Also in 1971/2, the Southern League and Northern Premier League joined forces to draw up concrete proposals concerning automatic promotion and relegation to the League. Their cause received an added boost at the 1972 Annual Meeting when another non-League club made the break into League football, helped in by an extremely unusual voting pattern. In all, twelve non-League clubs applied, but oddly the votes were concentrated on just four, of which three polled only one vote each. Rarely had the voting clubs been so single-minded.

Three of the four retiring clubs polled high votes: Northampton, just six seasons after being in the First Division (49), Crewe (46) and Stockport (46) were each re-elected. That left a straight fight between Barrow, third from bottom but making their second application in a row, and Southern League Hereford United, who had won the hearts of the nation with a 2–1 Cup win against First Division Newcastle.

In the first ballot, Barrow and Hereford finished level with 26 votes each. Bradford Park Avenue managed one vote, as did Cambridge City and Wimbledon. There were no votes for Bangor, Bedford, Boston, Hillingdon, Romford, Telford, Wigan or Yeovil.

In the second ballot, Barrow received 20 votes, Hereford 29. It was thus another breakthrough for the south at the expense of a remote northern club.

But it turned out to be another excellent boost for the non-League cause. Like Oxford and Cambridge, Hereford would soon find themselves in the Second Division.

The following year it was back to normal, as the pattern of voting yet again showed the futility of putting too many names into the hat. Although Colchester (48 votes), Northampton (43) and Crewe (36) were comfortably re-elected, Darlington, another distant northern club, managed only 26 votes, the lowest total for a re-elected club since the war. Had the remaining votes not been so divided, Darlington would almost certainly have gone the way of Barrow and Bradford Park Avenue (who both failed to win a single vote. Once out, it seemed, soon forgotten.)

Yeovil (14), Kettering (12) and Wigan (10) gained the most votes among the challengers in 1973 – enough if combined to have comfortably unseated Darlington – followed by Chelmsford (4), Cambridge City, Nuneaton and Telford (1 each), Bedford, Boston and Wimbledon (no votes).

In the elections for the Management Committee, there was success for another new, or rather old, familiar face in football circles. Louis Edwards, the Manchester United chairman, decided to stand down after five years, his place being taken by fellow director, Sir Matt Busby. Sir Matt was, surprisingly the first former manager and only the third former professional player of repute ever to sit on the committee, after William Bassett and Phil Bach.

In Bassett's era, a regular occurrence at Annual Meetings had been Derby County's attempt to amend Regulation 31 by introducing a system of four up and four down throughout the divisions. (Bradford City were the first to put forward the idea, in 1905.)

In the 1950s Tottenham carried on the crusade, and at one Annual Meeting managed to achieve a healthy majority. As celebrations broke out on the floor, Bob Smith of Man-

chester City stood up and amid the hubbub said: 'Before we all get too excited gentlemen, does this not need a three quarters majority?' Fred Howarth confirmed that it did, and the celebrations came to an instant halt.

In 1973 Derby tried yet again, and as usual, their motion was defeated. But this time the Management Committee refused to let the matter rest. Instead of four up and four down, the Committee proposed a compromise of three up and three down. Bristol City seconded the motion, and after sixty-eight years of resistance, the clubs finally gave their approval.

To some, the new system was a retrograde step. Among its critics was Liverpool's manager Bill Shankly, who commented that it would add to the fears already plaguing League football. If the First Division was to be of the highest order, he reckoned, then it would have to be as selective as possible.

He and others even suggested that only one club should be relegated from Division One. Of course, this might never actually affect *his* club, but statistically there is no evidence to show that the 'extra' third club, whether promoted or relegated, does any better or any worse than the first or second clubs. On the positive side, as Alan Hardaker had been arguing since 1961, the more clubs involved in promotion and relegation issues, the greater the public interest.

Sir Matt Busby's arrival at Management Committee meetings came shortly after that of another new participant, one R. H. G. Kelly, who in March 1973 had been appointed as Assistant Secretary to replace Eric Howarth. Then aged twenty-seven, Graham Kelly had been on the League staff since 1968 and was chiefly known to the Committee for his regular inspections of club books, alongside the long-serving Norman Thomas.

Graham Kelly's and Sir Matt Busby's first year with the Committee came at a difficult time for the nation, beset by fuel and power shortages in late 1973 – which hampered the use of floodlights, for example – and the imposition of a three-day working week. By January 1974, the ban on floodlighting was relaxed and those clubs who had stocks of fuel were allowed to use their own generators.

One direct consequence of the power shortages was a movement towards the staging of League matches on Sundays, an idea which had long been resisted for all kinds of moral and social reasons. Burnley's Bob Lord, who was by then a Vice President of the League, announced: 'If it happens I shall get out of football altogether.'

But however tempted some might have been to take Lord at his word, the fact was that apart from the power shortages, there was a genuine desire to discover whether the public would prefer games on Sundays, as they did in several European and Latin-American countries.

The first League clubs to play on a Sunday were Cambridge United and Oldham, who held their Third Round FA Cup tie on the morning of 6 January 1974. Three other games took place in the afternoon. A fortnight later, the first League match on a Sunday took place, when Millwall entertained Fulham.

At the next meeting of the Committee, Bob Lord asked that his strong objections to these events be recorded in the minutes, but he never did resign, and once the power crisis ended, Sunday football resumed its taboo status.

On the disciplinary front, Len Shipman and Alan Hardaker kept up their purge throughout 1973/4. Preston and Newport each had one point deducted for fielding ineligible players and were fined £200. Arsenal were fined £2000 for making illegal approaches to Phil Parkes and Gerry Francis of QPR.

But by far the most controversial decision of the season was a £5000 fine imposed on Exeter City, who had committed the League's cardinal sin of failing to turn up for a match. Moreover, in behaving in this way they had defied an order from the Management Committee.

In common with a handful of other Associate Members at this time, Exeter were struggling to maintain a large enough playing staff to cover injuries and illness. Both Southport and Halifax had recently been given permission to postpone matches for this reason, but they were warned 'to think very seriously about their position in the Football League if they were not able to fulfil their match commitments'.

When Exeter found themselves in a similar situation, they routinely applied to the League to postpone their fourth Division matches against Peterborough on 30 March and Scunthorpe on 2 April.

Nine of Exeter's players were reportedly unfit and had medical certificates to prove it, leaving the club with only nine able men, of whom two were goalkeepers. Surely it was a clear-cut case. The matches would have to be postponed.

To City's dismay, the League ordered Exeter to play on. Which they did, against Peterborough. But, still struggling, they decided to defy the Committee and not send a team to Scunthorpe. No club had ever done this in the entire history of the League, but Exeter stated that they had no choice. Their only alternative would have been to field ineligible players.

Exeter's punishment was swift and shattering. Three weeks after the cancelled match, the Committee decided to fine the Devon club £5000, a crippling amount for a small outfit, especially as they were ordered to pay it within five weeks. Exeter were further ordered to pay £1026, which represented Scunthorpe's net average home receipts, plus another £68 for the expenses incurred on the day of the match. Scunthorpe were also awarded the two points, so that, uniquely, the record for 1973/4 shows that both clubs played only forty-five games each that season.

Exeter were stunned. They couldn't deny their failure to fulfil the fixtures, but why had they been singled out for such apparently harsh treatment?

The answer was quite straightforward. Exeter's plight seemed to have broken the Committee's patience. The members were tired of smaller clubs pleading injuries and illness to get out of their commitments. If you can't stand the heat, they implied, get out of the kitchen. An appeal failed, despite the sympathetic support from other clubs, and Exeter had to dig deep into their pockets to pay up. (They appealed once more for clemency but were unsuccessful again ... in 1981!)

Two other matters of concern to the League in 1973/4 were the Safety of Sports Grounds Bill, which followed the Wheatley Report, and the renegotiations of television rights. In the latter discussions, the Committee were helped by Tommy Trinder, the Fulham chairman.

Essentially, the television companies wanted to maintain the existing levels of televised football at a fee increased by 10 per cent, to cover three years. In response, a majority of clubs preferred to reduce the coverage but increase the fees.

'Ask for £1 million a season', Trinder had once said, not entirely tongue-in-cheek. Middlesbrough reckoned £2 million was nearer the true value. West Ham pointed out that while televised football attracted high audiences, it cost the BBC and ITV only about a quarter of the money spent on other popular programmes. On the other hand, said Alan Hardaker, clubs did gain extra revenue from advertising when the cameras paid a visit. This was little consolation to those outside the First Division, however.

While the television negotiations reached a deadlock, various members of the Committee were also having to deal with the Commission of Industrial Relations, the VAT office, numerous groups of MPs, the College of Arms (which helped the League and its clubs register their badges and crests against commercial misuse) and, of course, the FA at Lancaster Gate. Alan Hardaker and Committee men Dick Wragg and Bob Lord were often to be seen along the corridors of power at Westminster.

Not surprisingly, therefore, in 1973 some clubs voiced their concern that the League, if not able to move from Lytham, might at least have a London office, especially as politicians were taking a deeper interest in the game.

One of the Government's concerns was the apparently unabated spread of hooliganism, which in 1974 reached new levels at Newcastle and Old Trafford. On 30 March, Newcastle's Sixth Round FA Cup tie against Nottingham Forest was held up by a pitch invasion (the match was subsequently replayed), then on 27 April, with five minutes remaining of Manchester United's vital match against neighbours Manchester City, former United hero Denis Law, now playing for City, back-heeled the ball into the net to put United down into the Second Division. It was his last goal in League football, and on his own admission the goal he least wanted to score. The United fans felt the same. They invaded the pitch and the match had to be abandoned.

Only three times before had League matches been abandoned for reasons other than poor conditions – at Burnley in 1891, at Middlesbrough in 1915 and at Forest in 1968, after a fire – but this was the first time a fixture had ever been unfinished because of crowd trouble.

It was with this incident hanging over the League that Len Shipman chaired his last Management Committee meeting on 6 June 1974. His health had suffered during the previous year, and he reluctantly handed over the reins after eight years in office. He would, however, stay on the Committee, as had his predecessor Sir Joe Richards.

One of Len Shipman's last formal duties as President was to present the Fourth Division trophy to Peterborough United, the club over whose demotion he had presided six years earlier. One could criticize the League for all kinds of failings during Shipman's period of office, but one could never accuse it of being afraid to make unpopular decisions.

Now it faced another decision. Who would succeed Len Shipman?

CHAPTER TWENTY-SEVEN

Bob Lord or Lord Bill?

*T*hat was the choice: Bob Lord of Burnley or Lord Westwood of Newcastle United. Bob Lord, the firebrand who had harassed the League for as many years as he had served it, and was, in 1974, the senior Vice President, or the real Lord, Bill Westwood, who had been on the Committee for four years and was the first peer of the realm to be actively associated with the League.

If anyone had suggested to the Management Committee in 1960 that Bob Lord would one day be a member of that Committee, let alone stand for the presidency, the members would have quaked with an uneasy mixture of laughter and fear. For Bob Lord to have become part of the League establishment was as improbable as Andrei Sakharov joining the Politburo or Ken Livingstone gaining membership of the Monday Club.

No individual had caused the Management Committee more trouble than Bob Lord. The League minutes first record his presence in August 1956, when he attacked the Committee for refusing to allow clubs to charge reduced prices for old-aged pensioners. Two years later he was in trouble for using abusive language to a linesman, having entered the match officials' dressing room (itself against the regulations).

In Bob Lord's opinion – 'in my 'umble estimation', as he would often say – the League was totally biased against his club. He resented the fact that Burnley were fined £1000 for fielding nine reserves in March 1961, just before a European Cup match and an FA Cup semi-final. He resented the fact so loudly and offensively that the Committee passed a resolution complaining that it 'could not tolerate the irresponsible comments of Mr Lord'.

That didn't muzzle him, however. He started writing letters to Lytham, objecting to almost everything the Committee said and did. He complained about referees, about fines, about the awarding of medals, the method for electing Vice Presidents, even the travelling expenses he received when he was hauled up before Committee to explain his behaviour. He argued about a tournament in New York that Burnley were invited to attend, he maintaind that Alan Hardaker and the *Daily Mail* had it in for him, and, most famously of all, at a charity dinner at the Adelphi Hotel in Liverpool he made an ill-informed attack on the Jews.

Considering that amongst his audience were Jewish fund raisers and Jewish club directors, and that League circles had always been free, on the surface at least, of any anti-Semitic or religious bias, Lord's speech caused a storm. The bread rolls were, literally, flying that night. So offensive were his remarks that, however he pleaded innocence afterwards, Lord would never really shake off the stigma of that speech or of his attacks against the Leeds directors, several of whom were Jewish.

But history, or at least this history, should not view Bob Lod unkindly simply because of his ill-chosen remarks. Lord was no anti-Semite. He was friends with various Jewish club chairmen, including Harry Zussman of Orient, and he worked closely with Jewish members on the Management Committee.

The fact is that Bob Lord was, like so many of his generation, the product of a culture which ignorantly categorized 'Jewishness' only in the stereotypical sense of 'meanness'. It is more than likely that he never even understood what a Jew was. He was like a child in the playground who accuses another of 'acting Jewish', and in later life never realized how racist or hurtful such comments can be.

Lord could treat any other group in the same manner. He would utter oaths about referees or 'continentals', then have a drink with them; rail against the players, then treat them to champagne. When he began: 'in my 'umble estimation', one knew that another attack was about to begin. And while those who knew him well, including Jews, referees, 'continentals' and players, usually humoured him, many did not. This did not help when it came to seeking the presidency in 1974.

Vice Presidents of the League have often been stormy characters. We have already looked at John Lewis and Fred Rinder. Both were rebellious, outspoken characters who eventually learned to harness their enthusiasm for the good of the League. Bob Lord was exactly the same.

He was born in 1908, and in best Lancashire tradition worked his way up from the bottom. The son of a Burnley barber, he started as a barrow boy for a butcher and ended up owning a chain of fourteen butchers' shops. Having watched Burnley from an early age, he first tried to get on the board in 1950 and met much the same sort of reception as he would later encounter from the League. But in 1951, a vacancy at Turf Moor arose, and Lord was the only nominee. 'Under the circumstances, gentleman, there is nothing we can do. We shall have to put up with him!' was the chairman's reaction.

Put up with him they did, with the result that he became chairman in 1955 and transformed Burnley into a shining example of what a small-town club could become with proper planning.

He bought eighty acres of land at Gawthorpe for a training ground when the other directors baulked at the cost (which was actually very low); he laid one of the first all-weather pitches in the North of England; he brought Harry Potts in as manager and began

a youth policy which was to transform the team into a major footballing force during the first half of the 1960s. The Burnley training facilities were the envy of the League.

Burnley did everything the modern way, almost as if Lord was being deliberately progressive just to annoy the Committee. When flying to League matches came into vogue in the late 1950s and early 1960s, Lord flew his team at every possible opportunity, even to relatively handy destinations such as Nottingham, Wolverhampton and Birmingham.

A dictator and a trouble maker he may have been, but his ideas worked. In a town of 81,500 people he brought an average gate of 28,000 to Turf Moor, the equivalent of 116,000 at Coventry or 42,000 at Oxford. One could take a dislike to Bob Lord, one could detest his attitudes, but one could not question his knowledge of football.

Nor could anyone accuse him of being totally autocratic. For example, during the PFA's campaign for the abolition of the maximum wage, Lord was one of the few, if not the only club chairman to take the trouble to consult his own players as to their views. They persuaded him, too. After meeting them he made a public declaration in support of the PFA. Of course, that could have been as much due to his irritation with the existing Management Committee as to his belief in the players' cause.

He accused the leaders of the game of being bumbling amateur legislators. How could they pick the England football team when they had so little or no experience of management? How could they reject the players' demands when no other profession in the world had a maximum wage?

The Management Committee was responsible for the decline in attendances, reckoned Lord. Their ideas were antiquated. What football needed was a paid dictator. 'The Football League is too big and too commercial to be run by amateur legislators. The time has come to appoint a highly-paid boss to the job', he wrote in 1963.

But Lord knew his own position only too well to claim that role for himself. In fact, he seemed to revel in being a rebel. 'Who was the butcher's boy to be telling the big shots how to run their mismanaged business?' he asked sarcastically in his autobiography.

There were many in the game who quietly agreed with him, but didn't dare admit it. When he was first nominated for the Management Committee in 1962, he received only 9 votes. A few months later he was up before the Committee again for making personal attacks on Leeds United's chairman, and then in 1963 he seemed to contradict all his beliefs in players' rights by brazenly suggesting that the League completely ignore Justice Wilberforce's judgement on the Eastham case.

In 1965, after he was reprimanded yet again for remarks he had made in the press, Joe Richards told Lord: 'It isn't as simple as you would think to run the League.' And when Lord finally made the Committee in 1967 – how the members must have winced when the votes were announced – one of the first things Lord did was to admit that Sir Joe was right. Life was a lot harder than he'd imagined on the other side of the fence. He had never, for example, realized just how much preparation and work had to be done for each Management Committee meeting.

In time, Bob Lord even came to an understanding with his former arch-opponent, Alan Hardaker, which was not really so surprising since they were both such similar characters; tough, forthright and dedicated.

By the time he stood for the presidency, it is probably true to say that no one apart from Hardaker knew or understood the League regulations better than Bob Lord. And no other member of the Committee worked harder than the Burnley chairman. 'His commitments seem to hang on him like an empty rucksack', commented the *Observer* in 1974.

On one occasion Lord even reported a manager for being abusive towards the match officials in their dressing room. The poacher had well and truly turned gamekeeper.

Not that he stopped complaining altogether. For example, he moaned so often about the catering at Management Committee meetings that the other members told him in exasperation to take charge of it himself. This he did, and the other members supped well thereafter. Lord was apparently meticulous, especially about the quality of the meat. One can well imagine the Burnley butcher reproaching some London chef for his choice of cuts.

Once, the hotel concerned was so annoyed by his complaints that they resolved to give him exactly what he had said he would prefer to their fancy cooking: fish and chips in newspapers were wheeled in, together with a bottle of beer. All the other members ate à la carte, while Bob Lord laughingly tucked into his offering. He could take a joke.

For this reason, and because of his dedication to the game, despite his moaning, his abrasiveness and his careless comments, Bob Lord is actually remembered very fondly in League circles today. He had his mellower side, which showed especially in his later life. He hated the thought of Sunday football, not because he was religious but because he was, for all his progressive ideas in football, at heart a traditionalist. He bitterly opposed televised football. He once told a journalist, almost plaintively, in 1974: 'I don't like this modern way of playing. It's taken all the glitter out of the game.'

In 1972 Bob Lord stood for the presidency against Len Shipman, but was forced to withdraw when he needed an operation on his ear. When Shipman eventually stood down in 1974, Lord was nominated again.

This was his best chance yet. No one on the Committee had his experience or his tenacity and energy. If he had been a rebel in the past, he was now very much part of the establishment. With his oiled hair and centre parting he resembled a centre-forward from the 1930s –

one of the old school.

But he could not escape his past. As the votes for him and Lord Westwood were counted, it became clear that the years had caught up with the butcher from Burnley. Some chairmen could not forgive him his abusive comments; some could not trust him to act as guardian of the League.

Lord Westwood received 41 votes, Bob Lord only 6. The scale of his defeat hurt, there could be no denying, but the decision was right, nevertheless. Like Fred Rinder and John Lewis before him, Bob Lord was a valued member of the Management Committee, but he was no League president.

Nor was he a quitter. He continued to serve the Management Committee faithfully and energetically under Lord Westwood's leadership. In 1979 he became president of the newly formed Alliance Premier League, and he gave his name to the League's knock-out cup, the Bob Lord Challenge Trophy. When Lord Westwood stood down from the presidency of the League in March 1981, Lord also served as Acting President until May of that year.

Burnley followers nowadays tend to remember Bob Lord as the man who transformed Turf Moor into a modern stadium, putting stands before players and precipitating the decline which eventually led to Burnley slipping down into the Fourth Division. The Bob Lord Stand, opened in September 1974, was dubbed the 'Martin Dobson Stand' by cynical supporters, after Dobson's £300,000 transfer to Everton had helped to pay for its erection. Lord was also accused of having engineered certain land deals to his own advantage.

But those same fans might note that, had Lord not replaced the old wooden stands, they would have soon been condemned under the Safety of Sports Grounds Act a few years later. Replacing them then would have been much more expensive.

It is also true that Burnley might never have become the force they were without Bob Lord.

As Bill Shankly wrote: 'Controversial he may be. But he is no hypocrite. Everything he has done has been with the interests of Burnley FC at heart. He is Burnley through and through. If you think of the club you think of him. The two are inseparable.'

Lord died on 8 December 1981, a few months short of Burnley's centenary. The club was then in the Third Division and over £300,000 in debt. Six years later they were almost relegated from the League when they finished a point away from the bottom of the Fourth Division. Some fans blamed Lord for the decline, but they were wrong. The same harsh economic facts of modern football also dragged down clubs like Preston, Blackpool and Bolton during the same period. The difference was that Bob Lord had given the Burnley supporters a taste of the big time, and the higher they rise, the harder they fall. Not even Bob Lord could argue about that.

*   *   *

The chance of becoming the tenth president of the Football League did not fall to Lord Westwood because of his title alone, but it certainly helped. If the FA could have their peers and knights, why couldn't the League also enjoy a touch of reflected nobility? Lord Bill, as he was known to Newcastle folk, was a charismatic man who commanded respect in both football and the business world.

Furthermore, his rise was quite unprecedented in the annals of the League. Before Westwood, John McKenna had risen most quickly to become President, serving eight years before his election; Charles Sutcliffe waited the longest – 38 years. Lord Westwood, however, served on the Committee for just four years before becoming President.

To look at the man it was not hard to understand why he attracted everyone's attention. Lord Westwood's appearance was, to say the least, quite distinctive. He was tall, he had gleaming silvery hair, and most noticeable of all he wore a black patch over his left eye. This, the unfortunate legacy of a car accident, gave him an almost buccaneerish aspect.

But there was more to Lord Westwood than simply an imposing physiognomy. He possessed great wit and charm. He was an urbane man, whose light approach to life belied an essentially serious nature.

No one was more delighted with his election than Alan Hardaker. Football in the mid 1970s needed a figurehead, a man who could argue the League's case in the corridors of power, and lead the clubs with a progressive outlook. Len Shipman, for all his other qualities, had not been able to do that, with the result that Hardaker was having to bear too much of both the public and the private burden on his own shoulders.

Lord Westwood was Hardaker's perfect ally, as Bob Lord knew only too well. Just before the election, the Burnley chairman had been arguing with Hardaker about the costs of producing the *Football League Review*, which Lord claimed was being used as Hardaker's mouthpiece (which it was). Lord suspected Hardaker of campaigning for Westwood and against him in the run-up to the Annual Meeting, and for a while he refused to eat with the other members of the Committee – fish and chips, à la carte or anything else.

It is easy to imagine how Bob Lord must have regarded the aristocratic figure of Lord Westwood, who had, in effect, overtaken him in the running for high office. Westwood's easy-going manner and his way with words were in direct contrast to Lord's.

Lord was a butcher whose outbursts filled the back pages of the press. Westwood was a director of several large companies, whose activities featured in the more rarefied columns of the business news. Lord knew that his knowledge of the game far outstripped that of the Newcastle chairman, but he also realized that that was not enough.

At one meeting, Lord's resentment came out into the open. Westwood, always quick off the mark, told him: 'You think I was born with a silver spoon in my mouth. Let me tell you something. You were born with a bloody shovel in yours!' It did the trick. Lord supported the new President thereafter.

In fact, Bill Westwood was not born with a silver spoon in his mouth at all. He was born in Dundee on Christmas Day 1907 (a fact in which he delighted). His father was a union leader in the shipyards, who was elevated to the House of Lords by Winston Churchill in 1944, in recognition of his contribution to wartime shipbuilding. His son had to make his own way in life, however. He started work as a clerk for the London Midland Scottish Railway in Glasgow shortly after the First World War, and then followed his parents to Newcastle around 1930, where he became secretary to a cinema group.

Like his father he soon rose up the ladder, eventually becoming managing director. From there he moved into the toy manufacturing business with a well respected firm called Dunbee-Combex-Marx, and took on several other directorships with a number of public and private companies.

About the only thing that was ever handed to Bill Westwood on a plate was his father's title, in 1953. The first Lord Westwood had also been a director of Newcastle United, and his son later followed the same path. He joined the board in 1960 and soon achieved prominence by being elected chairman of United in October 1964, a role he played until 1978, when he became club president.

Westwood was an establishment figure such as the League had never quite known before. Previous Presidents had achieved public prominence solely through football: Lord Westwood was already well known outside the game. Apart from his business interests and his seat in the House of Lords, he was also active in his local Conservative Association, was a magistrate and served as president on the North East's Publicity Association. His silver hair and black eye-patch were as familiar outside the game as within.

Lord Westwood's chief contribution to the

League before attaining the presidency had been to help negotiate the Lang Agreement between the League and the FA, whereby the League received a fairer share of the revenue earned from certain Cup and international matches. Those negotiations proved to Alan Hardaker that Westwood would be a good man to succeed Shipman; and Hardaker was right. The two men worked well together, Hardaker providing the facts, Westwood presenting them.

But as his years in office progressed, three factors overtook the President. Firstly, despite his popularity as a raconteur – he undertook speaking tours of America and was in frequent demand as an after-dinner speaker – he was not an authoritative chairman of Management Committee meetings. He could represent, but not necessarily dictate.

Secondly, both his business affairs and his health began to suffer during his seven years in office.

But thirdly, and most importantly, in 1980/1 his own club Newcastle faced a financial crisis. Westwood's period as chairman had seen United take two trips to Wembley and enjoy some success in Europe, but when he and his fellow directors were asked to invest around £50,000 towards United's overall debt of £500,000, Westwood decided the time was right to leave.

This did not go down too well with the St James's Park faithful. They assumed that with his title and business interests, Lord Westwood had plenty of reserves. Then aged seventy-three, Westwood responded by saying that he was 'too old to take on the mountainous problems' facing Newcastle. Between fifty and sixty board meetings a year, plus all his other League, FA and wide business commitments, added up to an intolerable workload. In addition, Dunbee-Combex-Marx were ailing at the time. But while Lord Westwood saw his departure as a chance to allow younger men to make their mark, many of the fans saw his sudden departure in March 1981 as treachery.

Local ramifications apart, resignation from the board at St James's Park gave Westwood no choice but to resign also from the presidency of the League. This was accepted with regret by the members of the Management Committee, who gladly agreed to allow Lord Westwood a couple of extra weeks in office to allow him one last honour as President: the presentation of the trophy to the League Cup winners on 14 March at Wembley.

Unfortunately, it was not to be. Liverpool and West Ham drew 1–1 at Wembley, and on the next morning Lord Westwood had to step down. 'Gentlemen, this is the last supper', he told the Committee. He was, he admitted later, rather relieved to be stepping down.

Lord Westwood remains a Life Member of the League, and now lives in retirement in Gosforth. But never has a League President parted company with the game in such an abrupt manner. At Wembley one day, in apparent obscurity the next. He has hardly been to a match since March 1981.

As fortune would have it, Bob Lord stepped into the breach as Acting resident, and must have glowed with pride as he travelled to Villa Park a couple of weeks later to present the League Cup to Liverpool after the replay. The fact that it was April Fool's Day will not have bothered Bob Lord. Lord Westwood, however, will have appreciated the irony. His great skill as President had always been to take the steam out of a situation. 'I enjoyed being President thoroughly,' he said in his retirement. 'I never lost any sleep over football, but then it was easy for me because Alan Hardaker was such a brilliant Secretary.'

'It doesn't matter what you do in football,' he remarked. 'Nine times out of ten you're wrong, and the one time you're right someone else takes the credit.'

Returning to 1974, however, Lord Westwood had yet to find that out.

CHAPTER TWENTY-EIGHT

Brave New Worlds

Lord Westwood's first task as President was to face concerted action by Midland clubs who were demanding an overhaul of the Management Committee's constitution. The League's greatest failing, claimed this caucus of nine clubs, was a lack of communication.

Underlying their anxiety was a thinly-veiled suggestion that somehow Alan Hardaker was making decisions without consulting the Management Committee. This was refuted on several occasions by the Committee members, who rather resented the implication that they were somehow being dominated by the Secretary. But the truth is that often they were.

Hardaker was a dominant personality and an administrative wizard. He was a professional, whereas the Committee men were, by necessity, part-time amateurs. It was still against the rules for directors to be paid or for a paid official to sit on a club board. Hardaker, on the other hand, had been in harness for nearly twenty years and knew the ropes better than any other man in English football.

Powerful though the Secretary was, however, he was still no dictator. Indeed, he tried to keep all ninety-two clubs informed by issuing a newsletter after each Management Committee meeting. But, as Lord Westwood reminded the clubs, 'Communication works two ways.' It was no use complaining about a lack of contact when so many chairmen left the circulars unopened on their desks.

Nevertheless, the Midland clubs' proposals were constructive and in line with recommendations made by the Commission on Industrial Relations (which first met to assess the football industry in 1972). At an Extraordinary General Meeting held immediately after Westwood's election in 1974, they suggested the introduction of regional representation on the Management Committee.

Beforehand, each member had been elected according to his merits and the status of his club. A regional system would allow each member to represent the clubs in his area, report back to them and, if necessary, carry their views forward. This, it was claimed, would ease the Committee's burden and speed up decisions, which would in turn help to improve the League's flagging image.

The Management Committee, and especially Alan Hardaker, opposed the idea on the grounds that members should represent the national interest and be elected on their personal merit. The counter-argument was that this often gave the Committee a northern bias, and depended too much on Hardaker to spread the word.

The root of the communication problem lay essentially, however, in personality clashes and the fact that League and football-related business was becoming ever more complex and time-consuming. Club chairmen and secretaries were being asked to absorb and deal with all kinds of new legislation governing players, ground safety, insurance, industrial relations and trading regulations. On the pitch, football remained a simple game. Off the pitch, it was anything but. Alan Hardaker coped easily with this new state of affairs; he lived, breathed and ate football administration. For unpaid, untrained directors it was harder to keep up.

So regionalization was touted as a solution and the Midland clubs (led by Birmingham, Coventry and Aston Villa), got their way with a substantial majority. Thus the Management Committee underwent the single greatest change in its constitution since 1892.

The offices of President and two Vice Presidents would survive, but from 1975 onwards the six Committee members would be elected from geographically arranged groups of between six and nine full member clubs.

There was also one other significant change.

For the first time ever, the Associate Members were given the right to elect on to the Committee their very own representative. This was an important concession and one for which the lower division clubs had been fighting since the 1920s (much to Charles Sutcliffe's annoyance at the time). In the past, directors of Third and Fourth Division clubs had sat on the Committee – Harold Shentall and Joe Richards for example – but only because at the time of their first election their clubs had been Full Members.

Voting under this newly agreed constitution had to wait until 1975. In the meantime, elections to the Management Committee in 1974 were as usual. Syd Collings' health was failing, so he was honoured as a Life Member. In his place the clubs elected one of the leading members of the Midland caucus, a man with a familiar surname in League circles; Jack Wiseman was David Wiseman's son, and thus he became the first member to have followed his father on to the Committee.

The election of Associate Members in 1974 was a close-run affair, with another remote northern club only just surviving a challenge from the south. Doncaster (46 votes), Stockport (38) and Crewe (37) were each re-elected, together with Workington, who polled only 21. Once again, had there been fewer non-League challengers the Cumbrians might well have lost their place. As it was, the vote was split between Kettering (16), Yeovil (14), Wigan (10) and Chelmsford (8). Other applicants were Nuneaton and Telford (1 each) and Cambridge City, who, hardly surprisingly, attracted no votes at all. (With their neighbours

United now established in the League, one wonders why City persisted in their forlorn quest.)

Lord Westwood's first season in office turned out to be a good one, full of interest and surprise. The First Division Championship, won by Derby County for the second time, saw only eight points separating the top ten clubs, while the Second Division enjoyed one of its best seasons for many a year. Manchester United strode back to Division One at the first attempt. Promoted with them were the long absent Aston Villa, plus Norwich City.

These last two teams contested the League Cup Final at Wembley, while another Second Division club, Fulham, reached Wembley for the FA Cup Final, against West Ham. Never before had the Second Division provided three of the four major finalists in domestic competitions. Sheffield Wednesday, meanwhile, slipped down into the Third Division for the first time.

'Despite all the gloomy forecasts from some critics both in the press and other media,' Lord Westwood told the 1975 Annual Meeting, 'the past season has not been unsuccessful.

Gates were up by nearly 600,000 (a rise of 2.4 per cent), and relations with the PFA had 'never been happier or more harmonious'. But change was imminent, warned the President. 'The report by the Commission on Industrial Relations contains the seed for reform in many aspects. Talks are continuing on what might be termed the "big" issues', said Lord Westwood, by which he meant freedom of contract – the abolition of all retention clauses at the end of a player's contract.

Most realists in football knew by then that freedom of contract was inevitable, but a large number of directors and managers were still terrified of its consequences. (In fact, as we shall see, the talks to which Lord Westwood referred would continue for another four years.)

Regionalized representation on the Management Committee took effect as from the 1975 Annual Meeting. Long-serving retiring members Arthur Would, Michael Gliksten and Sam Bolton each became Life Members, and Dick Wragg was elected a Vice President. Since Bob Lord and Lord Westwood stayed in office, this meant vacancies for six new members. After the votes were counted, however, three of the other sitting members kept their places.

The voting resulted as follows:

Group One (North West): sitting member Sir Matt Busby, Manchester United, was elected unopposed.

Group Two (North East and Yorkshire): Robert Strachan, York City, was elected after a second ballot.

Group Three (West Midlands): sitting member Jack Wiseman, Birmingham City, was elected in preference to Aston Villa's Doug Ellis by 36 votes to 13.

Group Four (East Midlands and East Anglia): Life Member and former President Len Shipman, Leicester City, was elected unopposed.

Group Five (South and South West): John Deacon, Portsmouth, was elected unopposed.

Group Six (London): Brian Mears, Chelsea, son of former League Vice President and FA chairman, Joe Mears, was elected unopposed.

Associate Members: their first ever representative on the Management Committee, Dr Clifford Grossmark, Gillingham, was elected unanimously.

Thus, the ten-strong Management Committee for 1975/6 comprised four new men, the single biggest change to the Committee ever made in one year.

As it transpired, two of the new intake would serve for only a year. Coincidentally, both Portsmouth and York City were relegated to Division Three at the end of the season, so John Deacon and Robert Strachan had to stand down at the 1976 Annual Meeting. Their places were taken by Robert Daniel of Plymouth

Argyle and Christopher Needler of Hull City.

Regionalization had its teething problems. Each Committee member would call together the clubs in his region to explain Committee decisions and discuss future issues; perfect in theory, but in practice there was a great deal of talking but not a lot more understanding or agreement.

At least life was looking up for the League competitions. The 1975/6 season had seen a marked return to the brand of attacking football which many believed had been stifled for good in the early 1970s. Fourth Division champions Lincoln City, for example, became the first club to score a century of League goals since QPR in 1966/7.

The following season would reflect the trend towards more open football with a 5 per cent rise in gates, the biggest increase since England had won the World Cup in 1966.

Lord Westwood reflected the new mood of optimism at the 1976 Annual Meeting when he turned to the press and said:

'It has often been argued whether football sells papers or whether papers sell football. I do not propose to re-open that argument today, because it is an argument that cannot be won. I would just like to say thank you for the many thousands of words you write about the League game, thank you for the many words spoken on radio, and thank you for the action shown on our television screens.

We do not always agree with one another; in fact, we often have to agree to differ. But we in the Football League respect your abilities, as I hope you respect ours. The League office is always open to you, to answer your queries, to check your stories, and I do sincerely express the hope that the telephone never stops ringing.'

No President since John Bentley had ever expressed so openly such a warm sense of regard for the press. But, of course, Westwood knew just how vital it was to have the support of the media if the League was to continue its apparent rise in popularity.

Westwood's optimistic and progressive approach was further illustrated by his eager embrace of the concept of automatic promotion and relegation from non-League football to the Fourth Division. To that end, he and Alan Hardaker continued negotiations with the Southern League and Northern Premier League over the formation of an Alliance. If nothing else, Westwood implied, it would be preferable to the large numbers of non-League clubs applying every year with little hope of success.

In 1975 another fourteen threw their names into the hat, the best effort coming from Kettering Town, who received 20 votes and would have succeeded had the other votes not been so divided, yet again. Kettering's total was just 8 short of Workington's (28). The Cumbrians were thus re-elected along with Swansea (43), who six years later would finish sixth in Division One, Scunthorpe (41) and Darlington (32).

Among the other unsuccessful challengers the results were: Yeovil (8), Wimbledon (4), Bedford, Goole Town and Scarborough (2 each), Gainsborough Trinity, Nuneaton, Telford and Weymouth (1 each), Boston and Chelmsford (no votes).

The following year, 1976, there were still nine non-League clubs up for election, and predictably the four retiring clubs were again able to capitalize on the spread of votes. However, the writing was now most clearly on the wall for Workington. While Stockport (42 votes), Newport (41) and Southport (38) were each comfortably returned, Workington scraped back in by the seat of their pants with just 21 votes, narrowly ahead of Southern League Yeovil (18). Next came Kettering (14).

But if either of these last two felt confident about their chances for 1977, the fickle nature of football emphatically put paid to that. Some way behind Kettering in the 1976 voting came two clubs, Wigan (6) and Wimbledon (3), each of whom would leapfrog over Kettering and Yeovil in the near future.

Other applicants in 1976 were Chelmsford (3), Nuneaton and Telford (2 each), Gainsborough and Scarborough (1 each).

But, as Lord Westwood was able to tell the 1976 Annual Meeting, long overdue change was on its way. A few months earlier, progress towards a more defined relationship had led both the Southern League and Northern Premier League to agree that from 1977 onwards they would each submit a list of applicants to be vetted by the Management Committee. From that list two approved clubs would be chosen to challenge the four retiring clubs, in return for which any club losing its League status would be guaranteed a place in either the Northern Premier or Southern Leagues.

Thus, 1976 was the last time that Full Members had to sift through a long list of totally unsuitable applicants. From then onwards, in theory at least, only six names would go forward each year.

Another welcome new measure agreed at the 1976 Annual Meeting was the abandonment of the much unloved system of goal averages. On the instigation of Arsenal, to whom the entire football-loving public and press should be eternally grateful, it was agreed:

● That if two clubs finished equal on points, the 'goals against' total should be deducted from the 'goals for' to determine 'goal difference'. A greater goal difference would merit a higher placing.

● In the event of goal differences being equal, the club scoring the most goals would rank higher.

● If both clubs scored the same number, the matter would then be decided by a play-off at a neutral ground (although this has yet to happen).

In addition to 'goal difference', another term entered the lexicon of modern football. This was the word 'designation'.

Goal Average versus Goal Difference

Statistical fiends might be interested to know that, had the goal difference system pertained before 1976, one League Championship would have been decided differently.

In 1923/4, Huddersfield won the first of their trio of League titles with a goal average of 1.818, a tiny fraction ahead of Cardiff, whose goal average was 1.794. Had goal difference been in operation, the Championship would have gone to Cardiff, and thus to Wales for the first and only time in League history. Both teams had a goal difference of 27, but Cardiff would have finished top, having scored 61 to Huddersfield's 60. Even with goal average, the finish was so close that had one of Cardiff's players not missed a penalty on the last day of the season the Welsh club would have won the Championship after all.

The Second Division promotion race that season would also have ended differently had goal difference applied.

Derby would have been promoted to Division One in place of Bury. Again in Division Two, in 1926/7 Manchester City would have been promoted in place of Portsmouth, and in 1949/50 Sheffield United would have gone up instead of local rivals Wednesday.

There are three other examples, all in the Fourth Division.

Carlisle would have won the Championship in 1963/4 instead of Gillingham; in 1965/6 Tranmere would have been promoted in place of Colchester, and in 1974/5 Lincoln would have gone up instead of Chester.

Since 1976, had goal average remained in use, only one important placing would have been different: in 1983/4 Hull City would have been promoted to Division Two in place of Sheffield United.

Following the introduction of the Safety of Sports Grounds Act in 1975, clubs in the First Division were required to have their grounds brought up to the standards recommended by the Wheatley Report, which had since 1973 been incorporated in the voluntary Green Code. Designation – that is, being brought under the Act's aegis – meant that if the Green Code's standards were not met, either a licence would be withheld or the capacity of the ground reduced accordingly.

For clubs like Manchester United and Arsenal who had always maintained their grounds under careful supervision, the designation order presented only a few headaches. But for other clubs, notably Newcastle and later Southampton, designation involved a huge expenditure on new crush barriers, improved ways of access, new lighting, surfacing and fire prevention . . . in fact, whatever the local licensing authority demanded.

No one could publicly decry the Safety Act. After the second Ibrox tragedy in 1971, in which sixty-six people died, everyone was aware of how narrow the divide between discomfort and disaster could be. And as almost every fatal incident at football matches had proven, most accidents could be avoided. It was no longer enough for club directors to throw up their hands in horror and claim that accidents were an inevitable consequence of large crowds gathering in confined spaces. Football clubs had to be seen to be making an effort to improve their own grounds. Gates were declining enough, without adding a fear for safety to the already potent fear of hooliganism.

Given two years to set their houses in order, the big question amongst First Division clubs in 1975 was this: how were they going to find the money for all the safety improvements?

Like a bolt from the heavens, the answer came from the Pool Promoters' Association. Alan Hardaker persuaded the pools companies that a percentage of their profits from spotting-the-ball competitions (which did not form a part of the fixtures agreement) should finance the setting up of a new body, the Football Grounds Improvement Trust.

Richly appreciated though the PPA's apparent generosity was, their offer was not entirely a voluntary gesture. While the tax on pools betting was set at a swingeing 42.5 per cent, compared with only 8 per cent on horse-race betting, spotting-the-ball competitions were not taxed at all (apart from VAT). In order that they should remain untaxed, it suited the PPA, therefore, to be seen to be making this valued contribution to football. Had they not made the offer, the Government might easily have changed its mind, especially after a recent Royal Commission on Gambling.

So the PPA was relieved, the Government was satisfied, the Football League was absolutely delighted and once again the credit for the arrangement had to go to Alan Hardaker.

The Football Grounds Improvement Trust is administered from the League headquarters. Among its six original trustees, all appointed by the League, were Sir Norman Chester and former Preston and England international Tom Finney OBE. Other trustees in 1987 include former secretary of the PFA, Cliff Lloyd, and the current League Secretary, Graham Kelly.

The first FGIT payment of £130,700 arrived in October 1975, a few months before the safety of Sports Grounds Act took effect on First Division clubs. Very welcome it was, too. The mid 1970s had seen a rapid rise in inflation, affecting building costs and ground improvements particularly, as far as football clubs were concerned.

The 1960s had seen the erection of many a new stand at League grounds, but thereafter costs rose so much that whereas Manchester United's fine cantilever stand built in 1963 had cost £350,000, Everton had to pay over £1 million for their new Main Stand in 1971, and Chelsea all but bankrupted themselves by spending twice as much again in 1974.

New stands or not, as in the inter-war period, the 1970s saw a spate of clubs falling into financial difficulties, amongst them Second Division Luton Town, who in December 1975 were reported to have been close to winding up altogether. Several other clubs owed transfer money to each other. So serious was the overall situation that in April 1976 the League set up a sub-committee to sit with members of the Chester Report Committee to make 'urgent investigations' into the financial state of League clubs.

Even with FGIT's money, in the first months of the Safety Act's operation the League was forced to divert some of its other income towards ground safety measures. Over £50,000, received from the FA under the Lang Agreement, went in late 1975 towards helping Second Division clubs, and that was just the tip of a huge iceberg.

Maintaining standards at League grounds would soon prove to be as difficult and time-consuming as keeping an old jalopy on the road; repair work was never-ending, accessories were expensive, and just when clubs thought they had it right, the licensing authority would make a check and point out another fault. To make it harder, some authorities were stricter than others.

As if all this extra expense were not enough, clubs had to prepare themselves for another potential rise in their costs following further negotiations with the PFA. These resulted in 1978 in agreement to introduce 'freedom of contract'.

Freedom of contract would have seemed like an impossible dream to the pioneers of the Players' Union at the turn of the century. It remained something of a pipe dream even in 1963 after the Eastham judgement, which still tied the player to his club under certain circumstances, dictated mainly by the scale of any wage offer or the fee being offered for him by another club. In either case, the club held the whip hand.

In 1968 the Chester Report recommended the complete abolition of the retention system, a view investigated further by the Commission on Industrial Relations, which was chaired by Professor Sir John Wood and delivered its report in 1974. The commission discovered a shocking lack of communication between the League and the players (so much for all the Ministry of Labour's recommendations in 1961).

Coinciding with Lord Westwood's election as President in 1974, therefore, a new start was made with the formation of the Professional Football Negotiating Committee. This brought together the League and the PFA under Wood's independent chairmanship, and was designed to discuss all aspects of players' conditions. It meets on a quarterly basis and has, since its inception, been one of the most influential and beneficial bodies professional football has ever known.

Sir John Wood acts as chairman in a purely voluntary capacity. A professor of law at Sheffield University and an expert in arbitration, he little knew in 1974 just how long and how tough his involvement was going to be.

Early meetings of the PFNC soon showed that the major issue separating the League and the players was the question of freedom of contract. This was an issue as important as the abolition of the maximum wage and of even greater potential significance than the Eastham case. Freedom of contract, if ever the clubs would accept it, meant that clubs would lose their automatic right to retain a player after his contract was over. Whatever they offered him, whatever any other club offered, he was free to do as he wished. He could negotiate for a further contract; he could find another club. He could, of course, also find himself on the street without a job.

George Eastham had loosened the chains, but freedom of contract threatened to break them altogether.

It was the most radical change ever proposed in the ninety-year-old professional relationship between a player and the League, so it was small wonder the clubs were terrified at first.

What made them particularly fearful was that the logical consequence of freedom of contract appeared to be the abolition of transfer fees.

When negotiations in 1974 began, the clubs were worried that if, for argument's sake, Eddie Grundy finished his contract with Borchester United, he was quite at liberty to sign for whoever wanted him. Borchester wouldn't receive a penny for his registration, no matter how much money they had invested in his training, wages or development.

The first hurdle in the long and tortuous negotiations which took place between 1974 and 1978, therefore, was the question of transfer fees. Could they continue to operate under freedom of contract? That there had to be some provision for financial recompense went without saying in League circles, whatever the Chester Report suggested to the contrary. The League system couldn't possibly operate without transfer fees, argued the clubs.

At that time, the ninety-two clubs were said to have had accumulated debts of £13 million. Only twenty-nine of them were in profit, and fees were seen as a means by which smaller clubs kept afloat by grooming stars for the top. Transfers kept money circulating within the game. If players were to move freely without fees, the financial structure of football would change beyond all recognition: all the rich and glamorous clubs would gain an unfettered choice of every available player, smaller clubs would have to turn part time or reduce their staffs to an absolute minimum. The League argued, therefore, that freedom of contract had to be allied to a system of compensation. If Liverpool wanted to sign Eddie Grundy at the end of his contract, they would have to compensate Borchester United.

The PFA accepted this. Although the Chester Report had implied that it was a myth that transfer fees helped smaller clubs, the union realized that the bank overdraft of many a club was in fact based upon the saleable value of its players. Borchester's bank manager was far more likely to tolerate a £100,000 overdraft if he knew that Eddie Grundy might fetch that amount from a First or Second Division club. The PFA concluded, therefore, that although it still smacked of dealing with players like cattle, a system of compensation fees would ultimately allow clubs to keep more players on their books. The problem for both the PFA and the League, a problem which took many months to resolve, was how this system of compensation was to work.

The plan first settled upon, largely by agreement between Alan Hardaker and Cliff Lloyd, was based on a similar agreement existing in Holland. It depended on a complex but pre-determined mathematical formula called the multiplier. The multiplier was like a ready reckoner which would calculate instantly a player's worth, based on his age, his wage, the division in which he played and his relative standing within the profession. Was he, for example, a twenty-one-year-old First Division player on his way up, chasing international honours, or a Third Division veteran with only a year or two left of his career?

There were several attractive features of the multiplier system. Among them, a player, his club and any interested club would know exactly how much he was worth when his contract expired. That, in turn, would help keep prices at a sensible level. 'The fervent wish was that in time this system would restore sanity to the transfer market', wrote Hardaker, at a time when the League record stood at over £300,000, three times the figure of only a decade earlier.

Ultimately, however, the multiplier system was not introduced. First the clubs turned against it, and then the PFA began to see its weaknesses – all this after some two years of negotiation. The main reason for its rejection was that it couldn't always be depended on to work out a satisfactory compensation fee. Did one base the players' value on his basic wage only, or on his overall contract, which perhaps included a car, a house, special bonuses and so on? Was the wage calculation based on the selling club's wages or the buying club's?

For example, using the multiplier and a hypothetical set of figures for 1974, a Fourth Division youth at Halifax on £50 a week could have been bought for only £30,000 by Liverpool. His age, his wage and his division determined a low price (which would be lower if a Second or Third division club wanted him). In reality, however, he may have been a young starlet – it was not Halifax's fault that they couldn't pay him more – so Liverpool would have made a real swoop and Halifax would have lost out.

Conversely, if Halifax wanted to buy a reserve player from Manchester United, where he was earning perhaps £200 a week, under the multiplier they might have to pay £20,000: more than they could afford if they wanted to offer him a decent wage.

The system had the same faults at the other end of the scale. A thirty-two-year-old First Division player on high wages with eighty caps to his credit might have been expected to drop down a division or two at a low price, as a reward for his long service. Under the multiplier system, however, he would have been rated very highly.

Even with the multiplier, therefore, there would have to have been some recourse to arbitration, ideally an independent appeals board. And if such a body were necessary, anyway, why not leave the bargaining to the clubs? The appeals board could then settle any outstanding disputes.

These were the issues at stake when the clubs first agreed, in principle only, to freedom of contract at the 1976 Annual Meeting. But if the events of the 1960s were anything to go by, the clubs would do all they could to delay the decision being enshrined in the regulations. This is exactly what happened. It took another two seasons for the details to be hammered out between the clubs and the PFA, before the Negotiating Committee could draw up a final draft agreement in October 1976. This then had to be presented at an Extraordinary

Arthur Drewry (right) helps Will Harrop with the FA Cup draw in 1952. Drewry always conveyed an air of casual elegance and good humour.

Jimmy Guthrie, the doughty chairman of the Players' Union, shortly before he was ousted and replaced by Jimmy Hill, in 1957.

League headquarters in Starkie Street, Preston: seat of the Charnley/Howarth dynasty, but 'a dump' in new-boy Hardaker's view.

Arthur Oakley – a sentimental appointment.

Fred Howarth.

LEFT

Joe Richards: on the day that the dapper Mr Football became Sir Joe, and thus the first League official ever to be knighted.

RIGHT

The League Cup trophy, donated by Joe Richards. One day, he predicted, the final would be played at Wembley, although not in his lifetime. Fortunately he was wrong and the League Cup came to Wembley in 1967.

BELOW

League headquarters in Lytham St Annes. Alan Hardaker, who lived in the house next door, later maintained that he would have preferred to base the League at Leamington Spa.

LEFT

Jimmy Hill and Cliff Lloyd arrive at the Ministry of Labour for talks in January 1961. Later that day Hill would have cause to curse the new fangled parking meters, having outstayed his allotted time because of the prolonged negotiations.

BELOW

After four and a half hours of tough bargaining the players' strike is off. Jimmy Hill and Joe Richards shake on it, with Labour Minister, John Hare (centre foreground), a relieved man.

ABOVE

The Management Committee at Bournemouth, July 1953. Back row (left to right): David Wiseman (B'ham), Norman Banks (Bolton), Joe Mears (Chelsea), Joe Richards (Barnsley), Fred Howarth (Secretary). Front row: Harry French (Middlesbrough), Arthur Oakley (Wolves), Arthur Drewry (President), Will Harrop (Liverpool), Harold Shentall (Chesterfield).

LEFT

Members of the Management Committee were often more conspicuous for their work at the FA. As Chairman of the FA Challenge Cup Committee, David Wiseman (left) was known to millions as the man who made the Cup draw. Joe Mears gives him a hand in February 1964.

A contrived memorial at Peel Park, a year after Accrington Stanley finally folded in January 1966. The pitch is now used by local schools, though Stanley have since revived.

The unlikely revolutionary: George Eastham, pictured with his new boss, Ernie Clay, in September 1960. So determined was Eastham to leave Newcastle that he spent five months as a salesman for Clay until Arsenal signed him up.

RIGHT

The Football League Review *ran from August 1966 to December 1974 and at its peak was inserted into the programmes of 73 clubs. It made no money but after tentative beginnings won plenty of friends.*

RIGHT

The Management Committee face an Extraordinary General Meeting at the Cafe Royal in December 1968. The issue at stake was, as usual, money. It was this Committee which proposed putting the clock back seven years by reintroducing the maximum wage. From left to right are Len Shipman (President), Wilf Taylor (Newcastle) and Sam Bolton (Leeds).

LEFT

Extra spice was added to the League Cup by televising the draw. Alan Hardaker, Sam Bolton and Bob Lord perform the honours on London Weekend Television in November 1972.

LEFT

Lord Westwood exported teddy bears to the USSR and brought a smile to the Management Committee.

BELOW

Alan Hardaker – the man who dragged the League into the modern era. With the exception only of Charles Sutcliffe, no man worked harder for the League than Hardaker. Had he really been a dictator, as he was so often portrayed, the whole structure of the League would have been radically altered in the early 1960s.

LEFT

Bob Lord, the Burnley butcher. From being the scourge of the Committee he turned into its elder statesman. His love for the game was unrivalled, but he seldom received a favourable press.

BELOW

The Management Committee at Lytham St Annes, August 1968. Back row (left to right): Alan Hardaker (Secretary), Arthur Would (Grimsby), Michael Gliksten (Charlton), Bob Lord (Burnley), Louis Edwards (Man Utd). Front row: David Wiseman (B'ham), Wilf Taylor (Newcastle), Len Shipman (President), Sam Bolton (Leeds), Syd Collings (Sunderland).

General Meeting in March 1977, which deferred the whole question for three months. 'The door has not been shut', Alan Hardaker told the press. The main sticking point was the method for assessing compensation fees.

'We have spent twenty-six months of negotiating to arrive at this position, and the game cannot afford to miss the opportunity, considering the state it is in', commented a very frustrated but determined Derek Dougan, chairman of the PFA at the time. A talkative, radical thinker, bubbling with ideas, Dougan had recently retired from a long career as centre-forward with six different clubs. He was backed by a particularly strong, well-briefed committee comprising Gordon Taylor (Dougan's eventual successor), then a winger with Blackburn, Terry Venables, the former England, Chelsea, Spurs, QPR and Palace wing-half (who went on to become a successful manager), and Bruce Bannister, an experienced striker then with Bristol Rovers. If Jimmy Hill had won much of the credit for the victory in 1961, the whole PFA committee deserved praise for its conduct between 1976 and 1978, as, of course, did Cliff Lloyd, as ever beavering calmly and effectively in the background.

For the League, Alan Hardaker was his usual steadfast self: sharp, superbly prepared and able to argue every clause if necessary. He urged the clubs to find a quick settlement, if only because the EEC was soon to review the whole question of players' movements within the European Community and it was therefore vital for the League to have agreed upon a system that could not then be challenged.

Meanwhile, Professor Wood sat in the middle; patient, anxious, and often shocked at how difficult it was to get the League chairmen to agree on anything. Ironically, one of the chief opponents of freedom of contract amongst the clubs was Sir Jack Scamp of Coventry, himself an experienced arbitrator in industrial disputes.

While the PFA reassessed their own tactics, the clubs discussed the matter further in their regional groups. It is worth noting, however, that throughout these vital stages the Management Committee was unanimous in its support for the PFNC's findings, a sure sign of realism on its side and efficacy on the part of the system. And although the clubs were concerned that every possible loophole be investigated in order to protect themselves, as a West Bromwich Albion director admitted: 'There is no foundation for the future in the League retaining the present system. Freedom of movement has to come, and come quickly.'

Interference from a government commission, pressure from Europe, an independent negotiator in the middle – men like Bentley and Sutcliffe would have been astounded. Whatever was wrong with good-old-fashioned bullying?

In the 1970s, however, League clubs had only one real trump card, and that was procrastination. In June 1977 the inevitable hold-up occurred. 'Nothing in football can be taken for granted', commented Alan Hardaker ruefully at the time. At another Extraordinary General Meeting, first the clubs approved the principles of the plan, then they voted against them becoming part of League regulations. As Hardaker wrote: 'It was a Gilbertian situation' – except that in this instance the players were not singing with delight. As in 1960, they threatened a strike.

But there was to be no repeat of the events surrounding the abolition of the maximum wage. For a start, the public was now largely indifferent to the issue. It was too complicated and much less emotive than the maximum wage issue. Secondly, the negotiations dragged on for so long that it was hard for outsiders to keep up with every twist and turn. Thirdly, there were no particular dramas for the media to seize upon, no deadlines and very few real threats. There was simply a lot of talking.

This seemed to have reached a conclusion in September 1977, when at a third Extraordinary General Meeting it was agreed overwhelmingly that: 'The clubs accept totally the player's right to move freely at the end of a contract and with every possible safeguard to ensure that right.'

But it was not to be. Still the small print wasn't right. More meetings took place, culminating in a fourth EGM in March 1978. The main point of contention was still the system of working out compensation fees.

So it was back to the negotiating table for Lord Westwood, and then on to a final EGM in April 1978. This time, the multiplier was taken out of the agreement, and at long last the much discussed, bruised and battered resolution was passed without a single vote of dissent. The marathon was over, leaving Hardaker exhausted and Lord Westwood bemused and bewildered.

A player of 1900 or even 1961 reading the new regulations concerning freedom of contract would have dismissed them as pure fantasy. Club directors would have laughed. But in 1978 freedom of contract became a reality, and, for better or worse, it revolutionized the relationship between club and player.

These were the main points of the new system, which remains in force today:

● If a player is transferred during the term of his contract, the previous conditions apply. That is, he can be sold for a transfer fee and the clubs must go through their usual bargaining procedures.

● If his contract is over and his club wants to keep him or receive a compensation fee, it must offer him the opportunity of another contract on at least as favourable terms as before. If the contract offered is worse, then the player is automatically entitled to a free transfer. If the club is expecting a compensation fee, it must continue to pay the player his former basic wage until another club signs him. If it wants him to carry on playing until that happens, it must negotiate weekly contracts.

● If, after the usual bargaining, the two clubs cannot agree on the level of compensation, the matter has then to be referred to the Appeals Committee.

● The four-man Football League Appeals Committee consists of the chairman (Professor Sir John Wood) plus a representative each from the League, PFA and the Secretaries' and Managers' Association. The function of this new committee is simply to determine compensation fees in the event of two clubs not reaching an agreement. It does not deal with disputes over transfer fees (as opposed to compensation fees).

The working of the system is simple in theory, though not always perfect in practice. At its best, if Borchester United valued Eddie Grundy at £200,000, while Liverpool want to buy him at £100,000, the Appeals Committee might well settle upon a fee of £150,000. Sometimes the buying club gets an unexpected bargain, sometimes the selling club gets a welcome bonus. As the chairman has often said, if both clubs leave the Appeals Committee feeling slightly aggrieved he knows the system has worked.

It has not, however, had much effect on keeping transfer fees at a sensible limit. When freedom of contract was agreed, the record fee between two British clubs stood at £440,000, paid by Liverpool for Celtic's Kenny Dalglish in August 1977. Eighteen months later, Trevor Francis became the first £1 million player when Nottingham Forest bought him from Birmingham City.

The reason why high fees continued to change hands was that not all clubs could wait until a player's contract had finished, while a club wanting to gain the maximum benefit from selling a player now simply put him on the market before his contract ended. Thus, if Borchester suspected that Grundy was worth a £100,000 compensation fee as a free agent, they might hope to get on average about £20–30,000 more as a transfer fee if they sold him in mid contract.

Dealing in players thus became a gamble for everyone, buying or selling: to wait or not to wait. Buy now at a high price, or delay a year but risk losing the player to another club. This 'lottery' has inevitably contributed to putting up players' wages, simply because the successful player now commands so much more bargaining power than beforehand.

The point is illustrated by the sale of the England strikers Gary Lineker and Peter Beardsley. When Lineker's contract with Leicester ended in 1985, they couldn't hope to match the wages a bigger club might offer. Leicester valued him at £800,000. Everton bid less. In the end, the Appeals Committee agreed with Leicester's valuation and stipulated that if Everton sold Lineker within two years, Leicester should receive a third of any profit. Everton did sell Lineker a year later, to Barcelona, at a total price reputed to have been £4.2 million.

Leicester could argue that the rich clubs get richer, the poor get poorer. Everton could respond by saying that the money they spend keeps other clubs in business. Market forces are market forces, and there have always been rich and poor in League football.

In 1987 Liverpool spent £1.9 million on Newcastle's Peter Beardsley, but he had a year to run on his contract. Had Liverpool waited a year they would undoubtedly have bought him for less, perhaps roughly the same price as Lineker had cost Everton (plus a bit extra to allow for inflation). But Liverpool wanted Beardsley in 1987, not 1988, and it was obviously in Newcastle's interest to sell him at the best possible price.

(Strictly speaking, Everton's £800,000 to Leicester should have been called a compensation fee, whereas Liverpool's £1.9 million to Newcastle was a transfer fee. Few people make the distinction, however.)

So the system introduced in 1978 did not keep down fees (other factors would see to that), but it did allow freedom of contract to be implemented without clubs losing their precious transfer system.

For the benefit of the player, freedom of contract now gave him the same rights as any other professional employee, after eighty years of waiting. It also opened him up to the same anxieties. He might, for example, find himself out on a limb at the end of a contract, unpaid and unwanted. But at least the negotiating machinery now existed to protect his interests, while the Appeals Committee has helped to prevent players being priced out of a job by greedy clubs.

Above all, the PFA's contribution to the negotiations between 1974 and 1978 signalled the beginning of a new era in League football. From 1978 onwards, the PFA was to be viewed as a responsible partner in the game, not as an unavoidable irritant. The PFA came of age in 1978, in the League's estimation at least.

Alan Hardaker himself was realistic about freedom of contract. He knew it was inevitable, but he understood the clubs' reservations. He also realized how few players it would benefit. 'Once there were 3500 players registered by the 92 clubs of the League,' he wrote in 1977. 'Now there are fewer than 2500. Freedom is a word with two faces.'

*　　*　　*

The 1977 Annual Meeting, Hardaker's twentieth since becoming Secretary, came as a great relief in one respect. As intended by Lord Westwood, just six clubs were listed as applying for Associate Membership, the smallest number since the First World War. Thus far, the new system had worked.

The two lucky non-League candidates, chosen from an original list of sixteen, were Altrincham, even though they failed to finish in the top four of the Northern Premier League, and Wimbledon, who had just won their third Southern League Championship in succession.

The new system paid immediate dividends for the non-League fraternity. When the votes were counted, Altrincham (12) were least favoured, Halifax (44 votes), Hartlepool (43) and Southport (37) were each re-elected, but Workington (21) were unable to improve on their previous year's showing (this was actually their fourth application in a row) and were displaced by Wimbledon (27). Thus, another northern club made way for a southern one, and in this case, an apparently unlikely one.

Wimbledon had turned professional as recently as 1964. Their ground was fairly basic, even by senior non-League standards, and they were in a part of London sandwiched between Fulham and Crystal Palace. Furthermore, in previous elections Wimbledon had fared badly compared with clubs such as Kettering and Yeovil. So could their inclusion really be merited, or were Wimbledon going to be another Thames FC?

Events, of course, have proved Wimbledon to be one of the two most successful recruits of the post-war era (along with Oxford). From the Southern League to the First Division in nine seasons is the kind of progress which even a comic-book editor might dismiss as far-fetched. But back in 1977 Wimbledon's achievement was a much simpler one. They had proved what most people had suspected for decades – that if the list of applicants at Annual Meetings was cut down, heads were bound to roll.

That Workington were the first to fall under this new system was really no surprise. In a rugby-dominated town with a population of less than 30,000, their gates were poor, their recent playing record had been miserable, and they were tucked away on the north-west coast, an hour's drive north of Barrow. Elected in 1951, Workington's zenith had been fifth place in Division three in 1966. Now it was down to the Northern Premier League, where they have remained ever since. Like Bradford Park Avenue, Barrow and Gateshead, Workington tried to win back their place the following year, but under the new system of vetting they weren't even chosen to go forward. In 1971 Cumbria had boasted three clubs. Now it had just one.

And if Southport felt sorry for ousted Workington as they left the Café Royal in June 1977, a year later it was their turn. A day after being fined £250 for belatedly handing in their list of re-engaged players, Southport found themselves locked in a tied vote with Northern Premier League runners-up Wigan Athletic. The first ballot resulted in York (49 votes), Rochdale (39) and Hartlepool (33) being re-elected. Southern League Bath City received 23 votes, but Southport and Wigan both polled 26 each. In the second ballot, Wigan eased ahead by 29 votes to 20.

Thus, while the Northern Premier League gained another ex-Fourth Division recruit, and Southport were offered the consolation of having their £250 returned, League football returned to the town of Wigan for the first time since Wigan Borough had dropped out in 1931. Southport had been Associate Members since 1921. Only four years earlier they had been in the Third Division, but three re-election campaigns in a row had proved too much.

First Workington, now Southport. Was this the way of the brave new world? No doubt a few non-League clubs rubbed their hands with glee at this second success in a row, but their celebrations were to prove a touch premature. From 1979 until 1987, not one non-League club managed to emulate Wigan or Wimbledon. The fortress doors were, in fact, as solidly impenetrable as ever.

And yet, at the time of Wigan's success, all the signs suggested that the drawbridge was coming down for good. Not only did the long-planned Alliance Premier League kick off in 1979, but the Management Committee behaved as if the Alliance were in actual fact a Fifth Division, no more, no less.

It did this, firstly, by vetting each of the twenty Alliance clubs' grounds, facilities and balance sheets, in order to grade their suitability for joining the League.

Secondly, Bob Lord accepted the presidency of the new competition.

Thirdly, George Readle, the League's Deputy Secretary, was appointed secretary of the Alliance, with further secretarial assistance being provided from Lytham St Annes; and finally, the League helped to appoint the referees and linesmen for all APL matches.

In short, the Committee appeared anxious to keep this infant league well and truly under its own tutelage. It even discussed the possibility of the top eight Alliance clubs entering the League Cup.

But if the Committee was enthusiastic as the APL prepared for its first season, at the League's Annual Meeting in 1979, the clubs decided to adopt a wait-and-see attitude. Having discarded Workington and Southport in the previous two years, it was again time to rally round the Old Pals.

Nineteen non-League clubs applied to join the League that year, from which the Committee selected two clubs to be put forward, neither of them winners of their respective competitions. Southern League champions Worcester City were deemed 'not up to the required standard', much to the Southern League's consternation. Kettering received the nomination instead. Similarly, NPL runners-up Altrincham were preferred to champions Mossley.

As it happened, neither stood a chance. Doncaster (50 votes), Crewe (49), Darlington (43) and Halifax (37) were re-elected. Altrincham polled 13 votes, Kettering 12.

The 1979 Annual Meeting was significant in

When the system of showing red and yellow cards to players being sent off or cautioned was first introduced in 1976, the first red card went to Blackburn's David Wagstaffe at Orient on 2 October. When the system was dropped in 1981, the last red cards were also shown at Orient, on 17 January, to Orient's Nigel Gray and Cardiff's Gary Stevens. Three months later, Luton Town devised a red card system of their own. During an eventful match against Oldham on 25 April 1981 the Kenilworth Road electronic scoreboard flashed up the message 'Send him off!' after an Oldham player had committed a foul. This time it was Luton who received a caution. Red and yellow cards were reintroduced in 1987 after pressure from FIFA.

---

one other respect. Alan Hardaker was now aged sixty-seven. Officially he should have retired in July 1977. But history was to repeat itself, for just as Fred Howarth had hung on to his position for as long as possible in the mid 1950s, so too was Hardaker reluctant to stand down when it came to the crunch.

Tragically, however, the 1979 Annual Meeting was to be Hardaker's last. For although Fred Howarth enjoyed a long, and relatively peaceful retirement after he left the League in 1956, Alan Hardaker had given his all to football, but left nothing for himself.

CHAPTER TWENTY-NINE
Alan Hardaker – Making Waves

Just as Charles Sutcliffe dominated the first half century of the Football League, Alan Hardaker stands out as the single most influential figure of the last fifty years, and perhaps also as one of the most misunderstood. Many people who had never dealt with him reviled him for being arrogant and difficult, but almost without exception those who knew him had nothing but respect for the man; for his dedication, his knowledge, his unquestionable abilities and also, it may surprise his detractors to learn, for his generosity and humour.

It would be tedious to list all his achievements – they are already recounted in earlier chapters – but equally it would be remiss not to emphasize the fact that Hardaker did not always get his way. Indeed, the description of him as a dictator stands up to little scrutiny.

Only in one sense was he all-powerful: he knew and understood more about League administration than any other man or woman, and thus hundreds of people depended on him for help, advice, information and opinion. He always gave this freely – sometimes abrasively, sometimes with a wry wit, but never without putting the League's interests first.

Lord Westwood wrote of him: 'He is forthright, honest and sometimes blunt ... he is often described by the media, the clubs, the managers and even the players as a dictator. Let me put the record straight – he is not a dictator. He abides by the Football League rules and regulations, and any decision he gives is in accord with the handbook or the instructions of the Management Committee.'

What Westwood did not say was that he, as President, and virtually every other member of the Management Committee, used to leave much of the League's business to Hardaker. He was not so much the power behind the throne as the power in front. And because many of the decisions he had to relay were unpalatable ones, Hardaker, and not the Committee members, took most of the flak.

Unlike his three predecessors, Hardaker came into football administration relatively late in life, but his credentials were perfectly in tune with League traditions. Born in July 1912 into a middle-class family in Hull, Hardaker was the son of a haulage contractor and one-time Rugby League player. His two main influences in early life were exactly those of the League's founder members: his father was a passionate Liberal, his mother a keen Methodist.

As a youth, Hardaker might have emulated Len Shipman by taking on the family haulage firm. Instead, he left the business soon after leaving school and went to work in the town clerk's office in Hull. He was a keen footballer, playing at centre forward in a works team before joining Hull City Reserves as an amateur. Hardaker was thus the first League Secretary to have been on the books of a League club.

He was exactly the sort of player one would have imagined: a hard tackler whose mouth was as potent as his shot. But he did have potential, and at twenty-three was offered professional terms. Knowing his own limitations and those of the profession only too well, he rejected the offer and remained at the town hall, where he was at the time the youngest Lord Mayor's secretary in Britain. This was 1935. (Had he signed as a professional, he later learned, the Hull manager had intended selling him immediately to Bradford PA for £750!)

After Hull Reserves, Hardaker switched to the Yorkshire League with Bridlington Town, and then to Yorkshire Amateurs. He nearly made the amateur international team. But, at the age of twenty-seven, war broke out and Hardaker enlisted with the navy – 'the best university in the world', as he called it.

Fortunately he graduated, with the rank of lieutenant commander, and by August 1946 was back at his old post of Lord Mayor's secretary, though in Portsmouth rather than Hull. It was a good time to be in the city, for Hardaker was able to sit in the directors' box at Fratton Park and see them win two Championships in succession.

It was shortly after their second triumph that Hardaker applied for the post of Assistant Secretary of the Football League. He was thirty-five, with an experience of the world far wider than Fred Howarth's, and used to shouldering all manner of duties, be they social, political, military or purely administrative. Yet apparently what impressed Howarth above all about Hardaker was that when asked to submit his travelling expenses after the first interview, he noted that Hardaker had travelled first-class.

What happened thereafter has already been told. Hardaker waited his turn, and waited. He was snubbed, ignored, and finally appointed Secretary in December 1956, after five years in the background. Indeed, one of the only references to him in the period 1951–6 was in November 1954, when the Committee commended him for his report on the clash of Doncaster Rovers' fixtures with race meetings. It was like congratulating Stanley Matthews for scoring a goal in a third team game.

Once in the hot seat, Hardaker's appetite for organization was insatiable. Backed by Joe Richards, he swept away the cobwebs and dragged the League into the modern era. He wrote in his autobiography: 'I must confess that whenever I smelt money for the League I usually jumped straight in and let everybody know about it later. In this respect I agree I have done things beyond the line of duty but, by way of mitigation, I estimate I have made the League about £12 million by my own efforts.'

Aside from his more public duties, one of Hardaker's greatest contributions to the League was to revamp completely its offices and procedures. Under his supervision the League moved to Lytham and expanded its staff from six to nearly thirty. True to the form of the naval officer he had once been, he was always cajoling, organizing and inspecting the staff and their work, making sure everything was ship-shape. Hardaker was also a traditionalist. Female members of staff, for example, were not allowed to come to work in trousers. He showed 'a degree of efficiency at times bordering on the ruthless', wrote David Lacey in the *Guardian*.

Undoubtedly Hardaker was too dedicated. He lived in a house next door to the League's offices and had only two escapes from football: his close-knit family (one of his four daughters worked at the League for a while), and fishing, a hobby he was rarely able to indulge. He had no really close friends, although he always enjoyed excellent relations with European administrators, who were for the most part younger, more progressive men than their English counterparts.

Hardaker admitted: 'I do not cultivate people', which was probably true also of his predecessors. Certainly, he shared Fred Howarth's rather frosty relationship with the FA secretary Stanley Rous. Howarth's antipathy, suggested Hardaker, was because he had applied for the FA job at the same time as Rous in 1934 and was disappointed at being passed over.

But between Hardaker and Rous the impasse

was more complex. It hinged upon power and influence and the often tortuous relationships which existed between UEFA, the FA and the League. For one period of six months Rous would not even talk to Hardaker. Furthermore, Rous was an avowed believer in the concept of a Super League and the eventual dream of a European League. Hardaker, on the other hand, was an implacable defender of the existing League framework. Although his 'Pattern for Football' – quite the most advanced and imaginative document the League had ever known – aimed to restructure the League, it never set out to trim the numbers or create an elite. (Like Sutcliffe, Hardaker was not only an ardent champion of small clubs, but also a restless innovator who never shrank from drawing up and testing theories and formulas. Had he been a dictator, had he enjoyed Sutcliffe's powers, there can be no doubt that the League would have been restructured sooner than 1986, and in a far more radical fashion.)

'It has never been part of my brief to please people and, in any case, I believe it is a mistake to tiptoe through life just to avoid treading on a few feet', he wrote. Thus he was variously described as 'football's godfather', 'a cross between Cagney and Caligula', 'St Alan of St Annes' and, most cruelly, 'Lytham's answer to Idi Amin'.

Much of this reputation derived from his words rather than his deeds. For example, he scored an embarrassing own goal by branding agent Bagenal Harvey as the sinister 'Mr X' behind the players' fight against the maximum wage in 1960/1. But he was also unfairly reproached by the players for being quoted in the *Daily Mail* as saying: 'I wouldn't hang a dog on the word of an ex-professional footballer.' What he had said was that he wouldn't like to see a certain type of vindictive player sitting on disciplinary committees because he wouldn't hang a dog on the evidence of people like that.

Not surprisingly, Hardaker's career was littered with writs against people who misquoted

him like this, and one might have sympathized had he decided to slap up a large sign reading 'No Comment' on his office door. But he was too outspoken a man to be silent for long.

He castigated club chairmen for making decisions which threatened to bring the roof down over their heads. He vehemently opposed the introduction of regionalized representation on the Management Committee, and he made no secret of the fact that he didn't trust clubs to deal with each other fairly.

These were not prejudices. They were opinions based on his daily experiences. Sometimes the machinations of the clubs left him in despair. They called him a dictator. 'If only I was...' he would sigh, looking enviously at the power some of his opponents enjoyed within their own clubs.

Managers who fought their way to the top and stayed there were, he wrote, 'devious and ruthless and selfish'. He took particular exception to Don Revie, who he said was forever telephoning him at Lytham to beg concessions from the League. When the FA appointed Revie as England manager, Hardaker told Ted Croker: 'You must be off your heads!'

Perhaps his most famous comment came a few weeks before England's vital game against Poland in 1974, which England had to win in order to qualify for the World Cup finals. Hardaker said: 'It is a football match, not a war. Let us keep our sense of perspective about this game. The game of football won't die if we lose. It will be a terrible thing for six weeks then everyone will forget about it.'

England did not qualify, and very few people did forget it. But the comment said more about Hardaker's attitude towards international football than it did about the role of football in the nation's life. He was hardly the man to say that football didn't matter. Rather, he believed that in the long run more people cared about the fact that Manchester United were just about to be relegated to Division Two, or that Peterborough were then top of Division Four, than they did about England's ability to do well in the World Cup.

On another occasion he dismissed Hungary's defeat of England at Wembley in 1953. 'The Hungarians created five and a half chances and scored six goals, while England made twenty chances and scored three goals.' One senses that he knew full well that such a statement was as fickle as it was provocative.

'I have never known anyone like Alan Hardaker for getting into trouble – but neither have I known anyone like him for getting out of trouble', said Sir Joe Richards. It was as if he enjoyed making waves, enjoyed the image which the media had made of him. If they wanted gut reactions, he would give them.

But whatever he said in the heat of the moment, there is no denying that when it came to the bread and butter of running the League, Hardaker was quite outstanding. 'He revelled in power but never abused it,' said Arthur Would. 'Everyone on the Committee admired him and trusted him completely.'

One quote from David Lacey of the *Guardian* remains especially apposite. 'Alan Hardaker represented the sort of binding force in the Football League which was not always loved but, like Tito in Yugoslavia, may become increasingly popular in his absence.'

Certainly a Football League without Alan Hardaker seemed inconceivable, at least while he was still alive and able to cope with the huge workload which had become his norm.

To satisfy all parties, therefore, in 1977 Hardaker was given a new title, that of Chief Executive and General Secretary – he loved titles, apparently – with a top salary to match his rank. Deputy Secretary George Readle was made Secretary–designate, Graham Kelly would rise to Deputy Secretary, and Norman Thomas, who had been at the League longer than anyone, would become the Assistant Secretary.

That, at least, was the plan. But after two years with Hardaker as General Secretary – two years in which he kept his same office at Lytham, maintained his authority, made a study trip to the North American Soccer League and represented the League at enough social functions to fill a Filofax – the Management Committee finally decided to grasp the nettle and make plans for the future. The simple truth was that Alan Hardaker could not be expected to carry on forever.

So it was that on 30 June 1979, the Committee overturned the plan drawn up in 1977 and appointed thirty-three-year-old Graham Kelly as the new Secretary of the Football League. This was an enormous blow to George Readle, who had been lined up for the job since 1973. His name had even been printed on new notepaper. But he was a dedicated man, and he stayed on at Lytham to serve as Deputy Secretary to Graham Kelly.

This was not the end of Alan Hardaker's involvement, by any means. Indeed, the idea of Hardaker disappearing into retirement was unthinkable to anyone who knew him. Instead, the League gave him yet another title, that of Director-General, and asked him to be a consultant. He didn't want the job. 'No one consults a consultant', he said. But all the same, he handed over the reins to Graham Kelly and told him: 'The job's yours. Make your own mistakes.' And with that he went off with enormous relief on a tour of Australia.

On his return, however, Hardaker could not resist being involved. He stayed in his large office at Lytham (meaning that Kelly had to work from the adjoining room) and the staff still thought of him as the boss. But in his own mind he was fidgety, unhappy, unsure of his role.

So he started to do what came naturally to him. He started to draw up plans for the reorganization of the League, and in December 1979 he was nominated as chairman of the Football Grounds Improvement Trust. He also became chairman of a company bidding for the independent radio franchise in Lancashire. But it wasn't enough for a man who had been so intimately involved with every facet of League affairs for over two decades. He craved activity.

Alan Hardaker's last Management Committee meeting was on Sunday, 10 February 1980, at the Great Western Hotel, London. Since becoming Secretary twenty-three years earlier, he had not missed a single Committee meeting. Then, at the beginning of March, he attended three regional meetings of clubs to explain his newly drafted ideas for 'Football in the 'Eighties'. It was to prove his last effort on behalf of the League.

On 4 March, he suffered a fatal a heart attack in his home next door to the League's offices. It was completely unexpected and an enormous blow to his wife, Irene. Her husband was only sixty-seven when he died. He should have been looking forward to a long and prosperous retirement.

At the League Cup Final a fortnight later, the flags flew at half-mast. Hardaker was dead, but his 'folly', his 'baby', his Cup, carried on.

But Hardaker's legacy was much greater than the League Cup. He had coaxed, dragged and bullied the Football League from its dusty, tradition-bound state in the mid-1950s into a tough, commercially-minded giant which stood a chance (but only a chance) of surviving the even harsher, tougher days which loomed ahead.

The ultimate tragedy of Alan Hardaker's life was that, although the League would learn to live without him, he never had the chance to live out the rest of his life without the League.

*   *   *

Hugely important though Alan Hardaker was, as football constantly teaches us, the team is always greater than the man. Hardaker's successor, Graham Kelly, had served his apprenticeship well since becoming number three at Lytham in 1973. He was already known to many in the game as the young man who accompanied Norman Thomas in conducting spot checks on club books. He had also been attending Management Committee meetings for some time.

Now he occupied Hardaker's huge office at Lytham, more aware than anyone what a hard act he had to follow. 'It would have been folly for me or for anyone to have attempted to emulate Alan Hardaker,' he later recalled. 'I told myself I'd do the job in my own way because that was how I got the job in the first place, by showing my own qualities.'

In one sense, however, Kelly has come to resemble Hardaker. He, too, is single-minded about the League, and no other man knows the regulations better or dedicates more time and effort to the League's cause. In most other respects, though, Graham Kelly has a completely different approach to that of Alan Hardaker. He is a quieter, less abrasive man with a much lower public profile, more in keeping with the traditions of Tom Charnley and Fred Howarth than Alan Hardaker's more confrontational style.

But then, football itself was changing and it is debatable whether Hardaker's style would have been appropriate for the 1980s in any case, if only because the role of the Management Committee had changed with regionalization. As Graham Kelly came to the fore, so too did a whole group of club chairmen who were no longer content to let the Committee get on with League business in isolation.

There was too much at stake. In Lord Westwood's last season as President, gates fell by 2.7 million, 11 per cent down on the previous year and the largest single drop since 1972. As attendances fell to record lows, unemployment rose to its highest levels since the early 1930s. And in the newly-elected Conservative Government led by Margaret Thatcher, football and sport in general had probably the least sympathetic hearing in Westminster than it had experienced since the Second World War. Harold Wilson had been a football fan, Edward Heath had been a personal friend of Bob Lord, and James Callaghan's cabinet had included several sporting enthusiasts; Sports Minister Denis Howell was himself a former League referee. Margaret Thatcher, on the other hand, gave sport very low priority in her first six years in office.

So, if the Football League was to change as it entered the new decade, this was as much because of forces outside the game as personnel changes within it.

A year after Alan Hardaker's death, the Committee lost another of its leading characters. According to the League's minutes, Lord Westwood announced that due to 'internal problems at Newcastle United he would be tendering his resignation from the club's board of directors, with effect from 16 March 1981. Consequently he would have to resign as President of the Football League as from that date.'

Although Lord Westwood's position at Newcastle was the immediate cause of his departure, it was also apparent that once Alan Hardaker died, Westwood was no longer entirely comfortable in office. Hardaker had been his right-hand man, the man upon whom he had depended for his facts (as had all members of the Management Committee) and largely for his opinions.

Bob Lord became Acting President for the three months preceding the Annual Meeting, but was barely able to settle into his new role or even to consider being nominated for the presidency before he was taken seriously ill. Dick Wragg of Sheffield United took the chair temporarily, and Lord eventually died the following December. In the same year, Brian Mears resigned from the board at Chelsea, so he, too, had to leave the Management Committee.

The election for a successor to Lord Westwood, who was made a Life Member, took place at the 1981 Annual Meeting. There were four nominations, more than ever before, and uniquely, two of the names put forward belonged to men who had not previously served on the Management Committee. No one had ever risen to the office of President without at least a few years' prior work on the Committee.

Despite this, it turned out to be a tight contest. In the first ballot, Fulham's blunt and controversial chairman, Ernie Clay, managed to poll 5 votes. Jack Wiseman of Birmingham, a member of the Management Committee, gained 7 votes. That left the Committee's newest recruit, Jack Dunnett of Notts County, to fight it out in a second ballot with Liverpool's chairman, John Smith.

Like several of his fellow First Division chairmen, Smith believed that the leading clubs were not properly represented on the Committee. He had a genuine case; of the ten-man Committee at the start of the 1980/1 season, half represented Third Division clubs (two of which would be relegated to Division Four in 1981), two were from the Second Division (including Westwood's Newcastle) and only three were from the First Division. This purely accidental imbalance became a theme for discussion for the next five years, until the First Division clubs finally won a greater voice on the Committee in 1986.

But in 1981, despite Liverpool's quite outstanding record on the pitch (they had just added the European Cup and League Cup to their long list of honours), the clubs narrowly preferred Jack Dunnett to John Smith, by 28 votes to 24.

Dunnett was under no illusions about his new job, however. 'We are in the position of a beleaguered garrison; the situation is very serious', was his first pronouncement to the press as President. Commenting on the fall in gates, he said: 'All the Management Committee know something is wrong. We are not idiots. But don't ask me the solution. I don't know it.'

Nor did anyone else. It was going to be a very difficult few years.

CHAPTER THIRTY
Jack Dunnett – Back-bencher Forward

'A new ball game kicks off as League swings to left.' That was *The Times*' headline which heralded Jack Dunnett's election as the eleventh president of the Football League.

There was no new ball game, and Dunnett, MP for Nottingham East, was by no means a member of the Labour left. He was, and is, a solicitor with extensive business and property interests. But he was the first Labour man to take office at the League and that in itself was a real break with the previous Liberal, then predominantly Conservative, tradition.

But then, the Tory Lord Westwood had been the first peer of the realm to hold office, so in true democratic spirit it was surely right and proper that the League appoint his successor not only from what the Lords call 'another place' – that is, the House of Commons – but also from the opposite side of the political divide. It was ironic, nevertheless, that while the rest of the country had turned so emphatically to the right in the 1979 election, the League should have chosen its president from the other side.

That Dunnett was a Labour MP was, in fact, irrelevant. What counted was that he was a seasoned campaigner in politics, business and football, a man used to wheeling and dealing. He was also highly ambitious.

Dunnett's political involvement was certainly far greater than Lord Westwood's had ever been. During his seven years as President, Lord Westwood attended the House of Lords on average only about ten times a year. Dunnett, on the other hand, spent nineteen years as an MP and had a good record of attendance in both debates and at committee level. He was also extremely active in his Not-

tingham constituency.

In fact, he was the archetypal back-bencher, whose behind-the-scenes work on committees never made news and was known only to people within the confines of Westminster. There are hundreds of MPs like Dunnett who beaver away in the corridors of power, lobbying, arguing, making deals. They know that the real work is done in committee rooms and maintaining a power base in the constituency party, not by making speeches in the Chamber. Dunnett himself decided not to speak in the Chamber after 1970, and in 1983 was picked out as one of ten 'silent' back-benchers.

But his attendance record was actually better than many other back-benchers, and he reduced his involvement only when, after fifteen years in the House, he became disillusioned with the direction the Labour Party was taking. In many respects his election as President of the League signalled the end of his Commons involvement.

A decade earlier, Dunnett had proved his usefulness to the League even before he was elected to the Management Committee in 1977 (as the Midland area's representative in place of the retiring Len Shipman). Apart from arranging introductions in Parliament, Dunnett lobbied consistently on behalf of the game. For example, he tried to gain tax relief for clubs forced to make ground improvements as a result of the 1975 Safety of Sports Grounds Act. He also acted as go-between in the League's negotiations with London Weekend Television in 1978–9 (of which more later), which subsequently led to an improved offer from the BBC.

This breadth of knowledge and experience

of the sharp end of the football business, plus the fact that he was a dab hand at winning elections, largely explains why Dunnett rose to the presidency after less than four years on the Management Committee.

Apart from being the first MP, Jack Dunnett was also the first Jewish president the League had elected. Before the 1960s, the Management Committee had been very much a bastion of Anglo-Saxon Protestantism, with a few Scots and Irish thrown in for good measure (though, strangely, no Welshmen).

Even so, in common with William McGregor and Lord Westwood, Jack Jacob Dunnett – the League's second 'JJ' – was actually born in Scotland, to where his family had fled from Poland and Lithuania. Jack was four when his unemployed father packed their bags yet again during the General Strike of 1926 and, like so many Scots, travelled south in search of work. His search ended in Croydon, south London, where Jack was brought up within a short distance of Selhurst Park.

It was at Stamford Bridge, however, that Dunnett saw his first match in 1933, and it was Chelsea who captured the eleven-year-old's initial interest. But only from afar. From Croydon his next stops were North Africa and Italy, where he served in the Cheshire Regiment between 1941 and 1946. On his return from the army it was on to Downing College, Cambridge, where he studied law, and, as luck would have it, in 1949 he found his first job with a firm of solicitors in King's Road, Chelsea.

As soon as work was over at lunchtime on Saturdays, he would take the short walk over to Stamford Bridge and stand behind one of the goals to watch players such as Roy Bentley and Eric 'The Rabbit' Parsons.

By the time Chelsea won their one and only League title in 1955, Dunnett had forsaken the terraces for a seat in the stand, and become an active member of his local Labour Party. In 1958 he was elected a county councillor for Brentford and Chiswick, and he spent the next

three years contentedly watching Chelsea and Third Division Brentford on alternate Saturdays, until finally he accepted an invitation to join Brentford's board in 1961. Neither of his favourite teams seemed to respond well to this decision: both were relegated. The following season they bounced back, however, while Dunnett himself stepped up another rung of the political ladder following his selection as prospective parliamentary candidate for Nottingham East. In 1964 he won the seat back from the Tories at his first attempt, and in the same year became a Greater London councillor for the Hounslow area.

Two areas to represent, a young family, a thriving business, a busy legal practice and a football club to run in west London; it was small wonder that Jack Dunnett gained a reputation for being hyper-active. Topped up with black coffee, and dashing up and down the country from match to meeting, Dunnett spent the swinging 'sixties as a go-getter. Not everyone was impressed with his ideas, however.

The relationship with Brentford ended in January 1967. A few miles away, Jim Gregory had just become chairman of Queen's Park Rangers. While Loftus Road at that time was in a dilapidated state, Gregory's team was running away with the Third Division Championship and was on course for a place in the first League Cup Final to be held at Wembley. Brentford, for their part, had a much better ground, but were going nowhere in the Fourth Division. Both clubs had debts which could have been wiped out had one of the grounds been sold. So the two chairmen made a deal, and Gregory announced that Rangers would move into Griffin Park at the end of the season. Dunnett insisted that the arrangement was to share the ground only, but the fans feared a merger and turned against both men.

In the end it was all academic. None of the other directors at either club agreed with the plan, so Dunnett resigned.

Within a month or two, Notts County lured him on to their board, but he was determined not to become a club chairman again; too much aggravation, too many other things to do. These were, after all, the Wilson years, when every Labour MP had to play his part in preserving the Government's narrow majority.

Then the Notts County chairman had a heart attack and asked Dunnett to take over. This wasn't in the Dunnett plan at all, but once he started to think about the challenge, the fact that the ground was on his patch and that his constituency surgeries were on Fridays...

He became chairman in August 1968, and not long afterwards invited Brentford's manager, Jimmy Sirrel, to take over at County. 'Who?' was the reaction of most County fans when they heard of the appointment, then 'What?' when they heard one of the doughty manager's broad Scottish utterances.

Dunnett told the awaiting press that he and Sirrel would get Notts County back into the First Division, where they had last been in 1926. Since County were then near the foot of the Fourth Division, his announcement was met with polite guffaws. But thirteen seasons later, Dunnett's promise was fulfilled, which for those who knew him was no surprise.

County might have done it quicker had Sirrel not left to join Sheffield United for two seasons, and had Dunnett not refused to plough money into the team simply to win quick success. 'We reached Division One by what I regard as prudent management', he says now. Debts were turned into profits, but costs were watched closely. Too closely for the fans, who became impatient for success, and criticized Dunnett for being too cautious (although he did put a great deal of his own money into the club).

But Dunnett had a policy and he was sticking to it. He did not want County to go up to the First Division and plummet down again as had clubs like Bolton and Carlisle in recent years.

So when County did finally go up, they had £150,000 in the bank and were aiming to survive on gates of 15,000. This was not such a wild expectation. In earlier years, County's gates had always outstripped those of Forest. But it was not to be. After three years of struggling on the lowest gates in the First Division, County dropped back down to the Third Division in successive seasons.

County's rise and fall notwithstanding, there aren't many other uncertainties in Jack Dunnett's life. He appears to have planned it with a precision which borders upon the presumption.

In 1979, after winning his Nottingham parliamentary seat for the sixth time, he decided to stand down at the next election in order to concentrate on football. To him that meant becoming President of the Football League.

As planned, he achieved that office two years later, a few weeks after Notts County had been promoted to the First Division. And had County stayed in the First Division, it is quite conceivable that Jack Dunnett would still have been President when the League began its centenary celebrations in 1987. But not after. That was not part of the Dunnett plan. He intended to stand down after two terms in office.

'A man of demonic energy', was one journalist's description of Jack Dunnett. He worked at a frenetic pace, he talked fast and he thought fast. Under Lord Westwood's jovial but often rather wayward chairmanship, remembered a former Committee man, Management Committee meetings would often take several hours. With Jack Dunnett in the chair, they were kept down to less than three hours. It is legendary within the football world that while he was chairman of Notts County (a position from which he resigned in June 1987 – again, according to plan), he would call only one board meeting a year, and that took only thirty minutes.

Instead, all the day-to-day business was conducted on the telephone and by using a reporting system. 'I was in London most of the time. My colleagues were busy men as well, and we found the system worked perfectly satisfactorily. We didn't want to sit around a table reading out minutes.'

Some people gained the impression that Dunnett didn't want to sit around a table at all. If he wanted to fight for a cause – his own or the League's – he was far happier doing deals in the corridor, just like in Westminster, than sitting round a negotiating table. But no one ever accused him of short-changing football because of his other commitments. As President he managed eighty games a year, and didn't miss a function.

One leading First Division manager said after witnessing a typical meeting with Dunnett: 'His knowledge of football impressed me very much. I listened to everything he said and all I heard was good, sound common sense. His performance as chairman left me speechless.' High praise indeed, especially as it came from the normally garrulous Brian Clough.

'I've been a chairman all my life,' said Dunnett, 'in business, in politics and in football. Meetings are held to make decisions. Everything else should be trimmed away, and if you want a cosy chat then have it afterwards.'

'He wanted to finish each meeting as soon as it started,' commented a friend. 'He always seemed to be on the edge of his seat, wanting to get away to another meeting. He was always one step ahead.'

Like it or lump it, that was how Jack Dunnett, and that is how he still does it. He had five years as President, and at the time of the centenary he is still on the Management Committee.

What he will do next is anyone's guess. One suspects, however, that Jack Dunnett knows exactly.

CHAPTER THIRTY-ONE

Crisis Points

*I*f there is one word that sums up the state of League football in the first half of the 1980s, that word is crisis.

Crisis is an overused, emotive word at the best of times, but in this context it is not used lightly. Before the 1980s, League football had survived enough low points in its history to suggest that it was a hardy beast, able to fight, or sometimes bungle, its way through the toughest of situations. But the crisis of the 1980s went deeper than ever before. Jack Dunnett described the position in 1981 as that of a 'beleaguered garrison'. It was an apt description; there appeared to be no reinforcements on the horizon, mutiny simmered within the ranks and, worst of all, at times it seemed as if the outside world was quite content for the garrison to fall.

The problem was not just one of declining attendances, although gates, having dropped 11 per cent in 1980/1, would drop steadily for the next five seasons to an all-time low aggregate of 16.4 million in 1985/6.

Nor was it just about standards on the pitch, which were in many instances very encouraging, especially in European competitions. Liverpool's almost total stranglehold on the League (eight Championships in twelve seasons) did not stifle all ambition.

Again it was not merely a question of economics, although at least fifteen League clubs had to be rescued from extinction between 1978 and 1986. Nor was the crisis simply one of hooliganism, be it on the terraces or on the streets of Britain and the Continent.

For every one of the above problems, there was always an exception: a team with rising gates, a manager experimenting with new tactics, a club establishing a firm financial footing, and a ground where the fans were impeccably behaved.

Deeper even than all these issues put together was a growing, nagging suspicion that not only were the difficulties facing football too great for its leading figures to handle alone, but that the English and Welsh public as a whole was turning away from League football and would have been quite happy to divert its attention to other forms of sport and entertainment, such as snooker, athletics, do-it-yourself, American football, theme parks, or whatever television and the commercial world could dangle in front of the consumer's eye.

Football, in short, was struggling to retain its previously undisputed right to the title of 'the national game'. It mattered not that more people than ever were now actually playing the game. If League football was in a bad way, if the England team was achieving very little, if most of the news emanating from professional football circles was negative, then 'the national game' was in danger of being disowned by the nation.

The 1980s have therefore been characterized by two great struggles.

Firstly, the League has had to learn how to deal with a whole range of problems which in previous years it had either ignored or failed to understand. Recognizing this only too clearly, Alan Hardaker said a few months before his death: 'We must sit down and talk.' He warned that unless the game in Britain and Europe agreed upon some serious changes, then the League would have to emulate the Scandinavians by going part-time.

Secondly, and this is a separate issue from

the first point, the League has had to win back the nation's trust, to prove that football is a worthwhile endeavour, despite the trail of wanton destruction left by rampaging youths across Europe and the tragedies at Birmingham, Bradford and Brussels in May 1985.

It has had to prove to millions of sceptics that football should still merit all the media coverage, money, passion and enthusiasm which had so characterized the game during the late 1940s and mid 1960s.

To achieve this, the Football League has had to take a crash course in learning how to sell itself. Not in a financial sense (though that would follow), but in terms of public relations. Not just to the public, but to the Government and to the commercial world.

This was no simple task. By 1980 the League had fallen behind in the communications revolution. There was a football press, there were numerous radio and television programmes devoted to the game, but the League's voice was seldom to be heard anywhere – except in a crisis. Alan Hardaker was a gift to the media whenever a crisis loomed, but when his much-loved *League Review* collapsed in 1975 there was nothing to replace it. In an age of mass communications, the League had allowed others to do the communicating on its behalf. (It hadn't always been that way. In the heyday of *Athletic News*, from 1888–1930, members of the Management Committee had flooded football's main source of information with informed debate and opinion.)

So, how could the League solve the myriad problems it faced? How could it restore the sullied name of football? These have been the two vital questions of the 1980s.

In this chapter we look at the first of them: the elements which made up the League's growing crisis, and the process by which the football authorities struggled to come up with solutions, one by one, meeting by meeting, year by year. As the centenary came and went, not all of those difficulties had been addressed,

and of those which had, not all had been totally eradicated. But the crucial point was this: the 'beleaguered garrison' did, after all, find hidden reserves of strength, and did start to fight back.

In Chapter 33 we will see how that struggle led in 1986 to the restructuring of the League in an attempt to put football back on to the paths of righteousness, respectability and, of course, prosperity.

Some may judge that the League sought the wrong solutions. Others may argue that, indeed, nothing and no one could halt the inevitable decline of the game of football. All we attempt to do here is relate what actually happened between 1980 and 1986. As John F. Kennedy once remarked: 'To state the facts frankly is not to despair for the future, nor indict the past.'

On 11 August 1980 a group of seven representatives from the Secretaries, Managers and Coaches Association unveiled a blueprint for the future. It was a charter entitled 'Soccer – the Fight for Survival'. This did not purport to be the answer to all football's worries, but it did contain several constructive proposals which, it was hoped, would restore some order and purpose to the flagging game.

The men responsible for this charter were Arsenal secretary Ken Friar, plus managers Alan Dicks (Bristol City), Harry Haslam (Sheffield United), Ron Saunders (Aston Villa), Graham Taylor (Watford), Terry Venables (Crystal Palace) and Bill Nicholson (formerly Tottenham).

Two months later, a large group of club chairmen met for a two-day seminar in Solihull, near Birmingham, and discussed the charter, among other issues. Prominent in this group was Jimmy Hill, the BBC's football expert and chairman of Coventry City. Twenty years earlier, Hill had been campaigning for the rights of players. Now he was on his soap box again, this time on behalf of the establishment.

The Solihull seminar was a key event in the history of the League. It was the first gathering of its kind in the modern era, an opportunity for chairmen to discuss the issues facing football without the imposed structure of resolutions, amendments and so forth.

It also yielded some relatively quick results. At an Extraordinary General Meeting of the League the following February – Lord West-wood's last official gathering as President, as it happened – the following resolutions were passed:

● *As an experiment to encourage more attacking football, in 1981/2 three points instead of two would be awarded for a win.*

This was the first successful attempt to alter the points system first agreed in November

Three Points for a Win

Various alterations to the points system were mooted before 'three points for a win' was introduced in 1981. Among the suggestions came two from the Management Committee. In 1965 it proposed that one quarter of a point be awarded for each goal scored, and in 1976 that a team be awarded an additional point if it won a game and scored three or more goals in the process.

Had the three-points-for-a-win system been in operation since 1888, the First Division Championship would have changed only once, in 1974/5. Ipswich, who finished third, would have displaced Derby at the top. Relegation from Division One would have changed sixteen times. In the Second Division, on three occasions the champions would not even have been promoted, and twelve times a different team would have gone up, including both Rotherham and Barnsley, neither of whom have ever reached Division One. In 1948/9 Leicester would have been relegated to the Third Division for the first time, and, curiously, in 1977/8, Orient, who finished fourteenth, would have been relegated. Lower down the League, Gateshead would have been promoted to Division Two in 1949/50, and we all know what happened to them ten seasons later. Overall, 6.35 per cent of all titles, 6.3 per cent of promotions and 10.5 per cent of relegation issues would have been dif-

ferent had the new system been in effect since 1888.

Of all the major national leagues only Algeria, Iceland and New Zealand have followed the Football League by adopting the three-points-for-a-win system. Statisticians should be grateful, however, that the new system found more support than an alternative scheme put forward by Leicester City in 1980. This was to award two points to the winners of each period of forty-five minutes, then an additional two points for the overall winners.

The 1980s have seen a number of experiments with points systems around the world. The North American Soccer League awarded six points for a win, four points for a victory obtained by a penalty shoot-out (that is, after a drawn game), and one bonus point for every goal scored per game to a maximum of three. Norway also abolished draws by introducing penalty shoot-outs. The Soviets decided that after a team had scored ten draws in a season it would no longer be awarded any points for drawn matches. Bulgaria tried awarding no points for goalless draws, which seemed to work well until it was realized that several games which were goalless until the final minutes suspiciously ended up as 1–1 draws. But the oddest system exists in Algeria, where three points are awarded for a win, two for a draw, and one point for any team defeated in a match which lasts the full ninety minutes!

1888. Opponents of the innovation predicted that, rather than encouraging attacking play, teams would have greater cause to defend a single-goal lead.

Statistical evidence, of which one must always be wary, certainly does not suggest that the new points system has produced more attacking football. Since 1980/1, when the goals-per-game average was 2.46, the figure has risen only very marginally and fluctuated around the 2.6–2.7 margin (compared with 3.44 in 1960/1, the best post-war season). Nevertheless, there have been no serious attempts to revert to the old system.

● *The limit on Friday-night and Sunday fixtures was raised from four to six games per club each season, in an attempt to boost attendances and avoid possible outbreaks of crowd violence.*

Bob Lord and the Lord's Day Observance Society (who were not related) both objected to the further relaxation of Sunday football, but attendance figures showed that for certain clubs and in certain circumstances, Sunday football was a worthwhile alternative. In 1987/8, holiday games and live televised matches apart, there were twenty-seven games scheduled for Sundays and 102 for Friday nights (just under 6 per cent of the total).

● *No club was to be permitted to sign any players until all outstanding transfer debts were settled.*

This rule was an attempt at self-regulation, but it had little effect.

The early 1980s was a period of great financial restraint in Britain, with the newly elected Government telling everyone to tighten their belts and live within their means. But if football's garrison was beleaguered, there was enough wheeling and dealing going on within its crumbling walls to suggest that, under the strain, some managers and chairmen were beginning to confuse piles of Monopoly money with the real thing.

Malcolm Allison's buying spree at Manchester City was the most extreme example of reckless spending during these troubled years. Despite investing £1.4 million on Steve Daley, £250,000 on untried youngster Steve Mackenzie, £1 million for Kevin Reeves, £765,000 for Michael Robinson ... the list goes on, Allison brought no honours to the club and left it reeling with debt. A wisecrack circulating in Manchester at the time held that if City's scouts were ever unsure as to which player they should sign up, they were to buy the whole team, just in case.

Allison's profligacy and that of several other managers – there were three transfers in excess of £1 million at the start of the 1980/1 season alone – did football's reputation great harm in the public arena. What made the spending seem worse was that so few of the £1 million players justified their price tags. How could they, when the pricing had been so arbitrary?

Steve Daley was sold after a year at City for a loss of £1 million. He cost the club nearly £21,000 per game. Garry Birtles, signed by Manchester United from Nottingham Forest for £1.25 million in 1980, returned to Forest nearly two years later for £300,000. His fee worked out at about £86,000 per goal. Forest themselves lost in excess of £1 million on deals involving Justin Fashanu and Ian Wallace.

Similar stories were repeated throughout the First and Second Divisions. Transfer fees simply went berserk at a time when the clubs could least afford them. There were calls for a transfer limit (shades of Charles Clegg and Sir Henry Norris), but as Jack Dunnett said in September 1981, 'There is no way you can stop clubs paying high fees. Good players are a limited commodity on the market and one club will always be willing to pay more than the rest to get the man they want. There is no point fixing a transfer limit, because clubs would only find illegal ways of getting around it.'

There was an alternative, however.

Both Dunnett and the PFA favoured the

introduction of the European multiplier system. Under this system, which priced players according to their age, wage and status, Nottingham Forest's Trevor Francis would have been valued at around £520,000 in 1981, instead of £1 million.

That was all very well for any buying club, but not so welcome for the sellers. For example, using the multiplier system, Everton would have paid only £50,000 for Bury's goal-keeper Neville Southall. Instead, Bury received £150,000.

The multiplier system did not, therefore, win many friends among club chairmen who, despite the above resolution passed in 1981, continued to buy players they couldn't afford. The Management Committee subsequently placed bans on any further signings at Bristol City, Swansea City and Hereford United in 1982, and Wolves in 1984.

The most publicized case of non-payment of transfer fees involved Charlton, who owed over £30,000 to Leeds United. Despite the League's urgent reminder that such disputes were covered by League regulations, in July 1983 Leeds went so far as to take legal action against Charlton, who, as a result, faced a winding-up order in the High Court unless they settled the debt. One can understand Leeds' frustration, but the League had in the past always tried to keep such quarrels 'within the family'. For a club to seek recourse from an outside body was to imply that the regulations were inadequate.

Since then, tougher controls have been introduced by the League.

Firstly, a club must now pay at least 50 per cent of the fee on signing, and the balance within a year. That applies whether the fee is £1000 or £1 million. Secondly, all cheques must be sent direct to the Football League's offices, to be cleared, before the money is passed on. Any club delaying their payments will be charged interest.

So far, the system has been successful in preventing abuse of the transfer system. But as

we shall see, just as effective in restoring sanity to the market was the economic recession. Bank managers were simply no longer prepared to extend overdrafts so that managers and chairmen could use bank resources to gamble on assets as unpredictable as footballers.

● *No club official, director or secretary was to be permitted to have an influence on the control or management of more than one League club.*

This rule, first introduced before the First World War when Henry Norris and William Hall were on the boards of both Arsenal and Fulham, was revived at the February 1981 EGM largely as a result of Wimbledon's chairman, Ron Noades, becoming involved in the affairs of Crystal Palace.

Noades had led Southern Leaguers Wimbledon into the Fourth Division after only a year at the helm, but reckoned that the club had a greater chance of success at a better ground. He proposed, therefore, to move Wimbledon in with Crystal Palace.

There was nothing new about the idea of ground-sharing in London. Henry Norris had tried to introduce it with Fulham and Arsenal in 1910. Jack Dunnett had considered it with Brentford and QPR in 1967. In each case, the fans' reaction had been one of abject horror. To lose one's ground was to lose all identity, they argued; besides which, surely it could only lead to a merger.

In the end, Noades led a consortium which bought up Palace for a reported £600,000 in January 1981, a few weeks before the EGM. After the resolution above was passed, he retained his shares in Wimbledon for a time but agreed not to play any part in the management of Wimbledon's affairs (there were no rules at that time to prevent an individual having shares in as many clubs as he or she liked).

Unwittingly, however, Noades did have some say in the Dons' fortunes. When he became chairman at Selhurst Park, he appointed Wimbledon's chirpy young manager, Dave Bassett, as the new Palace boss.

Bassett stayed one day before changing his mind – the shortest managerial appointment on record – and then returned to Wimbledon to lead Noades' former club straight up into the First Division, leapfrogging over Palace in the process (and, to rub salt in the wound, beating them 5–0 at Selhurst Park along the way). Football has a nasty habit of foiling even the boldest of men.

Noades' motivation had been to create as strong a footballing outfit in south London as north Londoners had at Tottenham and Arsenal. Other men's motives were not so clear. A millionaire businessman called Anton Johnson bought interests in three clubs during the early 1980s: Rotherham, Bournemouth and Southend. He was finally banned from the game in December 1984.

In 1986 the Walsall chairman, Ken Wheldon, bought control of Birmingham City and for a few months retained an influence in both clubs (he actually tried to move Walsall to Birmingham's ground) before the Management Committee finally put its foot down.

But some cases have presented the League with a real dilemma. For example, having rescued Oxford United from the brink and become club chairman in January 1982, in April 1983 millionaire publisher Robert Maxwell bought an interest in nearby struggling Reading. Maxwell then announced plans to merge the two clubs under the title of Thames Valley Royals, who would play in a new stadium mid-way between Oxford and Reading.

Protests and sit-ins ensued at each club, but the fans were wasting their time, announced Maxwell in a press conference at the FA. The merger would go ahead.

It didn't. Oxford reached the First Division, Reading reached the Second and Thames Valley Royals became a footnote in Maxwell's eventful and often controversial career.

He never seemed content merely with what had been achieved at the Manor Ground. In January 1984 he was reported as having bid £2 million to buy up Birmingham City. The following month it was Manchester United for £10 million. He retained, meanwhile, a shareholding in Reading. Then, in March 1984, Maxwell invested the money which saved Derby County from extinction (he actually bought the ground) and the following August installed his son Ian as chairman. When Ian stood down in 1987, Maxwell senior moved to Derby and another son, Kevin, took over at Oxford. Maxwell's daughter, was also on the Oxford board at the same time.

Since there was then no League rule to prevent members of the same family having a controlling interest in more than one club, in Maxwell's case there was nothing the Management Committee could have done. Nor did it wish to block the involvement of any wealthy man, if the alternative was to see a club die. All it could do was heed the words of William McGregor in 1909. 'Beware of the clever sharp men who are creeping into the game'. How shocked the founder would have been to know that in the 1980s so many impecunious clubs were crying out for a clever, sharp man to rescue them. And yet Robert Maxwell's involvement with the League had still to enter its stormiest phase, as we relate in Chapter 34.

● *The Associate Members' collective vote was increased from six votes to eight.*

This was a further boost for the Third and Fourth Division clubs, whose demands for extra voting power went back to the 1920s. Remember that in 1974 they had also gained representation on the Management Committee.

*   *   *

There was one other item of significance at the February 1981 EGM; that was the question of allowing each club to have one paid director. This had been another of the talking points at the Solihull seminar, originally at the instigation of Orient and Crystal Palace.

Orient's chairman, Brian Winston, argued that the FA rule which prohibited a club director from being remunerated for his services was a barrier to progress in modern professional football. A fully paid managing director, chief executive, call him what you will, stood a much better chance of handling the increasing responsibilities and pressures that the average football club now faced. Football was now too complicated a business to entrust to a group of unpaid amateurs backed up by an overworked club secretary.

Furthermore, that same overworked club secretary had exactly the sort of experience that was necessary at board level. Yet because he was a salaried official he was prevented by an outdated law from having a proper voice in club affairs.

The FA Council was not convinced by this argument. Voluntary service had, after all, been one of the cardinal virtues expected of a club director since the advent of professionalism in 1885. As feared, therefore, the FA's Annual Meeting in 1981 rejected the proposal (largely because Bob Lord made a powerful speech against it), although the Welsh FA gave its four League clubs permisson to appoint a paid director in August 1981. Encouraged by this, lobbying continued, and six months later FA approval was gained, but only on condition that the appointment of each paid director would be vetted by the League and FA.

Three League clubs immediately took up the option: Liverpool, Queen's Park Rangers and Fulham, where the manager, Malcolm Macdonald, was appointed a director. 'The fact is,' Macdonald said at the time, 'that there aren't enough people in the game who know it as a professional and have a right of say in the decision-making processes.'

As it happened, none of the early appointments involved any club in the outlay of an extra salary. Liverpool made a director of their long-serving secretary, Peter Robinson. Luton did the same with John Smith. At Loftus Road, Terry Venables, who was manager at the time, said that his elevation to the board was simply 'making official what I've been doing for the last few months anyway'.

Two years later, in October 1983, the League had its first player-director, when Terry Cooper, player-manager of Bristol City, was appointed to the board. (It is believed that the only other League player to have been a director was Tottenham's amateur international centre-forward, Vivian Woodward, in season 1908/9.) But Cooper could not have been elected to the Management Committee. A few months later, the League drew up a regulation which prohibited players from standing for office.

Not every club took up the option of appointing a paid director. By December 1986 there were nine in Division One, eight each in Divisions Two and Three and five in Division Four. Roughly two-thirds of the thirty individuals concerned were club secretaries or managers.

But the change in the FA regulations was more than just a cosmetic exercise. Suddenly, younger men who may previously have been preoccupied with establishing their own businesses now had a chance to concentrate on their clubs, without losing out. Indeed, a few could enjoy handsome salaries as a result of becoming paid directors.

A risk of exploitation by individuals was balanced, therefore, by the advantages of having professional expertise at board level. For years, the press and public alike had criticized football clubs for being old fashioned and amateurish. Now, at last, the professionals were being given a chance.

Which is more than can have been said for non-League clubs. Despite the success of the Alliance Premier League, and the League's early ties with it, the so-called 'Fifth Division' proved to be anything but a stepping stone to the League in its first seven seasons.

Looking back on our narrative, we left the non-League clubs full of bright hopes for an end to the League's 'closed shop' as the Alliance came into being in 1979. Alas for them, they would have to wait until 1987 to see their dreams come true.

The first straight contest between an Alliance club and the four retiring League clubs took place at the 1980 Annual Meeting. A close-run and desperately unfortunate affair it was, too. Darlington (49), Crewe (48) and Hereford (48) were comfortably returned, but Rochdale (26) just squeezed back in, one vote ahead of the Alliance's first champions, Altrincham.

To lose by one vote was frustrating enough, but after the meeting it transpired that two Full Members had not actually taken part in the election. Grimsby's representative at the AGM inadvertently sat in the wrong part of the meeting room, probably because his club had only just switched from Associate to Full Membership. Also absent from the vote was Luton's chairman, who got the time of the meeting wrong and arrived from lunch a few minutes after the election was over.

This was a sickening blow to Altrincham's hopes, since both Grimsby and Luton had promised to vote for them. Instead, having driven all over the country to canvass support and spent over £10,000 on an election campaign, Altrincham's hopes were scuppered by a misunderstanding and a miscalculation. That was all it had taken to change the course of soccer history.

If this seems like an overstatement, it is worth repeating that this was the first year in which a single Alliance club had been pitted against the four re-election candidates. Had Altrincham gained entry then, and done well, who knows how this would have influenced the voting pattern over the next few years?

Cruelly disappointing though the 1980 AGM was for Altrincham, their one crumb of comfort was the narrowness of the defeat. It boded well for the Alliance's future hopes.

A year later, Altrincham were back; Alliance champions once again, and more confident than ever of success. But this time they gained only 15 votes. Thus, Tranmere (48), York (46), Hereford (46) and Halifax (41) were each returned with barely a bead of perspiration.

Altrincham's manager was furious, and launched a bitter attack upon the whole re-election process. And in 1987 the club chairman, Gerry Berman, admitted that those two consecutive defeats in 1980 and 1981 had all but knocked the wind out of Altrincham's sails. They continued to knock out League clubs from the FA Cup, including First Division Birmingham City at St Andrew's in the Third Round in 1986. They continued to show better financial returns than the majority of Third and Fourth Division clubs. Yet that was still not enough.

They may call football 'a funny game', but in Altrincham in 1981 no one was laughing.

In 1982 the pattern was repeated. Telford United took up the challenge, only to win even fewer votes than Altrincham. Northampton (53), Crewe (50), Rochdale and Scunthorpe (both with 48) were each re-elected, way ahead of Telford (13).

Maidstone United reduced the gap in 1983, winning 26 votes compared with Blackpool (52), Crewe (49), Hereford (49) and Hartlepool (36). In 1984 the Kent club tried again, and, like Altrincham, saw their vote drop at the second attempt. Maidstone managed only 22 votes this time. The re-elected clubs were Chester (52), Halifax (52), Rochdale (50) and Hartlepool (32).

Alliance frustration built steadily, especially as Hartlepool's re-election application was their fourteenth, more than any other club in League history. Their penultimate home game of the previous season had attracted only 790 spectators. Not surprisingly therefore, pressure from the Alliance – now renamed the Gola League – concentrated on winning support for automatic promotion and relegation, a proposal first put forward seriously by non-

League clubs in 1959.

The Gola League's well-oiled publicity machine pointed out the excellent record of Alliance clubs when drawn against League clubs in the FA Cup. Indeed Altrincham, Enfield, Telford and Maidstone had all performed better in the early rounds of the Cup than several Fourth Division clubs who rarely progressed beyond the First or Second Rounds.

Attendance figures also showed that a handful of Alliance clubs, including Boston and Kettering, had, on occasions, attracted gates equal to or better than those of some Fourth Division clubs. Furthermore, while gates were falling in the League, they were rising in the Gola League.

This persistent lobbying soon told. In 1984 Oldham's chairman, Ian Stott, proposed a modified form of automatic promotion and relegation, in which the four bottom clubs would go to the vote and the one at the bottom of the poll would be automatically relegated to the Gola League. Its place would go to the highest-placed Gola League club whose ground and financial affairs best met the League's criteria.

Ian Jones of Doncaster countered this proposal. It was not, it could not be as simple as that, he warned, on behalf of the Associate Members, whom he represented on the Management Committee at the time. 'We, too, dislike intensely this annual vote for survival because we believe it brings the League into disrepute,' said Jones. 'But we also believe that the way forward and proposals for change should come from the clubs concerned and not be inflicted upon them by the First and Second Divisions.'

Jones argued that if a club was to be demoted, there would have to be financial safeguards. Just because a club was voted out of the League didn't mean that it could suddenly renege on all its financial commitments to players and staff.

If no recompense was available, how could any Fourth Division club risk offering its players long contracts or loyalty payments? Which director would risk giving an ongoing bank guarantee if he thought non-League football was on the horizon?

It was a long and eloquent speech, which reminded everyone present of just how much more thought had to be invested in the concept of automatic promotion and relegation. Indeed, so convincing was Ian Jones's argument that Oldham then agreed to withdraw their proposal for further studies.

The result of these studies was a revised set of proposals which the Associate Members unveiled during the 1984/5 season.

These were the main points:

• *There would be a straight election between the bottom Fourth Division club and the champions of the Gola League (or the next best club, subject to grading).*

The Gola League clubs could not accept this. They argued that since the formation of the Fourth Division in 1958, five clubs had failed to be re-elected. Of those, only two had actually finished at the bottom of Division Four. In other words, the proposal for a straight one-to-one contest would tend to make it even harder for a non-League club to gain entry.

• *Any club finishing bottom of the Fourth Division two seasons running would automatically be relegated to the Gola League and its place taken by the champions or next best graded club.*

Although this seemed like a concession, closer analysis of the twenty-six seasons of Division Four from 1958 to 1984 showed that only three clubs had ever finished bottom of the Fourth Division twice in succession: Chester (1961–2), Bradford Park Avenue (1967–9) and Workington (1976–7).

• *If and when two clubs do swap places, as recommended by the 1983 Chester Report, the allocation of League grants (comprising sponsorship, pools money and television fees – worth about £100,000 in 1984/5) would be divided as follows: in the first season, one-third to the promoted club, two-thirds to the relegated club; in the second season, two-thirds to the ex-Gola League club, one-third to the ex-League club.*

This proposal was designed to ease the blow of any club losing League status. The Gola League pointed out, however, that any promoted club would start out in the League with a considerable disadvantage, having approximately £60,000 less than its opponents.

In the end, the proposals failed to find approval at the 1985 Annual Meeting. Nor was there further movement on the election front. The year 1985 saw Bath City gain a paltry 8 votes, compared with Northampton (52), Stockport (50), Torquay (50) and Halifax (48).

Until and unless the system changed, it seemed as if an Alliance club's only hope was of being called in as a substitute; that is, to await the collapse of a League club and hope that the Management Committee would invite an outsider to make up the numbers. Between 1979 and 1985 that was indeed a very real possibility – in theory.

In practice, during the first part of Jack Dunnett's presidency the Committee adopted a different policy, one that favoured a process of 'natural wastage'. Thus, if a club was going bankrupt and couldn't be saved, the League would not replace it.

Between 1981 and 1985 the question was not 'if' but 'when' the League would announce the fall of the next Accrington Stanley.

There were certainly plenty of candidates: Bristol City, Hereford, Hull, Bradford City, Wolves (twice), Derby, Charlton (twice), Swansea, Middlesbrough, Hartlepool, Southend, Tranmere, Halifax, Newport and Rotherham. And these were just the cases where extinction threatened. At other clubs, such as Chelsea, Nottingham Forest, Manchester City, Leeds United and Aston Villa,

the debts ran into millions of pounds.

For every one of the ninety-two clubs, the biggest source of concern was the decline in attendances. When Jack Dunnett took on the leadership of this 'beleaguered garrison', crowds had just dropped by 11 per cent. For the next five seasons they would drop on average by just over one million spectators per season. No amount of sponsorship, pools money or even television money could compensate for the enormous deficit that this dramatic fall represented.

Unemployment was one major reason for the decline, but there were other factors, too: hooliganism, television coverage, the existence of many more diversionary activities – every expert had his own pet theory and there was, and still is, an element of truth in each hypothesis. It is not for this book to judge the issue. But the severe effect this catastrophic fall in gates had upon the League is undeniable. Even allowing for inflation, the plight of clubs in the early 1980s made the hardships of the 1920s seem like a minor cash flow problem.

Attendances were not the sole cause of this malaise, however. The prevailing economic climate of the early 1980s was unfavourable to any spendthrift, poorly managed business. Furthermore, there were circumstantial factors which had nothing to do with government policy or the international recession.

Bristol City and Swansea, for example, were victims of their own sudden decline. Each found themselves in the Fourth Division with several of the same highly paid, long-contract players they had signed when in the First Division only a few seasons earlier. In September 1979, Bristol were sixth in Division One. Exactly three years later they were bottom of the Fourth Division, saddled with a First Division wage bill.

Hull City also fell rapidly, despite investing heavily in a new manager and players. In the case of Wolves, who emulated Bristol by hurtling from the First to the Fourth Division in straight seasons, a debt of over £2 million,

A report on the financial state of the ninety-two clubs in 1981/2 found that the League as a whole was operating at a loss of £6 million, but that it received £5.9 million from outside sources (mainly pools, television and sponsorship).

Total match receipts in all four divisions amounted to £35 million, of which 60 per cent came from the First Division.

Just to police the 2028 League games cost the clubs £1.3 million, while the expenses of match officials, paid by the League, amounted to £454,000. Only fourteen League clubs had assets which exceeded their liabilities.

In the same season, transfer fees amounting to £22.2 million were paid to League clubs, of which £17.9 million was to First Division clubs. This figure has not been surpassed since, although it was not as high as the record season of 1979/80, when the total fees paid reached a staggering £32.8 million.

caused mainly by the building of a new stand, combined with apparently gross mis-management, led to the famous Old Golds coming within a hair's breadth of extinction on two occasions. Debts caused by new stands also brought wholesale changes at Chelsea and Tottenham.

In the majority of cases, economic reality caught up with clubs only because bank managers, VAT inspectors, tax collectors or major creditors finally lost patience. There were cases where League clubs were found to have been trading long after they should have gone into liquidation.

Everything in the early 1980s seemed to conspire against the survival of football. The Safety of Sports Grounds Act affected all First and Second Division clubs by 1979. By 1985, fifty League clubs were 'designated' under the Act, and although the Football Grounds Improvement Trust gave grants of up to 75 per cent for safety work, several clubs still struggled to find the balance.

Then there was the bill to be paid for trying to curb hooliganism. In August 1983, five South Yorkshire clubs were threatened with legal action over unpaid police bills. By 1984/5 it was estimated that for every 1000 spectators watching League football the clubs were having to pay £136 for policing. In the same season, the total policing bill for the Football League came to approximately £2.4 million.

Apart from the top dozen or so clubs in the League, the same deficiencies were common to every League club. As highlighted by a team of FA accountants, these were:

● *Gates receipts could no longer be depended on to pay wages.*

As a result, a few clubs decided to calculate their budgets on the basis of no gates at all. The wages were thus paid out of League grants, fund-raising activities, lotteries, social clubs, sponsorship and so on.

● *Although raised admission prices had brought in higher gate receipts, the rise had failed to keep pace with increased expenses.*

In 1979/80, using figures from all ninety-two clubs, players' wages represented 56 per cent of total match receipts. In 1982/3 the figure rose to a high of 80 per cent. That receipts exceeded wages at all was largely due to the much healthier state of the First Division clubs, despite the fact that they paid by far the highest wages.

A breakdown of the figures (compiled by the Football Trust) reveals that in the Fourth

Division, wages have outstripped match receipts for every season since at least 1979. Third Division comparisons show that the clubs can just meet their wage bills with match receipts, but with little to spare.

Predictably, the margin is greatest in the First Division, but even that is reducing as wages rise. In 1979/80, wages represented 44 per cent of total match receipts. In 1984/5 the figure had risen to 56 per cent. Of course, not all the surplus is profit. Overheads are also by far the highest in the First Division.

● *It was becoming increasingly difficult for clubs to meet their obligations under the Safety of Sports Grounds Act, let alone carry out routine maintenance of their grounds.*

In every case but one (Sheffield Wednesday), capacities have been cut throughout the 1980s. Clubs with large grounds could always afford to fence off large areas of unimproved terracing without affecting receipts – Chelsea, for example – but the overall effect of the Safety Act was to make smaller grounds more expensive.

As the above three factors began to take a grip upon struggling clubs in the early 1980s, the number of clubs at crisis point rose to an unprecedented level. A few random snippets from the *Rothmans Football Yearbook*'s diary of the 1981/2 season provide a flavour of the times:

'11.1.82 Bristol City losing £4000 a week ... 25.1.82 Darlington will fold unless they receive £50,000 within six weeks. They are £100,000 in debt and losing £1000 a week ... Bristol City players call in the PFA to thrash out the club's plan to give eight leading players immediate free transfers to cut the £350,000 annual wage bill ... 18.2.82 Chester announce loss of £137,000, they are losing more than £3000 a week ... 21.2.82 The 92 Football League chairmen, at a crisis meeting in Solihull, want to amend some of football laws to improve the product

and the image of the game ... 25.2.82 Hull City, with debts of £350,000 call in the receiver but hope to complete the season ... Derby owe £10,000 in tax bills ... 1.3.82 Halifax Town's playing staff go up for sale. Chairman Sam Rorke says: "If the financial position does not improve by the end of the month I will close the club down." They are losing £3000 a week and have debts of £254,000 ... 2.4.82 Aldershot announce a loss of £92,000 for the year ending June 1981, almost double the previous deficit ... Rochdale, expected to lose £30,000 this season, say they will close unless the next five home matches double their attendances ...'

And so on and so forth. This was the reality of the Football League; Aston Villa won the European Cup, the Milk Cup brought in £2 million to the game, Liverpool secured sponsorship worth £500,000 ... but Rochdale's home gates did not improve, and Halifax scrapped their reserve team. Nevertheless, the following season the League kicked off with all ninety-two clubs in place.

But how? How could these ailing clubs continue to defy all financial logic and survive? It most certainly wasn't through any financial help from the Management Committee. Had they given just one small grant to a club in need, then a dozen others would have demanded the same or more. The League's coffers would have been empty within a season.

But did that mean that the League was being heartless? To some people it did, not because financial assistance was refused, but because the Committee in this period seemed quite prepared for clubs to fall by the wayside.

This never happened, but the fact that it didn't was no miracle. It was the result of sheer hard work and sacrifice on the part of hundreds of people. Whenever a club reached the brink, somehow the directors, supporters, players, local businessmen and the community all rallied together to save the day. This was as it had been since the beginning of professional football.

But there was an added element in the 1980s.

In at least fifteen cases of threatened or actual liquidation, the PFA took over the wages of the players, negotiated deals which would help to save as many jobs as possible, or provided a straight loan. For three or four hectic seasons, the PFA secretary, Gordon Taylor, seemed to be the chief surgeon of football, dashing around the country to administer the kiss of life and bandage up clubs wounded by debt and despondency. Meanwhile, club chairmen seemed to spend as much time in the courts as they did in boardrooms – pleading their cases, or begging for a stay of execution.

Each one found a different way of averting the bank manager's noose, but the first option was usually to reduce the playing staff. In 1979 there were 2025 contract players registered with League clubs. By 1983, when it reached its lowest point, the figure was 1575.

Another indicator of how hard times were was the number of players allowed to leave without a fee, often simply to cut the wage bill. In the year ending June 1978 there were 224 free transfers registered by the Football League. By 1982 that number had reached a peak of 442. That represented something like 20 per cent of the profession.

What other methods did the clubs find to reduce their debts?

Preston, Wolves and Leeds won a reprieve by selling their grounds to the local council. Swansea's team played without wages for a while. At Derby the manager and coaching staff raised the money to buy £70,000 Bobby Campbell from Bradford City, and, ironically, that money helped, in turn, to save Bradford City.

Some clubs sold part of their land for redevelopment: supermarkets at Hull, Crystal Palace and Bolton, flats at Brentford, houses at Bournemouth, a pub at Tranmere. Others, such as Stoke, Birmingham and Walsall, wanted to sell land or their whole ground, but were scotched either by the local planning authorities or by the fact that no one wanted to buy the land anyway. Scunthorpe were suc-

cessful, however, and their Old Show Ground was due to become a supermarket in 1988.

Only a few clubs were able to add to their income by improving their own facilities. Jack Dunnett's club, Notts County, built a sports centre behind one of their goals; Bristol City installed bowling greens under a stand; Tottenham and Aston Villa built conference suites in their new stands. QPR tried another means of raising money – an artificial pitch – of which more later.

Meanwhile, their neighbours Chelsea and Fulham were inadvertently forced into a different sort of financial corner when the ownership of their grounds fell into the hands of a property developer. Their fate was still undecided as the League entered its centenary year.

Two clubs suffered the ignominy of losing their grounds. Bristol Rovers were forced out of Eastville by high rental charges in 1986 – they went to share Bath City's ground – and Charlton were given little choice but to leave the Valley. They moved in with Crystal Palace – the Football League's first ground-sharing arrangement. It was a good way of saving money, but a depressing outcome for Charlton's dwindling number of fans.

In 1986, at the same time as Wimbledon overtook Crystal Palace to reach Division One, poor Ron Noades' new tenants, Charlton, promptly did the same in their first season at Selhurst Park. Homeless Charlton's promotion was all the more remarkable in that the club had been so close to the wall on two previous occasions.

In 1984 the deadline was only twenty-five minutes away when the Charlton's new owners managed to sign the final agreement. But even that seemed positively laid-back by the standards of Wolves, who in July 1982 were reported to have been saved with just three minutes to spare. Only James Bond could have contrived a more timely *dénouement*.

The public's perception of this was that, while the PFA, the fans and local communities seemed to care enough to preserve that magical number of ninety-two clubs, the League itself was not bothered. Jack Dunnett remarked: 'It's true that I believed in natural wastage. If a community couldn't sustain its football club I didn't see why it should be propped up. We were quite prepared to see the League slimmed down to ninety or even seventy clubs. We certainly weren't going to provide special arrangements under which clubs who were teetering on the edge would have been allowed to avoid paying tax or their creditors.

Then gradually our policy changed and we decided that if a club did drop out we would replace it, because there were a lot of Alliance Premier League clubs quite capable of taking on League status.

But then the clubs kept confounding us and the ninety-two survived. Each year I said that a club will go broke, and each year they proved me wrong.'

We say it again. How many industries today have the same number of outlets as they had in 1950?

The astonishing aspect of football's financial woes of the early 1980s is not that so many clubs were in dire straits. It is that all ninety-two survived. Not one 'did an Accrington Stanley'.

* * *

Running parallel with this continual fight for survival at club level was a fight of a different nature on the terraces.

It is not this book's brief to chronicle the outbreaks of violence which plagued League football in the 1980s. Other accounts give the subject the kind of thorough treatment it both needs and deserves. To pay scant attention to the problem here would be only to indulge in platitudes. As always, we shall confine our comments to how the issue of hooliganism affected the League, and how it reacted to the challenge.

The first point to make is that football administrators were trained to run a sport, not to act as policemen or psychologists. If politicians, sociologists and community workers were needed to patch up the inner cities after riots in the summer of 1981, how on earth was football expected to solve its own behavioural problems of the same period without outside help?

The League's number one ally in this crucial battle against crowd disorder has always been the police. And the police recommended that segregation would be the best way to stop violence inside a ground.

Thus, the face of League football changed, fence by fence, barrier by barrier, during the 1970s and 1980s as it became sadly necessary to keep rival fans apart and all fans off the pitch.

The first fences at a League ground went up in 1972, at Chelsea. By 1980 most First and Second Division grounds were fenced, at least in the standing areas. Several grounds erected fences even in front of seated areas. The fences constituted an attempt, not always successful, to keep the hooligans back, but their main effect was to alienate the ordinary supporter. Football as seen through wire meshing is, quite literally, a pain in the neck.

After fencing and segregation, the authorities turned their attentions to other methods of control and deterrence. In conjunction with the newly formed Football Trust (which was formed to aid football at all levels, using money donated by the PPA from spotting-the-ball competitions), League Secretary Graham Kelly started investigating the possible use of closed-circuit television cameras inside grounds in 1980. In the same year the FA's own committee on crowd problems met with the Home Secretary to discuss various measures.

Alcohol was banned at Scottish grounds in 1981, while in Parliament Jack Dunnett tried to help through the Football Crowds (Control) Bill, an attempt at bringing government in on the fight against hooliganism both at home and abroad.

To try to reduce violent play on the pitch, the League chairmen gathered at Solihull in

1981 appointed a sub-committee, including Sir Matt Busby and Jimmy Hill, to look into the eradication of so-called 'cynical' or professional fouls. But a crackdown had already begun at the beginning of the season, which ended with sendings-off at an all-time high of 150.

Also in 1981, the Football Trust called in the experts for a one-day conference on hooliganism in football. What emerged was that fencing and segregation had reduced the problem within grounds, but that much remained to be done outside. There was no single answer.

Coventry City ran their own experiment by converting their Highfield Road ground into an all-seater stadium, in 1981. By 1985, after various pitch invasions and a fierce battle between Coventry and Leicester fans (in which the plastic seats were used as missiles), City reluctantly put back the security fences and stripped one of the terraces of its seats.

But the experiment had been worthwhile, if only to learn where it went wrong. The same can be said of developments at Loftus Road.

During the same summer as Coventry spent £400,000 on their new seats, Queen's Park Rangers spent £350,000 on laying down the first artificial pitch to be used for League football.

In fact, according to the League's minutes, Colchester United were actually the first club to apply for permission to lay a synthetic surface, in July 1980. Permission at that time was refused. The time was not right, said the Management Committee.

QPR's chairman, Jim Gregory bypassed the League when he announced his plans in March 1981, although he did attend a Management Committee meeting to keep everyone informed. (Remember that Messrs Gregory and Dunnett had been allies before, in 1967 when QPR had been about to move into Brentford's ground.) Gregory told the Committee that he would remove the synthetic pitch after a three-year trial period, but only if it proved to be a commercial failure or if improvements in technology led to a better surface becoming available. His eventual aim was to build a roof over the stadium.

Since there was nothing at the time in League regulations to prevent Rangers from going ahead with either of these plans (although there is now), all the Management Committee could do was to adopt a position of what it called 'benevolent neutrality'. Jack Dunnett was, however, a great believer in innovation, and, it has to be remembered, football at that time was searching for solutions to all kinds of problems. Maybe, just maybe, artificial pitches would provide some of the answers.

There were some reservations. QPR were in the Second Division at that time. What if they were promoted? Dunnett's response to this was that the best possible test for the new pitch would be to see the best possible players using it.

Soon after QPR had made their plans public, Charlton Athletic informed the Committee that they, too, intended to lay an artificial surface. This time the Committee demurred, and Charlton were politely informed that it would be best for them to await developments.

The first complaint arrived at Lytham in October 1981, from Blackburn Rovers, who had just been beaten 2–0 on Rangers' gleaming new pitch. Three weeks later, Leicester complained, having lost by the same score.

QPR complained about the complaints, and then had to pay additional hotel bills which Portsmouth had incurred through having to spend an extra day getting accustomed to the pitch. It did Pompey no good. They lost 5–0.

When Everton asked what action the Committee would take if any club refused to play at Loftus Road in the newly sponsored Milk Cup, the response was straightforward. The competition had to be preserved, so the tie would be awarded to QPR.

Artificial turf had few supporters in its early days, mainly because the pitch laid at Loftus

Road had been laid to unnecessarily hard speci-fications to cope with the other events Rangers hoped to stage. But to smaller, struggling clubs looking for new ways in which to increase their income, synthetic grass held many attractions. Thus, in time, an artificial pitch became regarded as something of a panacea – put one down and watch all your troubles disappear along with the grass cuttings.

Depite the many objections to QPR's pitch, Jim Gregory did not rip it up after three years. Rangers reached the First Division after two seasons with the new surface, and were pro-hibited from playing on it only when they qualified for the UEFA Cup in 1984/5 (they used Highbury instead).

Then, in 1985, Luton Town became the second League club to install a synthetic surface, but this time using a much more advanced variety which had greater 'give' and less bounce than the Loftus Road brand. Luton claimed that the new pitch earned them an extra £100,000 a year for various events and daily hire.

Before 1985 the League rules stated that any club wishing to install a plastic pitch would need a majority vote of approval from fellow League clubs. Tranmere was the first and only club to be outvoted under this rule, in 1983.

By 1985 the PFA and FA had expressed their views in no uncertain manner. The union announced that a ballot of members had come out overwhelmingly against artificial pitches. Then, in May 1985, the FA banned any club apart from Luton and QPR from playing Cup matches on a synthetic surface. At that time, Preston were just digging up their grass pitch to put in a plastic one.

At the League's Annual Meeting in 1986, Leicester City's Terry Shipman (son of the former President) led the anti-artificial-pitch brigade with a proposal 'that no First or Second Division match be played on plastic grass after 31 July 1988 except in exceptional circumstances'. Everton seconded the motion.

QPR and Luton never found out what Leicester meant by 'exceptional circum-stances', because the motion was defeated, much to their relief (see pp. 337 ff.). Immedi-ately, Second Division Oldham went ahead with their installation, so as the 1986/7 season began, there were four artificial pitches in the Football League.

Over the next year another six or so clubs applied and were given permission to install pitches, but none did. At about £300,000 a go it was beyond the pockets of most smaller clubs, unless they were given local council aid (as was the case at Preston). Finally, the League chairmen agreed on a three-year moratorium on artificial pitches – no more to be installed while the matter was given greater con-sideration.

QPR had by this time made up their mind. Their new chairman, David Bulstrode, decided to go back to nature in the summer of 1988 and install the same kind of natural pitch as Fulham possessed. This was a revolutionary grass surface called Cell System, developed in Switzerland and marketed initially in Britain by a firm whose chairman was Denis Thatcher, husband of the Prime Minister.

The development of more hard-wearing natural surfaces like the one at Fulham, and the vast improvements in pitch technology already made by the Sports Turf Research Institute at Bingley, Yorkshire, have suggested that real grass will have a stronger case than ever in the 1990s and beyond.

But during the present decade, and especially after the financial battering that smaller clubs took in the early and mid 1980s, many an anxious director has continued to view synthetic turf as the answer to their prob-lems – regardless of the quality of football played on them.

At the top end of the League there remains a solid conviction that football should be played on grass and grass alone. If a club cannot make football on grass pay for itself, then perhaps they should make way for another club which can.

The debate will go on for some time, no doubt. But money is at the heart of the matter. Artificial pitches have been seen as promising financial salvation; *ipso facto* they have been a key issue of the 1980s.

There were four other ways of bolstering up finances in the League: improving the revenue from the pools, creating new competitions, introducing sponsorship, and raising more money from the television companies. Each method was fraught with difficulties.

Firstly, the pools. In 1984 the League's existing agreement with the PPA ran out, and the Management Committee negotiated a new twelve-year agreement which increased the League's pools income by £1.3 million to £5.5 million annually. Although this seemed like an excellent deal, the fact that it was said to have been negotiated secretly and without the clubs' approval led Fulham's chairman, Ernie Clay – the Bob Lord of his time – to demand an EGM. He claimed that the Committee should have obtained better terms. Here again was the age-old conflict: the clubs elected the Management Committee to do a job, then complained when they did that job.

The result of this dispute was that a group of chairmen led by Crystal Palace's Ron Noades revived the idea of the League running its own pools competition. This had first been mooted in 1962 and several times since, but the problem was always the same: how could it compete with the well-established pools industry without damaging the substantial PPA contribution to the League? A complicating factor in the 1980s was the fact that the PPA was already funding the Football Grounds Improvement Trust and the Football Trust.

The League had already burnt its fingers in trying to foil the pools companies in 1936 – much to the clubs' anger – and yet now, almost half a century later, the clubs were preparing to mount a challenge of their own. The Management Committee was not amused. Nor was the PPA. But in truth, the clubs stood little chance of denting the PPA's supremacy. By 1985 the pools industry was worth about £550 million per year. Some 10–11,000,000 coupons were distributed each week. It was David *versus* Goliath, with Goliath holding all the stones.

Around seventy-five clubs on both sides of the border promised to participate in the proposed competition, 'Top Score', and winnings of £600,000 were promised. It was launched at the start of the 1985/6 season and lasted just three months.

What about raising cash by starting up new competitions? Here was another potential minefield. With attendances still falling and the number of unemployed at record levels, the last thing the public appeared to want was yet more football. Figures showed quite clearly that even committed supporters were becoming increasingly selective in the matches they chose to attend.

Alan Hardaker had long complained that there were already too many games in a season (although his creation, the League Cup, was partly responsible for this). England managers from Alf Ramsey to Bobby Robson had each made the same complaint. How could English football possibly compete at international level if its top footballers were playing over sixty games a season?

Nevertheless, during the 1980s the clubs agreed to the creation of two new competitions, the Associate Members' Cup and the Full Members' Cup (details in Appendices). Average gates for 1986/7 of 3361 in the former and of 5140 in the latter (excluding the final at Wembley) convinced few people outside the League that new competitions were the answer. But new sponsors Freight Rover and Simod respectively, and the ever-seductive promise of a Wembley final have ensured both competitions' survival, in the near future at least. Certainly, the Freight Rover Trophy has added a delightful dimension to the season for Third and Fourth Division clubs, for whom the nearest they might normally expect to get to Wembley would be a visit to Brentford's ground.

Another route to solvency chosen in the early 1980s was sponsorship. The League's first contact with sponsors had come in 1970 with the Texaco Cup, Watney Cup and Ford Sporting League (see Appendix Seven). Not everyone was happy about it, however. 'Sponsorship has to be watched carefully or it could grow too big and kill you', warned West Bromwich's chairman, Jim Gaunt, in September 1970. The comment cost him a rebuke from the Management Committee.

But the Committee did act cautiously, nevertheless. Several offers were received during the 1970s for various sponsored competitions, all of which either the Committee or the clubs rejected. And when QPR, for example, wanted to display their kit-makers' trade name prominently on their shirts in March 1977, the Committee refused permission. They reversed the decision six months later (although Rangers had to change their shirts in the event of television coverage).

Sponsorship became a major factor in football at the beginning of the 1980s. It took several forms: sponsorship of a competition, of a club, of an individual match, of part of a ground, of the match-ball, of a man-of-the-match award, even of different items of a player's kit, right down to his socks.

The Management Committee first considered the idea of attracting sponsors for the League and for the League Cup in 1980. Various companies showed interest in giving their name to the League Championship, among them two rather well-known multinational soft drink manufacturers, but the first actual deal was signed in March 1982 with the National Dairy Council. This was for the sponsorship of the League Cup (see Appendix Four).

Worth over £2 million for four years, the agreement represented a milestone in the League's history. The deals with Texaco, Watney Mann and Ford in 1970 related to peripheral competitions, whereas the League Cup was the third most important domestic competition in England and Wales.

There could certainly be no objections to football associating with such an everyday, innocuous and healthy product as milk. The Milk Cup was a delight for headline writers – 'Milk Shake-up', 'Cream of the Cup', 'Golden Top performance' and so on. It also inspired a memorable advertising campaign which attributed to milk 'a lotta bottle'. Another gift for the headlines.

The agreement with the National Dairy Council was arranged by a London firm called CSS Promotions, appointed by the League in December 1981 to seek out means by which the League and its ninety-two clubs might maximize their commercial potential.

It was no easy task, mainly because it was almost impossible to coax ninety-two separate companies into adopting the same products. For example, in the late 1970s Alan Hardaker tried to pesuade every club to use an official Football League ball, complete with its own special logo. This was an idea he'd seen used successfully in the United States and Australia. But because several clubs already had their own deals with other manufacturers, the potential benefits were never fully realized.

Nevertheless, in March 1984 the British company Mitre Sports signed the first of a series of agreements worth £500,000, by which any club using Mitre balls for all their matches would receive a share of the fee (plus, of course, free balls and other benefits). Since the agreement was made, around sixty clubs have taken up the offer, the remainder having concluded their own deals with different manufacturers.

Individual club sponsorship really took off in the early 1980s. As one would expect, clubs such as Liverpool and Manchester United attracted the best deals, reported to have been worth £500,000 over three seasons. This compared with, for example, £200,000 for West Ham and £150,000 for Norwich City. By 1987 every League club had become associated with a sponsor for one period or another.

Meanwhile, at Lytham St Annes and CSS,

next on the agenda was sponsorship of the League competition itself. It is interesting to note that non-League football provided a lead in this respect. The Isthmian League proved to be pioneers in the late 1970s when they arranged a cup sponsorship with the Japanese electronics company Hitachi and league sponsorship with the paint makers Berger. The Northern League was then sponsored by Drybroughs.

But the Football League – surely that was different: the oldest league in the world, a hallowed name, an institution. Would not sponsorship cheapen its image? There are, as always, two sides to this argument.

On one hand, there is hardly a branch of the entertainment or sporting industry not open to sponsorship or commercial tie-ups. Opera, concerts and the theatre, from the park bandstand to the Royal Festival Hall, from the fringe basement to the National Theatre, all now depend on donations and sponsorship.

Years before football became involved, cricket, rugby and especially motor racing were each becoming increasingly embroiled in the commercial world. The Grand National was saved by sponsorship, while snooker and darts were more or less thrust into the wider world by sponsorship. Cricket's embrace was particularly warm, despite the traditional conservatism which pervades the pavilion.

Given the precedents already set by other sports, therefore, it is surprising only that the League didn't take on sponsors earlier.

The counter-argument is that, although sponsorship might help individual clubs, its contribution to the League competition is minimal and demeaning and should therefore be discarded. Graham Kelly described sponsorship as 'the icing on a very substantial cake'. Opponents reckoned that the cake was good enough to eat without that icing.

In an ideal world, it is probably true to say that every sport would love to get by without sponsors. In the real world, that is no longer a practicality. But even if sport could survive happily unaided, the fact is that commercial interests would still be keen on becoming involved in sport. And who can blame them for pursuing the prospect of being involved in an immensely enjoyable activity, of entertaining colleagues and clients, of meeting the stars? In many respects sponsors are fans who have chosen a different way to show their support. How much more exciting and effective it is to have one's company name flashing across the television screens as a brilliant goal is scored than to see another dull advertisement in the local newspaper! Compared with television advertising, sponsorship of a televised sport is a veritable bargain.

So even had the League not wanted sponsors, there were several companies who wanted the League.

That raised the issue of the type of company or product with which the League should choose to be associated. Not tobacco, and preferably not beer or spirits. The company had to be well known, and be able to benefit from having ninety-two promotional outlets all over the nation.

The League's first deal was signed on 5 May 1983 with the Japanese camera, computer and photocopying-machine makers Canon. Canon was already a familiar name in football circles following its joint sponsorship of the 1982 World Cup in Spain. Other Japanese companies were among the first to sign club sponsorship deals: Hitachi at Liverpool, Ricoh at Stoke, JVC at Arsenal, and Pioneer at Ipswich, while the computer firm Atari sponsored a new indoor six-a-side competition called 'Soccer Six' at the Birmingham National Exhibition Centre.

The relative success of this tournament immediately led to reports that Atari were considering sponsoring the League Championship, but only if the League could sort out a deal with the television companies – which it had not done at the time – and make definite progress in the fight against hooliganism.

Television coverage is the biggest carrot of

all. All major sponsorship deals in football, at both League and club level, largely depend on how much exposure the League can negotiate with the television companies. For this reason, Canon had a clause in their agreement which enabled them to reduce the prize money if, for any reason, League matches were not shown on television.

The main provisions of Canon's sponsorship were as follows:

• Canon would invest £3.3 million in the League over three seasons. Prize money would be divided as follows:

First Division champions £50,000, runners-up £25,000, third place £15,000
Second Division champions £25,000, runners-up £15,000, third place £5,000
Third Division champions £15,000, runners-up £8000, third place £4000
Fourth Division champions £8000, runners-up £4000, third place £2000, fourth place £1000

• Canon would pay monthly awards for the team scoring the most goals in each division, from £1000 a month in the First Division down to £250 for the Fourth Division. At the end of each season there would be additional prizes for the top scorers from £6500 in the First Division down to £2000 in the Fourth Division.

• Canon would also contribute £50,000 towards Centres of Excellence (run for young footballers by various League clubs), £4000 for loyalty awards to players and club staff, and £16,000 to clubs making the best efforts to promote family attendance.

• In return for an additional facility payment from Canon, each League club was to provide:

two perimeter advertising boards at First Division grounds, one at other grounds;
one page of advertising or editorial material in match programmes;
ten complimentary tickets and ten tickets at cost plus hospitality.

One of the most contentious parts of the Canon deal was that the venerable old League Championship trophy, first awarded in 1891, plus the three other divisional trophies and shields, were to be consigned to a glass case in Graham Kelly's office in Lytham and be replaced by tall, thin trophies of modern design. Such was the price of sponsorship; football had now become a 'product' and its traditions a saleable commodity. The pioneers of the League would have been quite dumbfounded.

As it transpired, Canon's prize money was cut from £177,000 to £75,000 when televised football was off the screens for five months after the League had failed to reach an agreement with the television companies in February 1985. But this failure was not the reason for Canon's decision not to renew the contract at the end of the three years. Nor, according to Canon, were they withdrawing because of the battering that football's image had taken after the horrors of Bradford, Birmingham and Brussels in May 1985.

Instead, Canon calculated that the sponsorship had served its purpose. It had heightened the public's awareness of their name and products, and the decision to part company was purely a business one. This was announced in January 1986, giving the League plenty of time to find a new sponsor. But, until the League settled its differences with the television companies, this was easier said than done, as the next chapter will attempt to explain.

Are you sitting comfortably? Then let the great television saga begin.

CHAPTER THIRTY-TWO

The League Takes a Screen Test

A more baffling relationship than the one between English football and the television companies is hard to imagine. By 1985 it was like a marriage in which neither partner understood the other or could agree on the reasons for staying together. And yet it should have, and could have, been the perfect match.

Football has the reputation of being the 'national game' in Britain, but in the 1980s both the BBC and ITV have treated it more like a long-running soap opera character whom they want to kill off gently without upsetting too many of the viewers. They allowed televised football to rot, and then turned to the Football League and said: 'You see, no one wants to watch it any more!'

The League itself wasn't entirely blameless. In the early 1980s it lacked both the expertise to negotiate with the television companies and the confidence to wield its powers (for reasons we will discover later), and by the time it had mustered up its strength it was too late to influence the television moguls. So it was that the most popular spectator sport in Britain (and the world) ended up in 1987 being displaced from a peak-viewing slot by American basketball, while in Australia, viewers were able to watch more televised football than the British.

The seeds of this sorry decline were sown in the late 1970s. Since 1966 the viewing public had become accustomed to a regular diet of recorded highlights of League football: BBC's *Match of the Day* on Saturday nights, and ITV's regionalized programmes on Sunday afternoon. In addition, there were preview programmes on both channels around midday on Saturday, and late-night mid-week highlights

more often than not.

The League always felt that it was not being paid a realistic price for its wares. In 1969/70, broadcast and television fees were worth £220,000 to the League, which after various deductions yielded the paltry total of £1346 per club. Even at that time, such a sum wouldn't go much further than a new set of bulbs for the floodlights. Since it was generally agreed that television did have a detrimental effect on attendances, this level of recompense was small enough to persuade many clubs that television simply wasn't worth it. Armchair supporters, however, felt otherwise.

At its peak in the early 1970s, *Match of the Day*, with Jimmy Hill as presenter, was attracting twelve to thirteen million viewers. Brian Moore on London Weekend Television's *Big Match* played to an audience of about nine million. There were no video recorders at that time, but there were plenty of grannies wise to the blindside runs of Martin Peters.

During the 1970s the Management Committee tried to reduce the amount of coverage while increasing the fees. At the same time, audiences for televised football dropped, and ITV began to covet the BBC's sacred Saturday-night slot.

It was on a Thursday evening in 1978, a few months before the next television agreement was due for negotiation, that a junior member of the Management Committee, Jack Dunnett, sat drinking a cup of coffee as he waited to enter a winding-up debate in the House of Commons. A message was handed to him that one Michael Grade of London Weekend Television wished to have a word.

That night over a drink, Grade outlined to

Dunnett his company's desire to buy up the exclusive rights to televise League football. The figure he mentioned was far in excess of what the League was already receiving.

Dunnett took Grade's verbal offer to the Management Committee and was instructed to negotiate further – secretly though, because if the BBC discovered it was being kicked into touch all hell would erupt, and hell hath no fury like a Corporation executive scorned. Not to mention what Jimmy Hill would say when he found out. (In fact, he was reported to have exclaimed: 'Hooligans!', when the LWT deal was made public. 'That's show biz', said others, while the headlines bellowed 'Snatch of the Day!')

Of course, the clubs were delighted. Under the new proposed terms they would receive more than a threefold rise in television fees, from £5000 per club each year to £17,000.

But while a triumphant Michael Grade sucked contentedly on his cigar, the BBC was furious and sued the League, whose members apparently hadn't spotted some small print in the previous contract which prevented them from dealing with other companies without first talking to the BBC. The Office of Fair Trading supported the BBC's protest, and Grade's swoop took on the forlorn appearance of a daring smash-and-grab raid which had been foiled at the last moment by an avuncular Dixon of Dock Green.

But if the Management Committee was embarrassed at being caught red-handed in the arms of another, the settlement which followed made it seem as if 'Snatch of the Day' had been nothing less than a brilliant plot, hatched to extract more money from the television companies. From LWT's offer of £17,000 per club, the new agreement with both the BBC and ITV, negotiated without Jack Dunnett this time, promised £25,000 per club – an astonishing £20,000 rise on the previous terms.

Although this seemed perfect on the surface, as the Management Committee sat down to consider the new offer, Dunnett dismissed it as a recipe for disaster. Because inflation at that time was still in double figures, he reckoned that the agreement should have been for two years only, and properly index-linked. Instead, the television companies were offering a four-year term with a 10 per cent allowance for inflation in only the third and fourth years.

With the meeting only a few minutes old, Dunnett told the Committee that he would resign if the terms were not changed, and with that he marched out of the room. As Labour Party workers in Nottingham and directors at Notts County were to find out in subsequent years, when Jack Dunnett promised to resign, he always kept his word.

On this occasion, however, he was back on the Committee within weeks, re-elected by the clubs in the region he had represented.

Meanwhile, the clubs rejected Dunnett's warnings and accepted the four-year television deal, delighted with the new terms.

But there was a price to pay. Firstly, the League was now forced to deal with both television companies simultaneously. By forming what was in effect a cartel, they effectively ended the League's future bargaining power. This flew straight in the face of competition.

Secondly, the thirteen-year-long pattern of BBC on Saturdays, ITV on Sundays came to an end as part of the 1979 agreement. Now the two companies would take turns to fill the Saturday night slot. ITV increased their audiences marginally as a result, and boasted profits of £1.75 million from overseas sales of matches. But the head of ITV Sport warned that television fees would not increase when the current agreement ended in 1983, largely because the overall ratings in England and Wales had fallen steadily since 1979.

It was during this four-agreement that Jack Dunnett became President of the League.

One of the first obstacles he tried to overcome was the refusal of both television companies to show teams playing with sponsors' names on their shirts. In October 1981, for example, ATV refused to record highlights of Aston Villa's match against Brighton because Brighton refused to change their shirts, which bore the name of their sponsors British Caledonian (whose slogan, ironically, was 'never forget you have a choice').

Coventry City (chairman: Jimmy Hill) tried a novel way around the ban by attempting to change their name to Coventry Talbot (after the car company which sponsored them) and to display a large 'T' on the shirts as part of the design.

Television's ban on shirt advertising seemed quite preposterous when viewed alongside the rest of the sports coverage. The BBC quite happily broadcast the names of Gillette, and Benson and Hedges for their televised cricket coverage: Grand Prix races were broadcast despite the plethora of track-side and car-carrying adverts, while at Wimbledon every year there was never any suggestion that Bjorn Borg should erase the manufacturer's quite visible logo from his rackets.

Yet football clubs had to change their shirts if cameras were present, simply to avoid showing a name – written no more than a few inches high – which was often so local or obscure that it wouldn't have meant much to viewers anyway. But even if the sponsor was a well-known company, as in the case of British Caledonian, how was this different from a tennis star shown in close-up with a trade-name on his shirt sleeve?

The FA also banned shirt advertising for Cup matches, which was ironic since, in Don Revie's days as manager, the England strip had carried unusually visible emblems advertising the kit-manufacturers, Admiral.

In 1983 the deal signed in 1979 came up for renewal, and the League's specially appointed Television Negotiating Committee set about its difficult task. The members were Sir Arthur South (Norwich), Robert Daniel (Plymouth), Peter Robinson (Liverpool), and a man who was starting to have quite an influence in League circles, Philip Carter of Everton.

But after forty years in the retailing business, even Carter's bargaining powers would be sorely tried over the next two years. The sad and sorry wrangle over television, eventually to lead to the most sweeping reforms the League had ever experienced, began in February 1983.

The Negotiating Committee received a two-year offer from television, worth £5.3 million. On 1 February a meeting of club chairmen voted unanimously to reject it. Jack Dunnett's attitude was unequivocal: television could do what it liked with football coverage as long as shirt advertising was allowed and the price was right. £5.3 million, he agreed, was not right.

At this point the dispute took a completely unexpected turn. A company which ran pub entertainment offered the League a staggering £8 million for the right to show recorded League matches in pubs all over Britain every Monday night. They would do this by using large screens called Telejectors.

Was this really a serious offer? Or was it an attempt by Jack Dunnett to force the television companies' hand when it came to further negotiations?

On 30 March the Management Committee recommended acceptance of this unlikely package, even though it threatened to deprive millions of viewers of football while earning handsome profits for publicans, for whom Monday nights were traditionally very quiet.

Four clubs – Liverpool, Manchester United, Arsenal and Tottenham – came out against the Telejector deal. The public, meanwhile, was quite baffled. To confine football viewing to pubs seemed totally counter-productive at a time when clubs and the police were desperately concerned about drink-related hooliganism. And what about the viewers, young, old, infirm or teetotal, who couldn't or wouldn't go to a pub? Were they to lose out?

We were never to find out. Telejector pulled out of the reckoning almost as abruptly as they had entered it, in late April 1983, while the tortured negotiations with the BBC and ITV went on ... and on.

The television companies argued thus: recent viewing figures were down, therefore they had to experiment with a new package of predominantly live matches instead of recorded highlights only. In return for this, they offered £5.3 million, and agreed to drop their opposition to shirt advertising.

But did the public really want live football? Only thirteen million had watched the World Cup Final in 1982, compared with twenty-three million in 1978. Even the last, vital game involving England in 1982 had drawn only a thirteen-million audience. Perhaps viewers were just turning away from football *per se*.

The League's attitude was somewhat complicated at this juncture by the requirements of the Canon sponsorship deal, unveiled in May 1983. Before that deal the League had broadly accepted that a weekly barrage of recorded highlights was both excessive and counter-productive. Now, however, it was anxious to gain the maximum coverage – which meant more live matches than television was broadcasting – in order to satisfy Canon's demand for extensive television coverage.

By now the negotiations were turning into a sit-com with farcical undertones. The two sides couldn't agree even on shirt advertising. Television wanted to limit the display to an area no larger than 16 square inches. Fine, said the League, we'll have each name 8″ × 2″. No, replied the television companies, it must be 4″ × 4″. Imagine trying to squeeze the words British Caledonian into that small a square!

But the most contentious issue was the number of live games to be shown. At one stage the two parties seemed to have agreed on live coverage of seventy matches: eight full games and sixty-two second half only. The Television Negotiating Committee took this proposal back to the Full Members, who rejected it. Instead, they called for just four matches to be covered live, with recorded highlights to be shown the rest of the season as usual.

ITV's Head of Sport, John Bromley, was exasperated. 'We've wasted seven months talking to them. No wonder the sport is disintegrating in front of us.' But the clubs' reasoning was quite understandable. Live football was an unknown quantity, and it was best to tread warily at first, especially in order to monitor how it affected attendances.

Still anxious not to lose the Canon sponsorship, the League put the matter to a vote of all ninety-two clubs. This produced a majority in favour of a compromise two-year agreement which provided for ten live matches a season. Approved finally in July 1983, the details were as follows:

● *Ten matches to be televised live, five per channel, with the BBC taking Friday-night games, ITV Sunday afternoon. The Milk Cup Final also to be televised live on a Sunday.*

Thus, for the first time, the League was going to have to adjust its fixtures especially for television.

● *The existing format of recorded matches to continue, except on weekends when live games would be broadcast.*

Even with these recorded games, the deal represented the first reduction in the number of games shown since regular televised football had begun.

● *Shirt advertising to be permitted up to 16 square inches, but no lettering to exceed 2 inches in height.*

When Aston Villa exceeded this limit by a centimetre or two in March 1984, they were reprimanded by the Management Committee. The most important aspect of this long-awaited concession was that clubs competing in Europe would now be able to attract higher sponsorship fees because they could promise much wider television exposure (UEFA having lifted its ban on shirt advertising the year before).

• *In addition to the £4.6 million fee, a sum of £300,000 per annum to be made available to compensate clubs for any loss of gate receipts caused by live broadcasts. Also the overseas sales minimum guarantee to be increased to £500,000.*

Claims for compensation would be decided by a four-man committee chaired by Graham Kelly. Clubs would be given eight weeks' notice of their games being selected.

The deal wasn't perfect, but it was at least settled, and, crucially, the Canon deal had been preserved also. And when the first League match was televised live, on Sunday 2 October 1983, the crowd of 30,596 at White Hart Lane, to see Tottenham beat Nottingham Forest 2–1, was actually a fraction more than Tottenham's previous home attendance (and higher than the following match).

The alarm bells didn't sound until three weeks later, when a televised Friday-night game between Wolves and Aston Villa, which in normal circumstance should have drawn a higher than usual attendance, attracted only 13,202 spectators, some 4000 below Wolves' average. As the season progressed, it became apparent that most Friday games suffered similarly.

Nor did the Friday games enjoy large audiences at home. In 1984/5 they reached about seven million in the ratings, which for peak Friday evening viewing was poor by either channel's standards. Sunday games held their own, however, at around eleven million which, when contrasted with the viewing figures for traditional recorded matches, – four to six million (no better than *Ski Sunday*) – persuaded the television companies to push for more live Sunday games in the next agreement.

And so to the next round of talks and the beginning of 1985.

Sir Arthur South, Robert Daniel, Peter Robinson and Philip Carter must have gone back to the negotiating table with heavy hearts. They were representing a disunited body against the might of a determined duo. And no one knew better than Phillip Carter that if the committee failed to negotiate a good deal, or if the clubs turned against it, that the simmering discontent among the leading clubs was in grave danger of boiling over.

One could almost sense this rising tide of unrest as the clubs met on St Valentine's Day, 1985. First came the clubs' unfavourable response to the twelve-year pools agreement, to which reference has been made in the previous chapter. In the ensuing atmosphere of rancour, the chairmen then considered television.

On the table in front of them was an offer worth approximately £19 million over four years, a 46 per cent rise on the previous year's payments. If one added all the attendant benefits of television coverage – sponsorship and ground advertising in particular – the deal had the potential to bring League clubs a sum of up to £52 million.

In addition to nineteen live matches, there was an option for fifteen extra regionally broadcast live games and a guaranteed minimum of seventy-six recorded highlights.

The Management Committee approved the deal. The four members of the Television Negotiating Committee felt it to be the best they could possibly extract from the BBC and ITV. It offered more money for a longer period at a time when football was crying out for stability and respectability. What more could the League clubs want?

A lot more, it seemed.

Oxford United's chairman, Robert Maxwell, led the opposition on St Valentine's Day, citing the enormous sums American football received from television. The television offer was 'Mad, bad and sad', he said, and the League could get much more.

But how much more? Figures were bandied about the meeting room like an auction in Never-Never Land. Men with no experience of television negotiations started talking about £60 million. No, more! At one stage the stakes went as high as £90 million. 'As poker players they made the dumb mistake of trying to read the opposition's hand in a mirror that turned out to be clouded by the steam rising from fevered imaginations', wrote Hugh McIlvanney in the *Observer*.

The members of the Television Negotiating Committee could hardly believe what was happening. All their work. All their efforts. They had gained an agreement which might have doubled the television income, and yet still it wasn't enough. Philip Carter was livid, but what could he do?

While some chairmen cried out for more money, others maintained that televised football should be stopped altogether for a season. Said Jack Dunnett after the meeting: 'It seems that football is prepared to have a year or two with no television if it comes to that. We know the huge financial losses that would be involved but, on the other hand, we might induce more people to come through the turnstiles. We are not looking for outright war.'

So the deal was rejected. Robert Maxwell, who had a 21-per-cent shareholding in Central

TV and a greater interest in cable television, was co-opted on to the Television Negotiating Committee, along with Ken Bates of Chelsea and Irving Scholar of Tottenham. And while many a chairman prayed for these new men to bring home the bacon more plentifully than ever, managers Brian Clough and Jack Charlton said they were quite happy for there to be no football on television. Gates might rise as a result.

Both sets of hopes proved ill-founded. As time would soon tell, not only was the rejection of the television deal disastrous in financial terms, but it finally persuaded men such as Philip Carter that the time was ripe for a massive re-evaluation of the League, and of the place of clubs such as his own within that League.

St Valentine's Day 1985 saw more than just the massacre of a television deal. It saw the beginning of the end of the Football League as it had existed since the days of the real massacre in 1929, the complete revamp of the Management Committee and the method by which it was selected, and, ultimately, the end of Jack Dunnett's period of office as eleventh president of the Football League.

CHAPTER THIRTY-THREE

Beleaguered by the Super Leaguers

The year 1985 was the most devastating in the hundred years of the Football League. Almost every one of the issues which had plagued the game over the previous two decades came to a head with such force that by the time the League met in London for its ninety-seventh Annual Meeting there were serious doubts as to whether William McGregor's heritage would survive to celebrate its centenary.

That it did – and that we are here to tell the tale – was the result of eleven months of soul-searching meetings, tough negotiations and, above all, passionate belief on the part of a handful of individuals that the Football League was worth preserving at almost any cost.

But although the climax of this quite historic movement occurred during the year 1985, the rumblings had begun roughly five years earlier amongst the leading clubs of the First Division, as they began to sense that the structure and organization of the League no longer served their best interests. This was by no means the first time that top clubs had questioned the League set-up, but it was the first time that circumstances would lend such weight to their discontent as to make the movement for reform quite irresistible.

As ever, power and money were at the heart of the question. Why did the leading clubs want more power?

A group of clubs we will christen the 'Big Five' (Liverpool, Everton, Manchester United, Tottenham and Arsenal) – although there were others often just as involved – believed that whenever it came to sharing the revenue, or making decisions on rules or policy, the League's tail always seemed to be wagging the dog.

While they couldn't deny lesser clubs a voice in League affairs, they felt that the Second, Third and Fourth Division members wielded an influence way out of proportion with their relative strengths. Money was not the only issue at stake here. The Big Five were anxious that decisions on such matters as artificial pitches, the use of substitutes and television coverage should not be swayed by smaller clubs, who might survive by hanging on to the bigger clubs' coat-tails but who should not be allowed to slow them down any further.

Thus, the Big Five turned their attention to the League's voting system, and to the constitution of the Management Committee.

Voting was the most urgent and yet also the simplest area for reform. Firstly, the Big Five and many others felt that the majority needed to implement rule changes should be reduced from three-quarters to two-thirds. This was hardly a new demand. Derby County had proposed it first in 1895! Since then there had been numerous failed attempts to change the system, the latest being at the instigation of the Management Committee in 1983 (prompted by Sir Norman Chester's second report).

The Big Five were also unhappy about the structure of the Management Committee.

The switch to a regionalized system of representation in 1975 had, unintentionally, brought about an imbalance. In 1984/5 only one of the Big Five was represented on the Committee – Liverpool, whose chairman John Smith had become a member in 1982 after failing to be elected as president the year before. (In September 1982 Smith had been one of the first men to warn about the possibility of a Super League breakaway.) Of the other

Committee men, Jack Dunnett's club Notts County was in the Second Division relegation zone, Dick Wragg (Sheffield United) and Jack Wiseman (Birmingham) belonged to Second Division clubs, while Robert Daniel (who switched from Plymouth to Torquay), Christopher Needler (Hull) and Ian Jones (Doncaster) were each from the lower divisions. That left only Alan Everiss of West Bromwich, Sir Arthur South of Norwich (relegated that year) and Geoff Smith of Watford from the First Division.

As far as the leading clubs were concerned, four out of ten members, and that purely by chance, was not enough representation for the First Division. Instead, there ought to be some way of guaranteeing the First Division and, indeed, the Full Members, a majority on the Committee. So that was the basis of the power struggle: voting powers and the constitution of the Management Committee.

The Big Five's second area for concern was the League's financial arrangements. They argued that television and sponsorship deals were obtained on the strength and popularity of the leading clubs. With all due respect to their fellow Leaguers, they argued, the television companies were rarely interested in filming matches outside Division One. Nor were companies like Canon attracted towards football by the likes of Halifax. That wasn't being hard-hearted, it was simply being honest.

In view of this, the Big Five looked for a way in which the share of television and sponsorship money could be weighted in their favour.

Similarly, they objected to contributing 4 per cent of their gate receipts to the League pool (which was shared out at the end of the season ninety-two ways), because this amounted to a subsidy of the smaller clubs.

Of course, that's exactly what the pool was supposed to be. Ever since the First World War, when Charles Sutcliffe, the great Christian Liberal, had pioneered the system, it had provided a means by which the wealthy had supported the poor.

At the centre of the movement for reform was Everton's chairman, Philip Carter, who discounted any suggestion that greed was the big clubs' sole motivating factor. He felt particularly strongly that the Management Committee of the day was reacting to circumstances rather than taking the initiative itself, and that the system of regional groups inhibited rather than encouraged progress.

Because of this, in 1981/2 a group of six First Division chairmen gathered at Goodison Park, Philip Carter acting as host. More meetings followed, with the numbers in attendance rising from six to ten and eventually to all twenty-two of the First Division chairmen. It wasn't long before the Second Division clubs asked to be involved, too. Jimmy Hill (Coventry) was central to these discussions, as were Doug Ellis (Aston Villa) and Martin Edwards (Manchester United).

There could be no doubting the resolve of the so-called Super Leaguers. Martin Edwards was quoted as saying: 'The smaller clubs are bleeding the game dry. For the sake of the game they should be put to sleep.'

Tottenham's manager, Keith Burkinshaw, voiced a widely shared belief that a reduced First or Premier Division of sixteen or eighteen clubs would reduce the burden on top players and allow them to develop their skills, thus benefiting standards in both domestic and international competitions.

But even in 1982 there was vehement opposition to the Super League concept. Ron Noades, chairman of Crystal Palace, remarked of the Big Five: 'What they want is not a Super League, it's a selfish League.' Gordon Taylor, Secretary of the PFA, declared that his members were totally against the idea of a Super League breakaway, but if the leading clubs did manage to form one then the PFA would have no choice but to campaign for total freedom of contract – that is, the abolition of all transfer fees for players at the end of their contracts. Meanwhile, Jack Dunnett as

President was caught between the desire to appease the Big Five and therefore save the League, and the knowledge that his own club, Notts County, would not be among the candidates ever considered for a Super League.

There was nothing cloak and dagger about the Super League meetings. None of them ever took place behind the Management Committee's back, and Jack Dunnett often lent his voice and gave advice. He and Phil Carter were always on good terms. In fact, one might say that never in the League's history had there been such a frank exchange of views in such informal circumstances.

By April 1983 the debate was in full flow. A group of twenty-five First and Second Division chairmen attended a meeting in Coventry, with Jimmy Hill in the chair, and it afterwards emerged that the top clubs were still threatening a breakaway if they couldn't negotiate a larger share of gate receipts, television money and other League revenues.

But, as if to warn the Super Leaguers just how hard reform would be from within, if and when they tried to change the League regulations, in April 1983 Sir Norman Chester delivered his second report on the structure and finance of the Football League. Just like the reaction to his first report in 1968, to Alan Hardaker's 'Pattern for Football', and to the Gola League's thought-provoking proposals unveiled in January 1983, the majority of League clubs still showed a stubborn resistance to radical change.

Not all ears were deaf to Sir Norman's entreaties, however. Despite his report's lukewarm reception in 1983, within a year or two its findings became the basis for much of the leading clubs' thinking.

Apart from discussing the difficulties in voting and representation already outlined above, Sir Norman proposed in 1983 that the League be reduced to sixty-four full-time professional clubs, with the remainder linking up with the Gola League to form a separate, intermediate league. Rather than kill off the less

successful League clubs, argued Chester, the new set-up would allow them to flourish. It was pointless for a club like Scunthorpe, for example, to drain itself in an effort to keep up with the Joneses of the First and Second Divisions, when in reality it had much more in common with nearby non-League clubs such as Boston United. The relative prosperity of Boston, and others in the Gola League (including ex-Leaguers Barrow), proved that there was a good life to be had below stairs.

It was largely as a result of the Chester Report that the Management Committee proposed that the three-quarters voting majority be reduced to two-thirds, which as we noted earlier was rejected at the Annual Meeting in 1983.

But one rule change was approved at that meeting, and that was to allow clubs to keep all the receipts from their home matches (less the 4 per cent pool), rather than give a share to the visiting club as had formerly been the practice.

This was another potential bombshell. Smaller clubs saw it as another nail in their coffin, a chance for the rich to get richer, while supporters of the measure claimed that it would help clubs to gain maximum advantage from their investments in players and ground improvements. For example, Newcastle had taken an expensive gamble bringing Kevin Keegan to St James' Park but, having reaped the reward by attracting consistently high gates, they still had to share the receipts with other clubs.

At the other end of the scale, Crystal Palace argued that when less attractive clubs visited Selhurst Park, their own income was hit twice: firstly because attendance fell, and secondly because what little they earned still had to be shared. 'Clubs must stand or fall by their own income', said Palace chairman Ron Noades.

The first concerted attempt to change the constitution of the Management Committee came in September 1983 when the chairmen of Chelsea, Wolves, Crystal Palace, Charlton,

Derby and Fulham combined to requisition an Extraordinary General Meeting.

Their intention was threefold: to end regionalization, to prohibit any sitting member from standing – for re-election, that is – if his club ceased to be a Full Member during his term of office, and to enforce retirement on any member once he reached the age of seventy. The first proposal failed, but the latter two did not. (Since then, two members have had to step down under the seventy-year rule: Len Cearns (West Ham) in 1984 and Sir Arthur South (Norwich) in 1985. Both were given a new honorary title – Life Vice President.)

In view of all the meetings and machinations since 1981, it was no surprise when Philip Carter stood against Jack Dunnett for the presidency in 1984. Dunnett won, by 35 votes to 17, but the fact that someone from outside the Management Committee had made a bid for the leadership, that Notts County had just been relegated to the Second Division, and that Carter had recently taken early retirement and was now concentrating more of his energies on football, suggested that a further challenge could not be ruled out.

Carter, as we noted in the previous chapter, was by 1984 actively involved as a member of the Television Negotiating Committee, which brings us back to the St Valentine's Day Massacre of 1985.

Would the new seven-man committee fare any better than had its original four members in February? Would Robert Maxwell's influence and contacts within the television world be able to deliver the bounty?

Alas not. There was no pot of gold at the end of the rainbow. Angry at the League's rejection of their offer in February, the BBC and ITV dug in their heels. The League asked for more money, the television negotiators said there was no more. The League demanded more recorded matches, the television people said they weren't interested in recorded games, and even if they had been the buying price would be way below the original offer. Ken

Bates met a similar response when he tried to extract more fees from radio.

The talks subsided into silence, and as the 1984/5 season drew to a close, a black-out for the next season seemed more and more likely.

1985 went from bad to worse. While the TV talks reached deadlock, the hooligan gangs of England appeared to be trying to outdo each other in attracting the most headlines. Trouble broke out at both Milk Cup semi-finals between Sunderland and Chelsea and then, at Kenilworth Road on 13 March, there was one of the worst riots at a football match ever witnessed in this country.

After Luton's FA Cup tie against Millwall had been held up by overcrowded fans spilling on to the pitch, the match was followed by a quite horrific pitched battle between Millwall fans and the police, who were quite overwhelmed. Seats were torn out, innocent spectators terrorized, missiles hurled, and at one point a policeman, who was trying to administer the kiss of life to a colleague who had collapsed, was kicked by a couple of youths. In all, forty-seven people were injured, mostly policemen; damage worth £15,000 was caused to the ground, and marauding youths left a trail of destruction through the town which led, via a wrecked train, back to London.

If this had been an isolated incident, the subsequent response might have been different. But it wasn't. It was clearly part of a cycle of mounting violence which now, by association, cast football in the worst possible light.

Two weeks later the Prime Minister, Margaret Thatcher, held a cabinet meeting to discuss the incidents, and expressed dismay at how little she believed the clubs were doing to curb the menace. Unfair though this was – the football authorities had been working on the problem for at least four years – the sudden intervention of the Prime Minister was to have a crucial effect on the game. Her strident message was quite plain. Put your house in order and don't expect the Government to put up the money! The Home Secretary, Leon

Brittan, also indicated that the Government would follow Scotland's example by banning all alcohol at football grounds, a potentially devastating blow to the clubs' already ailing finances.

If there was to be no television, and therefore a reduction in sponsorship and advertising revenue, *and* a ban on alcohol sales, how could the clubs be expected to invest more money in making their grounds more safe and secure? It was a vicious circle.

Responses varied. Aston Villa announced the start of a membership scheme for one of their enclosures, to encourage more families to attend. Chelsea's chairman, Ken Bates, decided to erect a twelve-volt electric fence to keep fans off the pitch. He was prevented from switching it on by the local authority, and the fence was never used.

Then came the final day of the season, with football in a depressed mood and the League's reputation at a low point. Disunited within, attacked from without, perhaps at least it could lick its wounds during the close season and make a fresh start the following August?

Again, fate stepped in. About five minutes before half-time at the Third Division match between Bradford City and Lincoln at Valley Parade, someone in the seventy-seven-year-old wooden stand dropped a cigarette. No doubt thousands of cigarettes had been dropped in the stand over the years, but this one slipped down between the floorboards and set alight a pile of accumulated litter.

The result was the worst disaster in English sporting history, in which fifty-six people died. By chance there were television cameras present, and thus millions of viewers were able to view the scene only an hour or so later. Apart from the awful suffering, what made the Bradford fire so much more tragic was the fact that it could so easily have been avoided, and would have been had Third Division grounds been included in the provisions of the Safety of Sports Grounds Act.

In view of this, to add irony to tragedy,

before the fateful match Bradford had just been celebrating their promotion to Division Two, which meant that the ground would have become designated under the Safety Act the following season. Indeed, work was due to start on rebuilding the stand seventy-two hours after the match.

If Bradford came to represent all that was doom-laden and antediluvian in the lower reaches of professional football in Britain, on the same afternoon as the fire, events at Birmingham wore a starkly modern face.

In the game between Birmingham City and Leeds United, the visiting fans rioted on the pitch, injured ninety-six policemen and caused a wall to collapse. A teenage boy died under the rubble.

With that boy's fate, and the agonizing deaths of the fifty-six men, women and children at Bradford, the spirit of English football seemed to die also. Faced with such appalling events, who cared if the League appeared to have made a terrible error of judgement by rejecting the television offer? What did it matter whether football was to be televised or not the following season? Would many people want to watch it anyway?

But there was worse to come. On 29 May viewers all over Europe settled into their armchairs to watch Liverpool play Juventus in the final of the European Cup in Brussels. Instead, they watched in shocked bewilderment as two bands of hooligans, English and Italian, put on an orchestrated exhibition of senseless, petty violence.

The Liverpool 'supporters', those so-called witty, sportsmanlike lads from the Kop, joined by sundry youths from all over England, charged a group of Italian fans who, under strict UEFA regulations, should never have been allowed into that section of the ground. As at Birmingham a wall collapsed, only this time thirty-nine people died; crushed, trampled and asphyxiated under a wave of frightened fugitives.

The cameras were there. All the world saw

it. England's shame was complete.

Back in London the FA immediately banned all League clubs from competing in European competitions during the next season. Two days later UEFA placed an indefinite ban on all English clubs playing in Europe, and four days later FIFA extended the prohibition to the whole world, even Scotland (although not Wales, to allow the League to continue).

The following day the clubs met for the 1985 Annual Meeting in a sombre mood. A minute's silence was observed for the victims of the three fatal incidents of May and, as was customary, for those friends of the League who had died during the previous twelve months. Was it an omen that heading the obituary list was the name of Arsenal's former player, Bernard Joy? It really did seem on that June day in 1985 as if all the joy which he had personified had, indeed, been lost from the game.

The business of the meeting was fairly routine. A Management Committee proposal to introduce two substitutes per club for each game was defeated, as it would be the following year (it was eventually approved in 1987).

It was agreed that captains should wear distinguishing arm bands in future League games (as was the practice in Europe) and, as we have already noted, Bath City failed to oust any of the retiring clubs.

The Annual Meeting ended on a curious note, with the considerable presence of Robert Maxwell once again at the centre of things. Jack Dunnett asked the clubs to permit Sir Arthur South to continue his role as chairman of the Television Negotiating Committee, despite the fact that he had just retired from the Management Committee. A man of his experience and skill was too valuable to lose at this vital hour.

Maxwell opposed the suggestion, and suggested instead that Mr Philip 'Walker' of Everton be made chairman. Philip 'Carter' refused, and then pledged on record his support for Sir Arthur, at which point Maxwell resigned from the Television Committee. It had been but a brief association. In fact, for all his bravado on St Valentine's Day, the Oxford chairman had not even made it to the negotiating table.

Back in the outside world the walls were closing in on the beleaguered garrison. On 20 June, Liverpool learnt that their own ban from Europe would be extended for three years above and beyond any other period for which the remaining English clubs were barred. This would lose Liverpool an estimated £2 million in revenue, said a despondent John Smith.

The other five clubs who had been due to compete in Europe were angry. Norwich City, for example, had been so proud of getting into Europe for the first time in their history. Their fans were and are amongst the best behaved in the country, and yet here they were, along with Everton, Manchester United, Tottenham and Southampton, being made to pay for the lunacy of individuals completely beyond their control. They were like innocent primary schoolkids put in detention because of a fight among sixth-formers on the other side of town.

It was a desperate summer for the League. Criticism came from all sides, while Mrs Thatcher was pressing the League and FA to introduce a national membership scheme for all football supporters. The notion was widely regarded by both the police and the football authorities as being quite unworkable, as the League and FA argued repeatedly, but in the Prime Minister's characteristic fashion, 'the lady was not for turning'.

'Put your house in order!' she was ordering the football authorities, while at the same time placing upon them demands which would divert them from that very task.

The League's response was to ask the Government to lop 2.5 per cent off the 42.5 per cent betting tax imposed on the pools. With the £12 million so raised, the League could then bring every newly designated Third and Fourth Division ground up to required safety standards and install closed-circuit television cameras at all the major grounds, as Justice Popplewell had recommended in his interim report on the incidents at Bradford and Birmingham.

Again, the Prime Minister refused to budge. If football was so impecunious, how come Everton had just spent £800,000 on buying Gary Lineker from Leicester?

The ban on alcohol passed through Parliament on 25 July. Five days later, a compromise was reached with Downing Street whereby the football authorities at least promised to urge all clubs to implement membership schemes.

Meanwhile, in a desperate attempt to make up for all the lost revenue from television, the League clubs agreed to introduce two new competitions for the make-or-break season to come: the Super Cup for those six clubs banned from Europe, and the Full Members' Cup for all the other First and Second Division clubs (see Appendices).

To the public it seemed a baffling stance to adopt; why foist apparently meaningless football matches upon a dwindling number of supporters who were already anxious for the future, tired of violence and above all disillusioned by the whole state of English football?

The measure of the public's mood was shown on the first day of the following season, probably the most testing season the League had ever known both on and off the pitch. Gates were down by 10 per cent, and not a minute of the action was shown on television.

John Bromley, Head of Sport at ITV, told the *Sunday Times* in late September: 'A couple of weeks ago I said I'd had one letter complaining about the absence of League football. Since then I've been flooded with two more.' BBC's Jonathan Martin commented: 'Soccer is no longer at the heart of the television schedules, and it's never likely to be again.'

On Monday 30 September the Big Five made their move. They were going for the big one – the Super League.

Plans had been hatched at a secret meeting in Manchester on the Sunday evening and announced the following day. By Tuesday morning the back pages were buzzing, and a curious air of bewilderment settled upon Lytham St Annes. It would not lift for some months.

The Big Five plan was for Everton, Liverpool, Spurs, Arsenal and Manchester United to invite another thirteen to fifteen clubs to join them in a completely new Super League, free of control from Lytham St Annes and free to negotiate its own lucrative television and sponsorship deals. Why slice up the party cake ninety-two ways when eighteen bigger slices would be so much more appetizing?

'The mind boggles at the marketing possibilities of a small group,' said one representative from the Super Leaguers. 'We have no option but to do it, and there is no better time. It is not a question of greed. Unless we do it now we may all go down.'

That was their reasoning, and this was their dream: that only those clubs commanding large support would join and that any other club seeking membership, or promotion (the details of this were not clear), would have to fit in with the Super League's overall requirements. The inference was plain: they wanted big-city teams with good stadia and genuine marketing potential, and that did not include clubs like First Division Oxford or Luton.

Thus, the League family was to be broken up and its poorer relatives locked out in the cold. The Super League was to be a private party. Invitation only.

The *Daily Mail* drew up a list of the potential Super Leaguers. In addition to the Big Five there were six certainties: Chelsea, Sheffield Wednesday, Aston Villa, West Ham, Manchester City and Newcastle. Then came seven probables: Southampton, Ipswich, Watford, Nottingham Forest, Portsmouth, Sunderland and Leeds. That meant no place for the following First Division clubs: Leicester, Coventry, Luton, QPR, Birmingham, Oxford and West Bromwich Albion.

It was 1888 all over again. When McGregor and Bentley had drawn up their list of twelve clubs for the League, they had been met with howls of protest from clubs such as Nottingham Forest. Why include Everton, the sporting press had asked, when Bootle had much the better credentials?

And yet here was the chairman of Everton leading a movement which threatened to kill off McGregor's brainchild in its ninety-eighth year. Not only that, but according to some reports the Big Five intended handing over the running of the Super League to the FA secretary, Ted Croker. Within days of these reports Croker confirmed that he would, indeed, be prepared to take on the role. As the *Observer* remarked, the FA 'had severe trouble containing its delight at last week's rumblings', because the Super League plan offered the Association a perfect opportunity to restore its dominance over English football (a dominance which, with timely irony, the FA had abdicated exactly one hundred years earlier by reluctantly recognizing that evil phenomenon called professional football).

But would the top clubs find the FA a more sympathetic master? As the *Guardian* suggested caustically, leaving the family home at Lytham to bed down at Lancaster Gate was a bit like resigning from the Ottoman Empire only to join up with the Hapsburgs.

Another candidate for the supremo role was Liverpool's secretary and director, Peter Robinson, while in later weeks Gordon Taylor of the PFA became the media's favourite choice.

But in the days immediately following the Big Five's announcement, nothing was certain. Certainly, the League headquarters had very little idea about the Big Five's plans other than what had been printed in the newspapers. And most of that was speculative. Some reports said there would be a Second Division. Others suggested that the Second, Third and Fourth

Divisions would be left to sort out their own fate under the umbrella of the existing League, perhaps in amalgamation with the Gola League. What seemed certain was that the Milk Cup would be left to curdle while the Super Leaguers joined up with the top Scottish and Irish clubs to start a British Cup.

The advantages of the Super League were plain. New interest, fewer meaningless games and, because the fixture list would be reduced by perhaps ten games a season, the England manager Bobby Robson would at least have the luxury of calling his squad together for longer periods.

Sir Norman Chester appeared to have been vindicated at last. He told the *Daily Mirror*: 'A breakaway would be good for the game. A smaller League would mean better leadership.'

In the *Daily Mail* it was said that the Big Five were preparing to start the Super League the following season. But, and it was a very big but, would it really happen? Was this just a threat to force the League to give in to the demands of the Big Five? Would any one man dare to put himself forward as the axe-man who cut down the greatest football league in the world just two years short of its hundredth birthday? Would that man travel to Carrow Road and tell Norwich that their promotion campaign that season had all been a waste of time and money? And who would stand up to defend the ailing old League now that Alan Hardaker was no more and the ghost of Charlie Sutcliffe not even a memory? Besides which, was there not a Super League already? Only the previous Saturday the attendances at Highbury, Anfield and Old Trafford had amounted to 118,074 people. That was 10,000 more than all the other First Division games put together.

A saddened Graham Kelly could do little but stand by patiently and watch the family squabbling, hoping all the while that the machinery of the League would be equal to the bumpy ride ahead. He knew that if the traditional conservatism of the smaller clubs thwarted the Big Five's ambitions this time –

and it needed only six Second Division votes to scupper a three-quarter majority under the prevailing regulations – then the League would lose whatever degree of power it still clung on to.

'If we lost twenty members out of ninety-two, the biggest twenty, it would destroy the existing League,' said Kelly. 'Every single aspect of our operation would be affected by a major defection.'

But as an experienced observer in the corridors of power, Kelly also knew that forming a Super League was no simple matter. There were the pools to consider, the tax advantages gained from membership of the League, the PFA to settle with, and many other factors. Above all, how could the Super Leaguers decide fairly who was to join them and who was not? The longer there was speculation rather than a concrete plan, the more chance there was of settling the issue within the League framework.

Which, as it transpired, was exactly what did happen.

Within a week or so of the Big Five's announcement, it became increasingly apparent that none of the leading chairmen was actually prepared to take that historic step across the Rubicon. For another few weeks the whole question seemed to go rather quiet, and any soundings which did catch the press's attention were conciliatory rather than defiant.

But behind the scenes there was plenty going on, culminating in the first of a series of vital meetings of First and Second Division chairmen on 12 November at the Mount Royal Hotel in London.

Central to the discussions, which were held independently of the League, was a compromise plan for a twenty-club First Division and a twenty-four club Second Division. The remaining forty-eight Associate Members would stay under the League's umbrella, but under new conditions.

The compromise was essentially a modified version of Sir Norman Chester's proposals in 1983. 'Had his recommendations been adopted then,' said Tottenham's chairman, Irving Scholar, before the meeting, 'football would not be facing its most testing time this century.'

Crucial to the success of the compromise proposals discussed on 12 November was the majority approval of the First and Second Division clubs. Under the League's three-quarters majority rule, in order to become part of the regulations, thirty-nine of the forty-four Full Members would have to support it, assuming that the eight Associate Members' votes would be cast in opposition. If a majority was not attained, the Super Leaguers would then be bound to go their own way.

In effect, it all boiled down to the Second Division clubs. They could either accept the dictates of the Big Five and lose part of their power and income, and the chance to win three promotion places that season, or be left to an uncertain fate. Their votes held the key, but as the 12 November meeting showed, they were not prepared to be bullied into a deal. Far from lying down, they had ideas of their own.

These were as follows: that instead of a reduced First Division and an enlarged Second Division, the existing 22:22 ratio should remain. Instead of sponsorship money being divided 70:30, as the Super Leaguers had proposed, they suggested 55:45. On the question of voting power, the Second Division lobby supported one vote per club, while the Super Leaguers wanted a weighted system 2:1 in their favour.

'They have missed the point,' said an angry First Division director after the meeting. 'There's not a cat in hell's chance of us agreeing to their proposals.'

Only on one point did the two factions agree: the Third and Fourth Division clubs should be cast adrift.

By now, the various factions were well organized. The First Division clubs, with Philip Carter, Martin Edwards and Irving Scholar at the helm, were said to have been unanimous in their support of the Super

Leaguers' demands. How could it have been otherwise?

None of the twenty-two clubs wanted to be left behind, however distasteful some of them felt the Super Leaguers' demands to be. In public, therefore, the First Division appeared united. In private, there was great uneasiness. The Big Five were now the Big Twelve, but the remaining ten were like floating voters who saw the rescue ship preparing to sail away.

For the Second Division bloc, Ron Noades of Crystal Palace was elected as chairman, with Bill Fox (Blackburn) and Lawrie McMenemy (manager of Sunderland) as his co-negotiators.

To represent the Associate Members, who had the least clout of all, Reg Driver (Aldershot), Ian Jones (Doncaster) and Martin Lange (Brentford) were elected. Their position was quite categorical. They would not have their fates decided upon by other clubs. They accepted fully that the time had come to open up the League to non-League clubs through automatic promotion and relegation, but they would not have the door to the upper divisions slammed on them at the same time. As Martin Lange remarked, what businessman in his right mind would invest in one of their clubs if he knew there was little chance of reaching the top. Life in the lower divisions would be empty without incentives.

While the Super League debate progressed, there was still no football on the screens, Canon were on the verge of ending their sponsorship agreement, and with English clubs out of Europe there were increasing dangers of an exodus of top players to richer, continental clubs. Attendances were still falling, and Swansea and Wolves were on the point of collapse.

It was going to be a long, hard winter of discontent.

But there was a glimmer of hope and, in a historical context at least, it came from the most unlikely of sources. The day after the abortive Mount Royal meeting, Gordon Taylor of the PFA spoke up in defence of the League like a corporal from the trenches who was not prepared to see his best mates sacrificed just so that the generals could add more gold braid to their uniforms.

The PFA would not stand by idly and see the ninety-two-strong League breaking up, he said. If necessary, it would block such a move in the courts. 'I strongly believe that the leading players in the game will not sell their less well-paid colleagues down the river. Nothing can be done which affects the conditions and work of our members without our approval, and that will certainly not be forthcoming for the proposals that have been put forward.'

Taylor reminded the Super Leaguers that half the 18 million spectators who watched League football in 1984/5 were at games outside the First Division. 'The game's biggest sponsor is not the pools, television or any other commercial company, but the football public, who contributed £49 million to income last season. Every effort should be made to preserve professional football in every major town and city in England and Wales.'

It was as if the spirits of Sutcliffe and Hardaker were egging Taylor on, and yet how ironic, after all the years of antagonism between the union and the League, that in 1985 the most vocal champion of the League should turn out to be the union secretary.

As November turned into December, and a second meeting of First and Second Division clubs attempted to bring the two factions closer to agreement, the short stocky figure of Gordon Taylor began to wield a giant influence. He was arbitrator, peace-maker and message boy all rolled into one. The League could not have found a better champion.

On 2 December the PFA held its Annual Meeting in Manchester and, just as in the campaign for the abolition of the maximum wage twenty-five years earlier, the players showed a remarkable degree of cohesion. They did not support a breakaway league, nor were they prepared to see voting control of the League being handed to the First Division clubs. They were prepared, however, to call a strike if the clubs took any action which threatened the livelihoods of their members.

For their part, the clubs were far less united, with the Second Division clubs continuing to play hard to get and the Super Leaguers refusing to withdraw their threat to break away. In late November, Everton's Philip Carter spelt it out for the umpteenth time. 'It is not a question of bluff and counter bluff. We will break away if agreement on our proposals is not reached soon.' His patience was running out, and, more importantly, so was time.

The longer they delayed, the less chance there was of resolving the matter in time for the following season, and with football still off the television screens, the lack of advertising revenue was proving to be an acute loss to the potential Super Leaguers. Remember also that the ban on alcohol at football grounds still applied, which in the First Division placed a great threat to executive box sales. Two clubs, Watford and Tottenham, announced the shelving of plans for new stands because of the uncertain financial future. Something had to give, sooner or later.

The next major meeting took place at a hotel near Manchester Airport on 11 December, and after five hours of tough bargaining there appeared a crucial chink in the First Division clubs' armour.

On the vexed question of voting power, Messrs Carter, Edwards and Scholar conceded that no one division should have control over the destiny of the League. The price for this concession was to be a change in the distribution of League revenues so that the First Division clubs took the biggest slice but still left enough for the rest to survive on. There was also a hint that the Second Divison clubs were close to accepting a reduction in the First Division and therefore a limit on the number of teams being promoted, at least in the initial transition period.

'Football as we know it may yet survive',

declared Patrick Barclay in the *Guardian*.

And so to the most crucial meeting so far, a week later on 18 December at the Post House Hotel, Heathrow. It should be stressed that the agreements reached at this meeting did not end forever the threat of a breakaway or secure the future of the League. That could be done only by agreeing to change the regulations at an official meeting of the Football League. But the Heathrow Agreement did lay down a concrete basis for how those regulations should be changed, and for that reason 18 December 1985 represents a turning point in the history of the League.

There were ten men involved directly: three elected representatives from each of the First Division, Second Division and Associate Member groups. Liaising between them was Gordon Taylor, busy as ever in the central role of peacemaker which he had unwittingly taken on.

It took six hours to hammer out the settlement, and as an exhausted but elated Taylor said afterwards: 'We've had a helluva job, and there were times today when it looked difficult. Lots of points were thrashed out and we got there in the end.'

But it wasn't the end.

The clubs still had to vote on the package at an Extraordinary General Meeting of the Football League.

Philip Carter was optimistic, however: 'There has been considerable compromise by each division, and we feel the package is sufficiently rounded in all areas to be acceptable.'

The basic elements of the Heathrow Agreement were as follows:

● *The ninety-two-club League would be preserved, with a First Division of twenty clubs, a Second Division of twenty-four.*

Although the First Division would lose two clubs, the reduction didn't go as far as many observers had hoped. Most major European footballing nations had First Divisions of sixteen or eighteen clubs, so a twenty-strong division would still be relatively large. It meant thirty-eight games a season, the same as in France, compared with, for example, thirty-four in West Germany, Belgium, Holland, the Soviet Union and Spain, and thirty in Italy, Portugal, Switzerland and Denmark.

● *In order to make a fair and equitable transition, rather than relegate four clubs and promote two, there would be a system of staggered promotion and relegation, supplemented by a system of play-offs. The exact format for these had yet to be worked out, but they would be similar to those used in American leagues and would be tried in all divisions. Initially the play-offs would operate for two years, but if they proved popular with spectators they could become a permanent part of the calendar.*

The introduction of play-offs was a key element in the compromise. It would bring in extra revenue to the lower divisions, enable the First Division to be reduced progressively over the course of two seasons, and add extra spice to the League competition. After all the arguing of the previous three months, here at last was a genuinely imaginative development which would excite the public and satisfy the clubs.

And yet the idea for play-offs had come about in a rather unexpected manner. Martin Lange of Brentford was the chief proponent. He put forward the idea originally as a means of compensating Third and Fourth Division clubs for the losses in revenue they would suffer as a result of other parts of the agreement. But it was such a good idea that the Second Division clubs latched on to it as a means of rearranging the numbers in the First and Second Division. Inadvertently, therefore, Lange had helped to build a bridge between the First and Second Division factions.

But whoever deserves the credit, for the sake of historical accuracy we must add here that play-offs had in fact been mooted as early as

1972. Need we say by whom? Alan Hardaker, of course.

● *There would be automatic promotion and relegation between the Gola League and the Fourth Division.*

● *The majority required for changing League regulations would be reduced from three-quarters to two-thirds, but in future the First Division clubs would have two votes each, the rest remaining as before, that is, one each for Second Divison clubs and eight between the Associate Members.*

According to this plan, the First Division of the future would thus command 40 out of the total number of 72 votes. To obtain a two-thirds majority, therefore, the First Division bloc would still need another eight votes from the other clubs.

What worried many people about this system was that it allowed the First Division clubs to block any moves by the Second, Third and Fourth Division clubs, whose combined votes would amount to only 32. This weighted voting system was the biggest sticking point in the future negotiations.

● *The First Division to receive a 50 per cent share of all revenues earned from television and sponsorship. The Second Division would receive 25 per cent, the Associate Members 25 per cent, and both the League and the FA would be required to take a cut in the share they earned from Milk Cup and FA Cup games respectively.*

● *The 4 per cent League levy on match receipts to be reduced to 3 per cent.*

● *The constitution of the Management Committee to be changed so that First Division clubs were guaranteed four representatives, the Second Divison three and the Associate Members one.*

So far, so good. Or was it? The protagonists may have reached a settlement, but talks in private meant nothing if the League itself wasn't brought in on the act. Changing League regulations is no simple matter – it needs careful drafting and much preparation – and by mid-January the League was losing its patience with the reformers. As Jack Dunnett said: 'They have had two opportunities to let us know what they want, but we are still waiting. All we know is what we read in the newspapers. If we delay much longer it will cause chaos. Imagine if all this talking and meeting goes on into a second season.'

Dunnett's message took on a greater urgency when it was announced on 7 January that Canon were not going to extend their sponsorship at the end of the 1985/6 season. The time had come for the Management Committee to force the pace, if only to protect the League's chances of finding a new sponsor.

At least football was back on the television screens, albeit at a price some way short of the February 1985 offer. A five-month patched up deal was struck just before Christmas by which the League would receive £1.3 million for a series of live matches. Recorded games were still accorded little exposure, and the negotiations would have to start all over again in the summer.

Meanwhile, at Lytham St Annes a date of 4 March was pencilled in for an Extraordinary General Meeting. At this meeting the clubs would get the chance to consider the Management Committee's own set of proposals for reform, based upon those laid out in the Heathrow Agreement.

But when these proposals were circulated, they were not received kindly. 'We did not have time to draft our own set of proposals for the EGM,' Martin Edwards commented. 'The Management Committee have taken the basis of our plans, tinkered with them a little bit and presented them to the clubs. I think the League proposals will be thrown out and the majority of clubs will want to wait until our own proposals are put forward at a later meeting.'

Edwards pointed out that two of the main elements of the Heathrow Agreement had been omitted from the Management Committee's proposals: the change in the voting system and

the reconstitution of the Management Committee.

In response, Jack Dunnett explained that the First Division clubs could easily gain a majority voice on the Committee through the existing constitution. Dick Wragg was due to step down in a few months (having reached the age of seventy), Jack Wiseman would follow the year after, and Dunnett's own term of office was due to end in 1987. By voting in their own men to these and other casual vacancies over the next three years, said Dunnett, the First Division clubs could end up with nine out of the ten places on the Committee.

On 17 February the First Division chairmen met in Birmingham to consider the Management Committee's proposals for the 4 March meeting. They rejected them unanimously, and Philip Carter issued yet another warning. 'We hate bringing out the idea of a Super League or a breakaway, but if things stay the same there is no way the major clubs will allow themselves to be dragged down into obscurity.' The Everton chairman also made it clear that he had been assured of support from the Second Division clubs.

On 19 February the Associate Members met under the League's aegis to formulate their response. At this meeting it emerged that their own negotiating trio had agreed to the Heathrow Agreement only 'as the best of a bad job'. Ian Jones, a member of the Management Committee and of the Associate Members' negotiating team, told the press after the meeting:

'We are very concerned about the consequences for Third and Fourth Division clubs. Up to £3 million would be diverted from us, and that means up to 1000 employees, predominantly players, could find themselves out of work.

'The impact of losing so much money would be far more devastating to us than the advantages it will give First Division clubs. We are disappointed that there has still been no suggestion on how to improve the game or bring people back through the turnstiles.'

Inevitably, the EGM for 4 March was postponed. There was simply no point in holding it when all the factions were so publicly opposed to the League's proposals yet still unready to put forward their own.

By March, however, the First Division clubs' blueprint was complete, and a date for the final showdown was set for 28 April, when at long last the Super League movement would learn its fate.

To break away or not to break away, that was the question.

They were well prepared. All twenty-two First Division chairmen had agreed at a meeting at Villa Park on 24 March that if their ten-point package (based on the Heathrow Agreement) did not get the necessary three-quarters majority, they would walk out of the League *en bloc*. All for one and one for all. And to prove that this was really no idle threat, Philip Carter confirmed that a feasibility study for a Super League had already been undertaken.

D-Day for football, Carter called the forthcoming EGM. 'Vote yes or we break away!'

With only days remaining, however, there were still a few sticking points. The biggest concerned the proposal to give First Division clubs two votes each, and thus guarantee them the balance of power.

As the days and hours ticked by, there were some feverish talks to try to solve this dilemma, the best possible solution being proffered by that wily campaigner of old, Jimmy Hill. Hill was then a director of Charlton Athletic, who were at that time just on the verge of winning promotion to the First Division.

He suggested that instead of two votes, the First Division clubs should have one and a half votes each.

Thus, a twenty-strong First Division bloc would count for 30 votes out of a total of 62, and would still need 11 extra votes to secure a two-thirds majority. It was only a minor adjustment – with two votes each the First Division would have needed only an extra 8 votes for a majority – but in those fraught last few days of talks, any little concession here and there was worth pursuing in the cause of harmony.

Monday, 28 April arrived and still no one was clear what would happen at the Cumberland Hotel EGM. In the morning each faction held separate meetings, but while the Associate Members were almost entirely opposed to certain elements of the ten-point package, the real drama was taking place between the First and Second Division representatives.

The Second Division clubs had accepted the package on condition that Hill's compromise formula be accepted, but as the hour for the EGM approached, Gordon Taylor was still desperately trying to persuade a handful of still unconvinced First Division chairmen to accept the compromise. 'It really was touch and go up to mid-day,' Taylor recalled later. 'We literally didn't have an agreement until less than an hour before the EGM was due to start.'

And even when the EGM did begin in the early afternoon, there was extra uncertainty as it was discovered that all twenty-two First Division clubs had appointed Philip Carter as their proxy. Though quite unprecedented, it was a perfectly legal move. Besides which, the time for talking was over. It was time for the most crucial vote in the post-war history of the League. Rejection of the package would spark a breakaway. Acceptance would initiate the single most radical restructuring of the League in its ninety-eight years.

But as the hands went up, the outcome was plain for all to see. The ten-point package was accepted, by 43 votes to 10, and the world's oldest League had survived.

The collective sigh of relief was immense. 'This is a victory for common sense', said Gordon Taylor, whose own common sense had dominated the previous months of negotiations. Graham Kelly was perhaps more relieved and delighted than anyone. For the past seven months he had been placed in the most awkward position of all, caught in the middle between the Management Committee and the clubs. And yet the events leading up to that April EGM had vindicated his belief that the League structure was capable of reform from within. The family could live together after all.

The reactions of two club officials after the meeting summed it up. 'We are glad that it's all over at last', said one. 'Now at last we can get back to reading about football and not what goes on behind the scenes', said another.

For the ten members of the Management Committee, however, the meeting ended in sadness, for the acceptance of the ten-point package signalled an abrupt end to their terms of office. Under the new constitution, each member would have to stand down and new elections take place.

This had never happened before, and as the events of the previous seven months had foretold, the outgoing members would find it hard to win their seats back. Rightly or wrongly, they were seen as members of an old guard which had kept the besieged garrison alive, but never quite managed to hold back the foe. It was time for new men and radical thinking.

The following month, postal elections were held and the new order was confirmed. Out went Jack Wiseman after twelve years on the Committee, just one year away from his seventieth birthday. Out, too, went Christopher Needler and Robert Daniel after ten years of service. Only one member of the former Committee would survive – Jack Dunnett.

Under the new constitution, the Associate Members were to keep their one representative on the Committee, and in deference to Dunnett's greater experience, Ian Jones of Doncaster stood aside and let Dunnett take his place. It was the gesture of a good man, one of several to whom the League owes a debt for its preservation.

But would Dunnett be able to hold on to the presidency? No League president had ever been voted out of office before, and Dunnett himself had won many a difficult election before in the wider world. On the other hand, Notts County were now in the Third Division, and his challenger was Philip Carter of Everton, the man who had co-ordinated and led the movement for reconstruction. It was going to be the closest contest the League had ever seen.

But at least it would take place in an atmosphere of guarded optimism. The League had survived the traumas of 1985, and England's chances in the forthcoming Mexico World Cup were now brighter than many might have anticipated at the start of the season. Although League gates had fallen by 1.3 million (a drop of 7.6 per cent) – as had been expected after the events of May 1985 – on the field there was much to admire. In an exciting climax to the season, Liverpool won the Double, only the fourth club to do so in League history, and Swindon broke the points record by winning the Fourth Division with 102 points, thus beating York's record of 101 in 1983/4. The number of goals also rose, albeit only fractionally.

Crowd violence was much reduced, although by no means eradicated, and although the designation of Third and Fourth Division grounds after the Bradford fire was punishing to most Associate Members, no one club was crippled by the great demands placed upon them. The Football Trust and Football Grounds Improvement Trust had proved equal to the demands made upon their funds since May 1985 (and FGIT Chairman Tom Wharton was awarded the OBE in recognition of his contribution to ground safety).

Above all, the League remained a competition of enduring fascination. Charlton won promotion to the First Division in the same season as they were forced to leave their home and share with Crystal Palace. Their south London neighbours Wimbledon went up with them; this after only nine seasons in the League – a quite remarkable feat, unparalleled in League history. In the same year, those other former Southern Leaguers, Oxford United, won the Milk Cup.

While the minnows grew to maturity, former giants were humbled. West Bromwich were relegated to the Second Division, Middlesbrough to the Third and, most poignantly of all, founder members Wolves slipped down to the Fourth, where they joined Burnley and Preston. Amazingly, the 1986/7 season would kick off with more founder members in the Fourth Division than the First Division, the first time this had ever happened.

Clearly, nothing in football is sacred, although as the 1986 Annual Meeting showed, despite reconstruction, the innate conservatism of the majority of clubs remained a formidable force. Indeed, this meeting proved that the First Division clubs were neither united on every issue nor capable of getting all their own way.

It also saw the first use of the weighted voting system, which had seemed perfect in theory, but proved to be a real headache when it came to counting up the votes. There seemed to be half votes littered all over the place, and all kinds of problems working out the two-thirds majority. It took an agonizing ten minutes to count up and calculate the results of the last ever re-election poll (under the reconstruction plan, automatic promotion and relegation between the League and the GM Vauxhall Conference – formerly the Gola League – was due to operate from 1987 onwards).

In fact, the retiring clubs had little to worry about. Enfield received only $7\frac{1}{2}$ votes, compared with Torquay (61 votes), Cambridge (61), Exeter (64) and Preston – yes, Preston ($62\frac{1}{2}$). Double winners in 1889, League champions for the first two seasons, Major Sudell's Invincibles – Preston were the first founder members to seek re-election since Burnley in 1903.

The year 1986 was the last chance for a club, great or small, to show any sympathy or charity towards a fellow Leaguer down on its luck. From now on the bottom club in the Fourth Division would be out, whoever they were, regardless of their past. No other element of the reconstruction plan had such an enormous impact on the League as this one simple change in the rules.

There were three other decisions of note at the 1986 Annual Meeting.

Firstly, the clubs considered Leicester City's proposal to ban First and Second Division matches being played on an artificial surface after 31 July 1988. The anti-plastic-pitch lobby had already been given a boost a week earlier, when the FA had banned the playing of Cup matches on synthetic surfaces, except at those clubs where such pitches already existed (QPR and Luton). This caught out Preston, who had just started installing their own new plastic pitch.

Everton's chairman, Philip Carter, argued that if artificial surfaces were to be tried out, the experiment should be conducted outside the Football League. So was the great experiment about to come to an end?

There was a queue of clubs who had already gained the League's permission to replace their natural pitches. Among them, Oldham had workmen poised to start digging if Leicester's proposal was rejected. Not surprisingly, Ian Stott of Oldham was the first to voice his opposition. He stressed that the only way for clubs to reassert themselves in their communities was through the use of artificial pitches.

Jimmy Hill of Charlton also opposed the motion. 'I think every club has the right to fight for its life in every way it can,' he said. 'If that means using artificial pitches, so be it. The key question is: has the product been less palatable to the public at Luton and QPR? I believe crowds have gone up at both clubs and Luton have an appetizing surface for those clubs who believe in skill.'

Hill was backed by Luton's John Smith and by the findings of the recently issued Winterbottom Report on synthetic pitches, sponsored by the Sports Council. This report made several observations which contradicted the generally held belief that the new type of pitch resulted in more injuries. Luton's own experience seemed to prove that the pitch also transformed their relationship with the community, as well as earning them an extra £100,000 in its first season.

(John Smith's and Ian Stott's enthusiastic pro-plastic stance suggested that reconstitution of the Management Committee had not eliminated the probability of future internal disagreement. Stott and Smith were both members-elect of the new Committee, as were Philip Carter and Bert McGee, each of whom supported Leicester's proposal.)

Leicester failed to win the day, being defeated by $34\frac{1}{2}$ votes to $28\frac{1}{2}$ – the FA changed its mind about the ban the following October – and thus work began immediately at Boundary Park, where Oldham became the fourth League club to install a synthetic surface.

The second important issue was a proposal from the outgoing Management Committee for each team to have two substitutes in League matches. This was to bring the League into line with the FA Cup and other European competitions. And, as if to prove that despite reconsruction, the First Division clubs did not all speak with one voice, the move failed to win a two-thirds majority because nine First Division clubs were in opposition. (In August, however, an EGM sanctioned the use of two substitutes for the Littlewoods Challenge Cup, formerly the Milk Cup.)

But the most crucial moment of all at the 1986 Annual Meeting was the vote for the President. Remember, no President had ever been voted out in mid office, and no man had ever been elected to the post without having previously served on the Management Committee.

On 23 May 1986, all that changed. Philip Carter won the vote by $37\frac{1}{2}$ votes to Dunnett's $26\frac{1}{2}$, and thus the Super League leader was now the twelfth President of the League. In fact, the vote was closer than the First Division lobby might have expected. Apart from carrying the Associate Members' bloc of eight votes, Dunnett polled almost half the Second Division votes and perhaps five in the First Division, plus his own vote as President. Exact figures are unknown, since the voting was by secret ballot. Nevertheless, under the old system the result would have been extremely close. With weighted voting, however, the First Division clubs were easily able to carry Philip Carter into office.

There was no acrimony. Both men had worked together amicably in the past, and the level of support shown for Dunnett indicated that he would still be a popular and influential voice on the Management Committee. Even so, no politician likes to lose an election, and after congratulations and commiserations had been exchanged, Dunnett's disappointment was clear.

Joe Richards had been President when Barnsley were in the Third, and even the Fourth Division. There had been several Presidents whose clubs were in the Second Division. But power in the League was invested differently now. Notts County were in the Third Division, and that cost Jack Dunnett his office.

Only minutes after the 1986 AGM the new Management Committee met for the first time. There were eight members, of whom seven had never sat on the Management Committee before. Such was the scale of the bloodless coup of 1986.

Restructuring the League

Here are the main points of the restructuring plan accepted by the clubs in 1986, with an indication of how they affected the distribution of income. (Figures for 1987/8 are estimated.)

1 LEAGUE COMPETITION

Ninety-two-club composition to remain, the divisions to be divided as follows: First Division twenty clubs, Second Division twenty-four clubs, Third and Fourth Divisions twenty-four clubs each (that is, unchanged).

2 PLAY-OFFS

To compensate clubs outside the First Division for their loss of revenue under reconstruction, *and* to provide a fair means of reducing the First Division, play-offs to take place in seasons 1986/7 and 1987/8 to produce the numbers in each division outlined above (for full details of the first games, see next chapter). From 1988/9, if the clubs agree to continue with the experiment, the play-offs between the First and Second Divisions will operate similarly to those of the lower divisions. That is, they will decide upon one promotion and relegation place, but not change the numbers in each division.

Income from the play-offs to be divided thus:

25 per cent to each participating club
50 per cent to a pool, to be divided equally amongst all clubs in the division other than those promoted.

(In 1986/7, Second Division clubs earned approximately £11,000 each from the play-offs.)

3 VOTING

First Division clubs: $1\frac{1}{2}$ votes each
Second Division: 1 vote each
Associate Members: 8 votes collectively
The President to lose his vote
To change regulations, a majority of two-thirds required.

4 MANAGEMENT COMMITTEE

First Division: 4 representatives (including President)
Second Division: 3 representatives
Associate Members: 1 representative

Each representative to be eligible for re-election after two years in office (changed in 1988 to three years).

5 RELEGATION FROM FOURTH DIVISION

The ninety-second club in the League to change places automatically with the champions of the GM Vauxhall Conference (Alliance Premier League), provided the champions meet the League's criteria on finance, ground safety, facilities and so on.

In its first non-League season, the relegated club to receive its full share of pools income and the Pool Account (i.e. the 3 per cent levy on gates), but none of the income from sponsorship and television. (In 1987/8 these sources combined were worth £82,000 to each Fourth Division club. Thus, outgoing Lincoln received £50,000, incoming Scarborough £32,000.)

6 SPONSORSHIP MONEY

Income received from the two main sponsors (currently Barclays Bank and Littlewoods), not including prize money, to be divided up 50:25:25, that is:

First Division: 50 per cent of total divided between twenty clubs (twenty-one clubs still in 1987/88)
Second Division: 25 per cent of total divided between twenty-four clubs (twenty-three in 1987/8)

Third and Fourth Divisions: 25 per cent of total divided between forty-eight clubs

Before reconstruction, sponsorship had been worth £14,600 per League club (£1.3 million divided equally). Under the new system, the share-out was approximately thus:

First Division: £31,400 each
Second Division: £14,800 each
Third and Fourth Divisions: £7,200 each

It can be seen, therefore, that the First Division share more than doubled, the Second remained roughly the same, and the Associate Members' share halved.

7 TELEVISION

As with sponsorship, income to be divided 50:25:25. But before the money is shared out, the PFA to be given £200,000 (plus a reserve of £25,000 if needed), and 10 per cent of the total fee to be put aside for compensating those clubs showing live games but suffering a reduced gate.
    In 1987/8 the share-out of television fees was:

First Division: £61,000 each
Second Division: £29,750 each
Third and Fourth Division: £14,255 each

Had the previous system operated, each club would have received £28,800.

8 LEAGUE CUP

Previously, all League Cup receipts after Round One were divided 20:40:40; that is, 20 per cent being pooled for equal distribution among all ninety-two clubs, the remainder being divided equally between each team.
    The ratio changed under the new system to 10:45:45 for all rounds, the 10 per cent pool to be divided between the clubs (according to the 50:25:25 ratio used for sponsorship and television).
    In 1987/8 the projected share of the 10 per cent Littlewod Cup pool was:
        First Division: £10,250 each
        Second Division: £4675 each
        Third and Fourth Divisions: £2240 each

It should be noted, however, that each club enjoys a larger share of gate receipts than before.

9 FA CUP

As for the League Cup, the new share-out is 10:45:45, but only after Round Three. In the semi-final and final, the FA takes 25 per cent of the receipts for its own purposes, the remaining 75 per cent being divided again 10:45:45.

10 LEAGUE LEVY

The levy on all League match receipts to be reduced from 4 per cent to 3 per cent, this money going into the Pool Account, to be shared equally between the ninety-two clubs.
    The amount to be redistributed (the Pool Account) is calculated on the basis of the total number of spectators per season × 25p, or a similar sum to be decided upon by the Management Committee. The Pool Account still benefits the lower-division clubs at the First Division's expense.

11 POOLS CONTRACT

To be distributed as before, equally between all ninety-two clubs, after deduction of the League's administrative costs.
    The Pool Account (3 per cent levy) and the pools contract combined were worth approximately £50,000 per club in 1987/8.

CONCLUSION

First Division clubs have gained considerably from the reconstruction, in terms of both money and power. In this respect the Super League movement was a complete success for its leaders.

The Second Division clubs fought to maintain their own position in the League and largely succeeded, though without gaining any extra money and at the expense of having an equal voice with the First Division.

The Third and Fourth Division clubs' share of the vote, although held static, diminished in terms of the overall vote, and their share of League revenues fell, but not as drastically as they had originally feared. This was because the play-offs brought them in extra income and the overall amount received from television and sponsorship increased anyway. The Associate Members now have the most to lose from failure on the pitch, since ninety-second place guarantees an exit from the League.

CHAPTER THIRTY-FOUR

Towards the Centenary

*I*t didn't take long for the new Management Committee to realize that, like Hercules confronted by Hydra, each time it dealt with one problem, another popped up to take its place. Hercules triumphed in the end – at best, we can report here that the League *is* winning its battle to revive the game, but the monster problems are not over yet.

Ours is a story which has no fairy-tale ending, but which ends with a celebration, nevertheless. The League has reached its centenary, intact, strong, still alive and kicking, but characteristically never far from controversy. It was ever thus.

For example, ten days after taking office the new Management Committee was able to announce the signing of a two-year deal with the television companies worth £6.2 million, some £1.6 million per season below the rate which had been offered in February 1985. The deal allowed for fourteen live League games per season, plus live coverage of one leg of each Littlewoods Cup semi-final and the entire final. But significantly, there was no guarantee of recorded League highlights, only of Rounds 2–5 of the Littlewoods Cup, to be shown in mid week.

For years, a number of clubs had complained that there was too much football on television. Now, the lament was almost universal: there weren't enough recorded matches, and what live action there was had been bought for a song. An oft-quoted comparison was the case of France, where, since de-regulation by the Government, the television companies were paying £20 million for televising football.

Whether or not the comparison was justified – and certain experts reported that the League could not expect more from television than it was already receiving – what was certain was that the relationship between the League and the British television companies had to be improved.

Journalists Lynton Guest and Peter Law expressed this view in the *Observer*. 'The acrimony that has poisoned relationships between TV and many sporting bodies in Britain will not disappear until television re-examines its entrenched attitudes to sport and the consumer, and is prepared to pay a price that more fairly reflects the revenues and ratings achieved', they wrote. ITV in particular, they reported, easily recouped its outlay on football since each live match generated about £600,000 in advertising revenues. 'Compared with standards elsewhere,' Guest and Law concluded, 'British television's much-vaunted technical expertise and its public service commitment seem sadly threadbare when it comes to soccer.'

So, while the television schedules turned increasingly towards American football and other imported games (basketball and Australian rules football for example), the national game, soccer, became a sporadic, unpredictable offering confined largely to mid-week and Sunday afternoons. Those regular Saturday-night highlights were now well and truly part of the past. 'I never thought the day would ever come when I would miss the sight of Jimmy Hill on a Saturday night', wrote one typically anguished armchair viewer to a football magazine.

In 1987 the League began to formulate its own plan for the future by setting up a company called Worldwide Soccer Limited, which started operating in 1988. It was set up at the instigation of the League's executive to the Television Committee, Lee Walker, formerly at Lytham St Annes but now based at the League's new office at Wembley. The aim of Worldwide Soccer is to enhance the present overseas sales of recorded League football by packaging it into an attractive programme which will act as a vehicle for merchandising and sponsored programming, and thereby bring a greater reward to the League in terms of both profits and international prestige.

The League had already gained valuable experience in this field, and a steady profit, through several years' involvement with Thames Television International, who have marketed League matches to roughly forty countries. Thus, between 1985 to 1988, while courtesy of the League and TTI, viewers all over the world were watching League football quite contentedly, the English and Welsh viewer was deprived of regular televised League action, particularly during the period August 1985 to January 1986, when there was no televised football at all on either BBC or ITV. Nevertheless, given that League football is still the most popular football in the world when it comes to international television viewing, the future for Worldwide Soccer seems bright indeed. It signed its first British deal in January 1988 with Granada Television, based in Manchester, for five, one-hour local programmes of recorded highlights, and more contracts were expected to follow. Negotiations with both the BBC and ITV for a new contract with the League followed in February.

It is hard to predict how televised football will be presented in the not-too-distant future. Technical advances in cable and satellite television will offer the League and its audience all kinds of opportunities hitherto largely confined to the United States and parts of Europe. It is an exciting prospect, and one which the League now seems ready and able to face with a measure of expertise and confidence which would have seemed unthinkable only a decade

ago. Such is the power of marketing.

Settling the television deal was one of the new Management Committee's first tasks. Finding a new sponsor for the League proved to be a harder task.

Canon's contract ended at the end of the 1985/6 season, by which time the League was still recovering from the effects of May 1985. Crowds in 1985/6 were at an all-time low, and no one could be sure as to how effective the reconstruction plan would be in counteracting the decline. Consequently, companies were not exactly queuing up to take over from Canon, despite the fact that Canon had professed themselves to be extremely pleased with the results of their three-year contract.

In July there were reports that Guinness were considering taking Canon's place, but it wasn't until early October that the League managed to attract a definite sponsor, the *Today* newspaper.

In retrospect it is easy to criticize the deal by which *Today* agreed to invest £4 million in the League over two seasons, but at the time everything about the arrangement seemed perfectly marvellous. *Today* was seen as a young, modern publication – the first national tabloid to use colour printing and advanced newspaper technology – with access, in theory, to millions of homes around the nation.

The *Today* deal offered the champions of the First Division £50,000, the Second Division £25,000 (the same as Canon had paid) and the Third and Fourth Divisions £12,500 each. In addition, each League club was to receive £14,500 in the First Division, £7300 in the Second and £3300 in the Third and Fourth. There were also additional payments to reward clubs making efforts towards family spectators. 'We feel the time is ripe to stand up and support the national game', said *Today*'s managing director.

But the chemistry was never quite right. Rather than feeding off each other's strengths, both *Today* and the League were hampered by each other's frailties. *Today* needed to boost its circulation and find an identity. The League, needing to rehabilitate its own image, needed a shoulder to lean on, and the shoulder it chose was wavering.

There was another, more practical problem with *Today*. Whereas most newspapers had given some prominence to the words 'Canon League', they were loath to give any free publicity to one of their rivals. Even those newspapers whose interests did not directly clash with those of *Today* studiously avoided any reference to the sponsors.

Today's sponsorship did not last a year, let alone the agreed two-year period. With reported accumulated losses of £30 million, its recently arrived third proprietor, Rupert Murdoch (who already owned two other daily newspapers, *The Times* and the *Sun*), regarded the League deal, agreed by *Today*'s previous owners, Lonrho, as an expendable luxury.

In an effort to extract itself without loss of face, *Today* accused the League of breaking its promises, particularly by arranging for the centenary celebrations to be sponsored by another company, Mercantile Credit. '*Today* Boots Out Broken Promises League' went the newspaper's headline.

Murdoch could not have chosen a more punishing time for the announcement. Graham Kelly returned from his holiday to be faced by a barrage of press and the prospect not only of having to take legal action against *Today* for breach of contract, but also of having to find a new sponsor. There were eleven days left before the new season began, and just four days to go before the League opened its centenary celebrations with a banquet in London, followed by a star-studded representative match at Wembley.

But for once in the history of the League, misery was transformed into elation within a remarkably short period. The fact was that the League now represented a much more attractive proposition than it had a year earlier. Gates had risen, football had fought back from its despair in 1985, and the widely admired Cup Final between Coventry and Tottenham had reminded the nation that football was, after all, a precious commodity. Because of this, no sooner had *Today* dropped out than there were six major companies reported to have been interested in sponsoring the League. Nine days of hectic negotiations ensued, ending just two days before the first League matches of the centenary season, when the League's commercial director, Trevor Phillips, announced the signing up of new sponsors, Barclays Bank.

Barclays were the perfect sponsors: solid, prestigious and respected both on the local high street and internationally. Unlike *Today* they were also unlikely to change their minds in mid contract. Their agreement was for three years, from 1987–90, and was worth in total £4.55 million, the largest single sponsorship deal in British domestic sport.

Ultimately, therefore, one could say that the *Today* newspaper did the Football League a great favour by withdrawing their sponsorship. The League may have lost a purse, but it found a patron. A real patron.

As with the *Today* deal, the champions of the divisions were to receive £50,000 (First), £25,000 (Second) and £12,500 (Third and Fourth), but the pool, distributed amongst all

THE TODAY LEAGUE

It's a real winner from the top to the bottom

'In a League of our own' announced the Today newspaper. As the Guardian commented eleven months later, the sponsorship agreement 'must have seemed like good idea at the time'.

the clubs (on the 50:25:25 ratio), was worth approximately £900,000, compared with £638,000 from *Today*. Small change, no doubt, to a bank of Barclays' standing, but a welcome boost to most League clubs.

The Barclays deal was more than just a financial arrangement, however. It was a vote of confidence, a blue chip on the shoulder at a time when the League needed all the credibility it could muster in order to renegotiate a better television deal in 1988, attract other sponsors and, more importantly, to improve the chances of League clubs being readmitted to Europe by UEFA (which is based in Switzerland where, happily, big banks are regarded with great reverence).

In one respect Barclays had already been closely involved in football, as bearers of the bank accounts of approximately thirty-six of the ninety-two clubs. They were therefore under no illusions as to the stark financial realities facing the League.

Money problems still plagued clubs at every level of the League in the period 1986–8, and for no club more than Wolves, who in the summer of 1986 were £2.5 million in debt and yet again tottering on the brink. The new Management Committee adopted the same line as its predecessors by stating that if Wolves dropped out they would not be replaced.

Wolves did survive, of course, thanks to a £3 million buy-out by the local council. Other clubs were not so fortunate. From First Division Manchester City, £5 million in debt, to lowly Halifax Town, £424,000 in debt (and for a while without electricity), the recession of the early 1980s continued to plague League football.

Only a day before Barclays' sponsorship was announced, company information specialists Jordans, in association with the accountants Peat Marwick McLintock, issued a financial report on all ninety-two League clubs. The report made chilling reading.

If the definitions set down in the new Insolvency Act were applied strictly to League

According to the Football League, of the 1975 professional players registered with League clubs in January 1986, 9 per cent earned more than £30,000 but the majority earned less than half that amount; roughly 25 per cent from £10–15,000 per year, another 29 per cent from £5–10,000.

Although, obviously, bonuses and other benefits help to make a footballer's life more lucrative at the top of the scale, a surprising 40 per cent of all players at First Division clubs were on similar basic wages to their Fourth Division counterparts.

clubs, reported Jordans, eighty of the ninety-two would be technically insolvent (although in practice accounting procedures differed greatly). Two clubs (Hartlepool and Swansea) had not, at the time of the report, filed any company accounts since 1983, and another six not since 1984.

Average wage bills were £1.1 million in the First Division, £623,000 in the Second, £398,000 in the Third and £348,000 in the Fourth – a ratio of approximately 45:25:16:14 (compared with a distribution of League revenues of 50:25:12.5:12.5).

But the discrepancies between individual clubs were much greater. Average per capita wages at Tottenham were £37,000, compared with £3400 at Crewe (including all employees, not only playing staff). Only in the First Division and at a few Second Division clubs were players earning substantial wages.

One of the most curious findings in Jordans' survey related to Lincoln. Despite losing their League status at the end of the season, Lincoln were in a healthier financial state than any other club in the Fourth Division.

Most worrying was that throughout the League, gate receipts were falling as a proportion of total revenue and in some cases were insufficient to cover basic wages. As a result, many clubs were in debt and largely dependent on clearing banks (Barclays included) and the personal support of individual directors.

Apart from Wolves, the most serious case of collapse in the summer of 1986 was Middlesbrough, wound up by the Official Receiver in July with debts of over £1 million. As usually occurred, a new company was formed by those ubiquitous saviours otherwise known collectively as 'a consortium of businessmen'.

Reborn Middlesbrough had to kick off the new season at Hartlepool, however, because Ayresome Park was still in the hands of the Receiver. Although this had never happened before in League history, Middlesbrough's feelings of dislocation were not uncommon in the 1980s. At least sixteen other clubs were threatened with homelessness or loss of identity during this decade, for one reason or another.

Only two clubs were actually forced to move: Charlton to share a ground with Crystal Palace, Bristol Rovers to share with non-League Bath City. But it was not for want of trying on behalf of certain landlords and club chairmen.

February 1987 saw the revival of merger mania in London, with one of the new Management Committee members, Ron Noades, at the centre of attempts to merge Crystal Palace with his former club, Wimbledon. The managing director of First Division Wimbledon wanted to sell the club's rather basic Plough Lane ground and merge with Palace at Selhurst Park, which Palace were already sharing with First Division Charlton. It would be the first step towards forming one major force in south London capable of rivalling the north London giants, Tottenham and Arsenal. Only Selhurst Park in south London had the facilities and the catchment area from which to launch such a challenge.

Enticing though this concept was in theory, and inadequate though Plough Lane undoubtedly was by First Division standards (even by Third Division ones if one was being really harsh), in practice the merger idea won very

little support, particularly among Wimbledon's small but steadfast band of supporters. Having just reached the First Division in record time, they were loath to see this achievement snatched from under their noses.

As to the potential of a south London giant, Wimbledon enthusiasts asked: what was the point in having success if it wasn't your club any more? Besides which, Wimbledon had a place in the First Division. Why should Palace muscle in on their glory?

A few days after the merger plan was announced, in west London there was even more surprising news when it was announced that Fulham were to be merged with Queen's Park Rangers. The owners of Craven Cottage, a property company called Marler Estates, had bought up QPR lock, stock and barrel from chairman Jim Gregory, and wanted to redevelop Craven Cottage at a huge profit. Yet again, it was time for football's hardiest campaigners to click into gear – Jimmy Hill (himself a former Fulham player) and Gordon Taylor.

The issue at stake was not merely Fulham's survival but the growing fear of 'asset stripping'. This was the process by which a property developer or businessman bought up a football club and ran down its footballing assets – primarily by selling the best players – thus creating a situation in which crowds diminished to such a point that he could declare that the club was no longer viable and that not enough people cared anyway. What choice did he have but to sell the ground for development and merge with a neighbouring club?

The brief existence of Fulham Park Rangers – on paper at least – was a perfect example of this process, just as the reaction it caused was also illustrative of how deeply football supporters cared for their clubs and home grounds. Never mind that Fulham were struggling, that crowds were low and that Craven Cottage was one of the most valuable pieces of real estate in the League ... if cold logic had ever entered the argument there would have been only fifty clubs left in the League, with supermarkets and private housing on every other existing ground in the country.

(Lest future generations gain the impression that merger mania spread throughout the League in the 1980s, it should be stressed that the threat was greatest in London, where property prices were high enough to make buying up a football club a potentially profitable business. Elsewhere, several clubs were only too willing to sell their grounds for development so that they could move to newly built modern stadia in better locations. This was Scunthorpe's dream, answered in 1987 by a supermarket developer. Other clubs, such as Halifax, Northampton, Walsall and Chester, were thwarted by either a lack of funds, their local planning authority or by the fact that no one wanted their land anyway.)

The League's response to the London merger plans was almost immediate. After fans from all over the country had shown at mass meetings and by demonstrations at grounds their vehement opposition to mergers of any kind, the Management Committee blocked the attempts of QPR's chairman, David Bulstrode, to merge his new acquisition with Fulham, just as the Management Committee had done seventy-seven years earlier when Henry Norris had attempted to merge Woolwich Arsenal with Fulham.

Rather taken aback by the depth of anger he had aroused, Bulstrode gave up the merger plan when Jimmy Hill organized the usual 'consortium of businessmen' to take over the club, though not the ground. Marler still owned Craven Cottage and Loftus Road, and within the same London borough, 75 per cent of Stamford Bridge, where a battle of another kind was shaping up.

In April 1987, Management Committee member Ken Bates launched a £15-million 'Save the Bridge' appeal, aimed at buying the ground from Marler and thus staving off the very real possibility of Chelsea having to leave the ground in 1989. His fellow Committee man, Ron Noades, meanwhile abandoned his efforts to merge Palace with Wimbledon, a poll amongst the fans having rejected it by a large majority.

At a national level, outbreaks of hooliganism were still being reported, but now almost entirely outside the confines of League grounds, some of which had begun to resemble caged fortresses.

Again, the authorities were beginning to get a grip on the situation. The widespread use of CCTV cameras and specially adapted detector vans enabled the police to pinpoint the troublemakers and, during 1986/7, make a series of well-publicized arrests. All the police investigations concurred with the findings of sociologists at Leicester University: that the modern hooligan was not necessarily young nor unemployed. Indeed, some were married, with mortgages and in respectable jobs. Violence was their creed, not football, as the clubs had been telling the nation for many years.

On 9 October 1986 the Government renewed its pressure on the League when Sports Minister Richard Tracey gave the League six weeks to report on the progress clubs had made on implementing membership schemes.

League President Philip Carter did admit that more could be done. 'We have not conquered the problem of hooliganism', he agreed after meeting with Dick Tracey. But there was also a strong feeling that the Government had altered its attitude and now seemed to believe that not only should a blanket membership scheme be introduced, but also a complete ban on away supporters. As Graham Kelly commented: 'If in destroying hooliganism you destroy the game and end competition, then the hooligans will have won. We are as anxious as anyone to beat hooliganism, but this is a worrying shift of emphasis.'

'Politicians don't appreciate the problem,' responded Cardiff's managing director, Ron Jones, in a statement typical of the League's reaction. 'They are out of touch with football.'

Philip Carter was caught in the most difficult position. Despite his general sympathy with the Conservative administration, he was faced by a Minister for Sport who was, in the words of one club director, 'long on advice but short on action', and a Prime Minister who, in her utterances, appeared to have no understanding as to why the game of football might be important to millions of the electorate.

Recalling one of the many meetings with the Government between 1985 and 1986, FA secretary Ted Croker wrote in his auto-biography (see Bibliography): 'Mrs Thatcher knew little about professional football and nor did the people who were advising her.' Cro-ker's impression was confirmed, he wrote, when one of those advisers (self-appointed perhaps) turned out to be Robert Maxwell, whose involvement with football by then amounted to only two years.

The League's real Achilles' heel when it came to negotiations with the Government was Luton Town. Luton occupied much of the League's attention in the early months of the 1986/7 season, not because of their artificial pitch but because of their controversial decision to ban all away supporters from Kenilworth Road.

There were two main reasons for this decision.

Firstly, Luton wished to rid the town and the immediate vicinity of the ravages of fortnightly hooliganism. This in turn would help to improve their relations with the local council and community, and thus improve their chances of finding a new ground elsewhere in Luton. (Luton's ground was due to be hemmed in by a new road scheme which would severely limit their ability to stage first-class football. All attempts to find another site had, until then, failed.)

Secondly, in order to raise the funds to build a new ground, Luton had completely rede-signed Kenilworth Road to accommodate lucrative executive boxes. By doing this,

however, they had lost the ability to segregate rival supporters.

A ban on away fans therefore seemed the logical solution to both their public-relations difficulties and their ground limitations. The club also calculated that what they might lose on receipts – if anything – they would gain by much reduced policing costs.

As the experiment began in autumn 1986, all eyes were on Kenilworth Road. If the scheme worked, other clubs might follow and thus the real cause of hooliganism – clashes between home and away fans – would be eradicated. If it failed then Luton would be the main sufferers, since all their short-term plans depended on having no visiting supporters at the ground.

Initial reactions from neutral observers were mostly favourable. Patrick Collins in the *Mail on Sunday* wrote: 'By their brave and simple decision to ban away fans, Luton have restored the civilized Saturday afternoons of our youth.' Kenilworth Road was, wrote Collins, a perfect example of how the game used to be, with fathers and sons, all wearing club colours, attending happily, while local residents 'stood and nodded approvingly at the passing parade'.

On the other hand, the resultant atmosphere at Luton was quite different to anything else in the First Division. Away teams' efforts were met with only muted applause, and at times during games there seemed to be a deathly, if polite, silence. Combined with the already unusual nature of matches at Luton, due to the artificial pitch, it was almost as if football at Kenilworth Road was a new ball game alto-gether – a sort of sanitized, contrived version of the real thing, 'No blood, no mud!' sneered one reporter after a particularly soulless encounter.

Nor was the membership scheme infallible. Cunning visiting fans discovered various methods of beating the system – none of them ever publicized – and the computerized turn-stiles didn't always work.

Nevertheless, the League placed no objec-tions to the scheme being used for League matches. Instead, the main controversy arose when, shortly before the season began, the League stated that Luton would be banned from the Littlewoods Challenge Cup unless visiting clubs were allocated 25 per cent of available tickets, as required by the competition rules.

Graham Kelly put the League's view thus: 'What the Government seems to be saying is it doesn't matter if Luton have an advantage in the Cup. It doesn't matter if they are drawn at home and win every match if it means there are no hooligans on railway stations and public transport. We are saying, is it worth playing the competition if hooligans are allowed to distort the competition in this way?'

Luton, whose chairman David Evans was then a prospective parliamentary candidate for the Conservative Party and an avowed admirer of the Prime Minister, refused to concede, however, and so on 22 September the League banned Luton from the Littlewoods Cup.

Thus began a dispute which was to provide the new Management Committee with an unprecedented dilemma. Assailed by criticism from all sides – the media, the Sports Council, the Government and, the newspapers reckoned, public opinion (always a tenuous claim) – the League insisted on sticking to the rules.

As a compromise, Luton offered to play their Littlewoods Cup First Round tie against Cardiff City behind closed doors. Cardiff's own fans had recently been on the rampage at Exeter, and hardly won much sympathy for being excluded from Luton, but still the League refused to back down.

Philip Carter spelled out the League's stance in an interview with Joe Melling of the *Mail on Sunday*, published on 28 September 1986:

'*The Football League is dedicated to beating and banishing the mindless hooligans who have threatened to destroy our national sport.*

Let's make that clear from the very start. It's vital that this message is received and understood by all decent-minded people who love their football and wish to watch this game in peace and harmony.

Unfortunately, I am not convinced that our determination to fight this continual battle with all the means at our disposal has come across clearly to the public during the highly publicised dispute with Luton Town.

The situation has not been helped by the Prime Minister, Margaret Thatcher, appearing on television insisting that Luton must be backed in their fight against hooligans. She has conveyed the mistaken impression that no one else is doing anything about the problem.

The Football League Management Committee does not consist of doddering old men with their heads buried in the sand. We are the custodians of the game, elected by the 92 member clubs of the Football League. Our job is to protect the interest of all of those clubs. Nobody, be it Luton Town or Margaret Thatcher, is more concerned about the hooligan problem than we are.

The League Management Committee has supported fully Luton's experiment in banning away supporters from their ground in League matches. If other clubs wish to follow suit, they have every right to do so. But the rules of the Littlewoods Cup are different.

Since I became President in May, I have bent over backwards to accommodate Luton's wishes. It has to be said that they have been totally intransigent. They chose not to take advantage of several opportunities to propose official amendments to a change in the rules of the Littlewoods Cup competition.

We have offered to them six separate compromise situations which would have kept Luton within the rules.

Frankly I believe that if they had allowed season ticket holders from other clubs, it would have provided a sensible compromise which would have been in accord with the Prime Minister's wishes.'

Carter went on to describe how the League had offered a seventh compromise, allowing Luton to switch their home Cup ties to the opposition's venue, but this too had been rejected after a tough meeting at Lytham St

Annes. 'Compromise is not my sort of word', David Evans had declared. In future, he said, away fans may be readmitted to Kenilworth Road, but not during the current season.

Under pressure from the Minister for Sport, and public criticism, the Management Committee finally elected to put the whole matter to a meeting of all ninety-two clubs, due to take place at Villa Park on 6 October.

Should Luton be allowed to stay in the competition or not? The clubs would decide.

Margaret Thatcher had no doubts whatsoever. As soon as the meeting was announced, she applauded David Evans, praised the Luton scheme and urged the League to reinstate the club. This was quite without precedent in ninety-nine years of the League – a Prime Minister publicly intervening in the League's internal affairs (not even during the Pools War of 1936 had this happened).

But among the clubs and the football hierarchy there was a division. The FA supported Luton; the majority of clubs seemed opposed. Gordon Taylor of the PFA took the League's side. 'It could be argued that Luton are behaving in exactly the same way as the hooligans in trying to impose their anarchical rule on others.'

Diplomatic as ever, Philip Carter would say only that the Lytham meeting had made progress and that he looked forward to other experiments with membership schemes. For a man who had only just stepped into the presidency he was already exhibiting all the right qualities of League leadership; supporting his members in deed, yet adopting a carefully measured stance in his public utterances.

As fully expected, when the Birmingham meeting did take place, Luton did not win the vote. As a last-gasp measure, the League offered them a chance to play their home leg of the Cardiff tie on neutral ground, but Luton stuck to their guns and withdrew from the competition. They were fully within their rights, as was the League; a question of two rights making a wrong impression.

The dispute had several consequences, the most immediate being a change on the Management Committee. One of the newly elected members of the Committee in May 1986 had been was John Smith, chief executive of Luton Town. Amidst all the discussion over Luton's fate, Smith had been like an exam pupil sitting in on meetings of the marking committee.

The vote against Luton left him with little option. 'I didn't want to leave the Committee,' he said after the verdict at Birmingham, 'but I put it to the meeting that if I didn't have their confidence I would go. They voted on the issue and voted against me. I regret this has happened. I have been in the game for more than thirty years, and had reached the pinnacle of my career in football. I am supposed to represent the views of the League, but that would have meant going against my club, and this I clearly could not do.'

The dispute did not end there. Since Luton had withdrawn from the Littlewoods Cup they were asked to return their share of the Littlewoods sponsorship money, worth £5000. For their part, Cardiff City won a bye to the next round of the competition and demanded compensation for the loss of gate receipts (a claim not enhanced by the behaviour of Cardiff fans on the rampage in Exeter shortly before the dispute).

John Smith's departure meant another election for the Management Committee. Irving Scholar of Tottenham Hotspur, one of the original Super Leaguers who had only narrowly failed to be elected in the previous elections in May, was the strong favourite, but he quickly announced his unwillingness to stand. 'There are more politicians in football than there are in the House of Commons', he told *The Times*.

John Smith's replacement did come from north London, however, from Arsenal. The new man (in more senses than one) was David Dein, the club's vice chairman, who had claims to be one of the fastest climbers up the football ladder in League history, having joined the Arsenal board only three years earlier. Dein was also, at thirty-nine years old, the youngest member on the Committee.

Like every other Committee man, with the exception only of Jack Dunnett, Dein had little chance to learn the ropes before being thrust into the hurly burly of League affairs.

On 19 November the Government went back on the offensive on the question of identity cards. Mrs Thatcher was still insisting that she wanted to see a 100 per cent membership scheme. Dick Tracey told the press: 'We have been saying this for eighteen months and it is still our view.'

But with the League also still adamantly maintaining its stance, for a while it looked as if the Prime Minister might end all the discussion by making membership schemes part of Government legislation.

Given her record on other unpopular pieces of legislation, the threat was genuine enough, despite the fact that the League had widespread support for its rejection of the 100 per cent identity card scheme. 'If a plastic card is taken from a villain,' said Philip Carter, 'that is not the end of the villain.' Backing this view was the Association of Chief Police Officers and the House of Commons' All-Party Committee on Football, whose chairman, Tom Pendry MP, said: 'I urge the [Sports] Minister to cool it now, recognize that the League are at least looking at ways of improving their image, and have an inquiry into the best way of going forward.'

In the League's view, the way forward meant adhering to a twenty-point package of proposals put forward by its new anti-hooligan committee. Among the recommendations were calls for CCTV cameras at all ninety-two grounds, with more trained on areas outside the grounds; a target of 70 per cent controlled admissions (through season-ticket holders, members, family enclosures and so on); and strengthened police powers of arrest.

There was also strong support for schemes implemented by several clubs, including Leeds and Norwich, by which only season-ticket holders, Supporters Club members and shareholders were sold tickets to strictly defined parts of away grounds.

The debate over membership schemes continues to this day, but the Government did not carry out its threat to legislate. Instead, in February 1987 the League was able to work out a compromise with Sports Minister, Richard Tracey, by which clubs undertook to reach a target of 50 per cent membership schemes where ground conditions allowed (for Philip Carter's view on these developments, see Chapter 36).

But do any of these anti-hooligan measures work? Has the theory of membership schemes been successfully translated into practice?

According to all available statistics, the answer is emphatically positive. Ejections and arrests were down in 1986/7, dramatically in most instances, and there was more evidence that troublemakers were no longer bothering to travel to away games where detection by CCTV or the police was a significant risk. Police swoops on hooligan gangs in Cambridge, London and the West Midlands also indicated that at last the police were making genuine progress in tracking down the ringleaders.

But there was still much work to be done, as was shown graphically on the opening day of the centenary season, when Wolves fans caused havoc at Scarborough's very first game in the Football League.

The main conclusion we can reach at this, the closing stages in our history, is that by 1988 the League was winning the battle against hooliganism, possibly the most important battle it had ever faced in its hundred years. More families, mostly fathers with children, were taking advantage of family enclosures, and the atmosphere at many, although not all, grounds improved noticeably.

Above all, committed supporters did not prove hostile to the process of joining their clubs as fully paid-up members. Tottenham, for example, had 18,000 members by October 1986, out of an average gate that season of nearly 26,000, and only two other clubs decided to follow Luton's example by banning all away fans – Torquay and Colchester.

Whether or not the anti-hooligan and pro-membership trends were responsible for attracting more spectators during 1986/7 is hard to determine. A more peaceable atmosphere at grounds, higher standards on the pitch, the England team's admirable performance in Mexico and the prospect of the European Championships in West Germany in June 1988 – probably all these factors helped in proving that despite the doom of 1985, the decline in attendances was not irreversible. Just under 900,000 extra spectators attended the League programme (excluding play-offs) in 1986/7, a rise of 5.4 per cent and, incidentally, the first rise since 1979/80. The centenary season saw this upward trend continue.

Curiously, there was one factor which may well have had the effect of either increasing or reducing League attendances, and that was the continuing absence of English clubs from European competitions. Figures from the 1960s and 1970s show that in certain seasons those clubs competing in Europe actually attracted fewer people to League matches, because fans wanted to save their money for the big European games. And since these clubs were often those with the highest League attendances, this had the effect of lowering the aggregate.

Conversely, the ban from Europe had the undoubted effect of reducing the income of top clubs and therefore also their ability to hold on to star players. Hence the sales of Liverpool's top scorer Ian Rush to Juventus for £3 million and England's World Cup hero Gary Lineker from Everton to Barcelona for £4.2 million. A more surprising trend in 1986/7 saw more star English players moving to Scottish clubs (which continued to compete in Europe). England internationals Terry Butcher (Ipswich) and Chris Woods (Norwich) both signed for Glasgow Rangers, and thus began a steady stream of exports north of the border. This exodus was only marginally compensated by the arrival of players from abroad, such as Newcastle's £1 million signing of the Brazilian, Mirandinha.

There was one other development worth recording from the 1986/7 season, and that was a quite unexpected threat made in September 1986 that the whole reconstruction plan, so laboriously debated for so long the season before, should in fact be overturned. The League clubs' capacity for contrariness was never more alarmingly exhibited.

The cause of the unrest lay in the fact that one element of the reconstruction plan, the introduction of a British Cup, had not actually got off the ground. This meant that although, as planned, the First Division was going to be reduced to twenty clubs, there would be no extra matches to make up for the loss of revenue.

Two men therefore led a campaign to restore the First Division back to twenty-two clubs, which would in effect undo all the work and effort of the previous season's negotiations. The fact that those two men were the chairmen of Manchester City and Aston Villa, who would both lose their First Division places that season, was not, at that time, significant. Indeed, their views were supported by several other leading clubs.

As Liverpool's Peter Robinson told *The Times*: 'We negotiated the reduction on the understanding that there would be a British Cup. If that competition does not come about, in two seasons' time when the First Division is reduced to 20 teams we will be losing 10 per cent of our revenue, which is equivalent to £200,000.'

The Second Division lobby was incensed by this threatened *volte face*. One angry Management Committee member, Bill Fox of Blackburn Rovers, said:

'There is no way we are going back on what was agreed. We asked the First Division clubs several times: "Are you sure you want to cut your own division?", and they said "Yes!".

'Part of our agreeing to increase the top clubs' voting power was based on them cutting their clubs and the Second Division being increased to twenty-four. They can't have everything their own way. The changes are all linked. They can't pick out one and go back on it. If it does come up again then everything else must be discussed again – percentages, voting, television agreements, the lot!'

Thankfully for the League, and indeed for you, the wearied reader of our hundred years of family feuding, the reconstruction plan was neither dropped nor renegotiated. And nor did anything come of a proposal a month later, in October 1986, for the League to take over the FA. Apparently, two members of the new Management Committee had drawn up plans for the League to assume some of the FA's responsibilities. There was particular anger that while the League had banned Luton from the Littlewoods Cup, the FA had not barred them from the FA Cup. There was even talk of League clubs withdrawing from the FA Cup over the matter.

They did not, of course, which is just as well because the end of the 1986/7 season saw one of the best FA Cup Finals of the post-war period. Coventry's 3–2 extra-time victory over Tottenham did more for the game's image than a million words.

From the League's point of view also, the season ended on its highest note for years, as the play-offs and automatic promotion and relegation from the Fourth Division kept the fans on tenterhooks right up until the very last days of May.

This is how the historic events of 1987 unfolded.

By 29 April it was known who was going to be the first non-League club to gain automatic promotion to the Football League. It was GM Vauxhall Conference champions Scarborough, who had taken everyone by surprise with a superb late-season run.

But who would be fated to take their place? Incredibly, one of the leading contenders for the big drop was Burnley, founder members of the League, once the pride and joy of Charles Sutcliffe and Bob Lord and twice League champions. That they were now having to enter into a skirmish at the bottom of the Fourth Division for very League survival seemed quite unbelievable. Only a decade earlier they had been a First Division club.

Saturday, 9 May turned out to be the judgement day, and what a day it was, too! A crowd of 15,781 turned up at Turf Moor, the vast majority of them fearing a wake but praying for a miracle. As it happened they had to wait, because the kick-off was delayed by twenty minutes to allow late-comers to enter the ground. (Now there was a sign of the times, at a venue where the record crowd was 54,775.)

In an afternoon of high drama, Burnley went 2–1 up and played the last neurotic half hour in the knowledge that their opponents, Orient, needed to win to have a chance of promotion, and that victory for either Lincoln at Swansea or Torquay over Crewe would consign Burnley to an unenviable place in footballing history.

Lincoln lost 2–0, but might still have survived had Crewe held on to their 2–1 lead at Torquay. It was then that fate, or rather a dog, stepped in, biting Torquay defender Jim McNichol on the leg and thus causing injury time in this nail-biting finish. Those few extra minutes proved decisive. Torquay equalized, and thus Lincoln City, not Burnley, became the first club to be relegated from the Football League.

When the new system had been unveiled a year earlier, everyone had talked in terms of Hartlepools, Rochdale, Halifax or any of the perennial strugglers going down. Nobody dreamed that Burnley might come close, and few would have made a bet on Lincoln, who had been relegated to the Fourth Division only a year earlier and who hadn't appeared in the re-election zone since 1971. On the other hand, they had dropped out of the League more times than any other club, in 1908, 1911 and 1920. And now 1987.

While gloom descended over Lincoln, and the celebrations still reverberated around the seaside resort of Scarborough, the next stage of the reconstruction plan was only just beginning – the play-offs.

More great old names from the past were involved, including founder members Wolverhampton Wanderers, fighting to get out of the Fourth Division, and Bolton Wanderers, struggling to stay in the Third. In the end, neither club was successful, although Wolves had more cause than most to feel aggrieved by the new system. They had finished the season proper in fourth place, nine points above the next two clubs, Colchester (in fifth place) and Aldershot (sixth). Under the normal rules that would have seen them comfortably promoted to the Third Division and, who could have told, perhaps on the long trail back to the top. Instead, in their final play-off against Aldershot in front of a crowd of 19,962 at Molineux, they failed to overturn a 2–0 deficit from the first leg, meaning that Aldershot, the underdogs, went up at the Wolves' expense.

Bolton also had cause to curse Aldershot's good form. The Shots beat Bolton 3–2 on aggregate, and thus sent the Wanderers down to the Fourth Division for the first time (although in fairness, without the play-offs Bolton would still have been relegated).

Those other early pioneers of the League, Sunderland, meanwhile failed to overcome Gillingham and were thus relegated to the Third Division, also for the first time in their history. (Sunderland would have gone down also under the old system, just as Swindon, victors in the play-offs, would have gone up.)

Apart from Wolves, one other team had their promotion place sacrificed by the play-offs. Oldham had finished third in the Second Division, normally sufficient to gain automatic promotion. Instead, they were pipped in the play-offs by Leeds, who were in turn denied in a thrilling last-match replay with Charlton.

Altogether the twenty play-offs, involving twelve clubs, attracted a total audience of 310,317 (an average of 15,515), suggesting that they had exactly fulfilled their promise in terms of interest, excitement and financial return. Apart from the participating clubs and those who were promoted, a large slice of the receipts was shared out equally. For Second Division clubs this amounted to £11,500 each; for the Associate Members £4750 each. The play-offs looked as if they were here to stay.

A week later, with the football world still buzzing in the aftermath of May's scintillating matches, the last gathering of the League before the centenary celebrations took place at the National Exhibition Centre's Metropole Hotel, on 5 June 1987. This was the ninety-ninth Annual Meeting of the Football League, the first to be held outside London since the Second World War, and the first ever in peacetime not to feature a vote for the re-election of clubs.

Compared with the mood two years earlier, the League seemed to be in fine fettle: content (well, mostly) with the effects of the reconstruction plan, and full of anticipation for the centenary season ahead.

The meeting itself was quite routine, as many modern Annual Meetings are – most of the real talking takes place at divisional meetings beforehand. There were two deaths of particular note to report, those of Sir Norman Chester CBE, the architect of so much of the League's new thinking (after years of rebuttal), and Sir Stanley Rous CBE, former secretary of the FA and president of FIFA. The other notable absence was that of Liverpool from the honours list. Remarkably, it was only the third time in fifteen seasons that the Anfield club had not won a major honour.

A motion to ban plastic pitches for all Littlewoods Cup games was rejected, in view of the three-year moratorium on synthetic surfaces agreed the year before. This was a great relief for much-maligned Luton, who only the day before had announced their readiness to admit limited numbers of away fans to Littlewoods Cup matches (thereby enabling them to enter the competition). QPR had in the meantime announced that they were going to replace their prototype synthetic pitch with a natural surface in 1988.

Still on the subject of pitches, Tottenham Hotspur proposed that by 1989 all First Division clubs should have under-soil heating. This was rejected, but Spurs were more successful with their second proposal, that two substitutes per team be allowed for League matches.

There was disappointment for the League's new commercial director, Trevor Phillips, who prefaced the meeting with a slick audio-visual presentation on the forthcoming centenary celebrations, then stood in anguish as the clubs failed to vote through a proposal that the logo of the centenary sponsors, Mercantile Credit, be displayed on each player's shirt sleeve.

Otherwise, much of the business of the meeting would have been quite familiar to any one of the pioneers of the League ninety-nine years earlier. William McGregor would have nodded approvingly at a motion which laid down the punishment to clubs who failed to fulfil a fixture 'without just cause' – the deduction of two points plus possible expulsion from the League (with perhaps just a weary sigh that such cautions should still be necessary after all these years).

McGregor would also have approved a fine of £10,000 imposed on Tottenham Hotspur for fielding only two recognized first-teamers in their League match against Everton, five days before their Cup Final appearance against Coventry.

The fielding of a weak team was one of the first offences listed in the 1888 rules and, indeed, the only one of the original regulations to survive until today. (McGregor would have blanched at the size of Tottenham's punishment, however. The first large fine his contemporaries had imposed for this offence was

£50 against Everton in 1906.)

But there would have been no prouder man than McGregor had he known that his brain-child, the Football League, would still be around in the late twentieth century to celebrate its hundredth birthday.

The centenary celebrations, sponsored by the finance company Mercantile Credit, began in glittering fashion on 7 August 1987, with a huge banquet at the Grosvenor House Hotel on London's Park Lane (only a few doors away from where the 1938 Jubilee Banquet had been held at the Dorchester).

Among the 1000-plus guests were some of the leading figures of the game, including Jacques Georges, president of UEFA, England manager Bobby Robson, and guest of honour, Pele. Also attending proudly were representatives of Scarborough, the League's newest recruits, and Accrington Stanley, one of the former member clubs and successors to the founder club Accrington.

Every table included a familiar face, from the past and the present. There was Sir John

The centenary sponsors' logo for 1987–8.

Moores, former chairman of Everton and a character we first encountered in our history in 1936. In contrast, there was a modern-day club chairman, Elton John, the rock singer and number one Watford fan. Close by was snooker World Champion Steve Davis, and near the end of the proceedings a small, stocky Argentinian arrived in the banqueting hall, name of Maradona.

But this was just the beginning of what the sponsors dubbed 'a year-long party'.

The following day witnessed the gathering on Wembley's lush turf of some of the greatest players of the decade, as a Football League eleven managed by Bobby Robson took on a World eleven led by Barcelona manager Terry Venables.

A crowd of 61,000 and millions of viewers around the world purred with delight at a masterful performance from Michel Platini who, sadly, had resolved to retire from football after the game. Maradona, who was to receive £100,000 for his afternoon's work, had a more subdued ninety minutes, as the League eleven romped to a 3–0 win. (For details see Appendix Three.)

The next season, 1987/8, saw a whole series of centenary events. In September there was a Centenary Fun Run, in which League clubs all over the country – their players, staff and supporters – staged 2.5 mile sponsored runs in aid of local charities. On 25 November League champions Everton played the Bundesliga champions Bayern Munich at Goodison Park, Everton winning 3–1.

In December the League staged the indoor Guinness Soccer Sixes competition at the Manchester G-Mex exhibition centre. Nottingham Forest won in the final against Manchester United. Then in February there was a Gala Concert starring Elkie Brooks at the Royal Albert Hall in London, followed in April by four nights of pop concerts at the Wembley Arena, in which 40,000 fans were able to hear the music industry's own salute to the game.

On 13 April the City of Birmingham held a service in honour of William McGregor at Birmingham Cathedral, followed by the unveiling of a memorial plaque at the McGregor suite in Villa Park. In the afternoon Aston Villa played Birmingham City, with the players kitted out as they would have been in 1888.

On the actual anniversary of the League's formation, 17 April 1988, a Centenary Festival at Wembley was arranged in which sixteen clubs (eight from Division One, four from Division Two and two each from the lower divisions) took part in a family-oriented two-day tournament, with prize money of £385,000. Nottingham Forest beat Sheffield Wednesday in the final of what was, in the end, a disappointing competition for all but the minnows, Tranmere Rovers. They beat two First Division sides during the event.

Last, but by no means least, in this enormous centenary party, was the scheduled staging of the Mercantile Credit Football League Centenary Trophy, a tournament contested between the top eight clubs of the Barclays League First Division, according to the placings in 1987/8, with a *grande finale* held at Villa Park.

As in 1938, any profits from all the celebrations are to be directed towards the good of the game, through a specially formed charity, 'The Football League Centenary Appeal', which will be devoted to developing all areas of the game, from the coaching and training of young players to the possible establishment of a Centenary Centre. 'We have the world's best game,' the League President Philip Carter said proudly at the centenary launch. 'It deserves the best we can hand on to future generations.'

Indeed it does, and a Centenary Centre, be it in London, Manchester, Birmingham or wherever, would represent a perfect living monument to the Football League as it enters its second century. Provisional plans are for the centre to encompass outdoor and indoor training facilities, all-weather pitches, a centre where players may study, and perhaps even a new central office for the League.

All that is for the future. For the time being we must leave our history more or less as it began, in typical League tradition, with a contretemps.

When William McGregor former the League in 1888 the idea of one man having a stake in the fortunes of more than one club would have seemed quite anathema. Yet by the 1980s there were so many impecunious clubs crying out for a wealthy knight in shining armour that the hallowed concept of one man, one club, was in severe danger of being sacrificed in the name of survival.

And so to our last controversy. As the centenary season began, Robert Maxwell was chairman of Derby, but he also had an interest in Oxford, where his son was chairman, and in Reading, where he owned 29 per cent of the shares. Then in November 1987 Maxwell was presented with the opportunity of buying up rock-singer Elton John's majority share in Watford, for a sum of £2 million. Although Maxwell intended to buy this share in the name of his company, BPCC, and although he declared that the new Watford chairman would be a BPCC executive, and not himself, the League refused to sanction the sale.

Until then League Regulation 80 had forbidden anyone having a direct or indirect involvement in the running of one club. It was arguable whether Maxwell had already broken that rule by being involved with both Oxford and Reading while being chairman of Derby. Who was to say that he dictated his son's affairs at Oxford, or that he used his shareholding at Reading to influence the club's management?

This was a moot point, and as Philip Carter commented, 'It is virtually impossible to frame regulations that are 100 per cent legally binding.'

With the Watford issue, however, the League decided that it was time to toughen up the regulations. A line had to be drawn somewhere, and the prospect of Maxwell con-

trolling, directly or indirectly, 15 per cent of the First Division's voting power did not go down well with the Management Committee.

A war of words ensued, with Maxwell launching, via his newspaper, the *Daily Mirror*, the most vitriolic attack on the League ever seen in the press. He called the Committee 'the mismanagement committee' and even attacked the League for its dealings with television in 1985 (despite his own controversial involvement on St Valentine's Day). But, Maxwell did say publicly that if the Committee disapproved of his takeover at Watford, he would walk away from the deal.

The Committee did not approve and Maxwell did not walk away.

On 5 December Philip Carter struck a compromise deal with Maxwell. The League would withdraw its legal action preventing the transfer of Watford's share to BPCC if Maxwell severed all his family's ties with Oxford.

Ten days later the other members of the Management Committee voted 5–3 against Carter's compromise and Maxwell was told that he could only take over Watford if he disposed of his interests in all three of his other clubs.

Maxwell fumed again – 'The Football League is now being run by small men with even smaller minds' he announced – but the Committee's deliberations were backed up by the clubs at a subsequent Extraordinary General Meeting held, appropriately enough, in the Derby Room of the Royal Lancaster Hotel, London, on 19 January 1988.

This meeting voted 44–17$\frac{1}{2}$ in favour of a resolution limiting any one individual or his associates from owning more than 10 per cent of the shares in a club, if he or his associate is already a director or shareholder of another club.

That stopped Maxwell in his tracks – while Elton John eventually decided to stay on at Vicarage Road – but the route by which the League arrived at this settlement was littered with calumny and bitterness. Furthermore, the resolution was not designed to be retrospective, so that Maxwell's existing shareholdings were not affected, leaving supporters of Derby and Oxford wondering just what lay in store for their clubs if the millionaire publisher should suddenly decide to switch his loyalties elsewhere at a future date.

It was an unfortunate, and at times distasteful interlude in the centenary season, one which in many respects typified the stormy relationships and power struggles which have characterised the League's one hundred years.

But it would be wrong to end our tale on such a note of gloom. For while big men have often argued off the pitch, one must not lose sight of the enormity of the League's real achievement, in fostering the game of professional football.

From twelve clubs at the Royal Hotel, Manchester on 17 April 1888, to ninety-two clubs on 17 April 1988.

Millions upon millions of spectators, thousands of players, and hundreds of administrators, referees, linesmen, coaches, trainers, teachers, journalists, commentators, retailers, souvenir sellers, policemen, statisticians, historians, businessmen, financiers . . . all actively engaged in this one great obsession which came about because a draper in Birmingham wanted to revive professional football. 'A fixity of fixtures' he had called for, little realizing, no doubt, that it would all come to this.

As we said at the very beginning: such a simple concept, and all it needed was for someone to invent it.

CHAPTER THIRTY-FIVE
League Football and the Men – and Women – Who Make It

Graham Kelly – League Secretary

When Barclays Bank became sponsors of the Football League in August 1987, it was appropriate that one of the parties to the arrangement should have been Graham Kelly, since twenty years earlier the fifth Secretary of the League had served behind the counter in one of their branches in Blackpool.

With all due deference to Barclays, fortunately for the League Kelly never quite settled into the banking routine. Instead, after joining the Lytham staff in July 1968, he rose steadily through the ranks to succeed Alan Hardaker in 1979, which in League terms was a bit like taking over the number ten shirt for Brazil after Pele, or the manager's job at Liverpool after Bill Shankly.

But Graham Kelly had the best credentials a man could ever want in his position, and that was the endorsement of Alan Hardaker himself. No one recognized Kelly's qualities better than Hardaker. The former Secretary had, after all, worked closely with Kelly for six years and had instilled in his young apprentice a level of respect and familiarity with the League's regulations which had once been Hardaker's hallmark and is now, as a direct result, very much Graham Kelly's, too.

And yet on their first meeting the two men almost got off to a bad start. Kelly recalled his interview after he had applied for a post in the accounts department at Lytham. 'I almost lost the job when Alan Hardaker asked me if I followed much football. When I said, with

some pride, that I'd just driven back overnight from having seen Manchester United win the European Cup at Wembley, his immediate reaction was, "Oh no, not another bloody Manchester United supporter!"'

In fact, Kelly was as much a supporter of the small clubs as was Hardaker. Football clubs and golf clubs, as it happened.

Born two days before Christmas Day, 1945, Kelly was brought up next to a disused hotel at the Cleveleys Hydro, just north of Blackpool on the Lancashire coast. It was a children's paradise.

While his mother worked in the hotel trade and his father drove trams in Blackpool, Kelly junior had the run of the extensive grounds. He played football every waking moment on some old tennis courts or in a huge indoor garage, and took readily to golf when only five years old. The *Daily Mirror* came to write a feature about his golf. He was quite a child prodigy.

On Saturdays he started watching games at Bloomfield Road at the age of six. This was in the days of Blackpool's three Cup Final appearances in five years, when packed crowds watched legendary figures such as Matthews, Mudie, Mortensen and Perry.

Kelly plays down his own efforts on the pitch. 'Slow was not the word', he says of his days as a centre-forward. At other times he played in goal. 'I was tall, I could catch well, but I was never daft enough to be a good goalie.' Nevertheless, as a 'keeper he made the Blackpool Schoolboys Under-15s and kept out of the team a player who later turned professional. Another member of the side was John Hurst, who went on to enjoy a long career at Everton and Oldham.

For a period, Kelly was even on Accrington Stanley's books as a schoolboy, although he never actually played a game for them. The height of his footballing career came with a couple of trial matches for Blackpool's A team. Thereafter it was on to Blackpool Rangers as an outfield player in the West Lancashire League, and, after he had joined the League staff, into Sunday football.

Apart from playing, Kelly spent his teens on the Kop at Bloomfield Road, in the days when it had a roof, and following Blackpool around the country (hence his discomfort at Hardaker's suggestion that he was a Manchester United fan). Jimmy Armfield and Roy Gratrix were among his favourites; two stylish defenders. Alas, he was too young to have remembered Matthews at his prime.

After leaving Baines Grammar School in Poulton-le-Fylde with three 'A' levels under his belt, it hadn't occurred to Kelly to be involved further in the game, except perhaps as a sports journalist. He spent nearly four years at Barclays before seeing the League's advertisement in a local paper.

Once at the League, one of R. H. G. Kelly's first tasks in the accounts department was to accompany Norman Thomas on inspections of club books, as ordered by the Management Committee in the wake of the Peterborough and Port Vale scandals (see Chapter 24). Notts County was the first of forty clubs he visited over the course of the next five years.

Whenever possible, he and Thomas would take in a game during their tours of inspection. On one occasion he remembers seeing Kevin Keegan playing for Scunthorpe. On another he was chauffeured back to his hotel in Ipswich in the Cobbold Rolls Royce. For a young man fresh out of a bank it was an exciting, fascinating apprenticeship which gave him an invaluable insight into all aspects of administration at club level.

In the meantime he had married Liz, in 1970, started to study company secretaryship, and had already caught Alan Hardaker's eye. In 1973 Hardaker suggested that Kelly apply for the post of Deputy Secretary, a job which finally went to George Readle. Kelly was, however, appointed to the number three position in the League hierarchy, and was given the title Assistant Secretary shortly afterwards, when Eric Howarth, Fred's nephew, left the organization.

He was then aged twenty-seven and clearly destined for a leading role. For the next six years he and Readle held the fort at Lytham while Hardaker acted as the League's front man, and when the time came for Hardaker to step down, which he resisted for two years, it was Kelly rather than Readle who stepped into the great man's shoes. This was a great blow to Readle, as we noted in Chapter 29, but an indication of the respect with which the Management Committee regarded Graham Kelly.

When appointed in 1979, the new Secretary was just thirty-three years old, the youngest the League had ever had.

First impressions of Graham Kelly can be misleading. Although tall and well built, with his ginger mane, round features and spectacles he can convey the image of an innocent choirboy. In his manner at times it seems as if he wouldn't say 'boo' to a goose, let alone to an irate club chairman.

But confrontation is not Graham Kelly's style. Instead, he prefers to work by consensus in a calm rational manner. He has quite a startling eye for detail and, as many have said who have worked with him, an apparently insatiable appetite for the minutiae of League administration. In this respect he is very much Hardaker's star graduate.

Graham Kelly is not a naturally outgoing man. He can seem shy and is said to be hard to get to know. Yet since becoming Secretary he has commanded enormous respect in League circles and developed an unexpected gift for public speaking. A sense of humour is perhaps the most important prerequisite of the job. Without it, says Kelly, a League Secretary would be doomed.

He certainly needed both humour and patience during the tortuous negotiations concerning the reconstruction of 1985/6 when, as Secretary, he could do little more than await the deliberations of the clubs. Uncomfortable though this may have been, Kelly is the first man to defend the democratic system under which the League operates. He supports neither a change of emphasis nor the concept of a League supremo or commissioner.

'Giving one man, any man, power over the League would run totally against the tradition and strengths of the League. The present system does work. It isn't overloaded because of disputes, as some people might think. We resolve all our issues by negotiation, not by dictation or appealing to outside bodies or the courts.

'People have got to subscribe to League rules and regulations, otherwise where would it stop? Taking a disputed goal to be settled by outside jurisdiction? Critics of the League don't understand the complexities and the responsibilities of our administration.

'The key to being Secretary is to guard and apply the regulations which bind the clubs together. That was the whole purpose of forming a League, to create a framework in which professional football can thrive. To do that you must have rules, otherwise it all falls apart. As Secretary that often means making unpleasant decisions.'

But there have been some popular decisions, too, such as when the Management Committee met to consider the merger plan between Fulham and QPR in February 1987. Outside the meeting room, Fulham supporters had camped in readiness for a decision, while the Management Committee sent out sandwiches to keep them going. When the Committee finally emerged with the news that it would not sanction the merger, Kelly and the members were greeted like heroes.

'That was the Football League in effect flying in the face of the Chester Report, accepted economic rules, economies of scale, natural wastage, etc. etc. . . . ,' Kelly admitted. 'It was the Football League being soft. And that's partly because the League exists as a family, with all the strains and strengths that any family shares.'

Nowadays the League Secretary must bear an even greater burden in the family's affairs. He has to be a walking reference book, a counsellor, an executive and a media man all rolled into one. It is not enough to be a socialite or to make tough speeches; Kelly has to be the expert for everybody, from the President of the League to the office boy at a Fourth Division club.

Tom Charnley was thirty-one years in the job, Fred Howarth twenty-three and Alan Hardaker twenty-two, but each one started at a much later age than did Kelly. In theory, the fifth Secretary could still be at his post well into the twenty-first century. If this is the case, the League need have no fears for the future. It is in good hands: the hands of a man who as a goalkeeper was big enough for the job, rarely let the ball slip, but was never quite daft enough to throw himself about. Perfect credentials for a Secretary of the League.

Who's Who at League Headquarters

Having met the Secretary it is now high time to meet some of the unsung heroes behind the scenes – the men *and* women who make League football today.

With the benefit of modern communications technology, these dedicated workers at Lytham St Annes are not as far removed as they may seem in geographical terms. Nevertheless, as

One Hundred Years of the League:
Facts and Figures

- There have been eighty-nine full seasons of the League competition.
- A total of 134,980 games have been completed (not including play-offs, test matches, postponed or abandoned games, the aborted 1939/40 season, wartime fixtures, Wigan Borough's and Accrington Stanley's expunged records from 1931/2 and 1961/2 respectively, and the match in 1973/4 when Exeter failed to turn out against Scunthorpe).
- Just under 401,000 goals have been scored, giving an average per game of 2.97 goals.
- A total of 122 separate clubs has taken part in the League since 1888 (this is counting Leeds City as separate from Leeds United, South Shields from Gateshead, Accrington from Accrington Stanley and so on).
- Founder members Notts County have played more League games than any other club, with a total of 3566.
- Liverpool have won more League points than any other club, with a total of 4099 up to 17 April 1988.
- Aston Villa have scored more goals than any League club; up to 17 April 1988 their tally was 6049.
- Everton have played more seasons in Division One than any other club. In their eighty-nine seasons, eighty-five have been in Division One.

one approaches League headquarters along the promenade and down the tree-lined Clifton Drive South, it is hard to imagine that one is about to enter the nerve centre of the largest professional football league in the world. Yet it is not difficult to see why Joe Richards was so keen to set up shop here. Lytham St Annes is a genteel, unspoiled seaside resort, far removed from the bright lights of neighbouring Blackpool or the bustle of Preston.

As we enter the League's offices, our first port of call is to the press office, where press liaison officer Andy Williamson is assisted by Marion Ainge, herself a former journalist with the *West Lancashire Evening Gazette*.

Andy and Marion are responsible for the day-to-day contact with all sections of the news media, explaining League policy and providing information as required or appropriate. If ever you see the words 'League spokesmen' in an article, you can be pretty sure Andy Williamson was the speaker.

The press office also co-ordinates press conferences, provides press facilities at League events (such as Littlewoods Cup finals), and performs a hundred and one other duties concerned with information and club liaison. Suffice it to say that the phone seldom gets a rest in this office.

Andy, who joined the League in 1971, has taken on two other responsibilities in recent years, that of co-ordinator for the development of indoor football (the Guinness Soccer Six competition) and the League's anti-hooliganism policies. In both these fields Andy had just the right qualification: he is a Class One referee.

Helping him to combat crowd disorder is security adviser Jack Crawford, who joined the staff in August 1987 and is responsible for monitoring crowd control and anti-hooligan measures taken at League grounds. He also advises clubs on their safety problems. Again, Jack is fully qualified to take on such a role: he is the former Assistant Chief Constable of Merseyside.

In the League's general office we find a bevy of staff, all under the supervision of Sandra Whiteside, another of the League's long-serving stalwarts. Sandra joined in 1967 and since then has worked in almost every single department. She took over the general office in 1975 and by 1988 had served the League for 21 years.

The general office has two areas.

The post room is run by Liz Ashforth, with staff members Jannette Williams and Michael Southern (who in 1987 was also playing for Morecambe FC, having been a youth with Burnley). The room is a hive of activity, with printers printing, mailing machines processing letters and piles of League publications – minutes, handbooks, press releases and so on – stacked in readiness for circulation.

Two part-time telephonists, Lorna Parnell and Brenda Vause, make up the team. It is their unenviable task to juggle the calls and to know in which part of the building/country/world each member of staff happens to be, and to be pleasant at the same time. Needless to say, they always manage.

Liz Ashforth has an added responsibility – to look after the League's vast filing system, which is housed in the basement. It is here that you will find the minutes of every Management Committee meeting since 1888, plus heavy, leather-bound volumes containing records of players and attendances, and files full of correspondence, some of it going back to the First World War. Liz also looks after a small library of football books.

So when Graham Kelly needs to know who said what at an EGM in 1983, or what happened when Alan Hardaker asked clubs about admission prices in 1964, Liz finds the answer. She may also find in the basement the odd club statistician or centenary historian ploughing through some obscure League records as part of their researches. She guards a precious archive.

The second part of the general office is the special events section, formed a few years ago to look after the League's own cup competition finals (Littlewoods, Freight Rover, Simod) and the Guinness Soccer Six tournament. Sandra Whiteside runs this section with Jane Connaughton. Together they deal with ticket requests and all the numerous arrangements

necessary for the staging of a Wembley final. Sandra and Jane also bore the enormous responsibility of co-ordinating the Mercantile Credit centenary celebrations.

From the general office we climb the wide staircase at Lytham, past portraits of various Management Committees and former Presidents, to the upper storey of the League headquarters. On the landing, in a glass display case, is the ornate silver and enamelled casket presented to William McGregor when he was made a Life Member of the League in 1895. It was donated by William McGregor Junior in 1952.

The first office we come to is that of the Deputy Secretary, David Dent. Dent is one of the most experienced administrators in football, and is only the second senior member of the League's staff ever to have had experience at club level (Tom Charnley was the first).

From a farming family in Appleby, Cumbria, Dent was the youngest club secretary in the League when he joined Carlisle in 1960 at the age of twenty-three. After eighteen years at Brunton Park, he then moved to Coventry City, (he received the League's long service medal in 1981) and has been with the League since March 1984. He succeeded the late George Readle in October 1984.

As Deputy Secretary, his main task is to share the responsibility for running the League's affairs with Graham Kelly. He attends all Management Committee meetings and any other meetings which Kelly cannot manage. Dent is particularly involved with the Associate Members Advisory Committee, and is secretary to the Committee of Enquiry into Playing Surfaces, formed in 1986.

In addition, he liaises between the League and the members of the Management Committee (most of whom rarely visit Lytham), and is in overall charge of all office management and personnel arrangements at the League. Being a former club secretary himself, Dent is also a valuable source of information and advice for individual clubs.

Homes of the League

Before moving to Lytham St Annes in 1959/60, the League was based at nine different locations.

From 1892 to 1899 the office address was given as 27 Harley Street, Hanley, which was the small, unpretentious terraced home of Harry Lockett. The building no longer stands, although the street still exists. Lockett then moved to 8 Parker's Terrace, Etruria, the League's address moving with him. No trace of the street survives today.

Tom Charnley took over from the disgraced Lockett in 1902 and for a few months ran the League from his home at 248 St Paul's Road, Preston, which still stands today, a few hundred yards from Deepdale. But it was clear that the League needed an office of its own, and in 1903 Charnley found a room at 13 Winkley Street, a quiet, narrow street off the town's main shopping thoroughfare, Fishergate, close to the railway station. Also based in the building at that time was a barrister, a tailor and the Conservative Party Registration Office.

Only a year or so later, the League was on the move again. The new address was 47 Tithebarn Street, which it is thought may have belonged to a paper and rag merchant, for whom, in exchange for a peppercorn rent, Charnley was possibly able to do some part-time work. It was in Tithebarn Street that Charnley took the first step to modernity by purchasing a typewriter.

From 1913–26 the League was based at Castle Chambers, in an office which was formerly home to the Berlitz School of Languages and looked out across the Market Place to the Harris Library. When the League left, it became a Christian Science Reading Room. The League had its first telephone at this address, thus saving Charnley frequent trips over to the main post office across the street.

After Fred Howarth joined Charnley in 1921 and the League doubled in size from forty-four to eighty-eight clubs within three years, more staff became a priority, so bigger offices at the grand address of 30 Winckley Square were taken on in November 1926, at a rent of £90 per anum. A third staff member was then appointed, with a fourth arriving in 1930, and for the first time the offices were large enough to host occasional meetings of the Management Committee.

Unfortunately, the office, which faced the neatly laid-out square (where all the best offices in Preston were to be found), was requisitioned in 1941 and Fred Howarth, now in charge, hurriedly found much smaller premises round the corner at 102 Fishergate, for £55 per annum.

Immediately after the war, the League made its final move in Preston, again just around the corner, to a late Georgian terraced house at 6 Starkie Street. The house had previously been the vicarage of a nearby church, and still had a powder-room. By now the staff was growing, as were the League's responsibilities – the Provident Fund arrived in 1949, for example – but as Alan Hardaker discovered when he arrived in 1951, life at Starkie Street was still relaxed and unhurried.

Eventually, in 1958, as we related in Chapter 21, Joe Richards and Hardaker decided that the League needed more prestigious headquarters, and after converting the Sandown Hotel in Lytham St Annes, the cramped, old-fashioned Starkie Street building was sold for £3250 in 1959. The new owners then sued the League when they discovered that the hot water system didn't work.

Next to David Dent's office is that of Graham Kelly, and assisting both men is personal assistant Glynis Firth. Glynis and her assistant, Paula Barrington, deal with the daily correspondence and co-ordinate all Management Committee business. Glynis, who comes from Dewsbury, also organises AGMs, EGMs and any other divisional meetings, arranging hotel bookings and accommodation. Since joining the League in 1974, she has been one of the few women attending Annual Meetings, and understandably longs for the day when more women become involved at a higher level of the game. (At the last count, in 1987, there were in fact just two women directors in the League, both related to fellow directors, nine female club secretaries and seven female commercial managers – most of them in London and the South. Does this tell us anything about the North and Midlands?)

Both Glynis and Paula have an extra and highly important task, and that is to deal with all matters relating to the Football Grounds Improvement Trust, not only for the ninety-two League clubs but also the thirty-eight in Scotland and fourteen in Northern Ireland: their proposals, their claims, their payments and, of course, their regular enquiries. Next time you lean against a solid new crush barrier, remember that Glynis and Paula in Lytham helped to put it there.

Next along the corridor is the office of the recently formed commercial department. Here we find Doris Warren, personal assistant and secretary to Lee Walker, who is now based at the League's new office at the Wembley Conference Centre (of which more below). Doris joined the League only a few months after arriving in Britain from Canada, where she was a teacher for seven years and a legal assistant in Vancouver. Her job is to co-ordinate the League's commercial and television activities between the offices in Lytham and London.

Opposite the commercial department is the referees and fixtures department, run by ref-erees officer John Goggins, his assistant Ann Boothman, plus David Cookson and Louise Standing. We will look at the fixtures later.

The section's main job is to appoint referees, linesmen and assessors to all League matches, plus assessors to all FA Cup, Central League, Football Combination and GM Vauxhall Conference matches.

Goggins, a retired headmaster and former League referee, has 120 voluntary assessors to choose from – all former referees or linesmen. It is the task of each assessor to award marks from four to ten for each official. If a referee's performances are below average, he will be informed and advised on how to improve, but all markings are strictly confidential.

In 1987 the youngest League referee was twenty-nine and the oldest forty-eight. Although the official retiring age is forty-eight (formerly forty-seven), since 1956 from time to time the League has relaxed the age limit in order to maintain a number of experienced men on its list. In 1987/8, for example, four of the nine retiring referees were asked to stay on the list, which totalled ninety-one referees altogether.

But these men were exceptions. According to a League survey conducted in the mid 1960s, on average a referee reaches his peak between the ages of forty and forty-three, after which his marks begin to deteriorate. Furthermore, at the time of the survey, those referees who were kept on after retirement age showed a rapid decline during the following season.

Another reason for not extending the age limit is that the League needs to have a steady input of younger men. Every referee aspires to the League list, and like non-League clubs he must follow a definite system of promotion. His final staging post before the League will be one of the three feeder or 'panel' leagues: that is, the GM Vauxhall Conference, Central League or Football Combination.

The current fee for a referee is £60 per game, for linesmen £30 per game, plus expenses. Financing this costs the League approximately

£650,000 a season. But will there ever be full-time professional referees? Not if the League or, indeed, the referees have any say in it.

Firstly, many referees are already in well-paid jobs and would have to be offered handsome salaries to be tempted away. Secondly, most referees don't reach maturity until their early forties, just at the point where they have established themselves in their own careers. And even if they did give up their work to take up the whistle full time, they would still have to retire around the age of forty-eight.

Thirdly, if the best referees were professionals, they would have to be given all the prestigious matches, thus reducing the incentive for ordinary referees on their way up.

Finally, and most importantly, the League could pay a referee a million pounds per match and he might still make mistakes. Money would not improve his judgement. Indeed, it might even impair it if he fears for his job.

So there will be no professional referees in the Football League for many years to come.

Before we move into another department of the League's offices, another survey conducted by the League in the mid 1960s revealed that a League referee runs on average 8 miles and a linesman 4.74 miles in each game. Each official runs slightly more in the first half than the second, and altogether covers less distance in a higher-class game.

Next door to the referees section is John Goggins' other assistant, Carole Roberts, whose main concern is the fixtures. This means answering a barrage of enquiries from clubs, the public (often from overseas) and the press. If a club wishes to arrange a friendly match, it must consult Carole first, in case the date and venue clash with a nearby League game. If a League match is rearranged, then Carole's job is to inform the media.

But the most complex part of the process of arranging fixtures is not actually done by the League, as we shall now discover with a brief sortie back into history.

'Fixity of Fixtures'

When the League was born in 1888 there existed no mathematical method of putting into practice Mr McGregor's 'fixity of fixtures'. But since there were only twelve clubs, it was sufficient to hold a ballot to determine which clubs would play at home on the first Saturday. After that it was up to the clubs to workout dates between themselves.

Not surprisingly, the system often led to fierce arguments, and as the League expanded to two divisions and started accepting clubs from the same city or region, the need for outside help soon became apparent.

It arrived quite out of the blue from a Mr W. F. Fletcher of Birmingham, who attended a Management Committee meeting in March 1898 to demonstrate his system for fixture making. It was an almost immediate success, his first sample list being adopted with just a few amendments.

The Fletcher system was used by the League until 1914/15, after which Charles Sutcliffe perfected his own formula, adopted by the clubs when the League restarted in 1919. Mr Fletcher was apparently rather miffed about this – he had been paid around £25 a season before the war – and accused the League of using his system without paying for it. Eventually, in June 1924, he confronted the Committee with a claim for £120 for the copyright and the remaining charts which he had already printed.

On seeing Sutcliffe's formula, however, Fletcher had to admit that his copyright hadn't been infringed and that with the Third Division in operation his charts would not have been adequate. Nevertheless, the Committee did pay him, and the surplus Fletcher charts are still in the League's possession, gathering dust in their original brown paper wrapping in the basement at Lytham St Annes.

Sutcliffe's system was his pride and joy, and the jealously guarded charts with which he drew up the fixtures were assumed to possess almost magical significance (see Chapter 10).

Every summer, Sutcliffe would lock himself away with his son and daughter, working uninterruptedly for two or three days and nights to come up with the final fixture list. For his efforts the League paid him 150 guineas in 1922. His son Harold (heir to the charts) was also paid £100 for his 'exhaustive work' in typing up the lists.

Unfortunately, the Sutcliffe system was not entirely to the clubs' liking, however. They particularly objected to the fact that they would often face the same opponents, home and away, on successive Saturdays. In 1923, therefore, they voted to return to the Fletcher system, a great blow to Sutcliffe's morale.

But the little lawyer was loath to give up his new obsession. He adapted his charts accordingly, and won back the commission straight away. From 1919 to 1967, therefore, the League fixtures materialised courtesy of the Sutcliffe family. When Charles died in 1939, Harold took over.

Fans take fixture lists so much for granted that few appreciate the complexities of arranging some 2000 games to suit every single club. The astonishing aspect of Sutcliffe's system was that it generally came up with a first draft which needed only about eight changes a year. Not even the modern-day computer can better that.

According to journalist Eric Todd of the *Guardian*, who was once allowed a peek at the hallowed Sutcliffe charts, they resembled a chequerboard of 924 red and white squares. Every club was allocated a number, which Sutcliffe changed every year so that the fixtures would always be different.

That chart was used for the First and Second Division. Another chart with a few extra squares covered the remaining two Third Divisions. But before Sutcliffe could settle any of the fixtures, he had to refer to another chart which was divided into eight sections: all four divisions of the League, plus the four reserve competitions which, of course, had to be dovetailed with League fixtures.

The clubs were then divided into cities or regions: three in the Birmingham area, three in Liverpool and so on. Each club could choose one or more 'pairing', that is, another club whose fixtures should not clash with their own.

Altogether there were about 150 pairings, which change each year according to a club's status (see diagram for the current pairings).

Finally, the chart had eight separate lines set aside for holiday and mid-week dates. (In Harold Sutcliffe's era, this section was complicated by the introduction of floodlights. Some clubs had them, some didn't.)

It was not only League clubs who benefited from the charts. The Sutcliffes also used them for the Lancashire Combination and the Southern League, each of which had two divisions.

Working alone, Harold reckoned that the League fixtures took him 150 hours to complete, starting in March and finishing in July. He recalled making only one error, when he inadvertently mixed up Sheffield Wednesday with Sheffield United on one list.

He told Eric Todd: 'I learned everything from my father, who spent many hours perfecting his system, and I shall never forget his delight when he was satisfied he had found the answer. I was only a lad at the time, but the more I worked with him the more I was amazed at the simplicity of the fixture chart, although the allocation of numbers to the clubs is somewhat complicated.'

(Harold Sutcliffe followed his father in more than just the fixture making. He qualified as a solicitor in 1926 and practised in the family offices in Rawtenstall all his life. He was an active Methodist, and shortly after the Second World War sat as a Liberal councillor in the same ward as had his father before the First World War. He was even married twice, as was Charles, and inherited his father's dislike of the pools. But he smoked a pipe rather than cigarettes, and did not have his father's frail physique, nor, indeed, his passion for the game.)

Only in 1936 did the League start charging outsiders for the reproduction of the fixtures, as a result of the Pools War and Watson Hartley's promptings (see Chapter 14). There were two scales of charges. For advertising wall cards, pocket cards and annuals, the fee was five guineas plus one guinea for each club's list reproduced. For football and sports annuals issued by the press, there was no set fee but a donation was requested.

The pools, of course, paid nothing until 1959, so the income was relatively small. In 1949, for example, it reached £900, of which £264 went to Harold Sutcliffe to pay for his time and expenses.

If the system had a weakness it was that no one apart from Sutcliffe knew how it worked. For that reason, Alan Hardaker was most concerned that Harold should teach someone at Lytham how to use the charts before he died.

Once the League negotiated the pools agreement on copyright, however, the fixtures assumed an even greater importance. Indeed, they became the League's largest source of income. Hardaker therefore offered to buy the copyright of the charts from Sutcliffe in 1961. He offered £250 at first, but they settled on £400.

Harold drew up his last fixtures in 1967, after which he died in October, aged sixty-four, thus ending a family involvement with the League which spanned over seventy-five years. Harold missed not one single Annual Meeting between 1919 and 1967.

Sadly, the famous Sutcliffe charts have not survived. But Charles would have been the first man to show enthusiasm for the task facing his son's successors. This was to draw up a computer program which would take the charts' place.

Since 1967, various computer companies have worked on the fixtures, the present matchmakers being CAP Industry Limited of Alderley Edge, Cheshire, who have had the commission since 1982. Neville Hawkins was responsible for developing the program, which

fits quite comfortably on to one floppy disk, thin and small enough for Charles Sutcliffe to have easily lost in one of his voluminous, bulging briefcases.

Together with Janice Wood and Steve Richards of CAP, Hawkins explained the intricacies and problems facing the computer operators every year. In brief, these are the main points they have to consider.

● *Pairings. Each club fills in a questionnaire detailing which clubs it would like to be paired with. As the diagram shows (see page 370), it is not simply a question of pairing Manchester United with Manchester City. Neighbouring clubs like Bury, Rochdale and Stockport want to avoid clashes with the big clubs, too, although in many cases this is unavoidable unless games are switched to a Friday night, which the computer cannot arrange. That is up to the clubs concerned and to the fixtures office at Lytham.*

Pairing is not simply a matter of proximity. It can also hinge on local transport conditions, demography and policing arrangements. For example, Scarborough and York are forty-one miles apart, but they are covered by the same police department. They cannot have matches clashing, therefore. Pairings also change as clubs swap divisions.

Not all requests for pairing can be satisfied. In west London, for example, Chelsea, Fulham and QPR cannot avoid clashing, so one club, usually the one in the lowest division, must always suffer. The same applies with Tranmere, who can never avoid clashing with Liverpool or Everton except by switching to a Friday night or Sunday (which they can do no more than six times a season).

Whatever a club wants, if the police object to a certain pairing arrangement it will not be put into effect. For example, in London the police prefer certain clubs to be at home on the same afternoons, to keep their supporters apart.

● *Clashes with other events. Each area has counter-attractions which must not clash with home matches, to avoid overstretching the police and local transport as well as to protect attendance levels.*

For example: the Farnborough Air Show —

Fletcher's Simplex Tables for Arrangement of Fixtures.

Series for a League of 20 Clubs.

The numbers at head of columns are those of the Clubs forming the Association, and the numbers underneath show which of their fellow Clubs are played in the successive rounds of the Competition.

Number of Club.	1	2	3	4	5	6	7	8	9	10	11	12	13	14	15	16	17	18	19	20	Number of Club.
No. 1 Match	2	1	19	18	17	16	15	14	13	12	20	10	9	8	7	6	5	4	3	11	No. 1 Match
" 2 "	3	20	1	19	18	17	16	15	14	13	12	11	10	9	8	7	6	5	4	2	" 2 "
" 3 "	4	3	2	1	19	18	17	16	15	14	13	20	11	10	9	8	7	6	5	12	" 3 "
" 4 "	5	4	20	2	1	19	18	17	16	15	14	13	12	11	10	9	8	7	6	3	" 4 "
" 5 "	6	5	4	3	2	1	19	18	17	16	15	14	20	12	11	10	9	8	7	13	" 5 "
" 6 "	7	6	5	20	3	2	1	19	18	17	16	15	14	13	12	11	10	9	8	4	" 6 "
" 7 "	8	7	6	5	4	3	2	1	19	18	17	16	15	20	13	12	11	10	9	14	" 7 "
" 8 "	9	8	7	6	20	4	3	2	1	19	18	17	16	15	14	13	12	11	10	5	" 8 "
" 9 "	10	9	8	7	6	5	4	3	2	1	19	18	17	16	20	14	13	12	11	15	" 9 "
" 10 "	11	10	9	8	7	20	5	4	3	2	1	19	18	17	16	15	14	13	12	6	" 10 "
" 11 "	12	11	10	9	8	7	6	5	4	3	2	1	19	18	17	20	15	14	13	16	" 11 "
" 12 "	13	12	11	10	9	8	20	6	5	4	3	2	1	19	18	17	16	15	14	7	" 12 "
" 13 "	14	13	12	11	10	9	8	7	6	5	4	3	2	1	19	18	20	16	15	17	" 13 "
" 14 "	15	14	13	12	11	10	9	20	7	6	5	4	3	2	1	19	18	17	16	8	" 14 "
" 15 "	16	15	14	13	12	11	10	9	8	7	6	5	4	3	2	1	19	20	17	18	" 15 "
" 16 "	17	16	15	14	13	12	11	10	20	8	7	6	5	4	3	2	1	19	18	9	" 16 "
" 17 "	18	17	16	15	14	13	12	11	10	9	8	7	6	5	4	3	2	1	20	19	" 17 "
" 18 "	19	18	17	16	15	14	13	12	11	20	9	8	7	6	5	4	3	2	1	10	" 18 "
" 19 "	20	19	18	17	16	15	14	13	12	11	10	9	8	7	6	5	4	3	2	1	" 19 "

After the 19th Match, the Return Contests are play[ed]...

A special detailed fixture list for each of the [Clubs] — the return contests (as suggested by the Author) being arran[ged]... arrangement should be adhered to, it will be seen th[at]... alternate as it is possible to arrange them.

Mr Fletcher of Birmingham compiled the League's fixtures until Charles Sutcliffe came up with his magical charts during the First World War.

INSTRUCTIONS FOR THE USE OF FLETCHER'S SIMPLEX TABLES FOR ARRANGEMENT OF FIXTURES.

FOR CRICKET AND FOOTBALL LEAGUES, &c., &c.

The Table. The Table with the square block of figures in the centre is a complete plan of the competition, shewing the programme of all the Clubs.

Each number represents a club.

A Ballot is taken to decide which club each number shall represent.

This one Ballot arranges the whole fixtures of every Club in the League.

The Detailed Fixture Lists. Read the columns of the Table downwards. Each column is one Club's programme, the Club denoted by the number at the head of the column having to play its fellow Clubs in the same order as their respective numbers appear underneath.

As soon as the number of each Club has been fixed by the Ballot, the representative of each Club is supplied with the Detailed Fixture List numbered at top with the number drawn by his Club.

On each list the numbers of the opposing Clubs are printed, in the same order as they appear on the Table, and the Home and Away arrangements are planned ready.

When the names of the opposing Clubs are written opposite their respective numbers, the Fixture List is quite complete.

Dates. There must be a date fixed for each round of the Competition, and all the matches in a round must, as far as possible, be played on the date set out. If the date of any match has to be altered or postponed, the match must take place on some date which is not reserved for any of the other rounds.

Method of Ballot. Slips of paper bearing the names of the Clubs must be provided, and also as many slips of paper numbered 1 and up.

The name slips must be placed in one hat, and the number slips in another.

One slip at a time from each hat must be drawn, and the result of each draw must be called out by the Chairman.

The representative of each Club must carefully note down the numbers drawn for the various Clubs, and, when the Ballot is over, must obtain his own Club's Fixture List, and write thereon the names of the opposing Clubs ON THE SAME LINES AS THEIR RESPECTIVE NUMBERS ARE PRINTED.

Special method of Ballot to accommodate neighbouring Clubs who do not want their matches to clash. In Tables for Leagues of 8 Clubs (1 and 5), (2 and 6), (3 and 7), (4 and 8).

" 10 " (1 and 6), (2 and 7), (3 and 8), (4 and 9), (5 and 10).

" 12 " (1 and 7), (2 and 8), (3 and 9), (4 and 10), (5 and 11), (6 and 12).

" 14 " (1 and 8), (2 and 9), (3 and 10), (4 and 11), (5 and 12), (6 and 13), (7 and 14).

" 16 " (1 and 8), (2 and 9), (3 and 10), (4 and 10), (5 and 11), (6 and 12), (7 and 13), (8 and 15).

On every occasion when one of any of the above pairs plays at home, the other plays away, and vice versa. Consequently, when there is a pair of neighbouring Clubs in a League who do not want their Fixtures to clash, they must be fixed up with one of the above pairs of numbers.

It is necessary to pair such Clubs first.

When preparing for the Ballot, leave their name slips out of the name slip hat, but put all the number slips in the number slip hat. Draw one number, and allot it to one of the pair of neighbouring Clubs, and then give the opposite number, as specified above, to the other of such a pair of Clubs.

The number given to the second Club should be taken out of the hat.

When the neighbouring Clubs have been disposed of, the Ballot amongst the independent Clubs for the remaining numbers will be carried out.

Important Note for Leagues composed of an ODD number of Clubs. The independent Clubs will not in any way suffer through allowing a pair or pairs of neighbouring Clubs to have first draw.

N.B.—It will be observed that all the tables are mapped out for combinations of even numbers. In case an Association is composed of an odd number of clubs, the series of tables suitable for the next even number must be used.

For example, an Association of 9 clubs must use series of tables for 10 clubs, and in drawing lots for the numbers, one of the numbers, say No. 10, must be left out of the hat, and in each round of the competition the club which should play No. 10, or the dummy club, has an open date. Thus each of the 9 clubs has one open date in each half of the programme.

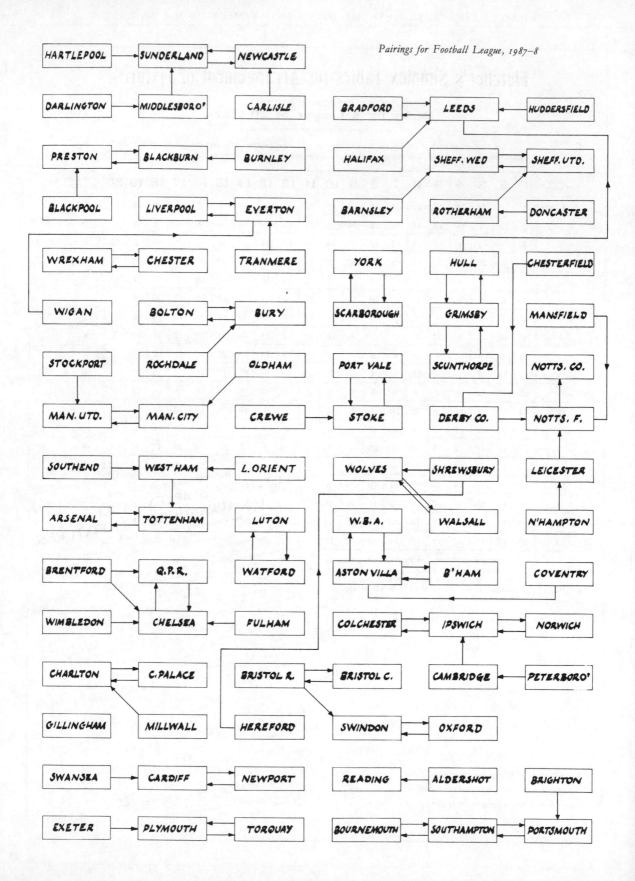

Aldershot; the Grand National – all Liverpool clubs; the Nottingham Goose Fair – Forest and County; political party conferences – Brighton, Blackpool and Bournemouth; county cricket matches – Northampton; St Leger – Doncaster; Twickenham rugby matches – Brentford.

Then there are clubs such as Cardiff, Swansea, Newport, Wigan and Hull who try to avoid clashes with neighbouring Rugby Union and Rugby League fixtures. Hull, however, like to be at home on the day of the Hull Fair, just as Fulham prefer to be at home on the day of the Boat Race.

● Midweek variations. According to local customs such as market days, early closing, industrial shifts and school holidays, each club has its own preference for mid-week fixtures. Most choose Tuesdays, but Port Vale prefer Monday nights. Distance has also to be considered in the lower divisions, where clubs prefer their longest journeys to be kept for evening kick-offs, as this obviates the need for an overnight hotel stop the night before the match.

● Holiday dates. Every club wants to be at home on a holiday, and no club wants to have to travel far on Boxing Day or at New Year. Equally, some towns have special Wakes weeks when they prefer to be at home. To be fair, the computer must alternate holiday fixtures so that, for example, Birmingham City don't get Boxing Day games at home two seasons in a row to the detriment of Aston Villa.

● Cash flow. The computer mustn't give any one club three or more home or away games in a row, for obvious financial reasons. Nor can it have a sequence with four out of any five games at home or away. Clubs also prefer to have strictly alternating home and away games at the beginning and end of each season, to balance their cash flow. No club wants a local derby on the first day of the season, since it is a waste of a traditionally lucrative home fixture.

Having stored in its memory bank all those factors, the computer can then start to weave its merry way through the fixture jungle. It starts tentatively around May, but cannot begin too seriously until the last games are over, which from 1987 onwards means after the play-offs.

After the computer prints out an initial dummy run, which takes a week, the CAP team then initiates 'a clash analysis', checking that pairing requests have been met whenever possible. They must use a certain amount of judgement, because where two sets of pairings are found to clash for one particular fixture, the computer is unable to establish which one should have priority. That is where human skills come in, interpreting a diagram like the one duplicated here.

By now it is mid June, and the list is ready to submit to the League.

At Lytham, John Goggins and Carole Roberts check through the entire list to make sure that Cup dates have been allowed for and that no important matches clash with later rounds of the cup competitions. The amended list is then fed back into the IBM.

The second draft is now ready for the scrutiny of the clubs, who between them, on average, request about ten changes each season. Other date changes might have to be made to accommodate the television companies or, in November 1987 for example, to accommodate the wishes of England manager Bobby Robson (who asked for his squad to have a Saturday off before the vital European Championship qualifying match in Yugoslavia).

Finally, the fixture list is completed and ready for the clubs and the public. It is now the last week of June, and the preparations for the new season can begin with even greater anticipation than ever.

All that remains is for Carole Roberts at Lytham to keep a beady eye on proceedings. After seventeen years at the League, Carole, a keen skier and marathon runner, has learnt to keep her fingers crossed for the weather and pray that there won't be too many drawn games in the cup competitions.

Such is the complexity of Mr McGregor's 'fixity of fixtures'.

From the main building at Lytham we now move across the driveway to an adjacent block where there are two more sections of the League (housed, incidentally, in the former home of Alan Hardaker).

Downstairs is the all-important accounts department, headed by the League's longest-serving member of staff, Assistant Secretary and accountant Norman Thomas. Norman first became involved in the late 1940s when he was working for the League's auditors in Preston. He then moved to Starkie Street to administer the Provident Fund shortly after it was established in 1949, and is thus the only current League official to have worked at the former offices. He was awarded a long-service medal in 1972.

Working with Norman are Christine Mooney and Angela Wyatt. Together, this trio deals with every single penny of the League's annual turnover – £10.6 million at the last count. Transactions range from £1.3 million, received from various sponsors, to £3400 paid out for substitute boards, or fifty pence for a referee's sandwich.

Upstairs is the registrations department, run by Mike Foster, his assistant Sheila Murphy, and Debbie Singleton. Mike has been with the League for fifteen years, Sheila and Debbie seven years each. Secretary Sue Baron helps out both here and in the accounts section below.

Registrations is perhaps one of the most intriguing sections at Lytham, for it is here that all transfers and new players are dealt with. In season 1986/7 the office had to process 231 temporary transfers, 374 full transfers, 529 trainees signing on and a further 604 new registrations. A particularly busy time is the transfer deadline, which falls on the fourth Thursday in March, when clubs make a last gasp effort to sign the player who will bring them to glory or save them from despair. In March 1987 eighty-two transfers went through on the day of the deadline, but even this figure has been surpassed on busy days in high summer.

Then there is the 5.00 p.m. deadline every Thursday afternoon when transfer forms have to be sent in order to allow a player to play for his new club on the following Saturday. Thanks to modern technology, the clubs no longer have to appear in person with the required documentation. These can be sent by fax machines, by telex or in the post, as long as they are dispatched before the Thursday deadline.

Even so, the registrations department must actually check the details before a newly-signed player can play, which means a skeleton staff operating on Saturdays to vet any last-minute problems.

Before the communications revolution, beating the deadline was a much more frantic affair, with mad dashes to Lytham being a common occurrence, and desperate managers or secretaries occasionally turning up on the doorstep with only minutes to spare. Staff still remember when Brian Clough made the trip to Lytham by helicopter but still missed the deadline.

In order to reduce the instances of clubs buying players they can't really afford, thus forcing other clubs to be chasing bad debts all around the country, the League now operates a system whereby every club must pay a minimum of 50 per cent of the transfer fee on signing, with the balance payable over the next twelve months (plus VAT and a 5 per cent levy, which goes towards the players' pension fund).

All fees have to be channelled through the registrations department, which makes sure that the payment is cleared, whether it be £1 million for a star player or £1000 for a veteran reserve. The League never discloses details of the actual fee. It is entirely up to the clubs to reveal the amount if they so desire.

Apart from the general excitement of transfers, the registrations department also oversees the re-engagement of players and the Associate Schoolboy Scheme, and is closely involved with the Football League Appeals Committee, the Professional Football Negotiating Committee and the Footballers' Further Education and Vocational Training Society, which itself incorporates the Youth Training Scheme.

A copy of every player's contract is kept in this office – each one has to be carefully vetted to make sure it adheres to the regulations – and also, records of every single player's appearances. This is in order to keep a check on such things as bonus payments.

Each club has to send in its team sheet from every match within seven days. The referee sends in one too, and each appearance is dutifully entered into the records. (Even so, discrepancies do occasionally arise, and every year statistician Jack Rollin comes to Lytham to check the League's records alongside his own.)

In this day and age one would have assumed that appearance records would have been kept by a computer. In fact, the registrations department did try this for a year before they went back to using the set of wonderful leatherbound ledgers which had been tried and trusted for decades. A comforting, fascinating place, the registrations department.

Finally, we leave Lytham St Annes for the Wembley Conference Centre, where we find the League's newest venture, the London branch of its commercial department. The idea for a League presence in the capital originated with Alan Hardaker, was tried briefly in the 1970s (by sharing an office with the League's insurers in the City of London), mulled over again by Jack Dunnett in the early 1980s, and finally found favour in 1987.

The advantages are obvious. London is the biggest centre of commercial activity, and with the League increasingly able and anxious to attract sponsorship and other commercial interest, it became imperative to have staff 'on the spot'.

Heading the new department is Trevor Phillips, the League's commercial director. Trevor's responsibility is to promote and enhance the image of League football, while using all his marketing guile to increase the revenue intake of both the League as a unit and the ninety-two clubs as a collection of outlets.

He must also help to guide clubs through the often perilous world of commercialdom, while accepting, often reluctantly, that he cannot always persuade them to accept his plans. An example of his difficulties came at the 1987 AGM, when the clubs voted against the proposal for players to sport the Mercantile Credit centenary logo on their club shirts.

But Trevor's defeats are far outweighed by his successes, which include the dramatic efforts to sign up a sponsor eleven days before the centenary season began, after the *Today* newspaper had abruptly withdrawn. 'The two most hectic weeks of my life', he confessed after proudly signing up Barclays.

Phillips is keen to promote the 'family' aspect of League football. He believes in tearing down fences, not building more, and sees the family enclosure as one positive way to encourage new supporters and create a new concept in football: that is, a ground where parents can drop off their kids, happy in the knowledge that they'll be safe; where women and children will find the kind of welcome which they have come to expect in other leisure facilities, and where youngsters can meet their heroes and feel part of the club.

Some people dismiss this kind of approach as pandering to American gimmickry and as being irrelevant to the traditions of the game. Trevor Phillips points to attendance figures and the game's image in recent years, and stresses that not only has change got to come, but it has to be in line with changes occurring throughout the leisure and entertainment industry.

If there is a deal to be struck or a commercial event to co-ordinate, be it with Barclays, Mercantile Credit, Littlewoods, Freight Rover, Simod, Mitre, Guinness or any number of other companies interested in the League, Trevor Phillips will be at the heart of the activity. He spent eighteen years as general sales manager for the Beecham Group, and is now a tonic all of his own to the League.

With Philips at the new Wembley offices is Lee Walker, one of the longest serving members of staff at the League. Lee started out his working life as a qualified bookbinder in Leicester. He then became a printer of the *Football League Review*, joining the League's staff when the magazine moved from Leicester to Lytham in 1967. Not only did he print the *Review*, but at weekends he ended up driving from Torquay to Newcastle to deliver it.

From circulation manager, Lee moved to the referees and linesmen's office, which he eventually took over when the late George Readle became Deputy Secretary in 1973. From there he moved to become fixtures secretary for ten years, and thereafter concentrated on the television and commercial aspects of the League.

Lee's current position is that of sales and marketing director. With twenty years' experience at Lytham behind him, no one, surely, knows the product better than Walker.

Also in the Wembley office are personal assistant Mo Widdecombe, who came to the League with over fifteen years' experience of working for the Canadian Government and, more recently, a major international construction company, and receptionist Lorraine Shuck, who joined the League in late 1987.

And that just about concludes our tour around the League's offices and its staff of thirty-one. There remains, however, just one of the Men Who Make League Football, and a rather important character he is, too.

Our history began with the first President of the League, William McGregor. It ends, a hundred years later, with President number twelve, Philip Carter.

CHAPTER THIRTY-SIX

Philip Carter – Past Tense but Future Perfect?

*T*he twelfth President of the Football League is the man who defied a ninety-eight-year-old tradition by becoming the first League President never to have served on the Management Committee before taking office.

In most other respects, however, Philip Carter fits perfectly into the distinguished line of League leaders. He is the third in succession to have been born in Scotland, the third to have come from the city of Liverpool, and the second to be associated with Everton. He also shares a similar background with the founder. William McGregor was born in Scotland and started out in life as a retailer. The same is true of Philip Carter.

Carter's days north of the border were brief, however, (as were Jack Dunnett's). Born in Glasgow in May 1927 he moved to Liverpool as a two-year-old, and like most Liverpudlians was blooded young. He saw his first match at Goodison Park at the age of four, and says he's been thinking about the game ever since.

As a youth at Waterloo Grammar School, he spent more time on the playing fields than on the Goodison terraces. Then, after the war, he was conscripted into the Fleet Air Arm as a pilot. Some might say that he has been piloting ever since. Once out of uniform he joined the retailing division of Littlewoods (the pools company), rising to store manager, then chief buyer and eventually, in 1976, to managing director.

From the 1950s onwards Littlewoods was practically a branch office of Everton. The company's millionaire owner, Sir John Moores, became chairman of Everton, and the two boards have been closely linked ever since. When Carter became managing director at Littlewoods in 1976, his predecessor had been an Everton director, then in 1987 his own successor at Littlewoods was also elected to the board. Carter himself made the inevitable progression on to the Everton board in 1973, and in 1977 became chairman, thus following in the footsteps of his mentor, Sir John Moores, who also led both Everton and Littlewoods at the same time.

Men from a pools company occupying Will Cuff's seat at Goodison? The old master would have been horrified. He fought the Pools War in 1936 to keep companies like Littlewoods out of football.

But no doubt even Cuff might have softened once he had espied the trophy cabinet. At one point it was empty. Everton had reached a low point, near the foot of the division and with crowds well below 20,000. Another chairman might have sacked the manager, but Philip Carter stuck with his man, and his man, Howard Kendall, responded.

In 1983 the Toffeemen put their sticky patch behind them and twice wrested the League Championship away from their neighbours at Anfield. Everton also won the FA Cup and the European Cup Winners' Cup, and were runners-up in the League, the FA Cup (twice) and the Milk Cup, all in the space of three hectic years.

Success at Goodison did Carter's prestige no harm at all as he embarked in 1982 upon the road which would eventually lead to the presidency. As we read in Chapter 33, he began chairing informal gatherings of First Division chairmen who were unhappy with League affairs. From an original group of six, the numbers grew to ten, and then Carter found himself chairing meetings of all the Full Members.

As the League lurched from one low point to another in 1985, Philip Carter soon emerged as the leader of the discontents. He was young (ish), successful (with a CBE to boot), and after taking early retirement from Littlewoods in 1983, he was also able to devote plenty of time to the League's cause.

'One has got to have a sense of purpose,' is Carter's creed. 'There's no point in actually being involved with an organization if you're merely turning up to rubber stamp somebody else's initiatives. One should try to improve any organization you're part of. I didn't make a conscious decision to lead a breakaway, but it was a conscious decision to lead, or to help to lead the First Division clubs who wanted to air their views.'

Before he became President, Carter's first official League duty was as a member of the Television Negotiating Committee which hammered out a four-year deal with the BBC and ITV, worth £19.8 million, only to see it tossed out by the clubs in February 1985. That experience alone would have given him some indication of the frustrations and difficulties of League management.

Then followed the disastrous events of May 1985 at Bradford, Birmingham and Brussels. Pressure on the existing leadership grew, and Carter became a focus of the so-called Super League movement. The leading clubs wanted a bigger slice of the cake, a bigger say in League affairs, and wanted it so badly that they threatened to form their own competition.

Not even Charles Sutcliffe or Will Cuff could have bullied their way out of a threat like this one. As we have seen, up until the last hours of the negotiations the very future of the dear old League hung in the balance; but tradition, the promptings of Gordon Taylor, good sense and compromise finally prevailed. Carter was no longer a Super Leaguer but a Football Leaguer, and in May 1986 he became the twelfth President. He had just turned fifty-nine.

Early retirement for Philip Carter has proved to be the equivalent of most people's idea of a full-time job. Apart from being President of the League, a Vice President of the FA and chairman of Everton, he is chairman of the Merseyside Tourism Board, chairman of the Croxteth Trust, chairman of the Empire Trust (a Liverpool theatre), and a member of the Merseyside Development Corporation. He also helps to raise money for Liverpool's disadvantaged communities.

From all this we can gather two things about Philip Carter. Firstly, he has rather a soft spot for Liverpool. A man of his achievements might easily have been lured to London. Secondly, he is not just a businessman. After leaving Littlewoods he could have joined any number of company boards. There were certainly offers. He could have concentrated on increasing his capital, or he could have simply put his feet up and enjoyed a well-earned break. Instead, he dashes around Merseyside and the country from meeting to meeting doing work for which he is paid not a penny.

William McGregor and Charles Sutcliffe would have approved of Philip Carter, except perhaps in one respect. They were both Liberals, while Carter is chairman of the Liverpool Conservative Association. But, as he admits himself, he has often backed unlikely causes. He took on Everton when they were at a low ebb, and he embraces Toryism in an age when the Government is about as popular in Liverpool as a blockage in the Mersey tunnel.

So Carter is a true blue, in both football and politics. But he can be said to be on the 'caring' side of modern Conservatism; a pragmatist who is quite willing to deal with Liverpool's

BELOW

*Sponsorship and new silverware — the
meaning of success in the modern era.*

Jack Dunnett, the young Labour activist, arrives at Brentford in January 1967. He and Jim Gregory of QPR planned the first ground-sharing arrangement in the League. The fans were not amused and Dunnett moved on to higher things at Notts County.

The Management Committee at Lytham St Annes, October 1984. Back row (left to right): Graham Kelly (Secretary), Sir Arthur South (Norwich), John Smith (Liverpool), Geoff Smith (Watford), Alan Everiss (WBA), Ian Jones (Doncaster), David Dent (Deputy Secretary). Front row: Robert Daniel (Torquay), Jack Wiseman (B'ham), Jack Dunnett (President), Dick Wragg (Sheff Utd), Christopher Needler (Hull).

ABOVE

11 May 1985: a day of celebration at Third Division champions Bradford City turned to tragedy as fire swept through the old wooden stand at Valley Parade, killing 56 people. It was the worst disaster to befall a Football League club, and like so many disasters, could have been avoided.

LEFT

Sir Norman Chester – his two major reports on football and the League, in 1968 and 1983, were dismissed by a majority of clubs. By 1985 he was vindicated. After his death, a football research centre was set up in his name at Leicester University in 1987.

Defenders of the League: Professor Sir John Wood (left) and Gordon Taylor. After all the years of antagonism between the union and the League, it was ironic that Taylor, as Secretary of the PFA, should play such a prominent role in saving the League. Wood, a tireless chairman of various independent tribunals, worked with the Commission on Industrial Relations to transform relationships between the players and the League.

The moment of truth for the Football League. Graham Kelly and Jack Dunnett listen intently at the historic EGM of 28 April 1986, at the Cumberland Hotel, London. The League was saved, but Dunnett became the first President to be voted out of office.

A galaxy of stars line up for the Mercantile Credit Centenary Classic at Wembley Stadium on 8 August 1987. Thirty-three players from 14 different countries took part. The League XI won 3–0, Diego Maradona (fifth from right, front row) received a reported £100,000 for appearing, but Michel Platini of France (second right, front row) playing his last game before retiring, won the applause. (For team line-ups see Appendix Three).

Charles Sutcliffe's charts are no more. Janice Wood, Neville Hawkins and Steve Richard of CAP feed in the vital floppy disk which will sort the fixtures for the League's Centenary season. As a youth, Harold Sutcliffe (inset) helped his father compile the fixtures, until inheriting the task in 1939. It took him 150 hours to complete one season's fixture lists. Sutcliffe attended every single Annual Meeting between 1919 and his death in 1967.

*The Management Committee, 1987–8.
Back row (left to right): Ken Bates
(Chelsea), Graham Kelly (Secretary),
Bill Fox (Blackburn), Ron Noades
(C. Palace), David Dent (Deputy
Secretary). Front row: Ian Stott
(Oldham), Bert McGee (Sheff Wed),
Philip Carter (President), Jack Dunnett
(Notts Co), David Dein (Arsenal).*

ABOVE

The Lytham St Annes team 1987. Back row (left to right): Chris Mooney, Doris Warren, Michael Southern, Andy Williamson, Jannette Williams, Sheila Murphy, Mike Foster, David Cookson, Carole Roberts, Debbie Singleton. Middle row: Marion Ainge, Lorna Parnell, Ann Boothman, Jane Connaughton, Lee Walker, Angela Wyatt, Sandra Whiteside, Brenda Vause, Glynis Firth. Front row: Jack Crawford, David Dent, Graham Kelly, Norman Thomas and John Goggins. (Not in picture; Paula Barrington, Liz Ashforth, Sue Baron and Louise Standing).

RIGHT

The League's new Commercial Department, based at Wembley (left to right): Lee Walker, Lorraine Chuck, Trevor Phillips and Mo Widdecombe.

LEFT

*Philip Carter – twelfth President of the
Football League.*

BELOW

*Tom Finney on behalf of Preston North
End, accompanied by representatives of the
eleven other founder member clubs, stand
outside the entrance to Birmingham
Cathedral before the service to celebrate the
founding of the Football League, 13 April
1988.*

left-wing council if it will benefit the city. And unlike Margaret Thatcher, says one who has dealt with Philip Carter, the man is for turning. He will listen to both sides of an argument, he will weigh up the evidence, and he will always come up with a decision. Sometimes, just sometimes, that decision will reflect a change of heart (as in the contretemps with Robert Maxwell in early 1988).

Carter is also a practised delegator, a team leader who likes a good argument only as long as his opponent is armed with the facts. If not, he becomes impatient and he will flatten the opposition with his own set of facts. (This, of course, was Charles Sutcliffe's forté.)

Philip Carter is very much a man of the modern age. He has learnt the efficacy of combining public charm with hard-nosed practicality. He speaks a language which men like Sutcliffe and McKenna would find quite incomprehensible. Football has become 'the product', clubs are now 'outlets'. These are the words of a man who has spent forty years in retailing, which is probably just as well, because a President of the League nowadays has to be as much a marketing expert as he also has to be a diplomat.

In private, Philip Carter is said to be a difficult man to get to know. Some of his critics call him 'a cold fish'. Others say he is actually quite shy. But amongst friends, the twelfth President is apparently the life and soul of a party. He loves good restaurants and he loves entertaining.

What little spare time he has from his 'early retirement' is spent with his wife and family (three children and four grandchildren, to whom he is patently devoted), in his garden, or at the opera, ballet or concerts (mostly the Liverpool Philharmonic and preferably Mozart, Wagner or Sibelius). His reputation is like his attire – always correct and quite spotless.

In short, Philip Carter is a thoroughly decent sort of chap who manages to be powerful and amicable at the same time. 'He's a winner', said one man with whom he had worked for thirty years.

This is just as well for the Football League as it enters its second century. Our hundred years of history have shown that whatever else the League desperately requires, leadership is of prime importance. All the great Presidents have led fearlessly and tirelessly. They have had to make unpleasant decisions and face a barrage of criticism from self-opinionated club chairmen, while at the same time putting on a brave face to the Management Committee and a friendly face to the world. This was as true in 1888 as it is in 1988.

Despite his being outvoted during the Maxwell affair and despite the disappointing reception given to some of the centenary events, few people close to the game doubt that Philip Carter has the energy and the self-confidence to tackle the difficult years ahead. Equally, few can deny that some of the issues facing football would be daunting in the extreme for whoever occupied the President's shoes. To conclude our tale of the past century, therefore, we asked the twelfth President for his views on the present state and future hopes of the oldest Football League in the world, in the earnest hope that his comments would be of interest not only now, but also when it comes to celebrating the bicentenary in 2088.

After numerous incidents involving spectators at League grounds between 1980 and 1985, culminating in the death of a boy at Birmingham and the thirty-nine deaths at the Heysel Stadium in Brussels, it might appear that the football hooligan has won. He has driven away thousands of spectators, forced most clubs to put up security fencing, persuaded three to ban all away fans (Luton, Torquay and Colchester), and caused such havoc in Europe that League clubs were banned from European competitions in 1985. Hooliganism has been on the League's agenda since 1963, but only in 1985 did the government take a serious interest, by ordering the League to implement membership schemes at each club. At first they called for 100 per cent membership, but in time the football authorities were able to convince them that this would be impossible to implement without killing the game. Now we have partial membership schemes, many of which have been unpopular not just with the fans, but with the police also. What is your personal view?

Philip Carter: We had consultations with the police, and came to the conclusion that membership schemes could help with crowd control. We also managed to agree with the Minister for Sport (at that time Richard Tracey) that rather than full membership we'd aim for a voluntary target of 50 per cent membership, that is, half of each ground being designated for members. That's not so different to the situation you find at cricket grounds.

Not every ground has the right lay-out to achieve the figure of 50 per cent. Equally, I think the clubs and the police in many cases are concerned that because they've had no crowd disorders for years, the introduction of something new may in actual fact cause problems.

So we've treated each case on its merits and local circumstances, and so far every club has given us its full co-operation. By September 1987 we had forty-one clubs able to enforce the 50 per cent members-only target, twenty-one clubs have reached between 40 and 50 per cent, and all the others have done what they can with the approval of their local police authorities.

Supporters must not think that it is some kind of gimmick, though. We've gone into the question very thoroughly. We've had in-depth discussions with all the parties concerned, and I feel supporters must give the membership schemes a fair trial.

But the Government's original concept that membership schemes were somehow the best way to combat hooliganism is quite erroneous. I think they're merely part of a total package of activities which is aimed at discouraging the hooligan element.

Let's also look at the positive side of these schemes. They can help to bring the club and the supporter much closer together. They enable the club to offer members all sorts of attractive advantages: preference for Cup tickets, better facilities, reductions on souvenirs and other goods.

Lots of people become members of organizations they support. Theatres, golf clubs, cricket clubs, whatever; there's a stronger relationship and tie than if you're just a casual attender. Ultimately, there may be a base that we in the Football League can develop collectively. A reciprocal membership scheme which covers all League clubs is one possibility for the future.

We are already looking into the possibility of a central computerized system for reciprocal membership, but at an estimated cost of £7 million (about £70,000 per club) we have to ask whether it would be really justified, especially as we cannot be sure it would solve the problem of football-related hooliganism.

We must be careful not to deter the casual spectator, and there are far more of these than there are trouble makers. Our aim is to attract customers, not to make it harder for them to attend.

We think we've driven most football hooliganism away from the grounds. Of course there are exceptions, but they are just that, exceptions rather than regular occurrences.

Of course, I'd rather have no restrictions at all. We are supposed to have a free society in which people have the choice to go to the cinema, the theatre, the bowling alley, and equally they should have the choice to go to football. That is the ideal scenario, and you can't get away from that. But the practical reality is maybe different entirely.

Every generation of football fans seems to complain that the game lacks the star players it used to have. It was no different in 1908, 1958 or 1988. But in recent years the loss of talented and popular individuals like Glenn Hoddle to Monaco and Ian Rush to Juventus has suggested that even the richest League clubs cannot guarantee to hold on to their best players. Will this 'skill drain' to Europe grow, or is it, as in the early 1960s, just a passing phase?

Philip Carter: At the moment, UEFA and FIFA rules state that each club can have only two foreign players in the team at any one time, although they can have more on their books. In 1986/7, for example, Barcelona had three British strikers – Mark Hughes, Gary Lineker and Steve Archibald – but only two could play in the first team. The EEC wants us to lift those restrictions as part of their 'harmonization' programme, so that footballers, like all other workers in Europe, will have free movement between member countries.

We in Britain, that is the League, FA and PFA, agree with other footballing bodies in Europe that free movement would be disastrous for the game, so we've suggested as an interim measure, to keep the EEC happy, that a limit of three foreign players per team be introduced. But the EEC might still call for the limit to be raised to five by 1992, and then maybe eventually to end all restrictions, which obviously football will resist vigorously.

As far as the Football League is concerned, our worry is that certain domestic leagues are going to be denuded of their major stars. You've only got to look at Denmark, where they've got no domestic league to speak of because all their best players are playing in other countries.

You've got major companies owning clubs in the Italian League, like Fiat at Juventus or Pirelli at AC Milan, using them as advertising vehicles as opposed to football vehicles, and therefore they have much greater muscle in attracting foreign stars.

It's not only skill we are losing. It's the fact that, as for a big-hit West End musical, once the star performer leaves the show it loses some of its gloss and attraction. I think the elimination of stars in any form of entertainment must reduce the appeal to the public. This applies to football just as much.

But the Football League is not going to stop producing star players just because they might eventually be going abroad for a year or two.

If you're a large company with a very sophisticated training scheme, you know that you're going to lose some of your people eventually to rival organizations. Therefore, you organize yourself accordingly. That happens all the time in football, not just because of transfers but through injury, loss of form and so on.

Nevertheless, our ultimate concern is to improve the quality of the game and make it more attractive to the public, and we cannot hide the fact that the loss of stars to Europe is a major concern both to us and to the PFA.

So far, not many foreign players have done well in the League. Mirandinha and Ossie Ardiles stand out as exceptions. Might the League be a more interesting competition if we followed the Spanish, French and Italians by importing more talent?

Philip Carter: As we are, theoretically, the most productive, or practically the most productive League in the world, I'd be concerned that by introducing more foreign players we might be hampering the development of our own.

Of course, the equivalent of a Platini or a Maradona would be welcome, to brighten up our ideas and excite the crowds. But if the imported player is merely a competent left-back or whatever, I'm not too sure if it's right to introduce him simply so people can say: 'My goodness, we've got a Brazilian here!' If that's the case, then marketing of the team is being put before the quality of its play.

At the same time, I think the League should be proud of supplying Europe with some of its top players. If you consider, we already supply the bulk of players for five national squads: England, Scotland, Wales, Northern Ireland and Eire. Maybe we should be worried if foreign clubs didn't covet our players.

Do you think part of the answer would be for major companies to take over leading clubs in the Football League and sponsor them in the more direct manner found on the Continent? Wouldn't League clubs then be able to keep their best players?

Philip Carter: That's perfectly feasible, but I think it's highly improbable. For a start, the whole structure of the League's organization would have to be changed, and that could happen only with a two-thirds majority vote. I think you'd find it very difficult to get the majority of smaller clubs to agree to letting in major companies like that.

A second major difficulty would be the tax situation in this country. I'm not sure, for example, that Newcastle United's sponsors would have been able to afford to attract Kevin Keegan as they did in 1982 had he been in his prime. I don't think a local sponsor or a national sponsor would necessarily have kept Gary Lineker here.

Because of the tax laws here, the cost of trying to match his real and potential earnings abroad would have been absolutely astronomical by comparison. Barcelona can afford the Linekers of this world because they have a stadium with a capacity of 108,000, and of that total perhaps 100,000 are members who all pay up front. They positively embrace the idea of membership. So Barcelona may have £10 million in the bank from season tickets and membership fees before they've kicked a ball.

We simply don't have that situation over here, and maybe we never will. Just to take my own club as an example, Everton has a capacity of just under 53,000, less than half Barcelona's. And the ticket prices are well under half the price.

Do you predict, therefore, that if League football is to maintain standards and hang on to its best players, the public is going to have to pay more to watch?

Philip Carter: By our standards, continental fans do pay much more. But equally, if people want to pay for entertainment in this country, they will. How much did they pay in 1987 to see the pop singer Madonna at Wembley? £16 for a place on the terraces. They could watch a match at Wembley for less than half that.

The difference is that with soccer we're talking about over two thousand games a season in the League alone, not including cup competitions, and these games can attract only so many million people at a certain price. It has to be good value, otherwise people won't go.

I think football is exceptionally good value, and I think that's why we still command the crowds. It's a marvellous entertainment, which is delivered to the public at a price which the majority, though I accept not all, can afford.

In 1981 Queen's Park Rangers were given permission to install an artificial pitch at Loftus Road. Bold though this experiment undoubtedly was, at the time the technology was insufficiently advanced to provide a suitable surface for football. Since then, substantial advances have been made in the development of artificial pitches, and three more League clubs have followed QPR's example: Luton, Preston and Oldham. Leicester City and your own club, Everton, led a move to ban these pitches from the First Division, and although this was unsuccessful, the League has placed a moratorium on further installations until at least 1990. Do you still feel that synthetic pitches are unsuitable for League football?

Philip Carter: First of all, I don't agree that artificial pitches have reached a level of quality which makes them nearly acceptable. I deplore the fact that in 1981 the League allowed their use in competitive matches before any proper study had been undertaken. Like any other research and development, testing should have taken place outside the mainstream of activity. A large department store wouldn't put a product on their shelves right round the country without having tested it somewhere else. Snooker players would never be asked to experiment with a new kind of baize in the course of an important competitive match.

The concern I have is that clubs may end up caring more about the financial advantages of an artificial pitch than about the quality of the product they're offering the public. The

Football League has an overall responsibility for football. We have to be sure that the type of product that the clubs are delivering is the type that the public wants.

The question is, do the public want the game of football as it is played on artificial pitches, which is, no one can deny, very different from the traditional game on grass? The fans obviously don't want it at QPR, because the club is digging it up in 1988 and putting down real grass. The fans simply didn't like what they saw.

Some clubs would argue, however, that they need to put down an artificial pitch in order to open up their facilities to the community and save themselves from financial ruin.

Philip Carter: I've yet to have it proven to me that these extra activities actually do produce sufficient revenue to be worthwhile. Nevertheless, if clubs do decide that they wish to take that route to financial survival, then all right, I don't wish to stop them.

But I don't think we can allow those clubs to impinge on other clubs who are producing the right quality and who are managing to cope without the need for plastic pitches.

As chairman of a First Division club, and as one partly responsible for the quality of League football, I would argue that if clubs in the lower divisions want plastic pitches then the First Division clubs can say: 'Sorry, we're grass only; if you want to be promoted you must lay grass.'

But there is a further element which concerns me just as much. I've never known a multi-purpose sports stadium anywhere in this country which has not been heavily subsidized by the local council. I've never known one to stand on its own two feet yet.

Essentially, therefore, you have local authorities trying to gain for themselves municipal sports centres on the cheap. They're saying: 'We'll bale you out or we'll take some equity in your football club and we'll put down an artificial pitch, but in return you must now do this, that and the other to satisfy our needs.' And suddenly you find that football is subservient to every other activity in that locality, and instead of them actually building their own custom-built, multi-purpose sports stadium, they've done it at a fraction of the price, simply by shelling out the cost of an artificial pitch.

But you see, the whole argument might have changed in ten or fifteen years. There have been tremendous advances in the development of natural grass pitches. And who's to say that in a few years we won't have the ability to cover stadia?

Do you think either the administration of the League or its public reputation suffers from the headquarters being sited at Lytham St Annes?

Philip Carter: Firstly, I think criticism of the League over this issue has died down considerably in recent years. Of course, if you were starting from scratch you wouldn't put the League offices in Lytham, but in this technological age you can have your office anywhere because communication between the outlets and the office is simplicity itself.

On the second point, however, I think from a public image point of view any large national organization, in sport, industry or any field, would automatically think of basing itself in one of the major centres: London, Birmingham, Manchester or any of the large cities.

Various presentations have been made by towns or cities wanting the League to set up shop within their boundaries, and a sub-committee from the Management Committee is looking into the possibilities. Birmingham is certainly one of the strongest candidates so far. Apart from its merits as a city, we can't forget the fact that the League's founder lived and worked in Birmingham. Manchester, too, has very strong links with our history and traditions.

Rather more important than the location of

the headquarters is the question of how the League can go forward into the next century. To help us resolve that question, during the centenary celebrations of 1987–8 we have set up a charitable trust which we hope will eventually enable us to raise sufficient money to enter into some sort of development which goes beyond simply moving the offices.

One of our ideas is to build a Centenary Centre. This would provide areas for meetings and conferences. There would also be all-weather outdoor and indoor training facilities for managers, coaches and players which would be available both to League clubs and to young players all year round. We would also consider a museum of football.

But we won't be rushing into any hasty decisions on this. The location has to be right and the price has to be acceptable to the clubs. We're not allowed by law to use money from the charitable trust to spend on new offices – it can be used only to finance the other social and educational developments – so we'd still have to find extra money if we wanted the offices to become part of this Centenary Centre. And we've got to make sure our planning and motives are sufficiently sound to make any new development worthy of carrying the League banner into the twenty-first century.

Most sporting events nowadays are sponsored, be they Test Matches, Grand Nationals or even sedate bridge championships. But purists would argue that the Football League, which has survived so long and has such a tremendous worldwide reputation, should maintain its dignity by steering clear of sponsorship. Having concluded the deal with Barclays Bank in August 1987, you presumably don't agree.

Philip Carter: Sport needs money from outside sources. That is a fact of life in a free country. The League simply cannot afford to turn down a good offer – providing, of course, that the company doing the offering is the right one – not just to help League football to survive, but to help it to improve.

Remember, we are talking about the national game. It is natural for us to want to preserve and improve it, just as it is natural for a commecial interest to want to become associated with us.

Barclays have branches all over the country; so does the Football League. And even in smaller towns with a Fourth Division club and gates of 2000, that club still has tremendous local importance. Through their branches, Barclays can get more people involved. And what a tremendous compliment to the League that such an important international bank should wish to tie its name to ours. I don't think sponsorship cheapens the League. I think it enhances football. It enhances both sides.

You were part of the Television Negotiating Committee whose efforts to reach an agreement with the television companies were scuppered by the clubs in February 1985. We have already looked at how damaging that rejection was to the League's interests, but what about the future? In your opinion, does football really need television, or does it damage the game?

Philip Carter: I'm quite clear about television. I think that a correctly balanced presentation of televised football, a blend of live and recorded games, is an essential part of projecting football to the public. It's a form of advertising, it promotes interest in the game. Rather like those trailers of films or shows, it whets people's appetites and provides a regular reminder that football is happening, live and exciting.

I think the whole question of TV is going to change dramatically in the next few years, because we face the gradual introduction of cable and satellite television. This will provide a form of competition to the existing channels. We could have a sport-only channel, for instance, with plenty of time for live or recorded football – not just League football, but from all over the world.

We may see greater regionalization, so that

each region shows its own games to a local audience, as happens in the United States; as happens now, in local radio.

Certainly, if those sorts of changes take place, then the sponsorship and advertising possibilities will be far greater than they are at the moment, and we in the League will have a wider scope for negotiating separate deals. It may well be that one channel or cable company will buy the rights to the Littlewoods Challenge Cup, for instance. It may well be that the League will, through its new outlet, World wide Soccer, be able to package its own programme and sell it to one of the main channels, as it is now doing overseas.

All those possibilities are there for the future, and I don't think they're that far away, frankly. We are already selling matches abroad through Thames Television International, who film selected games, edit and package them under our auspices. At the moment, the TTI package goes to more than forty countries, which shows how popular the League still is abroad.

We also have to be careful that the British public has enough of its own football to watch on television, before satellite television swamps them with games from around the world.

We have to persuade the television companies all over again that League football is worth a prime-time slot on a Saturday night. Football is the national game, and yet we have allowed ourselves to be manoeuvred into a situation in which the television companies are dictating the terms. We must regain the initiative.

Almost from the day it was born, the League has enjoyed a wavering relationship with the FA. Sometimes the two bodies have worked hand in hand, sometimes they've shaped up for a fight. In the latter event, someone has invariably come forward to suggest that the League should break out on its own, or even take over the Association altogether. Might this ever occur?

Philip Carter: Absolutely not. As guardians of the professional game in England, we could not possibly, nor would we want to, have any jurisdiction over the 40,000 other clubs around the country. The two organizations are complementary and interdependent, but they each have separate roles to play.

The FA is the major body representing football throughout England, and it's the body which represents us in the rest of the world, through UEFA and through FIFA. There is no way that the League could take on that responsibility, and any suggestion that we would even attempt to, is nonsense. We're not equipped to do it.

Of course, you're going to have differences of opinion and differences of emphasis. But the present FA chairman, Bert Millichip, has stated publicly that since the new Management Committee came into power in 1986, he feels that the League and FA have never worked so closely together.

I do think, however, that the League should be better represented at the FA in those areas which relate to the League. Beyond that, it should be represented only in areas in which the FA feels that a League presence would be beneficial. But these are minor quibbles. Otherwise, the League is totally bound up within the FA. I see no reason to change the nature of the relationship.

The fact is that we must work together for the mutual benefit of football. And I don't accept any argument that somehow the League's authority is being weakened. It is up to us to see that it isn't. If we're not strong enough to see that our particular battle is fought in the right quarters, then the problem is in our camp, not the FA's.

Part of the reason for restructuring the League, for which you campaigned so hard, was to increase public interest. That has certainly been the case with the end-of-season play-offs, but the public at large might argue that the introduction of the Full Members' Cup is hardly a great attraction.

Philip Carter: The main reasoning behind reducing the First Division to twenty clubs was to enable us to introduce a third cup competition. We already have the FA Cup and the Littlewoods Cup, so a third cup on the same lines would hardly be of interest to the public. I accept that, which is why we proposed the British Cup, involving English, Scottish and maybe Irish clubs, along the lines of the original Texaco Cup. But if we have a British Cup, then hostile elements in FIFA can turn round and say that in future Great Britain should send only one joint team to the World Cup. Or UEFA could restrict entry to the Cup Winners' Cup to one team, the winners of the British Cup. So we have to be careful there, and that is why we have been experimenting with the Full Members' (now Simod) Cup, and will continue to do so until we get the right formula.

The other point about reducing the First Division is that it will enable us to play every League game on a Saturday. Even with an extra cup competition, that should also give us two free weeks which the England team can use for pre-match preparations.

So the restructuring has two elements. A new competition to compensate for loss of League fixtures, plus a boost to our international prospects.

One of the ten demands made by the so-called 'Super Leaguers' was the introduction of automatic promotion and relegation from the Vauxhall Conference (or Alliance Premier League). Why, as chairman of a First Division club, were you so insistent on this?

Philip Carter: We wanted to complete the pyramid of football, so that any one of the 40,000 clubs in the country could, on merit, eventually make its way through the minor leagues up to the Football League itself. From that point of view, automatic promotion and relegation has put us in touch with the rest of football and helped revitalize the game. Now, in theory, any team, however humble, can try to 'do a Wimbledon', as it were. There's nothing like competition and incentive to improve football.

The old system of re-election was very difficult for the League clubs to handle, because it couldn't honestly be viewed as fair. It was extremely difficult for the chairmen to have the responsibility of deciding whether one of four clubs was going to be thrown out.

And let's be absolutely clear about this. Automatic promotion and relegation was in point of fact proposed first by the lower division clubs, not by me. I think that in the past, most First Division club chairmen hardly bothered whether one club or another stayed in or out of the Fourth Division, unless they were local. But the Associate Members cared sufficiently to suggest that we changed the system. The credit for the change must be theirs.

One hundred years is a long time for any organization to survive, especially one which has been subjected to such a constant stream of abuse and criticism from all quarters. Do you see any reason to believe that that criticism will abate in the future?

Philip Carter: I do feel optimistic about the future, because I think that everybody in football now, finally, realizes that we're facing a different challenge. The requirement of the past just to produce twenty-two players on a Saturday afternoon and expect people to roll up to watch them has long since disappeared.

We're being forced to become more professional in the projection of the game itself. We've now appointed a marketing director, and we're also examining ways in which we can remodel the League secretariat, not just to improve the competition but to improve the ways in which we relate to other organizations, be it concerning football, television, sponsorship, local government or whatever.

It all boils down to how we develop, use, promote and market our product. We have to be more aware on a collective as well as on a regional and local basis of what it is the public wants and demands out of football, apart from purely the match itself.

That means tailoring our stadia to the needs of ordinary people, not always to be thinking of how we can police a violent minority. We want to take fences down, not build more. For example, I think it's quite incredible that we've started this whole wave of family enclosures at football.

People talk glibly about how we've lost all the families. It's not true; we've never had families at football grounds. Fathers and sons maybe, but not families. But now we're actually attracting mothers, daughters, fathers and sons, in spite of all the adverse comment about the game. That must be a positive move as far as we're concerned.

I think it's also encouraging to see how we're attracting sponsors of repute; the media want our product, and at long last the Government is interested in us too. I know its interest was sparked off by the Bradford fire and the crowd problems in 1985, but I think that in time the Government's concern will grow once it starts to realize the benefits of the game itself.

So, overall, after we hit rock bottom in May 1985, I now get the impression that the public is getting behind the game again. It's difficult to quantify. One could argue that an extra one million through the turnstiles in 1986/7 is a measure of our success, but it goes beyond statistics. I think people generally talk about football rather more kindly in 1988 than they did in 1985, or even 1978 perhaps. They can see that we're trying as hard as we can to make football better all round.

Do you think football will ever attract back the so-called missing millions?

Philip Carter: Success in the League for the next decade or more will not, I think, be measured in terms of increased attendances. You see, we could attract a few million more spectators and yet still not solve our other more

basic problems. More fans won't necessarily help us to become more viable, though of course I'd love to see every ground in the League bulging to capacity.

The capacity of most grounds will continue to go down as we increase levels of comfort and add more seats and membership areas. We've been doing this for years, and while gates have declined, our income has steadily risen. So I don't think we necessarily want to use old-fashioned yardsticks. Just one example. Everyone loves the FA Cup, and rightly so. It will always be the most hallowed knock-out competition in England. But the economic facts are that in 1986/7 the Littlewoods Cup was more lucrative for most League clubs than the FA Cup.

A major thread running throughout our history has been the concept of the League as a family; sometimes living in perfect harmony, sometimes squabbling, but essentially united by a common interest. At one stage, you led a movement which almost culminated in the break-up of that family. Now that the internecine quarrel is over (for the time being at least), and you are now at the head of the family, do you see it surviving much longer?

Philip Carter: I think the family is safe. I'd like to think that the structure of ninety-two clubs can be maintained, for all the reasons which have been stated time and time again – that you've got the nurseries of the future and the dormitories of the past and so on – but I am concerned that other issues may emerge which would cause the structure to be changed. The obvious one is artificial pitches.

And as with attendances, we shouldn't be hampered by the old yardsticks. We can maintain the structure without necessarily adhering to that magic number of ninety-two. We must be practical about this. Some clubs will not survive for ever, and no club has a divine right to remain in business.

But I do believe in the structure of the League as it stands, and I would be wary of changing it for change's sake. The League has, after all, lasted throughout a hundred often very turbulent years. It has survived all kinds of financial crises, disasters, two world wars and, you could say, it has survived a countless number of poor decisions and mistakes made at every level.

The League is a tough nut, and it's got millions of supporters, so I don't doubt that William McGregor's idea will be around for a long time yet. And I daresay the next hundred years will be just as exciting, controversial and fascinating as the first century.

So I look forward to the future with confidence. There's no doubt in my mind that football will continue to be the game of the people, or that League football will remain the biggest spectator sport in the country, and I feel privileged to have been given the opportunity to contribute to the greatest game in the world, and to have been one of 'the Men Who Made it'.

League Secretaries and Management Committee Members 1888–1988

Secretaries

The Secretary of the Football League has four main areas of responsibility; to oversee administrative operations at Lytham St Annes, to keep a constant check on clubs and individuals to see that they adhere to League regulations, to implement the policies and wishes of the Management Committee and to communicate the Committee's views to the outside world.

Since 1890, the Secretary has had no vote at League meetings, and since 1902 he has been barred from having any ties with a League club.

The Football League has employed only five Secretaries. From 1888–92, Harry Lockett acted as Honorary Secretary.

Harry Lockett	1892–1902
Tom Charnley	1902–1933
Fred Howarth	1933–1956
Alan Hardaker	1957–1979
Graham Kelly	1979–1988

The Management Committee

The Management Committee is elected by the clubs to govern the affairs of the League. Although it has no direct powers to change any regulations, one of its prime functions is to propose new regulations and amend existing ones. But it can implement these changes only if the clubs grant their approval.

Current regulations allow for a Committee of eight members, including the President, each member to be elected for a period of three years. No one over the age of seventy is eligible, and in 1986 the office of Vice President was abolished.

Since 1930 every member of the Committee has automatically become a member of the FA Council, and every League President has been appointed a Vice President of the FA.

Altogether, eighty-six men from forty-five different clubs have served the Committee since 1888, including twelve Presidents. Everton, West Bromwich, Birmingham, Arsenal and Newcastle have between them provided the most members of the Committee.

Below is a list of Management Committee members and officers, in the order of their election.

W. McGregor (A Villa)	Chairman 1888–92
	President 1892–4
	Life Member 1895–1911
W. Sudell (Preston)	Hon. Treasurer 1888–92
H. Lockett (Stoke)	Hon. Secretary 1888–92
J. J. Bentley (Bolton)	Committee 1888–93, 1910–12
	Vice President 1893–4
	President 1894–1910
	Life Member 1912–18
W. Allt (Wolves)	Committee 1888–92
W. Starling (Small Heath)	Committee 1892–4
E. Browne (Notts Co)	Vice President 1893–5
L. Ford (WBA)	Committee 1893–4
	Vice President 1894–7
R. Molyneux (Everton)	Committee 1893–8
J. Parlby (Ardwick)	Committee 1893–9
J. Lewis (Blackburn)	Committee 1894–5, 1900–1
	Vice President 1901–26
J. H. Strawson (Lincoln)	Committee 1894–5
D. Haigh (Sheff Utd)	Vice President 1895–1901
J. Dunkley (A Villa)	Committee 1895–8
W. H. Bellamy (Grimsby)	Committee 1896–1900
T. H. Sidney (Wolves)	Vice President 1897–1905
H. S. Radford (Nottm F)	Committee 1898–1905
	Vice President 1905–8
C. E. Sutcliffe (Burnley)	Committee 1898–1902, 1903–27
	Vice President 1927–36
	President 1936–9
	Life Member 1938–9
W. W. Hart (Small Heath)	Committee 1899–1903
G. H. Leavey (W Arsenal)	Committee 1901–4
J. McKenna (Liverpool)	Committee 1902–8
	Vice President 1908–10
	President 1910–36
	Life Member 1923–36
Dr J. C. Baxter (Everton)	Committee 1904–19
H. Keys (WBA)	Committee 1905–10
	Vice President 1910–29
J. Cameron (Newcastle)	Committee 1907–16
A. J. Dickinson (Sheff Wed)	Committee 1909–30
	Vice President 1929–30
T. E. Harris (Notts Co)	Committee 1909–17
T. Houghton (Preston)	Committee 1912–13
W. Hall (Arsenal)	Committee 1913–27
J. P. Oliver (Newcastle)	Committee 1917–28
F. W. Rinder (A Villa)	Committee 1917–30
	Vice President 1930–8
	Life Member 1938
T. A. Barcroft (Blackpool)	Committee 1919–25, 1926–43
W. C. Cuff (Everton)	Committee 1925–36
	Vice President 1936–9
	President 1939–49
	Life Member 1945–9
M. F. Cadman (Tottenham)	Committee 1927–39
	Vice President 1939–41

P. Bach (Middlesbrough)	Committee 1929–37
W. I. Bassett (WBA)	Committee 1930–7
A. Brook Hirst (H'field)	Committee 1931–9
	Vice President 1939–41
J. J. Edwards (Arsenal)	Committee 1936–40
A. H. Oakley (Wolves)	Committee 1937–41
	Vice President 1941–55
	Acting President 1949
	President 1955–7
W. Tempest (Blackburn)	Committee 1939–41
W. J. Cearns (West Ham)	Committee 1939–50
A. Drewry (Grimsby)	Committee 1940–9
	President 1949–55
G. F. Rutherford (N'castle)	Committee 1938–42
	Vice President 1942–9
D. F. Wiseman (B'ham)	Committee 1941–2, 1949–71
	Life Member 1971–8
W. J. Harrop (Liverpool)	Committee 1941–50
	Vice President 1950–6
H. Shentall (Chesterfield)	Committee 1942–56
	Vice President 1956–63
H. French (Middlesbrough)	Committee 1942–63
P. Wood (Huddersfield)	Committee 1943–7
J. Richards (Barnsley)	Committee 1948–55
	Vice President 1955–7
	President 1957–66
	Vice President and Life
	Member 1966–8
J. H. W. Mears (Chelsea)	Committee 1950–7
	Vice President 1957–63
C. N. Banks (Bolton)	Committee 1950–64
L. T. Shipman (Leicester)	Committee 1955–63
	Vice President 1963–6
	President 1966–74
	Committee 1974–7
	Life Member 1978–
W. B. Taylor (Newcastle)	Committee 1956–64
	Vice President 1964–70
	Life Member 1970–1
Dr A. Stephen (Sheff Wed)	Committee 1957–67
S. S. Collings (Sunderland)	Committee 1963–74
	Life Member 1974–6
F. A. Would (Grimsby)	Committee 1963–75
	Life Member 1975–
S. Bolton (Leeds Utd)	Committee 1964–8
	Vice President 1968–75
	Life Member 1975–6

E. M. Gliksten (Charlton)	Committee 1964–75
	Life Member 1975–
R. W. Lord (Burnley)	Committee 1967–70
	Vice President 1970–81
L. C. Edwards (Man Utd)	Committee 1968–73
Lord Westwood (Newcastle)	Committee 1970–4
	President 1974–81
	Life Member 1981–
R. Wragg (Sheffield Utd)	Committee 1971–5
	Vice President 1975–86
	Life Vice President 1986–
Sir Matt Busby (Man Utd)	Committee 1973–82
	Vice President 1982–3
	Life Member 1983–
J. F. Wiseman (B'ham City)	Committee 1974–83
	Vice President 1983–6
	Life Member 1986–
Dr C. S. Grossmark (G'ham)	Committee 1975–84
R. B. Strachan (York City)	Committee 1975–6
B. J. Deacon (Portsmouth)	Committee 1975–6
J. B. Mears (Chelsea)	Committee 1975–81
R. Daniel (Plymouth)	Committee 1976–86
G. H. C. Needler (Hull City)	Committee 1976–86
J. J. Dunnett (Notts Co)	Committee 1977–81
	President 1981–6
	Committee 1986–
Sir Arthur South (Norwich)	Committee 1981–5
	Life Vice President 1985–
B. B. Winston (Orient)	Committee 1981–3
J. W. Smith (Liverpool)	Committee 1982–6
P. Axon (Stoke City)	Committee 1982–3
A. Everiss (WBA)	Committee 1983–6
L. C. Cearns (West Ham)	Committee 1983–4
	Life Vice President 1984–
I. M. Jones (Doncaster)	Committee 1984–6
G. A. Smith (Watford)	Committee 1984–6
M. Roworth (Nottm F)	Committee 1985–6
P. D. Carter (Everton)	**President 1986–**
J. R. Smith (Luton)	Committee 1986
K. W. Bates (Chelsea)	Committee 1986–8
H. E. McGee (Sheff Wed)	Committee 1986–8
I. H. Stott (Oldham)	Committee 1986–
R. G. Noades (Crystal P)	Committee 1986–
W. Fox (Blackburn)	Committee 1986–
D. B. Dein (Arsenal)	Committee 1986–
D. Bulstrode (QPR)	Committee 1988–
G. McKeag (Newcastle)	Committee 1988–

Short Biographies of the Men Who Made It

For all the arguments and intrigue over the years, The Men Who Made It were team-mates, enjoying a bond which develops only through many a long hour of collective work. Looking at a photo of the Management Committee in which he had served, one former member warmly recalled, 'Ah! They were a grand bunch!' He did not know then that every other man in the picture had made almost exactly the same comment.

Here follows short pen-pictures of those more prominent members of the Management Committee who have not already been featured in the main text, starting with the first formally elected Committee in 1893.

In the period 1893–1900 we have little information about four committeemen. W. Starling was a founder of Small Heath who may have been a restauranteur in Birmingham. John Strawson of Lincoln was a former League referee who served as the League's auditor for 24 years, David Haigh was a FA Council member and close associate of Charles Clegg, and all we know of John Dunkley was that he was a director of Aston Villa.

Sixteen men served on the Management Committee between the two world wars. Of these, six were businessmen, four were solicitors, three were council officials and two were in the licensed trade. They also numbered two passionate teetotallers (who were both former League referees), two former international footballers, two former racing cyclists and two men who would later become chairmen of the FA.

Of the fifteen men who served between 1945 and 1961, four were in building related trades, three were in coal and two were fruit merchants. Unlike previous Committees, and perhaps crucially in view of the negotiations with the players between 1960–3, there were no solicitors on the Committee during this period. Indeed there was only one representative from the professions – Dr Andrew Stephen.

From 1961 to 1985 a total of twenty-six men were elected to the Committee. They were predominantly businessmen, of whom half a dozen represented the new breed of younger, wealthier club chairmen. They were also mainly from that generation of men who served during the Second World War or performed National Service afterwards. In this respect they shared a bond with Alan Hardaker, who was in reality the dominant influence at all Management Committee meetings during his period as Secretary.

The advent of regionalized representation in 1975 (six regional groups each electing their own man) brought a much greater turnover of Committee men than ever before, with the result that some members served for only a year or two (these are not included in this section). A further change in the constitution came in 1983 when it was decided that members should retire at the age of seventy.

The Management Committee member of today plays a quite different role to that of his predecessors. Whereas up to the 1960s the Committee was primarily concerned with 'the game' and making sure that clubs stayed within the regulations (often a forlorn hope), the modern Committee man has to delve into matters far beyond the boundaries of mere sport. He must be able to handle meetings with politicians and policemen, marketing men and the media.

He can no longer be a silent onlooker. He has to fight for his patch and the clubs of the division he represents. There is no room on the Committee of the 1980s for bland yes-men or happy-go-lucky jokers. The League needs workers now; hard-headed businessmen with ideas and commitment. And whereas once the average director ran his business with care and his football club with abandon, nowadays he must exercise caution.

He may no longer pick the team, but he does still call the shots. And if he does plough in his own money, he loses control of it at his peril. The football gravy train has ground to a halt. Now, everyone must get results.

Except that he is more likely to be younger and therefore more energetic, the Committee man of the 1980s is as powerful and self-opinionated as his counterpart in the 1880s or 1930s. The present generation would not be overawed or outgunned by a John Bentley or a Fred Rinder, and tempting though it might be to suggest that somehow the modern football man is a different animal altogether from his antecedents, in truth there are as many similarities as differences.

Behind the scenes politicking was as endemic within football in 1938 as it is in 1988. There were rebel-rousers then, as now. There were even big-money, sharp talkers too (although none of them was ever interested in running or owning more than one club).

So just as we praise, or chide, the current generation, we should remember that the likes of John McKenna and Charles Sutcliffe were no paragons of virtue. They craved power and success as fervently as any of their successors.

Becoming a member of the Management Committee is a much tougher business nowadays, however. Sentiment was often sufficient to gain election in the past, but not now. And serving on the Committee demands a much higher degree of time and energy than ever before, if only because the issues facing football are so much more complex. Not that you'll find any of the members ever complaining. Serving the League is still as much a privilege as it is a headache.

Edwin Browne (*Notts County*) – *Vice President 1893–5*

Described as 'a man of tact and influence', Browne was assist-ant secretary of Nottinghamshire CCC at Trent Bridge when in 1883 Notts Co FC moved in to share the ground and Browne became their secretary too. Ten years later County could no longer afford his services, but this at least allowed him more time for the League. Browne sat on the Committee for two years, with the League paying £25 towards his testimonial in May 1895. He is chiefly remembered for having written a history of Nottinghamshire Cricket Club. Also, in 1879 he led a tour of cricketers to North America, writing a journal which is still preserved at Trent Bridge.

Louis Ford (*West Bromwich*) – *Committee 1893–4, Vice President 1894–77*

A League referee until 1892, as Albion's secretary Ford took an active and often contrary view on many questions facing the League. Indeed, as we have seen, had Ford's radical proposals on gate-sharing and the awarding of points been carried in the early years, the subsequent history of League football might well have been totally different.

Described as 'a shrewd judge of football ability', Ford later joined Walsall, becoming a publican in Rugeley. To ease his financial worries, in 1910 the League sent him £10, which must have kept him going, since we next read of him in 1938 being granted a further £21 for his failing health. Also in that year, Ford sent a note of congratulations to the League on its jubilee celebrations. 'Fifty years is a long time to look back, and we little thought when we started the League it would reach to such proportions, embracing so many counties. I have always watched it with keen pleasure.'

Dick Molyneux (*Everton*) – *Committee 1893–8*

Everton's first full-time secretary, appointed in 1889 in succession to W. E. Barclay, Molyneux was reportedly a shrewd fellow who didn't talk much, had a keen sense of humour and was an athletics enthusiast. He resigned in 1901, and shortly after was appointed secretary at Brentford.

Joshua Parlby (*Ardwick*) – *Committee 1893–9*

Known as 'Falstaff' because of his beard, girth and loud humour, Parlby started with Stoke, first as a player, then as a committee man. He moved to Manchester in 1892 to take over the Wellington Hotel on Stockport Road, and immediately teamed up with nearby Ardwick, many of whose members were also in the brewery trade. As the club's first full-time secretary, it was largely thanks to Parlby's persuasive powers that Ardwick kept their place in the Second Division in 1894 only a few months after going bankrupt.

Parlby also managed to talk round a young Welshman called Billy Meredith into signing for the club. 'There are some men whose silver tongues are said to have the power of charming song-birds from the trees, and I believe Josh Parlby was one of them', wrote Meredith.

City historian Andrew Ward described Parlby as: 'never a skilled tactician – a supreme amateur in many respects – it was his enthusiasm and energy in organising the club's affairs that proved most valuable. He was affectionately remembered for the artful way he would smuggle half the Ardwick team up and down the railway system to away fixtures for free, and

for the way he would promise the team win bonuses that, it later transpired, he could not pay.'

Considered to be the father of Manchester City, Parlby eventually left his post as secretary in 1895 to run another public house in Bolton, although he remained a club director until 1904, when along with two fellow directors he was banned by the FA for three years in a scandal over illegal payments.

William Bellamy (*Grimsby*) – *Committee 1896–1900*

A League linesman who was well known in Grimsby as a partner in his family's mineral water business, Bellamy became a director of Town in 1890 and later the club's honorary secretary. At one stage, in 1894, he helped to rescue Grimsby with a personal loan of £150. After joining the Management Committee, Bellamy became an FA councillor, rising to FA vice president in 1921 and life vice president in 1941. He died, aged eighty-four, in 1945.

T. H. Sidney (*Wolves*) – *Vice President 1897–1905*

Tom Sidney was the type of committee man who served both his club and the town in which he lived. He could be supervising a training session at Molineux in the morning, then chairing a session of the town council's education committee in the afternoon. Eventually, however, his municipal duties became too burdensome, and he was forced to resign from the League.

Judging by the effusive messages of appreciation which accompanied his departure, Sidney was clearly a valued member. Later on that year, after he developed eye trouble and couldn't attend the 1905 Annual Meeting, he was presented with an illuminated address and album by President J. J. Bentley.

But there was plenty of fight left in Sidney, as he showed at the FA's annual meeting in 1908, when he vigorously opposed abolition of restrictions on wages and bonuses. 'Everything in football must not be sacrificed to money, and clubs with little money, but any amount of enthusiasm, must have a chance', he urged. His words still ring true today.

Harry Radford (*Nottingham Forest*) – *Committee 1898–1905, Vice President 1905–8*

Honorary secretary Harry Radford was the man who helped steer Forest towards professionalism in 1889, and then co-founded the Football Alliance, which later became Division Two. Like Tom Sidney, he was a corporation official. Unlike Sidney, it was declining health which forced him to stand down in 1908. The Committee granted him £20 during his illness, but he died early the following year. He was the father of the Nottingham bass singer Bob Radford.

Walter Hart (*Small Heath*) – *Committee 1899–1903*

Hart was a true Brummie. He worked at the family firm of tinware manufacturers in Hockley, at the heart of Birmingham's metal-bashing district, just around the corner from McGregor's shop on Summer Lane. As president of the Birmingham FA and an early honorary secretary of Small Heath,

Hart would have been very much part of McGregor's circle. He shared McGregor's and John Lewis's teetotal habit, having signed the pledge when he was thirteen.

Known as the father of Birmingham City, it was Hart's suggestion in 1888 that Small Heath be the first club to become a limited liability company, despite attracting capital of just £150. Hart's lifelong abstinence, and his devotion to Birmingham football, lasted until his death at the age of eighty-three in 1940. Thus, only Joe Tillotson remained of that original band of Summer Lane enthusiasts.

George Leavey (Woolwich Arsenal) – Committee 1901–4

The first Southerner to sit on the Management Committee, Leavey came to prominence in May 1900 when he brought representatives of the League and Southern League together for a meeting at the Liberal Club in London. Nothing came of this, or any of his subsequent attempts to amalgamate the two leagues nor of his rather forlorn attempt to oust J J Bentley from the presidency in 1904. He lost the vote by 33 votes to 4, and then lost his seat on the Committee. Back in Plumstead, Leavey ran a men's outfitters in Hare Street, and was known as a pioneering motorist.

Dr James C Baxter (Everton) – Committee 1904–19

A Catholic in a club dominated at the time by Protestants, Dr Baxter had two obsessions – football and medicine. *Porcupine* magazine described him 'as one of the busiest men in Liverpool [whose] beneficence amongst the poor is almost unbounded'.

Dr Baxter was a cheerful, sunny man; an optimist who was popular with patients and with city institutions. He was a magistrate, a local councillor with a particular interest in tramways, electric power and housing – he worked at one time with J A Brodie, city engineer and inventor of goalnets – while in the remaining moments left over from his busy Robson Street surgery he found time to sit on Everton's board from 1889–1928.

In 1892 Dr Baxter gave the club a massive £1000 interest-free loan to help purchase Goodison Park, and throughout his period on the board he acted as Everton's medical officer.

This left just enough time for him to serve in the same capacity at an orphanage, a seminary, a dramatic society and on behalf of several insurance companies. Small wonder that the good doctor was never known to take a holiday, unless, of course, it was to a place where Everton happened to be playing.

After missing many Management Committee meetings during the First World War because of his medical commitments, Dr Baxter was very disappointed to lose his seat to Tom Barcroft in 1919.

He died in January 1928, and so missed seeing Everton win the Championship that season. But Dixie Dean's precious limbs were not unprotected, for Dr Baxter's son, Dr Cecil Baxter, carried on his father's role as both team doctor and club director.

A lasting reminder of Dr James Baxter is a stained glass window dedicated to his memory at the Church of Our Lady Immaculate, St Domingo Road.

Henry 'Harry' Keys (West Bromwich) – Committee 1905–10, Vice President 1910–29

Harry Keys was one of the most popular men of his time in football circles. He came from a well-known West Bromwich family, his father being a town councillor and his three brothers all achieving great sporting and commercial success. Harry was no different. As a youth he won fame as a prize-winning cyclist for the Midland Cycling and Athletic Club (of which he later became president). He once cycled twenty miles in one hour (no mean feat on the older machines), and was also a three-wheeler expert. On one occasion, Keys nearly won the National Tricycle Championship in Bristol. Sadly, he later lost all his trophies to a burglar. When not on two wheels, he was turning out for Sandwell FC.

At the age of twenty-one, Keys set up as a bicycle agent in Livery Street, Birmingham, later moving to Colmore Row. He joined Albion's board in 1896, and was chairman when they moved to The Hawthorns, from 1899 until 1903, when he resigned over 'unfortunate differences'. Soon afterwards, the club faced extinction and when asked, Keys didn't hesitate to return to form a new board with former Albion winger Billy Bassett. Together, they rescued the club (and Bassett succeeded Keys on to the Management Committee).

The *West Bromwich Free Press* said of Keys and the Albion: 'In its periods of crisis he never despaired, and in its hours of triumph he was always modest. A man of forceful personality, he expressed his views decisively, but he was eminently fair.' In fact, he was known to give the players some pretty stern dressings down; they called him John Bull. Unusually, he seldom sat in the directors' box at The Hawthorns, preferring instead the company of journalists in the press box. But then, he was once described as 'a genial companion, a racy raconteur and an appreciative listener'.

There was a softer side to Harry Keys. Outside football, his two passions were gardening and drawing, especially in pen and ink. Many examples of his work adorned The Hawthorns' boardroom.

Keys had two sons. The younger was killed in the First World War, a loss from which he was said never to have quite recovered. His elder son was Major Harry Wilson Keys, who became chairman of Albion from 1948–70 and was often outspoken in League affairs. He once threatened to start up an organization for club directors independent of the Management Committeee. His father would not have approved.

Harry Keys died on 22 August 1929, aged sixty-eight, and drew hundreds to his funeral, including men such as Joe Tillotson, Howard Vaughton and Leslie Knighton. He was, according to the *Midland Chronicle*, 'the soul of honour and straight dealing'.

John Cameron (Newcastle) – Committee 1907–16

Like McGregor, Cameron was born in Perthshire, came south to seek work, and found it in the clothing trade. He was also a well-known lay preacher and chairman of Newcastle from 1903–8. But although United won two Championships during this spell, no amount of prayer could make them win at the Crystal Palace, where they lost three Cup Finals in four seasons.

In early 1916 Cameron gave up his trade and became a

publican in Jarrow, but he died the following July, leaving a wife and eight children at the mercy of the brewery. So popular had Cameron been that offers of help flooded in from clubs and individuals, raising £768 for the family within a few weeks. Cameron's chief legacy to football was the North-Eastern League, of which he was the founder and first chairman.

Arthur Dickinson (*Sheffield Wednesday*) – *Committee 1909–30, Vice President 1929–30*

According to the Sheffield 'Green 'Un', what Arthur Dickinson didn't known about football and the laws of the game wasn't worth knowing. 'A statement by him was accepted as the last word in accuracy.' He was said to have had a photographic memory, and was an exceptionally fit man. He took a brisk walk every day, rarely ate lunch, and always kept his age a secret, perhaps because during the inter-war period he was the oldest member on the Committee.

His other little weakness was public speaking. He hated it, but if given no option he would always choose his words extremely carefully. Hence, he was greatly respected, but often regarded as a touch brusque.

Round-faced, with a distinctive white goatee, Dickinson was born in 1851 and was a Sheffield man through and through. He spent the summer at Bramall Lane watching cricket, and the winter at Hillsborough. Apart from his League and club duties, he was chairman of the Sheffield Amateur League, was active in the Sheffield and Hallamshire FA and was for a while vice president of the Midland League. And naturally, he was in the cutlery business, travelling the country and crossing the Atlantic often three or four times a year to sell Sheffield produce. But he always squeezed in time to do a bit of scouting for the Wednesday, who were his chief passion.

Like his close friend and fellow Committee man Harry Keys, Dickinson was a keen cyclist in his youth. He joined Wednesday in 1876, became financial secretary in 1887 when the club turned professional, and was honorary secretary from 1891–1920. No other club retained an honorary secretary for so long.

Dickinson claimed to have been the first man to have introduced a Scot to an English club, when he brought Lang of Clydesdale to Wednesday in 1876, no doubt after spotting him while 'on business'. When the club had to leave Olive Grove, Dickinson was put in charge of dismantling the old club and setting up a new limited company to start up at Owlerton.

Before the move, the supporters had voted in favour of an alternative site, at Carbrook, but when Dickinson went to Alderman George Senior for his opinion, Senior told him: 'Do as tha' likes, lad. I breathe sulphur all the week, and I'm sure not goin' to Carbrook to suck it in!' Owlerton was, on the other hand, in the country, and thus free from pollution.

With the Clegg brothers (Charles and William), Dickinson was on Wednesday's first board of directors, which numbered twenty-two men! Like the Cleggs, he had a foot in both camps, being also a shareholder of Sheffield United.

In 1920, at the age of sixty-nine and after a disastrous season, Dickinson relinquished his duties at Wednesday, where he had effectively been team manager. When the club gave him a testimonial, it was said that he kept the cheque in his desk and never cashed it.

Made a Vice President of the League in 1929 on the death of his great friend Harry Keys, Dickinson died half an hour before a Management Committee meeting in London on 4 November 1930. He had been at Hillsborough for a match the day before, and was chatting happily with journalist Ivan Sharpe and Will Cuff in the Euston Hotel lobby when he suddenly collapsed, without making a sound, and died on the floor. Still no one, not even his close friends, knew how old he was.

Tom E Harris (*Notts County*) – *Committee 1909–17*

Tom Harris knew football administration better than most of his fellow Committee men. Having joined the Notts County board in 1892, he became honorary secretary a year later and full-time secretary in 1902, until forced to resign through ill-health in 1913. The League sent him £50 to speed his recovery – he would accept only £20 – while the clubs showed their esteem by re-electing him to the Committee for the next three seasons, despite the fact that he was absent from meetings for nearly a year. The two Nottingham clubs also staged a benefit match for him in December 1913.

An avid and meticulous chronicler of County's games, Harris died in 1917.

Tom Houghton (*Preston*) – *Committee 1912–13*

Houghton was thrown into the deep end as chairman of Preston when William Sudell left Deepdale in 1893. His occupation was given as 'traveller' and, indeed, he was known to have travelled thousands of miles both on business and to scout for players. But in 1906 he apparently went too far, and was suspended from football management for one month after being found guilty of improper conduct towards spectators during a post-match fracas at Owlerton.

In his public life, however, he was much less controversial; a Freemason and a Tory councillor, Houghton was well respected for his efforts to create local amenities such as parks and swimming pools. Described by contemporaries as genial and always willing to assist good causes, his sudden death at the age of forty-nine was a great shock both to the Committee and to the town of Preston.

William Hall (*Arsenal*) – *Committee 1913–27*

William Hall was Sir Henry Norris's eyes and ears on the Management Committee. One can easily imagine the comments made about this unlikely duo. Both sported fine, white, bushy moustaches, but Hall was a tiny man over whom Norris appeared to tower both physically and mentally.

A 'metal merchant' from Putney, Hall was first a director at Craven Cottage, but when the powerful Fulham chairman Henry Norris turned his attentions to Woolwich Arsenal, Hall stepped into his mentor's shoes. For three years, from 1910–13, Norris ran both clubs using Hall almost as his agent, a situation which was subsequently barred by the League as a result of their activities.

It was Norris and Hall who suggested that Fulham and Arsenal merge, and Hall who helped to search London for a new site for Arsenal. After the move to Highbury, both men concentrated on the Gunners (though remaining on Fulham's board for some years still), and there can be no doubt that without Norris's sponsorship, Hall would not have been elected on to the Committee.

Hall's football career ended as it had begun, hanging on to Norris's coat-tails. When Norris was suspended by the FA for financial irregularities, Hall inevitably went into purdah with him. He resigned from the Management Committee in September 1927, and died about five years later.

John Peel Oliver (Newcastle) – Committee 1917–28

Despite his honourable name, Oliver seems to have made little impression on the Committee, or on the world in general. A wine and spirit merchant, he was appointed chairman of Newcastle in 1918 after having been a director of the club from its early days, and was still in charge when he returned from St James' Park on the evening of 19 December 1928, never to return.

Tom Barcroft (Blackpool) – Committee 1919–25, 1927–43

Tom Barcroft was the joker in the pack, providing those vital moments of light relief so necessary during long, hard Management Committee meetings. Known as 'the man in the straw hat', Barcroft was a much-loved, cheery man, a constant fund of anecdotes. This might explain why, despite twenty-two years on the Committee, he never achieved nor apparently sought higher office either at the League or at the FA. On the other hand, after losing his seat to Will Cuff in 1925, he did bounce back two years later, which suggests some commitment on his part.

After starting out as a bank clerk, Barcroft joined Blackpool as secretary on a temporary basis, then stayed thirty years, until 1924. A favourite Barcroft yarn told of how Blackpool, once en route to Leicester, failed to meet up with their goalkeeper at Preston station because of a crush of well-wishers seeing off troops to the Boer War. So Barcroft took his place between the posts and gave a humorous running commentary to the fans throughout the game.

The man in the straw hat died on 27 September 1946, aged seventy-five.

Morton Cadman (Tottenham) – Committee 1927–39, Vice President 1939–41

Morton Cadman was closely connected with Spurs for sixty of his eighty-two years. A proud possessor of one of the club's original membership cards from 1882, he joined the committee in 1891 as an amateur playing member. Captain of the reserves during the following decade, he saw the club turn professional and move to White Hart Lane, and was said to have been reluctant when first invited to join the board just before Tottenham's famous Cup-winning season of 1900–1. Once in harness, however, he worked hard for the club, and was partly instrumental in gaining Spurs' election to the League in 1908.

Cadman was well known in the Edmonton area of London as a rate collector and council official. He lived close to White Hart Lane in Brettenham Road, until selling his house to the council to make way for a new school (which still survives). He retired in 1929.

A small, dapper man, rather like William Hall, he was a great advocate of all-English teams in the League, so the modern cosmopolitan scene at Spurs would come as a great shock to him.

After election as Vice President just before the Second World War, Cadman became a widower (like so many Committee men), and was absent for several months until being forced to resign in March 1941 due to his failing eyesight. He died on 4 December 1948, aged eighty-two.

Phil Bach (Middlesbrough) – Committee 1929–37

While Billy Bassett brought a touch of celebrity to the Committee, Phil Bach brought with him experience of the bread-and-butter side of professional football. As a Sunderland fullback, Bach won a single cap for England against Ireland in 1899, largely because the match was being played at the newly opened Roker Park. Unfortunately, the honour cost him dear, because Sunderland had a League match on the same day and his deputy, Andy McCombie, performed so well that Bach was unable to win back his place. He spent the rest of his career with Southern League Reading.

On returning to his native North East, Bach became a licensed victualler and was elected a director and then chairman of Middlesbrough. He was a much-respected international selector for the FA, was president of the North-Eastern League, vice president of North Ridings League and, in common with McKenna and Rinder, was also a Freemason.

League clubs held the burly figure of Bach in such esteem that, although too ill to attend Committee meetings for a year, he was re-elected in his absence in June 1937. He died, however, six months later, aged sixty-five.

William Bassett (West Bromwich) – Committee 1930–7

With the single exception of Sir Matt Busby, Billy Bassett was the most illustrious former footballer ever to sit on the Management Committee. As a 5 foot 5 inches tall seventeen-year-old, he was an unlikely prospect on his debut in 1886, but he soon won the hearts of Albion fans with his darting runs from the wing, his pinpoint centres and his blistering shot. He played in twenty-one of Albion's first twenty-two League matches in 1888/9, scoring eleven goals, and went on to win sixteen England caps (seven goals). Overall, he made about 450 appearances in thirteen years for Albion, with the remarkable tally (for a winger) of 125 goals.

Ironically, one of the most frequently recalled moments of Bassett's career took place after he had hung up his boots for Albion, when he travelled to Berlin for a friendly against Germany in 1900. A defender was marking him so closely, much to his annoyance, that he ran round the back of the goal to see if the German would follow. He did! Bassett said later; 'Had I gone up in a balloon, I think I should have found him treading on my toes along the Milky Way.'

After retiring from the game, Bassett profited from his wide popularity by becoming a successful businessman. He helped Harry Keys and Fred Everiss to rescue Albion in 1905, became a director of the club, and later of three other companies, including the Imperial Picture Palace in West Bromwich. No doubt he and Fred Rinder had much to talk about concerning the cinema industry, since it was Rinder's job to inspect the buildings.

In 1908 Bassett became Albion's chairman, and two years later both he and Keys had to give personal guarantees when the club was ailing once more. He kept a watchful eye on everything at the club, including training and tactics, and until his health began to deteriorate in the 1930s, he didn't miss a single Albion board meeting for twenty-seven years.

Bassett's election to the Management Committee in place of his late friend Harry Keys was essentially an emotional gesture. He was ill for long spells, and missed Albion's finest moment, when they won the Cup in 1931. But shortly afterwards, the Prince of Wales visited The Hawthorns, and so Bassett was able to share at least some of the honour.

He was taken ill again in August 1932 on his way to an Albion match at Highbury, had to rest for six months, and never fully recovered. But when the Albion lost to Sheffield Wednesday in the 1935 Cup Final, the players hoisted him on their shoulders and sang 'For he's a jolly good fellow'.

He was undoubtedly one of the most popular men in the Midlands; successful, dashing and manly in rather the same mould as Harry Keys. But, because of his illness, he was never more than a celebrity member of the Management Committee.

Bassett died on 8 April 1937, aged sixty-eight. He had been at St Andrew's the day before, and had just been presented with a silver casket to mark his fifty years with Albion. 'No one has had anything like so great an influence upon the Albion Club', said one newspaper.

At his funeral he was described as a hero in the town. Thousands lined the streets, forty Albion players attended, and a former Albion amateur international centre-forward, the Reverend W. C. Jordan, officiated at the service. Fred Rinder, Charles Sutcliffe, Stanley Rous, Will Cuff, Steve Bloomer and Jesse Pennington were just a few of the famous names at the graveside.

This was his obituary: 'Mr Bassett was much more than a distinguished football player and legislator – he was a man.'

Amos Brook Hirst (Huddersfield) – Committee 1931–9, Vice President 1939–41

Amos Brook Hirst was one of several men who served their apprenticeship on the Management Committee before going on to higher office at the FA.

A tall, commanding figure, Brook Hirst was a prominent Huddersfield lawyer who played a leading role in saving the club from being moved to Leeds in 1919. During those tension-filled months, Brook Hirst often came into direct confrontation with the Management Committee, whom he felt favoured the pro-Leeds contingent. He also clashed with the FA over the arrangements for semi-finals during Huddersfield's 'double' attempt in 1928.

But, as we have seen with so many of our country's leading characters, keen critics from the back benches have often ended up as establishment figures in government.

Rugby was his first love, but when injury put an end to his playing career he switched to organizing local soccer. He

became one of Town's first directors in 1908, resigned in 1911, but returned as chairman in 1920 to steer the club, under Herbert Chapman's management, to a record three Championship wins between 1923 and 1926. Elected president of the club in 1941, in October of that year he resigned from the Management Committee 'with much regret', after being elected chairman of the FA Council. Brook Hirst was knighted in 1954, and died a year later.

John James Edwards (Arsenal) – Committee 1936–40

Very little is known of the League's second 'JJ' apart from the fact that he was a solicitor in London's Piccadilly, and after the Norris era was Arsenal's largest single shareholder. He made little impact on the Committee before asking to be excused in January 1940, following his suspension by the Law Society for alleged professional misconduct.

Walter Tempest (Blackburn) – Committee 1939–41

Tempest was the ideal Lancashire self-made man. Chairman of Blackburn Rovers from 1933–8, he was the managing director of a firm making window blinds, having started out in life as a Rovers reserve player and a railway ticket collector. Tempest had the typical Management Committee profile for the period; a magistrate, a Freemason and a town councillor (first Liberal, then Tory). As Lord Mayor of Blackburn he invited the Committee to a reception at the town hall in 1940, a unique occasion at that time. He died, aged fifty-nine, in May 1941 after a short illness.

Bill Cearns (West Ham) – Committee 1939–50

A prominent East London building contractor, Bill Cearns was born in Canning Town. He started as a junior clerk in Smithfield Market, then joined the Thames Ironworks shortly after its proprietor Arnold Hills had set up the team which would eventually become West Ham United. At seventeen, Cearns joined a Stratford building firm which he later bought up.

His father James, who also worked at Thames Ironworks, was one of the founder directors of West Ham. Bill succeeded him on to the Hammers' board in 1925, and his firm built all the stands at Upton Park, including in 1925 the double-decker main stand which was completed in just one summer (the company built a replica at Filbert Street also).

Bill Cearns was an innovator. Apart from his building firm he once tried to start an ice-cream sales company, and in 1928 he introduced speedway racing to this country from Australia. The first meeting was at High Beech, near Epping. Also in 1928, Cearns' company built the Wimbledon greyhound stadium, and he became a director of the South London Greyhound Association. He was also responsible for building the greyhound stadium at Southend (where the football club played until 1955). Among his other building credits were the first permanent buildings at Hendon aerodrome.

Cearns became chairman of West Ham in 1934 and president of the Football Combination in 1936. A modest man of a kindly disposition, he was part of a family whose history is almost indivisible from that of West Ham.

At the time of his death in February 1950 at the age of sixty-seven, Bill's younger brother Frank was the club secretary and his son Len was on the board. And just take a look at the board at Upton Park in 1986: chairman, Len Cearns, who also happens to be a Life Vice President of the League; vice chairman, Bill Cearns Junior; directors, Brian Cearns and Martin Cearns. That is, three of Bill Cearns' four sons (the fourth son concentrated on greyhounds) and his grandson. That left only Jack Petchey on the board who was not a member of the clan which in four generations helped to form West Ham, build its ground, and run the club for its entire history. No other club in the League can boast such continuity.

Family enclosures are all the rage in modern football, but as supporters of West Ham might joke, they've had them for years at Upton Park. They just call it the directors' box instead.

George F. Rutherford (Newcastle) – Committee 1938–42, Vice President 1942–9

In common with Arthur Oakley, Rutherford was a coal merchant. He joined the Newcastle board in 1925 when John Oliver was chairman, and was remembered as an unselfish, hospitable man and a steadying influence on the Committee.

Following in his father-in-law's footsteps, he was chairman of Newcastle from 1941 until his death in 1949 at the age of sixty-six. After George came his brother, Dr R. Rutherford, chairman from 1951–4, and then George's grandson, Robert J. Rutherford, chairman from 1978–81.

David Wiseman (Birmingham) – Committee 1941–2 and 1949–71, Life Member 1971–8

David 'Curly' Wiseman was the life and soul of the party, a born comic who had no ambitions to rise up the football ladder, but who could be serious when it mattered. Born in Small Heath in 1895, he left school at thirteen, started as a dishwasher in a restaurant at half-a-crown a week plus board and lodgings, then became apprenticed to a plumber. Eventually, he set up on his own account and built up one of the biggest plumbing businesses in the Midlands.

Wiseman joined Birmingham's board in 1928, and after election to the Management Committee became an international selector. But it was as a member of the Challenge Cup Committee that he achieved widest fame, his Birmingham accent becoming known to millions of radio listeners who tuned in to the draw.

Wiseman was elected a life member of the FA in 1969, was awarded an OBE in 1970, and became a Life Member of the Football League in 1971.

There is much by which to remember him: his own brand of rhyming slang, which soon became familiar to his fellow committee men, many of whom he gave nicknames; his sense of humour; his Charlie Chaplin imitations. As a youth, Wiseman had been a tap dancer and comedian in variety halls, and even in later life he would stand up at parties to sing or do impersonations. He was still playing golf at the age of eighty.

But whatever Curly Wiseman was doing, wherever he was, everything had to stop at exactly eleven o'clock. After an operation on an ulcer, Wiseman's doctor had recommended that he drink a glass of champagne each morning during his convalescence. Wiseman soon recovered, but refused to give up his morning tipple. If he was on the motorway he would pull over and get the usual half-bottle out of the boot. On planes he carried it in a bag. Only the best champagne would do, and nor was it always confined to elevenses. There was hardly a boardroom in the country without a bottle ready and waiting for Curly Wiseman. Small wonder he was so widely mourned when he died in November 1978 at the age of ninety-three.

But the bubbles haven't gone entirely flat since his passing. One of Curly's sons, Alan, is chairman of Southern League's Alvechurch, while another, Jack, is still on Birmingham City's board and joined the Management Committee in 1974 (see page 399).

Will J. Harrop (Liverpool) – Committee 1941–50, Vice President 1950–6

Alan Hardaker called Will Harrop 'One of the kindest men I've ever known'. He was a quiet, rather serious man who would sit and talk for hours on how the League should be conducted. He gave much sound advice to up-and-coming men like Hardaker and Len Shipman.

Yet for all his apparent calm, he wielded considerable influence. Harrop worked for a firm of accountants and estate agents. He joined Liverpool's board in 1926, becoming chairman until 1941, when he stood down to take up his seat on the Management Committee and FA Council. He rose to be chairman of the Challenge Cup Committee, then returned to Anfield as chairman in 1953.

Like so many other Committee members, Harrop was a magistrate, a staunch Methodist and also a long-standing town councillor. And since he was Tory councillor for the Anfield Ward, he really did rule that patch of Liverpool quite effectively. Indeed, so loyal was he to the club that he once turned down the nomination for League President because he didn't want to spent too much time away from Anfield.

Harrop was seventy-six when he died after returning to Liverpool on the train from meetings of the FA and League in London, in February 1956.

Harold Shentall (Chesterfield) – Committee 1942–56, Vice President 1956–63

Despite his twenty-one years on the Management Committee, jovial Harry Shentall, the Chesterfield fruit wholesaler, was more remembered for his work with the FA. He was a friend of Sir Stanley Rous, a vice chairman of the FA after 1962, and a life vice president from 1969. During his long spell with the League, he was often absent from Committee meetings while on tour with the England party.

Shentall joined the Chesterfield board in 1923, becoming chairman in 1928. He was also president of the Derbyshire FA and in 1957 was awarded the OBE for his work with National Savings. Though he retired from the Committee with a long-service medal in 1963, he didn't retire from the family fruit business until 1967, when he was aged eighty. He was another magistrate, a parish councillor, a Rotary president and a Freeman of the City of London (because of his fruit connections). Shentall died in April 1972, aged eighty-five.

Henry 'Harry' French (Middlesbrough) – Committee 1942–63

Like his close friend Harry Shentall, French was a fruit merchant who was often known to leave his hotel early on Monday mornings after Management Committee meetings in order to buy fruit at Covent Garden. But he was a very different man to Shentall, being blunt, direct and difficult to budge.

French followed in the footsteps of his father and elder brother by becoming a Middlesbrough director, and followed the team whenever he could, despite his recurrent ill health. A big man with a gruff voice, French died just days before he was due to be awarded the League's long-service medal, in May 1963.

Philip Wood (Huddersfield) – Committee 1943–7

Phil Wood and Harry French shared the sorrow of having lost a son during the Second World War. Wood was the managing director of the family firm of woollen and worsted manufacturers based at Bradley Mill, which used to stand behind the open end at Leeds Road. Wood joined Huddersfield's board in 1938 and became chairman in 1941 when Amos Brook Hirst was elected chairman of the FA. He died in July 1947 at the age of fifty-seven, only a fortnight after being re-elected to the Committee.

Joe Mears (Chelsea) – Committee 1950–7, Vice President 1957–63

Joe Mears was a real gentleman. A former public schoolboy and officer in the Marines, he was remembered as one of the only members of the Committee ever prepared to sit down and chat with players, even if he didn't always share their views.

Born in the same year as Chelsea, the club his uncle Gus had helped to found, Mears went into the family business (which then was mainly wharfing, garage and motor distribution), and became the youngest director in football when he joined the board at Stamford Bridge in 1931 at the age of twenty-six. Nine years later, in 1940, he also became the youngest chairman, but was almost immediately commissioned in the Royal Marines, with whom he saw service in Crete, Egypt and Ceylon. At one time during the war, Mears was in charge of security at Sir Winston Churchill's underground operation room in Whitehall.

After the war he returned as Chelsea's chairman, and saw them win their only Championship to date in 1955.

Regarded as a quiet, astute man, he apparently wanted to be President of the League but was instead elected to the chairmanship of the FA in 1963. His proudest moment in this capacity should have been as host for the 1966 World Cup. In March 1966, however, he suffered a heart attack after the Jules Rimet Trophy was stolen from an exhibition in London. Mears recovered, and was able to join the England team's preparations in Oslo. Then, just before the group was about to leave for Copenhagen, Mears collapsed in a park and died at the feet of Len Shipman, just ten days before the World Cup was due to open.

Norman Banks (Bolton) – Committee 1950–64

A man in the same mould as Joe Richards, Banks was a tough man who liked to say his piece, and took a pride in working hard, but also playing hard. He was never bothered about promotion within the Committee, but didn't miss one single meeting in his fourteen years in office.

As a youth, Banks was a prominent amateur goalkeeper in Bolton and was for years active in local and junior football circles. He joined his father's paint-manufacturing business, and was elected as a Bolton director in 1924, being chairman twice during his forty-four years on the board. He was also active in the local Conservative club.

When he retired in 1950, the same year as he joined the Committee, Banks emulated his Bolton predecessor John Bentley by retiring to Fairhaven, Lytham. In 1959 he was therefore a keen supporter of the League's move to Lytham St Annes.

Among his many football offices, Banks was chairman of the Central League and president of the West Lancashire League. He died in December 1969, aged seventy-eight.

Wilf Taylor (Newcastle) – Committee 1956–64, Vice President 1964–70, Life Member 1970–1

In common with Fred Howarth, Wilf Taylor was as old as the League. His original intention had been to become a farmer. At the age of fourteen, however, he went to stay with his uncle, the first Lord Mayor of Newcastle, who enlisted his help at the local milling firm of Hindhaugh's, where they were short-handed owing to an outbreak of 'flu. Young Wilf stayed for fifty years and became a director of the firm.

Only in his latter years did he become involved in football administration. As a youth he had tried the game, but was too often afflicted by bronchitis, although he did recall how, as a boy, he had once had to mark Jackie Rutherford, who only a few years later became a great star for Newcastle and England. He was dropped from his school team as a result of that encounter, and concentrated his sporting efforts thereafter on golf.

He joined the Newcastle board during the war, and after retiring from business was elected chairman in 1956, shortly after United had just won their third FA Cup in five years. In the same year he was elected to the Management Committee, where his first task was to defend United's entry into the Anglo-Scottish Floodlit League, which was then about as welcome in Committee circles as a portrait of Jimmy Guthrie.

Taylor's maxim was simple: keep your mouth shut and your ears open. He bemoaned the lack of incentive facing players in the late 1950s, yet opposed the abolition of the maximum wage. He tried to persuade the rest of the Newcastle board to let George Eastham leave in 1960, but three years later defended the club's position in court.

One contemporary described Taylor as a thin, crotchety and daunting man. Another called him small, full of fun and very likeable. He was certainly one of the old school; a 'solid Geordie character'.

After fourteen years on the Committee, his bronchial condition finally caught up with him and he stood down in 1970. Taylor died in February 1971.

Dr Andrew Stephen (*Sheffield Wednesday*) – *Committee 1957–67*

Andrew Stephen was, incredibly, only the second Scot to sit on the Management Committee since William McGregor. He was also the second doctor (Dr James Baxter, 1904–19, having been the first) and a chainsmoking one at that. The softly-spoken Dr Stephen initially became involved with football when he succeeded his partner as club doctor at Hillsborough. He took such an interest that he joined the board in 1949 and was chairman between 1956–73.

For years he accompanied the England party as team doctor, and retained the role even after he was elected chairman of the FA to succeed Joe Mears, in January 1967. He was the first Scot ever to fulfil that role. His medical knowledge proved invaluable soon after he joined the Management Committee, when Wilf Taylor was taken ill just before a Committee meeting and Dr Stephen was able to treat him before taking him to hospital.

Knighted in 1972, Dr Stephen retired from the FA a year later. He was regarded as 'a perfect gentleman' whose quiet, gentle character must have provided quite a counterbalance during some of the more fraught Committee meetings during the early 1960s. He died in February 1980, aged seventy-three.

Syd Collings (*Sunderland*) – *Committee 1963–74, Life Member 1974–6*

In a period dominated by powerful men, Syd Collings was a good, solid committee worker, if not himself a great instigator. A wine and spirit merchant who later bought up a chain of laundries, Collings joined the Sunderland board in the late 1940s, becoming chairman a few years after a scandal involving illegal payments at the club had been revealed by Alan Hardaker, causing a boardroom shake-up at Roker Park. By that time Collings was already active in FA circles, and closely allied to Sir Stanley Rous.

As chairman of the International Committee, he appointed Alf Ramsey as England manager, and then found himself in overall charge of the FA's organization of the 1966 World Cup, when chairman Joe Mears died a few weeks before the tournament began.

A tall, popular man, he stepped down as chairman of Sunderland in 1970 – his son Keith later succeeded him – and when his health deteriorated quite rapidly, left the Management Committee in 1974, a year after Sunderland's historic victory over Leeds in the FA Cup Final. Collings died in the summer of 1976, aged seventy-three, having just celebrated the return of his beloved Rokerites to the First Division.

Arthur Would (*Grimsby*) – *Committee 1963–75, Life Member 1975–*

It was that other Lincolnshire gentleman of the old school, Arthur Drewry, who persuaded Arthur Would to join the board of Grimsby Town during the Second World War. Not that Would needed too much prodding. His father had also been a director.

Would ran a large building company and had interests in the motor trade and holiday camps. He was a gifted, articulate and wealthy man, who for Management Committee meetings would sometimes stay at the Dorchester Hotel while the rest of the members slummed it at the Great Western in Paddington! Wary of the PFA, and protective towards smaller clubs, his major contribution was as a member of the FA Disciplinary Committee, which often necessitated two or three trips to London a week.

Chairman of Grimsby from 1959 to 1973, he was also president of the Lincolnshire FA for twenty-five years, a church warden in his local parish and an independent county councillor for twenty years, eventually becoming chairman of Humberside County Council. At the age of seventy-two he stood down from the Management Committee when regionalization began in 1975, having just lost out in the election for Vice President to Dick Wragg of Sheffield United.

Sam Bolton (*Leeds United*) – *Committee 1964–8, Vice President 1968–75, Life Member 1975–6*

In complete contrast to Would, Sam Bolton was the archetypal blunt, hard-hitting Yorkshireman who, in common with Len Shipman, made good in the haulage business. It was in the air that he first made his mark, however, as a member of the Royal Flying Corps during the First World War and as a captain in the RAF during the Second World War, when he piloted Sunderland flying boats and won the DFC. Immediately after the war, Bolton joined the board at Elland Road, and was elected as a Tory councillor. He later served as deputy mayor and honorary alderman.

Chairman of Leeds United from 1948 to 1962, he laid the ground work for his successors by bringing Don Revie to the club as player-manager in 1961, thus beginning the club's transformation from a modest outfit into a European giant. No director served Leeds longer or more energetically. He would drive enormous distances on football business and think nothing of the effort – as long as it didn't keep him from his beloved golf. Many of his fellow Committee men during this period were keen golfers.

Bolton supported Don Revie to the hilt and, like his manager, was forever telephoning Alan Hardaker to try to win concessions for Leeds. The Secretary's response was invariably the same, and not for printing here.

A tall martinet of a man, Bolton could become animated and frightening if roused. 'Tub-thumping Sam', Joe Richards called him, after Bolton had banged his fist on the table so hard that a pot of ink flew all over the President's notes. A fastidious man in all his habits, Richards was not amused.

Bolton never hid his own feelings, and didn't stop at upsetting others. He once took such exception to the 'fancy London prices' being charged at the Great Western Hotel that he sent a porter out to buy him a bottle of milk.

He was also a stickler for punctuality. After one Management Committee meeting in London, his wife was just a few minutes late in coming to meet him, so he drove back to Leeds without her.

Bolton was a prominent figure in FA circles, too, especially as chairman of the Challenge Cup Committee. He was made a life member of the FA in 1975, the same year as he stood down from the Management Committee when regionalization was introduced. Eighteen months later, he died at the age of eighty-one.

Michael Gliksten (*Charlton*) – *Committee 1964–75, Life Member 1975–*

Michael Gliksten was the William Pitt of football. On the board at Charlton when he was only nineteen, he came to the notice of his elders as a vocal supporter of the PFA during the fight for the maximum wage in 1960/1, and as a result of his audacity was elected to the Management Committee four years later. At twenty-five, he was the youngest man ever to sit on the League's ruling body. Two years earlier, he had become the League's youngest chairman.

Imagine the striking effect this 6 foot 4 inches tall, red-haired youth must have had upon the much older men sitting around the table, some of them old enough to be his grandfather. He was confident, he was rich and he was cultured. But his footballing background was unquestionable, and they respected him in as an equal.

Gliksten was born in 1938, with a silver spoon in one hand and a Charlton rosette in the other. His father Albert and uncle Stanley, who rescued Charlton in 1932, had originally been on the board at Clapton Orient, when the East London club was under the temporary wing of Arsenal. By the time Michael came on the scene, the Glikstens and their manager Jimmy Seed had lifted Charlton from Third Division uncertainty to First Division fame.

The family fortune was carved out of a hugely successful timber company based in the East End. There were also property and farming interests. Gliksten junior attended Marlborough Public School and caused a sensation by starting up a soccer team. After school he studied in France and Germany, and then in 1958 joined his father on the board as the youngest director in the League (possibly the youngest ever).

His organizing skills were soon in evidence. He re-formed the London Mid-Week League for reserve teams, and formed two other junior leagues. He also became president of the Kent FA. On the Management Committee he was known as an 'astute individualist' who was energetic, efficient and a formidable presence, both physically and in debate.

Regionalization in 1975 put an end to his eleven years on the Committee, then, sadly, Gliksten's involvement with Charlton turned sour in the 1980s. Having left the board in 1982, he still owned The Valley and was paying interest on Charlton's old debts, which amounted to around £1 million. Charlton '84, the re-formed company, meanwhile moved across South London to share Selhurst Park with Crystal Palace.

So The Valley, once the biggest ground in the League, now lies overgrown and neglected; a court settlement is awaited between Gliksten, the landlord, and Charlton, the departed tenants; and the fans have been left, bewildered, in the void in between.

Michael Gliksten himself moved on to pastures new – literally. He left the timber business, went to the Royal Agricultural College as a mature student, and now runs a large livestock, agricultural and farming enterprise based in Suffolk and New South Wales, Australia.

In football he has returned almost to his family roots. He is now president of Clapton FC, an East End amateur club which plays in the Isthmian League a few miles from where his father and uncle first started out all those years ago with Clapton Orient.

Louis Edwards (*Manchester United*) – *Committee 1968–73*

Known as 'Champagne Louis', Edwards joined the Management Committee at the time of Manchester United's European Cup triumph in 1968. It was the climax of an eventful decade for Edwards, who joined the board at Old Trafford on the day after the Munich disaster and was made chairman in 1965 when United won the Championship.

A powerful but immensely sociable man, Edwards, like Bob Lord, was in the meat business, although on a somewhat grander scale. He drove a Rolls-Royce, and used his money to build United into the richest club in the land, with a modern, rebuilt stadium to house the expanding empire.

In his heart and soul Edwards was no committee man, and he was quite happy to move aside in 1973 to allow Sir Matt Busby to stand for election instead. Edwards died in 1980, aged sixty-five, and his son Martin is now chairman and chief executive at Old Trafford.

Dick Wragg (*Sheffield United*) – *Committee 1971–5, Vice President 1975–86, Life Member 1986–*

The last of a long line of tough and capable Vice Presidents (the office was abolished in 1986), Dick Wragg is one of the elder statesmen of football. His grandfather was a shareholder of Sheffield United, and his father, also Richard Wragg, was on United's books before the First World War. Dick's own son, Michael, is now on the board, so the Wragg time devoted to United now spans over eighty years.

Dick himself harboured ambitions to play at senior level, but after studying architecture at Sheffield University had to be content playing as an amateur for the Blades Reserves, then later with Macclesfield, Altrincham and Gainsborough Trinity. By that time he had gone into the family building and construction company, and after breaking an ankle in a match his father gave him an ultimatum: play football or work in the business. Young Dick chose the latter, and rose to prominence as president of both the National Federation of Roofing Contractors and the National Federation of Building Contractors. Through his work he also became a Freeman of the City of London.

In the days when United had both a cricket and a football section, Wragg joined the board in 1953 and was elected chairman of the Football Committee in 1960. He then became chairman of the whole club in 1968, and three years later had to perform the most difficult task of his life. United had just returned to the First Division and wanted a four-sided ground; the cricket club was earning very little, so after much discussion he was delegated as chairman to give the cricketers two years' notice to quit. The cricket pitch made way for a new cantilever stand, the pavilion was demolished in 1975, and over the next six years United promptly dropped to the Fourth Division.

A blunt Yorkshireman like Sam Bolton and Alan Hardaker, Wragg was always very much the traditional club director: ambitious, affable, always full of bonhomie and always ready to speak his mind. And like so many members in this period, he arrived on the Committee sporting not only his golf clubs but also some solid years of experience at the FA, where he became a most respected chairman of the International Committee. He also succeeded Len Shipman on the organizing committee for UEFA club competitions.

These duties have taken him and his trusty pipe all over the world. In Europe there are only two countries that he has yet to visit – Albania and Iceland. Any invitations?

Sir Matt Busby (Manchester United) – Committee 1973–82, Vice President 1982–3, Life Member 1985–

A man who hardly needs an introduction, Sir Matt was one of the best loved and respected managers of all time. He raised Manchester United from the status of a quite unremarkable First Division club into a world-renowned legend. Twice he rebuilt their hopes, from the bombed-out ruins of Old Trafford in 1945, and once again from the cruelly broken dreams of the Munich air crash. He was badly injured himself in that crash, and had to fight for his life for several days.

Under Busby's astute management, United won the FA Cup twice (in four Final appearances) and the League Championship on five occasions. His legendary 'Busby Babes' also won the FA Youth Cup six times in the 1950s. Busby's zenith came in 1968 when he was deservedly knighted after leading United to their famous European Cup victory over Benfica at Wembley. Many tears were shed that night, both of joy and of sorrow for all the friends he had lost at Munich a decade earlier.

Born in a Lanarkshire mining village in 1909, Sir Matt played for Manchester City and Liverpool, where he was in the same side as Cliff Lloyd, later to become secretary of the Players' Union. On the field he was described as a creative wing-half who was the master of deception.

Off the pitch he was incapable of deception. 'There is nothing wrong in trying to win, so long as you don't set the prize above the game', he would tell his players. He was like a father to them. Yet with his board of directors he could be as stern as a hospital matron. In this respect, and in his tracksuit style of management, he was very much a break from the pre-war tradition of managers.

After handing over team matters at Old Trafford in 1969, Sir Matt served on UEFA's Technical Committee, then in 1973 joined the Management Committee in succession to his chairman, Louis Edwards.

A quiet man in committee, he served as a valuable bridge between the League and the players during the negotiations for freedom of contract. But as someone said of Sir Matt, who is now president of Manchester United: 'He was just too nice a man to argue.'

Jack Wiseman (Birmingham City) – Committee 1974–83, Vice President 1983–6, Life Member 1986–

Son of David 'Curly' Wiseman (see page 395), Jack was the first man to follow his father on to the Management Committee. It was a tough act to follow.

First he joined his father's plumbing business, then in 1958, at the age of forty-one, he joined the Birmingham City board. After years of telling his father what was wrong with the game, now was his chance.

The 1960s were a time of great innovation at St Andrew's: new stands, large crowds, exciting players and a lively approach to marketing. While neighbours Villa appeared to be slumbering under a heavy quilt of tradition, the Blues buzzed. But it didn't get them anywhere, and City were soon eclipsed again.

In common with his fellow Vice President Dick Wragg, Wiseman cut his teeth at the FA, as divisional representative for the Birmingham FA. At the time of his election to the Management Committee in 1974, the Midland clubs, led by Sir Jack Scamp and Doug Ellis, were agitating for a regionalized system of representation, and Wiseman, somewhat caught in the middle, became their spokesman on the Committee. But when the new system did begin a year later, it was Wiseman who kept his seat.

Always loyal to the League, it looked as if he would serve out his term of office until his seventieth birthday. Instead, another change in the Committee's constitution in 1986 saw him ousted with just a year to go. But 'Tin Tack', as his father called him, remained cheerful, and a month later won back his place on the FA Council as divisional representative.

One of Wiseman's most significant contributions as a Committee member was to work closely with Gordon Taylor of the PFA on the complex business of players' insurance. But there were few jobs he wouldn't gladly take on, which was perhaps both his strength and his weakness. Said one former colleague: 'Jack was always available for advice, always willing to do a job. He just couldn't say no.'

Dr Clifford Grossmark (Gillingham) – Committee 1975–83

Dr Grossmark was of that rare breed of committee men: a loner. This was partly as a result of his character – he hated the social side of football and was a real worrier – and partly because of the nature of his role as the first Associate Members' representative to serve on the Committee. He said that he felt a bit of an interloper at times.

Despite his diffidence and the subsequent difficulties he had in chairing meetings of the Third and Fourth Division clubs, 'The Doc' was an extremely popular man who was twice re-elected after his first term of three years. His knowledge of players in the lower divisions was quite encyclopaedic, and he worked hard with Dick Wragg and Bertie Mee to build up contacts with schoolboy football.

Oddly for a club chairman, he never believed that his team would ever win a game. Television commentator and fellow Gills director Brian Moore recalled how, after a particularly bad run of results, Gillingham won a game 4–1. Moore rang up 'The Doc' that evening, full of relief and excitement. 'What a great result!' he said, to which the good doctor replied gloomily: 'We could have been three down in the first thirteen minutes.'

'The world's greatest pessimist,' remembered Moore, 'but lovable with it.'

He was a particularly kind person. Graham Kelly recalls that every Christmas Dr Grossmark would hand him a parcel to deliver to two old ladies in Blackpool. Sadly, this mystery duo had to go without in 1983, for on 12 November that year their benefactor died en route to see Gillingham play at

Fellows Park. As 'The Doc' might have expected, Walsall won 3–1, but football was the real loser that day.

Brian Mears (Chelsea) – Committee 1975–81

Although Brian Mears was also thought of as a somewhat diffident man, he managed to represent one of the most difficult regional groups, which included the tough-talking duo, Ernie Clay of Fulham and Jim Gregory of QPR.

Brian was the son of Joe Mears, a former member of the Management Committee and chairman of the FA, whose uncle Gus had been the founder of Chelsea. Brian joined the board in 1958 at the tender age of twenty-seven and followed in the family tradition by becoming chairman in 1969. He had already entered the family business, a Ford Motor distributorship, but in 1970 changed tack and went into advertising.

The next eleven years at Stamford Bridge were eventful, to say the least. Mears saw his team plummet from the euphoria of victory in the European Cup Winners' Cup in 1971 to the depths of debt and despair in Division Two by 1979. The huge debt – the result of building a colossal new stand – led ultimately to Mears resigning the chair in 1981. His half brother David also left the board soon after, having sold the family share of the ownership of the ground to a property developer for a reputed £1.25 million.

Chelsea's new chairman, Ken Bates, was not amused, and has been struggling with the consequences ever since. What the Mears family had given in 1905, the Mears family had appeared to take away seventy-seven years later.

Robert Daniel (Plymouth) – Committee 1976–86

The first Devonian to serve on the Committee, Robert Daniel was another 'bright young thing' who became wealthy enough at an early age to devote his prime years to the League. Born in Plymouth in 1934, he started his own cash-and-carry firm at the age of twenty, and by the time he was thirty-nine had earned enough to retire.

He became chairman of Argyle in 1964, when he was still an active player in Sunday football, and on election to the Committee in 1976 had an immediate impact as chairman of the League's new commercial department. Working alongside Graham Walker, the League's first marketing manager, Daniel was able to help many clubs set up profitable lotteries like the one he had already established at Plymouth.

He also helped to negotiate the League's first sponsorship deals with Canon, the National Dairy Council, Mitre and Atari (for the indoor Soccer Sixes), and was a member of the sorely tried Television Negotiating Committee from 1981 to 1986.

Commercial whizz-kid though he was, the constant travelling from Plymouth was a great drain upon Daniel, and in 1982 he stood down from the chairmanship at Home Park so that he could recover his health and concentrate more on League affairs.

But the lure of the game was too much, and he gladly accepted an invitation to join the board of Torquay United in 1984. Nowadays he divides his time between the calmer climes of Plainmoor, a house in Portugal and a home in Devon.

Christopher Needler (Hull City) – Committee 1976–86

In common with Messrs Gliksten, Wiseman and Mears, Christopher Needler's role in life was largely influenced by his father. Harold Needler and his brothers, John and Henry, had turned Hull City into virtually a family business in 1946, had built a completely new stadium at Boothferry Park and, with player-manager Raich Carter's goals and guidance, had launched a new set of hopes for the post-war era.

Christopher was born in 1944, just before the beginning of this dream, but if there were any family hopes that the prodigal son may one day have helped Hull out on the pitch, they were soon abandoned when he attended Repton. 'I was the worst footballer in the school', he freely admits.

Back in Hull he studied chartered accountancy before joining both the family quarrying firm and the Hull board in 1971. He was twenty-seven, another of football's growing breed of precocious young directors. Four years later he took over the chair at Boothferry Park, and was elected to succeed Dick Wragg as divisional representative at the FA. A year after that, he joined the Management Committee. He had, meanwhile, managed to take in a masters degree in law and economics at Trinity College, Cambridge.

Unfortunately, the laws of economics in football were somewhat harder to master. Having stood down from the chair in 1979 through pressure of work, Needler ploughed more of the family fortune into the club, but the only return he got was seeing City drop to the Fourth Division and the club fall to its knees. The fans called for his head, while he nursed the debts.

In the meantime, the family business had been sold, and as a new chairman, Don Robinson, picked up the pieces at Hull, Chris Needler moved to London and into insurance and the leisure industry. He remains on Hull's board, however, and is as closely involved as the motorway will allow. His brother-in-law is a fellow director, and his mother still won't miss a game. You don't give up a dream too easily.

Sir Arthur South (Norwich) – Committee 1981–5, Life Vice President 1985–

After a lifetime in local government, business and health administration, when Sir Arthur South joined the Management Committee at the age of sixty-five he might have thought he'd seen it all. Instead, he became chairman of the Television Negotiating Committee, one of the toughest jobs in football.

Sir Arthur was forty-one when he first became actively involved in the game, in rather unusual circumstances. He was attending a function in his official capacity as Lord Mayor when word came through that the chairman of Norwich City was waiting down in the foyer in a heightened state of anxiety. Having just finished bottom of the Third Division South, City apparently had no money left to pay the wages and would go to the wall unless someone came to their rescue.

South himself was not a wealthy man, although because he was in the fur trade everyone assumed he must be. But his reputation in the city was second to none, and within weeks of the chairman's desperate entreaty South had galvanized the town into action.

He set up a trust, and a committee to investigate why the

club had come to such a pretty pass, and in return for his rescue efforts was made a vice president at Carrow Road. That was as far as he intended to go, but when a director died in 1966 South took the plunge and joined the board. Even then he told people he wouldn't stay long because he knew little about football and didn't especially enjoy the game.

That was soon to change.

As someone who had been a Labour Party activist for thirty years and a tireless worker for the city's hospitals, South found the altogether different world of directors' boxes and boardrooms quite intriguing. He recalled watching a match one afternoon and overhearing Jim Gregory, the QPR chairman, and the Norwich chairman, Geoff Watling, discussing the idea of swapping their Rolls-Royces. 'They actually did a deal during the game!' Sir Arthur recalled.

But he learnt the ropes quickly enough, and after becoming chairman himself in 1973 led the club to some of its best years in Division One. He commanded enormous respect, with forty-eight years in local government and twenty years on the City board under his belt. His gruff, no-nonsense voice was often heard on BBC Radio's *Any Questions*.

The knighthood was conferred in 1974, in recognition of his public service. He received the honour at Buckingham Palace on the same day in June as Liverpool's manager Bill Shankly was made an OBE. Both were men of the people, in their different ways.

Sir Arthur is a man who likes a tussle. On the Management Committee he would often play devil's advocate, and never hesitated to speak his mind. He was the perfect man to lead the television negotiations. From 1970 to 1974 he had sat on a committee which looked into the regional affairs of the BBC, and he was also a practised negotiator as chairman of the area health authority (in which capacity he often came across his opposite number from Preston, Tom Finney, the former England winger).

'You always knew where you stood with Sir Arthur', said one of his colleagues. But in all his years of negotiations, party politics and public life, nothing had prepared him for the clubs' rejection of the television deal he and his committee had extracted from the BBC and ITV in February 1985. 'It was one of the most harrowing experiences I've had', remembered Sir Arthur.

John Smith (Liverpool) – Committee 1982–6

When the First Division clubs started to agitate for reconstruction of the League, around 1982, John Smith was often their spokesman. He stood for the presidency in 1981, coming second to Jack Dunnett, then joined the Committee a year later.

As chairman of the most successful club in the League, and one of the top five clubs in Europe, his was always a voice worth listening to.

Born in Toxteth, Liverpool in 1920, Smith started out in Walker's brewery, eventually rising to become a director of the brewing giant Tetley Walker. He was fifty-one when he joined the Anfield board, by which time Liverpool had won a mere seven Championships, the Cup only once, the League Cup not at all, and there was not a single European trophy in the cabinet.

After only two years on the board, Smith became chairman in 1973, and the rest is statistics: ten more Championships up till 1988 (making a record total of seventeen), two FA Cup wins, four League and Milk Cup wins (in a row), the European Cup four times and the UEFA Cup twice. As the man whom Smith appointed as Bill Shankly's successor, Bob Paisley, once remarked: 'I've been here in the bad times too. Some years we came second.'

So John Smith, as chairman of such a great club, must surely be some kind of wealthy mogul with an iron grip. Aren't all chairmen of successful clubs like that? Not a bit of it. Liverpool's very strength is their ability to work as a team, both off the field and on it.

Thus, while chairmen such as Ernie Clay and Bob Lord were earning all the headlines, Smith was simply allowing his team to get on with the job.

He can be tough if the mood takes him. He can also attend at the bar and enjoy a drink and a laugh with the fans. He seeks very little attention.

But he gets it all the same. In 1985 he was chosen to become head of the Sports Council, the first 'football man' to hold the office. But it was not through football that he won the wider recognition. Nor golf (yes, another golfer on the Management Committee). It was, in fact, through tennis. What Sir Norman Chester was to football, John Smith became to lawn tennis in 1980, having been chairman of a committee of enquiry into the sport.

Smith also sits on the Football Trust, is a JP, a deputy Lieutenant of the County of Merseyside and president of the Merseyside Development Corporation. Philip Carter of Everton is a member of the same body, and in some ways the two club chairmen are similar. They are both retired company directors, both Conservatives, both passionate believers in their city, and both hold the CBE.

They might have been sitting together on the Management Committee today. Both Merseyside giants had been represented together on the Committee twice before: John McKenna and Will Cuff between 1925 and 1936, Cuff and Will Harrop between 1941 and 1949. But Smith decided that the Sports Council needed his full energies, so he decided not to stand for re-election to the Committee after the reconstruction of 1986.

Not everyone realized this, however, and when they saw John Smith's name on the ballot paper, they voted for him. And that, cynics have suggested, was how John Smith of Luton came to be a member of the Management Committee.

Alan Everiss (West Bromwich) – Committee 1983–6

Although there have been more members of the Cearns clan at West Ham, no single family has enjoyed a longer association with a club than the Everiss crew at West Bromwich.

Alan's father, Fred, joined the Albion in 1894, became secretary in 1902 and served until 1948. After him came his brother-in-law, Ephraim Smith, who in turn handed over to Alan in 1960. The three men's total service to Albion amounts to 150 years.

Everiss Junior began as an office boy at The Hawthorns in 1933, spent the war in the RAF (as did Sir Arthur South and Sam Bolton), retired as secretary in 1980, and then joined the

West Bromwich board. A magistrate, as so many committee men have been, he also served as president of FLESA (the Football League Executive Staffs Association), an organization for managers, coaches and secretaries which his father founded in 1912.

Few men in the game had Alan Everiss's wealth of experience, and it was therefore no surprise when he was elected to the Management Committee as the Midland group's representative in 1983. Indeed, seldom had the Midlands been so well represented, for there was also Jack Dunnett as President of the League and Albion's chairman, Bert Millichip, leading the FA. Alan Everiss was hard working, dependable, avuncular and, in the words of one of his colleagues, 'a thoroughly decent man'.

Ian Jones (Doncaster) – Committee 1984–6

Here was another high flier. A successful young solicitor who would leave his office at midday on Saturdays, pick up his plane at Doncaster airport and fly to his club's away games.

Jones joined Doncaster's board in 1977 when he was aged thirty-three, and took the chair three years later. As successor to Dr Grossmark he was a tireless and effective campaigner for the Associate Members, especially in the delicate negotiations which led, over the course of two years, to the introduction of automatic promotion and relegation between the Fourth Division and the then Gola League. The Associate Members had good cause to thank him for his tactical manœuvres.

A qualified squash coach, Jones was a fine speaker and a lively presence on the Committee. But when the restructuring of the Management Committee took place in 1986, he made a gallant gesture and stood down to allow the outgoing President, Jack Dunnett, a chance to remain on the Committee as representative of the Associate Members. There is still, however, plenty of high flying left in Ian Jones, and one suspects that he won't be grounded for long.

Ken Bates (Chelsea) – Committee 1986–8

However one views Ken Bates, for sure the Football League is a livelier beast for his presence. Bates is the maverick on the Management Committee, a man charged up with ideas and energy, never hesitating to stir up a hornets' nest or challenge the status quo. He loves a battle, and usually finds one.

His first direct involvement with the League came as a co-opted member of the Television Negotiating Committee in February 1985, and he has been prominent in the commercial, marketing and broadcasting fields ever since.

To many people both inside and outside the game, Ken Bates is known as the man who once installed electric fences around the perimeter at Stamford Bridge. They worked on his dairy farm, so why not at a football ground? He also won notoriety on Fleet Street by sending members of the press packing from their complimentary seats in Chelsea's East Stand to a roof-top perch on the opposite side of the ground.

And yet behind his white beard, Ken Bates is not always the tough, shoot-first-ask-questions-later sort of man he often appears. In 1986–7 he stuck by his manager, John Hollins, during an abysmal run of results on the pitch, when other chairmen might easily have wielded the axe.

At the same time, Chelsea's financial turnaround under Bates has been remarkable. He transformed a club with a deficit of £2 million and losses of £12,000 a week in 1982 into a viable proposition within five years. In this achievement he has much in common with fellow Committee men Noades, McGee and Fox – strict housekeepers and Thatcherite economists all.

Born in Richmond, Surrey, fifty-six years ago, Bates recalls that as a toddler his first and only ambition was to become a professional footballer, a quest he pursued as far as one of Arsenal's nursery clubs, Chase of Chertsey FC.

After initial training in accountancy, he went into ventures as varied as sugar-cane growing in Queensland to land development in the Caribbean. In between he also became involved in venture-capital projects, quarrying, Irish banking, a building company in Burnley, a hotel in South Africa, travel and property. In recent years he has found a niche in dairy farming in Beaconsfield (his farm provided the ice-cream at the Centenary banquet).

Bates's football life has been almost as varied as his business career, though not so far-flung. In 1965 he was invited to join Oldham Athletic's board, at a time when the club was bankrupt and struggling at the foot of the Third Division.

Three years later he resigned from Boundary Park, but returned, via the West Indies, to Wigan Athletic in 1981. A year later, in April 1982, he took over as chairman of Chelsea. (Several past members of the Management Committee have had two clubs during their careers, but Bates is the first to have been involved with three.)

Since his election in May 1986, Bates has been a dominant figure, as chairman of the Centenary Committee and the Commercial and Marketing Committee and as a member of the Finance Committee. In the latter role he played a leading part in signing up Mercantile Credit (to the *Today* newspaper's ire) and in August 1987, Barclays Bank. His priority, he says, is to put the League on to a business-like footing and to make sure that money made on the back of the game by outside interests is channelled to the benefit of the clubs.

Ken Bates's toughest challenge lies beyond the Management Committee, however, and that is to keep Chelsea at Stamford Bridge, a ground which the Mears family sold to a property company, Marler Estates, rather than sell it to Bates. Bates has until 1989 to find the capital to buy Stamford Bridge – at anything from £15–85 million, depending on whose valuation you believe – or face the prospect of a move to another ground.

He lost his place on the Committee in 1988 when Chelsea were relegated to the Second Division.

David Dein (Arsenal) – Committee 1986–

When David Dein spent around £350,000 on Arsenal shares in 1983 and took a seat on the board, he caused quite a stir in North London. Then, within four months, he was elevated to the position of Vice Chairman, and less than three years later was elected to the Management Committee, having already joined the FA Council a short time before.

By any standards it was a quite meteoric rise to office, possibly the fastest of any of the Men Who Made It, and since Dein was thirty-nine at the time of his election, he also became the youngest man on the Committee.

Born in London, Dein's love affair with the Gunners began when he was five. He represented Hendon Schoolboys as a young player, before succumbing to that common curse of Management Committee members past and present, the dreaded knee injury. He then went on to graduate in economics and French before making an extremely successful career as a commodity broker, principally in sugar.

On arrival in the Highbury boardroom, Dein typified the growing breed of businessmen who were wealthy enough to

---

Apart from attending monthly Management Committee meetings, there are numerous other committees and League sub-committees involving anything from two to four members. In 1987–88 Philip Carter had the heaviest workload, sitting on nine of these committees. In 1987–8, Management Committee members participated in the following bodies:

● International Football League Board (to co-ordinate with the Scottish, Northern Irish and Eire Leagues)

● Joint Liaison Committee (to co-ordinate with the FA)

● Professional Football Negotiating Committee, and the Footballer's Further Education and Vocational Training Society Limited (each with the PFA, under the independent chairmanship of Professor Sir John Wood)

● Football League Appeals Committee (with the PFA and Football League Executive Staffs Association, also under Sir John's chairmanship, to determine transfer disputes if called upon)

● Trustees of the Football League Pension Scheme (with Ken Friar and Alan Bennett of FLESA and Bert Millichip of the FA)

● Players' Benefit Scheme (with Gordon Taylor and insurance expert SW Taylor)

● Players' Retirement Scheme

● Football League Jubilee Benevolent Fund

● Committee of Enquiry into Playing Surfaces (set up in 1986 to study all types of pitches, synthetic and real, while the three-year moratorium on artificial surfaces was in operation. David Dein of Arsenal is chairman, the other members being Ian Stott (Oldham) Gordon Taylor (PFA), Sir Walter Winterbottom, Tom Hughes (Middlesbrough), David Pleat (Leicester), Dr Steve Baker (Sports Turf Research Institute), David Thomson (Scottish League) and David Dent (Football League))

In addition, only Management Committee members and League staff sit on any of the following League sub-committees:

Referees, Commercial/Marketing, Television and Radio, Finance, Forward Planning, Centenary, Anti-Hooliganism.

---

devote their prime years to football, yet who were not much older than some of the senior players at the club.

But far from disturbing the steady, traditional tenor of life in Arsenal's marble halls, Dein soon settled down to become an establishment figure in his own right. For example, he played an important mediating role in Fulham's battle for survival in February 1987, and is also chairman of the League's Committee of Enquiry into Playing Surfaces. He is sharp, he is bright, and he clearly loves every minute of his involvement. Dein is the fourth Arsenal representative on the Management Committee, and his election meant that London clubs had three representatives on the Committee for the first time in League history.

Bill Fox (*Blackburn Rovers*) – *Committee 1986–*

In common with former members Harry French and Harold Shentall, the chairman of Blackburn Rovers, Bill Fox, is a fruit and vegetable wholesaler. He joined the family business on leaving grammar school in 1943, and is now chairman of the company and a prominent figure in the potato marketing and import industry. He is also managing director of his own commercial vehicles company.

A Rovers supporter from 1938, he has been ever present since, apart from two years' national service as a small-arms instructor in the East Lancashire Regiment. He joined the board at Ewood Park in 1976 and became chairman in 1982, when he was largely responsible for keeping the club alive through careful management of the finances.

In 1985 Fox was, with Ron Noades, one of the Second Division's negotiating team during a long-running debate over reconstruction. He was, therefore, a natural candidate for the Committee in the May 1986 elections.

In certain respects, Bill Fox follows in the tradition of Bob Lord (although don't mention deadly rivals Burnley to him!). He is a confident, outspoken man who 'calls a spade a spade' (or should that be 'a spud a spud'?), and always has his club's interest at heart. After John Lewis and Walter Tempest, he is the third Rovers man to sit on the Committee.

Bert McGee (*Sheffield Wednesday*) – *Committee 1986–8*

Bert McGee first caught the Wednesday bug as a young boy, but like so many Committee members his own amateur playing career ended with an injury. He then rose rapidly up the business ladder after starting with Presto Tools as an engineer in 1952. He is now the company chairmàn.

McGee became a director of Wednesday in 1973 and chairman in 1975, when he took a lead role in resurrecting the clubs from terrible debt, despair and the depths of the Third Division, not by free spending but by no-nonsense common sense and the application of strict financial control.

Apart from steering Wednesday's return to their rightful place in the First Division in 1984, in 1986 he fulfilled a life-long ambition by building a £1-million cover over the famous Hillsborough Kop, where he had first stood, in rain and shine, forty years earlier.

McGee is the third Wednesday man to sit on the Committee, after Arthur Dickinson and Dr Andrew Stephen, and as a Sheffield traditionalist he is very much in the Dickinson

Each Management Committee member automatically has a seat on the FA Council, which itself has thirty-one standing and other committees. As President of the League, Philip Carter is automatically a vice president of the FA and thus sits on the International FA Board, the FA Emergency Committee and the FA Executive Committee.

In 1987–8, Management Committee members were active on the following FA committees: Challenge Cup (Messrs Bates, Fox and McGee); Finance and General Purposes (Carter and Dunnett); Instructional (Stott); International (Bates, Carter, Dein and Dunnett); Match and Grounds (Fox and Noades); Referees (Dein and Noades); Rules Revision (Stott); Disciplinary (Dunnett, Fox, McGee and Stott).

Former Management Committee members Dick Wragg, Jack Wiseman, Len Shipman and Bob Strachan were also on various FA committees during 1987–8, most notably Dick Wragg as chairman of the all-important International Committee.

mould. A keen disciplinarian, McGee is much opposed to the exploitation of football clubs by wealthy outsiders. 'Football clubs shouldn't be used as ego trips or possessions by individuals,' he says. McGee retired from the Committee in 1988.

Ron Noades (*Crystal Palace*) – *Committee 1986–*

If Ron Noades had done nothing else in football, he would still have gone down in history as the man who almost single-handedly won Wimbledon a place in the League in 1977, by personally canvassing thirty-eight of the forty-four Full Members and visiting almost every major newspaper office to put over Wimbledon's case.

He is a man accustomed to having to fight for his cause. Born into a large and poor family in Kilburn, London, he was a tough kid who was always running one football team or another. His first job was as a trainee accountant with the Rank Organization, with a two-year interlude in the RAF working for NATO in Paris. Thereafter, he became a successful salesman, then a newsagent, then a property dealer.

In the meantime, he had stopped playing football and begun to rise up the ladder as a referee. He reached Grade Two and might have made it to League level had lung disease not ended his ambitions in his early thirties. Of the present Management Committee he is the only member to have refereeing experience, or, indeed, to hold an FA coaching badge, which he earned at Bisham Abbey.

Although a keen Derby fan at the time (a team he had chosen purely arbitrarily as a boy), in 1974 he took over Isthmian League Southall, turned the club inside out and steered them to promotion. Within two years he was at Wimbledon, a struggling non-League outfit whom he bought for a mere £2782 and who then went on to win their third Southern League title in a row and, as is now history, a place in the Fourth Division within a year of Noades taking over.

In the same way as property developer Henry Norris switched from Fulham to Arsenal in 1910 because he saw more potential in Plumstead, in January 1981 Noades moved across South London to Crystal Palace, who were then nearly £2 million in debt and at the foot of the First Division. But their potential was, and still is, enormous when one considers their ground and the vast catchment area they command.

Initially, Noades wanted to merge Wimbledon with Palace and create a South London giant. Instead, football being the fickle game it is, he then had to suffer the shock of seeing the young players he had brought to Plough Lane lift Wimbledon over the heads of Palace and into the First Division. Another attempt to merge the two clubs failed in 1987.

In common with Messrs Bates, Fox and McGee, Noades has brought spending at his club to within sensible limits after the profligacy of his predecessors. He also invited Charlton to share Selhurst Park, the first ever ground-sharing arrangement in the League, and brought about the £2 million redevelopment of one section of the ground into a supermarket.

At a national level, Noades has had his failures and his successes. His plan for a League pools competition, called Top Score, did not take off, but as chairman of the Second Division's representative group during the restructuring negotiations (along with Bill Fox), Noades conducted a shrewd campaign, fighting for the Second Division's interests yet not going so far as to provoke a split with the Super Leaguers. With Martin Lange of Brentford, Noades was also responsible for devising the play-off system, which as we have noted, was a vital element of the eventual Heathrow Agreement.

Since his election to the Management Committee – the first Palace man to be a member – Noades has been closely involved in many new schemes, including the revival of the *Football League Official Yearbook* (see Bibliography), the launching of Worldwide Soccer, the League's own television company, and the setting up of the League's commercial and marketing department.

Everything he urges for the League he practises in his own club. His record in football speaks for itself, and since Ron Noades was never afraid of speaking for himself anyway, it is as well that he is on the League's side.

Ian Stott (*Oldham*) – *Committee 1986–*

Oldham's managing director and chairman, Ian Stott is the first representative of the club to sit on the Management Committee, where he is at present the second-youngest

Although the Third and Fourth Division clubs have one representative on the Management Committee (in 1988 Jack Dunnett), there is also an Associate Members Advisory Committee. In 1987–8 this committee was chaired by Reg Driver (Aldershot). Other members were Jack Dunnett (Notts County), MDB Sinclair (York), K Chadwick (Blackpool), PS Hill (Hereford), JW Pratt (Mansfield), N Rowlinson (Crewe) and DA Ruston (Cambridge).

member. Born in Oldham in 1934, he attended a private boarding school near Rugby before moving to Shrewsbury Public School. A real all-rounder on the playing fields, he played hockey, cricket, rugby and soccer for various school teams before spending his national service in the Green Jackets and Lancashire Fusiliers.

He was then due to read law at Cambridge, but chose instead to enter the family cotton business, which owned four mills in Oldham. In the 1960s, the mills having been sold, Stott changed tack and built up a successful garage business, then diversified by building and running a hotel, a discotheque in Cheshire and a caravan park in North Wales. He is also chairman of the governors of his former preparatory school.

Invited to join the Oldham board in 1974, just after the club had won promotion to Division Two, he was elected chairman in 1982, and in League circles became a vocal sup- porter of automatic promotion and relegation from the Alliance Premier League to the Fourth Division.

His gift for both negotiation and oratory was frequently to the fore during the reconstruction discussions of 1985–6.

An expansive, articulate man, Stott became a leading cham- pion of artificial pitches after Oldham installed one in 1986. Stott himself made an extensive study of the new pitches, travelling all over Europe to see them in use. He is now on the League's Committee of Enquiry into Playing Surfaces.

Stott is known to be a shrewd man, full of confidence and authority, who, typical of his generation, believes in running his club as a business, not as a hobby to be bolstered up by continual hand-outs. Perhaps most significantly, he revels in committee work. All things considered – age, experience and abilities – Ian Stott is a man who should go far in the League. Watch this space.

APPENDIX THREE

Inter-League Matches

This section covers all the matches played under the direct auspices of the League; that is, Inter-League matches and other games (mainly benefits) played by teams selected by the Management Committee.

League regulations in January 1889 stated that funds for the organization would be raised by staging matches between teams selected by the Committee. In fact, the first such match played was against the Football Alliance in April 1891, but only because, a month earlier, the FA had refused permission for the League to play a Scottish League eleven.

With Harry Lockett acting as matchmaker, the League v. Alliance game was played at Olive Grove, Sheffield on 20 April 1891, the League claiming 60 per cent of the takings.

In 1892 the League managed to win the FA's approval to play the Scottish League, and the first of many games in this series took place at Bolton in April 1892. Later that year, however, the League was desperate for funds and hoped to arrange a return match, but when the Scottish League failed to respond, the Committee decided instead to arrange a North v. Midlands match at Bramall Lane (on condition that Sheffield United did not charge the League for hiring the ground). Committee men Bentley and Starling ran the lines, and each player received £1 for playing, but had to bring his own shorts, socks and boots.

The next match versus the Scottish League was eventually arranged for 8 April 1893 in Glasgow, and from then on, Inter-League matches were regular events, forming the largest single source of income for the League until 1939.

The League didn't trust its Scottish counterparts at first, it would seem. At Celtic Park in April 1893, a member of the Committee was asked to 'assist' at the gates. But when the League's share turned out to be £364 1s 9d – a huge amount then – the Committee called for 'a hearty vote of thanks' to the Scots and the players, each of whom was awarded a gold medal.

The Inter-League game in Belfast in 1902 is of particular note. In view of the recent Ibrox disaster, Tom Charnley wrote to the Irish League suggesting that an expert examine the stands before the match. The Committee also asked to be excused from the Irish FA's invitation to dinner after the game, which was just as well because, as the team were leaving Belfast docks, former Stoke goalkeeper Ezekiel Johnston (then playing in Ireland) spotted a passenger fall from the ship into the water. He leapt in to the rescue, and as a result the League decided to present him with a gold medal 'for his courageous act'.

The Belfast match had another consequence. Inside-forward Charlie Sagar of Bury needed treatment after the game, as a result of which his club claimed £37 19s 4d worth of expenses and wages. The League refused, but thereafter all Inter-League players were fully insured.

Sagar at least came away from Belfast with a photo. For the first time, the League commissioned a portrait of the team, one for each player (at a total cost to the Committee of £2 1s).

By 1904 it was customary for the team trainer also to be given a medal. He was usually the trainer of the club playing host, but for away games a member of the Management Committee sometimes took the job. For the match at Belfast in October 1904, for example, Charles Sutcliffe was linesman and John Lewis acted as trainer.

The revenue gained from Inter-League matches varied enormously. In November 1910 the League earned only £76 (after expenses) from the game at White Hart Lane against the Southern League. Four months later it took home £787 from Ibrox. In March 1913, the importance of Glasgow matches was shown again when the League's share of receipts amounted to £842, compared with £147 for the previous match in Belfast and £89 for the one before at Old Trafford.

The League could be extremely generous when it came to benefit matches, especially in the 1920s. For example, Tommy Meehan had played for the League XI three times between 1922 and 1923, but died in 1924. His benefit at Stamford Bridge raised £1416 towards the fund. *Athletic News* added £283 and League clubs raised a further £591. Hardly surprisingly, the League received several requests to stage benefit matches after this.

One of them, for the family of Burnley's late secretary, J. Howarth, at Turf Moor in April 1925, was used as an experiment to test the proposed alteration to the offside law. It didn't turn out to be much of a test – there was only one offside decision in the entire game!

Most games up until November 1929 were played on Saturday afternoons, but opposition from the clubs meant that, with just three exceptions, all future League representative games were played in mid-week, usually on Wednesdays. Both the Scottish and Irish Leagues objected to this strongly, because it harmed their potential revenues.

After the Second World War, Inter-League games lost much of their value to the League, whose main revenue now came from the 4 per cent levy on gates. But there was still new ground to be covered.

In April 1947 the League played its first game in Dublin, against the League of Ireland (known as the Free State League until 1936). In October 1955 the first Inter-League match was played under floodlights, at Hillsborough, specifically because the second half of the game was being televised.

Between October 1956 and July 1960 the League XI fell under the direct influence of the England manager Walter Winterbottom, who leaned even more heavily than before on English-born players, in order to test his own international selections. In September 1960, however, the Management Committee decided to appoint the manager of the League champions as honorary team manager of the League XI. Harry Potts of Burnley was the first to take on the role, followed six months later by Stan Cullis of Wolves.

But with the World Cup looming, Winterbottom was invited to resume his control in July 1961, and from then on every Inter-League match was regarded as an international preparation match. Winterbottom, and then Alf Ramsey, would include such players as Scots Dave Mackay and Denis Law, the Irish Peter McParland and the Welsh Cliff Jones, only if their appearances were calculated to add to the gate. Denis Law had already played against the Football League for the Italian League, in November 1961. Alongside him then was Gerry Hitchens, who had also played for the League. After the 1966 World Cup, Inter-League matches gradually lost their appeal and the series effectively ended in March 1976 when a crowd of less than 9000 at Hampden resulted in a loss to the League of over £3000. Only one Inter-League match has been played since, at Belfast in September 1987.

Taking only those games against the Southern League, Scottish League, Irish League and League of Ireland, the Football League's playing record was:

Played: 163 Won: 117 Drew: 22 Lost: 24 For: 544 Against: 211

Of those twenty-four defeats, all but five were against the Scottish League. The League's top score was 12–0 against the Irish League shortly after the World Cup win in 1966. They scored nine goals on a further four occasions.

There was never an official 'championship' as such, although some football annuals published tables and nominated champions. The Football League omitted to play only the Welsh League.

Here, in chronological order, are the details of the League's representative games:

20.4.91 at Olive Grove, Sheffield (6000)

Football Alliance   1 (Davis)
Football League   1 (Chadwick)

ALLIANCE: R Roberts (Sunderland Alb), T Clare (Stoke), J Rae (Sunderland Alb), H Brandon (Sheff Wed), H Clifford (Stoke), P McCracken (Sunderland Alb), H Davis (B'ham St George's), W Smith (Nottm F), J Devey (B'ham St George's), D Hannah (Sunderland Alb), T Edge (Stoke)
FL: J Trainer (Preston), T Brandon (Blackburn), N Ross (Preston), D Calderhead (Notts Co), G Dewar (Blackburn), H Wilson (Sunderland), C Athersmith (Villa), T McInnes (Notts Co), J Goodall (Derby), E Chadwick (Everton), H Daft (Notts Co)

11.4.92 at Pike's Lane, Bolton (9500)

Football League   2 (Bassett, McInnes)
Scottish League   2 (McMahon, Taylor)

FL: J Reader (WBA), R Holmes (Preston), D Gow (Sunderland), J Reynolds (WBA), H Gardiner (Bolton), W Groves (WBA), W Bassett (WBA), T McInnes (Notts Co), J Goodall (Derby), E Chadwick (Everton), H Daft (Notts Co)

24.10.92 at Bramall Lane (6000)

North   2 (Hannah, Campbell)
Midlands   3 (Goodall, Dowds, Brown)

NORTH: J Sutcliffe (Bolton), R Holmes (Preston), Orr (Darwen), Wilson (Sunderland), H Gardiner (Bolton), McEvoy (Darwen), D Hannah (Sunderland), N Ross (Preston), Campbell (Sunderland), E Chadwick (Everton), Hill (Burnley)
MIDLANDS: C Charsley (Small Heath), H Brandon (Sheff Wed), Hendry (Notts Co), J Reynolds (WBA), Hendry (Sheff Utd), Dowds (Villa), W Bassett (WBA), Brown (Sheff Wed), J Goodall (Derby), H Wood (Wolves), D Hodgetts (Villa)

8.4.93 at Celtic Park (31,500)

Scottish League   3 (Taylor, Madden, McMahon)
Football League   4 (Begbie og, Wood, Geary, Bassett)

FL: W Rowley (Stoke), T Clare (Stoke), R Howarth (Everton), J Reynolds (WBA), C Perry (WBA), E Needham (Sheff Utd), W Bassett (WBA), F Geary (Everton), J Southworth (Blackburn), H Wood (Wolves), J Schofield (Stoke)

10.2.94 at Ulster Grounds, Belfast (5000)

Irish League   2 (Barron, Gibson)
Football League   4 (Wheldon 2, Geary, Wykes)

FL: J Reader (WBA), R Howarth (Everton), H Thickett (Sheff Utd), T Perry (WBA), J Holt (Everton), J Crabtree (Burnley), D Wykes (Wolves), W Hammond (Sheff Utd), F Geary (Everton), C Wheldon (Small Heath), H Wood (Wolves)

21.4.94 at Goodison Park (28,300)

Football League 1 (Goodall)
Scottish League 1 (Oswald)

FL: J Sutcliffe (Bolton), J Crabtree (Burnley), R Holmes (Preston), J Reynolds (Villa), J Holt (Everton), E Needham (Sheff Utd), C Athersmith (Villa), J Goodall (Derby), J Devey (Villa), G Wheldon (Small Heath), F Spiksley (Sheff Wed)

24.9.94 William McGregor testimonial at Perry Barr (3000)

Aston Villa 1 (Gordon)
Football League 3 (J Goodall, Ross, another)

VILLA: W Dunning, H Spencer, J Welford, J Reynolds, J Cowan, G Kinsey, W Athersmith, C Hare, J Devey, R Gordon, S Smith
FL: J Reader (WBA), J Somerville (Bolton), A Scott (Nottm F), T Perry (WBA), A Goodall (Derby), E Needham (Sheff Utd), W Bassett (WBA), J Ross (Liverpool), J Goodall (Derby), G Wheldon (Small Heath), J Schofield (Stoke)

13.4.95 at Celtic Park (30,000)

Scottish League 1 (Oswald)
Football League 4 (Devey, Becton 3)

FL: H Storer (W Arsenal), R Holmes (Preston), J Crabtree (Burnley), J Reynolds (Villa), T Crawshaw (Sheff Wed), E Needham (Sheff Utd), C Athersmith (Villa), F Becton (Liverpool), J Devey (Villa), D Hodgetts (Villa), S Smith (Villa)

9.11.95 at Victoria Ground, Stoke (3000)

Football League 2 (Williams, Finnerhan)
Irish League 2 (Kelly 2)

FL: T Baddeley (B Port Vale), C Eccles (B Port Vale), G Swift (Loughboro), J Turner (Stoke), R Chatt (Villa), T Chapman (Man City), W Williams (Everton), P Finnerhan (Man City), T McCairns (Grimsby), A Flewitt (Everton), W Dorrell (Villa)

11.4.96 at Goodison Park (21,280)

Football League 5 (Devey, Athersmith, Becton 2, Goodall)
Scottish League 1 (Oswald)

FL: J Sutcliffe (Bolton), H Spencer (Villa), W Williams (WBA), T Perry (WBA), J Higgins (WBA), J Crabtree (Villa), C Athersmith (Villa), J Devey (Villa), J Goodall (Derby), F Becton (Liverpool), A Milward (Everton)

7.11.96 at The Oval, Belfast (12,000)

Irish League 0
Football League 2 (Beats, Bloomer)

FL: J Reader (WBA), H Spencer (Villa), W Williams (WBA), W Higgins (Grimsby), J Higgins (WBA), A Malpass (Wolves), W Bassett (WBA), S Bloomer (Derby), W Beats (Wolves), H Wood (Wolves), T Bradshaw (Liverpool)

24.4.97 at Ibrox Park (34,651)

Scottish League 3 (Low, McPherson 2)
Football League 0

FL: J Sutcliffe (Bolton), H Spencer (Villa), W Williams (WBA), J Crabtree (Villa), T Crawshaw (Sheff Wed), E Needham (Sheff Utd), C Athersmith (Villa), S Bloomer (Derby), J Devey (Villa), E Chadwick (Everton), T Bradshaw (Liverpool)

6.11.97 at Hyde Road, Manchester (10,000)

Football League 8 (Bloomer 2, Beats 2, Wheldon 2, Schofield 2)
Irish League 1 (Campbell)

FL: C Williams (Man City), M Earp (Sheff Wed), B Pumphrey (Gainsboro), T Booth (Blackburn), T Morren (Sheff Utd), W Holmes (Man City), W Bryant (Newton Heath), S Bloomer (Derby), W Beats (Wolves), G Wheldon (Villa), J Schofield (Stoke)

9.4.98 at Villa Park (22,000)

Football League 1 (Beats)
Scottish League 2 (Hamilton 2)

FL: W Foulke (Sheff Utd), H Thickett (Sheff Utd), A Langley (Sheff Wed), T Perry (WBA), T Morren (Sheff Utd), E Needham (Sheff Utd), C Athersmith (Villa), H Wood (Wolves), W Beats (Wolves), G Wheldon (Villa), S Smith (Villa)

5.11.98 at Grosvenor Park, Belfast (8000)

Irish League 1 (Darling)
Football League 5 (Bloomer, Farrell 2, Fletcher, Needham)

FL: J Sutcliffe (Bolton), J Crabtree (Villa), W Williams (WBA), T Booth (Blackburn), T Crawshaw (Sheff Wed), E Needham (Sheff Utd), W Williams (Blackburn), S Bloomer (Derby), J Farrell (Stoke), H Fletcher (Notts Co), J Turner (Stoke)

1.4.99 at Celtic Park (35,000)

Scottish League 1 (Campbell)
Football League 4 (Athersmith 2, Bloomer, Settle)

FL: J Hillman (Burnley), T Prescott (Notts Co), J Eccles (Stoke), F Forman (Nottm F), T Crawshaw (Sheff Wed), J Crabtree (Villa), C Athersmith (Villa), S Bloomer (Derby), W Toman (Burnley), J Settle (Bury), J Turner (Stoke)

11.1.99 at Burnden Park (5372)

Football League 3 (Bloomer 2, Settle)
Irish League 1 (Spencer og)

FL: H Birchenough (Port Vale), H Spencer (Villa), W Williams (WBA), J Fitchett (Bolton), J Leeming (Bury), E Needham (Sheff Utd), F Johnson (Stoke), S Bloomer (Derby), W Beats (Wolves), J Settle (Everton), D Hurst (Blackburn)

31.3.1900 at Crystal Palace (7500)

Football League 2 (Bloomer, Hedley)
Scottish League 2 (Walker, Norris og)

FL: W Foulke (Sheff Utd), H Spencer (Villa), J Crabtree (Villa), H Griffiths (Wolves), W Wigmore (Small Heath), R Norris (Nottm F), C Athersmith (Villa), S Bloomer (Derby), G Hedley (Sheff Utd), J Settle (Everton), T Miller (Wolves)

10.11.1900 at Cliftonville, Belfast (7000)

Irish League 2 (Clarke, Worrall)
Football League 4 (Hogg 3, Bloomer)

FL: M Kingsley (Newcastle), W Layton (Sheff Wed), A Evans (Villa), J Fitchett (Bolton), F Forman (Nottm F), E Needham (Sheff Utd), J Sharp (Everton), S Bloomer (Derby), R Hogg (Sunderland), C Sagar (Bury), J Cox (Liverpool)

16.3.01 at Ibrox Park   (37,668)

Scottish League   6 (Hamilton 3, A Smith, Walker,
                        McColl)
Football League   2 (Athersmith, Raybould)

FL: M Kingsley (Newcastle), W Balmer (Everton), J Crabtree (Villa),
W Bull (Notts Co), W Bannister (Burnley), E Needham (Sheff Utd),
A Whittaker (Blackburn), C Athersmith (Villa), S Raybould (Liver-
pool), C Sagar (Bury), F Blackburn (Blackburn)

9.11.01 at the Manor Ground, Plumstead   (12,000)

Football League   9 (Bloomer 4, Wooldridge 3, Wood 2)
Irish League   o

FL: W George (Villa), J Glover (Liverpool), J Iremonger (Nottm F),
J Fitchett (Bolton), T Crawshaw (Sheff Wed), W Abbott (Everton),
A Goddard (Glossop), S Bloomer (Derby), W Wood (Bury), W
Wooldridge (Wolves), S Wharton (Small Heath)

8.3.02 at St James's Park, Newcastle   (11,000)

Football League   6 (Bloomer 2, Cox, Hogg 3)
Scottish League   3 (Campbell 3)

FL: M Kingsley (Newcastle), R Crompton (Blackburn), J Iremonger
(Nottm F), S Wolstenholme (Everton), W Bannister (Bolton), A
Houlker (Blackburn), W Hogg (Sunderland), S Bloomer (Derby), W
Beats (Wolves), J Settle (Everton), J Cox (Liverpool)

11.10.02 at Cliftonville, Belfast   (10,000)

Irish League   2 (Darling, Kirkwood)
Football League   3 (Bloomer 2, Calvey)

FL: T Baddeley (Wolves), J Glover (Liverpool), J Iremonger (Nottm
F), D Nurse (WBA), T Booth (Everton), E McDonald (Notts Co),
W Hogg (Sunderland), S Bloomer (Derby), J Calvey (Nottm F), C
Sagar (Bury), H Lipsham (Sheff Utd)

14.3.03 at Celtic Park   (39,000)

Scottish League   o
Football League   3 (Spiksley, Raybould, Davis)

FL: T Baddeley (Wolves), H Spencer (Villa), R Crompton (Blackburn),
W Johnson (Sheff Utd), T Booth (Everton), W Abbott (Everton), H
Davis (Sheff Wed), P Humphreys (Notts Co), S Raybould (Liverpool),
A Capes (Stoke), F Spiksley (Sheff Wed)

10.10.03 at Valley Parade   (17,000)

Football League   2 (Bloomer, Sagar)
Irish League   1 (Waddington)

FL: J Sutcliffe (Man Utd), H Spencer (Villa), J Iremonger (Nottm F),
S Frost (Man City), T Crawshaw (Sheff Wed), E Needham (Sheff
Utd), J Sharp (Everton), S Bloomer (Derby), W Hogg (Sunderland),
C Sagar (Bury), A Lockett (Villa)

4.4.04 at Bank Street, Manchester   (25,000)

Football League   2 (Bloomer, Raybould)
Scottish League   1 (Robertson)

FL: T Baddeley (Wolves), R Crompton (Blackburn), H Burgess (Man
City), S Frost (Man City), S Greenhalgh (Bolton), W Abbott
(Everton), J Rutherford (Newcastle), S Bloomer (Derby), S Raybould
(Liverpool), W Shearman (Nottm F), J Cox (Liverpool)

15.10.04 at Grosvenor Park, Belfast   (12,000)

Irish League   o
Football League   2 (Stokes, W Jones)

FL: J Ashcroft (W Arsenal), J Jones (Wolves), H Burgess (Man
City), S Ashworth (Everton), T Crawshaw (Sheff Wed), W Bradshaw
(Blackburn), D Stokes (Bolton), W Shearman (Nottm F), W Jones
(Small Heath), H Munday (Chesterfield T), A Bridgett (Sunderland)

11.3.05 at Hampden Park   (36,000)

Scottish League   2 (Quinn, C Thomson)
Football League   3 (Roberts, Bloomer, Parkinson)

FL: J Linacre (Nottm F), H Spencer (Villa), H Burgess (Man City), S
Wolstenholme (Blackburn), C Roberts (Man Utd), A Leake (Villa),
D Stokes (Bolton), S Bloomer (Derby), J Parkinson (Liverpool), J
Bache (Villa), H Hardman (Everton)

14.10.05 at Hyde Road, Manchester   (13,000)

Football League   4 (Hampton 2, Veitch 2)
Irish League   o

FL: H Maskrey (Derby), J Glover (B'ham), H Burgess (Man City), W
Makepeace (Everton), P Sands (W Arsenal), W Bradshaw (Blackburn),
G Dorsett (Man City), F Rouse (Stoke), H Hampton (Villa), C Veitch
(Newcastle), H Lipsham (Sheff Utd)

24.3.06 at Stamford Bridge   (18,000)

Football League   6 (Shepherd 4, Common, Bache)
Scottish League   2 (Kyle, Thomson)

FL: J Ashcroft (W Arsenal), J Glover (B'ham), H Burgess (Man City),
B Warren (Derby), C Veitch (Newcastle), J Bradley (Liverpool), R
Bond (Preston), A Common (Middlesbrough), A Shepherd (Bolton),
J Bache (Villa), J Conlin (Bradford C)

13.10.06 at Cliftonville, Belfast   (10,500)

Irish League   o
Football League   6 (Sharp, Coleman, Hilsdon 3, Rouse)

FL: A Robinson (B'ham), H Spencer (Villa), J Carr (Newcastle), B
Warren (Derby), C Roberts (Man Utd), R Craythorne (Notts Co), J
Sharp (Everton), J Coleman (W Arsenal), G Hilsdon (Chelsea), F
Rouse (Stoke), A Bridgett (Sunderland)

2.3.07 at Ibrox Park   (50,000)

Scottish League   o
Football League   o

FL: A Robinson (B'ham), R Crompton (Blackburn), J Pennington
(WBA), B Warren (Derby), C Roberts (Man Utd), W Abbott
(Everton), D Stokes (Bolton), J Coleman (W Arsenal), I Thornley
(Man City), J Bache (Villa), A Hall (Villa)

12.10.07 at Roker Park   (6000)

Football League   6 (Hibbert, Crawshaw 2, Thornley,
                        Bache, Hilton)
Irish League   3 (Andrews, Wilson, Young)

FL: R Williamson (Middlesbrough), R Crompton (Blackburn), H
Burgess (Man Utd), S Greenhalgh (Bolton), T Crawshaw (Sheff Wed),
W Makepeace (Everton), J Raine (Sunderland), W Hibbert (Bury), I
Thornley (Man City), J Bache (Villa), F Hilton (Bristol C)

29.2.08 at Villa Park (11,000)

Football League 2 (Hilsdon, Greenhalgh)
Scottish League 0

FL: S Hardy (Liverpool), R Crompton (Blackburn), H Burgess (Man Utd), B Warren (Derby), W Wedlock (Bristol C), S Greenhalgh (Bolton), C Tickle (B'ham), J Smith (Hull City), G Hilsdon (Chelsea), E West (Nottm F), A Hall (Villa)

10.10.08 at Cliftonville, Belfast (12,000)

Irish League 0
Football League 5 (Woodward 2, Mordue, Warren, Halse)

FL: S Hardy (Liverpool), R Crompton (Blackburn), G Maltby (Nottm F), B Warren (Chelsea), W Wedlock (Bristol C), W Makepeace (Everton), C Wallace (Villa), H Halse (Man Utd), V Woodward (Spurs), F Bradshaw (Sheff Wed), J Mordue (Sunderland)

27.2.09 at Celtic Park (46,000)

Scottish League 3 (Quinn 2, Paul)
Football League 1 (Woodward)

FL: S Hardy (Liverpool), R Crompton (Blackburn), T Whitson (Newcastle), K Hunt (Wolves), C Roberts (Man Utd), W Makepeace (Everton), D Stokes (Bolton), E Latheron (Blackburn), V Woodward (Spurs), F Bradshaw (Sheff Wed), A Smith (Bradford PA)

9.10.09 at Boundary Park (10,000)

Football League 8 (Freeman 4, Lintott, Stewart, Benson, Holley)
Irish League 1 (Macauley)

FL: W Matthews (Oldham), R Benson (Sheff Utd), A Cowell (Blackburn), S Greenhalgh (Bolton), W Wedlock (Bristol C), E Lintott (Bradford C), A Goddard (Liverpool), G Holley (Sunderland), B Freeman (Everton), J Stewart (Newcastle), G Wall (Man Utd)

26.2.10 at Ewood Park (30,000)

Football League 2 (Parkinson, Brittleton)
Scottish League 3 (Quinn, Devine, Templeton)

FL: J Dawson (Burnley), R Crompton (Blackburn), J Hayes (Man Utd), J Brittleton (Sheff Wed), J Harrop (Liverpool), W Makepeace (Everton), W Garbutt (Blackburn), G Holley (Sunderland), J Parkinson (Liverpool), J Bache (Villa), G Wall (Man Utd)

11.4.10 at Stamford Bridge (7000)

Football League 2 (Stewart, Parkinson)
Southern League 2 (Lewis, Fleming)

FL: J Lievesley (Sheff Utd), R Downs (Barnsley), T Rodway (Preston), F Taylor (Chelsea), J Harrop (Liverpool), H Moffat (Burnley), A Goddard (Liverpool), J Stewart (Newcastle), J Parkinson (Liverpool), J Bache (Villa), H Middlemiss (Spurs)
SOUTHERN: J Johnson (Crystal P), F Blackman (Brighton), J Bulcock (Crystal P), J Mahon (New Brompton), A Hartwell (QPR), A Trueman (Southampton), R Jefferson (Swindon), H Fleming (Swindon), W Steer (QPR), A Lewis (Northampton T), H Buckle (Coventry C)

8.10.10 at Celtic Park, Belfast (20,000)

Irish League 2 (Hunter, Andrews)
Football League 6 (Holley, Hibbert, Stewart 2, Conlin 2)

FL: R Williamson (Middlesbrough), R Balmer (Everton), G Maltby (Nottm F), R Duckworth (Man Utd), C Buckley (Villa), C Veitch (Newcastle), T Broad (Oldham), G Holley (Sunderland), W Hibbert (Bury), J Stewart (Newcastle), J Conlin (Man City)

14.11.10 at White Hart Lane (5000)

Football League 2 (Hibbert, Bradshaw)
Southern League 3 (Fleming, Reid, Trueman)

FL: T Lunn (Spurs), G Maltby (Nottm F), J Johnston (Clapton O), R Duckworth (Man Utd), C Buckley (Villa), W Bradshaw (Blackburn), J Mordue (Sunderland), J Coleman (Sunderland), W Hibbert (Bury), J Stewart (Newcastle), G Wall (Man Utd)
SOUTHERN: G Kitchen (West Ham), F Blackman (Brighton), J Walker (Swindon), W Booth (Brighton), A Hartwell (QPR), A Trueman (Southampton), R Jefferson (Swindon), H Fleming (Swindon), G Reid (Brentford), H Moody (Luton), H Lipsham (Millwall)

4.3.11 at Ibrox Park (65,000)

Scottish League 1 (Reid)
Football League 1 (Henshall)

FL: J Dawson (Burnley), R Crompton (Blackburn), J Pennington (WBA), C Veitch (Newcastle), C Roberts (Man Utd), W Bradshaw (Blackburn), J Simpson (Blackburn), S Bloomer (Derby), A Shepherd (Newcastle), J Bache (Villa), H Henshall (Villa)

9.10.11 at the Victoria Ground, Stoke (10,000)

Southern League 1 (Bradley)
Football League 2 (Roberts, Hampton)

SOUTHERN: C Shaw (QPR), R Brittan (Northampton T), J Robertson (Southampton), S Frost (Millwall), E Bradley (Coventry C), T Randall (West Ham), R Jefferson (Swindon), H Fleming (Swindon), J Peart (Stoke), F Bradshaw (Northampton T), E Freeman (Northampton T)
FL: A Iremonger (Notts Co), L Hofton (Man Utd), J Pennington (WBA), R Duckworth (Man Utd), C Roberts (Man Utd), G Hunter (Villa), J Simpson (Blackburn), H Halse (Man Utd), H Hampton (Villa), F Buck (WBA), B Shearman (WBA)

16.10.11 at Anfield (10,000)

Football League 4 (Hampton 4)
Irish League 0

FL: A Iremonger (Notts Co), L Hofton (Man Utd), J Pennington (WBA), R Duckworth (Man Utd), C Roberts (Man Utd), G Hunter (Villa), J Simpson (Blackburn), H Halse (Man Utd), H Hampton (Villa), F Buck (WBA), B Shearman (WBA)

17.2.12 at Ayresome Park (25,000)

Football League 2 (Freeman, Mordue)
Scottish League 0

FL: R Williamson (Middlesbrough), R Crompton (Blackburn), J Pennington (WBA), R Duckworth (Man Utd), T Boyle (Burnley), J Fay (Bolton), C Wallace (Villa), C Buchan (Sunderland), B Freeman (Burnley), G Holley (Sunderland), J Mordue (Sunderland)

30.9.12 at Old Trafford (10,000)

Football League 2 (Buchan, Bradshaw)
Southern League 1 (Webb)

FL: R Williamson (Middlesbrough), E Longworth (Liverpool), E Fletcher (Man City), H Moffat (Oldham), J Fay (Bolton), R McNeal (WBA), A Goddard (Liverpool), C Buchan (Sunderland), E West (Man Utd), F Bradshaw (Everton), G Wall (Man Utd)
SOUTHERN: C Shaw (QPR), H Collyer (Crystal P), J Walker (Swindon), R Spottiswood (Crystal P), J Hughes (Crystal P), T Randall (West Ham), F Walden (Northampton T), D Shea (West Ham), W Davis (Millwall), C Webb (Brighton), S Lamb (Swindon)

23.10.12 at The Oval, Belfast (11,500)

Irish League 0
Football League 0

FL: R Williamson (Middlesbrough), R Crompton (Blackburn), J Pennington (WBA), J Brittleton (Sheff Wed), C Roberts (Man Utd), R McNeal (WBA), J Simpson (Blackburn), C Buchan (Sunderland), B Freeman (Burnley), F Bradshaw (Everton), G Wall (Man Utd)

1.3.13 at Hampden Park (65,000)

Scottish League 4 (Reid 2, Dodds, Mercer)
Football League 1 (Logan og)

FL: R Beale (Man Utd), R Downs (Barnsley), E Fletcher (Man City), F Cuggy (Sunderland), T Boyle (Burnley), G Utley (Barnsley), C Wallace (Villa), C Buchan (Sunderland), H Halse (Villa), V Woodward (Chelsea), J Hodkinson (Blackburn)

1.10.13 at Cliftonville, Belfast (12,000)

Irish League 0
Football League 2 (Watson, Holley)

FL: S Hardy (Villa), R Crompton (Blackburn), J Pennington (WBA), F Cuggy (Sunderland), A Whalley (Man Utd), W Watson (Burnley), C Wallace (Villa), D Shea (Blackburn), B Freeman (Burnley), G Holley (Sunderland), H Martin (Sunderland)

10.12.13 Tom Harris (Notts Co and Management Committee) testimonial at Meadow Lane (7000)

Nottingham XI 1 (Richards)
Football League 1 (Vizard)

FL: S Hardy (Villa), R Crompton (Blackburn), F Womack (B'ham), M Hamill (Man Utd), J McCall (Preston), James Campbell (Sheff Wed), W Meredith (Man Utd), S Fazackerley (Sheff Utd), J Moore (Derby), E Hodgson (Burnley), E Vizard (Bolton)

9.2.14 at The Den (13,000)

Southern League 1 (Davis)
Football League 3 (Shea 3)

SOUTHERN: T Thorpe (Northampton T), J Fort (Exeter C), H Colclough (Crystal P), W Booth (Brighton), A Mitchell (QPR), R Liddell (Millwall), R Jefferson (Swindon), W Batty (Swindon), W Davis (Millwall), B Bowler (Plymouth Arg), E Hendren (Brentford)
FL: S Hardy (Villa), R Crompton (Blackburn), J Pennington (WBA), F Cuggy (Sunderland), J Harrop (Villa), R McNeal (WBA), C Wallace (Villa), D Shea (Blackburn), G Elliott (Middlesbrough), E Latheron (Blackburn), H Martin (Sunderland)

21.3.14 at Turf Moor (38,000)

Football League 2 (Boyle, Nellies og)
Scottish League 3 (Reid, Croal 2)

FL: S Hardy (Villa), R Crompton (Blackburn), I Boocock (Bradford C), T Barber (Villa), T Boyle (Burnley), R McNeal (WBA), A Jephcott (WBA), C Stephenson (Villa), J Peart (Notts Co), E Hodgson (Burnley), E Mosscrop (Burnley)

7.10.14 at The Hawthorns (9250)

Football League 2 (Latheron 2)
Irish League 1 (Nixon)

FL: H Pearson (WBA), R Crompton (Blackburn), I Boocock (Bradford C), T Fleetwood (Everton), J Harrop (Villa), W Watson (Burnley), J Simpson (Blackburn), C Buchan (Sunderland), H Bache (WBA), E Latheron (Blackburn), S Brooks (Wolves)

26.10.14 at Highbury (11,000)

Football League 2 (Stephenson 2)
Southern League 1 (Moody)

FL: A Reynolds (Fulham), R Crompton (Blackburn), I Boocock (Bradford C), J Harrow (Chelsea), T Fleetwood (Everton), W Watson (Burnley), F Walden (Spurs), C Stephenson (Villa), H Halse (Chelsea), E Latheron (Blackburn), J Hodkinson (Blackburn)
SOUTHERN: T Thorpe (Northampton T), J Kirkwood (Millwall), H Colclough (Crystal P), V Gregory (Watford), A Mitchell (QPR), R Liddell (Millwall), W Thompson (QPR), W Batty (Swindon), S Puddefoot (West Ham), H Moody (Millwall), R Hughes (Northampton T)

20.3.15 at Celtic Park (44,000)

Scottish League 1 (Dodds)
Football League 4 (Chedgzoy, Elliott, Latheron, Martin)

FL: W Smith (Man City), E Longworth (Liverpool), J English (Sheff Utd), T Fleetwood (Everton), C Roberts (Oldham), R McNeal (WBA), S Chedgzoy (Everton), C Buchan (Sunderland), G Elliott (Middlesbrough), E Latheron (Blackburn), H Martin (Sunderland)

22.2.19 Victory match at St Andrew's (22,000)

Football League 3 (Whittingham 2, Clennell)
Scottish League 1 (Culley)

FL: S Hardy (Villa), E Longworth (Liverpool), F Womack (B'ham), T Fleetwood (Everton), C Parker (Stoke), A Grenyer (Everton), W Harrison (Wolves), R Whittingham (Chelsea), J Cock (Huddersfield), J Clennell (Everton), W Morgan (B'ham)

5.4.19 Victory match at Ibrox Park (70,000)

Scottish League 3 (Richardson 2, McMenemy)
Football League 2 (Clennell, Elliott)

FL: S Hardy (Villa), E Longworth (Liverpool), F Womack (B'ham), T Fleetwood (Everton), T Boyle (Burnley), J Fay (Bolton), W Harrison (Wolves), C Buchan (Sunderland), G Elliott (Middlesbrough), J Clennell (Everton), E Mosscrop (Burnley)

22.9.19 E. Hodgson (Burnley) benefit at Turf Moor   (4000)

Burnley   **1 (Walden)**
Football League **5 (Smith 3, Chambers, Cook)**

FL: J Mew (Man Utd), F Potts (Bradford C), E Fletcher (Man City), T Fleetwood (Everton), C Hilditch (Man Utd), A Grenyer (Everton), R Turnbull (Bradford PA), H Chambers (Liverpool), J Cock (Huddersfield), J Smith (Bolton), J Hodkinson (Blackburn)

19.11.19 at Anfield   (20,000)

Football League **2 (Clennell, Stephenson)**
Irish League   **2 (Robinson, Reid)**

FL: S Hardy (Villa), E Longworth (Liverpool), W Cook (Oldham), T Curry (Newcastle), J McCall (Preston), W Watson (Burnley), A Jephcott (WBA), C Stephenson (Villa), T Browell (Man City), J Clennell (Everton), J Crisp (WBA)

20.3.20 at Celtic Park   (83,000)

Scottish League **0**
Football League **4 (Kelly, Cock, Morris 2)**

FL: S Hardy (Villa), E Longworth (Liverpool), J Pennington (WBA), J Bamber (Liverpool), J McCall (Preston), A Grimsdell (Spurs), S Chedgzoy (Everton), R Kelly (Burnley), J Cock (Chelsea), F Morris (WBA), W Smith (Huddersfield)

12.3.21 at Highbury   (35,000)

Football League **1 (Buchan)**
Scottish League **0**

FL: J Mew (Man Utd), W Cresswell (South Shields), J Silcock (Man Utd), J Bamber (Liverpool), G Wilson (Sheff Wed), T Bromilow (Liverpool), S Chedgzoy (Everton), R Kelly (Burnley), C Buchan (Sunderland), H Chambers (Liverpool), J Paterson (Arsenal)

1.10.21 at The Oval, Belfast   (10,000)

Irish League   **0**
Football League **1 (Chedgzoy)**

FL: J Dawson (Burnley), T Lucas (Liverpool), J Silcock (Man Utd), S Richardson (WBA), A McClure (B'ham), W Watson (Burnley), S Chedgzoy (Everton), C Buchan (Sunderland), W Walker (Villa), H Barnes (Man City), F Tunstall (Sheff Utd)

10.11.21 at County Cricket Ground, Leyton   (5000)

Army   **1 (Prince)**
Football League **4 (O'Brien 2, Seed, Puddefoot)**

FL: L Hill (QPR), J Fort (Millwall), E Rhodes (Crystal P), A Ducat (Fulham), A Mitchell (Brentford), B Dunn (Charlton Ath), J Rutherford (Arsenal), J Seed (Spurs), S Puddefoot (West Ham), M O'Brien (QPR), O Williams (Clapton O)

8.3.22 late John Robson (Man Utd) benefit at Old Trafford (20,000)

Whites   **1 (Chambers)**
Reds   **1 (Freeman og)**

WHITES: J Mew (Man Utd), T Lucas (Liverpool), R Freeman (Oldham), J Bamber (Liverpool), M Woosnam (Man City), T Bromilow (Liverpool), J Carr (Middlesbrough), J Spavin (Nottm F), H Chambers (Liverpool), C Stephenson (Huddersfield), W Smith (Huddersfield)

REDS: E Taylor (Oldham), R Downs (Everton), S Wadsworth (Hud-

dersfield), J Peacock (Everton), T Wilson (Huddersfield), D Mercer (Sheff Utd), R Kelly (Burnley), T Browell (Man City), H Barnes (Man City), F Hopkin (Liverpool)

18.3.22 at Ibrox Park   (60,000)

Scottish League **0**
Football League **3 (Chambers 2, W Smith)**

FL: J Dawson (Burnley), T Lucas (Liverpool), S Wadsworth (Huddersfield), B Smith (Spurs), G Wilson (Sheff Wed), T Bromilow (Liverpool), W Grimshaw (Cardiff), R Kelly (Burnley), H Chambers (Liverpool), H Barnes (Man City), W Smith (Huddersfield)

4.10.22 at Burnden Park   (10,000)

Football League **5 (Jack 2, Roberts 2, Cross)**
Irish League   **1 (McKenzie)**

FL: H Pearson (WBA), T Clay (Spurs), A Maitland (South Shields), F Kean (Sheff Wed), W Wadsworth (Liverpool), T Meehan (Chelsea), J Carr (Middlesbrough), D Jack (Bolton), W Roberts (Preston), B Cross (Burnley), A Dorrell (Villa)

17.2.23 at St James's Park, Newcastle   (30,000)

Football League **2 (Bullock, Chambers)**
Scottish League **1 (White)**

FL: E Taylor (Huddersfield), W Cresswell (Sunderland), S Wadsworth (Huddersfield), F Moss (Villa), G Wilson (Sheff Wed), T Bromilow (Liverpool), J Carr (Middlesbrough), C Buchan (Sunderland), N Bullock (Bury), H Chambers (Liverpool), F Tunstall (Sheff Utd)

29.9.23 at Windsor Park, Belfast   (15,000)

Irish League   **2 (Allen 2)**
Football League **6 (Bradford 4, Chambers, Tunstall)**

FL: R Pym (Bolton), W Ashurst (Notts Co), H Jones (Nottm F), H Healless (Blackburn), G Wilson (Sheff Wed), T Meehan (Chelsea), S Chedgzoy (Everton), R Kelly (Burnley), J Bradford (B'ham), H Chambers (Liverpool), F Tunstall (Sheff Utd)

15.3.24 at Ibrox Park   (63,050)

Scottish League **1 (Morton)**
Football League **1 (Chambers)**

FL: E Taylor (Huddersfield), W Cresswell (Sunderland), S Wadsworth (Huddersfield), F Moss (Villa), J Hill (Burnley), T Bromilow (Liverpool), D Mercer (Sheff Utd), R Kelly (Burnley), J Bradford (B'ham), H Chambers (Liverpool), F Tunstall (Sheff Utd)

11.10.24 at Cliftonville, Belfast   (12,000)

Irish League   **0**
Football League **5 (Bedford 4, Kelly)**

FL: H Hardy (Stockport Co), A Baker (Arsenal), S Wadsworth (Huddersfield), F Kean (Sheff Wed), T Wilson (Huddersfield), T Bromilow (Liverpool), J Spencer (WBA), R Kelly (Burnley), H Bedford (Blackpool), J Elkes (Spurs), W Ellis (Sunderland)

20.10.24 late T Meehan (Chelsea) benefit at Stamford Bridge (7500)

Chelsea   **2 (Whitton 2)**
Football League **0**

FL: A Wood (Clapton O), J Mackie (Arsenal), A Chaplin (Fulham),

Knowles (QPR), A Gomm (Millwall), R John (Arsenal), A Harry (Crystal P), S Earle (West Ham), A Pape (Clapton O), J Elkes (Spurs), F Penn (Fulham)

14.3.25 at Goodison Park (40,929)

Football League 4 (Roberts 2, Elkes, Puddefoot)
Scottish League 3 (Russell 2, Gallacher)

FL: R Pym (Bolton), T Lucas (Liverpool), J Jones (B'ham), J Hill (Burnley), T Wilson (Huddersfield), L Graham (Millwall), R Kelly (Burnley), F Roberts (Man City), S Puddefoot (Blackburn), J Elkes (Spurs), G Seymour (Newcastle)

27.4.25 late J Haworth (Burnley) benefit at Turf Moor (to experiment with new offside law) (6000)

Lancashire 3 (Puddefoot 2, Roberts pen.)
Yorkshire 4 (Wainscoat 3, Dixon)

LANCS: R Pym (Bolton), G Waterfield (Burnley), H Jones (Blackpool), E Braidwood (Nelson), T Bradshaw (Bury), F Mann (Man Utd), R Kelly (Burnley), F Roberts (Man City), S Puddefoot (Blackburn), H Barnes (Preston), Cameron (Nelson)
YORKS: J McLaren (Bradford C), A McCluggage (Bradford), G Shaw (Huddersfield), M Webster (Middlesbrough), O Levick (Sheff Wed), W Edwards (Leeds), G Donkin (Barnsley), E Dixon (Halifax), B Mills (Hull), R Wainscoat (Leeds), N Winn (Bradford C)

7.10.25 at Anfield (15,000)

Football League 5 (Walker 2, Kirkham 2, Dorrell)
Irish League 1 (Curran)

FL: B Baker (Chelsea), T Lucas (Liverpool), S Wadsworth (Huddersfield), A Baker (Arsenal), C Spencer (Newcastle), T Bromilow (Liverpool), R York (Villa), S Puddefoot (Blackburn), W Kirkham (Port Vale), W Walker (Villa), A Dorrell (Villa)

13.3.26 at Celtic Park (49,000)

Scottish League 0
Football League 2 (Bedford, Ruffell)

FL: H Hardy (Everton), F Goodall (Huddersfield), J Silcock (Man Utd), W Edwards (Leeds), J Hill (Burnley), G Green (Sheff Utd), R York (Villa), G Brown (Huddersfield), H Bedford (Derby), W Walker (Villa), J Ruffell (West Ham)

9.10.26 at Celtic Park, Belfast (14,000)

Irish League 1 (Kinsler)
Football League 6 (Roberts 3, Amos, Spence, Walker)

FL: D Tremelling (B'ham), T Cooper (Derby), S Wadsworth (Huddersfield), W Edwards (Leeds), F Kean (Sheff Wed), G Green (Sheff Utd), J Spence (Man Utd), E Hine (Leicester), W Roberts (Preston), W Walker (Villa), W Amos (Bury)

28.10.26 at The Den (2000)

Football League 4 (Hulme, Parker 2, Buchan)
Army 1 (Long)

FL: W Callender (Crystal P), M Forster (Spurs), W McConnell (Reading), L Oliver (Fulham), J Townrow (Clapton O), L Graham (Millwall), J Hulme (Arsenal), C Buchan (Arsenal), R Parker (Millwall), H Miller (Chelsea), F Penn (Fulham)

19.3.27 at Filbert Street (26,000)

Football League 2 (Elkes, Walker)
Scottish League 2 (McGrory, McPhail)

FL: J Brown (Sheff Wed), F Goodall (Huddersfield), H Jones (Blackburn), W Edwards (Leeds), J Elkes (Spurs), G Green (Sheff Utd), T Urwin (Newcastle), B Cross (Burnley), A Chandler (Leicester), W Walker (Villa), J Ruffell (West Ham)

2.5.27 Late John Lewis (Bolton and Management Committee) hospital benefit at Ewood Park (unknown)

Blackburn 3 (Whyte, Harper 2)
Football League 4 (Jack, Dean 2, Butler)

FL: A Gray (Man City), C Moore (Man Utd), J Silcock (Man Utd), A Watson (Blackpool), T Bradshaw (Bury), T Bromilow (Liverpool), W Butler (Bolton), D Jack (Bolton), W Dean (Everton), J Devine (Burnley), L Page (Burnley)

21.9.27 at St James's Park, Newcastle (1122)

Football League 9 (Dean 4, Hulme, Johnson 3, Seymour)
Irish League 1 (McCaw)

FL: D Tremelling (B'ham), F Goodall (Huddersfield), A Finney (Bolton), W Edwards (Leeds), C Spencer (Newcastle), W Hardy (Cardiff), J Hulme (Arsenal), H Johnson (Sheff Utd), W Dean (Everton), J Carr (Middlesbrough), G Seymour (Newcastle)

10.3.28 at Ibrox Park (60,000)

Scottish League 2 (McGrory 2)
Football League 6 (Dean 2, Hulme 2, Smith, McStay og)

FL: J Hacking (Oldham), F Goodall (Huddersfield), H Jones (Blackburn), W Edwards (Leeds), F Kean (Sheff Wed), S Bishop (Leicester), J Hulme (Arsenal), D Jack (Bolton), W Dean (Everton), J Bradford (B'ham), W Smith (Huddersfield)

22.9.28 at Windsor Park, Belfast (15,000)

Irish League 0
Football League 5 (Dean 2, Johnson 2, Jack)

FL: D Tremelling (B'ham), T Cooper (Derby), E Blenkinsop (Sheff Wed), W Edwards (Leeds), T Wilson (Huddersfield), A Campbell (Blackburn), J Bruton (Burnley), D Jack (Bolton), W Dean (Everton), T Johnson (Man City), Ruffell (West Ham)

7.11.28 at Villa Park (25,000)

Football League 2 (Hine, Dean)
Scottish League 1 (Archibald)

FL: J Hacking (Oldham), T Smart (Villa), E Blenkinsop (Sheff Wed), W Edwards (Leeds), E Hart (Leeds), A Campbell (Blackburn), J Hulme (Arsenal), E Hine (Leicester), W Dean (Everton), J Bradford (B'ham), A Rigby (Blackburn)

25.9.29 at Goodison Park (18,000)

Football League 7 (Bradford 5, Hampson, Hine)
Irish League 2 (J Mahood 2)

FL: A Davies (Everton), W Cresswell (Everton), H Jones (Blackburn), W Edwards (Leeds), E Hart (Leeds), A Campbell (Huddersfield),

E Toseland (Man City), E Hine (Leicester), J Hampson (Blackpool), J Bradford (B'ham), L Page (Burnley)

2.11.29 at Ibrox Park (40,000)

Scottish League 2 (Muirhead, Stevenson)
Football League 1 (Jack)

FL: H Hibbs (B'ham), W Cresswell (Everton), E Blenkinsop (Sheff Wed), W Edwards (Leeds), E Hart (Leeds), W Marsden (Sheff Wed), H Adcock (Leicester), E Hine (Leicester), D Jack (Arsenal), T Johnson (Man City), E Brook (Man City)

24.9.30 at Windsor Park, Belfast (12,000)

Irish League 2 (Bambrick 2)
Football League 2 (Hampson 2)

FL: J Brown (Sheff Wed), F Goodall (Huddersfield), E Hapgood (Arsenal), A Strange (Sheff Wed), M Webster (Middlesbrough), A Cadwell (West Ham), S Crooks (Derby), D Jack (Arsenal), J Hampson (Blackpool), W Walker (Villa), W Houghton (Villa)

5.11.30 at White Hart Lane (21,738)

Football League 7 (Hampson 3, Crooks 2, Campbell,
Hodgson)
Scottish League 3 (Ferrier 2, Battles)

FL: C Spiers (Spurs), F Goodall (Huddersfield), E Blenkinsop (Sheff Wed), A Strange (Sheff Wed), T Leach (Sheff Wed), A Campbell (Huddersfield), S Crooks (Derby), G Hodgson (Liverpool), J Hampson (Blackpool), J Carter (WBA), W Houghton (Villa)

23.9.31 at Bloomfield Road (15,233)

Football League 4 (Hampson 3, Houghton)
Irish League 0

FL: H Turner (Huddersfield), J Jackson (Liverpool), A Keeping (Southampton), W Edwards (Leeds), T Graham (Nottm F), J Tate (Villa), J Hulme (Arsenal), J Beresford (Villa), J Hampson (Blackpool), J Bestall (Grimsby), W Houghton (Villa)

7.11.31 at Celtic Park (51,000)

Scottish League 4 (McGrory 2, McPhail, McGonagle)
Football League 3 (Bastin 2, Smith)

FL: H Hibbs (B'ham), F Goodall (Huddersfield), E Blenkinsop (Sheff Wed), W Edwards (Leeds), T Graham (Nottm F), J Edwards (WBA), S Crooks (Derby), J Smith (Portsmouth), W Dean (Everton), J Bestall (Grimsby), C Bastin (Arsenal)

1.10.32 at Windsor Park, Belfast (17,000)

Irish League 2 (Bambrick, Devan)
Football League 5 (Brown 3, Worrall, Wood)

FL: F Moss (Arsenal), T Cooper (Derby), E Blenkinsop (Sheff Wed), L Stoker (B'ham), J O'Dowd (Chelsea), S Weaver (Newcastle), F Worrall (Portsmouth), E Hine (Huddersfield), G Brown (Villa), J Pickering (Sheff Utd), S Wood (WBA)

9.11.32 at Maine Road (29,603)

Football League 0
Scottish League 3 (Napier 2, Dewar)

FL: H Hibbs (B'ham), F Goodall (Huddersfield), E Blenkinsop (Sheff

Wed), A Strange (Sheff Wed), A Talbot (Villa), A Campbell (Huddersfield), J Hulme (Arsenal), J Smith (Portsmouth), G Brown (Villa), T Johnson (Everton), W Houghton (Villa)

4.10.33 at Deepdale (14,400)

Football League 4 (Bowers 2, Bastin, Crooks)
Irish League 0

FL: E Sagar (Everton), G Beeson (Sheff Wed), H Trentham (WBA), C Britton (Everton), J Allen (Portsmouth), W Copping (Leeds), S Crooks (Derby), A Grosvenor (B'ham), J Bowers (Derby), C Bastin (Arsenal), E Brook (Man City)

10.2.34 at Ibrox Park (59,000)

Scottish League 2 (Simpson, McPhail)
Football League 2 (Bowers, Beresford)

FL: E Sagar (Everton), G Shaw (WBA), E Blenkinsop (Sheff Wed), C Willingham (Huddersfield), J Allen (Portsmouth), W Copping (Leeds), J Bruton (Blackburn), J Beresford (Villa), J Bowers (Derby), S Weaver (Newcastle), C Bastin (Arsenal)

19.9.34 at The Oval, Belfast (13,500)

Irish League 1 (Brown)
Football League 6 (Tilson 2, Brook 2, Matthews,
Westwood)

FL: E Sagar (Everton), T Cooper (Derby), W Roughton (Huddersfield), C Britton (Everton), S Cowan (Man City), A Robinson (Burnley), S Matthews (Stoke C), H Carter (Sunderland), S Tilson (Man City), R Westwood (Bolton W), E Brook (Man City)

31.10.34 at Stamford Bridge (20,000)

Football League 2 (Brook 2)
Scottish League 1 (McCulloch)

FL: F Moss (Arsenal), T Cooper (Derby), E Hapgood (Arsenal), C Britton (Everton), J Barker (Derby), J Bray (Man City), S Matthews (Stoke C), E Bowden (Arsenal), S Tilson (Man City), G Hall (Spurs), E Brook (Man City)

8.5.35 George V Jubilee at The Hawthorns. Two referees trial
(unknown)

Football League 9 (Dix 3, Alsop 4, Hartill 2)
West Bromwich 6 (Sandford, Edwards, Boyes 2,
W G Richardson 2)

FL: H Morton (Villa), Mills (Notts Co), S Barkas (Man City), T Gardner (Villa), J Barker (Derby), Calladine (B'ham), S Crooks (Derby), Hartill (Wolves), G Alsop (Walsall), R Dix (Villa), Simpson (Nottm F)

11.5.35 George V Jubilee at Goodison Park. Two referees trial
(9000)

Football League 10 (Hampson 5, Leyfield, Eastham 2,
Geldard, Westwood)
Wales & Ireland 2 (Astley 2)

FL: G Holdcroft (Preston), R Smith (Bolton), W Cresswell (Everton), C Britton (Everton), J Atkinson (Bolton), A Robinson (Burnley), A Geldard (Everton), G Eastham (Bolton), J Hampson (Blackpool), R Westwood (Bolton), C Leyfield (Everton)

25.9.35 at Bloomfield Road (26,000)

Football League   1 (Boyes)
Irish League   2 (McNally, Kelly)

FL: F Swift (Man City), G Beeson (Villa), S Barkas (Man City), W Crayston (Arsenal), J Barker (Derby), A Robinson (Burnley), F Worrall (Portsmouth), H Carter (Sunderland), A Lythgoe (Huddersfield), R Westwood (Bolton), W Boyes (WBA)

30.10.35 at Ibrox Park (25,000)

Scottish League   2 (Massie, Brown)
Football League   2 (Camsell, Bowden)

FL: E Sagar (Everton), G Male (Arsenal), E Hapgood (Arsenal), S Smith (Leicester), A Young (Huddersfield), J Bray (Man City), R Birkett (Middlesbrough), E Bowden (Arsenal), G Camsell (Middlesbrough), S Tilson (Man City), E Brook (Man City)

23.9.36 at Windsor Park, Belfast (16,000)

Irish League   3 (Kelly 3)
Football League   2 (Steele, Westwood)

FL: E Sagar (Everton), W Rochford (Portsmouth), C Shaw (Wolves), C Willingham (Huddersfield), J Barker (Derby), J Bray (Man City), R Birkett (Middlesbrough), J Bestall (Grimsby), F Steele (Stoke C), R Westwood (Bolton), E Brook (Man City)

21.10.36 at Goodison Park (34,000)

Football League   2 (Westwood, Bastin)
Scottish League   0

FL: G Holdcroft (Preston), G Male (Arsenal), A Catlin (Sheff Wed), C Britton (Everton), C Gee (Everton), E Keen (Derby), S Crooks (Derby), J Richardson (Huddersfield), W Dean (Everton), R Westwood (Bolton), C Bastin (Arsenal)

22.9.37 at Ibrox Park (40,000)

Scottish League   1 (Delaney)
Football League   0

FL: V Woodley (Chelsea), B Sproston (Leeds), S Barkas (Man City), C Willingham (Huddersfield), S Cullis (Wolves), J Bray (Man City), S Matthews (Stoke C), T Galley (Wolves), F Steele (Stoke C), R Westwood (Bolton), G Ashall (Wolves)

6.10.37 at Bloomfield Road (14,700)

Football League   3 (Hall, Mills, Goulden)
Irish League   0

FL: V Woodley (Chelsea), B Sproston (Leeds), S Barkas (Man City), C Willingham (Huddersfield), A Young (Huddersfield), J Bray (Man City), A Geldard (Everton), G Hall (Spurs), G Mills (Chelsea), L Goulden (West Ham), E Brook (Man City)

21.9.38 at Windsor Park, Belfast (14,000)

Irish League   2 (McIvor, Shearer)
Football League   8 (Lawton 4, Morton, Welsh, Goulden, Robinson)

FL: V Woodley (Chelsea), B Sproston (Spurs), E Hapgood (Arsenal), C Willingham (Huddersfield), S Cullis (Wolves), D Welsh (Charlton Ath), S Matthews (Stoke C), J Robinson (Sheff Wed), T Lawton (Everton), L Goulden (West Ham), J Morton (West Ham)

2.11.38 at Molineux (28,389)

Football League   3 (Dix 2, Boyes)
Scottish League   1 (Walker)

FL: V Woodley (Chelsea), B Sproston (Spurs), N Greenhalgh (Everton), C Willingham (Huddersfield), S Cullis (Wolves), J Gardiner (Wolves), S Matthews (Stoke C), G Hall (Spurs), T Lawton (Everton), R Dix (Derby), W Boyes (Everton)

11.10.41 RAF benefit at Bloomfield Road (20,000)

Football League   3 (Mannion, Doherty, Rowley)
Scottish League   2 (Wallace, Bremner)

FL: J Fairbrother (Preston), J Bacuzzi (Fulham), W Cook (Everton), C Willingham (Huddersfield), R Pryde (Blackburn), J Mercer (Everton), S Matthews (Stoke C), W Mannion (Middlesbrough), J Rowley (Man Utd), P Doherty (Man City), T Pearson (Newcastle)

19.2.47 at Goodison Park (36,000)

Football League   4 (Lawton 2, Kippax 2)
Irish League   2 (McMorran, Wright)

FL: F Swift (Man City), L Scott (Arsenal), G Hardwick (Middlesbrough), W Wright (Wolves), C Franklin (Stoke C), H Johnston (Blackpool), S Matthews (Stoke C), W Mannion (Middlesbrough), T Lawton (Chelsea), J Hagan (Sheff Utd), F Kippax (Burnley)

12.3.47 at Hampden Park (84,714)

Scottish League   1 (Flavell)
Football League   3 (Westcott, Mannion 2)

FL: E Ditchburn (Spurs), L Scott (Arsenal), G Hardwick (Middlesbrough), P Taylor (Liverpool), C Franklin (Stoke C), W Burgess (Spurs), S Matthews (Stoke C), H Carter (Derby), D Westcott (Wolves), W Mannion (Middlesbrough), F Kippax (Burnley)

30.4.47 at Dalymount Park, Dublin (unknown)

League of Ireland   1 (Kelly)
Football League   3 (Stubbins, Hagan, Mortensen)

FL: E Ditchburn (Spurs), A Woodruff (Burnley), R Robinson (Middlesbrough), P Taylor (Liverpool), R Pryde (Blackburn), J Mercer (Arsenal), S Matthews (Stoke C), S Mortensen (Blackpool), A Stubbins (Newcastle), J Hagan (Sheff Utd), A Ormston (Stoke C)

22.10.47 at Windsor Park, Belfast (20,000)

Irish League   3 (McDowell 2, Bradford)
Football League   4 (McMillan og, Pye, Stubbins, Hagan)

FL: G Merrick (B'ham), A Woodruff (Burnley), R Robinson (Middlesbrough), P Taylor (Liverpool), A Brown (Burnley), A Emptage (Man City), S Matthews (Blackpool), J Pye (Wolves), A Stubbins (Liverpool), J Hagan (Sheff Utd), R Langton (Blackburn)

17.3.48 at St James's Park, Newcastle (64,000)

Football League   1 (Mortensen)
Scottish League   1 (Young)

FL: E Ditchburn (Spurs), B Mozley (Derby), G Hardwick (Middlesbrough), J Harvey (Newcastle), L Leuty (Derby), J Taylor

(Fulham), S Matthews (Blackpool), J Morris (Man Utd), S Mortensen (Blackpool), W Mannion (Middlesbrough), R Langton (Blackburn)

14.4.48 at Deepdale (35,000)

Football League   4 (Rowley 2, Stubbins 2)
League of Ireland   0

FL: E Ditchburn (Spurs), L Scott (Arsenal), J Walton (Preston), P Taylor (Liverpool), L Compton (Arsenal), T Blenkinsopp (Grimsby), T Finney (Preston), H Carter (Hull C), A Stubbins (Liverpool), J Rowley (Man Utd), A Ormston (Stoke C).

20.9.48 at Anfield (27,263)

Football League   5 (Milburn 3, Shackleton, Morris)
Irish League   1 (Jones)

FL: E Ditchburn (Spurs), A Ramsey (Southampton), R Robinson (Middlesbrough), T Blenkinsopp (Middlesbrough), W Jones (Liverpool), A Wright (Sunderland), S Matthews (Blackpool), J Morris (Man Utd), J Milburn (Newcastle), L Shackleton (Sunderland), R Langton (Preston).

23.3.49 at Ibrox Park (90,000)

Scottish League   0
Football League   3 (Mortensen 2, Finney)

FL: F Swift (Man City), L Scott (Arsenal), E Westwood (Man City), R Attwell (Burnley), C Franklin (Stoke C), F Harris (B'ham), T Finney (Preston), S Mortensen (Blackpool), J Milburn (Newcastle), W Mannion (Middlesbrough), R Langton (Preston).

4.5.49 at Dalymount Park, Dublin (30,000)

League of Ireland   0
Football League   5 (Shackleton 2, Bentley 2, Harris)

FL: G Merrick (B'ham), W Ellerington (Southampton), E Westwood (Man City), H Johnston (Blackpool), L Leuty (Derby), A Wright (Sunderland), P Harris (Portsmouth), C Gibson (Villa), R Bentley (Chelsea), L Shackleton (Sunderland), A Ormston (Stoke C).

15.2.50 at Molineux (14,523)

Football League   7 (Mannion 3, Baily, Lofthouse 2, Finney)
League of Ireland   0

FL: G Merrick (B'ham), L Scott (Arsenal), W Eckersley (Blackburn), W Nicholson (Spurs), C Franklin (Stoke C), J Bell (Blackburn), T Finney (Preston), W Mannion (Middlesbrough), N Lofthouse (Bolton), E Baily (Spurs), R Langton (Bolton).

22.3.50 at Ayresome Park (39,352)

Football League   3 (Mortensen 2, Baily)
Scottish League   1 (Young)

FL: B Williams (Wolves), A Ramsey (Spurs), J Aston (Man Utd), W Wright (Wolves), C Franklin (Stoke C), J Dickinson (Portsmouth), J Hancocks (Wolves), W Mannion (Middlesbrough), S Mortensen (Blackpool), E Baily (Spurs), R Langton (Bolton).

26.4.50 at Windsor Park, Belfast (20,000)

Irish League   1 (McMillen)
Football League   3 (Milburn 3)

FL: G Merrick (B'ham), S Milburn (Chesterfield), W Eckersley (Blackburn), J Harvey (Newcastle), W Whitaker (Middlesbrough), W Musson (Derby), P Harris (Portsmouth), J Morris (Derby), J Milburn (Newcastle), E Wainwright (Everton), V Metcalfe (Huddersfield).

18.10.50 at Bloomfield Road (30,000)

Football League   6 (Stubbins 5, Morris)
Irish League   3 (McGarry 2, Corr)

FL: R Allen (Man Utd), S Milburn (Chesterfield), G Pallister (Barnsley), H Johnston (Blackpool), T Cummings (Burnley), J Bell (Blackburn), T Finney (Preston), J Morris (Derby), A Stubbins (Liverpool), E Baily (Spurs), R Langton (Bolton).

29.11.50 at Ibrox Park (72,000)

Scottish League   1 (McPhail)
Football League   0

FL: E Ditchburn (Spurs), R Robinson (Middlesbrough), J Aston (Man Utd), W Wright (Wolves), J Taylor (Fulham), H Cockburn (Man Utd), J Hancocks (Wolves), S Mortensen (Blackpool), N Lofthouse (Bolton), J Morris (Derby), T Finney (Preston).

4.4.51 at Dalymount Park, Dublin (30,000)

League of Ireland   0
Football League   1 (Lofthouse)

FL: B Williams (Wolves), A Ramsey (Spurs), W Eckersley (Blackburn), W Wright (Wolves), J Taylor (Fulham), J Dickinson (Portsmouth), G Hurst (Charlton Ath), W Mannion (Middlesbrough), N Lofthouse (Bolton), E Baily (Spurs), R Langton (Bolton).

10.10.51 at Goodison Park (28,572)

Football League   9 (Thompson 4, Finney, Langton, Lofthouse 2, Coffey og)
League of Ireland   1 (Carberry)

FL: R Allen (Man Utd), R Robinson (Middlesbrough), L Smith (Arsenal), J Harvey (Newcastle), M Barrass (Bolton), J Dickinson (Portsmouth), T Finney (Preston), T Thompson (Villa), N Lofthouse (Bolton), H Hassall (Huddersfield), R Langton (Bolton).

31.10.51 at Hillsborough (49,075)

Football League   2 (Lofthouse, Finney)
Scottish League   1 (Hamilton)

FL: G Merrick (B'ham), A Ramsey (Spurs), L Smith (Arsenal), W Wright (Wolves), M Barrass (Bolton), J Dickinson (Portsmouth), T Finney (Preston), J Sewell (Sheff Wed), N Lofthouse (Bolton), L Phillips (Portsmouth), L Medley (Spurs).

26.3.52 at Windsor Park, Belfast (20,000)

Irish League   0
Football League   9 (Lofthouse 3, Pearson 3, Finney 2, Broadis)

FL: G Merrick (B'ham), J Ball (Bolton), T Garrett (Blackpool), W Wright (Wolves), J Froggatt (Portsmouth), J Dickinson (Portsmouth),

T Finney (Preston), I Broadis (Man City), N Lofthouse (Bolton), S Pearson (Man Utd), J Rowley (Man Utd)

24.9.52 at Molineux (15,161)

Football League 7 (Lofthouse 6, Ramsey)
Irish League 1 (Doherty)

FL: G Merrick (B'ham), A Ramsey (Spurs), T Garrett (Blackpool), W Wright (Wolves), J Froggatt (Portsmouth), J Dickinson (Portsmouth), T Finney (Preston), J Sewell (Sheff Wed), N Lofthouse (Bolton), E Baily (Spurs), W Elliott (Burnley)

17.3.53 at Dalymount Park, Dublin (40,000)

League of Ireland 0
Football League 2 (Bentley 2)

FL: B Williams (Wolves), S Wade (Arsenal), W Eckersley (Blackburn), W Wright (Wolves), J Froggatt (Portsmouth), J Dickinson (Portsmouth), T Finney (Preston), R Bentley (Chelsea), B Jezzard (Fulham), I Broadis (Man City), W Elliott (Burnley)

25.3.53 at Ibrox Park (60,000)

Scottish League 1 (Reilly)
Football League 0

FL: G Merrick (B'ham), K Green (B'ham), L Smith (Arsenal), W Wright (Wolves), J Froggatt (Portsmouth), J Dickinson (Portsmouth), T Finney (Preston), I Broadis (Man City), N Lofthouse (Bolton), R Froggatt (Sheff Wed), W Elliott (Burnley)

5.5.53 at Idraetspark, Copenhagen (32,600)

Danish Combination 0
Football League 4 (Lishman 2, Jezzard, Wright)

FL: B Williams (Wolves), A Ramsey (Spurs), W Eckersley (Blackburn), W Wright (Wolves), S Owen (Luton), R Barlow (WBA), P Harris (Portsmouth), J Sewell (Sheff Wed), B Jezzard (Fulham), D Lishman (Arsenal), D Roper (Arsenal)

23.9.53 at Windsor Park, Belfast (23,000)

Irish League 0
Football League 5 (Lofthouse 3, Hassall 2)

FL: G Merrick (B'ham), K Green (B'ham), W Eckersley (Blackburn), W Wright (Wolves), H Johnston (Blackpool), J Dickinson (Portsmouth), T Finney (Preston), A Quixall (Sheff Wed), N Lofthouse (Bolton), H Hassall (Bolton), G Robb (Spurs)

10.2.54 at Maine Road (18,208)

Football League 9 (Revie 3, Sewell 3, Berry 2, Lofthouse)
League of Ireland 1 (McQuade)

FL: G Merrick (B'ham), S Rickaby (WBA), R Byrne (Man Utd), W Wright (Wolves), J Dugdale (WBA), R Barlow (WBA), J Berry (Man Utd), D Revie (Man City), N Lofthouse (Bolton), J Sewell (Sheff Wed), V Metcalfe (Huddersfield)

28.4.54 at Stamford Bridge (49,182)

Football League 4 (Sewell, Jezzard 2, Haynes)
Scottish League 0

FL: G Merrick (B'ham), J Ball (Bolton), S Willemse (Chelsea), W Wright (Wolves), S Owen (Luton), E Bell (Bolton), P Harris (Ports-

mouth), J Sewell (Sheff Wed), B Jezzard (Fulham), J Haynes (Fulham), J Mullen (Wolves)

22.9.54 at Dalymount Park, Dublin (35,000)

League of Ireland 0
Football League 6 (Revie 3, Haynes, Matthews, Lofthouse)

FL: R Wood (Man Utd), W Foulkes (Man Utd), J Mansell (Portsmouth), J Wheeler (Bolton), W Wright (Wolves), R Barlow (WBA), S Matthews (Blackpool), D Revie (Man City), N Lofthouse (Bolton), J Haynes (Fulham), T Finney (Preston)

20.10.54 at Anfield (22,323)

Football League 4 (Hooper, Hassall, Lofthouse, Elliott)
Irish League 2 (Jones 2)

FL: R Wood (Man Utd), J Meadows (Man City), R Byrne (Man Utd), L Phillips (Portsmouth), W Wright (Wolves), D Edwards (Man Utd), H Hooper (West Ham), E Baily (Spurs), N Lofthouse (Bolton), H Hassall (Bolton), W Elliott (Sunderland)

16.3.55 at Hampden Park (29,394)

Scottish League 3 (Collins, Haddock, Marston og)
Football League 2 (Evans, Bentley)

FL: R Matthews (Coventry C), W Foulkes (Man Utd), J Mansell (Portsmouth), K Armstrong (Chelsea), J Marston (Preston), D Edwards (Man Utd), H Hooper (West Ham), P Atyeo (Bristol C), R Bentley (Chelsea), J Evans (Liverpool), F Blunstone (Chelsea)

26.10.55 at Hillsborough (37,788)

Football League 4 (Turner, Lofthouse 2, Finney)
Scottish League 2 (Smith, Collins)

FL: B Williams (Wolves), J Hall (B'ham), R Byrne (Man Utd), W McGarry (Huddersfield), W Wright (Wolves), J Dickinson (Portsmouth), T Finney (Preston), G Turner (Luton), N Lofthouse (Bolton), J Haynes (Fulham), D Hogg (Leicester)

7.12.55 at Goodison Park (25,000)

Football League 5 (Perry, Mackey og, Atyeo, Clayton, Byrne)
League of Ireland 1 (Gibbons)

FL: R Baynham (Luton), J Hall (B'ham), R Byrne (Man Utd), R Clayton (Blackburn), W Wright (Wolves), J Dickinson (Portsmouth), T Finney (Preston), P Atyeo (Bristol C), N Lofthouse (Bolton), J Haynes (Fulham), W Perry (Blackpool)

25.4.56 at Windsor Park, Belfast (20,000)

Irish League 5 (Dickson 2, Hill, Weatherup, Eastham)
Football League 2 (Davis og, Taylor)

FL: R Baynham (Luton), J Armfield (Blackpool), R Byrne (Man Utd), R Clayton (Blackburn), M Wicks (Chelsea), J Iley (Sheff Utd), P Harris (Portsmouth), A Quixall (Sheff Wed), T Taylor (Man Utd), J Haynes (Fulham), C Grainger (Sheff Utd)

19.9.56 at Dalymount Park, Dublin (32,000)

League of Ireland 3 (Hamilton, Tuohy, Curtis)
Football League 3 (Quixall, Taylor, Viollet)

FL: R Matthews (Coventry C), J Hall (B'ham), R Byrne (Man Utd), R Clayton (Blackburn), W Wright (Wolves), D Edwards (Man Utd), G Astall (B'ham), A Quixall (Sheff Wed), T Taylor (Man Utd), D Viollet (Man Utd), C Grainger (Sheff Utd)

31.10.56 at St James's Park, Newcastle (34,000)

Football League 3 (Lofthouse, Grainger, Haynes)
Irish League 2 (Dickson, Hill)

FL: R Wood (Man Utd), J Hall (B'ham), E Langley (Brighton), R Clayton (Blackburn), W Wright (Wolves), R Flowers (Wolves), S Matthews (Blackpool), J Haynes (Fulham), N Lofthouse (Bolton), G Rowley (Leicester), C Grainger (Sheff Utd)

13.3.57 at Ibrox Park (60,000)

Scottish League 3 (Fernie, Ring, Collins)
Football League 2 (Pilkington, Thompson)

FL: A Hodgkinson (Sheff Utd), D Howe (WBA), R Sillett (Chelsea), R Clayton (Blackburn), W Wright (Wolves), D Edwards (Man Utd), H Hooper (Wolves), T Thompson (Preston), T Finney (Preston), A Stokes (Spurs), B Pilkington (Burnley)

9.10.57 at Elland Road (13,000)

Football League 3 (Parry 2, Broadbent)
League of Ireland 1 (Nolan)

FL: N Sims (Villa), J Armfield (Blackpool), R Moran (Liverpool), R Barlow (WBA), J Charlton (Leeds), R Pearce (Luton), A Kaye (Barnsley), P Broadbent (Wolves), R Tindall (Chelsea), R Parry (Bolton), P Hooper (Bristol R)

30.10.57 at Windsor Park, Belfast (18,000)

Irish League 2 (Campbell, Dickson)
Football League 4 (Haynes, Murray, A'Court, Brabrook)

FL: E Hopkinson (Bolton), J Bond (West Ham), T Garrett (Blackpool), R Clayton (Blackburn), T Smith (B'ham), R Flowers (Wolves), P Brabrook (Chelsea), D Stevens (Bolton), J Murray (Wolves), J Haynes (Fulham), A A'Court (Liverpool)

26.3.58 at St James's Park, Newcastle (48,800)

Football League 4 (Kevan 3, Allen)
Scottish League 1 (Gemmell)

FL: C McDonald (Burnley), D Howe (WBA), T Banks (Bolton), E Clamp (Wolves), W Wright (Wolves), R Pearce (Sunderland), B Douglas (Blackburn), R Robson (WBA), R Allen (WBA), D Kevan (WBA), T Finney (Preston)

8.10.58 at Ibrox Park (50,000)

Scottish League 1 (Baird)
Football League 1 (Clough)

FL: E Hopkinson (Bolton), J Bond (West Ham), G Shaw (Sheff Utd), A Malcolm (West Ham), J Shaw (Sheff Utd), J Iley (Spurs), D Wilkinson (Sheff Wed), A Quixall (Man Utd), B Clough (Middlesbrough), J Greaves (Chelsea), B Pilkington (Burnley)

12.11.58 at Anfield (30,717)

Football League 5 (White 3, Haynes, A'Court)
Irish League 2 (Thompson, Russell)

FL: C McDonald (Burnley), L Hartle (Bolton), G Shaw (Sheff Utd), J Wheeler (Liverpool), J Shaw (Sheff Utd), W McGuinness (Man Utd), D Clapton (Arsenal), J Harris (Everton), L White (Newcastle), J Haynes (Fulham), A A'Court (Liverpool)

17.3.59 at Dalymount Park, Dublin (45,000)

League of Ireland 0
Football League 0

FL: C McDonald (Burnley), D Howe (WBA), G Shaw (Sheff Utd), R Clayton (Blackburn), R Gratrix (Blackpool), R Flowers (Wolves), D Wilkinson (Sheff Wed), P Broadbent (Wolves), D Viollet (Man Utd), J Haynes (Fulham), A Holden (Bolton)

23.9.59 at Windsor Park, Belfast (18,000)

Irish League 0
Football League 5 (Clough 5)

FL: R Springett (Sheff Wed), D Howe (WBA), R Wilson (Huddersfield), R Clayton (Blackburn), T Smith (B'ham), R Flowers (Wolves), J Connelly (Burnley), P Dobing (Blackburn), B Clough (Middlesbrough), G Eastham (Newcastle), A Scanlon (Man Utd)

4.11.59 at Ewood Park (20,300)

Football League 2 (Viollet, Connelly)
League of Ireland 0

FL: R Springett (Sheff Wed), J Armfield (Blackpool), A Allen (Stoke C), R Clayton (Blackburn), P Swan (Sheff Wed), A Kay (Sheff Wed), J Connelly (Burnley), P Dobing (Blackburn), D Viollet (Man Utd), R Parry (Bolton), E Holliday (Middlesbrough)

23.3.60 at Highbury (35,508)

Football League 1 (Hooper)
Scottish League 0

FL: A Kelsey (Arsenal), J Armfield (Blackpool), R Moran (Liverpool), R Robson (WBA), T Knapp (Leicester), D Mackay (Spurs), H Hooper (B'ham), J Bloomfield (Arsenal), L White (Newcastle), J Greaves (Chelsea), C Jones (Spurs)

14.9.60 at Dalymount Park, Dublin (18,000)

League of Ireland 0
Football League 4 (Dobing 3, Greaves)

FL: N Sims (Villa), J Sillett (Chelsea), A Allen (Stoke C), R Clayton (Blackburn), M Woods (Blackburn), M McGrath (Blackburn), P Brabrook (Chelsea), P Dobing (Blackburn), G Moore (Cardiff), J Greaves (Chelsea), F Blunstone (Chelsea)

12.10.60 at Bloomfield Road (19,066)

Football League 5 (Blanchflower, Law 2, Connelly, McIlroy)
Irish League 2 (Coyle 2)

FL: B Trautmann (Man City), J Angus (Burnley), J Armfield (Blackpool), R Blanchflower (Spurs), J Adamson (Burnley), D Mackay (Spurs), C Jones (Spurs), J White (Spurs), D Law (Man City), J McIlroy (Burnley), J Connelly (Burnley)

1.11.60 at San Siro Stadium, Milan (40,000)

Italian League   4 (Altafini 2, Tacchi, Hamrin)
Football League   2 (Law, McParland)

FL: R Springett (Sheff Wed), J Armfield (Blackpool), D Megson (Sheff Wed), R Robson (WBA), P Swan (Sheff Wed), R Flowers (Wolves), C Jones (Spurs), J McIlroy (Burnley), D Law (Man City), J Haynes (Fulham), P McParland (Villa); Subs: B Trautmann (Man City) for Springett, A Woosnam (West Ham) for Jones

22.3.61 at Ibrox Park (50,000)

Scottish League   3 (McCann, St John, Caldow)
Football League   2 (Hitchens, Swan)

FL: R Springett (Sheff Wed), D Howe (WBA), M McNeil (Middlesbrough), R Robson (WBA), P Swan (Sheff Wed), R Flowers (Wolves), P Brabrook (Chelsea), J Greaves (Chelsea), G Hitchens (Villa), J Fantham (Sheff Wed), R Charlton (Man Utd)

11.10.61 at Eastville (31,959)

Football League   5 (Douglas 2, Haynes, Connelly, Nolan og)
League of Ireland   2 (Morrissey, Eglington)

FL: R Springett (Sheff Wed), J Armfield (Blackpool), R Wilson (Huddersfield), R Robson (WBA), P Swan (Sheff Wed), R Flowers (Wolves), J Connelly (Burnley), B Douglas (Blackburn), R Pointer (Burnley), J Haynes (Fulham), R Charlton (Man Utd)

1.11.61 at Windsor Park, Belfast (15,000)

Irish League   1 (Morrison)
Football League   6 (Harris, Kay, Crawford 2, Fantham, Miller)

FL: G Banks (Leicester), D Howe (WBA), G Shaw (Sheff Utd), B Miller (Burnley), B Labone (Everton), A Kay (Sheff Wed), J Connelly (Burnley), F Hill (Bolton), R Crawford (Ipswich), J Fantham (Sheff Wed), G Harris (Burnley)

8.11.61 at Old Trafford (31,911)

Football League   0
Italian League   2 (Lojacono, Hitchens)

FL: R Springett (Sheff Wed), J Armfield (Blackpool), R Wilson (Huddersfield), A Kay (Sheff Wed), P Swan (Sheff Wed), R Flowers (Wolves), J Connelly (Burnley), J Fantham (Sheff Wed), R Pointer (Burnley), J Haynes (Fulham), R Charlton (Man Utd)

21.3.62 at Villa Park (18,459)

Football League   3 (Haynes, Hunt 2)
Scottish League   4 (Wilson 3, Brand)

FL: R Springett (Sheff Wed), J Armfield (Blackpool), R Wilson (Huddersfield), B Miller (Burnley), P Swan (Sheff Wed), R Flowers (Wolves), A Jackson (WBA), R Hunt (Liverpool), R Crawford (Ipswich), J Haynes (Fulham), R Charlton (Man Utd)

31.10.62 at Carrow Road (15,000)

Football League   3 (Crawford 3)
Irish League   1 (Meldrum)

FL: G Banks (Leicester), J Armfield (Blackpool), R Wilson (Huddersfield), R Moore (West Ham), J Sleeuwenhoek (Villa), C Appleton

(Leicester), B Douglas (Blackburn), F Hill (Bolton), R Crawford (Ipswich), J Byrne (West Ham), M O'Grady (Huddersfield)

29.11.62 at Highbury (35,699)

Football League   3 (O'Grady, Allen, Greaves)
Italian League   2 (Charles 2)

FL: R Springett (Sheff Wed), J Armfield (Blackpool), R Wilson (Huddersfield), R Moore (West Ham), B Labone (Everton), R Flowers (Wolves), J Connelly (Burnley), J Greaves (Spurs), L Allen (Spurs), B Douglas (Blackburn), M O'Grady (Huddersfield)

24.5.63 FA Centenary/FL 75th Anniversary at Highbury
(26,994)

England   3 (Greaves, Hinton, Byrne)
Football League   3 (Hunt, Hurst, Kay)

ENGLAND: R Springett (Sheff Wed), J Armfield (Blackpool), R Wilson (Huddersfield), R Moore (West Ham), M Norman (Spurs), G Milne (Liverpool), B Douglas (Blackburn), J Greaves (Spurs), J Byrne (West Ham), G Eastham (Arsenal), A Hinton (Wolves); Sub: A Marchi (Spurs) for Armfield
FL: P Bonetti (Chelsea), K Shellito (Chelsea), G Shaw (Sheff Utd), R Flowers (Wolves), B Labone (Everton), A Kay (Everton), T Paine (Southampton), R Hunt (Liverpool), G Hurst (West Ham), J Melia (Liverpool), C Dobson (Sheff Wed)

2.10.63 at Dalymount Park, Dublin (30,000)

League of Ireland   2 (Bailham, Whelan)
Football League   1 (Byrne)

FL: A Waiters (Blackpool), J Armfield (Blackpool), R Wilson (Huddersfield), G Milne (Liverpool), R Moore (West Ham), M Peters (West Ham), I Callaghan (Liverpool), R Hunt (Liverpool), J Byrne (West Ham), J Melia (Liverpool), M O'Grady (Huddersfield)

18.3.64 at Roker Park (9,513)

Football League   2 (Byrne, Greaves)
Scottish League   2 (McBride, Martin)

FL: A Waiters (Blackpool), G Cohen (Fulham), R Thomson (Wolves), G Milne (Liverpool), R Flowers (Wolves), R Moore (West Ham), T Paine (Southampton), J Greaves (Spurs), J Byrne (West Ham), A Kay (Everton), P Thompson (Liverpool)

9.5.64 at San Siro Stadium, Milan (13,390)

Italian League   1 (Suarez)
Football League   0

FL: A Waiters (Blackpool), G Cohen (Fulham), R Thomson (Wolves), A Mullery (Spurs), M Norman (Spurs), R Flowers (Wolves), T Paine (Southampton), R Hunt (Liverpool), F Pickering (Everton), R Charlton (Man Utd), P Thompson (Liverpool); Sub: G Banks (Leicester) for Waiters

28.10.64 at The Oval, Belfast (20,000)

Irish League   0
Football League   4 (Paine, Wignall 3)

FL: A Waiters (Blackpool), L Badger (Sheff Utd), K Newton (Blackburn), A Mullery (Spurs), R Flowers (Wolves), N Hunter (Leeds), T Paine (Southampton), R Hunt (Liverpool), F Wignall (Nottm F), T Venables (Chelsea), D Temple (Everton)

17.3.65 at Hampden Park (38,409)

Scottish League   2 (Hughes 2)
Football League   2 (J Charlton, Bridges)

FL: A Waiters (Blackpool), R Thomson (Wolves), R Wilson (Everton), N Stiles (Man Utd), J Charlton (Leeds), N Hunter (Leeds), T Paine (Southampton), J Greaves (Spurs), B Bridges (Chelsea), A Ball (Blackpool), R Charlton (Man Utd)

27.10.65 at Boothferry Park (28,283)

Football League   5 (Ball 2, Kaye 2, Charlton)
League of Ireland   0

FL: G Banks (Leicester), G Cohen (Fulham), K Newton (Blackburn), B O'Neil (Burnley), J Charlton (Leeds), N Hunter (Leeds), P Thompson (Liverpool), A Ball (Blackpool), J Kaye (WBA), G Harris (Burnley), D Temple (Everton)

16.3.66 at St James's Park, Newcastle (32,900)

Football League   1 (Greaves)
Scottish League   3 (Penman, McBride 2)

FL: R Springett (Sheff Wed), P Reaney (Leeds), K Newton (Blackburn), N Stiles (Man Utd), J Charlton (Leeds), N Hunter (Leeds), A Ball (Blackpool), J Greaves (Spurs), J Kaye (WBA), G Eastham (Arsenal), R Charlton (Man Utd)

21.9.66 at Home Park (35,458)

Football League   12 (Byrne 4, Hurst 2, Eastham 2,
                               Connelly 2, Paine 2)
Irish League   0

FL: P Bonetti (Chelsea), G Cohen (Fulham), R Wilson (Everton), M Peters (West Ham), J Charlton (Leeds), R Moore (West Ham), T Paine (Southampton), J Byrne (West Ham), G Hurst (West Ham), G Eastham (Stoke C), J Connelly (Man Utd)

15.3.67 at Hampden Park (29,066)

Scottish League   0
Football League   3 (Clarke 2, Hurst)

FL: P Bonetti (Chelsea), L Badger (Sheff Utd), K Newton (Blackburn), J Hollins (Chelsea), B Labone (Everton), R Moore (West Ham), I Callaghan (Liverpool), J Greaves (Spurs), A Clarke (Fulham), G Hurst (West Ham), P Thompson (Liverpool)

27.9.67 at Brussels (35,000)

Belgian League   2 (Puis, Van Himst)
Football League   2 (Peters, Clarke)

FL: G Banks (Stoke C), L Badger (Sheff Utd), N Hunter (Leeds), M Peters (West Ham), J Charlton (Leeds), R Moore (West Ham), A Ball (Everton), F Wignall (Nottm F), A Clarke (Fulham), G Hurst (West Ham), J Hollins (Chelsea)

8.11.67 at Dalymount Park, Dublin (27,000)

League of Ireland   2 (McEvoy, O'Neill)
Football League   7 (Greaves, Chivers 3, Ritchie 2,
                               Sammels)

FL: P Grummitt (Nottm F), W Smith (Sheff Wed), R Wilson (Everton), M Bailey (Wolves), V Mobley (Sheff Wed), R Moore (West Ham), J Sammels (Arsenal), J Greaves (Spurs), J Ritchie (Sheff Wed), M Chivers (Southampton), C Bell (Man City)

20.3.68 at Ayresome Park (34,190)

Football League   2 (Hunt, Newton)
Scottish League   0

FL: A Stepney (Man Utd), K Newton (Blackburn), C Knowles (Spurs), N Stiles (Man Utd), B Labone (Everton), R Moore (West Ham), A Ball (Everton), R Hunt (Liverpool), R Charlton (Man Utd), G Hurst (West Ham), M Peters (West Ham)

27.11.68 at Windsor Park, Belfast (12,000)

Irish League   0
Football League   1 (Hurst)

FL: G West (Everton), R Thomson (Wolves), R McNab (Arsenal), M Bailey (Wolves), B Labone (Everton), T Smith (Liverpool), J Radford (Arsenal), C Bell (Man City), P Osgood (Chelsea), G Hurst (West Ham), P Thompson (Liverpool)

26.3.69 at Hampden Park (23,582)

Scottish League   1 (Wallace)
Football League   3 (Casper, Ball, Tambling)

FL: P Bonetti (Chelsea), W Smith (Sheff Wed), E Hughes (Liverpool), P Osgood (Chelsea), J McGrath (Southampton), A Oakes (Man City), R Coates (Burnley), F Casper (Burnley), J Royle (Everton), A Ball (Everton), R Tambling (Chelsea)

10.9.69 at Oakwell (11,939)

Football League   3 (Robson, Bailey, Summerbee)
League of Ireland   0

FL: P Bonetti (Chelsea), P Reaney (Leeds), F Clark (Newcastle), C Harvey (Everton), P Madeley (Leeds), N Hunter (Leeds), B Robson (Newcastle), M Bailey (Wolves), M Summerbee (Man City), F Lee (Man City), J Morrissey (Everton); Sub: A Woodward (Sheff Utd) for Harvey

18.3.70 at Highfield Road (26,693)

Football League   3 (Astle 2, Rogers)
Scottish League   2 (Cormack, Graham)

FL: A Stepney (Man Utd), W Smith (Sheff Wed), E Hughes (Liverpool), H Newton (Nottm F), R McFarland (Derby), C Todd (Sunderland), R Coates (Burnley), B Kidd (Man Utd), J Astle (WBA), C Harvey (Everton), D Rogers (Swindon); Subs: W Glazier (Coventry C) for Stepney, M Peters (Spurs) for Kidd

23.9.70 at Carrow Road (20,743)

Football League   5 (Peters, Astle 2, Brown, Hector)
Irish League   0

FL: P Shilton (Leicester), P Edwards (Man Utd), J Robson (Derby), D Nish (Leicester), D Sadler (Man Utd), C Harvey (Everton), M Peters (Spurs), R Coates (Burnley), K Hector (Derby), J Astle (WBA), I Storey-Moore (Nottm F); Subs: D Smith (Stoke C) for Edwards, A Brown (WBA) for Storey-Moore, J Jackson (Crystal P) for Shilton

17.3.71 at Hampden Park (17,657)

Scottish League   0
Football League   1 (Coates)

FL: J Jackson (Crystal P), P Reaney (Leeds), D Parkin (Wolves), J Hollins (Chelsea), R McFarland (Derby), R Moore (West Ham),

R Coates (Burnley), A Brown (WBA), G Hurst (West Ham), B O'Neill (Southampton), I Storey-Moore (Nottm F)

22.9.71 at Lansdowne Road, Dublin   (20,000)

League of Ireland   1 (Matthews)
Football League   2 (Osgood, Radford)

FL: G Banks (Stoke C), C Lawler (Liverpool), D Nish (Leicester), P Storey (Arsenal), R McFarland (Derby), D Sadler (Man Utd), A Woodward (Sheff Utd), K Hector (Derby), J Radford (Arsenal), P Osgood (Chelsea), E Hughes (Liverpool); Sub: C Todd (Derby) for Lawler

15.3.72 at Ayresome Park   (19,996)

Football League   3 (Currie 2, Doyle)
Scottish League   2 (Stein, McQuade)

FL: R Clemence (Liverpool), C Lawler (Liverpool), D Nish (Leicester), M Doyle (Man City), J Blockley (Coventry C), R Moore (West Ham), E Hughes (Liverpool), A Currie (Sheff Utd), M Macdonald (Newcastle), G Hurst (West Ham), D Wagstaffe (Wolves)

27.3.73 at Hampden Park   (18,857)

Scottish League   2 (Duncan 2)
Football League   2 (Channon 2)

FL: P Shilton (Leicester), M Mills (Ipswich), D Nish (Derby), H Kendall (Everton), R McFarland (Derby), R Moore (West Ham), K Weller (Leicester), M Channon (Southampton), F Worthington (Leicester), J Richards (Wolves), C Bell (Man City); Sub: A Currie (Sheff Utd) for Kendall

20.3.74 at Maine Road   (11,471)

Football League   5 (Bell, Brown og, Tueart, Brooking, Bowles)
Scottish League   0

FL: R Clemence (Liverpool), P Storey (Arsenal), D Nish (Derby), J Dobson (Burnley), R McFarland (Derby), C Todd (Derby), S Bowles (QPR), C Bell (Man City), R Latchford (Everton), T Brooking (West Ham), D Tueart (Man City); Sub: K Hector (Derby) for Latchford

17.3.76 at Hampden Park   (8,874)

Scottish League   0
Football League   1 (Cherry)

FL: P Shilton (Stoke C), T Cherry (Leeds), M Mills (Ipswich), M Doyle (Man City), R McFarland (Derby), A Dodd (Stoke C), R Wilkins (Chelsea), M Channon (Southampton), J Greenhoff (Stoke C), A Currie (Sheff Utd), D Tueart (Man City)

17.5.77 Glasgow Jubilee Appeal at Hampden Park   (28,380)

Glasgow Select   2 (Jardine, Dalglish)
Football League   1 (Tueart)

FL: J Corrigan (Man City), K Clements (Man City), D Peach (Southampton), G Stanley (Chelsea), D Watson (Man City), R Wilkins (Chelsea), T Francis (B'ham), M Channon (Southampton), J Royle (Man City), G Owen (Man City), D Tueart (Man City); Sub: P Barnes (Man City) for Royle

8.8.87 Mercantile Credit Centenary Classic at Wembley (61,000)

Football League   3 (Robson 2, Whiteside)
Rest of the World 0

FL: P Shilton (Derby), R Gough (Spurs), K Sansom (Arsenal), J McClelland (Watford), P McGrath (Man Utd), L Brady (West Ham), N Webb (Nottm F), C Allen (Spurs), P Beardsley (Liverpool), C Waddle (Spurs); Subs: O Ardiles (Spurs) for Webb, A Smith (Arsenal) for Allen, S Ogrizovic (Coventry) for Shilton, S Clarke (Chelsea) for Gough, P Nevin (Chelsea) for Brady

R OF W: R Dassayev (Moscow Spartak), Josimar (Botafogo), Celso (Porto), Julio Alberto (Barcelona), G Hysen (Fiorentina), S Bagni (Napoli), T Berthold (Verona), G Lineker (Barcelona), M Platini (France), D Maradona (Napoli), P Futre (Athletico Madrid);. Subs: A Zubizarreta (Barcelona) for Dassayev, P Elkjaer (Verona) for Lineker, L Detari (E Frankfurt) for Josimar, I Belanov (Dynamo Kiev) for Bagni, D Stojkovic (Red Star Belgrade) for Celso, A Zavarov (Dynamo Kiev) for Futre.

8.9.87 at Windsor Park, Belfast   (3000)

Irish League   2 (Burrows, Caskey)
Football League   2 (Gibson, Mirandinha)

FL: B Grobbelaar (Liverpool), M Sterland (Sheff Wed), S Bruce (Norwich), J McClelland (Watford), N Winterburn (Arsenal), W Fereday (QPR), O Ardiles (Spurs), C Gibson (Man Utd), K Drinkell (Norwich), Mirandinha (Newcastle)

The League Cup and its Forerunners

The idea for a cup competition contested solely by League clubs was first mooted in February 1892 by a firm called Messrs Hudson and Co., who offered to donate a trophy worth £500 for the winners. The Committee declined the offer. Apart from the lack of spare dates, the League had no desire to antagonize the FA by instituting a rival knock-out tournament.

The idea was partially revived in 1932 with a suggestion that each Third Division section hold a cup competition (see Appendix Five), and during the Second World War the League operated its own cup competition from 1939 to 1941. The results were:

1939/40
West Ham 1 Blackburn 0 (8.6.40 at Wembley, att. 42,399)

1940/1
Preston 1 Arsenal 1 (10.5.41 at Wembley, att. 60,000)
Preston 2 Arsenal 1 (31.5.41 at Blackburn, att. 45,000)

In 1941/2 the London clubs played their own tournament, with a final at Wembley, in which Brentford beat Portsmouth 2–0 (30.5.42, att. 72,000), while the League's Northern clubs ran a League Cup with a two-legged final. Wolves beat Sunderland on aggregate 6–3. This was then followed by a Cup Winners' match at Stamford Bridge. This pattern was repeated in 1942, by which time the London clubs had returned to the League fold, and continued until 1945. Southern finals were played at Wembley, Northern finals were played on a two-legged basis.

Again, Cup Winners' matches were played at Stamford Bridge, as follows:

1941/2
Brentford 1 Wolves 1 (6.6.42, att. 20,174)

1942/3
Blackpool 4 Arsenal 2 (15.5.43, att. 55,195)

1943/4
Aston Villa 1 Charlton 1 (20.5.44, att. 38,540)

1944/5
Bolton 2 Chelsea 1 (2.6.45, att. 35,000)

There was also a Western Cup, but this involved non-League clubs.

The revival of the FA Cup in 1945/6 (played on a two-legged basis until the final) and the need to consolidate after the war signalled the shelving of the concept for the time being, but the wartime competition certainly served as a basis for the League Cup when finally introduced in 1960.

In the mid 1940s, a group called the Post-War Reconstruction Committee was formed to consider ideas for reviving football in peacetime. The idea of a League Cup was originally that of Stanley Rous, then FA secretary, who saw it as a consolation for those League clubs knocked out in the early rounds of the FA Cup.

The principal obstacle was a lack of space on the fixture list, but during the 1950s this was overcome by the gradual introduction of floodlighting. Even then, it took a couple of trial competitions to establish the feasibility of a League Cup.

In 1955, two mid-week competitions started. One was the Anglo-Scottish Floodlit League, which the Management Committee opposed, and the other, the Southern Professional Floodlit Cup.

The League Cup as we know it today was born in 1960 and immediately became dubbed 'Hardaker's baby' or 'Hardaker's folly'. In fact, Hardaker, with Joe Richards' support, merely revived the idea of the Post-War Reconstruction Committee and incorporated it into his 'Pattern for Football'. He saw the League Cup as being played on the Scottish model, at the beginning of the season, but more importantly, he suggested it primarily as a means of compensating clubs for the fixtures they would lose by reducing the size of each division to twenty clubs.

As we have noted earlier, the clubs liked the idea of the cup, but not the rest of the package. As a result, when the League Cup was finally agreed upon at the Annual Meeting in 1960 it had many critics, who saw it as a poor man's FA Cup and an unnecessary addition to the crowded fixture list. Joe Richards believed in it so strongly that he bought the trophy with his own funds and predicted that one day the final would be played at Wembley.

Entry to the Cup was not compulsory, and crowds initially were poor. Virtually all the top First Division clubs boycotted the League Cup in its first six seasons. West Bromwich Albion didn't enter until 1965, while Tottenham, Arsenal, Sheffield Wednesday and Wolves didn't enter until 1966. Liverpool and Everton also remained aloof for most of the early years.

Two factors helped to bring respectability (and therefore profitability) to the competition. Firstly, the League negotiated with Wembley to hold the final there in 1967. Entries rose as a result from eighty-three to ninety that year.

Secondly, after Hardaker had pressed UEFA and threatened a boycott of the Fairs Cup if his wishes were not satisfied, the League Cup winners were granted an automatic place in Europe. Unfortunately for subsequent winners QPR and Swindon Town (both then in the Third Division), this applied only to First Division clubs. In fact, the first club to take its place in Europe solely on the basis of winning the League Cup was Spurs in 1971 (Leeds, winners in 1968, qualified by dint of finishing fourth in Division One. Manchester City, winners in 1970, were otherwise engaged in defending the European Cup Winners' Cup).

Nevertheless, once automatic entry to Europe was confirmed, those clubs who had held aloof joined the competition, and since 1967 every League club has entered, with only one or two exceptions. Everton, for example, didn't compete in 1970/1 so that they could concentrate on the European Cup.

There have been various chages to the format. Since 1975 the first round has been played over two legs. The second round was also made two legged in 1979. In 1983 seeding was introduced to give lower division clubs a better chance of playing the top clubs (as a result of which, second round gates rose by 50,000).

In the first year, 1960/1, there were eighty-seven entries and gates averaged 10,755. The lowest number of clubs entering was eighty in 1962/3, and the lowest average gate was 9089 in 1963/4. After 1967, attendances rose to a peak of around 19,000 on average in 1971/2, but then declined gradually until 1985/6 when there were ninety-two entries and an average gate of 9719.

The first offer to sponsor the competition came in 1971. This was rejected. The Milk Marketing Board sponsored the League Cup from 1982 to 1986. The current sponsor is the retail division of pools company Littlewoods (of which Philip Carter used to be managing director), who pay the following: to each Associate Member entering £2500, to Second Division clubs £5000, to First Division clubs £10,000. Losing semi-finalists receive £7500 each, the runners-up £25,000 and the winners £75,000.

League Cup Finals

1960/1

Aston Villa beat Rotherham United on aggregate 3–2

First leg
22.8.61 at Millmoor   (12,226)

Rotherham United   2 (Webster, Kirkman)
Aston Villa   0

Rotherham United: Ironside, Perry, Morgan, Lambert, Madden, Waterhouse, Webster, Weston, Houghton, Kirkman, Bambridge.
Aston Villa: Sims, Lynn, Lee, Crowe, Dugdale, Deakin, MacEwan, Thomson, Brown, Wylie, McParland.
Referee: K Collinge (Altrincham)

Second leg
5.9.61 at Villa Park   (31,202)

Aston Villa   3 (O'Neill, Burrows, McParland)
Rotherham United   0 (a.e.t.)

Rotherham United: unchanged
Aston Villa: Sidebottom, Neal, Lee, Crowe, Dugdale, Deakin, MacEwan, O'Neill, McParland, Thomson, Burrows.
Referee: C Kingston (Newport)

1961/2

Norwich City beat Rochdale on aggregate 4–0

First leg
26.4.62 at Spotland   (11,123)

Rochdale   0
Norwich City   3 (Lythgoe 2, Punton)

Rochdale: Burgin, Milburn, Winton, Bodell, Aspden, Thompson, Wragg, Hepton, Bimpson, Cairns, Whitaker.
Norwich City: Kennon, McCrohan, Ashman, Burton, Butler, Mullett, Mannion, Lythgoe, Scott, Hill, Punton.
Referee: A Holland (Barnsley)

Second leg
1.5.62 at Carrow Road   (19,708)

Norwich City   1 (Hill)
Rochdale   0

Norwich City: unchanged
Rochdale: Burgin, Milburn, Winton, Bodell, Aspden, Thompson, Whyke, Richardson, Bimpson, Cairns, Whitaker.
Referee: R Mann (Worcs)

1962/3

Birmingham City beat Aston Villa on aggregate 3–1

First leg
23.5.63 at St Andrew's   (31,850)

Birmingham City   3 (Leek 2, Bloomfield)
Aston Villa   1 (Thomson)

Birmingham City: Scofield, Lynn, Green, Hennessey, Smith, Beard, Hellawell, Bloomfield, Harris, Leek, Auld.
Aston Villa: Sims, Fraser, Aitken, Crowe, Sleeuwenhoek, Lee, Baker, Graham, Thomson, Wylie, Burrows.
Referee: E Crawford (Doncaster)

Second leg
27.5.63 at Villa Park   (37,921)

Aston Villa   0
Birmingham City   0

Aston Villa: Sims, Fraser, Aitken, Crowe, Chatterley, Lee, Baker, Graham, Thomson, Wylie, Burrows.
Birmingham City: unchanged
Referee: A Sparling (Grimsby)

1963/4

Leicester City beat Stoke City on aggregate 4–3

First leg
15.4.64 at the Victoria Ground   (22,309)

Stoke City   1 (Bebbington)
Leicester City   1 (Gibson)

Stoke City: Leslie, Asprey, Allen, Palmer, Kinnell, Skeels, Dobing, Viollet, Ritchie, McIlroy, Bebbington.
Leicester City: Banks, Sjoberg, Appleton, Dougan, King, Cross, Riley, Heath, Keyworth, Gibson, Stringfellow.
Referee: W Clements (West Bromwich)

Second leg
22.4.64 at Filbert Street   (25,372)

Leicester City   3 (Stringfellow, Gibson, Riley)
Stoke City   2 (Viollet, Kinnell)

Leicester City: Banks, Sjoberg, Norman, Cross, King, Appleton, Riley, Gibson, Keyworth, Sweenie, Stringfellow.
Stoke City: Irvine, Asprey, Allen, Palmer, Kinnell, Skeels, Dobing, Viollet, Ritchie, McIlroy, Bebbington.
Referee: A Jobling (Grimsby)

1964/5

Chelsea beat Leicester City on aggregate 3–2

First leg

15.3.65 at Stamford Bridge (20,690)

Chelsea 3 (Tambling, Venables pen, McCreadie)
Leicester City 2 (Appleton, Goodfellow)

Chelsea: Bonetti, Hinton, Harris, Hollins, Young, Boyle, Murray, Graham, McCreadie, Venables, Tambling.
Leicester City: Banks, Sjoberg, Norman, Chalmers, King, Appleton, Hodgson, Cross, Goodfellow, Gibson, Sweenie.
Referee: J Finney (Hereford)

Second leg

5.4.65 at Filbert Street (26,958)

Leicester City 0
Chelsea 0

Leicester City: Banks, Walker, Norman, Roberts, Sjoberg, Appleton, Hodgson, Cross, Goodfellow, Gibson, Stringfellow.
Chelsea: Bonetti, Hinton, McCreadie, Harris, Mortimore, Upton, Murray, Boyle, Bridges, Venables, Tambling.
Referee: K Howley (Middlesbrough)

1965/6

West Bromwich Albion beat West Ham Utd on aggregate 5–3

First leg

9.3.66 at Upton Park (28,341)

West Ham Utd 2 (Moore, Byrne)
West Bromwich Albion 1 (Astle)

West Ham Utd: Standen, Burnett, Burkett, Peters, Brown, Moore, Brabrook, Boyce, Byrne, Hurst, Dear.
WBA: Potter, Cram, Fairfax, Fraser, Campbell, Williams, Brown, Astle, Kaye, Lovett, Clark.
Referee: D Smith (Stonehouse)

Second leg

23.3.66 at The Hawthorns (31,925)

West Bromwich Albion 4 (Kaye, Brown, Clark, Williams)
West Ham Utd 1 (Peters)

WBA: Potter, Cram, Fairfax, Fraser, Campbell, Williams, Brown, Astle, Kaye, Hope, Clark.
West Ham Utd: Standen, Burnett, Peters, Bovington, Brown, Moore, Brabrook, Boyce, Byrne, Hurst, Sissons.
Referee: J Mitchell (Whiston)

1966/7

4.3.67 at Wembley (97,952)

Queen's Park Rangers 3 (R Morgan, Marsh, Lazarus
West Bromwich Albion 2 (Clark 2)

QPR: Springett, Hazell, Langley, Sibley, Hunt, Keen, Lazarus, Sanderson, Allen, Marsh, R Morgan. Sub: I Morgan.
WBA: Sheppard, Cram, Williams, Collard, Clarke, Fraser, Brown, Astle, Kaye, Hope, Clark. Sub: Foggo.
Referee: W Crossley (Lancaster)

1967/8

2.3.68 at Wembley (97,887)

Leeds United 1 (Cooper)
Arsenal 0

Leeds United: Sprake, Reaney, Cooper, Bremner, Charlton, Hunter, Greenhoff, Lorimer, Madeley, Giles, Gray (sub: Belfitt).
Arsenal: Furnell, Storey, McNab, McLintock, Simpson, Ure, Simpson (sub: Graham), Radford, Sammels, Court, Gould, Armstrong.
Referee: L Hamer (Norfolk)

1968/9

15.3.69 at Wembley (98,189)

Arsenal 1 (Gould)
Swindon Town 3 (Smart, Rogers 2)

Arsenal: Wilson, Storey, McNab, McLintock, Ure, Simpson (sub: Graham), Radford, Sammels, Court, Gould, Armstrong.
Swindon Town: Downsborough, Thomas, Trollope, Butler, Burrows, Harland, Heath, Smart, Smith (sub: Penman), Noble, Rogers.
Referee: W Handley (Cannock)

1969/70

7.3.70 at Wembley (97,963)

Manchester City 2 (Doyle, Pardoe)
West Bromwich Albion 1 (Astle) (a.e.t.)

Manchester City: Corrigan, Book, Mann, Doyle, Booth, Oakes, Heslop, Bell, Summerbee (sub: Bowyer), Lee, Pardoe.
WBA: Osborne, Fraser, Wilson, Brown, Talbut, Kaye, Cantello, Suggett, Astle, Hartford (sub: Krzywicki), Hope.
Referee: J James (York)

1970/1

27.2.71 at Wembley (100,000)

Tottenham Hotspur 2 (Chivers 2)
Aston Villa 0

Tottenham Hotspur: Jennings, Kinnear, Knowles, Mullery, Collins, Beal, Gilzean, Perryman, Chivers, Peters, Neighbour (sub not used: Pearce).
Aston Villa: Dunn, Bradley, Aitken, Godfrey, Turnbill, Tiler, McMahon, Rioch, Lochhead, Hamilton, Anderson (sub not used: Gibson)
Referee: J Finney (Hereford)

1971/2

4.3.72 at Wembley (100,000)

Stoke City 2 (Conroy, Eastham)
Chelsea 1 (Osgood)

Stoke City: Marsh, Banks, Pejic, Bernard, Smith, Bloor, Conroy, Greenhoff (sub: Mahoney), Ritchie, Dobing, Eastham.
Chelsea: Bonetti, Mulligan (sub: Baldwin), Harris, Hollins, Dempsey, Webb, Cooke, Garland, Osgood, Hudson, Houseman.
Referee: N Burtenshaw (Great Yarmouth)

1972/3

3.3.73 at Wembley (100,000)

Tottenham Hotspur 1 (Coates)
Norwich City 0

Tottenham Hotspur: Jennings, Kinnear, Knowles, Pratt (sub: Coates), England, Beal, Gilzean, Perryman, Chivers, Peters, Pearce.
Norwich City: Keelan, Payne, Butler, Stringer, Forbes, Briggs, Livermore, Blair (sub: Howard), Cross, Paddon, Anderson.
Referee: D Smith (Gloucester)

1973/4

2.3.74 at Wembley (100,000)

Wolverhampton Wanderers 2 (Hibbitt, Richards)
Manchester City 1 (Bell)

Wolverhampton: Pierce, Palmer, Parkin, Bailey, Munro, McAlle, Sunderland, Hibbitt, Richards, Dougan, Wagstaffe (sub: Powell).
Manchester City: MacRae, Pardoe, Donachie, Doyle, Booth, Towers, Summerbee, Bell, Lee, Law, Marsh.
Referee: E Wallace (Crewe)

1974/5

1.3.75 at Wembley (100,000)

Aston Villa 1 (Graydon)
Norwich City 0

Aston Villa: Cumbes, Robson, Aitken, Ross, Nicholl, McDonald, Graydon, Little, Leonard, Hamilton, Carrodus.
Norwich City: Keelan, Machin, Sullivan, Morris, Forbes, Stringer, Miller, MacDougall, Boyer, Suggett, Powell.
Referee: G Hill (Lancs)

1975/6

28.2.76 at Wembley (100,000)

Manchester City 2 (Barnes, Tueart)
Newcastle United 1 (Gowling)

Manchester City: Corrigan, Keegan, Donachie, Doyle, Watson, Oakes, Barnes, Booth, Royle, Hartford, Tueart.
Newcastle United: Mahoney, Nattrass, Kennedy, Barrowclough, Keeley, Howard, Burns, Cassidy, MacDonald, Gowling, Craig.
Referee: J Taylor (Wolverhampton)

1976/7

12.3.77 at Wembley (100,000)

Aston Villa 0
Everton 0

Aston Villa: Burridge, Gidman, Robson, Phillips, Nicholl, Mortimer, Deehan, Little, Gray, Cropley, Carrodus.
Everton: Lawson, Jones, Darracott, Lyons, McNaught, King, Hamilton, Dobson, Latchford, McKenzie, Goodlass.
Referee: G Kew (Worcs)

Replay

16.3.77 at Hillsborough (55,000)

Aston Villa 1 (Kenyon og)
Everton 1 (Latchford) (a.e.t.)

Aston Villa: Burridge, Gidman, Robson, Phillips, Nicholl, Mortimer, Deehan, Little, Gray, Cowans, Carrodus.
Everton: Lawson, Bernard, Darracott, Lyons, McNaught, King, Hamilton (sub: Pearson), Kenyon, Latchford, McKenzie, Goodlass.
Referee: G Kew (Worcs)

Second Replay

13.4.77 at Old Trafford (54,749)

Aston Villa 3 (Little 2, Nicholl)
Everton 2 (Latchford, Lyons) (a.e.t.)

Aston Villa: Burridge, Gidman (sub: Smith), Robson, Phillips, Nicholl, Mortimer, Graydon, Little, Deehan, Cropley, Cowans.
Everton: Lawson, Robinson, Darracott, Lyons, McNaught, King, Hamilton, Dobson, Latchford, Pearson (sub: Seargeant), Goodlass.
Referee: G Kew (Worcs)

1977/8

18.3.78 at Wembley (100,000)

Nottingham Forest 0
Liverpool 0 (a.e.t.)

Nottingham Forest: Woods, Anderson, Clark, McGovern (sub: O'Hare), Lloyd, Burns, O'Neill, Bowyer, Withe, Woodcock, Robertson.
Liverpool: Clemence, Neal, Smith, Thompson, Kennedy (sub: Fairclough), Hughes, Dalglish, Case, Heighway, McDermott, Callaghan.
Referee: P Partridge (Durham)

Replay

22.3.78 at Old Trafford (54,375)

Nottingham Forest 1 (Robertson pen.)
Liverpool 0

Nottingham Forest: Woods, Anderson, Clark, O'Hare, Lloyd, Burns, O'Neill, Bowyer, Withe, Woodcock, Robertson.
Liverpool: Clemence, Neal, Smith, Thompson, Kennedy, Hughes, Dalglish, Case (sub: Fairclough), Heighway, McDermott, Callaghan.
Referee: P Partridge (Durham)

1978/9

17.3.79 at Wembley (100,000)

Nottingham Forest 3 (Birtles 2, Woodcock)
Southampton 2 (Peach, Holmes)

Nottingham Forest: Shilton, Barrett, Clark, McGovern, Lloyd, Needham, O'Neill, Gemmill, Birtles, Woodcock, Robertson.
Southampton: Gennoe, Golac, Peach, Williams, Nicholl, Waldron, Ball, Boyer, Hayes (sub: Sealy), Holmes, Curran.
Referee: P Reeves (Leicester)

1979/80

15.3.80 at Wembley (100,000)

Wolverhampton Wanderers 1 (Gray)
Nottingham Forest 0

Wolverhampton Wanderers: Bradshaw, Palmer, Parkin, Daniel, Berry, Hughes, Carr, Hibbitt, Gray, Richards, Eves.
Nottingham Forest: Shilton, Anderson, Gray, McGovern, Needham, Burns, O'Neill, Bowyer, Birtles, Francis, Robertson.
Referee: D Richardson (Great Harwood)

1980/1

14.3.81 at Wembley (100,000)

Liverpool 1 (A Kennedy)
West Ham United 1 (Stewart pen) (a.e.t.)

Liverpool: Clemence, Neal, A Kennedy, Irwin, R Kennedy, Hansen, Dalglish, Lee, Heighway (sub: Case), McDermott, Souness.
West Ham United: Parkes, Stewart, Lampard, Bonds, Martin, Devonshire, Neighbour, Goddard (sub: Pearson), Cross, Brooking, Pike.
Referee: C Thomas (Porthcawl)

Replay

1.4.81 at Villa Park (36,693)

Liverpool 2 (Dalglish, Hansen)
West Ham United 1 (Goddard)

Liverpool: Clemence, Neal, A Kennedy, Thompson, R Kennedy, Hansen, Dalglish, Lee, Rush, McDermott, Case.
West Ham United: Parkes, Stewart, Lampard, Bonds, Martin, Devonshire, Neighbour, Goddard, Cross, Brooking, Pike (sub: Pearson).
Referee: C Thomas (Porthcawl)

1981/2 Milk Cup
13.3.82 at Wembley (100,000)

Liverpool 3 (Whelan 2, Rush)
Tottenham Hotspur 1 (Archibald) (a.e.t.)

Liverpool: Grobbelaar, Neal, Kennedy, Thompson, Whelan, Lawrenson, Dalglish, Lee, Rush, McDermott (sub: Johnston), Souness.
Tottenham Hotspur: Clemence, Hughton, Miller, Price, Hazard (sub: Villa), Perryman, Ardiles, Archibald, Galvin, Hoddle, Crooks.
Referee: P Willis (Co. Durham)

1982/3 Milk Cup
26.3.83 at Wembley (100,000)

Liverpool 2 (Kennedy, Whelan)
Manchester United 1 (Whiteside) (a.e.t.)

Liverpool: Grobbelaar, Neal, Kennedy, Lawrenson, Whelan, Hansen, Dalglish, Lee, Rush, Johnston (sub: Fairclough), Souness.
Manchester United: Bailey, Duxbury, Albiston, Moses, Moran (sub: Macari), McQueen, Wilkins, Muhren, Stapleton, Whiteside, Coppell.
Referee: G Courtney (Co. Durham)

1983/4 Milk Cup
25.3.84 at Wembley (100,000)

Liverpool 0
Everton 0 (a.e.t.)

Liverpool: Grobbelaar, Neal, Kennedy, Lawrenson, Whelan, Hansen, Dalglish, Lee, Rush, Johnston (sub: Robinson), Souness.
Everton: Southall, Stevens, Bailey, Ratcliffe, Mountfield, Reid, Irvine, Heath, Sharp, Richardson, Sheedy (sub: Harper).
Referee: A Robinson (Portsmouth)

Replay

28.3.84 at Maine Road (52,089)

Liverpool 1 (Souness)
Everton 0

Liverpool: Grobbelaar, Neal, Kennedy, Lawrenson, Whelan, Hansen, Dalglish, Lee, Rush, Johnston, Souness.
Everton: Southall, Stevens, Bailey, Ratcliffe, Mountfield, Reid, Irvine (sub: King), Heath, Sharp, Richardson, Harper.
Referee: A Robinson (Portsmouth)

1984/5 Milk Cup
24.3.85 at Wembley (100,000)

Norwich City 1 (Chisholm og)
Sunderland 0

Norwich: Woods, Haylock, Van Wyk, Bruce, Mendham, Watson, Barham, Channon, Deehan, Hartford, Donowa.
Sunderland: Turner, Venison, Pickering, Bennett, Chisholm, Corner (sub: Gayle), Daniel, Wallace, Hodgson, Berry, Walker.
Referee: N Midgley (Salford)

1985/6 Milk Cup
20.4.86 at Wembley (90,396)

Oxford United 3 (Hebberd, Houghton, Charles)
Queen's Park Rangers 0

Oxford: Judge, Langan, Trewick, Phillips, Briggs, Shotton, Houghton, Aldridge, Charles, Hebberd, Brock.
QPR: Barron, McDonald, Dawes, Neill, Wicks, Fenwick, Allen (sub: Rosenior), James, Bannister, Byrne, Robinson.
Referee: K Hackett (Sheffield)

1986/7 Littlewoods Challenge Cup
5.4.87 at Wembley (96,000)

Arsenal 2 (Nicholas 2)
Liverpool 1 (Rush)

Arsenal: Lukic, Anderson, Sansom, Williams, O'Leary, Adams, Rocastle, Davis, Quinn (sub: Groves), Nicholas, Hayes (sub: Thomas).
Liverpool: Grobbelaar, Gillespie, Venison, Spackman, Whelan, Hansen, Walsh (sub: Dalglish), Johnston, Rush, Molby, McMahon (sub: Wark).
Referee: L Shapter (Torquay)

A P P E N D I X F I V E

Full Members' Cup

This is a knock-out competition involving First and Second Division clubs. It was introduced after English League clubs were banned from Europe in 1985. Until the sports shoe manufacturers Simod took on the competition in September 1987, it was known rather awkwardly as the Full Members' Cup (a term not readily clear to the public). The major incentive, as ever, is a trip to Wembley, but after 1987 to this was added extra prize money from the sponsors. The Simod Cup winners in 1988 and 1989 will receive £60,000. Runners-up will collect £30,000 and the losing semi-finalists £15,000.

In its first year, 1985/6, this much-maligned competition attracted only twenty-one of the forty-four Full Members, and of those a mere five were from the First Division. Average gates were 4223 until the final, which fortunately for all concerned was exciting and lucrative enough (receipts of £508,000) to rescue the Full Members' Cup from an early demise.

The second year, thirty-seven of the forty-four Full Members participated, including every Second Division club, and before the final, gates were marginally improved at an average of 5140. But the absence of several top clubs, the lack of a sponsor and an already crowded fixture list made this competition the least attractive of all the experiments tried by the League in the modern era. Gates of 821 and 817 at First Division Charlton, and only three attendances reaching five figures (apart from the final) in 1986/7 suggested an uncertain future for the Full Members' Cup.

That was, until sponsorship by Simod invested new life

into the concept and guaranteed its survival for a further two seasons. As a result, the list of entries was up to forty clubs in 1987/8, and aggregate attendances (including the final) showed an increase of 33 per cent (16 per cent on average).

The three finals have been as follows:

1985/6
23.3.86 at Wembley (68,000)

| Chelsea | 5 (Speedie 3, Lee 2) |
| Manchester City | 4 (Kinsey, Lillis 2 (1 pen), Rougvie og) |

1986/7
29.3.87 at Wembley (40,000)

| Blackburn Rovers | 1 (Hendry) |
| Charlton Athletic | 0 |

1987/8
27.3.88 at Wembley (61,740)

| Luton Town | 1 (Harford) |
| Reading | 4 (Gilkes, Beaven pen, Tait, Smillie) |

APPENDIX SIX

Associate Member Competitions

Third Division Cup 1933–46

The concept of a separate cup competition among Third Division clubs was first considered in 1932. When it began a year later interest was slow to build, and the competition took a further knock in June 1936 when one of the organizers resigned, leaving some unexplained omissions in the accounts.

By 1938/9, gates were so low – partly because clubs often played weak teams – that a complete revamp was required. Instead of every club competing, the second and third clubs in each section were scheduled to play each other, with the winners meeting in a final. However, war broke out before this rather meaningless new competition could begin, and the idea was revived for only one season, 1945/6.

From the match details which follow, note that the winners of each section, North and South, did not play each other as in the modern Sherpa Van Trophy. Also, the Southern Section Finals from 1935 to 1938 were played over two legs, delayed in 1937, 1938 and 1939 until the following season. The 1939 Southern Final was never played. Unless stated below, the attendances were not recorded.

The Third Division Cup Finalists were:

1933/4
Southern Section
Torquay 0 Exeter 1 (2.5.34 at Plymouth, att. 6198)
Northern Section
Darlington 4 Stockport 3 (1.5.34 at Old Trafford)

1934/5
Southern Section
Bristol Rovers 3 Watford 2 (15.4.35 at Millwall)
Northern Section
Stockport 2 Walsall 0 (1.5.35 at Maine Road)

1935/6
Southern Section
Two legs – Swindon 0 Coventry 2 (25.3.36, att. 3610)
Coventry 3 Swindon 2 (2.4.36 att. 2000)

Northern Section
Darlington 1 Chester 2 (27.4.36)

1936/7
Southern Section
Two legs – Watford 2 Millwall 2 (29.9.37, att. 2714)
Millwall 1 Watford 1 (18.10.37)
(Each club shared trophy for six months)
Northern Section
Southport 1 Chester 3 (27.4.37 at Southport, att. 6000)

1937/8
Southern Section
Two legs – Reading 6 Bristol City 1 (28.9.38, att. 1097)
Bristol City 1 Reading 0 (12.10.38, att. 718)
Northern Section
Southport 4 Bradford City 1 (4.5.38, att. 4642)

1938/9
(Clubs qualifying for the FA Cup third round were excluded)
Southern Section
Torquay *v.* QPR or Port Vale – war prevented the final or semi-final replay being played.
Northern Section
Bradford City 3 Accrington 0 (1.5.39, att. 3117)

1945/6
Southern Section
Bournemouth 1 Walsall 0 (4.5.46 at Chelsea, att. 19,715)
Northern Section
Rotherham 2 Chester 2 (27.4.46, att. 12,000)
Chester 2 Rotherham 3 (4.5.46, att. 12,650)

Third Division North v. South 1955–8

This series of six representative matches was played between selected sides from each Third Division section. The novelty of floodlighting, combined with the long-standing rivalry between the two regions, made these games quite attractive, and some were televised by the BBC.

The results were:

16.3.55 at Elm Park (10,424)

South 2 (Rainford, Wilson)
North 0

South: K Oxford (Norwich), M McDonnell (Coventry), J Langley (Brighton), B Nicholas (QPR), J Crosland (Bournemouth), G Hughes (Northampton), W Hinshelwood (Reading), J Rainford (Brentford), E Day (Southampton), D Mills (Torquay), M Grice (Colchester). Sub: G Wilson (Brighton) for Hughes.
North: R Minshull (Southport), R Jackson (Oldham), J Harrower (Accrington), K Furphy (Darlington), T Callender (Gateshead), F Clempson, K Finney (both Stockport), J Prescott (Southport), G Stewart (Accrington), G Darwin (Mansfield), M Jones (Scunthorpe).

13.10.55 at Peel Park, Accrington (10,521)

North 3 (Connor 2, Ryan pen)
South 3 (Morgan 2, Mills)

North: R Minshull (Southport), J Fleming (Workington), V Kenny (Carlisle), D Stokoe (Workington), J Ryden (Accrington), R Ryan (Derby), R Webb (Bradford C), I Broadis (Carlisle), J Connor (Stockport), G Smith, D Woodhead (both Chesterfield).
South: R Matthews (Coventry), A Jardine (Millwall), S Charlton (Orient), N Simpson (Coventry), D Rees (Ipswich), R Ashman (Norwich), R Mills (Northampton), D Mills (Torquay), M Cook (Watford), S Morgan (Orient), J Wheeler (Reading).

8.10.56 at Highfield Road (14,156)

South 2 (Newsham, Hollis)
North 1 (Johnson)

South: R Matthews (Coventry), A Jardine (Millwall), J Langley (Brighton), J Belcher (Crystal P), P Parker (Southampton), J Elsworthy (Ipswich), J Gavin (Norwich), S Newsham (Bournemouth), R Hollis (Southend), D Mills (Torquay), K Flint (Aldershot). Sub: M Cook (Watford) for Newsham.
North: M Newlands (Workington), M Currie (Bradford C), J Brownsword (Scunthorpe), A Mays (Derby), W Moore (Hartlepool), C Sneddon (Accrington), G Burrell (Chesterfield), R Hewitt (Wrexham), K Johnson (Hartlepools), G Smith (Chesterfield), J Simm (Bradford C)

2.4.57 at Edgeley Park (12,372)

North 2 (Holden, Ackerman)
South 1 (Langman)

North: R Gray (Gateshead), R Brown (Workington), T Cahill (Barrow), E Hunter (Accrington), R Greener (Darlington), B Hutchinson (Chesterfield), K Finney (Stockport), I Broadis, A Ackerman (both Carlisle), W Holden (Stockport), B Cripsey (Hull).
South: P Pickering (Northampton), A Jardine (Millwall), G Fisher (Colchester), G Wilson (Brighton), P Parker (Southampton), J Elsworthy (Ipswich), M Hellawell (QPR), D Dorman (Walsall), N Langman (Plymouth), D Mills (Torquay), R Cutler (Bournemouth).

30.10.57 at Selhurst Park (12,688)

South 2 (Steele 2)
North 2 (Luke, Tomlinson)

South: R Springett (QPR), J Bannister (Shrewsbury), A Sherwood (Newport), G Veitch (Millwall), K Harvey (Exeter), G Wilson (Brighton), B Harrison (Crystal P), J Shepherd (Millwall), R Hollis (Southend), F Steele (Port Vale), P Wright (Colchester).
North: R McLaren, E Robertson (both Bury), P Feasey (Hull), J Bertolini (Workington), W Taylor (Southport), C Crowe (Mansfield), J Tomlinson (Chesterfield), I Broadis (Carlisle), G Stewart (Accrington), W Holden (Stockport), G Luke (Hartlepool).

18.3.58 at Brunton Park (13,000)

North 0
South 1 (Harburn)

North: W Bly (Hull), E Robertson (Bury), J Brownsword, F Marshall (both Scunthorpe), D Blakey (Chesterfield), R Thompson (Carlisle), W Stephens (Hull), I Broadis, A Ackerman (both Carlisle), J Reid, M Bakes (both Bradford C).
South: J Savage (Walsall), J Neal (Swindon), A Ingham (QPR), R Yeoman (Northampton), W Davies (Reading), K Coote (Brentford), E Crossan (Southend), D Harris (Newport), P Harburn, D Sexton (both Brighton), J Hoskins (Southampton). Sub: F Howard (Brighton) for Harris.

Sherpa Van Trophy

A revival of the pre-war Third Division Cup was first proposed in 1959 by the FA, but since the League already had plans for the League Cup, the Management Committee told the Associate Members to ignore the approach. Then, in 1972, the Pool Promoters' Association offered to put up £100,000 for a competition to be played in May between clubs from the Third and Fourth Divisions, the Southern League and the Northern Premier League. The idea was dropped when the Associate Members refused to compete against non-League clubs and demanded a £5,000 minimum guarantee.

A purely Associate Members' Cup was reconsidered again in June 1981, but not started until January 1984. After a disappointing first season (average gate 2661, highest gate 6544 for the final), the competition was successfully revamped as the sponsored Freight Rover Trophy, with every Third and Fourth Division club entering, all matches played regionally and, as before the war, two regional finals (played over two legs). It was retitled the Sherpa Van Trophy in 1987/8.

As with the League Cup and the Full Members' Cup, the great bait is a Wembley final. Sherpa Van's five-year sponsorship is worth £350,000, divided each year among the entrants. The finalist clubs each receive a mini-bus.

In 1986/7 the average attendance was 3361, mainly owing to low gates in the early rounds. Nevertheless, the lure of Wembley is still sufficient to suggest a healthy future for the competition, and in 1987/8 gates rose by 25 per cent.

So far, Third Division clubs have dominated the tournament, and the Freight Rover finals have developed a deserved reputation for providing a friendly, wholesome atmosphere.

The finals have been as follows:

Associate Members' Cup
1983/4 24.5.84 at Hull (6544)
Hull City 1 Bournemouth 2

Freight Rover Trophy
1984/5 1.6.85 at Wembley (39,897)
Brentford 1 Wigan Athletic 3

1985/6 24.5.86 at Wembley (54,000)
Bolton 0 Bristol C 3

1986/7 24.5.87 at Wembley (58,586)
Bristol C 1 Mansfield 1 (a.e.t.) (Mansfield won 6–5 on penalties)

Sponsored and Miscellaneous Competitions

Long before sponsorship became an accepted part of the game, from as early as 1892, the Management Committee received offers from commercial interests wanting to enhance their own reputations by association with the Football League. Every overture was politely declined until 1970, when the Management Committee had a sudden change of heart and signed not one but three sponsorship agreements in the space of a few months. None of the resultant competitions was to survive the decade, but they each paved the way for sponsorship of the League Cup in 1982 and the League itself in 1983.

Ford Sporting League 1970/1

In 1970 Ford Motors and the League signed an agreement whereby a separate league table would be drawn up, based on League results but with additional points awarded for goals, and points deducted for sendings off and cautions. The idea was to provide an incentive for cleaning up the game and rewarding smaller clubs.

£100,000 prize money was made available; £50,000 for the winners, £30,000 for the runners-up and £20,000 to be divided up into eight monthly awards of £2500 each. In addition, Ford were to spend £30,000 on advertisements in the *Football League Review* and donate £20,000 a year to charities.

As it happened, Fourth Division Oldham waltzed away with £70,000 of the prize money. Crewe, from the same division, took the rest. But the rules of the Ford Sporting League stipulated that all the proceeds had to go towards ground improvements, so Oldham were placed in the rather awkward position of building themselves a 1400-seater stand while simultaneously being kept afloat by a loan from the local council. Crewe spent their money on rebuilding their Popular Side terrace.

The Ford agreement was terminated after one season.

Watney Mann Invitation Cup 1970–73

Known as the Watney Cup, this was a popular and well publicized pre-season knock-out tournament played among eight clubs: the two top scoring teams from each division (other than those promoted or competing in Europe).

The Watney Cup had two distinctions. It was the first ever separate sponsored competition organized by the League, and was the first to use penalty kicks as a method of settling games drawn after extra time (an idea borrowed from the North American Soccer League, and subsequently extended to all the major European cup competitions).

The success of the penalty kick system in 1970 was followed in 1971 by the experimental restriction of offside to the penalty area only. Opinion on this trial proved widely favourable;

games flowed more freely, there were fewer stoppages and less defensive football.

Prize money was as follows: £4000 to each participating club, £500 for first round winners, £500 for winning semi-finalists and £1000 for winners. In addition, the League and FA shared £50,000 from the sponsors plus a share of the gates, with a further smaller payment for the county associations in the areas of the clubs taking part. Clubs also received television fees and, of course, a share of the gate.

The Watney Cup had a bright beginning. Played over eight days in early August 1970 and covered fully by the BBC, the seven games produced thirty-one goals and an average attendance of 21,020 – a perfect curtain raiser for the season at a time when the League needed all the goals and favourable publicity it could muster (especially since the League's goals-per-game average the previous season had been the lowest – at 2·53 per game – since changes in the offside law in 1925).

The following three years saw gates fluctuate, but receipts remained healthy and it was unfortunate that the innovative spirit and occasional acts of giant killing were not be repeated after 1973.

The finals, all played in August, were as follows:

1970
Derby Co 4 Man Utd 1 (32,049)

1971
West Bromwich 4 Colchester 4 (19,009)
(Colchester won 4–3 on penalties)

1972
Bristol R 0 Sheffield U 0 (19,768)
(Rovers won 7–6 on penalties)

1973
Stoke City 2 Hull 0 (18,159)

Texaco Cup (1970–75)

Originally entitled the International League Board Competition, mercifully Texaco stepped in with sponsorship to save the public a mouthful and give credibility to a potentially fascinating competition which might have developed into the much vaunted British Cup.

Unfortunately, the Texaco Cup never quite lived up to its billing, and with its demise in 1975 it was reduced to becoming the relatively unattractive Anglo-Scottish Cup (see page 429). In England the Texaco Cup was lambasted by the press as being a dumping ground for middle-of-the-table sides, but in Scotland, where attendances were above average, it was welcomed. Even so, some Scottish clubs complained that the

League clubs entering were not of sufficiently high calibre (although a Scottish club never actually won the cup!).

Nevertheless, in 1970 hopes were high as sixteen clubs kicked off the competition. There were six clubs each from the Football League and Scottish League, plus two each from Northern Ireland and Eire. They were all clubs with no European commitments.

Each entrant received £1000, plus £1500 for first round winners, £2000 second round, £2500 runners-up, £3500 winners. The League received £22,500 and the Scottish League £17,500. The Irish League and League of Ireland each received £5000.

In the first round, Scottish clubs played English clubs while the Irish had their own North–South contest. Every round was played over two legs.

Owing to security problems in Northern Ireland during 1972–3, the Irish clubs withdrew, leaving nine English and seven Scottish sides in the tournament. The result was, contrary to the spirit of the competition, an all-English final, a pattern repeated over the following two years until the Scottish clubs' withdrawal.

The Texaco Cup finals were as follows:

1970/1
Hearts 1 Wolves 3 (26,000)
Wolves 0 Hearts 1 (28,462)

1971/2
Airdrie 0 Derby 0 (16,000)
Derby 2 Airdrie 1 (25,102)

1972/3
Ipswich 2 Norwich 1 (29,698)
Norwich 1 Ipswich 2 (35,798)

1973/4
Newcastle 2 Burnley 1 (34,540)
(one leg only)

1974/5
Southampton 1 Newcastle 0 (17,100)
Newcastle 3 Southampton 0 a.e.t. (19,288)

Anglo-Scottish Cup 1975–81

Once Texaco had withdrawn their sponsorship, the competition continued under varying rules, but it emerged as the preserve of Second Division clubs. In eleven seasons of the Texaco, then Anglo-Scottish Cups, only one Scottish club won the competition: St Mirren in 1980. The series ended in 1981 when Scottish clubs withdrew.

The Anglo-Scottish Cup finals were as follows:

1975/6
Middlesbrough 1 Fulham 0 (15,000)
Fulham 0 Middlesbrough 0 (13,723)

1976/7
Orient 1 Nottm F 1 (5058)
Nottm F 4 Orient 0 (12,717)

1977/8
St Mirren 1 Bristol C 2 (8000)
Bristol C 1 St Mirren 1 (16,110)

1978/9
Oldham 0 Burnley 4 (10,456)
Burnley 0 Oldham 1 (10,865)

1979/80
Bristol C 0 St Mirren 2 (3731)
St Mirren 3 Bristol C 1 (12,500)

1980/1
Chesterfield 1 Notts Co 0 (10,190)
Notts Co 1 Chesterfield 1 (12,951)

Football League Group Cup 1981/2

Despite the withdrawal of Scottish clubs in 1981, the format was continued among twenty-four League clubs from the Second, Third and Fourth Divisions. Six regional groups of four clubs played three games each, the winners going forward to knock-out rounds. An average gate of 2616 indicates the level of interest in the competition.

The final, on 6 April 1982, was as follows:

Grimsby 3 Wimbledon 2 (3423)

Football League Trophy 1982/3

A change of name and the introduction of two First Division clubs (Watford and Norwich) did little to enhance this flagging concept. This time, thirty-two clubs were divided into eight regional groups of four, and to add interest a bonus point was awarded for any team scoring three or more goals in a match. An average gate of 2051 did not suggest any bonus for the fans.

The final, on 20 April 1983, was as follows:

Lincoln 2 Millwall 3 (3142)

In 1983 the Third and Fourth Division clubs formed their own knock-out competition (see Appendix Six), followed by the Full Members in 1985 (see Appendix Five).

Screen Sport Super Cup

This was a competition held for one season only among the six League clubs who would have been competing in the European competitions in 1985/6 had it not been for the FIFA ban on English clubs competing in Europe, imposed after the Heysel Stadium riot of May 1985. Sponsorship came from European satellite sports channel Screen Sport, and was worth £254,000.

The competition was played as a mini-league between Everton (who should have been competing in the European Cup), Manchester United (Cup Winners' Cup), and Liverpool, Tottenham, Southampton and Norwich (all UEFA Cup). The top four teams then played two-leg semi-finals, with the two-leg final being held over to season 1986/7.

The final results were:

Liverpool 3 Everton 1 (20,660)
Everton 1 Liverpool 4 (26,068)

Attendances

The League

British football supporters and observers have long been fascinated, and anxious, about attendances. They are held to be the best measure we have to determine the popularity and the health of the game. However, they do not always tell us much about the wealth of the game. Since the Second World War, gate receipts have in many cases risen steadily despite the fall in attendances, simply because admission prices have increased and there are now more higher-priced admissions, that is, a higher ratio of people sitting to standing.

Accurate records for attendances do not exist before about 1934, and the League itself started keeping records only in 1946 (in order to keep tabs on the 4 per cent levy each club contributed towards the League's running costs).

From newspaper reports we can make the following very approximate estimates.

In the first season of the League the total number of spectators reached about 602,000. That is, an average gate of 4560.

In 1895/6 the total for the First Division was roughly 1,900,000, giving an average gate of about 7900.

Thereafter crowds grew steadily, and although gates above 25,000 were the exception rather than the rule, it is thought that the first 50,000 League attendance was at Villa Park in April 1900 (when Villa and their opponents Sheffield United were both challenging for the Championship).

Between about 1905 and 1915, gates were not greatly different from those of the 1980s. The aggregate for 1906/7 has been given as 10,929,000, an average of 14,380. Taking several typical Saturdays from season 1907/8, newspaper estimates (not always reliable) give us an average First Division attendance of 15,200. The following season, 1908/9, one football annual gave the First Division average as 15,800. Even allowing for mistakes, weather and differing fixtures, this is still below the 1980s norm (average First Division gates in 1986/7 were 19,794).

Taking another sample of typical Saturdays in 1910/11, the First Division average was 17,100, the Second Division average 10,400 and the Southern League average 6000.

FA Cup gates were, as now, marginally higher. The average for games in the last sixteen of the FA Cup in 1907/8 was 26,500. This compares with 24,630 in 1986/7.

Right up until the First World War, these very approximate averages do not vary greatly, and they do not suggest a higher level than today's, even at the League's lowest point in 1985/6.

After the First World War, gates rose considerably. For example, taking a few typical Saturdays in season 1919/20, the First Division average was 22,090, the Second Division 12,100 and the Southern League 8900.

League attendances then dropped in the mid 1920s, but rose again so that by the early and mid 1930s, newspaper reports suggest that average attendances were roughly at the same level as they would reach around the late 1950s. The only accurate figures we have for pre-1945 are from 1937/8, when the aggregate was 28,132,933. That was roughly the same figure recorded around 1964 and again in 1971.

From those figures we can guess (but only guess) that there was not an even, upward curve during the 1930s (leading towards the post-war boom), but rather a mid-1930s peak which started to fall again towards the outbreak of war.

It is only after the Second World War that we gain a truly accurate picture. We can make from the graph (see page 431) the following observations.

Although the overall trend is downward since the peak in 1949, there have been periods of recovery, most notably between 1966 and 1968 (undoubtedly as a result of England's World Cup win in 1966), and from 1986 to 1988.

The worst drops have occurred in 1960/1 (12 per cent), 1972/3 (11.4 per cent) and 1980/1 (11 per cent).

Highest aggregate and average attendances by season show that not all the divisions peaked at the same time:

● The highest seasonal aggregate attendance in the Football League was in 1948/9, when there were 41.2 million spectators.

● The highest seasonal aggregate for Division One was also in 1948/9, when 17,914,667 attended, more than attended all League games in 1986/7. The average First Division attendance in 1948/9 was 38,776.

● The aggregate for Division Two was highest in 1947/8 (12,286,350 – average 26,594).

● The aggregate for Division Three South was highest in 1950/1 (7,367,884 – average 15,947).

● The aggregate for Division Three North was highest in 1948/9 (5,005,081 – average 10,833).

Comparison of highest with lowest aggregates and averages shows that the greatest proportional drop has been in the Fourth Division. As one would expect, the First Division's share of the diminishing cake has increased since the Second World War. For example, in 1961/2 the First Division's share of the total was 43 per cent. In 1985/6 this share had risen to 55 per cent. In 1964/5 the Fourth Division's share of the total was 13 per cent; in 1984/5 it was down to 8 per cent.

League attendances sunk to an all-time low in 1985/6, in the wake of events at Bradford, Birmingham and Brussels, but in the two following seasons rose marginally to a level approaching the 1983/4 aggregate by 1988. Due to reconstruction of the League, the number of matches played in the First Division was reduced after 1986 and therefore exact comparisons cannot be made. Overall, however, the trend was upward.

The League Cup

Since League Cup finals were held at Wembley, the attendance totals for League Cup matches have held reasonably steady. Obviously, in both the League Cup and the FA Cup the luck of the draw largely determines the scale of attendances. Peaks in League attendances do not therefore always coincide with peaks in Cup attendances.

From its shaky beginnings in 1960/1 until the present day the League Cup has established a total audience of between 1.5 and 2 million per season. During the same period aggregate attendances at FA Cup matches have dropped sharply, so that currently each competition attracts roughly the same total audience (based on all rounds of the League Cup and Round One onwards of the FA Cup).

For example, when the League Cup Final was first held at Wembley in 1966/7 the League Cup attracted 1.395 million spectators compared with 3.967 million in the FA Cup.

At its peak in 1971/2 the League Cup drew 2.397 million, compared with 3.159 million in the FA Cup.

However in 1981/2 the League Cup actually attracted more spectators than the FA Cup (1.88 million as compared with 1.84 million). As is the case with the League's other competitions, gates in the League Cup have risen in recent seasons. In 1987/8 the increase was approximately 5 per cent (while FA Cup attendances in the same period rose by about 24 per cent).

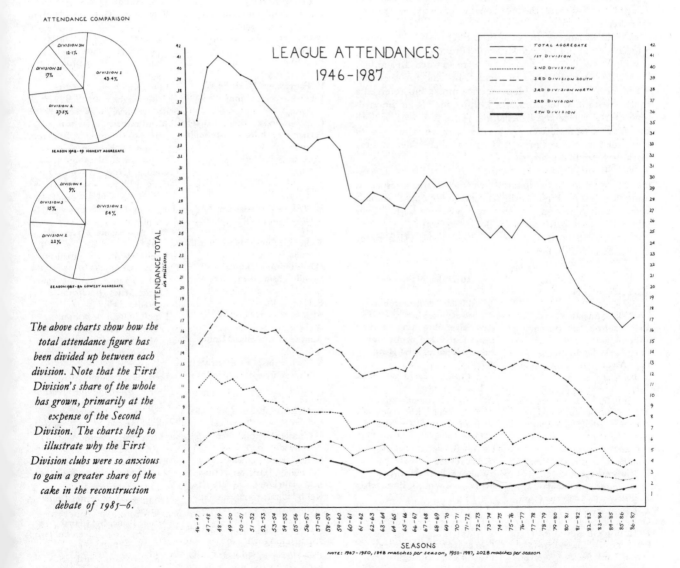

The above charts show how the total attendance figure has been divided up between each division. Note that the First Division's share of the whole has grown, primarily at the expense of the Second Division. The charts help to illustrate why the First Division clubs were so anxious to gain a greater share of the cake in the reconstruction debate of 1985–6.

LEAGUE ATTENDANCES
1946–1987

ATTENDANCE TOTAL in millions

SEASONS
NOTE: 1967–1950, 1848 matches per season, 1950–1987, 2028 matches per season

Long-Service Awards

The following is a list of those individuals who have been presented with the League's long-service award for twenty-one years or more service to their clubs. Most of the recipients were secretaries, directors or managers. In several cases, at the time of the award the period of service was actually much longer than twenty-one years, but application had been delayed. In most cases, the individual went on to serve several more years.

In three instances – those of Fred Everiss (WBA), George Ramsay (Villa) and George Howarth (Preston) – two medals, spanning over forty years' service, were awarded. In another, Charlie Paynter of West Ham served his club for over fifty years, did not apply for a long-service medal, but received a silver cigarette case from the League on his testimonial. Charles Maley received a medal in 1942 for his work at both Bradford clubs, then twenty-one years later, when he was with Leicester City, he was presented with an illuminated address marking forty-two years' total service.

Ivan Sharpe, the former Watford, Glossop, Derby, Leicester and amateur international player who became a respected journalist after the First World War and author of the League's seventy-fifth anniversary history, was presented with a silver salver in 1958 to mark his contribution to football.

An asterisk denotes member of the Management Committee at time of award (in brackets).

H. Abbotts, Bolton (1951)
John Addenbrooke, Wolves (1909)
Sam Allen, Swindon (1941)
Bill Anderson, Nottingham Forest (1968)
C. Annable, Derby (1968)
Fred Archer, Aston Villa (1961)
T. Bailey, Crewe (1948)
J. Bain, Brentford (1956)
*Tom Barcroft, Blackpool (1924)
Ted Bates, Southampton (1977)
John Battersby, Chelsea (1970)
Harry Beever, Huddersfield (1942)
Alan Bennett, Chelsea, Villa, Leicester (1983)
*John Bentley, Bolton (1913)
E. Blackburn, Tranmere (1951)
E. Blount, Swindon (1950)
Gordon Borland, Millwall (1977)
G. H. Brigg, Bradford PA (1959)
Frank Brown, Chester (1954)
Major Frank Buckley, Wolves (1945)

Sir Matt Busby, Manchester United (1967)
David Calderhead, Lincoln, Chelsea (1922)
Ken Calver, Brighton (1987)
Harry Catterick, Everton (1973)
Eddie Chapman, West Ham (1978)
Tom Charnley, Preston, Football League (1918)
A. H. Cole, Plymouth (1952)
W. R. Commins, Rochdale (1963)
Walter Crickmer, Manchester United (1942)
George Crow, Sunderland (1951)
C. A. Crowther, Leeds (1949)
*Will Cuff, Everton (1932)
Stan Cullis, Wolves, Birmingham (1970)
H. C. Curtis, Brentford (1944)
J. E. Davison, Sheffield United (1950)
Cornelius Dean, Orient (1927)
David Dent, Carlisle, Coventry (1981)

*Arthur Dickinson, Sheffield Wednesday (1914)
Bill Dickinson, Everton (1962)
A. Scott Duncan, Ipswich (1957)
Joe Eaton, Mansfield (1976)
J. Edelston, Leyton Orient (1951)
F. Emery, Carlisle (1959)
Eric England, Sheffield Wednesday (1967)
Alan Everiss, West Bromwich (1969)
Fred Everiss, West Bromwich (1923, 1944)
H. Fairclough, Leeds (1923)
Eddie Fletcher, Gillingham (1959)
C. E. Foweraker, Bolton (1938)
*Harry French, Middlesbrough (1963)
Tony Galvin, Huddersfield (1970)
Harry Glasper, Middlesbrough (1939)
Wally Gray, Ipswich (1968)
Tom Green, Middlesbrough (1970)
Walter Griffiths, Manchester City (1969)
*Dr Clifford Grossmark, Gillingham (1982)
E. Hall, Newcastle (1951)
F. Hamer, Bury (1939)
Alan Hardaker, Football League (1972)
John Harris, Sheffield United (1979)
S. E. Hawkins, Orient, Bristol Rovers, Charlton, Bristol City (1954)
W. Heald, Rotherham (1944)
R. Hewison, Bristol City (1943)
Charles Hewitt, Wrexham, Chester, Leyton Orient, Millwall (1954)
George Hicks, Orient (1970)
Bill Hillan, Hartlepool (1982)
B. W. Hitchiner, Coventry (1956)
Keith Holmes, Southend (1982)
Herbert Horsley, Workington (1972)
Graham Hortop, Brighton, Fulham, Millwall (1982)
Eric Howarth, Football League (1972)

Fred Howarth, Football League (1942)
George Howarth, Preston (1956, 1973)
Jack Howley, Wolves (1963)
C. G. Hunt, Southport (1951)
G. L. Hurley, QPR (1955)
R. S. Jarvis, Tottenham Hotspur (1968)
Norman Jones, Port Vale (1966)
Theo Kelly, Everton (1951)
*Harry Keys, West Bromwich (1926)
Leslie Knighton, Arsenal, Birmingham, Chelsea (1952)
Robert Kyle, Sunderland (1927)
Alan Leather, Tottenham Hotspur, Coventry, Brighton, Crystal Palace (1979)
*John Lewis, Blackburn (1920)
Graham Little, Plymouth (1986)
Clifford Lloyd, Wrexham (1968)
J. B. McClelland, Lincoln (1945)
Thomas McIntosh, Middlesbrough (1932)
*John McKenna, Liverpool (1923)
Peter McWilliam, Tottenham Hotspur (1939)
Albert Maddox, Burnley (1969)
Charles Maley, Bradford PA, Bradford City (1942)
Ernest Mangnall, Bolton, Burnley, Manchester United, Manchester City (1921)
Dennis Marshall, Notts County (1972)
Fred May, Reading (1969)
Robert Mellor, Oldham (1936)
A. Miller, Derby (1968)
W. S. Moore, Derby (1928)
Trevor Morris, Cardiff, Swansea, Wrexham, Newport, Wales FA (1971)
Ron Morse, Swindon (1974)
Arnold Newton, Sheffield United (1970)
Les Olive, Manchester United (1976)
Arthur Paine, Bury (1944)
G. S. Patterson, Liverpool (1937)
Jack Peart, Fulham (1945)
F. S. Perryman, Hartlepools (1950)

John Peters, Arsenal (1939)
W. P. Peters, Chester (1955)
J. Phillips, Charlton (1953)
Denis Piggott, Brentford (1968)
Eddie Plumley, Birmingham,
  Leicester, Coventry (1976)
Harry Potts, Burnley (1978)
George Ramsay, Aston Villa
  (1909, 1927)
Bob Redhead, Luton (1971)
S. F. L. Richards, Birmingham
  (1939)
Bill Ridding, Bolton (1967)
Les Rimmer, Shrewsbury (1969)
*Fred Rinder, Aston Villa (1938)
Peter Robinson, Liverpool (1978)
Ron Rollitt, Watford (1976)
David Rose, Ipswich (1984)
Ted Rothwell, Bolton (1978)
J. C. Rouse, Liverpool (1951)
Dave Russell, Tranmere (1972)
Keith Saunders, Newport (1971)
Angus Seed, Barnsley (1953)
Jimmy Seed, Charlton (1953)
R. Seed, Blackpool (1962)
Bill Shankly, Liverpool (1971)
Phil Shaw, Wolves (1978)
*Harold Shentall, Chesterfield
  (1963)
G. W. Sherrington, York (1951)
T. L. Simmons, Watford (1948)
Ken Smales, Nottingham Forest
  (1980)
Cecil Smith, Torquay (1972)
Ephraim Smith, West Bromwich
  (1939)
H. Smith, Burnley (1961)
Joe Smith, Blackpool (1952)
John Smith, QPR, Orient,
  Leicester, Luton (1980)
W. J. Smith, Aston Villa (1950)
Harry Stace, Bournemouth (1971)
John Steele, Barnsley (1981)
F. Stewart, Stockport, Cardiff
  (1932)

Alec Stock, Luton (1971)
Bob Stokoe, Bury, Charlton,
  Rochdale, Carlisle, Blackpool,
  Sunderland (1984)
*John Strawson, Lincoln, League
  auditor (1918)
Ronnie Suart, Chelsea (1978)
*Charles E. Sutcliffe, Burnley
  (1920)
Arthur Sutherland, Chesterfield
  (1971)
R. F. Swann, Gillingham (1971)
Bert Tann, Bristol Rovers (1971)
Eric Taylor, Sheffield Wednesday
  (1956)
R. H. Taylor, Preston (1943)
Norman Thomas, Football
  League (1972)
Jack Tinn, Portsmouth (1940)
W. R. Tulip, Gateshead (1956)
Arthur Turner, Tottenham
  Hotspur (1928)
Ray Vicary, Barnsley (1958)
Billy Walker, Nottingham Forest
  (1956)
G. Noel Watson, Nottingham
  Forest (1953)
Tom Watson, Sunderland,
  Liverpool (1910)
Frank Watt, Newcastle (1939)
C. G. Webb, Brighton (1941)
F. Westgarth, Hartlepools (1953)
Bert Westwood, Norwich (1980)
Jack Wigglesworth, Accrington
  (1952)
Wilfred Wild, Manchester City
  (1941)
Bill Williams, Stoke (1957)
Ernest Wilson, Walsall (1956)
Norman Wilson, Tranmere
  (1986)
*David Wiseman, Birmingham
  (1970)

Achievements on the pitch were rarely marked by the League. Harold Bell was presented with an illuminated address to mark his 401 consecutive League games for Tranmere Rovers between 1946 and 1955. Arthur Rowley received a similar award in 1966 to commemorate his record total of 434 goals, scored for WBA, Fulham, Leicester and Shrewsbury in the course of 619 appearances. In 1963, in addition to his long-service award, Jimmy Dickinson of Portsmouth was presented with an inscribed silver salver to mark his then record number of League appearances – 764 for Portsmouth..

Similar presentations were made to the former Southampton and England winger Terry Paine, then with Hereford United, when he passed Dickinson's total in 1975, and to Swindon's John Trollope in 1981 when he passed Dickinson's total. Trollope played 770 games for Swindon, a record for one club.

Players' long service was first rewarded in 1961, a statuette being presented to honour twenty years' loyalty to one club. The recipients were:

Ron Ashman, Norwich (1964)
David Blakey, Chesterfield (1967)
Billy Bly, Hull (1961)
Peter Bonetti, Chelsea (1978)
Frank Bowyer, Stoke (1961)
Bobby Charlton, Manchester
  United (1973)
Jack Charlton, Leeds (1972)
Ronnie Clayton, Blackburn
  (1969)
Andy Davidson, Hull (1969)
Jimmy Dickinson, Portsmouth
  (1963)
Tom Finney, Preston (1961)
Bill Foulkes, Manchester United
  (1971)
Redfern Froggat, Sheffield
  Wednesday (1962)
Ernie Gregory, West Ham (1961)

John P. Hart, Manchester City
  (1969)
Johnny Haynes, Fulham (1969)
Billy Liddell, Liverpool (1961)
Nat Lofthouse, Bolton (1961)
John McCue, Stoke (1961)
Bob McKinlay, Nottingham
  Forest (1969)
Gil Merrick, Birmingham (1961)
Jimmy Mullen, Wolves (1961)
Tommy Powell, Derby (1962)
Joe Shaw, Sheffield United (1966)
Roy Sproson, Port Vale (1970)
Ron Stitfall, Cardiff (1964)
John Trollope, Swindon (1981)
Ray Wilcox, Newport (1961)
Laurie Woodward, Bournemouth
  (1961)
Billy Wright, Wolves (1961)

BIBLIOGRAPHY

Alcock, A. W., ed., *The Book of Football* (Carmelite House, 1906)

Appleton, Arthur, *The Story of Sunderland* (Sunderland, 1979)

Berry, Harry and Allman, Geoffrey, *One Hundred Years at Deepdale* (Preston, 1981)

Binns, George, *Huddersfield Town 75 Years On* (HTFC, 1984)

Book of Football, Marshall Cavendish (6 vols, 1972)

Brown, Harry, *Soccer Who's Who* (Arthur Barker, 1970)

Buxton, Peter, *Stoke City Centenary Handbook* (Pyramid Press, London 1963)

Catton, J. A. H., ('Tityrus'), 'Rise of the Leaguers' (*Sporting Chronicle*, 1897)

Catton, J. A. H., *Wickets and Goals* (Chapman and Hall, 1926)

Denis, Stuart, ed., *People of the Potteries* (Keele, 1985)

Digest of Football Statistics (Football Trust, 1986)

Douglas, Peter, *The Football Industry* (Allen and Unwin, 1973)

Eastham, George, *Determined to Win* (Sportsman Book Club, 1966)

Ekburg, Charles and Woodhead, Sid, *The Mariners* (Sport and Leisure Press, 1983)

Fabian, A. H. and Green, G. *Association Football* (4 vols, Caxton, 1960)

Football League Handbook (Football League, annually 1888–1988)

Football League Yearbook 1987–88 (Facer Publishing, 1987)

Francis, Lionel, *75 Years of Southern League Football* (Pelham, 1969)

Gibson, Alfred and Pickford, William, *Association Football and the Men Who Made It* (4 vols, 1906)

Golesworthy, Maurice, *Encyclopaedia of Association Football* (Robert Hale, various editions 1956–76)

Green, Geoffrey, *The History of the Football Association* (Naldrett Press, 1953)

Green, Geoffrey, *There's Only One United* (Hodder and Stoughton, 1978)

Guthrie, Jimmy, *Soccer Rebel* (Davis Foster, 1976)

Hardaker, Alan, *Hardaker of the League* (Pelham Books, 1977)

Harding, John, *Football Wizard – the Story of Billy Meredith* (Breedon, 1985)

Hill, Jimmy, *Striking for Soccer* (Peter Davies, 1961)

Hugman, Barry, *A–Z Football League Players Records 1946–81* (Rothmans, 1981)

Inglis, Simon, *Soccer in the Dock – a History of British Football Scandals 1900–65* (Collins Willow, 1985)

Inglis, Simon, *The Football Grounds of Great Britain* (Collins Willow, 1987)

Joannou, Paul, *The History of Newcastle United* (Inkerman, 1980)

Keates, Thomas, *History of Everton Football Club 1878–1929* (Thomas Brakell, 1929)

Kaufman, Neil, *One Hundred Years of Orient* (Orient FC, 1981)

Lord, Bob, *My Fight for Football* (Stanley Paul, 1963)

Mason, Tony, *Association Football and English Society 1863–1915* (Harvester Press, 1981)

Morris, Peter, *Aston Villa 1874–1960* (Naldrett Press, 1960)

Pickford, William, *A Glance Back at the F.A. Council* (Bournemouth, 1938)

Radford, Brian, *Through Open Doors* (Harrap, 1984)

Rippon, Anton, *Soccer: The Road to Crisis* (Moorland, 1983)

Roberts, John, *Everton: The Official Centenary History* (Mayflower Books, 1978)

Rollin, Jack, *Soccer at War 1939–45* (Collins Willow, 1985)

Rothmans Football Yearbook, eds Jack Rollin, Tony Williams and Peter Dunk (annually 1970–87)

Seed, Jimmy, *The Jimmy Seed Story* (Sportsman Book Club, 1958)

Sharpe, Ivan, *Forty Years in Football* (Hutchinson, 1952)

Sharpe, Ivan, *The Football League Jubilee Book* (Stanley Paul, 1963)

Soar, Phil, *A–Z of British Football Records* (Hamlyn, 1984)

Soar, Phil, *And the Spurs Go Marching On . . .* (Hamlyn, 1982)

Soar, Phil, *Encyclopaedia of British Football* (Collins Willow, 1987)

Soar, Phil and Tyler, Martin, *Arsenal 1886–1986* (Hamlyn, 1986)

Speake, Robert, *One Hundred Years of County Football* (Staffs FA, 1977)

Sutcliffe, C. E., Brierley, J. A. and Howarth, Fred, *The Story of the Football League* (Preston, 1938)

Sutcliffe, C. E. and Hargreaves, F., *History of the Lancashire F.A. 1878–1928* (Blackburn 1928)

Turner, A. J., *Nottingham Forest 1865–1965* (Nottingham, 1965)

Wall, Sir Frederick, *Fifty Years of Football* (Cassell, 1935)

Walvin, James, *Football and the Decline of Britain* (Macmillan, 1986)

Ward, Andrew, *The Manchester City Story* (Breedon Books, 1984)

Young, P. M., *The Wolves* (1959)

Young, P. M., *Bolton Wanderers* (Sportsman Book Club, 1965)

Newspapers

Accrington Observer; Accrington Times; Athletic News; Barnsley Chronicle and South Yorkshire Post; Birmingham Daily Gazette; Birmingham Evening Mail; Blackburn Weekly Telegraph; Blackpool Gazette and Herald; Bolton Journal and Guardian; Daily Express; Daily Mail; Daily Mirror; Edmonton Weekly Herald; Football Field; Football League Review; The Guardian; Grimsby Evening Telegraph; Hexham Courant; Huddersfield Examiner; The Independent; Lancashire Daily Post; Lancashire Evening Post; Lancashire Review; Liverpool Review; Manchester Evening Chronicle; Manchester Evening News; Match Weekly; Midland Chronicle; Newcastle Evening Chronicle; The Observer; Preston Guardian; Rossendale Free Press; Sheffield Daily Telegraph; Sheffield Morning Telegraph; Sheffield Green 'Un; Shoot; Sports Argus (Birmingham); Staffordshire Advertiser; The Times; West Bromwich Free Press; Windsor Magazine; World Soccer; Yorkshire Post; Yorkshire Telegraph and Star